CANADIAN
INDUSTRIALRELATIONS
THIRD EDITION

JON PEIRCE

Professional Institute of the Public Service of Canada

KAREN JOY BENTHAM

Centre for Industrial Relations, University of Toronto

PEARSON

Prentice
Hall

Toronto

Library and Archives Canada Cataloguing in Publication

Peirce, Jon
    Canadian industrial relations / Jon Peirce, Karen Joy Bentham.—3rd ed.

Includes bibliographical references and index.
ISBN 0-13-127793-6

1. Industrial relations—Canada—Textbooks. I. Bentham, Karen Joy, 1957–
II. Title.

HD8106.5.P45 2007   331'.0971   C2005-905752-1

ISBN 0-13-127793-6

Vice-President, Editorial Director: Michael J. Young
Editor-in-Chief: Gary Bennett
Acquisitions Editor: Karen Elliott
Executive Marketing Manager: Cas Shields
Senior Developmental Editor: Pamela Voves
Production Editor: Laura Price
Production Coordinator: Patricia Ciardullo
Copy Editor: Trish O'Reilly
Proofreader: John Firth
Photo and Permissions Researcher: Christina Beamish
Indexer: Nancy Mucklow
Page Layout: Laserwords Private Limited
Art Director: Julia Hall
Cover and Interior Design: Gillian Tsintziras
Cover Images: Photodisc

Statistics Canada information is used with the permission of Statistics Canada. Users are forbidden to copy the data and redisseminate them, in an original or modified form, for commercial purposes, without permission from Statistics Canada. Information on the availability of the wide range of data from Statistics Canada can be obtained from Statistics Canada's Regional Offices, its World Wide Web site at http://www.statcan.ca, and its toll-free access number 1-800-263-1136.

4 5   11 10 09

Printed and bound in the USA.

Contents

Preface

We are very pleased that Karen Bentham has joined the writing team of *Canadian Industrial Relations* for this third edition. In addition to extensive teaching experience, Karen brings a broad range of practical industrial relations experience to the team, including her previous role as an Employee Relations Consultant for the Saskatchewan Health Care Association. Karen's wealth of practical knowledge is clearly reflected in the new features described below.

FEATURES

The third edition of *Canadian Industrial Relations* has retained the readability that was the hallmark of the first two editions, while dramatically increasing the number of concrete, real-world examples and practical learning aids. Adopting an institutional approach, each chapter focuses on a specific component of the Canadian industrial relations system, building upon and referencing previous chapters. The result is a unified, comprehensive picture of the structure and functioning of today's industrial relations system and a thorough canvassing of the challenges, controversies, and issues facing industrial relations scholars, practitioners, and unionists alike. As in previous editions, *Canadian Industrial Relations* works well as an introduction to the Canadian industrial relations system—using a practical, applied approach—but does not sacrifice the academic analysis so pivotal to a course.

The third edition's special features include:

- A set of learning objectives for each chapter;
- A "Current Issues" feature in each chapter provides real-life illustrations of the concepts discussed in the text;
- An end-of-chapter case, including questions for discussion, for each chapter;
- Key terms highlighted in the text and definitions provided in page margins;
- The combination of the previous edition's chapters on the economy and management into a single chapter;
- The separation of the previous edition's combined chapter on negotiation and the collective agreement into two distinct chapters;
- A detailed examination in Chapter 12 of the expanded scope of grievance arbitration, such as the broader range of issues that arbitrators are now expected to consider; and
- A streamlining of the international and comparative industrial relations chapter (Chapter 13).

Like the two previous editions, the third edition provides a concluding chapter on key themes that tie the course together.

WHAT THE BOOK COVERS

- Chapter 1 (Introduction) discusses the importance of the world of work, defines the term "industrial relations," considers some of the most important industrial relations theories, and looks at five different perspectives on the employment relationship.

- Chapter 2 first considers the environmental contexts of the industrial relations system, with special attention paid to the economic environment, including recent labour force trends. The chapter then goes on to focus on management as an actor in the industrial relations system, paying attention to both the evolution of Canadian management practice and the identification and description of the various types of management industrial relations strategies currently practised.

- The three subsequent chapters deal with labour's role. Chapter 3 takes a historical perspective and offers a more in-depth treatment of Canadian labour history than many other industrial relations texts. Since the historical focus had been arguably both a strength and a weakness of previous editions, this edition amalgamates some of the historical analysis formerly spread throughout several chapters into one comprehensive chapter.

- Chapters 4 and 5 focus more specifically on the role and activities of unions. Chapter 4 examines union membership and density, some recent changes in composition of the Canadian labour movement, and the basic structure and function of Canadian unions and labour federations. Finally, the chapter considers the vexing issue of union democracy.

- Chapter 5, which deals with union actions and impacts, describes the range of actions in which unions engage in pursuit of their political and economic goals and how those actions have changed in recent years. The chapter goes on to consider unions' impacts on wages, productivity, and management of organizations before concluding with a discussion of their broader effects on Canadian society as a whole.

- The following group of chapters is devoted to the industrial relations system's legal aspects. Chapter 6 begins by introducing the concept of the common law of employment and discussing the protections afforded in this regime as compared to those afforded unionized employees. Employment legislation is discussed next, specifically employment standards, the statues that govern equity in employment, and the system used in Canada to regulate occupational health and safety.

- Chapter 7 deals with private sector labour relations legislation, describing its major functions and some of the interprovincial commonalities and variations. Card majority and mandatory vote certification systems are discussed as are the difficulties and controversies associated with definition of the bargaining unit and exclusion of employees from collective bargaining legislation.

- Chapter 8 considers collective bargaining and labour legislation in the public sector. A major focus here is the current state of public sector collective bargaining, which many have argued is in a state of profound crisis. The chapter also considers the evolution of public sector collective bargaining and some distinctive features of public sector labour relations legislation.

From here, it is a fairly natural progression to our next group of chapters, which deal with the bargaining process supported by public and private sector labour legislation, with the results of that process, and with the conflict that often arises during collective bargaining.

- Chapter 9 examines bargaining structures, which make up an important element of the environment in which bargaining takes place, and then goes on to examine the negotiation process itself. Preparations for bargaining, the four sub-processes of negotiations, various process innovations, the concept of a settlement zone, and the factors that affect unions' and employers' bargaining power are all discussed.

- Chapter 10 is devoted to an examination of collective agreements and provides an overview of the main types of collective agreement provisions as well as a brief analysis of what insight collective agreements can provide into the nature of the union–management relationship.

- No IR text would be complete without a discussion of strikes and lockouts—the most talked about, but perhaps least understood, aspect of the industrial relations system. Chapter 11 examines some trends in strike activity, discusses the significance of strikes in the Canadian industrial relations system, considers the causes of strikes and lockouts, and explains some of the policy measures used to control them; in addition, three recent Canadian strikes are described and analyzed.

- Chapter 12 considers grievances and features a detailed examination of an actual grievance case. A key element of this chapter is its discussion of major criticisms of the conventional grievance process and of alternatives to conventional arbitration, including expedited arbitration, grievance mediation, and preventive mediation. For the third edition, we have, as noted earlier under "Features," added a detailed examination of the expanded scope of arbitration.

- Chapter 13, the international chapter, features an examination of industrial relations systems in both developed and developing countries, and pays special attention to the changes these systems have been undergoing in recent years. In the third edition, special emphasis has been placed on the growing links between workers and workers' organizations in developed and developing countries and on publicity campaigns designed to draw attention to the plight of workers in the latter.

- Chapter 14, the book's conclusion, will "pull the pieces together." This chapter looks at the Canadian industrial relations system as a whole in the light of recent developments such as globalization, trade liberalization, and the growth of a contingent work force. This examination focuses on five key themes and some of the most important findings and policy suggestions related to those themes.

Although the book does not contain a separate chapter on Quebec, a discussion of key features of that province's quite distinctive industrial relations system, such as the extension of collective agreements to non-unionized firms through the decree system, has been incorporated into the text where appropriate.

PEDAGOGY

The book incorporates a number of practical learning aids that will assist in making the book's content clear and accessible to students and provide them with a range of resources to draw on.

- **Specific Learning Objectives** Each chapter starts with a list of learning objectives directly related to the key concepts presented in the chapter. These objectives serve to focus students' learning and assist instructors in developing assignments and exams.

- **Chapter Overview** Each chapter is preceded by an overview of the major topics covered in the chapter, again focusing students and also allowing instructors to easily determine the chapter's completeness and appropriateness for their particular course.

- **Key Terms** Key terms are highlighted within the text and defined in page margins. A complete glossary is also provided at the end of the text.

- **Current Issues Feature** These boxed inserts provide real-life, current illustrations of the principles and theories discussed in each chapter. Each Current Issues box is designed to bring industrial relations to life using examples from companies or labour disputes with which students will be familiar, or by detailing industrial relations issues that students may have read or heard about in the news.

- **End-of-Chapter Case** At the end of every chapter, a relevant case offers an alternative pedagogical approach to the subject matter. Most cases draw on real companies or cases, and many can serve as the basis for further student research and analysis. The end-of-case questions spotlight the key concepts illustrated in each case and lend themselves well to student assignments.

- **Questions for Further Discussion** The end-of-chapter questions are designed to focus on key concepts and encourage students to apply these concepts to real-life situations. Use of these questions for exams facilitates and focuses students' studying.

LEARNING OBJECTIVES

After studying this chapter, you should be able to:

1. Explain the overall significance of the world of work.
2. Discuss the interdisciplinary nature of the field of industrial relations (IR).
3. Identify and explain various definitions of IR.
4. Discuss some well-known theories of IR.
5. Describe five different perspectives on IR.

The first part of this chapter considers the significance of work in most Canadians' lives. After a brief discussion of the interdisciplinary nature of our field of study, some definitions for the term "industrial relations" (IR) are offered. A discussion of some of the best-known theories of industrial relations, including the systems framework and the strategic choice theory, follows. Five perspectives for the study of IR are examined, and the chapter concludes with a brief outline of what the rest of the book will cover.

---

strike A cessation of work by employees, in combination, in concert, or in accordance with a common understanding. May include a slowdown designed to restrict output.

Current Issues 1.1

SPIN-OFF EFFECTS: THE NHL LOCKOUT

As the National Hockey League lockout entered its fifth month with no end in sight, players and coaches weren't the only people suffering economically from the effects of the dispute. Many people who indirectly rely on the NHL for their bread and butter were also suffering.

For example, in Sherbrooke, Quebec, InGlasCo, the official supplier of the 300 000 or so pucks the NHL normally uses each year, was forced to lay off about half of its 40 employees. Explained Denis Drolet, president of InGlasCo's parent company, "We sell to teams, we sell to the retail side. Retailers have no reason to buy NHL product. They have no interest and no demand for it." Fortunately for InGlasCo and its remaining employees, the NHL makes up only half of the company's business. Minor and junior league teams make up the other half.

Nor is the puck supplier the only business that's suffering because of the lockout. The effects of the dispute are being felt as far away as Barbados. At Bert's Bar in Christ Church, a place where Ottawa Senators' owner has sometimes been known to hang out, business is down 10 percent. The reason? According to owner Bert Inniss, it's simply because, with no hockey games to watch on the satellite TV, vacationing Canadians and embassy staff aren't stopping in as much.

Closer to home, the Last Call liquor delivery service of Ottawa, which for a modest fee will bring booze to people's homes, is also reporting a decline in business, particularly on Saturday nights when *Hockey Night in Canada* would usually be broadcast. Owner Francis Butler says Saturday night calls are down 25 to 40 percent. What isn't clear is what hockey fans are doing instead of playing hockey—and drinking.

Sources: Adami, Hugh. (2005). "Tales from the Lockout," *Ottawa Citizen*, January 19, p. A1, column 1; Associated Press. (2005). "Feeling the Squeeze," January 16, from CNN website.

Case 2.1

WESTJET: A CANADIAN SUCCESS STORY

On February 29, 1996, WestJet airlines began operations out of Calgary with 220 employees, three aircraft, and routes to five cities in western Canada. Nine years later, WestJet has 4800 employees and 56 airplanes and operates scheduled flights to 32 North American cities, and charter flights to 26 destinations in eight countries. WestJet's CEO, Clive Beddoe, has been named one of Canada's most respected CEOs, and his company, which was named one of Calgary's best places to work and placed among Canada's Top 100 Employers, ranks as the country's best customer service organization and the second most respected company, behind only Royal Bank.

QUESTIONS FOR DISCUSSION

1. Visit the Canadian Autoworkers' (CAW) website and the Canadian website of the United Steelworkers. Take a look at the variety of causes the CAW's Social Justice Fund (SJW) and the Steelworkers' Humanity Fund support. What motivates these unions to put their time and money toward these causes?
2. At which points did Canadian union membership increase significantly? At which points did it decrease? What were the reasons?
3. Explain how and why the mix of men and women within Canadian unions has changed.
4. In which provinces is union membership highest? In which is it lowest? Explain the reasons for this variation.

- **Case Appendix** The Case Appendix provides additional case materials that focus on some emerging trends. Health and safety and human rights cases have been included, as well as labour board and arbitration cases addressing such topics as certification procedures for bargaining units composed mainly of part-time workers and the use of volunteers by non-profit organizations.

- **Annotated List of Websites** This list provides students with resources available on the Internet and describes some of the information available on government and union websites.

- **Glossary** A glossary provides a list of the principal key terms and definitions used in the text and commonly used in the industrial relations field.

> ### Annotated List of Websites Related to Labour and Employment
>
> **Canadian Sites**
>
> Statistics Canada
>
> (www.statcan.ca) If what you're after is basic economic and employment-related data, this is an excellent and very user-friendly site. The home page gives you the choice of an alphabetical index or a subject-related index. From there, it's easy to obtain basic data on such subjects as the unemployment and inflation rates, the labour force, earnings, and the incidence of full-time and part-time work. You can also, without much difficulty, find information on employment by industry or occupation and comparative international data on strikes and lockouts.
>
> If you're looking for more detailed information or for historical data, the site becomes more problematic. In recent years, Statistics Canada has begun to operate on a "cost-recovery" basis, which means, in plainer English, that you have to pay for much of the data the agency has to offer. If you aren't careful, a search could end up costing you quite a bit of money. For historical data, you are best advised to start by consulting Statistics Canada's collection of hard-copy publications.

SUPPLEMENTS

Canadian Industrial Relations is accompanied by a comprehensive supplements package.

Instructor's Resource CD-ROM (ISBN 0-13-204316-5)

This resource CD includes the following instructor supplements:

Instructor's Resource Manual with Video Guide This comprehensive guide contains a detailed lecture outline of each chapter, suggested answers to discussion questions, and helpful case notes. The manual also provides video cases, discussion questions, and teaching notes, linking the video segments to chapter content.

Pearson TestGen The Pearson TestGen is a special computerized version of the Test Item File that enables instructors to view and edit the testbank questions, generate tests, and print the tests in a variety of formats. Powerful search and sort functions make it easy to locate questions and arrange them in any order desired. TestGen also enables instructors to administer tests on a local area network, have the tests graded electronically, and have the results prepared in electronic or printed reports. Issued on a CD-ROM, the Pearson TestGen is compatible with IBM and Macintosh systems.

PowerPoint Slides A collection of over 300 slides, culled from the textbook or specifically designed to complement chapter content, is also available electronically in PowerPoint format on the Instructor's Resource CD-ROM.

These instructor supplements, offered on CD-ROM, are also available for download from a password protected section of Pearson Education Canada's online catalogue (http://vig.pearsoned.ca). Navigate to your book's catalogue page to view a list of the supplements that are available. See your local sales representative for details and access.

CBC/Pearson Education Canada Video Library (VHS: ISBN 0-13-149445-7; DVD: ISBN 0-13-228627-0)

Pearson Education Canada and the CBC have worked together to bring you segments from the CBC series *Venture* and *The National*. Designed specifically to complement the text, this case collection is an excellent tool for bringing students in contact with the world outside the classroom. These programs have extremely high production quality and have been chosen to relate directly to chapter content. Teaching notes are provided in the Instructor's Resource Manual with Video Guide. Please contact your Pearson Education Canada sales representative for details.

ACKNOWLEDGMENTS

As was the case with the first two editions, Pearson staff have been extremely helpful throughout the long and sometimes difficult process of preparing this third edition. The authors are grateful to James Bosma for his wise guidance in developing the second edition and for his help in bringing Karen Bentham on board for the third, and to Acquisitions Editor Karen Elliott for her continued support. We would also like to acknowledge the valuable contributions made by Laura Price, Production Editor, and Trish O'Reilly, Copy Editor. Our greatest thanks go to Developmental Editor Pam Voves, who has at various times played the role of literary critic, den mother, psychologist, and confessor—always with encouragement and good grace. Without her friendly assistance and gentle perseverance throughout the revision process, it is unlikely that this third edition would have seen the light of day.

We would also like to acknowledge the help of the staff at the Public Service Labour Relations Board library, particularly Head Librarian Margo Jeske, who provided invaluable research assistance. Karen would also like to extend her sincere appreciation to the Librarians at the University of Toronto, Centre for Industrial Relations library, especially Bruce Pearce, whose patience, persistence, and research expertise are second to none.

Reviewer Acknowledgments

The authors would like to thank the following reviewers for their feedback: Danielle Baker, George Brown College; Dan Cameron, University of Regina; J.J. Collins, St. Clair College of Applied Arts and Technology; Rob Dawson, Nipissing University; John Fakouri, Algonquin College; Doug Fletcher, Kwantlen University College; Eleanor Gallant, University of Prince Edward Island; Thomas R. Knight, University of British Columbia; Joseph B. Rose, DeGroote School of Business; Ian Sakinofsky, Ryerson University; Carol Ann Samhaber, Algonquin College; Lynne Siemens, Malaspina University College; Craig Stephenson, Mohawk College. These reviewers' comments have done much to strengthen this book. Naturally, we assume sole responsibility for any errors that remain.

J.P. and K.B.
Ottawa and Toronto, August 2005

CHAPTER 1

INTRODUCTION TO INDUSTRIAL RELATIONS

Today's Canadian workforce includes a large number of women and members of ethnic minority groups.

LEARNING OBJECTIVES

After studying this chapter, you should be able to:

1. Explain the overall significance of the world of work.
2. Discuss the interdisciplinary nature of the field of industrial relations (IR).
3. Identify and explain various definitions of IR.
4. Discuss some well-known theories of IR.
5. Describe five different perspectives on IR.

The first part of this chapter considers the significance of work in most Canadians' lives. After a brief discussion of the interdisciplinary nature of our field of study, some definitions for the term "industrial relations" (IR) are offered. A discussion of some of the best-known theories of industrial relations, including the systems framework and the strategic choice theory, follows. Five perspectives for the study of IR are examined, and the chapter concludes with a brief outline of what the rest of the book will cover.

THE SIGNIFICANCE OF WORK

Welcome to the study of industrial relations!

Industrial relations is about the world of work: its joys and sorrows, its satisfactions and frustrations. The importance of work in the lives of most Canadians is immense. Most of us spend about one-quarter of our time working, which is more than we spend doing anything else, except sleeping. Through work, we seek to live our dreams and realize our ambitions. To a large extent, our adult identity is shaped by the work we do and the jobs we hold. We meet many of our friends at work; a good many of us meet our life partners there. A fulfilling job, working among congenial people in pleasant surroundings, can be the source of immense satisfaction. By the same token, unfulfilling work performed in the company of people one finds indifferent or hostile can be the source of such intense frustration that it can affect one's mental health. And as we see in Chapter 6, work can also pose physical risks.

Landing a job is often an occasion for celebration. Losing one can lead to feelings of inadequacy, guilt, or anger that can last for months or even years. Those people who don't have jobs—for whatever reason—often feel like second-class citizens who aren't contributing to society. Work is addictive to some, so much so that they feel more comfortable at the plant or the office than at home. Even when they're supposed to be on vacation, such people try to maintain constant connection with their work through faxes, long-distance phone calls, or email. Others develop such strong attachment to their work and to their places of work that when they retire (especially if the retirement has been abrupt or involuntary), they find themselves unable to cope with the separation. It isn't uncommon for these retirees to suffer heart attacks or develop severe depression.

Work's economic impact is equally important. The majority of Canadians—except for those lucky few who inherit fortunes or draw winning lottery tickets—derive almost all their income from work-based earnings. Those who lose their jobs generally suffer severely reduced buying power, despite the existence of social support programs like Employment Insurance (EI). When a large number of people in the same community lose their jobs, as when a plant closes or relocates, that community's very existence may be imperilled.

At an even more basic level, work is essential to produce the goods and services, like food, housing, telephone service, and electric power, on which we all depend. If people didn't work, or hadn't worked in the past, such goods and services wouldn't be available for our use. When work is interrupted, whether because of a labour dispute or because of a natural disaster like a fire, power blackout, or ice storm, the disruption of people's daily lives can be severe.

Current Issues 1.1

SPIN-OFF EFFECTS: THE NHL LOCKOUT

As the 2004–5 National Hockey League lockout entered its fifth month with no end in sight, players and coaches weren't the only people suffering economically from the effects of the dispute. Many people who indirectly rely on the NHL for their bread and butter were also suffering. ▶

For example, in Sherbrooke, Quebec, InGlasCo, the official supplier of the 300 000 or so pucks the NHL normally uses each year, was forced to lay off about half of its 40 employees. Denis Drolet, president of InGlasCo's parent company, explained that demand for their product had dropped precipitously due to the lockout: "We sell to teams, we sell to the retail side. Retailers have no reason to buy NHL product. They have no interest and no demand for it." Fortunately for InGlasCo and its remaining employees, the NHL makes up only half of the company's business. Minor and junior league teams make up the other half.

Nor is the puck supplier the only business that's suffering because of the lockout. The effects of the dispute are being felt as far away as Barbados. At Bert's Bar in Christ Church, a place where Ottawa Senators' owner Eugene Melnyk has sometimes been known to hang out, business is down 10 percent. The reason? According to owner Bert Inniss, it's simply because, with no hockey games to watch on the satellite TV, vacationing Canadians and embassy staff aren't stopping in as much.

Closer to home, the Last Call liquor delivery service of Ottawa, which for a modest fee will bring booze to people's homes, is also reporting a decline in business, particularly on Saturday nights when *Hockey Night in Canada* would usually be broadcast. Owner Francis Butler says Saturday night calls are down 25 to 40 percent. What isn't clear is what hockey fans are doing instead of playing hockey—and drinking.

Sources: Adami, Hugh. (2005). "Tales from the Lockout," *Ottawa Citizen*, January 19, p. A1, column 1; Associated Press. (2005). "Feeling the Squeeze," January 16, from CNN website.

The Changing World of Work

Of late, the world of work has been changing quite dramatically. Until quite recently, most jobs in Canada were full-time and full-year. Most people worked on a regular schedule—typically from 9 to 5, Monday through Friday. Once you found a job, you could generally expect to keep it for a while, assuming that your performance and attendance remained satisfactory. Many people stayed with one employer, or at most two or three, throughout their entire working lives. While changes in occupation weren't unknown, they were the exception rather than the rule.

Today, far too many people are working part-time, often in coffee shops like this one, because it is the only work they can find.

Over the past quarter century, the incidence of "atypical" forms of employment has increased dramatically. These include regular part-time work; casual work; work done on a short-term contractual basis; work performed at home rather than on the employer's premises; and self-employment.[1]

These atypical employment patterns have increased so much that, according to the most recent Statistics Canada data, barely a majority of Canadian workers work under "standard" arrangements. Such dramatically shifting work patterns pose a major challenge for individual workers, for the unions that represent or seek to represent their interests, and for public policy makers responsible for regulating working conditions. The Canadian workforce has been changing no less dramatically. Once predominantly male and almost all white, our workforce now reflects the diversity of a country with a multicultural population. About 46 percent of all Canadian workers are women, and the country's workforce includes people from many different ethnic and religious backgrounds.

An increasing number of women are balancing work and family responsibilities. Between 1978 and 2003, the proportion of women participating in the labour force increased from 45 percent to just under 62 percent.

Our workforce also includes people with varying types and degrees of physical and mental disabilities. This new, more diverse workforce has also brought new challenges to unions and policy makers, but especially to employers. For a variety of reasons (some of which are the result of recent legislation), employers are under increasing pressure to provide various physical facilities, like wheelchair-accessible entrances, to meet the needs of workers with physical disabilities; to provide same-sex medical benefits to meet the needs of gay and lesbian couples; or to provide flexible work schedules to meet the needs of single parents or members of religious minorities. As we will see in more detail in Chapters 10 and 12, this "duty to accommodate" is now increasingly considered in negotiating collective agreements.

Few young people entering today's work world can realistically expect to stay with one employer, or even one occupation, throughout their entire careers, as many of their parents and grandparents did. The traditional "implicit contract" whereby the employer provides employees with job security in return for their loyalty and continuing commitment has, for the most part, been rescinded. This has its advantages and disadvantages: On the one hand, people who frequently change employers or occupations may be less apt to become bored and may achieve more job satisfaction than people who stay in the same place for many years. On the other hand, there is no question that today's increasingly fluid arrangements breed considerable insecurity.[2] As well, generating loyalty and commitment from workers becomes extremely difficult when few of these workers have any assurance that they will still be on the payroll in six months' time.

WHAT IS INDUSTRIAL RELATIONS?

Industrial relations is an interdisciplinary subject. It draws on fields as diverse as economics, law, history, business management, political science, psychology, and sociology in analyzing, and proposing solutions for, workplace problems (Dunlop, 1958).

A simple example may help illustrate why many different academic disciplines are necessary to study problems arising out of the world of work. Let's suppose we're trying to explain why union membership rates are higher in Canada than in the United States. (This isn't simply a hypothetical exercise. Union-growth analysts have been trying to get at this question for many years.) What "tools" would we need to answer this question?

Union growth is clearly related to broad trends in the economy, like unemployment and inflation. Obviously, anyone looking at the question would need to have some understanding of economics. But this only gets us part of the way. In recent years, union membership rates in Canada and the United States have diverged quite sharply, despite generally similar economic conditions. Clearly, we need more than economics to answer the question fully.

Legislation regarding how unions are certified and who is allowed to join unions can have an important effect on membership rates. If, for example, one government allows unions to become certified through a simple count of signed membership cards while another requires a formal vote, membership rates will likely be higher under the first government, because it's more difficult for a union to become certified where there is a formal election process. Since the United States (where private sector labour legislation is under federal jurisdiction) requires a vote and many Canadian jurisdictions allow certification through signed membership cards, membership rates will likely be higher in Canada, other things being equal (see Figure 1.1). In addition, some governments allow most workers, other than managers, to join unions; while other governments may exclude members of specific groups, like professionals, domestics, and agricultural workers. Other things being equal, the jurisdiction that allows a greater number of occupational groups of

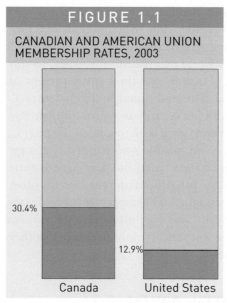

FIGURE 1.1

CANADIAN AND AMERICAN UNION MEMBERSHIP RATES, 2003

30.4%

12.9%

Canada   United States

Source: for Canada, *Workplace Gazette*, 7:3 (2004); for U.S., drawn from the Web site of Department of Labor's Bureau of Workplace Statistics.

workers to belong to unions is likely to have significantly higher union-membership rates (Peirce, 1989). Since American law, as currently interpreted, excludes more potential union members than Canadian law, our country's membership rates again should be higher.

In addition, different political arrangements may be more or less conducive to union growth. Union-growth analysts have generally found that rates go up when a labour or social democratic government is in power and down when a conservative government holds sway (Maki, 1982; Bruce, 1989). Indeed, a labour-oriented party can influence union membership growth even from a balance-of-power or strong opposition position. In Canada, threat of defeat by the CCF party, which was the forerunner to the NDP, was a primary factor inducing Prime Minister Mackenzie King to introduce *PC 1003*, the bill first granting collective bargaining rights to Canadian workers (Morton, 1995). Without such a political party, the possibility of using the political arena to enhance union growth is significantly diminished. The fact that Canada does have such a party (the NDP), while the United States doesn't, arguably contributes to higher membership rates here (Meltz, 1985; Bruce, 1989). So does Canada's multiparty parliamentary system, which has made it much easier for a party like the NDP to get started here than it would be in the United States (Bruce, 1989).

History also plays a role, as well as law and political science. In regions where there is a history of strong, positive labour organizations, unions are likely to have an easier time recruiting new members than in regions lacking such a history. Since union membership involves a group dynamic, the values attached by a given community to union membership may also play a role. Those communities in which union membership is looked on favourably will likely see better success in organizing drives than those where a more individualistic ethic prevails, like high-tech communities. Here, the study of sociology will prove helpful, and psychology is useful in determining what motivates some individuals to join unions, but not others (Kervin, 1988).

Depending on the industrial relations issue we're looking at, many other academic disciplines could come into play. For example, a knowledge of literature would be helpful in analyzing the writings of working people (often an important source of IR knowledge). A knowledge of music and folklore could be very useful in studying work songs, which in turn may offer some important clues to the work process in a given occupation or community (Seeger, 1972). Today, a knowledge of ergonomics could prove extremely useful in understanding contemporary health and safety issues, like the growing incidence of carpal tunnel syndrome among grocery cashiers and secretaries.

Industrial relations is obviously a subject requiring many different kinds of knowledge. To many (including the authors), this is one of the field's enduring fascinations. To others (Laffer, 1974), it is a source of frustration, as is the apparent lack of a single, overarching theory (Heneman, 1969), comparable to, for example, the law of supply and demand in economics. The debate over what the field of industrial relations should include has been raging for some time and seems unlikely to end soon. Suffice it to say that, for now, experience suggests the world of work isn't always a neat and tidy place, and that attempts to analyze it as if it were are probably doomed to fail.

Defining Industrial Relations

How should we define "industrial relations"? A possible starting point might be, "the relations between unions and management." That is all right, as far as it goes. Union–management relations *are* at the core of our field. But as we will soon see, and as some of you may have sensed already, the field takes in a good deal more than that.

To begin with, union–management relations in Canada, as in most other industrialized countries, are conducted within a legislative framework devised by government—in this case, both provincial and federal governments, since both have jurisdiction over various aspects of the IR system. Any definition of IR that fails to take governments' role into account is seriously deficient. It's also inaccurate to confine any definition to the unionized part of the workforce. Fewer than one-third of all Canadian workers are union members. We can't simply fail to consider the remaining two-thirds.

In a broader sense, the IR system affects the lives of almost all Canadians, including those who aren't themselves workers, such as children or retired people. If a private-sector firm undergoes a **strike**, not only are its employees, managers, and their families affected, so are its customers, its suppliers, and not infrequently the entire community in which the firm is located. This is particularly true if that firm happens to be the community's only employer or one of its major ones. In the case of a public sector dispute involving groups like transit workers or sanitation workers, the entire community may feel the effects very quickly, particularly if the service that the striking workers normally provide is one for which there is no readily available substitute. In the case of a big-city transit strike, even people who normally drive to work will be affected because many of those who can't take the subway will also be driving, making traffic heavier and progress slower.

strike A cessation of work by employees, in combination, in concert, or in accordance with a common understanding. May include a slowdown designed to restrict output.

Clearly, then, a broad definition is needed if we are to take into account all the ways in which the IR system affects people: as workers or managers, as taxpayers, and as consumers. We have not seen a better definition of IR than the one put forward by Thomas Kochan (1980:1): "All aspects of the employment relationship."[3] Almost every other definition—and there are a good many—leaves out one or more important aspects.

To be sure, other disciplines also deal with the world of work. These disciplines include, among others, organizational behaviour (OB), human resource management (HRM), sociology, labour economics, and labour studies. Where industrial relations differs from other disciplines is in what Noah Meltz (1989a) describes as its concern for balancing efficiency and equity, the interests of management and those of workers, as well as its interdisciplinary approach. Thus, while OB and HRM courses tend to take a pro-management approach, and labour studies courses take a pro-labour and often pro-union approach, IR courses seek to make students aware of the needs and interests of both workers and management. While labour economics courses focus on the economic aspects of work, and sociology courses focus on the behavioural and psychic aspects, IR courses treat the different aspects of work as interrelated. In these ways, industrial relations has a valuable, perhaps even unique, contribution to make to the study of work-related issues.[4]

THEORIES OF INDUSTRIAL RELATIONS
Dunlop's Systems Theory

As noted previously, few industrial relations experts would maintain that the field possesses a single, strong explanatory theory. Nonetheless, there have been several attempts at developing such a theory. The most important of these theories is that of John Dunlop (1958). Dunlop (1958:5) defines an **industrial relations system** as "an analytical subsystem of an industrial society." In his view, the IR system is equally as important as the economic subsystem, but not a part of it. This will be an important point to remember throughout this book, especially when we begin to consider elements of behaviour, like certain types of strikes, that appear to be economically irrational. As we shall soon see, actors in the IR system may and often do have concerns beyond purely economic ones. Economic theory (Dunlop, 1958:5) can't be expected to explain all aspects of these concerns, though it can explain some of them. While there are areas of overlap between the economic and IR subsystems, there are some aspects of the IR system (such as elements of workplace rule making) that fall outside the scope of the economic subsystem.

At any one time, says Dunlop (1958:7), an IR system comprises certain actors, certain contexts, a body or web of rules governing the actors' workplace behaviour, and a common ideology binding the system together. The actors include managers, workers and their representatives, and government or specialized private agencies (e.g., arbitration panels) appointed by workers and management to handle certain aspects of their relationship. The workers may be unionized or not. It is their job to do the work, following instructions given to them by management, whose job is to provide such instructions (Dunlop, 1958). Government's primary interest is as a peacekeeper and rule maker, though within the public sector government also wears a second hat as employer. The complications resulting from government's dual role here will be discussed in more detail in the public sector chapter (Chapter 8).

The contexts within which the actors operate include market (economic), technical, and power (political) ones. To a considerable extent, these contexts determine the balance of power between the two most important actors (workers and management). Changes in these contexts are likely to produce shifts in that balance of power. Each of the contexts has its greatest impact on a subset of the rules. For example, the market context affects pay and benefit levels, while the power context

industrial relations system An "analytical subsystem of an industrial society" (John Dunlop) governing individuals' workplace behaviour.

affects legislation governing union **certification** and strike procedures (Anderson and Gunderson, 1982).

Web of Rules

The web of rules includes substantive rules regarding system outcomes such as pay, benefits, hours of work, and workplace safety, and procedural rules on such matters as collective bargaining, grievance procedures, and transfer or promotion procedures (Dunlop, 1958; Anderson and Gunderson, 1982). For the most part, labour relations legislation (discussed in Chapter 7), or the web of rules established to govern behaviour in unionized workplaces, is of a procedural nature. On the one hand, the assumption here is that as long as the parties are placed on a relatively level playing field through the establishment of appropriate procedures for collective bargaining, the handling of impasses, and the like, they'll negotiate better outcomes than the government could. On the other hand, employment standards legislation (discussed in Chapter 6), or the web of rules applied to all workers but of particular importance in non-unionized establishments, does prescribe certain outcomes. These include minimum wages, maximum hours of work, minimum vacation entitlements, and safety regulations governing the maximum permissible level of discharge of certain substances into the air or water.

It's customary to speak of these two sets of rules as separate entities, and to a large extent they are indeed distinct from one another. At the same time, the two complement each other in some important ways. To begin with, employment standards legislation applies to all workplaces (unionized as well as non-unionized). It is, therefore, illegal for a union and an employer to negotiate any terms and conditions poorer than those provided in employment standards legislation (e.g., a wage below the provincial minimum). Employment standards legislation thus serves as the floor on which collective bargaining can begin. Unions also have an important role to play in enforcing employment legislation in the workplace, in educating workers about their rights under this legislation, and in enhancing minimum legislated standards through the collective bargaining process. Again, these points are discussed in more detail in Chapter 6.

The notion of a common ideology between the actors in the IR system has led to some confusion and a fair amount of debate. By "ideology" Dunlop (1958:16–17) means "a body of common ideas that defines the role and place of each actor and that defines the ideas which each actor holds toward the place and function of the others in the system." He further suggests (1958:17) that "[t]he ideology or philosophy of a stable system involves a congruence or compatibility among these views and the rest of the system." What has never been clear is just how far the idea of a "common ideology" should be taken. It would probably be fair to say that most North American employers and workers share a common preference for a democratic, capitalist system of government, rather than a totalitarian one like Communism or fascism. This assumption doesn't, however, take us very far towards understanding the extent to which workplace conflict would be restrained or modified as a result of that common ideology. Confusion about this point and various others has led to a number of criticisms of the systems framework over the years.

certification The process through which a union is designated the sole and exclusive bargaining agent for a given group of workers, normally by a labour relations board or some similar government agency.

Criticisms of the Systems Framework

Dunlop's systems framework offers useful insights into the interdisciplinary nature of industrial relations. It also offers a convenient introductory approach to the study of foreign IR systems with which a researcher is unfamiliar. By looking at the actors, the contexts in which they operate, and the web of rules governing the actors' behaviour, one can learn a good deal about such systems.

In many other ways, however, the systems framework has proved disappointing. Dunlop (1958:6) had anticipated that his approach would provide IR with a theoretical core and turn it into "a genuine discipline." While most industrial relationists today would probably agree that IR is a genuine discipline, few would agree that the systems framework has provided a theoretical core that can generate testable research hypotheses. As Anderson and Gunderson (1982:5) note, the most common criticism has been that it is "only a taxonomy which has resulted in descriptive rather than explanatory research."

Another problem is that, by viewing the IR subsystem in at least relative isolation (1958:2), Dunlop tends to minimize the importance of various environmental inputs beyond the three contexts he identifies. But the most serious problem with the systems framework has to do with the role of conflict. Granted, Dunlop doesn't ignore the role of conflict; indeed, he suggests that at times, when the actors don't share a common ideology (1958:17), the system will lack stability and may require major changes. He doesn't, however, distinguish between relatively positive or "cathartic" conflict, of the type that can be worked out through collective bargaining and other such activities, and destructive or dysfunctional conflict, which could impair or even permanently destroy the actors' relationship. Dunlop also doesn't indicate to what extent conflict is inherent within the employment relationship—or, for that matter, if any kind of conflict at all is inherent. This seems a serious omission, particularly given that his view of the employment relationship is an extremely traditional one in which managers give orders and workers execute them. More generally, Dunlop seems to assume that IR systems possess a greater degree of stability than most actually do. His inadequate treatment of conflict has been criticized by earlier writers like Singh (1976) and by more recent ones like Kochan, McKersie, and Cappelli (1984).

Some of the problems just noted were solved when Alton Craig (1967, 1986) put Dunlop's model into more conventional systems form with the use of an input-output framework and a feedback loop (Anderson and Gunderson, 1982:6). Among other things, the input-output framework allows for the use of a broader range of inputs. It also provides a fuller representation of the inputs' role in shaping the IR system's outputs, through various conversion processes, and helps to show the system's connection to and interdependence with other systems instead of representing it in isolation as Dunlop does. Finally, on the important question of conflict, Craig is somewhat more explicit than Dunlop. By identifying the **grievance** process, strikes, and **lockouts** as conversion processes, and the latter two also as system outputs, Craig (1986) indicates that some degree of conflict is inherent in the IR system, but that much of it can be worked out through the system's normal operations.

While in many ways an improvement on Dunlop's original framework, Craig's model (see Figure 1.2) isn't without its own problems. To begin with, Craig pays little attention to the role of management. Profit, market share, and the good or service being produced aren't even listed as outputs. The only "organizational" outputs

grievance An allegation by either party (union or management) that the other has violated the collective agreement.

lockout Closing of a place of employment or a suspension of work by an employer done to compel employees to agree to terms or conditions of employment.

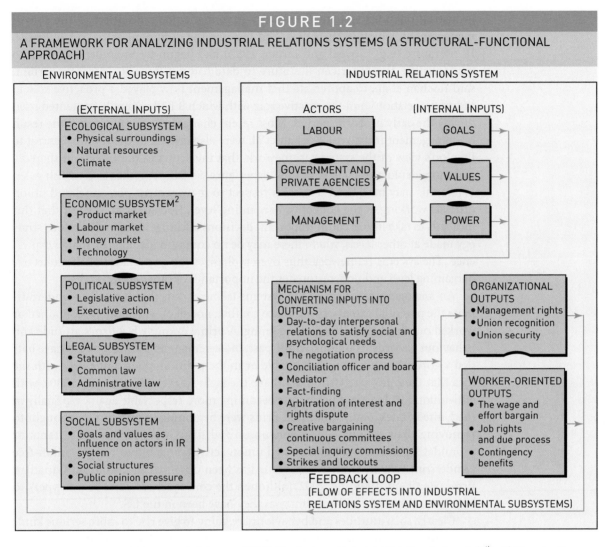

FIGURE 1.2

A FRAMEWORK FOR ANALYZING INDUSTRIAL RELATIONS SYSTEMS (A STRUCTURAL-FUNCTIONAL APPROACH)

Source: Craig, Alton J. and Norman A. Solomon. (1996). *The System of Industrial Relations in Canada* (5th ed.). Toronto: Pearson Education Canada.

listed are collective agreement provisions. Second, although Craig doesn't explicitly limit his model to unionized workplaces, almost all his conversion processes and system outputs presuppose a collective bargaining process, severely limiting the model's applicability in non-unionized settings. Implicitly at least, the model appears to presuppose a strategy of union acceptance on the part of management. Third, although again Craig isn't explicit on this point, the model appears to assume that most workplace conflict can be contained within, if not worked out through, the IR system. Developments in the past quarter century have cast increasing doubt on such an assumption.

The Strategic Choice Theory

The "**strategic choice**" perspective on industrial relations arose out of concerns of Thomas Kochan and his associates (Kochan et al., 1984) that the then-dominant

strategic choice framework (or theory) An industrial relations theory developed in the US by Thomas Kochan and his associates that stresses the linkages between a firm's industrial relations and human resources policies and strategies and its overall competitive strategies, and distinguishes three levels of industrial relations activity.

industrial relations systems framework gave inadequate attention to the role of management, which in their view had become the dominant actor. While British IR literature (e.g., Gospel and Littler, 1982) had begun to pay more attention to management, the American literature to date had not done so. It was important, said Kochan et al., to appreciate that management now played a proactive role in industrial relations, not the reactive role with which it had generally contented itself during the early post-war period. Most recent changes, they argued, were the result of management initiatives. Kochan et al. were also critical of the notion, central to Dunlop's view of the systems framework, that the actors in the IR system shared a common ideology as a result of their experience working together to establish rules. While this may have been true with respect to management personnel and union officials working at the collective bargaining level, Kochan et al. suggest that this idea fails to take into account important decisions affecting industrial relations strategy made at other levels, where there may be no common ideology or shared experience. The systems framework thus overemphasizes the importance of the collective bargaining level and underestimates the importance of other levels.

An analogous criticism of the systems framework is that it tends to underestimate the potential extent of workplace conflict, not all of which can be contained or worked out through collective bargaining. A prime example is a firm's attitude and behaviour towards its unions. In the past, management and unions might have battled vigorously at the bargaining table or in the political arena, but rarely with the idea that the other party shouldn't have the right to exist. By the early 1980s, with anti-union ideology and behaviour becoming more respectable again, especially in the United States, many unionized firms were beginning to give serious thought to removing their unions, while non-unionized firms were hiring consultants or intimidating and harassing suspected union activists in a bid to remain union-free (Anderson, 1989a). Similar behaviour has been observed in unionized Canadian firms (Bentham, 1999 and 2002), although the consequences don't as yet appear to have been as serious in this country as they have been in the US.

Clearly, such attitudes and behaviour are going to give rise to more serious kinds of conflict than simple bargaining-table disputes over wages,[5] and it is no longer possible to assume that the IR system will be able to effectively resolve this kind of conflict. Collective bargaining is the IR system's main mechanism for resolving conflict; however, by their actions, the managements of the organizations in question have indicated their unwillingness, if not their outright refusal, to engage in the process. In such circumstances, it becomes extremely difficult to speak of any sort of "shared ideology" between management and unions.

Kochan and his associates were also concerned that industrial relations developments had, in the past, generally been considered in isolation from other developments within unions, governments, and especially within firms.[6] Thus, a key element of the strategic choice theory is that industrial relations and human resources policies and strategies are not made in isolation, most especially not in isolation from firms' overall competitive strategies. The human resource strategies a firm follows and the stance it takes towards unions, for example, are directly related to such strategic decisions as what product line it will enter or remain in, where it will establish new plants, and in what type of new technology it will invest. To help readers visualize such linkages, Kochan et al. propose a three-level industrial relations strategy matrix (1984:23) comprising a macro or global level, an employment relationship or collective bargaining level, and a workplace or shop-floor level. The matrix outlines the nature of the IR-related decisions to be made by all three main actors (employers, unions, and government). The authors hypothesize (36) that more effective and lasting changes will occur when there is consistency in strategies across the three levels and a match between the strategies of different actors. Instability is more likely to occur when strategies at different levels are inconsistent.

Another key element of the strategic choice model is that environmental contexts affect the range of strategic options available to management, and this range of options will be further constrained by management's values, beliefs, and ideologies. These values, beliefs, and ideologies differ between organizations but within an organization, they tend to be relatively stable over time. Indeed, the policies and practices that embody them tend to become institutionalized and somewhat self-fulfilling. Only when environment pressures grow sufficiently strong will management question and adapt their values, beliefs, and ideologies. Thus, management practices are characterized by long periods of relative stability periodically interrupted by major transformation. While the framework can apply to unions and governments as well as management, it is of particular importance in explaining management behaviour.

Strategic Choice in Canada

Dunlop's systems framework continues to have some applicability within a comparative context; however, the strategic choice theory seems to offer a fuller and more accurate explanation of recent North American developments. Since the strategic choice theory was developed specifically to address observed industrial relations changes in the United States, opinions diverge regarding its applicability to Canada, partially due to the fact that fewer Canadian employers have aggressively pursued consistent strategies aimed at resisting, avoiding, or replacing unions. However, this is most likely not because Canadian employers' attitudes toward unions are dramatically different. Rather, contextual and environmental differences affect the suitability and feasibility of various strategies for many employers.

One of the most important environmental differences is the existence, in the United States, of virtual "union-free" zones, particularly in the South and West. These zones were created as a result of the "right-to-work" provisions of the 1947 **Taft-Hartley** amendments to the *National Labor Relations Act*, which allowed any state that so wished to opt out of union security provisions. From a strategic perspective the existence of "**right-to-work states**" has made union-replacement strategies, a viable option for US employers. In addition, even employers not immediately seeking to drive their unions out can always use the threat of relocation to extract greater concessions at the bargaining table. Lacking the equivalent of a union-free, low-wage zone, Canadian employers have historically found it far more difficult to use union-replacement strategies. The generally stricter Canadian labour board enforcement of unfair labour practice legislation (Bruce, 1990) also makes such strategies more problematic for Canadian employers.

Another important difference is the existence in Canada—in large measure as the result of past efforts of the labour movement and its political allies—of publicly funded medical care and various social programs, including a more generous

Taft-Hartley Act Legislation, passed in the US in 1947 as a series of amendments to the Wagner Act, which severely limited the powers of the American labour movement. The most significant feature was the "right-to-work" provision, which allowed states to outlaw union security provisions.

right-to-work states States which have passed legislation banning union security provisions. Most such states are in the southern or midwestern US.

employment insurance program. Canada's more generous social safety net has arguably allowed Canadian unions to resist employer demands for concessions more firmly than their American counterparts realistically can, thereby making concession bargaining likelier in the United States than here.[7]

PERSPECTIVES ON INDUSTRIAL RELATIONS

Another reason to question Dunlop's notion of a shared ideology within the IR system is the existence of a number of different perspectives among industrial relations scholars and practitioners (Anderson, Gunderson, and Ponak, 1989; Godard, 1994). Even within unions or management organizations, different individuals may hold different views on key issues. The five perspectives we'll be discussing apply to such things as the individual's primary research focus, the importance individuals attach to unions, the extent to which a person believes conflict is inherent in the IR system, and the individual's location on the political spectrum (right to left). While, as Godard notes (1994:26), not all industrial relationists can be consistently identified with one of the five perspectives, these perspectives nonetheless help to highlight differing opinions within the field on such issues as the role of unions or the appropriate managerial policies to follow to maximize efficiency and productivity. They will thus be useful throughout the book.

Neoclassical Perspective

Strictly speaking, the right-wing neoclassical perspective is more of a pure economics perspective than an IR perspective. Indeed, the discipline of industrial relations really began in North America as a result of the University of Wisconsin's John R. Commons' recognition that neoclassical economics was inadequate for explaining real-life problems such as poverty and unemployment and for providing practical solutions to those problems. Throughout the post-war period, few if any leading Canadian industrial relationists adopted the neoclassical perspective, though with the return of competitive labour markets and the ascendancy of the political right in recent years, there have been an increasing number of attempts to apply elements of that perspective to the IR system (Peirce, 1996). Generally, a desire to increase competitiveness has been the rationale behind such attempts. The neoclassical approach has been more popular in the United States, where, in recent years, it has been adopted by such prominent writers as Leo Troy (1992).

Neoclassicists believe, above all else, in the free and unfettered operation of markets, especially labour markets (Ehrenberg and Smith, 1985). In their view, the labour–management relationship is, in the words of John Godard (1994:27), "a free and equal exchange between two parties with different yet compatible interests." Neoclassicists also believe that managers should have unfettered authority to run their enterprises as they see fit. If workers don't like the way management is running the enterprise, they are always free to quit and find a job more to their liking. Members of this school have little or no use for unions, which they view as organizations that can only increase inefficiency and unemployment by raising wages above the "equilibrium point" at which labour markets clear and there is full employment. Those adopting the "**coercive drive**" **approach** to management, discussed in more detail in Chapter 2, are generally of a neoclassical persuasion and tend to take what Adell (1988a) has described as a "unitary" or "unchained entrepreneurship" perspective on labour law.

Within IR, neoclassicists' primary research focus is on labour markets. Logically enough, since they believe that unions and the government agencies that regulate them shouldn't exist in the first place, they tend to have little or no interest in the practical workings of these organizations. Their research tends to be highly quantitative and statistical, to make heavy use of large databases, and to focus on such issues as unions' impact on wages (Anderson et al., 1989). For the most part, members of this school tend not to concern themselves with questions of conflict, since they believe all such questions can be resolved through the operation of market forces (Godard, 1994:27).

Managerial Perspective

While the neoclassical perspective is closely linked to the discipline of economics, the managerial one is related to organizational behaviour. It arose out of the work of such varied people as F.W. Taylor and Elton Mayo (Gunderson and Ponak, 1995). Many working in personnel and human resource departments take this perspective.

Managerialists' main concern is the motivation of workers, both individually and in small groups. They believe that properly motivated workers will be more productive. Unlike the neoclassicists, they seek to motivate through positive incentives rather than through fear. However, they tend to be, at best, ambivalent towards unions, many viewing unionization as a sort of failure on the part of management. Where unions exist already, they'll often seek to establish a co-operative relationship (Gunderson and Ponak, 1995). For the most part, however, they believe that if intelligent and progressive human resource management policies are followed, unions should be unnecessary, and that while the interests of workers and managers may diverge in the short term, over the longer term they'll converge, again assuming appropriate management techniques are used to link the company's interests to individual workers' needs (Gunderson and Ponak, 1995). Managerialists tend to be particularly interested in employee involvement and other quality of worklife programs, as well as in a variety of incentive-based compensation schemes. Much research conducted from this perspective has focused on such issues as why some employees are more likely than others to go on strike or take industrial action and what management techniques and organizational structures will reduce an individual's propensity to engage in industrial conflict (Kervin, 1988:219). While much of this research has been valuable, in general it has paid little attention to the role of unions (Kervin, 1984, 1988; Gunderson and Ponak, 1995). The omission seems somewhat surprising, given that, in Canada at least, only a duly certified union can legally call a strike.

Institutional Perspective

The institutional perspective has generally been the one adopted by most mainstream industrial relationists. Arising out of the work of people like John R. Commons,

coercive drive approach A management approach most common in the nineteenth century that sought to "motivate" employees primarily through fear and intimidation, with the aim of extracting the maximum possible amount of work from them.

this perspective holds that in a competitive marketplace, individual workers are unable to resist the demands of powerful employers. Unions and collective bargaining are, therefore, needed to balance what would otherwise be a seriously uneven playing field (Barbash, 1984). This perspective entails more government intervention than the two perspectives already discussed, since government is needed to establish and administer labour relations legislation, without which most unions would be unable to function (see Chapter 7). Institutionalists believe that, while workplace conflict exists, much if not all of it can be dissipated through collective bargaining and other activities of the IR system. Overall, their aim is to strike a balance between economic efficiency and equity, while providing employees with some degree of say in what goes on in the workplace.

As their name suggests, institutionalists have a strong interest in real-world IR institutions—unions, management organizations, and the government agencies that regulate the IR system. Much of their research tends to be of a practical nature and most institutionalists have a keen interest in public labour-policy issues. While members of this school don't confine themselves to a single research approach, in general (Anderson et al., 1989) they tend to rely more heavily on interviews and case studies and less heavily on statistical analysis than do neoclassicists. Noted Canadian institutionalists have included H.D. Woods, chairman of a well-known federal task force on labour relations, and the Abbé Gérard Dion, founder of the industrial relations program at Laval University and long-time editor of the Canadian journal *Relations Industrielles*.

Reformist Perspective

Members of the reformist school think that collective bargaining and labour relations legislation *could* work, under the right circumstances, but that as things stand, the odds are weighted too heavily in favour of employers and the rich and powerful in general. While they are supportive of unions in principle (Godard, 1994), they are critical of a system that, all too often, doesn't allow unions to offer workers any real protection, especially in small organizations. Accordingly, reformists seek major economic redistribution, such as changes in the tax system, as well as pay and employment equity and other employment law reforms designed to correct what many of them view as widespread structural and political inequality (Godard, 1994).

One group of reformists, represented most notably by David Beatty (1983, 1987; Adell, 1988a), takes what Adell describes as an "egalitarian individualist" approach to issues of labour law and social justice more generally. In Adell's words, Beatty believes "that the justice of social institutions should be appraised on the basis of their effects on the worst-off members of society" (1988a:116). Beatty would use the *Charter of Rights and Freedoms* to bring about fairer labour relations legislation. For example, he would use it to remove existing exclusions from this legislation (such as those of management personnel, agricultural workers, and domestics), on the grounds that all workers should have the right to join a union, whether or not they choose to exercise that right (Beatty, 1987; Adell, 1988a).[8] More generally, Beatty views the Charter as providing a constitutional guarantee of the right to join a union and to strike (Beatty and Kennett, 1988).[9] But his program for labour law reform doesn't stop with the Charter. While this would guarantee fair procedures, he believes workers also need substantive legislative protection of the type provided by human rights and employment standards legislation (Beatty, 1987; Adell, 1988a).

A second group comprises mainly academics in such disciplines as history, sociology, and political science, as well as a few industrial relationists of progressive bent (Haiven, McBride, and Shields, 1990). This group's work focuses quite strongly on issues of power in the workplace and in Canadian society at large. Often they have been critical of the role of the state in maintaining or even fostering existing power imbalances (Haiven et al., 1990). Others have focused on such issues as discrimination, unsafe working conditions, **layoffs** and plant closures, and wage inequities (Godard, 1994:31). For example, Canadian legal scholar Harry Glassbeek has long been interested in the issue of corporations' legal liability for workplace injuries and illnesses (Glassbeek and Rowland, 1979).

layoff Separation from employment as a result of a lack of work.

Radical/Political Economy Perspective

Those holding the radical/political economy perspective, unlike those holding the previous four, believe that widespread inequality is an integral part of capitalist society and can't be overcome under existing economic and political arrangements. In the past, most radicals were of a Marxist or quasi-Marxist bent.[10] They believed that all members of society are divided into two classes: the working class, or proletariat, and the capitalist class, or bourgeoisie. The bourgeoisie, in this view, own the means of production, while members of the working class don't, and are thus forced to sell their labour to those who do. Most workers produce goods or services of far greater value than their wages and the costs of production put together. The difference between the value of the goods or services produced and the total costs of production (including wages) is kept by the capitalists as profits, and is referred to by Marxists as "surplus value."

To the Marxist, trade unions are at best a Band-Aid solution, at worst a distraction from what should be the working class's main mission: to overthrow capitalist society.[11] Classical Marxists thought this would happen through a combination of political means and direct action. Syndicalists (represented in North America mainly by the Industrial Workers of the World) had little use for politics, believing that a giant general strike would eventually bring the capitalist class to its knees. The failure of the Winnipeg General Strike (described in Chapter 3) meant the end of serious syndicalism in Canada. Classical Marxism hung on somewhat longer, as Communists continued to play a significant role in the Canadian labour movement through the early fifties (Morton, 1995). Marxist scholarship, however, has played a far smaller role in North American than it has in European industrial relations (Hyman, 1975). One notable exception is the work of Harry Braverman (1974). Taking a Marxist perspective on technological change, Braverman argues that the major effect of such change is to "deskill" workers, thus further increasing managers' and employers' control over the labour process.

Over the past few years, a new political economy school has arisen in North American industrial relations.[12] Members of this school agree with traditional Marxists about the centrality of power issues and the importance of relating IR to larger developments in the economy and society (Godard, 1994; Lipsig-Mumme,

1995). Their prescriptions for change are, however, generally quite different. In place of traditional Marxist calls for the violent overthrow of capitalist society, one hears calls for employee ownership and management of business enterprises (Godard, 1994). In place of calls for unions to serve as foot soldiers in the giant revolution, one hears calls for them to reach out to the communities in which their members live (Lipsig-Mumme, 1995:216) and, at the same time, to operate in a more genuinely international fashion (Lipsig-Mumme, 1995:218) to better serve the workers of transnational enterprises affected by recent North American trade agreements.

Most industrial relationists who take a political economy perspective would agree that there are serious problems with the Canadian IR system as presently constituted. Particular difficulties include the inadequate representation of women (Forrest, 1997) and of workers in small firms and peripheral areas of the economy (Lipsig-Mumme, 1995). Few, however, have gone so far as to call for the outright dismantling of the present Canadian IR system. Most appear to believe that, imperfect though that system may be, workers are still better served with it than they would be without it.

WHAT THE BOOK WILL COVER

This chapter has offered a very basic introduction to industrial relations: what it is, what some leading theories say, and what some different perspectives on the field have to say about such issues as the role of unions and the importance of power and conflict in the workplace. The next group of chapters is devoted to studying the roles of management and labour, the two major actors in the IR system. We start, in Chapter 2, with management, which most industrial relations experts agree is now the IR system's single most important actor. A key element of this chapter is its discussion of the historical evolution of Canadian management practice. The historical evolution of the Canadian labour movement and industrial relations systems is covered in Chapter 3. The structure of the Canadian labour movement and changing patterns of union membership and density are discussed in Chapter 4 while Chapter 5 examines the actions unions take in support of their objectives and the economic and social impacts of these.

The following group of chapters examines the legal aspects of the Canadian industrial relations system. Chapter 6 discusses employment legislation affecting all workers, while Chapter 7 focuses on private sector labour relations legislation. Chapter 8 considers collective bargaining and labour legislation in the public sector, with special emphasis on the federal public service.

The next three chapters are primarily concerned with the bargaining process and with the conflict that often arises during that process. In Chapter 9 we look at the negotiation process in some detail and in Chapter 10 we discuss the product of the negotiation process, the collective agreement. Chapter 11 examines strikes and lockouts, another potential outcome of the bargaining process.

The administration of the collective agreement is discussed in Chapter 12, which focuses on grievances and the grievance process. Chapter 13, on comparative industrial relations, starts with a brief look at some broad international IR models, before taking a closer look at some countries of special interest to Canada, including Germany, Japan, and the US. In the final chapter, Chapter 14, we revisit the Canadian IR system as a whole in light of important recent developments like globalization, liberalized trade, increased work hours, and the growth of a **contingent workforce.**

Although this book contains a chapter on comparative IR, we have also continued our earlier practice of using evidence from foreign IR systems to show the Canadian system in a comparative perspective. Likewise, a discussion of key features of Quebec's quite distinctive IR system has been incorporated into the chapters where appropriate.

contingent work-force Individuals who enjoy little or no job security because they are employed on a temporary, part-time, or contractual basis and can generally be laid off with little or no notice.

QUESTIONS FOR DISCUSSION

1. What has your experience of work been to this point? What have you liked best (and least) about it? How has that experience compared with that of your parents, or with that of people of your parents' generation?

2. What are some of the major strengths of the systems framework? What are some of its major weaknesses?

3. How have Thomas Kochan and his associates sought to address the systems framework's perceived problems through their strategic choice theory?

4. What are the key features of each of the five major perspectives on IR? Which do you find most convincing, and why?

5. How does IR differ from other disciplines that deal with the world of work, such as labour history or organizational behaviour? What has been IR's distinctive contribution to the study of work?

6. What are some new areas that you would expect IR to include within the next few years?

Suggestions for Further Reading

Adams, Scott. Dilbert cartoons (in most newspapers, particularly on Saturdays). The Dilbert strip offers a funny and often extremely penetrating look at the follies and foibles of North American workplaces. It's particularly good on management practice. In addition, Adams has written a number of "Dilbert" books.

Godard, John. (2005). *Industrial Relations: The Economy and Society* (3rd ed.). Toronto: Captus. Third edition of an excellent and very readable textbook written from a political economy perspective.

Terkel, Studs. (c. 1975 [1972]). *Working.* New York: Avon. Though possibly a bit dated by now, this series of interviews with more than 100 Americans about their jobs (from business executives to hookers) remains a classic.

CHAPTER 2

THE ENVIRONMENT AND MANAGEMENT OF INDUSTRIAL RELATIONS

In today's climate, no group is immune from layoffs—including high-tech workers like the ones shown here. In 2001, the high-tech industry lost about 15 000 jobs in the Ottawa area alone.

LEARNING OBJECTIVES

After studying this chapter, you should be able to:

1. Describe the political, social, and economic contexts of Canadian industrial relations.

2. Summarize the impact of the economic environment on workers' desire to unionize and propensity to strike.

3. Identify recent trends in the Canadian labour force.

4. Summarize some recent impacts of the economic environment on the management of industrial relations.

5. Identify and describe the five basic eras through which industrial relations management practices have evolved.

6. Identify and describe four current management strategies toward unionization.

This chapter opens with a look at the economic, political, and social contexts of industrial relations. Each contextual factor uniquely influences the bargaining power and decisions of both management and labour, shaping the interactions within, and the outcomes of, the Canadian industrial relations system. The chapter then goes on to take a closer look at the management of industrial relations, both the growing role of management within the industrial relations system and the evolution of management practices. We also discuss the search for alternative management practices and the various industrial relations strategies employers typically pursue.

As discussed in Chapter 1, our industrial relations system operates within, and is influenced by, various contextual factors. Dunlop characterized the important environmental considerations as the technological, market, budgetary, and power contexts but more recent adaptations of the systems model expand environmental considerations to include ecological, economic, political, legal, and social subsystems (Craig, 1986). A society's physical surroundings, and its adaptations to these, comprise the ecological subsystem. Thus, Canada's vast spaces and natural resources would influence, for example, what types of industries operate within our borders. Unlike other subsystems, however, the ecological subsystem does not consciously adapt to industrial relations outputs or modify subsequent system inputs (Craig, 1986). The legal subsystem is discussed in Chapters 6 and 7; accordingly, this chapter will focus on the political, social, and economic subsystems.

THE POLITICAL CONTEXT OF INDUSTRIAL RELATIONS

The Canadian Confederation of provinces was created by the *British North America Act, 1867 (BNA Act)*, which later became part of the *Constitution Act, 1982*. Among other things, the *BNA Act* outlined how powers of governance were to be divided between the federal and provincial governments. Until 1925, authority over industrial relations was considered a federal responsibility; however, a British Privy Council decision in that year determined that industrial relations fell within the category of property and civil rights, something section 92 of the *BNA Act* declared to be within provincial purview. Since then, provinces have been empowered to pass, enforce, and administer laws governing industrial relations within their province. The federal government remains responsible for industrial relations matters regarding federally regulated industries and federal undertakings.

The decentralization of Canadian industrial relations that resulted from this regulatory fragmentation is unique in the world. Only Australia grants similar levels of authority to sub-national states, and even there national intervention is permitted at the request of either of the parties (Thompson, Rose, and Smith, 2003). Thus, Canada's industrial relations system can be said to be made up of eleven—or more—unique subsystems. The ten provinces and the federal jurisdiction had, until recently, been considered the eleven subsystems; however, the creation of Nunavut, and the fact that both Nunavut and the Northwest Territories have their own Labour Standards Acts, suggests that the three territories should no longer be considered completely subsumed under the federal jurisdiction.

As subsystems of the larger Canadian industrial relations system, each jurisdiction arguably shares a similar ideology and is subject to similar contextual influences.

However, as unique subsystems, jurisdictions are subject to different contextual influences and nowhere is this more apparent than with regard to the political context. As regulators, provincial and federal governments enact and enforce legislation that provides the legal context for all industrial relations within their jurisdiction—and that reflects the political parties' perspectives regarding the appropriate protection of rights and balance of power between labour and management. In addition, in their role as employers, governments implement policies and practices that affect all public and para-public sector workers, who comprise almost a quarter of Canadian workers (Godard, 2005). The provincial and federal governments also attempt to shape the values and beliefs of all the industrial relations actors within their jurisdiction and provide various programs and mechanisms to support preferred industrial relations and management practices. Finally, the governments are responsible for broader social, economic, fiscal, and constitutional policies that shape the industrial relations environments (Godard, 2005).

THE SOCIAL CONTEXT OF INDUSTRIAL RELATIONS

As members of the same society, all the actors in an industrial relations system are conditioned by their social or cultural subsystem. Canadians, for example, are subject to somewhat different social and cultural influences than Americans. Differences between Canadians and our southern neighbours have been of particular interest to researchers, who have investigated, for example, differences in our views on government, unions, and corporations (Lipset and Meltz, 1998). Recent research regarding preference for union representation (Lipset, Meltz, and Gomez, 2004) revealed a paradox: even though unionization rates in the United States have dropped precipitously while Canadian unionization rates have remained relatively stable, workers in the United States express greater interest in union joining.

Of perhaps more interest for Canadian industrial relations are the differences that exist within our own country. Within every society, considerable variation exists between the goals and values of various sub-groups (Craig, 1986), and this may be especially true in the cultural mosaic that is Canada. Attitudes, values, and beliefs regarding the role of unions or the rights of employers and workers, for example, might vary depending on one's background, life experiences, and political orientation. Attitudes toward unions are also influenced by such things as the attitudes of one's peers and whether or not a member of one's family belongs to a union. Younger workers, whose attitudes tend to be more malleable, tend to be more responsive to these social-capital factors and research suggests Canadian youth currently express a stronger preference for unionization than adults (Gomez, Gunderson, and Meltz, 2002). Attitudes toward unionization are also affected by initial workplace experiences, perspectives on traditional union policies such as pay standardization and layoffs based on seniority, a preference for collective versus authoritarian solutions to workplace problems, political orientation, working conditions, and job characteristics (Gomez et al., 2002).

Factors that impact the social context of industrial relations extend well beyond such things as attitudes about unions, corporations, and government. Furthermore, the attitudes, beliefs, and values of the actors in an industrial relations system both influence and are influenced by the other subsystems (Craig, 1986). This articulation amongst the various subsystems makes it difficult to assess the individual impact of each subsystem. Indeed, to the degree to which the social subsystem has influence on an industrial relations system independent of its influence on the other contextual subsystems is arguable.

Rather than isolating social, political, or other influences, some recent research has taken a more holistic approach and analyzed regional differences in Canadian industrial relations systems. Arguing that regions are intellectual constructs that vary by discipline, Thompson, Rose, and Smith (2003) use provincial boundaries as logical demarcations between regions for the purposes of industrial relations. Provinces, the authors argue, are spatial and cultural divides that provide frames of reference and incubate values; they also have political structures and organizations of interest groups. Following an analysis of eight provinces, the authors conclude that with respect to Canadian industrial relations, regions are not merely spatial; they are also historical and psychological, and variations in political and social forces affect each province's industrial relations in ways above and beyond those that can be explained simply by differences in industrial structure.

THE ECONOMIC CONTEXT OF INDUSTRIAL RELATIONS

While all contextual factors influence the actors in an industrial relations system to some degree, the economic subsystem is perhaps the most important factor influencing the balance of power between the parties. Both macroeconomic conditions, such as inflation, unemployment, and interest rates, and microeconomic factors, such as labour intensity of production, and the degree to which demand for a product or service is affected by its price—the so-called **price elasticity of demand**—exercise a multitude of direct and indirect influences on the parties, their interactions, and the outcomes of industrial relations systems. Within the constraints imposed by the legal context, the economic environment most fundamentally affects system outcomes, especially the degree to which workers and their unions will be able to improve compensation and benefits and the relative ability of employers to restrain labour costs and increase profits. A review of introductory economic theory is beyond the scope of this text; thus, students are encouraged to consult some of the readings listed at the end of this chapter. What will be discussed in the following sections are some basic dynamics and current labour market trends.

price elasticity of demand The degree to which demand for a product or service is affected by its price.

Basic Dynamics

The business cycle dictates some basic dynamics regarding the balance of power between actors within an industrial relations system. When product demand is high prices and wages usually rise and workers may want to join unions to help protect their real wage levels. Furthermore, workers already in unions are more likely to strike in support of wage demands since they know their employers will want to get them back to work as soon as possible in order to avoid losing business and are, therefore, more likely to meet their wage demands. Moreover, even if some unionized workers lose their jobs because employers believe they cannot meet the union's wage demands without layoffs, at the high end of the business cycle, when the demand for goods and labour is high, it is usually relatively easy for them to find other work.

By the same token, at the low end of the business cycle when the general demand for goods and labour is low, workers are less apt to seek to join unions for the purpose of protecting their real wages. As well, those already in unions are less likely to go on strike over wages. At such times, it may not be that important for employers to get their workers back on the job, as they may not have a backlog of unfilled orders. Indeed, they sometimes have large unsold inventories and may even welcome a strike as a way of reducing their wage bill. Unions are less likely to press wage demands during these troughs in the business cycle for two reasons. First, any strike that does occur may last longer, since employers have less incentive to settle than they would in good times. Second, if workers get laid off because the employer cannot meet the union's wage demands without cutting jobs, it may be difficult if not impossible for them to find other jobs, since demand for labour will be low and unemployment generally high. Again, this does not mean that strikes will not occur in bad times. What it does mean is that strikes are less likely to be over wages and more likely to be over other issues. Granted, the preceding picture has been painted with an extremely broad brush. In the final analysis, each workplace is unique, with its own history, politics, and cast of characters; however, economic factors such as unemployment and inflation rates and other indices of the business cycle exercise considerable influence on the inputs and outputs of industrial relations systems.

Labour Force Trends

labour force All persons 15 years of age and over who are either employed or are unemployed but actively seeking employment.

The **labour force** includes all employed workers and all unemployed ones who are looking for work. Today's Canadian labour force differs in some important ways from the labour force of a generation or two ago. Over the years, the proportion of Canadians working in primary industries like agriculture, forestry, and fishing has declined substantially. Throughout most of the post-war period (Craig and Solomon, 1996), the proportion working in secondary industries like manufacturing has also been declining. In contrast, the proportion working in tertiary or service industries like utilities, trade, finance, education, and public administration has risen steadily. However, it is more recent trends that present the most pressing challenges for Canadian workers and their unions, employers, and governments. For example, the aging of the workforce has significant implications for pension funding and the availability of skilled workers. The fact that the Canadian labour force includes more women and members of ethnic minorities highlights the importance of government, employer, and union initiatives aimed at ensuring equity. The rapid growth of non-standard employment not only has implications for workplace equity but also challenges public policies that are predicated on the norm of full-time, full-year, long-term employment contracts.

Aging of the Labour Force

In 1971, only 8 percent of the Canadian population was 65 or older; by 2011 this figure is projected to reach 15 percent, an increasing number of whom will choose to continue to work into their senior years (Duchesne, 2004a). Simultaneously, the proportion of the workforce between the ages of 45 and 64 is increasing and by 2015, it is expected that this group of workers will constitute 48 percent of the working age population (FLMM, 2003). The special problems this demographic trend presents include fewer working taxpayers to support a larger dependent population, skills shortages, especially in some highly skilled occupations (Schetagne, 2001; Dohm, 2000), and escalating wage rates.

Fortunately, increasing life expectancies and medical advancements mean more seniors are living healthy, productive lives, and many are electing to work beyond normal retirement age. This trend is seen across a wide variety of occupations but is especially prevalent among more highly educated, male workers (Duchesne, 2004b). These demographic trends and projected consequences have put pressure on both employers and governments to reconsider the traditional retirement age, and especially rules regarding **mandatory retirement** at age 65. Manitoba and Quebec have already retired the concept, so to speak, and Ontario has pledged to follow suit; however, even if mandatory retirement is eliminated throughout Canada, most workers will likely still choose to retire at 65 or even earlier, thus leading to growing pressure on pension funds, which will have fewer younger workers paying into them and more retirees drawing benefits from them (see Sunter, 2001).

mandatory retirement Compelling employees to retire upon reaching a certain age, normally 65.

Mandatory retirement? It may create jobs for younger workers, but it may also create skills shortages. Furthermore, for many older people, their work is their life.

More Women and Minorities at Work

The increasing proportion of women in the labour force, especially married women with children, has been cited as one of the most profound changes in the Canadian workplace in the past half century. In 1950, just 22 percent of labour force participants were female (Leacy, 1999). By 2004, that number had risen to 47 percent (Stats Can, 2004b) and the expectation of workforce participation, except for a period following the birth of children, is now the norm. As their presence in the labour force increased, so too did women's presence in unions, albeit with somewhat of a lag. In 1951, fewer than 1 in 10 union members were female (Bain and Price, 1980). By 1975, however, 26 percent of union members were female (Stats Can, 1999) and by 2002, women comprised 48.6 percent of Canadian union members (Stats Can, 2002).

The growing presence of women in Canadian workplaces reflects their changing role in society and has presented a number of challenges for both employers and unions. Women's increased presence within unions, especially following widespread unionization of public sector workers in the 1960s (White, 1993), brought increased scrutiny regarding the representativeness and inclusiveness of union leadership, internal decision-making structures, and collective bargaining agendas. Employers faced similar scrutiny regarding the representativeness of their workforce, and governments responded with legislation aimed at eliminating both direct and systemic workplace discrimination. Beyond basic equity issues, women's increased presence in the Canadian workforce has highlighted the need for a national child-care program and for workplace policies and practices that facilitate work–life balance, such as parental leaves, flexible work scheduling, and rights and protections for part-time workers.

Equity issues and human rights protections have also increased in importance due to the increasing ethnic and religious diversity of the Canadian labour force. While it remains true that the majority of Canada's working age population was born in Canada, the proportion of foreign-born workers is increasing, especially in major urban centres (Reid, Meltz, and Gomez, 2005). People who immigrated in the 1990s were more likely to be visible minorities than people who had immigrated the decade before, but they were also more highly educated. Unfortunately, these recent immigrants, especially female immigrants, face far higher rates of unemployment than native-born Canadians. Recent immigrants also tend to earn considerably less than workers born in Canada—as much as 20 percent less for females. Fortunately, as their tenure in Canada increases, so too do employment rates; immigrants who have been in Canada for 16 or more years have a slightly higher chance of being employed than their Canadian-born counterparts (Stats Can, 2004a). Whether immigrants are recent arrivals or have been in Canada for 10 years or more, those with university educations are often underemployed in positions requiring little education (Stats Can, 2004c). Workforce disadvantages for recent immigrants include devaluation of foreign work experience (Swidinsky and Swidinsky, 2002), difficulties in equating foreign qualifications and training to Canadian standards, and outright discrimination. Wise employers will wish to take advantage of the skills of visible minorities and recent immigrants and, therefore, must ensure that their recruiting and other human resource practices do not inadvertently favour native-born Canadians.

Rapid Growth in Non-Standard Employment

Beginning in the mid-1970s, global economic changes, technological advancements, and demographic changes combined in such a way that more and more employers sought alternatives to standard full-time, full-year employment contracts (Kalleberg, 2000). Since then, part-time, limited-term, and casual employment, which allows employers greater flexibility and lower labour costs, have dramatically increased in prevalence. Such forms of work are often grouped under the moniker of **non-standard employment**. In fact, there is no generally accepted definition of non-standard employment; it can encompass virtually any form of employment other than the traditional full-time, full-year contracts of indefinite term. It can also encompass self-employment, **moonlighting**, and home-work, all of which have also increased in prevalence in the last few decades. In fact, many researchers eschew the term non-standard employment because it fails to capture the diversity of work arrangements that have evolved over the last two decades.

Regardless of the term that is used, the trend away from full-time, full-year, single-employer jobs is clear. In 1990, about one quarter of the Canadian workforce could be described as employed in non-standard arrangements. By 2000, that proportion increased to 34 percent (Townson, 2003). Self-employment, in particular, has expanded significantly, accounting for over three-quarters of Canadian job growth between 1989 and 1996. Multiple job holding has also increased, with many workers holding various combinations of part-time, full-time, and temporary jobs (Townson, 2003). Part-time work increased from 13.8 percent of those employed in 1979 to 19.1 percent in 1993 (Stats Can, 1998b). Since the mid-1990s, however, the percentage of part-time workers has declined somewhat, dipping to 18.4 percent by 2004 (Stats Can, 2005c), and very recent data suggest a slight decline in the proportion of self-employed. Overall, however, both part-time work and self-employment are increasing as a proportion of total employment (Townson, 2003). This trend away from full-time, full-year employment contracts of indefinite term presents a number of challenges to all parties to the industrial relations system, several of which are discussed in Current Issues box 2.1.

non-standard employment A term generally used to describe any type of employment other than full-time, full-year employment contracts of indefinite term.

moonlighting A situation where an individual holds more than one paid job at the same time.

Current Issues 2.1

THE GENDER OF NON-STANDARD EMPLOYMENT IN CANADA

In the post World War II era, a norm developed with regard to employment: The standard employment relationship involved a worker who worked full-time, year-round on one employer's premises, expected to continue to be employed for an indefinite period of time, and received a variety of statutory benefits and entitlements. Typically, the worker was male and supported a family. Women, who in 1950 made up only 22 percent of the labour force, were less likely to be engaged in standard employment and more likely to be engaged in part-time or seasonal work. In the 1970s, the standard employment relationship began to erode and in the 1980s, the growth of other types of employment outpaced the growth of full-time, full-year jobs. ▶

Employment legislation and public policy such as Employment Insurance (EI), public pensions, and child-care programs have been slow to respond to these job growth trends and, for the most part, remain predicated upon the notion of standard forms of employment. Indeed, the greater protections and benefits legislation confers on workers in standard employment relationships is one of the reasons employers have favoured the creation of non-standard jobs. For example, rather than providing notice and severance pay to permanent workers laid off for short periods on a seasonal basis, employers can save money by employing a contingent workforce on multiple short-term contracts. Savings are also realized through lower benefit costs since part-time and contract workers are often not provided the same benefits as their full-time counterparts.

While both men and women have been affected by the trend toward contract, temporary, and part-time work, women appear to be disproportionately disadvantaged. Women are overrepresented in almost all forms of "non-standard" employment, and especially in the forms of employment that offer inadequate regulatory protection and the lowest levels of pay, benefits, pensions, and job security. And, while many women may elect to work part-time, the vast majority of involuntary part-timers, those who would prefer but cannot find full-time work, are women.

Recent research suggests that the hazards extend well beyond the obvious and long-term financial consequences; non-standard employment often results in increased stress due to irregular and unpredictable work schedules, juggling the requirements of two or more jobs with personal responsibilities, inability to gain seniority or security, and lack of respect and support from employers. The results of this increased stress for women in non-standard employment include an increased incidence of musculoskeletal disorders, migraines, and headaches, as well as absenteeism, high turnover rates, and workplace conflict.

Recommendations to address these workplace inequities include: legislating full coverage of non-standard workers under employment standards legislation and ensuring that these rules are enforced through periodic inspections of workplaces; mandating equitable treatment of all workers with regard to pay, benefits, and training; reducing the number of hours required for Employment Insurance benefits; and bringing self-employed workers into the EI program.

Sources: Cranford, Cynthia J., Leah F. Vosko, and Nancy Zukewich. (2003). "The Gender of Precarious Employment in Canada," *Relations Industrielles* 58:3, pp. 454–483; Zeytinoglu, Isik Urla, Josefina Moruz, M. Bianca Seaton, and Waheeda Lillevik. (2003). *Occupational Health of Women in Non-Standard Employment*, Ottawa: Status of Women Canada.

Unemployment

An important measure of the Canadian labour force is the availability of employment. According to Statistics Canada, which conducts a monthly Labour Force survey, an individual is unemployed if he or she does not have a job during any given week, but has looked for work at some point during the four weeks preceding the survey. Note that unemployment is not measured by the number of people drawing Employment Insurance (EI) benefits. Some EI recipients are in fact employed, albeit only part-time.[1] Moreover, many unemployed individuals are ineligible for EI benefits, most notably those who have just entered the labour force, those who have exhausted their benefits, and most self-employed workers.

In 2004, the overall rate of unemployment in Canada stood at 7.2 percent (Stats Can, 2005c). Unfortunately, this figure does little to help us understand the sources of unemployment or the reasons people are unable to find work. Thus, it is useful to distinguish between different types of unemployment, since solving them requires different types of government policy. The three types of unemployment we will discuss are frictional, structural, and demand-deficient.

Frictional Unemployment

Frictional unemployment affects those who are changing jobs and have a certain period of time between their departure from the first job and arrival at the second. A certain amount of this type of unemployment, perhaps about 2 percent, is normal in dynamic labour markets. Indeed, its incidence may be higher in a strong economy than in a weak one, since people are more willing to leave jobs they do not really like in good times than in bad. Most economists agree that no special government policies are needed to deal with this type of unemployment, which is usually quite brief, often voluntary, and almost certainly represents a small portion of the total amount of unemployment in Canada today.

frictional unemployment Temporary unemployment due to time lost switching between jobs.

Structural Unemployment

Structural unemployment refers to a situation in which there is a mismatch of available jobs and skills, or in which unemployed workers live in different locations from the places where jobs are available. For example, there may be a shortage of skilled computer technicians in Ottawa, while at the same time there is extremely high unemployment among fishers in British Columbia. It would seem that the logical solution here would be to retrain the unemployed fishers as computer technicians and then help them move to Ottawa but this is often more easily said than done. The unemployed fishers may lack the aptitude, the desire, or the education needed to become computer programmers, and in any case, family considerations and the expenses and trauma involved with moving may make this an impractical idea for many of them. To the extent that moving is a practical and economically rational solution, education and training, along with relocation assistance, are the government policies that best address structural unemployment; however, it is important to recognize that in a country as large and geographically and culturally diverse as Canada, structural unemployment will never be easy to overcome.

structural unemployment A situation in which there is a mismatch of available jobs and skills, or in which unemployed workers live in different locations from those where jobs are available.

Demand-Deficient Unemployment

Demand-deficient unemployment refers to an overall lack of jobs. It is this type of unemployment that is most prevalent during depressions like that of the 1930s, or major recessions like those of the early 1980s and early 1990s. In dealing with this type of unemployment, governments find that education and training by themselves are not enough, though general training in basic literacy and numeracy can certainly help unemployed workers take advantage of what vacancies there are. Governments have two options available to them here. The first is broad, macroeconomic stimulation to increase demand. This is typically achieved through major

demand-deficient unemployment An overall lack of jobs in the economy.

changes in monetary, fiscal, and taxation policies or major public works spending, and was the approach taken in the United States and, to a much lesser degree, in Canada during the depression of the 1930s. Another option is to reduce work hours to spread the available work around more evenly (Donner, 1994; O'Hara, 1993).

IMPACT OF THE ECONOMIC ENVIRONMENT ON THE MANAGEMENT OF IR

Continuing high unemployment,[2] especially demand-deficient unemployment, has been one of the important factors driving a long-term shift, especially in the last three decades, in the balance of workplace power away from workers and unions and towards management. Other important factors driving the shift in the balance of workplace power include the privatization of many formerly government-owned enterprises, the deregulation of many previously highly regulated ones, trade liberalization, growing foreign competition, and technological change. Taken together, these forces have led to the emergence of an increasingly market-oriented economy. At the same time, provincial and federal governments, under growing pressure to attack deficit and debt levels, have weakened the social safety net. For example, Canadian employment insurance benefits have declined over time as a percentage of the unemployed worker's weekly salary. At the same time, eligibility rules have tightened so that many unemployed part-time workers who would formerly have qualified for employment insurance now do not.

Obviously, today's economic environment has made life more difficult for workers and their unions. But in many respects it has also complicated managers' lives. To begin with, managers have been no less immune from the effects of downsizing and restructuring than the workers reporting to them. Beginning with the recession of the 1980s, and continuing through to the present, many organizations flattened their management structures. While this may have improved internal communication and productivity, it also meant that many middle managers lost their jobs (Osterman, 1988), while others found their responsibilities significantly changed. Like the workers under them, surviving managers have had to "do more with less."

Nor are these the only pressures facing managers in the first decade of the new millennium. Globalization, combined with the almost instantaneous availability of information and the free movement of capital from country to country, means that the pace of decision making has stepped up considerably. Changes in technology have meant that competitive advantages, which once could be counted on to last years, may now last only a few months, or even weeks. Growing foreign competition, resulting in large measure from recent trade agreements, has put even more pressure on management to contain labour costs without compromising product quality. The combination of these contextual pressures has resulted in at least a partial reversion from accommodationist post-war management practices to the more hard-line approach typical of the twentieth century's first decades. Furthermore, recent years have seen management adopt a much more proactive approach to industrial relations, especially in the United States. Since we can better understand recent management trends if we view them in the broader context of the historical evolution of management industrial relations practice in Canada, it is this evolution to which we now turn.

THE EVOLUTION OF INDUSTRIAL RELATIONS MANAGEMENT PRACTICE

Management's major aims are to make a profit and to maintain control of the enterprise. The development of industrial relations management practices reflect management's attempt to achieve these objectives in the face of varying degrees of resistance from workers, and sometimes unions, seeking to maximize their wages and maintain or increase job security—objectives that most managers have seen as largely incompatible with their agendas. When worker/union resistance has been relatively effective, management has often had to compromise on one or both of its main objectives. There have, however, always been some organizations that have largely succeeded at reconciling their objectives with those of their employees, and some industries where a co-operative approach is more common than in others. There have also been periods when worker–management co-operation was easier to achieve and was thus more widely practised than at other times. But even though there have been variations, it is possible to trace the broad outlines of management industrial relations practice, most of which has taken five basic forms: **pre-industrial**, **coercive drive**, scientific management, **welfare capitalist**, and **bureaucratic**.

Pre-Industrial Era

In Canada, prior to the country's first industrial revolution, relatively few people worked for others, at least on a permanent basis. Most Canadians were self-employed farmers, fishers, or artisans. Manufacturing establishments were extremely small by today's standards, with an average of only five employees per firm (Godard, 1994). Those who did work for someone else generally worked for a family member, friend, or neighbour; apprentices might well live in the master's house. In most cases, the owner of a business was also its manager and personally oversaw all work done on its premises. The mode of control most employers exercised over their employees in this period is best described as **paternalistic**, meaning that they tended to assume responsibility for employees as a parent would for a child; they believed and behaved as if they knew what was best for employees.

Legally, workers had virtually no rights; servants who left their masters' employ without permission could be imprisoned (Morton, 1995:133). Still, while working for a relative or neighbour was no guarantee against arbitrary or even abusive treatment, craft traditions, community norms, and peer pressure probably provided some check on at least the more extreme forms of abuse and exploitation that characterized work in the early industrial period in Canada, Britain, and the United States. More importantly, most firms used limited technology and few sought to serve markets beyond their immediate local areas (see Commons, 1909). Indeed, most probably did not seek to compete on the basis of price, relying more on reputation and quality. For these reasons, the profit motive as such did not play the same role in pre-industrial business that it was to play starting in the industrial period

pre-industrial management A system of management used in pre-industrial societies—when most of those in employee status worked for friends or relatives—that operates on the basis of personal supervision, often by an owner-manager working alongside his or her employees.

coercive drive system A management approach most common in the nineteenth century, which sought to "motivate" employees primarily through fear and intimidation, in the interest of extracting the maximum possible amount of work from them.

welfare capitalist management A system of management, most common between the two world wars, in which companies sought to cement employees' loyalty and remain union-free by providing a broad range of benefits and establishing in-house consultation systems.

bureaucratic management Specialized, professionalized administration, in this case the IR and HR departments, where decision making is centralized and authority flows through multiple layers of management.

paternalistic management Human resource practices based on the notion that it is an employer's responsibility to take care of employees and determine what is in their best interests.

(Godard, 1994), and thus it was not necessary for managers to seek to extract the maximum possible "value" from workers—the critical assumption of the "coercive drive" system.

Coercive Drive System

With the growth of factories during the early industrial period, many more people entered into employee status, and many began working for people they had not previously known. The early factory system also saw the growth of a new management class between owners and workers (Yoder, 1962) as factories grew large enough that in most cases owners could no longer personally oversee all their workers. The result was the rise of a new supervisory class whose sole raison d'être was to extract the maximum possible production from the workers under them (George, 1968). A plentiful supply of labour and an almost total absence of protective government intervention (Yoder, 1962) made it possible for employers and managers to exercise virtually unfettered sway. The one partial exception here was skilled tradespeople, like printers and coopers, who might not always be easy to replace and who, in good times, could often set their own rates (Morton, 1995). However, women and children were often preferred to experienced adult male workers (Yoder, 1962), because their wages were lower and because they were generally considered more tractable.

Fear was what motivated workers, in a system where work was irregular and there was no employment security (Yoder, 1962), where most were paid barely enough to keep body and soul together (Morton, 1984), and where the six-day week and ten-hour or even twelve-hour day were the norm. Managerial control was exercised through ever-stricter monitoring of output and enforced through fines and even, on occasion, beatings (Heron, 1989). Not surprisingly, perhaps, such management practices and working conditions led to increased labour–management conflict, as workers sought to beat a system that appeared bent on extracting the last possible ounce of effort from them (George, 1968). With the formation of some of the craft unions described in Chapter 3, and with the Canadian government's growing if grudging recognition of working-class political power, some of this conflict began to be carried out in more organized fashion than had typically been the case in the pre-industrial period.

Scientific Management

scientific management (also known as **Taylorism**) A system of management launched by F.W. Taylor whereby tasks were broken down into their smallest possible components and quotas set on the basis of elaborate time-motion studies.

The **scientific management** approach (**Taylorism**) pioneered by F.W. Taylor is commonly treated in industrial relations courses and texts as part of, or indeed the culmination of, the coercive drive system. Further examination of scientific management suggests that, when viewed as a whole, the system is both more comprehensive and more complex than it generally has been perceived to be. Viewed from this broader perspective, Taylorism does indeed contain some elements consistent with the coercive drive system; however, it also contains other elements much more consistent with the welfare capitalism approach of the early twentieth century, which in many ways it undergirded (Anderson, Gunderson, and Ponak, 1989:6–7).

Taylor's aim was nothing short of a rationalization of the entire work process. Through detailed time-motion studies, he sought to break individual jobs down into their smallest and simplest components, simplifying each worker's task to allow each worker to achieve the maximum possible output from any given amount of effort. An appropriate quota, based on the results of those time-motion studies, would be set for each job. Those who exceeded it would be rewarded through incentive pay; those who did not meet it would be penalized (George, 1968). Nor was the scientific approach to be confined to job processes; it was also to be applied to such matters as worker selection, job determination, and the creation of a proper working environment. Only if workers and management co-operated in applying this scientific approach to all aspects of work, Taylor believed, could society reap the maximum benefits.

A crucial if highly controversial element of Taylor's program was his rigid separation of managerial work from that performed by ordinary workers. As he saw it, both inefficiency and frustration resulted when labour was asked to take on tasks properly within management's domain, such as "planning, organizing, controlling, methods determination, and the like" (George, 1968:90). Everyone would be happier and things would get done far more efficiently if management took care of all planning and control functions and workers simply executed the orders given to them by management—a situation referred to by Godard (2005:92) as the "think-do" dichotomy.

Like managers under coercive drive, Taylor sought to maximize worker output, and his system provided managers with the means to do so to a far greater degree than had previously been possible. The deskilling of workers associated with his "think-do" dichotomy was also consistent with earlier deskilling brought about, less systematically, during the early industrial period. Beyond that, Taylorism provided a basis for industrial innovations, like the moving automobile assembly line (Godard, 2005; Radforth, 1991), which essentially forced human workers to adapt their pace to that of machines.

In other ways, Taylorism differed significantly from coercive drive management. Taylor's aim was a harmonious workplace and also one in which workers would be rewarded for superior effort and would share in their firms' gains. In these respects, his system represented a significant advance over conventional nineteenth-century management practice. Particularly notable was scientific management's concern for the total workplace environment—psychological as well as physical. Such concern was especially true among one group of scientific managers initially known as the behavioural school. This school arose out of early efforts to "recognize the centrality of the individual in any cooperative endeavor" (George, 1968:141–142). This school of thought became much more prominent as a result of the now-famous experiments conducted by Elton Mayo and his Harvard colleagues at the Western Electric Company's Hawthorne plant. These experiments had interesting and somewhat surprising results. They revealed that workers' productivity went up not only when lighting was increased, but also when it was *decreased*. Mayo's conclusion was that if firms wished to increase productivity, they should pay more attention to their workers' needs (Anderson et al., 1989). Accordingly, the behaviourists, now known as the human relations school, started to do just that, focusing much of their attention on such things as individual motivation, group dynamics, and social support for employees (George, 1968; Anderson et al., 1989). Their work eventually led to the development of organizational behaviour as an independent field of study (Anderson et al., 1989).

Welfare Capitalist Management

The link between worker morale and efficiency established by scientific management, broadly applied, provided the rationale for many of the far-reaching changes in management philosophy and practice that occurred between 1900 and 1930. These changes ranged from the provision of employment security and company-paid benefits like pensions, to the establishment of various types of worker-representation systems and company athletic teams and recreational facilities.

A key development was the launching of large numbers of personnel departments in US and Canadian firms. Initially, these departments performed mainly employee welfare functions, as they had in Britain as early as the 1890s (Niven, 1967; George, 1968). Over time, they came to play a larger and more proactive role within organizations. As early as 1903 some writers were suggesting that, in the interest of maintaining labour peace, personnel departments should address any worker complaints that could not be resolved between workers and their foremen—in effect serving as informal arbitrators (Carpenter, 1903). Spurred on by the example of innovators like National Cash Register's John Patterson, a number of firms set up departments to do just that. In addition to handling employee welfare issues and resolving disputes, some of the new departments were also used to administer suggestion box systems—another turn-of-the-century innovation (Holman, 1904; Patterson, 1901).

During and after the First World War, many firms transferred all or at least a great deal of hiring and firing authority away from line supervisors to the new personnel departments (Slichter, 1929). The move corresponded with a growing shift away from the old temporary employment system to one of relatively permanent job tenure—something that the more enlightened sort of manager had been advocating for some time (Fitch, 1917; Erskine and Cleveland, 1917). If a firm was going to make the substantial investment in workers implied by the provision of job security, it would make sense to use professionally trained people to screen and select those workers.

Personnel departments grew in size and sophistication during the 1920s. A survey conducted in 1930 (Mathewson, 1931–1932) showed that more than 80 percent of all firms were keeping labour turnover records by the end of the decade, and about 40 percent were conducting regular job analyses. In addition, personnel departments were responsible for administering a broad range of employee benefits, including paid vacations, pensions, life and accident insurance plans, stock purchase plans, employee savings plans, low-cost loans, and home-ownership assistance plans. On the development front, personnel departments provided or arranged for on-the-job training for new hires and orientation courses for recent immigrants, helped set up sports teams and other recreational organizations, and arranged night school or correspondence courses for those in need of them (Mathewson, 1931–1932; Slichter, 1929). Many authors refer to the array of human resources practices that developed as "paternalistic management" since they were often based upon the pre-industrial notion that management was responsible for taking care of employees and determining what was in their best interests (Godard, 2005).

A number of First World War–era scientific management experiments had found little or no drop in productivity resulting from shorter hours (Nyland, 1989). Supported by those experiments, most major employers in the United States brought in the eight-hour day during the 1920s (Hunnicutt, 1988). Canadian workers also saw their hours shortened, though not to the same extent (Malles, 1976). At the same time, many firms established "works councils" or other worker representation bodies, while others established internal promotion ladders based on merit or converted wage-earning positions to salaried status (Slichter, 1929). Like the benefit plans, the reductions in hours, works councils, and internal promotion ladders were designed to increase workers' loyalty and reduce costly turnover. Another equally important objective was becoming, or remaining, union-free. To this end, many firms used hard tactics to drive out unions in the first place, but then adopted softer paternalistic welfare capitalist practices to keep them from returning later on (Slichter, 1929:349).

The evidence suggests that welfare capitalist firms in the 1920s were generally successful in achieving their two major objectives. The decade was marked by a large increase in productivity and substantial declines in union membership rates, strikes,

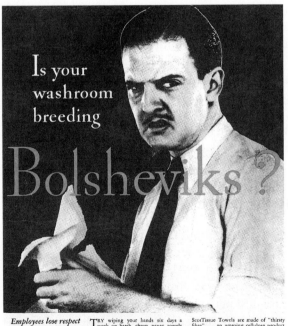

During the 1920s, the Scott Paper Company took advantage of employers' fear of militant employee action to sell its then-new disposable paper towels.

and turnover (Slichter, 1929).[3] Some contemporary observers (e.g., Slichter) feared that company benefits had become so pervasive as to sap workers' individual initiative and their drive towards co-operative self-help. Whether or not this was the case, few employers made any bones about the anti-union animus underlying their welfare capitalist practices. This animus, too, troubled thoughtful contemporary observers like Slichter, but by and large those working under welfare capitalist systems in the 1920s appear to have been happy enough to accept an implicit contract providing them with job security and relatively good pay and benefits in return for loyalty, commitment, and union-free status.

What is not clear is how many, even among male workers, were in fact working under such systems. Observers like Epstein (1932) have suggested that the proportion was small—perhaps 10 to 15 percent. Undoubtedly many workers, especially in peripheral regions like the American South (Hunnicutt, 1988) or Canada's Maritimes, continued to work under authoritarian coercive drive conditions.[4] There is also little evidence to suggest that welfare capitalist provisions were ever applied to any significant number of women. Nonetheless, welfare capitalism did have a lasting impact, as evidenced by the degree of conflict that ensued when firms started to abandon it during the 1930s.

With the advent of the Great Depression, many firms, unable to maintain their welfare capitalist practices, reverted to the hard-line coercive drive approach (Osterman, 1988). No better example of the change in thinking can be found than Henry Ford. Ford, known in the 1920s as the pioneer of the eight-hour day and $5 minimum daily wage, and as an employer willing to hire workers with partial disabilities, during the 1930s became notorious for hiring avowed criminals to beat up United Auto Workers organizers seeking to unionize his plant (Gannon, 1972; Lacey, 1986).

In the short term, reversion to coercive drive management led to increased workplace conflict. In the longer term, the result was large-scale unionization (see Osterman, 1988), which in turn led to yet another transformation of management practice, as management organizations were forced to adapt their practices to conform to the new labour relations legislation and the collective agreements made possible by that legislation.

Bureaucratic Management Practice

There is some disagreement in the literature about the extent of change in personnel practice during the early Depression years, prior to the legalization of collective bargaining in the United States. Some (Epstein, 1932) see the abandonment of welfare capitalism as total; others (Balderston, 1933; Brown, 1934–1935) indicate that a significant number of welfare capitalist personnel practices remained in place.

In any event, by the mid-1930s collective bargaining had become a major concern of personnel departments (Cowdrick, 1934–1935). In a parallel development, renewed emphasis was placed on supervisor training, since they would have to be the ones to administer the new collective agreements on a day-to-day basis (Cowdrick, 1935). With the legalization of collective bargaining and the signing of large numbers of collective agreements, many firms set up industrial relations departments to carry out collective bargaining and related activities, like grievance handling. The growth of such departments in turn spurred the growth of large numbers of academic industrial relations departments in the early post-war years.

Under collective bargaining, management practice was based on having workers adhere to two sets of formal, codified rules: those contained in company personnel manuals, developed by management, and those contained in collective agreements, developed jointly by management and unions. Of necessity, personnel practice in unionized firms became quite legalistic, since collective bargaining is a process tightly regulated by legislation. Non-union personnel policy, already quite bureaucratic in large firms, also became more legalistic during the 1930s and 1940s, as firms were expected to adhere to a growing body of employment standards legislation covering such diverse issues as wages, hours of work, overtime policies, and health and safety procedures. Some unionized practices, like seniority-based promotion, spilled over into the non-unionized sector, as non-unionized firms sometimes found these practices convenient. In other cases, like that of Dofasco Steel, some of those practices, along with high wage levels, were adopted as part of a broader union-avoidance strategy (Storey, 1983).

Collective bargaining certainly did not do away with worker–management conflict. The very early post-war period in particular saw a huge wave of strikes in Canada and the United States. However, with workers now able to strike legally and union recognition no longer at issue, these strikes were generally conducted in a more civilized fashion than pre-war strikes had been (see Heron, 1989), and seldom resulted in bloodshed. Meanwhile, industrial relations departments grew significantly during the post-war period as more firms were unionized and as collective bargaining was conducted over a broader range of issues, making both bargaining and contract administration more complex. A similar pattern of growth occurred in personnel departments, charged with administering an increasingly broad range of benefits, from pensions to insurance plans. Such developments were part of a broader pattern of growth of specialized management staff that was, perhaps, inevitable given many firms' increasing size and complexity during this period.

While burgeoning benefit plans gave personnel departments plenty to do, there was growing concern that, stripped of their earlier conflict-resolution roles, which had generally been taken over by industrial relations departments, personnel staff were becoming "managers of records" rather than of people (Owen, 1940–1941; Worthy, 1948). Such concerns continued into the 1960s (Heneman, 1960; Dunnette and Bass, 1963; Sokolik, 1969). By this time, however, others (Fischer, 1968) were predicting a more creative and proactive role for personnel departments. Anticipating to some extent the approach taken in the 1980s by Thomas Kochan and his associates, Fischer suggested that, in the future, the personnel function would assume a more strategic role in the overall management of the enterprise; that it would be responsible for furthering the organization, not just maintaining it; and that top management would become directly involved in the development and deployment of human resources.

A series of economic, social, and political developments beginning around 1970 was to create a quite different industrial relations environment and lead to yet another transformation of management practice. The economic environment had become increasingly difficult as a result of inflation arising out of the Vietnam War and the energy shock of 1973. These new economic pressures meant that management could no longer "buy off" union discontent with large wage and benefit packages, as it often had during the early post-war period (MacDonald, 1967). In any case, a new, more highly educated generation of workers had also come to look for more from their jobs than a paycheque. Riots at General Motors' Lordstown, Ohio, plant in 1970 demonstrated the need for management to attend to workers' intrinsic as well as extrinsic motivation. In the wake of Lordstown and a broad wave of both active and passive rebellion by discontented younger workers (Murray, 1971), many firms began instituting various **quality of worklife (QWL)** schemes aimed at addressing their workers' intrinsic needs. Some unions signed on. Others resisted, feeling that the QWL programs intruded on their authority to represent workers' interests in the workplace. That debate continues today.

In the meantime, complicating matters for extremely busy industrial relations and human resources staff was a new wave of litigation, arising from the broad range of civil rights and employment-related legislation passed during the 1960s and early 1970s. Such legislation, in the view of Arnold Deutsch (1979), amounted to nothing less than a human resources revolution, and meant that human resources would now affect every aspect of the organization, from hiring to marketing to investor attitudes. The legislation would also lead to the increased application of strategic planning and analysis to human resource management (Kochan and Barocci, 1985).

While all this was going on, the American labour movement was running out of steam. Largely as a result of lack of attention to organizing new members, by the 1970s it represented an ever-declining share of that country's workers. Decreasing numbers, combined with decreasing political clout, led to a much more management-oriented type of industrial relations. This move to a "new industrial relations" was less widely adopted in Canada than in the United States. In both countries, though, some of the limitations of the bureaucratic approach to management were becoming apparent. While many firms continue to use the older approach, in whole or in part, many others have spent much of the intervening period searching for alternatives.

The Search for Alternatives

In recent years, no single type of management practice has predominated as bureaucratic management did during the first quarter century after the First World War. Writing in 1971, Marvin Dunnette confessed to being unsure about the future direction of industrial psychology and personnel practice. Later, Paul Osterman (1988) would arrive at a similar conclusion. Noting the emergence of a broad range of diverse, even contradictory, human resource policies during the previous decade, Osterman said that while the human resource management system of many firms was clearly being transformed, the overall direction of that transformation was difficult to determine. After extensive study and observation, he could do no better than conclude that "something is happening and that the 'something' is extensive" (1988:61–62).

The quest to cut labour costs led many employers to go in for tough **concession bargaining**, resulting in some cases in **two-tier wage systems**. Other employers engaged in even more hard-line practices such as layoffs of previously secure

quality of working life (QWL) A process using joint problem-solving approaches that is focused on improving labour-management relations, organizational effectiveness, and employees' work satisfaction.

concession bargaining Situations in which the union is forced to agree to a wage freeze, wage reduction, or reduction in existing benefit levels in order to conclude a collective agreement.

two-tier wage systems Systems in which newly hired employees receive significantly lower wages than existing employees.

employees, shifts of employment to outside the firm (often to non-unionized establishments), the increased use of temporary and casual workers, the substitution of
machinery for human labour, or the relocation of plants to "union-free" areas like
the American South (Osterman, 1988; Kochan, McKersie, and Cappelli, 1984).
Other employers took an approach focusing on increasing employees' productivity
by increasing their loyalty and commitment to the firm. Such employers might
adopt employee-involvement or participation schemes, sometimes in connection
with new job-security commitments. They also tended to go in for a variety of joint
labour–management training programs. Other employers eliminated or reduced
traditional distinctions between white-collar and blue-collar work (Kochan et al.,
1984). In certain cases, firms simultaneously adopted hard-line practices (concession bargaining or the use of layoffs and the threat of relocation) together with
more participative shop-floor practices (Kochan et al., 1984), thus adding to the
apparent confusion as to the overall direction of industrial relations and human
resources practices.

CURRENT MANAGEMENT PRACTICES IN CANADA

While no single form of management industrial relations practice can be said to be
dominant in Canada today, the last few decades have seen a trend toward increased
employee involvement in decision making. **High performance work systems**,
which are sometimes called high-commitment, high-involvement, innovative work
systems, or alternative work practices, bundle together sets of practices designed to
empower employees, increase their discretionary effort, and improve both organizational and employee outcomes. There is no specific or defining set of practices
included in high performance work systems but they often include rigorous recruitment and selection procedures, incentive-base compensation, intensive training
and development, and reductions in pay and status differentials. Employees are
granted greater autonomy over job tasks and methods of work, sometimes by reor-
ganizing employees into self-directed or **autonomous work teams**. Employees also
help solve production problems and participate in quality control through **quality
circles**, and **total quality management (TQM)**. Many of the practices are not particularly new; what is new is the bundling of these practices.

   Debate surrounds both the prevalence and effectiveness of high performance
work systems. One survey suggests that in 1999, approximately 30 percent of Canadian firms had some sort of merit- or skill-based pay; only 10 percent utilized
autonomous work teams; and only a very few—at most 5 percent—combined
teamwork, flexible job design, performance-based pay systems, and formal team-
work-related training (Morissette and Rosa, 2003). While there is some evidence
that high performance work practices have positive impacts on organizational outcomes such as productivity, the research results are mixed, partially due to the fact
that many firms do not fully implement complementary bundles of practices and,
therefore, do not achieve their synergistic advantages. There is also some evidence of
improved outcomes for employees such as increased job satisfaction, empowerment
and task involvement. However, high performance work systems have also been

**high performance
work systems** A sys-
tem of work practices
designed to empower
employees, facilitate
their participation in
decision making, and
grant them greater
autonomy over job tasks
and methods of work.

**autonomous work
teams** A team of
employees empowered
to make decisions typi-
cally made by managers
or supervisors. The
level of authority and
responsibility can vary
from simply ordering
raw materials to being
empowered to dis-
charge team members.

quality circles A
gathering of employees
for the purpose of iden-
tifying the root cause of
a problem and finding a
solution.

**total quality
management** A
philosophy and set of
practices aimed at
continual improvement
in managing quality,
meeting customer
requirements, improving
production processes,
and reducing costs.

shown to increase both stress and the pace and intensity of work. The actual impact depends on how high performance work systems are implemented, with the most positive employee outcomes resulting from systems that fully implement bundles of practices, including genuine employee empowerment and truly autonomous work teams performing enriched tasks.

Industrial Relations Strategy

A recent development in the evolution of managerial industrial relations practices is the degree to which management has adopted a proactive, rather than reactive, approach to industrial relations. Indeed, as discussed in Chapter 1, the strategic choice theory arose out of concerns that Dunlop's systems framework was inadequate in explaining industrial relations changes occurring in the United States in the early 1980s. These changes, it was argued, were primarily the result of managerial initiatives, especially managerial initiatives concerning unions and workforce unionization. A key assumption behind macro-level management decisions under strategic choice is that union acceptance is no longer a given as it is in the systems framework. Strategic decisions may be designed quite deliberately to avoid the unionization of a workforce, weaken the union's influence where it does exist, or even drive it out altogether. Kochan et al.'s strategic choice model does not categorize the range of potential employers' strategies toward unions; however, one typology that is commonly used outlines the following strategies:

1. Union acceptance
2. Union resistance
3. Union removal
4. Union substitution/avoidance (Thompson, 1995a).

Some research suggests that for Canadian employers with at least a portion of their workforce already unionized, **union acceptance** appears to be the dominant industrial relations strategy. Employers adopting this approach base their strategic decisions upon the recognition that remaining non-union, or ridding themselves of a union that already exists, is neither feasible nor realistic. Either for philosophical or practical reasons, these employers remain neutral if their employees attempt to unionize. Strategic decisions focus on negotiating the best possible collective agreement terms and, in many instances, limiting the influence of unions (Thompson and Ponak, 2005). It is important to note that this category includes a wide range of employers from those who only grudgingly accept the presence of the union to those who embrace co-operative partnerships.

More recent research suggests that while it may be true that the majority of Canadian employers accept unions once they are certified, few remain neutral during the crucial organizing phase (Bentham, 2002). These employers may have adopted a **union resistance strategy**, which is characterized by acceptance of already existent unions but vigorous opposition to additional certifications or expansion of coverage of existing unions. These employers often seek to decrease their non-unionized employees' desire to unionize by adopting strategies such as extending union-negotiated pay and benefits to all employees, whether unionized or not (Thompson and Ponak, 2005). If faced with a union certification campaign,

union acceptance strategy An industrial relations strategy in which employers do not actively resist becoming unionized or make attempts to rid themselves of existing unions.

union resistance strategy An industrial relations strategy characterized by acceptance of already existent unions but vigorous opposition to additional certifications or expansion of coverage of existing unions.

these employers might aggressively communicate their displeasure to employees, threaten closure or relocation if certification is successful, promise increased pay and benefits if the certification fails, or engage in protracted legal battles to thwart unionization.

Employers adopting a **union removal strategy**, on the other hand, go to great lengths to eliminate any unions that already exist within their operation and avoid any new certifications. Thus, they adopt a range of human resource practices designed to decrease employees' motivation to unionize and to demonstrate to employees the limited role unions will be permitted to play within the organization. While few Canadian employers explicitly admit to embracing this industrial relations strategy, financial institutions and service-sector employers, especially fast food and retail, are well-known for adopting tactics that would fall within this category. For example, these employers often provide wage increases to non-unionized employees but deny similar increases to unionized workers or offer these conditions only after very protracted negotiations (Thompson and Ponak, 2005). Should a unionized store or branch go on strike, the employer simply directs customers to the store or branch down the street. Should they be faced with a union organizing campaign, these employers embrace aggressive resistance tactics. To limit the effectiveness of unions that already exist in the organization, these employers may engage in hard bargaining, insist on concessions, and use lockouts as a bargaining tool. To eventually eliminate these unions, employers using a union removal strategy may, for example, invest only in their non-unionized locations, making them increasingly productive, thereby rendering their unionized plants eventually obsolete. Another common tactic is to transfer operations to locations less likely to become unionized such as countries or states with low union density.

The goal of a **union substitution/avoidance strategy** is to remain union free in situations where workers are not yet unionized. Toward that end, employers establish formal non-union representation systems and often provide pay and benefits slightly superior to the unionized norm in their industry. Several employers in the Canadian petroleum industry have embraced this strategy: Imperial Oil, for example, has had "joint industrial councils" since 1919 (Thompson and Ponak, 2005). Dofasco remains the only non-unionized major Canadian steel producer, most likely due to the union substitution/avoidance strategy they have pursued since the 1930s (Thompson and Ponak, 2005). WestJet also endeavours to remain union-free, in order to preserve its labour cost advantage in the highly unionized airline industry.

Union avoidance tactics might include locating in low-density countries or states, careful employee screening, fostering employee identification with the company, providing union-level pay and benefits, and implementing non-union grievance systems. Alternately, tactics might include extensive use of contingent or temporary labour, aggressive opposition to certification campaigns, and shutting down operations that do become unionized.

Beyond managerial attitudes toward unions, a broad range of factors underlie a firm's choice of industrial relations strategy. These include management's business strategy, the degree of unionization within the firm, current collective agreement provisions, and relevant labour laws (Thompson and Ponak, 2005). Furthermore, relative union power, the union's receptivity toward co-operative endeavours, and

union removal strategy An industrial relations strategy in which employers aggressively try to eliminate any unions that already exist within their operation and avoid any new certifications.

union substitution/ avoidance strategy An industrial relations strategy in which the goal is to remain union free. This strategy usually involves implementing practices designed to substitute for union protections.

its militancy, especially with regard to its willingness to strike, also affect management's choice of an industrial relations strategy (Thompson and Ponak, 2005). It must also be recognized that not all employers' strategies fall neatly within one category or another. For example, retailers such as Wal-Mart and the fast-foot giant, McDonalds, have long pursued union avoidance strategies, engaging in protracted, expensive legal battles to defeat union certification applications. However, they are not known for pursuing other, "high-road" union avoidance strategies such as providing union-level pay and benefits or empowering employees through non-union representation schemes.

THE ENVIRONMENT AND MANAGEMENT OF INDUSTRIAL RELATIONS IN CANADA

The political, social, and economic contexts discussed at the beginning of the chapter affect and constrain managerial industrial relations strategies. For example, the statutory limits on employer behaviour during union certification campaigns that are both stricter and more strictly enforced in Canada than in the United States, mean that union resistance or avoidance may be less viable options for many Canadian employers. A combination of contextual factors has resulted in higher union density in Canada than the United States, as well as higher union density in certain industries—again limiting the feasibility of becoming or remaining union free or of limiting existing unions' influence on workplace policies and practices. Both macroeconomic and industry- or firm-specific economic factors also affect the feasibility of certain strategies and increase the instrumentality of others. Thus, different employers—even those in the same industry and in seemingly similar circumstances—may adopt different industrial relations strategies.

This chapter has described some of the contextual factors affecting the Canadian industrial relations system and the strategies and practices adopted by Canadian firms and managers. The next chapter focuses not on management but on another party to the industrial relations system—labour—and traces the historical development of the Canadian labour movement.

Case 2.1

WESTJET: A CANADIAN SUCCESS STORY

On February 29, 1996, WestJet airlines began operations out of Calgary with 220 employees, three aircraft, and routes to five cities in western Canada. Nine years later, WestJet has 4800 employees and 56 airplanes and operates scheduled flights to 32 North American cities, and charter flights to 26 destinations in eight countries. WestJet's CEO, Clive Beddoe, has been named one of Canada's most respected CEOs, and his company, which was named one of Calgary's best places to work and placed among Canada's Top 100 Employers, ranks as the country's best customer service organization and the second most respected company, behind only Royal Bank.

In the mid-1990s, Clive Beddoe and his three partners saw a market for a low-fare, no-frills airline to compete against Air Canada, which in their opinion delivered poor service at outrageously high prices. Drawing upon the success of other low-fare carriers in the United States, such as Southwest, JetBlue, and Valujet, and Europe's low-fare carrier, Ryanair, for inspiration, Beddoe and his partners drew up a solid business plan, which they pitched to wealthy and familiar contacts. Increasing investors' confidence by investing hundreds of thousands of their own money, they raised $8 million in seed money within 27 days. One of the early keys to West-Jet's success in the mature, high-cost airline industry was this solid financing, which enabled it to buy its first three Boeing 737s outright. Other keys to WestJet's success include its willingness to embrace technology and find novel ways to ensure full use of existing assets in order to keep costs low.

WestJet's most important key to success, however, is its commitment to the concept of putting employees first. Beddoe sees the relationship with employees as even more critical to success than the airline's relationship with customers. Good relations with customers, the CEO maintains, are the byproduct of good relations with employees. Although WestJet's salaries are considerably below industry average, employees participate in a profit-sharing plan and also have the option of participating in an employee share-purchase plan where WestJet matches employee contributions dollar for dollar, to a maximum of 20 percent of the employee's annual salary. This generous plan is designed to give employees a genuine interest in the company and to encourage them to think like owners, or as Beddoe puts it "filthy capitalists," and drive the company to success.

In order for all employees to feel like owners, WestJet avoids any class boundaries within the company. The sign outside the executive offices reads "Big Shots." The accountants' area is called "Beanland." Beddoe doesn't have a reserved parking spot and proudly boasts that WestJet's conference table was purchased second-hand. While his desk is relatively luxurious, Beddoe is quick to add that he bought it with his own funds. Everyone, including the CEO, is expected to pitch in and do whatever is necessary to make the airline successful. Pilots help clean the cabins during turnarounds, as do Beddoe and his wife and kids when they fly. Beddoe leads by example, pitching in to carry suitcases, or helping to change an airplane's tires or engines when needed.

Beddoe believes work should be fun and, toward that end, he encourages employees to enjoy their jobs and deal with customers with humour and a positive attitude. Employees are also encouraged to rely on their own ingenuity and take whatever steps are necessary to solve problems that may arise. In 2002, WestJet employees gave away almost $16 million in "guest credits" to compensate their customers for such things as delays and overbookings. Empowering employees to this degree could be risky but WestJet eliminates most of the risk by hiring the right front-line people, screening for disposition and attitude through peer-group interviews during which job candidates are expected to tell stories and jokes and participate in games.

Hiring the right people and aligning their interests with those of the company are not the only keys to WestJet's success. Remaining union-free, in an industry where unionization often means dramatically increased costs, is also pivotal. While there have been several union drives over the past nine years, WestJet remains union-free even in a highly unionized industry, due in part to their creation of a non-union association, the Pro-Active Communication Team (PACT). PACT represents employees in discussion with management and is empowered to go to the board of directors if these discussions are unsatisfactory. Indeed, the company's board includes a PACT representative. PACT's constitution requires that an overwhelming percentage of workers must vote to leave the association before they can be represented by a union, making it quite unlikely a union will gain a foothold in the company. Decreased costs are not the only motivation for remaining union-free; labour flexibility is also key to WestJet's success and would almost certainly be compromised by some union practices, such as seniority and strict adherence to detailed job descriptions. Industry analysts warn that while a union might not affect WestJet's bottom line too adversely while it continues to grow, it would certainly limit the company's ability to shed costs in a downturn.

Sources: Davis, Anthony A. (2004). "Sky High," *Profit* 23:1, pp. 20–24; Holloway, Andy. (2004). "Clive Beddoe," *Canadian Business* 77:9, pp. 42–43; Pederson, Susan. (2002). *Calgary's 10 Best Places to Work*, Macleod Dixon, www.macleoddixon.com/best_places_to_work_v2.pdf [March 19, 2005]; Thompson Okanagan Tourism Association. (2005). *WestJet Airlines*, www.thompsonokanagan.com/trellis/transporation/378 [March 19, 2005]; Jet Thrust Pilot Network. (2002). *Union drive begins at WestJet*, www.jetthrust.com/news/news.php?topicid=94 [March 19, 2005].

Case Questions

1. What industrial relations strategy toward unions has WestJet adopted? Explain which practices point to this strategy and which practices do not seem entirely consistent with this strategy.
2. What factors affected WestJet's decision regarding which industrial relations strategy to adopt?
3. Reflecting on the discussion regarding current management practices, explain the ways in which WestJet's human resource practices resemble a high performance work system.

QUESTIONS FOR DISCUSSION

1. Discuss some of the similarities and differences between the political and social contexts of industrial relations in your home province and in provinces in other regions of Canada.
2. Describe three key labour force trends and their implications for governments, employers, and unions.
3. Distinguish between frictional, structural, and demand-deficient unemployment and discuss some policy solutions appropriate for each.
4. In his book *Working Harder Isn't Working*, Bruce O'Hara (1993) proposes a legislated four-day week at a little over 90 percent of the worker's previous salary as the solution for continuing high unemployment. Discuss the pros and cons of O'Hara's suggestion. If you agree that shorter hours are needed in Canada, but don't think legislation will work, how do you think shorter hours could best be achieved?

5. Describe the main stages in the development of management thought and give some reasons for the changes in management approach between one stage and another.

6. Describe four industrial relations strategies towards unions and discuss the factors that affect which strategy management will adopt.

7. To what extent has the organization for which you work adopted practices associated with high performance work systems? Which of these practices has it adopted? How well have they worked? What have been some of the barriers to successful adoption?

Suggestions for Further Reading

Benjamin, Dwayne, Morley Gunderson, and W. Craig Riddell. (2002). "Introduction to Labour Market Economics." In *Labour Market Economics* (5th ed.), Toronto: McGraw-Hill Ryerson Limited, pp. 1–30. Introduces the actors in the labour market and explains their roles. Discusses factors affecting demand and supply of labour and explains the neoclassical model of the labour market and some alternative approaches.

Betcherman, Gordon. (1999). "Workplace Change in Canada: The Broad Context." In A. Verma and R. Chaykowsi (Eds.), *Contract and Commitment: Employment Relations in the New Economy*. Kingston: Queen's IRC Press. A thorough and very thoughtful overview of recent management trends in Canada.

Kochan, Thomas, Robert McKersie, and Peter Cappelli. (1984). "Strategic Choice and Industrial Relations Theory," *Industrial Relations* 23:1. Perhaps the single most important article on management and IR to have appeared in the past twenty years.

Lipsey, Richard G. and Christopher T.S. Ragan. (2001). *Economics* (10th Cdn. ed.). Toronto: Addison Wesley Longman. An excellent introductory economics text that covers all the basics either for students lacking formal training in economics or those who simply need a refresher. Chapters are divided into independent topics allowing students to focus where needed.

Thompson, Mark, Joseph B. Rose, and Anthony E. Smith. (2003). *Beyond the National Divide: Regional Dimensions of Industrial Relations*. Kingston: Queen's University School of Policy Studies. An interesting analysis of the similarities and differences in industrial relations structures and the historical, legal, political, and social factors that influence industrial relations in eight Canadian provinces. Chapters are organized by province, allowing students to focus on as few or as many provinces as they wish.

CHAPTER 3

THE HISTORY OF THE CANADIAN LABOUR MOVEMENT

Canadian labour has come a long way since 1900, when many people were still self-employed farmers working their land with horses or mules and simple hand tools.

LEARNING OBJECTIVES

After studying this chapter, you should be able to:

1. Explain some of the early barriers faced by the Canadian labour movement.
2. Distinguish the special difficulties faced by the labour movement in Quebec.
3. Identify the role played by government in the development of Canada's labour movement.
4. Explain the significance of the Canadian labour movement's work in the political arena.
5. Describe the role played by international (i.e., US-based) unions in the development of the Canadian labour movement.
6. Identify some of the most severe challenges faced by the Canadian labour movement today.

Like unions in all countries, the Canadian unions we know today are the product of eco-nomic, social, and political circumstances, as well as being (at least in part) the shapers of their own destinies. In this chapter, we trace Canadian unions through three stages of development—from craft through industrial to public service unionism. Along the way, we also consider the role of government in the development of Canada's labour move-ment, the nature of the political involvement entered into by Canadian unions, and the role played by international unions—or unions headquartered in the United States but with branches in this country. The chapter ends with a discussion of the challenges fac-ing the Canadian labour movement at the start of the new millennium.

THE DEVELOPMENT OF CANADIAN UNIONS: A BRIEF OVERVIEW

Very broadly, today's Canadian labour movement can be described as one that seeks to strike a balance between the pragmatic, economically-oriented approach characteristic of American unions and the more politically and socially conscious approach generally taken by European unions. Numerically, too, Canada's union movement, with membership rates of just under one-third of the country's work-force, holds an intermediate position between the heavily unionized countries such as Sweden and Denmark, and those with low membership rates such as the United States and Japan (Bamber and Lansbury, 1993; Adams, 1995a).

The movement has come a long way from the small, locally-based movement of the early-to-mid-nineteenth century. But the evolution has been a difficult and often tortuous one. In addition to overcoming obstacles common to most Western labour movements, such as employer and government opposition (Adams, 1995a), the Canadian movement has had to contend with problems peculiar to this coun-try, such as sparse population, a high degree of outside control over the Canadian economy, general economic underdevelopment (Lipton, 1973), and severe regional imbalances (Heron, 1989). These factors tended to retard the development of an independent Canadian labour movement, as did heavy waves of out-migration of Canadian workers to the United States (Drache, 1984) and the fragmentation of Canadian labour into separate English-Canadian and French-Canadian move-ments (Drache, 1984; Lipsig-Mumme, 1995).

An even greater obstacle was the tendency of many Canadian workers to affili-ate with the US-based **international unions** (Heron, 1989). There were good rea-sons why Canadian workers often found the internationals attractive. For one thing, American unions were generally bigger, stronger, and wealthier, with larger strike funds and more experienced organizers (Logan, 1948). For another, an American union card was a valuable possession for a Canadian worker who, due to the seasonal nature of work in much of the country, might well find himself forced to move to Massachusetts or Ohio for at least part of the year (Lipton, 1973; McKay, 1983:137). Still, there were inherent problems with a situation in which Canada's labour movement did not really control its own affairs. After surfacing periodically throughout much of the nineteenth century, these problems would come to a head just after the turn of the century, just before the First World War, and then again during the 1960s and 1970s.

international union A union headquartered in the United States but with members in Canada.

Despite these and other obstacles, the Canadian labour movement has, over time, managed to achieve impressive gains, both for its members and for society at large. Unionized workers have benefited greatly from the higher wages and benefits, safer workplaces, and generally improved working conditions that have resulted from collective bargaining. Almost all Canadians have benefited from the minimum wage and other employment standards legislation and from the social programs and universal health care insurance achieved largely through the labour movement's work in the political arena (Richardson, 1985). Canadian unions continue to fight to maintain these social programs today, even as ongoing globalization, trade liberalization, economic restructuring, and deindustrialization have made it increasingly difficult for them to maintain their members' jobs and incomes.

Heron (1989:xvi) identifies four key periods during which the Canadian labour movement expanded its membership and goals. These four periods were the 1880s, the end of each of the world wars, and the decade after 1965. Each of the four saw an upsurge of labour activity during a time of economic transformation; in each, workers were able to "coalesce into a united force capable of articulating and pursuing common goals" (Heron, 1989). In three of these periods (all but the 1880s), the role of government was also important. During the First World War, the government used the *Industrial Disputes Investigation Act* to prevent employers from discharging workers for union activity, which would have hindered the war effort. This encouraged union organization (Morton, 1995), although workers in war industries were still barred from striking. Later, Canada's first general collective bargaining legislation (*PC 1003*) spurred post–Second World War union growth, while the growth of unions in the 1960s and 1970s was mainly the result of public sector legislation such as the *Public Service Staff Relations Act*. In all three cases, the passage or extension of the legislation in question was a direct government response to labour militancy, albeit one designed to channel if not blunt that militancy (see Godard, 1994:260–261).

The Pre-Industrial Period (to 1850)

The earliest recorded strikes in Canada appear to have taken place in the eighteenth century at the royal shipyard in Quebec City (Moogk, 1976:33) and in the fur trade at Lac la Pluie (Lipton, 1973:1). But such disputes were rare in the early pre-industrial period. Most Canadians were self-employed farmers, fishers, or artisans. Those who did work for hire generally did so on a seasonal basis or for a relatively short period of time; few expected to remain employees indefinitely. Employees worked under a paternalistic system (often one of formal apprenticeship) and would normally work side-by-side with their employers and eat with the family (Heron, 1989:2–3).

The first significant wave of worker organization appears to have taken place shortly after the War of 1812. By the 1830s, there was significant organization in a number of towns, including Halifax, Quebec City, Montreal, Toronto, Hamilton, and Saint John (Forsey, 1982:9–18). To avoid harsh anti-conspiracy legislation, such as Nova Scotia's 1816 law that provided three-month jail terms for those entering into union contracts (Morton and Copp, 1980; Forsey, 1982; Heron, 1989),[1] unions generally operated as "friendly societies" providing members with a degree of mutual insurance against death, accidents, sickness, or unemployment (Forsey,

1982; Heron, 1989). Most early unions were purely local organizations involving skilled craftspeople such as tailors, shoemakers, carpenters, printers, bricklayers, and masons (Forsey, 1982:30–31). Few were confrontational. Shared craft traditions tended to blur the distinctions between masters, on the one hand, and journeymen and apprentices, on the other (Heron, 1989:7).

Beginning in the 1830s, with the arrival of large numbers of unskilled Irish, Scottish, and English immigrants, "crowd" behaviour became a factor during times of labour strife (Heron, 1989:5). Such behaviour typically involved direct action against the perpetrator of an alleged wrong, such as the burning of effigies or attacks on business owners' homes. Violence would often ensue, especially if police or troops were called in (Heron, 1989).

"Crowd" behaviour evolved into a more organized form of labour strife with the arrival, in the 1840s, of even larger numbers of Irish immigrants, many of whom found work as canal labourers. These labourers were incensed at the conditions they were expected to endure, including 14-hour days, payment in goods rather than money, grossly inadequate wages, and long waits between paydays (Bleasdale, 1981:124). In response, they took desperate measures. Their tactics ranged from more or less conventional work stoppages to more extreme measures, such as patrolling the canals and driving off other potential job hunters and halting navigation on the Welland Canal—or even attacking vessels and their passengers (Bleasdale, 1981:130–136). Although these tactics led to harsh reprisals from both employers and the government, they did often result in higher wages.

Early Labour Organization in Quebec

Effective labour organization was generally slower to develop in Quebec than in the rest of British North America. Like their English-Canadian counterparts, French-Canadian workers did not relish employee status. Most sought to become self-employed and economically independent (Moogk, 1976:15) and would remain employees only until they had saved enough money to achieve that end. Like the Nova Scotia and Canada West legislatures, the royal administration in Quebec had banned workers' associations for fear they would restrain competition in commerce and force up prices (Moogk, 1976:5). Both the courts and public officials persistently rebuffed workers' associations in their quest for economic protection and sought to limit their powers (Moogk, 1976:5).

But the Quebec authorities' suppression of collective activity went well beyond English Canada's criminal conspiracy laws against unions. Public protests over high prices and shortages were treated as sedition (Moogk, 1976). While expressions of craft fellowship were tolerated, they were channelled into the harmless (from the administration's perspective) form of religious confraternities, subordinated to the Roman Catholic Church, whose activities were limited to devotions and banquets (Moogk, 1976:7). Later, their powers were further limited by a French parliamentary decree that denied them the powers of discipline and compulsion over their members. With no meaningful economic or political role, the confraternities didn't provide Quebec workers with the sort of training in collective organization that English Canada's friendly societies did. The result was that, in the industrial era, Quebec workers lacked such training and were far slower to unionize than workers in the rest of Canada (Moogk, 1976:34–35).

In addition, French-Canadian workers often faced discrimination when they sought work elsewhere in British North America. Often passed over in favour of Irish labourers for canal work, in part because of the Lower Canada Legislative Assembly's desire to "anglicize Quebec by means of immigration" (Drache, 1984:20), they responded by migrating in droves to New England. When they were hired in English Canada, they were often given low-end jobs, which again led many to seek their fortune in New England rather than in English Canada (Drache, 1984:21). Quebec workers' tendency to try to improve their lot through emigration proved to be yet another obstacle to union growth in that province.

Labour in the First Industrial Revolution

What is known as Canada's "First Industrial Revolution" began shortly after 1850. Craft shops expanded into sizeable factories, and employers built lumber mills, canneries, and large coal mines (Heron, 1989:8). Instead of the handful of people employed by traditional craft establishments, these new enterprises often employed hundreds. They also needed to draw on wider markets beyond strictly local areas in order to stay in business.

With factories selling to expanded markets, profits became all-important. As manufacturers began to sell their goods to people they had never met, they could often compete only on the basis of cost (Commons, 1918). Profits were also necessary to enable employers to pay for all their costly new machinery.

To make profits, employers had to control their costs. Since they could generally do little about the costs of raw materials, land, or capital equipment, they focused their attention on controlling the cost of labour, which they could do something about. To this end, they brought in strict time-scheduling and monitoring of workers' output. Bells and clocks became common in factories, and the new, stricter schedules were enforced through fines and even beatings (Heron, 1989; Trofimenkoff, 1977:213). Work was sped up, mechanized, and simplified as much as possible so that more could be produced in less time with fewer people. With an eye to saving on wages, employers relied less on skilled artisans, flooding the market with cheaper, less skilled workers, including boys and women (Heron, 1989:8–9), and replacing skilled workers with machines where possible (Morton and Copp, 1980:22; Bercuson and Bright, 1994:78). Many employers were especially partial to female employees because, in addition to commanding lower wages than men, they were seen as docile, clean, quick, and sober (Trofimenkoff, 1977:220).

craft union A union that limits its membership to a single craft (e.g., brickmaking).

In reaction to harsher workplace conditions and employers' frequent attempts to deskill their jobs and cut their wages, workers began increasingly to form **craft unions**, some of which began to affiliate with American internationals (Heron, 1989:10–11). Cigar makers, coopers, molders, machinists, iron-puddlers, and locomotive engineers were among the groups that began to form unions after 1850. By the 1870s, coal miners were also starting to organize (Heron, 1989:10). Inspired by British "New Model" unionism, the new Canadian craft unions sought to formalize their relations with employers and to put themselves on a more secure footing through high dues and strong, centralized leadership (Heron, 1989; Morton and Copp, 1980). A union's bargaining strategy typically consisted of posting its wage demands on the factory or shop doors. If times were good and demand for the product high, the employer might well meet the demands. Otherwise, he would generally refuse the demands, and a strike or lockout might then ensue. Often such a dispute would result in the workers' dismissal; sometimes it would even lead to the union's dissolution. As Morton and Copp (1980:10) note, nineteenth century unions could generally succeed only when there were lasting labour shortages. Still, though strikes remained a very risky business at a time when merely belonging to a union could leave a worker open to criminal conspiracy charges, they became more and more frequent as industrialization progressed (Heron, 1989:12).

Beyond the Workplace: Making Common Cause

Confederation, increased industrialization, the growth of central labour organizations in Ontario and Quebec, and growing international awareness of the industrial system's abuses led Canadian workers in the 1870s to mobilize around issues of broad interest to all workers, such as shorter working hours and improved workplace safety (Godard, 1994; Morton, 1995). Nine-Hour Leagues in Hamilton and Montreal marked the beginning of broader workers' solidarity in Canada (Heron, 1989:14–15), with their strategy based on a series of strikes to support the demand for shorter work days (Godard, 1994:105). In the short run, the strategy failed, as Toronto printers struck George Brown's *Globe* ahead of schedule in 1872, causing Brown to charge the strikers with conspiracy and preventing the achievement of the nine-hour day for the time being (Morton, 1995:134). But the incident did provide politicians with some evidence of working people's potential political power and may well have been partly responsible for the Macdonald government's 1872 enactment of a *Trade Union Act*.

Through much of the nineteenth century, unions had been regarded as conspiracies in restraint of trade in Canada and in many European countries (Adams, 1995a:496). In Canada, this notion ended with the *Trade Union Act* of 1872, which declared that the purposes of unions were not to be considered unlawful simply because they might be in restraint of trade (Carter, 1989:30) and sheltered peaceful picketing from criminal prosecution (Heron, 1989:17). However, the protections of the Act applied only to those unions that took the trouble to register with the government, which few if any apparently did, thereby rendering it all but meaningless in practice (Morton, 1990:27). While the law gave unions little in the way of substantive protection, since employers still had recourse to civil conspiracy actions (Heron, 1989:18) and could still use any number of union-busting techniques (Lipton, 1973:65), it did provide unions with some measure of political legitimacy (Godard, 1994:106). In the years to come, the *Trade Union Act* was followed by more substantive legislation, such as the repeal (subject to certain limitations)[2] of the harsh *Masters and Servants Act* prohibitions on strikes (Morton and Copp, 1980; Godard, 1994), which meant that employees could no longer be sent to jail for striking or leaving their employers' service (Morton, 1990:34). Various provincial *Factory Acts*, which applied mainly to women and children (Morton and Copp, 1980:84), were also passed. Another, though short-lived, legacy of the period was the Canadian Labour Union, formed in Toronto in 1873 to address larger political issues and serve as a kind of national labour federation (Morton, 1995:134).

The Knights of Labor

The expansion of industrialization and strong growth in the manufacturing sector led to a new wave of unionization in the 1880s. The decade saw a revival of the craft unions and the formation of the Provincial Workmen's Association, a Nova Scotia miners' union (Heron, 1989:20). Antagonism between workers and employers became more pronounced during this period, as employers sped up assembly lines and sought to impose even stricter controls on workers in an attempt to extract still higher levels of production from them (Kealey and Palmer, 1981:240–241).

At this juncture, with the social costs of industrialization becoming ever more apparent (Kealey and Palmer, 1981:241), the **Knights of Labor** appeared on the Canadian scene, starting their first Canadian local assembly in Hamilton in 1875 (Craig and Solomon, 1996:115). This organization, which had been founded in Philadelphia in 1869 (Godard, 1994:107), was quite unlike any previous labour organization. As their leaders often said (Kealey and Palmer, 1982), they did not seek to make richer people, but better people. While conventional craft unions sought to improve the terms and conditions of employment at individual workplaces, the Knights aimed at nothing less than a moral and social transformation of industrial society (Kealey and Palmer, 1982).

In pursuit of such transformation, the Knights relied mainly on education and political action. During their brief time in Canada, they opened reading rooms and libraries and supported weekly newspapers, as well as developing producer and consumer cooperatives (Heron, 1989:25–27; Kealey and Palmer, 1981:250). Unlike most other labour organizations of their day (McKay, 1983:125), the Knights admitted women as well as men and unskilled as well as skilled workers, excluding only the Chinese (Kealey and Palmer, 1981; 1982). So broad and so persuasive was their appeal that in Ontario alone they organized at least 21 800 members over their history (Kealey and Palmer, 1981:245).

Politically, they achieved their greatest gains at the municipal level, including earlier store closing hours, union wages for municipal workers, and improved public transit (Kealey and Palmer, 1981:256). At provincial and national levels, while unable to achieve their goal of creating an independent working-class party (Kealey and Palmer, 1981), they did succeed in getting labour's voice heard by the politicians. During the 1890s, both the federal and the Ontario provincial governments implemented many of the Knights' recommendations, including factory acts, bureaus of labour statistics, arbitration measures, extension of the suffrage, and employers' liability acts (Kealey and Palmer, 1981:265). Perhaps most noteworthy of all, the first Monday in September was established as a holiday in 1894 in recognition of the dignity of labour (Morton, 1995:135).

The Knights' role in strikes has generated considerable controversy (Morton, 1995; Kealey and Palmer, 1981;1982). Undeniably they were less enthusiastic about strikes than were most conventional craft unions, generally preferring to resolve disputes through conciliation or arbitration instead. At the same time, the record shows that they took part in and even led a good many strikes in Ontario during the 1880s (Kealey and Palmer, 1981:258). It also shows that after a downturn in the economy in the late 1880s, the Knights became more cautious about striking, and that during a London cigar makers' strike, they signed up scab cigar makers and allowed them to use the Knights' label in competition with the cigar makers' union

Knights of Labor
Idealistic early labour federation, which organized on an industry-wide rather than craft basis.

(Heron, 1989:26–27). This action outraged international unionists and caused many to leave the order (Heron, 1989:28). Essentially, it was the beginning of the end for the Knights, though they were to linger on in Canada until the Berlin Convention of 1902. But whether or not the Knights' conception of broad-based **industrial unionism** was wildly ahead of its time, as Morton (1995:135) suggests, their vision of a genuine alternative culture would inspire former members until well into the twentieth century (Kealey and Palmer, 1981:229–230).

industrial unionism Broad-based, politically conscious unionism that seeks to organize all workers in an industry.

Trades and Labour Congress

The rise and fall of the Knights of Labor were far from the only significant developments on the Canadian labour scene during the 1880s. A more lasting development was the formation, in 1886, of the **Trades and Labour Congress** of Canada (TLC). This organization, which would remain Canada's major labour confederation until its 1956 merger with the Canadian Congress of Labour, met annually to address such labour-related issues as immigration policy, enforcement of factory acts, free education for children, and shorter work hours (Forsey, 1982; Morton and Copp, 1980). Like Samuel Gompers' American Federation of Labor, it did not affiliate itself with any political party, instead lobbying governments on an issue-by-issue basis.

Trades and Labour Congress Canada's first major labour federation, founded in 1886.

Labour in the Second Industrial Revolution

American Federation of Labor

A second industrial revolution began in Canada during the 1890s. Factories became larger and more capital-intensive (Heron, 1989:30–31; Kealey and Palmer, 1981:235), and supervision grew even stricter under the coercive drive system (discussed in detail in Chapter 2). Not surprisingly, worker–management struggles for workplace control intensified (Heron, 1989). Meanwhile, wages for most workers remained low despite the period's vast accumulation of capital. As late as 1890, Toronto printers were earning $12 for a 54-hour week (Lipton, 1973:79); less-skilled adult male workers generally earned far less—and women and children still less (Morton and Copp, 1980; Lipton, 1973; Bullen, 1986; McIntosh, 1987).

Conditions were clearly ripe for a new wave of union organizing. As in the past, Canadian workers found help south of the border. In the middle of his own organizing drive, **American Federation of Labor (AFL)** president, Samuel Gompers, realized that if Canada were not organized, all the AFL's efforts might be futile, since American employers would be able to procure cheaper Canadian labour (Morton, 1995:136). To prevent this from happening, Gompers enlisted the services of John Flett, a Hamilton carpenter and one-time socialist. Flett's turn-of-the-century campaign proved astoundingly successful: He was responsible for 57 new AFL locals in Canada in 1901 and for most of the 50 new locals added the following year (Morton and Copp, 1980:70). This wave of AFL organizing transformed the Canadian labour movement, setting it firmly on an international path. By 1902, fully 95 percent of all Canadian unionists belonged to international unions. The international direction of the Canadian labour movement was confirmed by Flett's election to the TLC

American Federation of Labor (AFL) US-based labour federation, the forerunner of the current AFL-CIO.

presidency at the organization's 1902 convention, held in Berlin, Ontario[3] (Morton and Copp, 1980).

The Berlin Convention

Berlin Convention
Crucial 1902 convention of the Trades and Labour Congress, which banned dual unionism and affiliated Canadian and American unions more closely.

Up until the **Berlin Convention**, the TLC had been less doctrinally rigid about its unionism than had the AFL. It had included local assemblies of the Knights of Labor alongside traditional craft unions—a practice that the AFL, and Gompers in particular, loathed.[4] Berlin changed all that. After the convention, no national union would be recognized by the TLC when a corresponding international union existed, and in no case would more than one central body be chartered in any city or town (Morton and Copp, 1980:74). This prohibition of "dual" unionism (i.e., the existence of more than one union per craft or trade) led the TLC to expel its remaining Knights assemblies, as well as other national unions organizing the same industries as AFL unions. The 33 expelled unions comprised about one-fifth of the TLC's total membership (Drache, 1984:27).

Historians and industrial relations experts differ on the significance of the Berlin Convention. To some (Morton, 1995:137), the linkage between American and Canadian labour movements established at Berlin was only common sense, since Canadian unionists "wanted to share a North American standard of living." To others (Drache, 1984:26–28), the move effectively split the Canadian labour movement by tying it to an American federation actively seeking to hinder its development as an independent, nationalist, and progressive force. Most likely, the truth lies somewhere in between. While Berlin did, to a degree, split the Canadian movement (especially insofar as it maintained TLC control in central Canada, leaving eastern and western unions out in the cold), it did not and could not destroy a persistent nationalist spirit within that movement. That spirit would find expression in a series of nationally-oriented labour federations, from the National Trades and Labour Congress (later known as the Canadian Federation of Labour) in the first quarter of the twentieth century through the **All-Canadian Congress of Labour (ACCL)** (1927–1940) to the **Canadian Congress of Labour (CCL)** (1940–1956). Unlike the TLC, the ACCL and CCL would both seek to organize workers on an industry-wide rather than craft basis and would place considerable emphasis on political action (Craig and Solomon, 1996:120–123).

All-Canadian Congress of Labour (ACCL) and Canadian Congress of Labour (CCL) Small Canadian labour federations that sought to organize workers on an industry-wide basis and emphasized political action.

Radical Unionism

While the Berlin Convention appeared to set the Canadian labour movement on a moderate as well as international course, there were a good many radical unions operating in Canada during the first two decades of this century. Berlin may even have heightened some unions' radicalism, by confirming that there was no place for them within the mainstream labour movement.

The century's first decade saw a series of increasingly violent strikes, often involving the use of police and volunteer militia to suppress them. Many of these disputes involved street-railway workers. Indeed, it seems that almost every Ontario city of any size had at least one major street-railway strike between 1895 and 1910 (Morton and Copp, 1980:77). These strikes helped develop strong public support for the labour movement (Heron, 1989:34–36), since both workers and railway-riding members of the general public were seeking to have the monopolies placed under public ownership, as most eventually were. Many other strikes occurred in the coal mines of Nova Scotia (McKay, 1983; Frank, 1983; McIntosh, 1987) and in BC's mines, logging camps, and railway gangs (McCormack, 1975; Mouat, 1990). On the railway gangs, for instance, a 12-hour day and seven-day week were standard. The work was backbreaking, and accidents, including fatal ones, were far from uncommon. Foremen often drove the men with their fists, and in some cases workers were watched by armed guards (McCormack, 1975:327).

Given such conditions, it is hardly surprising that the largely unskilled and immigrant workers should have turned to a radical union like the **Industrial Workers of the World (IWW)** for help. Like some other unions of its day, the IWW had a syndicalist philosophy. It placed little faith in either collective bargaining or political action, believing instead in a huge general strike that would destroy capitalism (McCormack, 1975:329–330). Meanwhile, the "Wobblies" were able to provide their members with much practical help in the here and now. Their organizing was done in at least 10 different languages, and their union halls served as mail drops and dormitories, as employment agencies, infirmaries, and classrooms (McCormack, 1975:328).

Industrial Workers of the World (IWW, or Wobblies) Radical, Western-based union of the early twentieth century.

Conciliation Legislation: *The IDI Act* (1907)

It was a coal strike that led Parliament to pass, in 1907, the *Industrial Disputes Investigation Act*, arguably the most significant piece of labour legislation Canada had yet seen. A nine-month strike of coal miners in the Lethbridge district in 1906 had come close to leaving residents facing a prairie winter without heat (Baker, 1983; Morton and Copp, 1980). Appalled by the near miss in Lethbridge, and by the increasing violence of other disputes—such as a strike in a suburban Ottawa lumber yard that left three dead that same year (Morton and Copp, 1980:88)—the public demanded government action to help stem the increasing labour bloodshed.

The use of conciliation to assist in the settlement of labour disputes was not a new concept in Canada. In 1900, the government had created a Department of Labour with a conciliation service (Heron, 1989:46). At the same time, it passed the *Dominion Conciliation Act*, allowing the labour minister to appoint a conciliation board either at one of the parties' request or on his own initiative (Carter, 1989:30). The idea behind the conciliation process, which initially was voluntary, was that once people became aware of the issues of labour disputes from reading the conciliation board's published report, public pressure would compel the two sides to settle those disputes (Carter, 1989). Similar principles were written into the *Railway Labour Disputes Act* of 1903 (Carter, 1989).

In 1907, with the passage of the *Industrial Disputes Investigation Act*, conciliation became compulsory. The Act required all workers and employers in transportation, resources, and utilities industries to submit their disputes to a three-person conciliation board before starting a strike or lockout. Even after the board had issued its report, a further "cooling-off" period was required before any strike or lockout could become legal (Heron, 1989:47). Compulsory conciliation has remained a cornerstone of most Canadian collective bargaining legislation to this day—although three-person board reports are now rare and the process has evolved into something much more closely resembling mediation in most cases (Carter, 1989).

The TLC initially gave the *IDI Act* cautious approval, but quickly changed its mind (Morton and Copp, 1980:89–90). The Act's greatest benefit to unions may have been in legitimizing very weak unions, which would otherwise have had little hope of getting their point across to the general public (Morton, 1990). More often, though, the time delays simply gave employers the opportunity to stockpile production, fire and blacklist union activists, or hire strikebreakers and private police (Morton, 1990; Heron, 1989). The Act did not require employers to participate in collective bargaining, nor did it prevent employers from imposing yellow-dog contracts barring employees from union membership. Since it did not provide such basic rights as the right to join a union or go on strike, the Act not only failed to put an end to the kind of bitter, violent recognition disputes that had led to its enactment in the first place but, in the view of industrial relations author Stuart Jamieson, it actually delayed the evolution of mature collective bargaining in Canada (see Morton and Copp, 1980:90).[5]

Even the immediate effects of the *IDI* probably did little to improve labour–management relations. The period just before the First World War continued to be marked by bitter workplace struggles, as managers schooled in the newly fashionable scientific management approach (discussed in detail in Chapter 2) sought to speed up production lines and extract ever more effort from their workers. Meanwhile, the workers affected by these new management practices were, like their European counterparts, turning to socialism or other forms of radicalism in increasing numbers (see Adams, 1995a; Heron, 1989:49–51; 1984). More and more, workers and managers were on a collision course and these conflicts were too profound to be solved by the simple requirements for a conciliation board report and a cooling-off period before a legal strike.

The First World War and Its Aftermath

The First World War saw a rapid increase in union membership, an increase spurred both by rising prices and by wartime labour shortages. Between 1914 and 1919, Canadian union membership more than doubled (Godard, 1994:95) as the wartime organizational surge brought unskilled workers, municipal government employees, and even teachers and other white-collar workers into the labour movement for the first time (Heron, 1989:53–54). These new unionists had grievances that went beyond soaring wartime prices. Unlike the British, French, and American governments, the Canadian government made no attempt to consult with union leaders or socialist politicians during the war, even though the TLC had obediently endorsed the war effort in 1914 (Heron, 1989:53; Morton and Copp, 1980:103). Further frustrated by their inability to elect members to Parliament on a labour ticket (Heron, 1989:56), Canadian unionists turned to radical protest and direct action. The period from 1917 to 1920 saw a wave of strike activity across Canada, inspired at least in part by a worldwide workers' revolt set in motion by the Russian Revolution of 1917 (Heron, 1989:55).

After the largely Western-based radicals lost out to the conservative craft unionists at the 1918 TLC convention, they launched a new industrial union known as the **"One Big Union" (OBU)** with socialist leadership. Their aim was to create a

One Big Union (OBU)
Short-lived Western-based socialist industrial union launched in 1918.

broad-based union free of traditional craft jurisdictional barriers. One of their key demands was for a six-hour day to reduce unemployment (Heron, 1989:57–58). The launching of the new union was, however, quickly overshadowed by some dramatic events taking place in Winnipeg and a number of other Canadian cities during the spring of 1919.

The Winnipeg General Strike

In April 1918, Winnipeg's workers had successfully staged a general strike over the issue of city workers' right to strike (Morton and Copp, 1980:115). Just over a year later, on May 15, 1919, they tried the same tactic to show sympathy with the building and metal trades unions, which had been denied collective bargaining rights (Heron, 1989:59). On that day, more than 25 000 workers walked off their jobs, launching a six-week strike (Morton and Copp, 1980:119). The Winnipeg strike would spark a wave of 30 sympathy strikes extending eastward to Amherst, Nova Scotia, and westward to Vancouver (Kealey, 1984:203–206). It proved a colossal failure in the end, however, as all three levels of government combined to crush it (Heron, 1989:60–61)—continuing a pattern of government repression that had begun during the war with the banning of socialist and radical organizations and the closure of foreign-language newspapers (Morton and Copp, 1980:113). Strike leaders were arrested and threatened with deportation (Morton and Copp, 1980), and the city's police force was dismissed for its pro-strike leanings and replaced by untrained special constables. Then, on "Bloody Saturday" (June 21, 1919), the RCMP charged a crowd of strikers, using bullets as well as their horses to suppress the crowd in the most authoritative way possible. By day's end, two strikers were dead and at least thirty were injured. Four days later, the strike was over (Morton and Copp, 1980:122).

For all intents and purposes, the Winnipeg General Strike's collapse marked the end of the radical labour movement in Canada (Morton and Copp, 1980:122–123). Even as many of the Winnipeg strike leaders went off to prison, the OBU was being reduced to insignificance, weakened both by employers who refused to have anything to do with it and by craft unionists who collaborated in undermining its strikes (Heron, 1989:59).

The Post-war Retreat

Ushered in by a severe depression that led to massive layoffs and hopeless strikes against draconian wage cuts (Heron, 1989:60), the 1920s were to prove extraordinarily difficult years for the Canadian labour movement. Continuing government repression, a renewed employer offensive against labour, and deep schisms within the movement itself combined to weaken labour's position dramatically and to bring "fearfulness, fatalism and cynicism" back into the working-class consciousness (Heron, 1989). Throughout most of the decade, union membership fell sharply (Morton and Copp, 1980:125–126). Ongoing waves of immigration throughout the decade helped ensure that unemployment levels remained relatively high and that unskilled and semi-skilled workers would continue to be easy to replace (Godard, 1994:117).

Having failed at radical industrial action, at the start of the decade the labour movement returned to more conventional electoral politics. In Ontario and Alberta, labour parties elected enough members to form coalitions with farmers' parties, but basic disagreements over such issues as work hours, prohibition, free trade, and taxation levels prevented the alliances from lasting very long (Heron, 1989:61–62). By the decade's end, most mainstream TLC unionists had reverted to the old Sam Gompers method of lobbying politicians on single issues of direct concern to unions (Morton, 1995:140).

With working people so clearly on the defensive, many early post-war employers found it easy to simply crush unions by intimidating and harassing any workers known or suspected to have had anything to do with them. For those who disliked such heavy-handed tactics, there was the new paternalistic management, or "American Plan" as it was often called.[6] The main idea here was to reduce workers' desire to join unions by providing company-dominated unions, or industrial councils, as channels through which workers could voice their concerns without posing any fundamental challenge to management's authority (Godard, 1994:113–115; Morton and Copp, 1980:130–131; Slichter, 1929). It isn't clear just how widely paternalistic management practices were adopted in Canada. But where they were adopted, they appear to have been fairly successful at keeping unions out (Godard, 1994:117; Slichter, 1929).

The period was not without its bitter struggles, particularly in Nova Scotia's coal-mining industry, where the military intervened three times to repress strike action. But the struggles were rarely successful, their failure underscoring the need for basic legislation protecting workers' rights to organize and to go on strike.

Catholic and Communist Unionism

As if the challenges from without weren't difficult enough, the 1920s saw the Canadian labour movement split in several different directions. We've already discussed the emergence of a number of different nationalist labour federations unhappy with the TLC's strong ties to the AFL. More serious, perhaps, because it pointed to new schisms within the labour movement, was the emergence of Catholic confessional and Communist union federations. The former had its roots in traditional Quebec nationalism, heightened by the First World War conscription crisis, and in a long-standing tradition of Church involvement in settling labour disputes in the province (Morton and Copp, 1980:131). Since early in the century, Quebec's Catholic hierarchy had been working for a distinctly Catholic unionism that would promote Catholic and francophone values, rather than the secular and socialistic values they saw arising out of the then-dominant international unions (Heron, 1989:60; Boivin, 1982 [see Déom and Boivin, 2001]:426–427).

Their efforts bore fruit in 1921 with the establishment of the **Confédération des travailleurs catholique du Canada (CTCC)**, which claimed to represent some 26 000 members (Boivin, 1982 [see Déom and Boivin, 2001]:427). A key aspect of confessional unionism was the attachment of a priest to each local, ostensibly as an adviser, but more often than not as its de facto president. The CTCC also stressed the common interests of workers and employers, shunning strikes in favour of less confrontational approaches such as conciliation and arbitration.[7] The new Catholic

Confédération des travailleurs du Canada (CTCC)
Catholic confessional union federation launched in 1921.

unions represented a serious challenge to the internationals and the TLC (Morton and Copp, 1980:131), since they were often competing for members with the older federations.

The challenge posed by the Communists, who launched their new party in Ontario in 1921, was equally severe. Since the Canadian party took its orders from Moscow, its labour strategies underwent a number of bizarre, even embarrassing, shifts resulting from Soviet policy changes (Morton and Copp, 1980:133–134). Early in the decade, the orders were to "bore from within," taking over the conservative AFL and TLC and transforming them into radical bodies. Unsuccessful in this attempt, the Communists in 1927 turned their attention to the new, more progressive ACCL and sought to bring in a number of like-minded unions in a bid to wrest control of the federation from its founder, Aaron Mosher. All this did was to earn the Communists the enmity of the non-Communist nationalist unions (Heron, 1989:70) and get them expelled from the ACCL (Morton and Copp, 1980:134). In 1930, the Communists formed their own labour federation, the **Workers' Unity League (WUL)**, dedicated to "militant industrial unionism and socialist revolution" (Heron, 1989:70). Finally, in 1935, still under orders from Moscow, the Communists changed their strategy yet again, disbanded the WUL, and rejoined the mainstream labour movement with an eye to forming broad-based anti-fascist alliances.

The WUL did much useful work within the Canadian labour movement, particularly by assuming leadership of the great majority of Canadian strikes carried out during the early 1930s (Heron, 1989:70–71). But by fragmenting the already small left-wing opposition within Canada's labour movement to the American-dominated TLC, the Communists also helped delay the emergence of strong, progressive national unionism.

Workers' Unity League (WUL)
Depression-era Communist labour federation.

Judicial Fragmentation

The final cause of fragmentation within the Canadian labour movement was neither a union nor a political party, but the British Privy Council, which in the Snider case of 1925 overruled a solid majority of Canadian judges to declare the *IDI Act* unconstitutional because labour relations was a matter of civil and property rights and, therefore, fell within provincial—not the federal—jurisdiction (Craig and Solomon, 1996:206). Since then, labour law, except in the case of undertakings clearly of a federal nature, has been held to be under provincial jurisdiction. In addition to making life more complicated for all actors in the IR system by in effect establishing multiple IR jurisdictions instead of one,[8] provincial jurisdiction has arguably promoted a decentralized union structure (Murray, 1995) that has made it more difficult for the Canadian labour movement to pursue coordinated national economic and political strategies.

Labour During the Depression

The Great Depression of the 1930s offered conclusive evidence of the failure of conventional approaches to economic and political problems. Like many other groups at this time, the Canadian labour movement began to try out a variety of new approaches both in workplaces and in the political arena. It was helped greatly by the American movement, which used a politically sympathetic government to achieve gains it had previously only dreamed of, including the granting of collective bargaining rights.

By 1933, one worker in four was unemployed, an increase of over 300 percent in the national unemployment rate since 1929, and 15 percent of the population was on relief (Morton and Copp, 1980:139–140). For those leaving school, job prospects were poor to non-existent. Many would be condemned to a life of "riding the rods" in search of any work they could get, or an even harder life in the government-sponsored relief camps established in 1932, which provided their inmates with room and board and 20 cents a day in return for six days a week of hard labour (Morton and Copp, 1980; Brown, 1970).

Few had really secure jobs. Both in the resource industries and in manufacturing, massive layoffs were the order of the day. At Ford Motor Company, employment fell from 7100 to 2174 between 1929 and 1932. Workers often had to bribe their way into even low-paying menial jobs (Manley, 1986:556).

Worker Unity League Activity

Under such conditions, most conventional union organizing and strike activity was out of the question, as the major federations hunkered down to protect existing members (Morton and Copp, 1980:142; Manley, 1986:557). The one big exception was the Communists' Worker Unity League (WUL), for whom the Depression was tailor-made, since it seemed to confirm the Communists' thesis of the need for broader class struggle (Morton and Copp, 1980:142). In Flin Flon, Manitoba, and Estevan, Saskatchewan, the WUL led bitter and ultimately unsuccessful mining strikes. Though the strikes failed, the courage shown by the workers would inspire many others over the years. The WUL's efforts were more successful in Ontario, where it managed to organize a fair number of furniture, textile, and garment workers despite ferocious redbaiting and frequent repression by provincial police and troops (Morton and Copp, 1980; Heron, 1989).

Government Repression

Government repression was by no means confined to strikers. A common enough feature of 1930s' life generally, it was applied most often and most brutally to the hordes of single, unemployed men who were the Depression's worst victims, and from whom governments seemed to feel they had most to fear (Morton and Copp, 1980:145–146). While the relief camp inmates didn't wear uniforms (Morton and Copp, 1980:147), in most other ways they lived and worked under military-style discipline. Inmates were barred from filing group petitions to seek improvement of their wretched conditions, or from making speeches, writing letters to newspapers, or doing anything else "to bring accusations before the tribunal of public opinion" (Brown, 1970:606–607). In 1933, authorities banned May Day parades in Regina and Saskatoon and had the RCMP raid a union hall in Moose Jaw and seize a list of names of "troublemakers" who had refused to work in the relief camps (Brown, 1970:600). Two years later, when unemployed workers made an "On-to-Ottawa" trek to press such radical demands as relief camp workers' right to vote and the removal of the camps from Defence Department control, they were met with RCMP billy clubs in what became a bloody riot on July 1 in Regina (Brown, 1970:610–611; Scott, 1945).

Though anti-Communist laws were not new to Canada (Scott, 1932), the Conservative government of R.B. Bennett applied them with particular rigour, as did Bennett's provincial allies such as Ontario Premier Howard Ferguson. In 1931, the Communists' Toronto office was raided and eight of its leaders arrested; seven were later imprisoned (Morton and Copp, 1980:145). Other Communist leaders were deported (Morton and Copp, 1980), a phenomenon that had become increasingly common since the First World War (White, 1932).[9] As the decade wore on, similar— or even harsher—treatment would be meted out to Communists, social democrats, and unionists by the authoritarian governments of Quebec Premier Maurice Duplessis and Ontario Premier Mitch Hepburn, who replaced Ferguson later in the decade (Morton and Copp, 1980:158–160, 163, 191).

Hopeful American Developments

South of the border, however, things were beginning to look more hopeful, particularly after 1933 when Franklin D. Roosevelt took office as President. Roosevelt's "New Deal" launched huge public works projects and provided significant stimulation for the US economy, leading to a substantial reduction in unemployment rates by the mid-1930s.

Influenced by business lobbying and by conservatives within his administration, Roosevelt didn't give the labour movement the legislated six-hour day and 30-hour week it had been seeking as a means of reducing unemployment (Hunnicutt, 1988). But he saw that he would have to give the labour movement a good deal to make up for the loss of the six-hour law. As a result, his broad package of reforms eventually included a social security plan generous enough to allow older workers to retire with dignity, and employment standards legislation providing for an eight-hour day and 40-hour week. Although this was a longer workweek than the labour movement had been campaigning for, it was still far shorter than that worked by most workers in industrialized countries (Hunnicutt, 1988).

The centrepiece of Roosevelt's labour policy was the 1935 *National Labor Relations Act (NLRA)*, or *"Wagner Act,"* as it is colloquially known.[10] This bill allowed most American private sector workers[11] to bargain collectively and to strike without fear of employer reprisal. The Act also defined standards for employer unfair labour practice—including prohibiting such practices as intimidation or harassment of union members or the formation of a management-dominated company union. The National Labor Relations Board (NLRB) was established to administer and enforce the act (Carter, 1989:32). This tribunal was particularly welcomed by unionists, since, in the past, labour matters had customarily been dealt with by the courts, which in general were not well disposed towards unions (Carter, 1989). Free of the fear that hostile employers could fire union organizers and members, American unions signed up hundreds of thousands of new members in the years immediately following passage of the *Wagner Act*.

Between 1937 and 1943, a number of Canadian jurisdictions did adopt certain features of the American legislation, the most comprehensive of these being Ontario's Labour Court, which came into effect in 1943. This mechanism was in

National Labor Relations Act (NLRA) or Wagner Act First American collective bargaining legislation, passed in 1935.

many ways similar to Wagner's National Labor Relations Board but it failed to meet with the labour movement's full approval because administration was left to the courts rather than being turned over to a separate administrative agency, as it was in the United States (Carter, 1989:32–33).

Industrial Unionism

A particularly important consequence of the *Wagner Act* was that it facilitated unionization of unskilled and semi-skilled workers, who would otherwise have had difficulty forming unions, since their skills were not scarce enough to enable them to withstand employer anti-union initiatives. Many of the more farsighted American union leaders, such as the United Mine Workers' John L. Lewis, were quick to recognize the huge growth the labour movement might achieve by organizing unskilled and semi-skilled workers in mass-production industries. Unlike traditional craft unionism, the industrial unionism envisaged by Lewis and his allies would seek to organize all workers in an industry and would use political action and mass worker mobilization, as well as collective bargaining, to achieve its objectives.

Disgusted with what they saw as the AFL craft unions' conservative, elitist, and defeatist strategy, Lewis and other industrial unionists launched a Committee for Industrial Organization within the AFL (Abella, 1975). When its members were expelled from that federation two years later (Morton and Copp, 1980:153), the Committee became the **Congress of Industrial Organizations**, or **CIO** (Heron, 1989:73). The CIO's efforts would quickly bear fruit, with the organization of such mass-production industries as automotive, steel, rubber, and meatpacking.

Industrial unionism spread more slowly in Canada, in large measure because Canadian workers still didn't enjoy basic bargaining rights. But CIO organizers nonetheless began working in Ontario and, in February 1937, a proposed 20 percent speed-up of the General Motors Oshawa plant assembly line led to a plant-wide strike under the auspices of the CIO that resulted in a compromise settlement in which the union won most of its substantive demands—still without gaining formal recognition (Morton and Copp, 1980; Abella, 1975). With this victory, the Canadian industrial union movement was launched, though it would continue to find the going tough in the absence of legislation protecting basic union organizing rights (Morton and Copp, 1980; Abella, 1975). Over the next few years, CIO unions would be established in Kitchener's rubber plants, Sault Ste. Marie's steel mills, and Montreal's dress factories (Morton and Copp, 1980:160–163). In 1939, the TLC would follow the AFL's lead and expel its CIO unions (Heron, 1989:73), which then merged with Aaron Mosher's ACCL to form the Canadian Congress of Labour, or CCL (Morton, 1995:143).

The Founding of the CCF

Desperate for solutions to the economic problems of the Depression, Canadians tried out a broad range of schemes ranging from social credit and religious fundamentalism to varying degrees of socialism (Morton, 1995, 141; Ferguson, 1935). The period's most important political development was arguably the founding of the **Co-Operative Commonwealth Federation**, or **CCF**, launched in Calgary and

Congress of Industrial Organizations (CIO) Industrial union federation established during the Depression to compete with the AFL.

Co-Operative Commonwealth Federation (CCF) Social democratic party formed during the Depression, the forerunner to the present New Democratic Party (NDP).

Regina in 1932–1933 under the leadership of J.S. Woodsworth. The party was made up of socialists, progressive farmers, old-style labourites, and urban intellectuals (Morton, 1995; Underhill, 1932). Its eight-point program included a planned system of social economy, the socialization of the banking sector, public ownership of the natural resource sector, socialized medical care, and adequate work or unemployment insurance for the unemployed under federal government auspices (Underhill, 1932).

Though many in the labour movement were initially cool to the new party (Morton, 1995:141), it gained increasing union support over time. By the late 1930s it was winning large numbers of seats in BC and Saskatchewan and in 1944, it formed the government in the latter province, under the strong leadership of Tommy Douglas (see Current Issues box below) (King, 1944). By this time, it was so strong both federally and in Ontario that it posed a serious threat to both governments. Canada's labour movement finally had an effective political party of its own.

Current Issues 3.1

TOMMY DOUGLAS: THE GREATEST CANADIAN

In November 2004, Canadians participating in the Canadian Broadcasting Corporation's (CBC) nationwide contest voted Tommy Douglas the Greatest Canadian of all time. The diminutive politician, described as the most influential politician never elected Prime Minister, earned the admiration and respect of Canadians as a tirelessly devoted advocate of the idea that humanity, or the common good, should supersede private interests. The Scottish-born Baptist minister led the Cooperative Commonwealth Federation (CCF) to victory in Saskatchewan, forming the first social democratic government in North America. After serving 17 years as Premier of Saskatchewan, he went on to serve as the federal leader of the New Democratic Party (NDP).

Tommy Douglas was a gifted orator, a charismatic leader, and a visionary, whose radical ideas later gained such popular acceptance that other politicians often claimed them as their own. He is best remembered for the many innovative social programs his government introduced, including North America's first government-run medical insurance program, which became the blueprint for Canada's national medicare program. Other innovations are almost too numerous to mention but included public crop insurance, government-run auto insurance, and the extension of phone and electrical services to rural communities through Crown Corporations.

Tommy Douglas also innovated on the labour front. Profoundly affected by the events of "Bloody Saturday," when the then 14-year-old watched as the RCMP fired into the crowd of striking Winnipeg workers, he was a staunch supporter of union rights. He saw no legitimate reason to deny government employees the same freedom of association granted their private sector counterparts. In 1944, the CCF government passed the Saskatchewan *Trade Union Act*, which, at the time, was "the most pro-union legislation in the democratic capitalist world" (Lipset, 1968:279). Among the many innovations contained within that Act was the extension of the right to unionize—including the unfettered right to strike—to public sector employees, something that would not occur in the rest of Canada for more than 20 years.

The Saskatchewan *Trade Union Act* was also the first legislation to introduce union security provisions mandating that if a union was certified in the workplace, new employees were required ▶

to join and the employer was required to deduct union dues. Unique in Canada, the Act also permitted work stoppages during the term of a collective agreement. Between 1944 and 1983, when the *Trade Union Act* was amended, Saskatchewan was the only jurisdiction in Canada to allow mid-contract strikes.

Sources: CBC Archives. (2005). "Tommy Douglas and the NDP," http://archives.cbc.ca/IDD-1-73-851/politics_economy/tommy_douglas/, [February 2005]; Weyburn Credit Union. (1987). Tommy Douglas Website, http://www.weyburnreview.com, [February 2005]; Lipset, Seymour Martin. (1968). *Agrarian Socialism: The Cooperative Commonwealth Federation in Saskatchewan*. New York: Anchor Books, Doubleday & Company, Inc.; Thompson, Mark, Joseph B. Rose, and Anthony E. Smith. (2003). *Beyond the National Divide: Regional Dimensions of Industrial Relations*. Kingston and Montreal: McGill-Queen's University Press.

Labour During the War Years

During World War II, the lack of basic bargaining rights became an issue uniting the long-divided Canadian labour movement, which had grown considerably stronger due to wartime labour shortages (Carter, 1989; Heron, 1989:78). By 1943, one Canadian union member in three was on strike—a rate that exceeded that of 1919, the year of the Winnipeg General Strike (Heron, 1989:78). For the Canadian labour movement, the pivotal event of the war years was undoubtedly the enactment, in 1944, of *PC 1003*, the bill granting Canadian workers such basic rights as the right to join a union, bargain collectively, and strike. The achievement of basic bargaining rights didn't come easily, however. Though wartime labour shortages and government orders-in-council curbing employers' right to fire workers again spurred union organization, Prime Minister King remained convinced of the perfection of the *IDI Act* and unwilling to move beyond it.

In a bid to maintain labour peace, the government did, in 1940, put forward an order-in-council urging employers to recognize unions voluntarily. But as L.S. Mac-Dowell notes, this policy was "ignored by employers and never followed by the government itself in the industries under its own control" (1978:662). In the absence of any legislation compelling them to deal with unions, many employers continued to refuse to do so. In a situation of wartime labour shortage, where wages were strictly controlled but prices generally weren't (MacDowell, 1978), serious labour strife was virtually guaranteed. A bitter gold mining strike at Kirkland Lake, Ontario, in 1942 and an equally bitter steel strike the following year united the formerly divided labour movement against the government. Both major labour federations (the TLC and the CCL) demanded that workers be given the same basic bargaining rights American workers had long enjoyed under the *Wagner Act* (MacDowell, 1978:669). A similar conclusion was reached by the National War Labour Board in 1943, in a report prepared by Mr. Justice C.P. McTague, who had been the conciliator in the Kirkland Lake dispute. Still King did not act (Morton and Copp, 1980:183).

What the McTague report could not do, however, the growing threat from the left could. In August 1943, the Liberals lost four federal by-elections, two to the CCF (Morton and Copp, 1980). The defeats and the CCF's high poll standings elsewhere appear to have convinced King that if he didn't move the Liberals to the left, he might well lose the next election. Accordingly, he established a system of family allowances and promised full post-war employment and universal medical care

(Morton, 1995:143). Most important of all, he finally granted Canadian workers their long-awaited collective bargaining rights.

Collective Bargaining Legislation: *PC 1003*

The federal legislation providing for those rights, the *Wartime Labour Relations Regulations* or Order-in-Council *PC 1003*, was proclaimed in February 1944. The fact that the country was at war granted the federal government the authority to extend the legislation throughout both federal and provincial jurisdictions even though similar legislation was already in effect in Ontario and BC (Heron, 1989:80) and similar, even stronger, legislation would take effect in Saskatchewan later that year. Following the enactment of *PC 1003*, employers were legislatively compelled to bargain with unions that could prove to the new labour relations board that they had the majority support of workers in any given workplace. This meant that strikes for union recognition were no longer necessary; in fact they were illegal. Otherwise, the right to strike, within limits, was protected, but the *IDI's* conciliation process (including the "cooling-off" period) still had to be observed before any strike or lockout was legal (Heron, 1989:80–81). The Act also prohibited strikes during the term of the collective agreement; instead, every collective agreement was assumed to contain a grievance procedure, culminating in binding arbitration, for the handling of disputes over contract interpretation (Craig and Solomon, 1996:207). A new board, the Canada Labour Relations Board, was charged with overseeing certifications and ruling on unfair labour practices (Heron, 1989:80).

Thanks to favourable wartime conditions, union membership rates had already risen dramatically. Between 1939 and 1945, the number of Canadian union members doubled, while union density increased from 17 to 24 percent of paid non-agricultural workers (Godard, 1994:96). Now, thanks to *PC 1003*, the unions would be able to maintain those gains during the post-war period. Indeed, membership rates continued to rise during the late 1940s, aided both by the legislation and by a booming post-war economy that proved conducive to union growth.

When the war ended, the federal government could no longer maintain its jurisdiction over labour legislation. In 1948, it enacted a slightly modified version of the wartime order, the *Industrial Relations and Disputes Investigation Act of 1948* (Morton and Copp, 1980:198), which later became known as the Canada Labour Code and which applied to workers within the federal jurisdiction. Within two years, every province adopted some version of the federal legislation. Many provincial acts, however, particularly those of the Atlantic provinces and Alberta, were significantly more restrictive than the federal one.[12] The one area of uniformity was the compulsory conciliation provision, a holdover from the old *IDI Act*, which was adopted in every province except Saskatchewan.

Maintaining Union Security: The "Rand Formula"

Another development that may have contributed to post-war union growth by enhancing unions' security was the landmark legal decision that introduced the so-called "**Rand Formula**," in 1945. The formula, devised by Justice Ivan Rand to help settle a Ford Motor Company dispute he was arbitrating, didn't require employees to join unions that had been certified for their bargaining units, but did require

Rand Formula Union security provision whereby no worker is required to join the union but all must pay it an amount equal to its dues as a condition of employment.

As this photo suggests, logging could be an extremely dangerous business.

An illustration from Dante's *Inferno*? Actually, it's a rather typical scene from a nineteenth century factory.

Brutal suppression of strike activity, as in the case of the Winnipeg General Strike, was more the rule than the exception before Canadian workers received official bargaining rights.

Fig. 18-3 How does this advertisement of 1943 reflect values of the 1940s? How different is it from ads today?

Even before World War II was over, advertisers were campaigning hard to ensure that "Rosie the Rivetter" would turn back into "Henrietta the Home-maker" as soon as possible after the end of hostilities.

Quebec workers take to the streets in a demonstration against the authoritarian regime of Premier Maurice Duplessis.

Like many generations of garment workers before them, these garment workers, many of whom are recent immigrants to Canada, must work long hours at very low wages.

United Food and Commercial Workers urge a boycott of Gainer's meats during their now-famous 1986 strike in Edmonton.

them to pay union dues, since all bargaining-unit employees, whether union members or not, benefited from the union's efforts on their behalf. Free of the threat of compulsory union membership, which they bitterly opposed, most employers adopted the **dues** "**checkoff**" whereby employees' union dues were deducted at the source. This gave unions a solid financial basis of support and helped ensure their survival (Heron, 1989:85).

dues checkoff
Employer deduction of union dues at the source.

Post-war Strikes

The Ford strike just mentioned was just one of a huge wave sweeping across Canada during the early post-war years. Workers needed substantial wage increases to keep pace with post-war inflation. And thanks to the new labour legislation, even the unskilled could now strike to support wage demands without risking dismissal or harassment from their employers. In 1946 alone, a year that saw the highest level of Canadian strike activity since 1919, strikes shut down the entire BC logging industry, the Ontario rubber industry, the entire steel industry, the Southam newspaper chain, and central Canadian ports (Heron, 1989:84). Though often long and sometimes bitter, these strikes were of a different character than the ones that had swept Canada after the First World War. With union recognition as such no longer at issue, the primary aim now was not mass mobilization, but the winning of specific contract demands. While picket lines continued to be tense places, bloodshed and loss of life were far rarer than in pre-war strikes. Thanks again to the new legislation, the strike had become less of a political weapon and more of an economic one (see Heron, 1989:85 and Morton, 1995:145).

Women: The Forgotten Minority

While *PC 1003* and the Rand Formula were certainly of great benefit to male workers, especially blue-collar workers in industries important to the war effort, this legislation proved of little immediate benefit to most female workers. The legislation didn't apply to public sector workers (except in Saskatchewan) and by and large these workers continued to be legally barred from joining unions. In the private service sector, where many other women worked, any significant degree of unionization would simply not be in the cards for the foreseeable future.[13]

Since most heavy industries had been unionized, the new labour legislation might have benefited the sizeable contingent of women who had left their homes to take wartime defence plant jobs—except for one minor detail: With the end of the war, women were leaving those plants in droves. To help ensure that the exodus continued, governments closed workplace daycare centres and cancelled wartime tax concessions (Roberts and Bullen, 1985:387). Not surprisingly, the female proportion of the labour force dropped from 31 to 23 percent between 1945 and 1946 (Bland, 1983:681), while marriage and birth rates soared. After the war, the country's advertisers did their part to complete the metamorphosis of "Rosie the Rivetter" into "Henrietta the Homemaker" by painting bright pictures of an appliance-filled future in which women were portrayed primarily as consumers (Bland, 1983:707). At home with her washer and dryer and high-gloss paste wax, a woman would have little reason to concern herself with such things as unions and labour legislation.

Labour During the 1950s

After the radicalism of the 1930s and rapid expansion of the 1940s, the 1950s was a decade of consolidation and stabilization, if not stagnation, for the labour movement. Overall, it was an era of economic and political conservatism. Few people, within the labour movement or outside of it, cared to rock the boat. While unions were generally accepted throughout most of Canada, they had to operate within fairly narrow bounds. In general, they were expected to concentrate on wages and benefits and not concern themselves with more fundamental questions of control or management of the enterprise (Heron, 1989:86–87). In addition, they'd lost the mid-term strike and other traditional tools of direct action (Heron, 1989:91–92). With the mid-term strike barred in favour of the grievance procedure, many believed union leaders were increasingly being made to function as the managers of discontent. Whether or not this was the case, it was definitely true that they now had to function in an increasingly bureaucratic and legalistic environment, one in which administrative and negotiating skills were more important than the ability to mobilize workers or move a crowd (Heron, 1989:86–89).

At the bargaining table, unions racked up impressive gains for their members. Wages increased dramatically, and the eight-hour day and five-day week became the norm. Paid vacations, pensions, and medical plans were all brought in (Roberts and Bullen, 1985:393–394). For the first time, ordinary workers were able to buy cars, appliances, TV sets, and other items of which they had previously only dreamed (Heron, 1989:99). At the same time, more and more union members tended to view their unions instrumentally, as essentially their business agents. Attendance at union meetings dwindled, except at negotiation time (Heron, 1989).

Union membership rates edged up to 34 percent in 1958, then started a slow drop towards the trough of 28 percent they would reach six years later. There were a number of possible explanations: public perception that union leaders had become "fat cats" and that unions had lost touch with "the little guy"; negative fallout from disclosures of union corruption and violence in the United States;[14] the apparent saturation of unions' traditional power bases in manufacturing, mining, construction, and transportation; and an unsympathetic Conservative government headed by John Diefenbaker.

With the onset of the Cold War, Communists had gradually been pushed to the sidelines. By 1950, CCFers and others had rid the CCL of any remaining Communist influence (Morton, 1995:145). The TLC had been slower to get in on the Cold War hysteria, but in 1949 it suspended its largest Communist organization, the Canadian Seamen's Union (Heron, 1989:90); five years later it also got rid of the West Coast fishermen's union (Heron, 1989). In hindsight, the TLC may have come to regret expelling the Seamen's Union, which was replaced with the gangster-ridden Seafarers' International Union (SIU), leading to one of the sorriest chapters in Canadian labour history (Heron, 1989). Using intimidation, beatings, and sweetheart deals with companies to defeat other unions, SIU leader Hal Banks would leave a black mark on the Canadian labour movement for years to come. Only after six years and 75 proven instances of violence would the **Canadian Labour Congress** (successor to the TLC) expel the SIU (Morton and Copp, 1980:233–236).

Canadian Labour Congress Canada's national labour federation.

Surprisingly, the Communist purges didn't seem to benefit the social democratic CCF, now the only remaining labour-oriented party on the left. Far from growing as a result of its old rival's demise, it fared poorly in most federal and provincial elections through the 1950s (Morton and Copp, 1980:227). Only after the party modernized itself, diluting its socialist agenda and broadening its appeal to middle-class voters after the fashion of the British Labour Party (Heron, 1989:110), would it do better at the polls. This new, more centrist party, known after 1961 as the New Democratic Party (NDP), would play a critical role in the expansion of collective bargaining to the public service and the liberalization of federal labour legislation by virtue of the balance-of-power position it held in several Liberal minority governments (Heron, 1989:110–112). Provincially, its impact would be even greater, as NDP governments elected in three Western provinces between 1969 and 1972 introduced a broad range of progressive labour legislation on issues ranging from health and safety to technological change (Heron, 1989:112).

Federation Mergers

The decade's major event, in terms of labour politics, was the merger of the two great federations, the TLC and CCL, which took place in 1956, just a year after the American AFL and CIO had merged under the presidency of George Meany. The two longstanding rivals formed a new organization, under the presidency of Montrealer Claude Jodoin, known as the Canadian Labour Congress. The merger appeared to make a good deal of sense, since it would end the union raiding that had become common during the post-war period and would also allow for the pooling of scarce organizational resources (Morton and Copp, 1980:216–220).

Amid the labour movement's growing bureaucratization, there were a few reminders of its stormier past. In 1957, Quebec Premier Maurice Duplessis crushed an illegal strike at Murdochville, Quebec, that resulted when the Gaspé Copper Company refused to recognize a duly certified Steelworkers' local. Provincial police stood by as **strikebreakers** stoned picketers and hoodlums ransacked the union office. Eventually, two-thirds of the strikers lost their jobs and the union was sued for nearly $3 million (Morton and Copp, 1980:228). In 1959, Newfoundland Premier Joey Smallwood, himself a former socialist and union organizer, decertified the International Woodworkers of America (IWA) during a bitter, but legal, loggers' strike in Badger. A few days later, after vigilantes had smashed the IWA headquarters in Grand Falls, employers signed agreements with a new local union created by Smallwood himself (Morton and Copp, 1980:230–231).

strikebreakers Those continuing to work during a strike or replacing striking workers.

Automation

Fears that technological change, or automation as it was then known, would displace and deskill large numbers of workers resurfaced at the end of the 1950s. The switch from steam to diesel locomotives threatened the jobs of thousands of railway firemen. The switch to computerized typesetting was an even greater threat to printers' jobs. In numerous other occupations, from mining and logging to banking and postal work, rapidly emerging new technologies transformed the way work was done, in the process putting thousands of workers' jobs and skills at risk.

In a few cases, such as longshoring in Montreal, comprehensive modernization agreements were worked out. Like a similar agreement on the Pacific Coast, the Montreal agreement allowed employers to proceed with mechanization and automation of longshoring work in return for job protection for those working full time on the docks (Picard, 1967). Others weren't so lucky. Many Toronto printers lost "their jobs, their savings, and … their craft" (Morton and Copp, 1980:240) in a lengthy, bitter, and ultimately hopeless strike against computerized typesetting at the city's daily newspapers. During the early 1970s, both the federal government and the three Western provinces with NDP governments wrote modest protection against the effects of technological change into their labour acts. But the legislation proved largely ineffectual, mainly because labour boards were extremely reluctant to intervene, even in cases where the legislation had clearly been violated (Peirce, 1987).[15]

The Canadian Labour Movement's New Face

The 1960s was a decade of renewed radicalism and questioning of conventional wisdom and received authority in most areas of Canadian life, from economics and politics to music and personal morality. The labour movement was no exception. By the end of the decade, it wore a very different face, mainly as a result of something previously considered unthinkable—full-scale unionization of the public sector, including federal and provincial government employees.

Unlike private sector unionization, which had evolved gradually, public sector unionization came very quickly to Canada once the forces leading to it had been set in motion. Through the 1950s and into the 1960s, the notion of parliamentary sovereignty had been used to deny public sector workers collective bargaining rights. As the sovereignty argument eroded and public sector workers became more militant, there were growing demands that they be allowed to join unions.

By the end of 1964, full collective bargaining rights, including the right to strike, had been granted to most of Quebec's public sector workers (Hébert, 1995:202). Meanwhile, federal government employees, frustrated with years of lagging pay, the transformation of their workplaces into large impersonal bureaucracies (Heron, 1989:106), and an unsympathetic Conservative federal government, were demanding similar rights. Elected in 1963, Lester Pearson's Liberal government initially promised to grant its employees collective bargaining rights with binding arbitration (Swimmer, 1995:369). A nationwide postal strike in 1965 and the Liberals' tenuous minority position, in which the pro-labour NDP held the balance of power, pushed them to go further than that. The result was a piece of comprehensive collective bargaining legislation, the *Public Service Staff Relations Act (PSSRA)*, which broke new ground in a number of different ways. Most notably, the bill, passed in 1967, gave the union the right to choose between binding arbitration and the conventional conciliation-strike route of resolving disputes (Swimmer, 1995). A Public Service Staff Relations Board was set up to administer the act and determine appropriate bargaining units (Swimmer, 1995:370). To safeguard the public health and welfare during public service strikes, the bill also established a procedure for designating employees whose services were deemed essential (Swimmer, 1995:377).

The *PSSRA* had a number of significant impacts on the labour movement all across the country. To begin with, a number of provinces (including Newfoundland and New Brunswick) soon followed the federal government's lead, passing their own "mini-*PSSRA*" bills legalizing full public sector collective bargaining, including the right to strike. Other provinces (including Ontario and Alberta) granted public employees bargaining rights, but substituted binding arbitration for the right to strike. In a class by itself, Saskatchewan had long treated government employees no differently than their private sector counterparts, covering both under the *Trade Union Act* of 1944. By the early 1970s, some form of collective bargaining covered every provincial government worker in Canada (Fryer, 1995:343–346). By decade's end, collective bargaining rights had likewise been extended to all the country's teachers and health care workers. The *PSSRA* and its provincial counterparts also facilitated unionization of professionals and other private sector white-collar workers. Once they saw their public sector colleagues benefiting from unionization, they came to realize that they could as well. By the 1970s, an increasing number of private sector professionals were taking out union membership (Thompson, 1982).

Even more important, the *PSSRA* and the various provincial laws brought large numbers of women into the Canadian labour movement for the first time, since women made up a large proportion of the public sector workforce. Among other things, this development would have a significant impact on the public sector unions' bargaining agendas. Unions with large female memberships soon began to demand improved maternity leave provisions, provisions allowing for more flexible working hours, and other benefits reflecting the reality of women's dual responsibilities to work and family. The relatively greater concentration of professionals in public sector unions led to a greater emphasis on intrinsic working conditions than one would find in most blue-collar unions, and bargaining table demands for in-service training and joint labour–management committees (Ponak, 1982:351–353).

Private Sector Militancy and the Woods Commission

wildcat strike A work stoppage carried out during the term of a collective agreement, normally without the union's authorization.

rank-and-file Ordinary union members, as opposed to the leadership.

The 1960s also saw increased militancy in Canada's private sector unions. In 1966, strikes had reached their highest level in 20 years (Godard, 1994:96), spurred by rising inflation. The middle of the decade saw the previously mentioned postal strike, the country's first national railway strike, a strike along the St. Lawrence Seaway, and disputes at Heinz Foods, Canada Packers, International Nickel, and in BC's logging industry (Morton and Copp, 1980:248–251). Across the country there was a wave of **wildcat strikes** (in 1966 these amounted to one-third the total number of strikes) and increasing **rank-and-file** rejection of contracts negotiated by union leaders (Heron, 1989:104; Morton, 1995:109). Alarmed at the growing turbulence in the country's industrial relations system, Prime Minister Pearson struck a Royal Commission under the direction of Dean H.D. (Buzz) Woods of McGill University (Morton and Copp, 1980:253–254). The Woods Task Force report, released in early 1969, recommended relatively minor changes such as the formation of employer associations to balance unions and the creation of a public interest disputes commission to deal with strikes in essential industries. Overall, its message was that the

Canadian IR system was, if not perfect, probably among the least of possible evils and that industrial conflict was an inevitable price to be paid for living in a democratic society (Morton and Copp, 1980:262–264).[16]

Changes in Quebec

Nowhere did the Canadian labour movement change more quickly during the 1960s than in the province of Quebec. The changes were greatest of all within the former confessional union movement, which by this time had gone through a number of different metamorphoses to emerge as the leading exponent of radicalism in the province.

Forced to become more militant to compete with other federations that were actively organizing in the province, the CTCC had, during the Second World War, dropped its "Catholic-only" clause and its opposition to strikes and started operating more like a conventional trade union (Boivin, 1982 [see Déom and Boivin, 2001]:427). Later, under the leadership of Jean Marchand, it played a leading role in the Asbestos strike of 1949 and the opposition to the Duplessis regime during the 1950s. In 1960, it severed its remaining ties with the Catholic Church and renamed itself the **Confédération des syndicats nationaux (CSN)**. Buoyed by Duplessis' replacement by Liberal premier Jean Lesage, the CSN grew rapidly in both size and influence during the 1960s. A key player during the "Quiet Revolution," the federation benefited particularly from the unionization of public sector workers (Boivin, 1982:429–430).

After Marchand's departure in 1965, the federation took an increasingly radical and separatist course under Marcel Pépin, losing much of its mainstream public support as the result of a major hospital strike in 1966 and a Montreal Transit strike during Expo 1967 (Boivin, 1982). By 1968, the CSN had expanded its efforts to the quest for a "Second Front" outside collective bargaining, which sought alliances between the labour movement and other progressive organizations such as tenants' groups and credit unions in local "political action committees" (Heron, 1989:117). With other provincial labour organizations, such as the **Quebec Federation of Labour (QFL)** and teachers' union (CEQ) also taking an increasingly radical stance (Heron, 1989), the CSN in 1971 published two radical manifestos that made the case for an independent and socialist Quebec (Boivin, 1982:430).

Brought together, at least for the time being, by their radicalism, the three major Quebec federations in 1972 established a "Common Front" for public sector negotiations with the provincial government involving some 250 000 workers (Boivin, 1982). The failure of those negotiations led to a massive public sector strike, the largest in Canadian history, which would eventually result in the jailing of the leaders of all three federations for defying back-to-work orders (Heron, 1989:118). Though the strike spread to the private sector, becoming a general strike in some parts of the province, it ended about a week later (Heron, 1989). The "Common Front" days were to be the high-water mark for both labour radicalism and labour unity in the province. Within two years of the great strike, dislike of the CSN's radicalism had prompted three large groups to break away from the federation and adopt a much more moderate political course (Déom and Boivin, 1995). The election of a separatist and pro-labour Parti Québécois (PQ) government in 1976 also

Confédération des syndicates nationaux (CSN) Quebec labour federation originating in the confessional unions of the early twentieth century.

Quebec Federation of Labour (QFL) Quebec division of the Canadian Labour Congress.

helped reduce Quebec labour radicalism, although there would be resurgences, especially in the PQ's second term, when it froze the right to strike and rolled back public sector salaries by almost 20 percent (Heron, 1989:128).

A New Breed of Worker

The young people entering the workforce for the first time during the 1960s posed problems both for employers and for the unions seeking to represent their interests. More highly educated than their parents had been, these young people had been raised in a culture of permissiveness and brought up to believe there should be a good deal more to a job than a paycheque. With their disdain for dress codes and traditional social mores generally, they found it hard to adjust to life in mainstream organizations with conventional top-down management practices.[17]

Often they gave their union leaders nearly as hard a time as their employers. Many were impatient with unions' often bureaucratic ways of doing things and with seniority-based systems that left them at the bottom of the ladder. Also, their bargaining agenda often conflicted with that of older, more established workers. Many of the older workers had bought into the post-war compromise whereby unions simply negotiated for wages and benefits and intrinsic concerns were, in effect, left outside the factory gate or office door. For young people raised with high expectations of work and life, and who had seldom known real, grinding poverty, the old compromise simply wasn't good enough. It wasn't enough that a job be secure and pay a decent wage; it had to be interesting and socially worthwhile as well.

Younger workers' unhappiness with established ways of doing things was probably a factor in the high rate of wildcat strikes and contract rejections during the 1960s. Later (as we noted in Chapter 2), it would prove a stimulus to the broad range of quality of worklife initiatives introduced during that decade—often in the face of union leaders' indifference or outright hostility.

Those Left Behind

Again, many didn't share in the general prosperity of the 1960s and early 1970s. In big cities like Montreal, immigrant workers, mainly women, continued to toil 50 to 60 hours a week or even longer, exposing themselves to heat, cold, toxic chemicals, and grossly inadequate sanitation in abattoirs, factories, hotels, and restaurants. If they were lucky, they would receive the minimum wage. Many did not. Fearing deportation or dismissal, most of those who didn't were afraid to complain. Even the few who did had no guarantee of success, given the lack of inspectors and of political will to enforce minimum wage and health and safety legislation (Arnopoulos, 1974). For Ontario's farm workers, conditions were little better. At a time when the average industrial wage was $3.17 an hour and the Ontario minimum wage $1.60, the top 54 percent of farm workers were averaging $1.71 an hour; fully 94 percent of all fruit and vegetable workers were getting less than the provincial minimum (Ward, 1974:302). Despite such pathetically low wages and primitive working conditions, the provincial government did not extend the minimum wage or other basic employment standards to farm workers (Ward, 1974).

A New Era of Restraint

With the 1973–1974 energy crisis and the subsequent wave of inflation and unemployment, the country's economic and political climate turned notably more conservative. The 1974 federal election was an omen of hard times to come. In that election, the NDP lost half its seats and its balance-of-power position as Pierre Trudeau's Liberals swept to a strong majority. The next year, BC's NDP government was defeated, and in 1977, the party lost power in Manitoba.

Though he'd ridiculed wage-price controls during his 1974 election campaign, on Thanksgiving Day, 1975, Trudeau introduced a comprehensive three-year program to control wages and prices (Reid, 1982). The labour movement was outraged. In protest, it withdrew labour representatives from most tripartite government bodies, such as the Economic Council of Canada, and staged a one-day general strike in 1976 against the controls and the government's Anti-Inflation Board. To some (e.g., Panitch and Swartz, 1988), the controls mark the beginning of the end of free collective bargaining in Canada. Even those (e.g. Reid, 1982:501) who believed the labour movement's fear about the controls had been largely unfounded admitted that the program "had imposed severe strains on both the social fabric and the industrial-relations system."

When "normal" collective bargaining resumed in 1978, it was in an environment increasingly hostile to workers and their unions, particularly the public sector unions. A wave of public sector strikes, particularly a series of lengthy disputes involving Canada Post (Swimmer, 1995:385–386) and the Montreal Transit system, had soured many Canadians on the whole idea of free collective bargaining in the public sector. By the late 1970s, there were numerous calls for the federal government to abolish its workers' right to strike. Despite strong public pressure, it didn't do that. But it did severely restrict its workers' right to strike in two other ways: by increasing the proportion of workers designated as "essential" and thus compelled to work during a strike (Swimmer, 1995; Panitch and Swartz, 1988), and through an increased use of back-to-work legislation (Panitch and Swartz, 1988:31), a device also used by provincial governments.

A second energy crisis, starting in 1979, launched the country into a new inflationary spiral as serious as the 1973–1974 one had been. Federal and provincial governments responded, once again, with wage control legislation—legislation this time aimed exclusively at the public sector. Federal wage restraint legislation limited increases to 6 percent in the first year and 5 percent in the second (Swimmer, 1995). Some provinces' legislation was even more restrictive. This was especially true in Quebec, where the PQ government in 1982 imposed a 20 percent reduction on public sector workers' salaries (Hébert, 1995:222–223), and in BC, where wage restraint legislation was accompanied by legislation effectively giving the provincial cabinet the authority to terminate any public sector worker unilaterally, under the guise of restraint (Panitch and Swartz, 1988:41).

The 1980s Recession and Its Aftermath

Beginning in 1981, Canada plunged into its most serious recession since the Second World War. In 1983, some 1.3 million Canadians (or more than 12 percent of the country's workforce) were officially unemployed (Heron, 1989:125; Morton, 1995:151). In some parts of the country, such as Newfoundland, the official unemployment rate was over 20 percent.[18] Food banks, which hadn't been seen since the Great Depression, began to appear in major Canadian cities as unemployment increased and more and more people exhausted their unemployment benefits (Heron, 1989:125–127).

Many of the high-paying jobs lost in manufacturing and resources never came back. Thereafter, high unemployment would be a more or less permanent feature of the Canadian labour market (Heron, 1989:125; Morton, 1995:151–152). The new jobs that replaced those well-paying jobs were mainly in the low-paying, hard-to-organize private service sector. Knowing they had few other options if they wanted to replace the thousands of members lost in manufacturing and resources during the recession, the unions made a valiant effort to organize the service industries, focusing their attention on the chartered banks and on retail giants like Eaton's. But Eaton's refused to sign a first collective agreement (Morton, 1995:152), and the bid to unionize the banks proved largely unsuccessful due to determined employer resistance marked by the frequent intimidation, harassment, and transfer of union activists (Lowe, 1980).

A Harder Management Line

In such a difficult economic environment, workers and unions were reluctant to press demands too hard, while management felt it could safely take a tougher stance in dealing with unions. By the early 1980s, management was starting to bring its own list of demands to the bargaining table. These demands often included outright wage freezes or even rollbacks, reductions in paid holiday time, and cuts in employer-paid benefit plans (Heron, 1989:136–137). By the mid 1980s, some employers were demanding that unions accept **two-tier wage schemes**, whereby new hires were paid far less than experienced workers. To back up their demands for concessions, employers often forced a strike or locked out their workers. Increasingly, they used the threat of closing down or relocating the plant to achieve concessions (Heron, 1989). Given the tough economic environment and increasingly unsympathetic political climate, such threats seemed all too real to most workers. The new employer militancy approach was used most often in historically anti-union Alberta. There, construction employers virtually destroyed the building trade unions in 1984 by means of a lockout that enabled them to break an expired collective agreement legally (Heron, 1989:136), while Peter Pocklington tried and failed to break the United Food and Commercial Workers (UFCW) union at his Gainer's meat-packing plant in Edmonton during a bitter strike that attracted nationwide attention (Godard, 1994:380–381).

two-tier wage schemes Wage arrangements whereby newly-hired workers are paid substantially less than experienced ones.

The Mulroney Years

Life became even more difficult for the Canadian labour movement following the 1984 landslide election of a Conservative federal government under Brian Mulroney. Sharing much of US President Ronald Reagan's political ideology, if not his personal dislike of unions, Mulroney pushed an agenda featuring large-scale privatization of public enterprises, deregulation of regulated ones, free trade with the United States, and relaxation of foreign investment controls. The effect of this agenda was to greatly increase foreign competition for Canadian businesses, thereby putting even more pressure on employers to cut labour costs. This in turn led to even more plant closures, a proliferation of mergers and acquisitions, large-scale layoffs, the substitution of technology for human labour, and harder work and longer hours for those who remained—all in the name of "rationalization" (Heron, 1989:134).

Schisms and Breakaways

As if it didn't face difficult enough challenges in its battles with employers and governments, the Canadian labour movement during this period was becoming increasingly divided against itself. The period was marked by major schisms within labour federations, a growing number of breakaways of Canadian branches from US-based international unions, and a number of serious incidents of union raiding, or attempts by one union to sign up members of another (Godard, 1994:244).

The Canadian Federation of Labour (CFL) Traditionally more conservative than most other unions, the building trade unions had long been unhappy with the Canadian Labour Congress (CLC). But nothing upset these labour traditionalists more than the CLC's granting of partial autonomy to its Quebec arm, the Quebec Federation of Labour, which allowed construction unions that had broken away from the internationals to remain affiliated. CLC leaders, reluctant to aggravate an already difficult situation in Quebec, didn't act despite the building trades' protests that the dual unions violated the CLC's constitution, whereupon 12 of the construction unions, representing about 350 000 workers, withheld their congress dues in 1980 (Morton, 1995). Two years later, having meanwhile been suspended from the CLC, the building trade unions formed their own federation, a new Canadian Federation of Labour based on internationalism and the apolitical, bread-and-butter approach of Samuel Gompers (see McCambly, 1990). The CFL operated quite successfully for 15 years. But in 1997, crippled by the loss of 40 percent of its members after the International Brotherhood of Electrical Workers returned to the CLC, it folded (McKinley, 1997).

Breakaways from US Internationals The secession of the Canadian branches of US international unions from their parent organizations was not new in the 1980s; however, the trend towards Canadianization of the labour movement gained a higher public profile as the result of several widely publicized breakaways, including most notably that of the **Canadian Auto Workers (CAW)** from the United Auto Workers (UAW) in 1985.

By the late 1960s and early 1970s, the Canadian branches of US-based international unions had begun breaking away from their parent unions and forming independent unions. The reasons ranged from dislike of US control over the Canadian labour movement and resentment at the poor servicing of Canadian branches, to more specific disagreements over bargaining strategy and political issues, such as

Canadian Auto Workers Industrial union representing Canadian auto workers, which split away from the United Auto Workers in 1985.

Canadian unionists' support for the NDP or the Americans' support for the Vietnam War (Heron, 1989:149).

The growing number of secessions from the internationals led the CLC to establish a number of autonomy guidelines for the Canadian branches of US internationals in 1970 and 1974. But despite these guidelines, the wave of secessions continued apace. The communications workers left their American parent in 1972, the paper workers in 1974, and energy and chemical workers in 1980 (Heron, 1989:152).

The Canadian Auto Workers' 1985 secession from the United Auto Workers was based to a large extent on bargaining strategy. The Canadian division had refused to go along with the international's concession bargaining approach in the previous round of negotiations and eventually reached a settlement differing significantly from the American one. The bitter dispute that resulted eventually became a major factor in the CAW's departure from the UAW (Craig and Solomon, 1996:186–18; Godard, 1994: 248–249).

Union Mergers and Raiding To make up for the membership lost through economic restructuring and deindustrialization, many of the big industrial unions, such as the steelworkers and autoworkers, were forced to look farther afield, to workers in totally unrelated industries. Often they turned to the unorganized; occasionally, however, they turned to workers already represented by a union, as in the now-celebrated dispute between the CAW and the **United Food and Commercial Workers (UFCW)** over the right to represent fisheries workers in Atlantic Canada.

In 1987, the 23 000-member Newfoundland branch of the UFCW announced its decision to affiliate with the CAW. The ensuing battle between the two unions, eventually won by the CAW, went before the courts as well as the labour boards and proved a major embarrassment to the labour movement (Craig and Solomon, 1996:170; Heron, 1989:152). In 1992, the CLC's executive committee imposed heavy sanctions on the International Woodworkers of America's Canadian division for raiding the Canadian Paperworkers Union (Craig and Solomon, 1996:170–171). More recently, a bitter dispute between the CAW and the Service Employees' International Union over the former's alleged raiding of the latter prompted the CLC to impose sanctions on the CAW. The dispute continued until sanctions were lifted in May 2001 (CNW, 2001). Nor was raiding confined to the private sector. In the federal public service, corrections officers left the **Public Service Alliance** in 2001 in favour of the CSN, in a bitter dispute that eventually wound up before the Public Service Staff Relations Board (PSSRB, 2000 and 2001).

Canadian Labour in the 1990s

As we noted in the first edition of this book (see especially Chapter 2), the 1990s was a decade of fundamental change in the economic and political environment. These changes led to equally major changes in the way work is organized and scheduled, in unions' strategies, and in national governments' willingness and ability to regulate economic and IR-related issues. For the most part, these changes left the Canadian labour movement in an even weaker position than it had been in at the start of the decade. Among the most crucial developments of the period were the implementation of comprehensive free trade agreements, a squeeze on public sector workers, a wave

United Food and Commercial Workers (UFCW) International union representing large numbers of Canadian retail workers.

Public Service Alliance Canada's largest federal public service union, representing mainly secretarial, administrative, and operational employees.

of union consolidation and mergers, and a questioning of labour's traditional links with its longstanding political partner, the NDP.

Free Trade and Its Implications

The period's single most important development was arguably the formation of a North American trading bloc (Lipsig-Mumme, 1995), following the implementation of Canada–US and North American free trade agreements in 1989 and 1994, respectively. In a related move (Reid and Meltz, 1995:47), Canada in 1994 signed on to a broad range of worldwide tariff reductions resulting from a new round of negotiations under the General Agreement on Trade and Tariffs (GATT). Over the past five years, Canada has been a party to further moves to liberalize trade throughout the western hemisphere. The wave of globalization and trade liberalization had the effect of intensifying the wave of restructuring begun during the late 1980s, leading to heavy job losses in the manufacturing sector and, by the end of the decade, the financial sector as well.

Workers' job security was a major casualty of economic restructuring, as many firms adopted a "lean production" mode whereby they retain only a small core of permanent workers, using short-term, temporary, or contractual workers to meet peak-period demands. Those remaining more or less steadily employed must often work longer and harder than in the past, since there are now so many fewer regular employees. The result is a situation where many workers are putting in long overtime hours while others remain unemployed or underemployed (O'Hara, 1993), as well as an increase in "atypical" part-time and temporary work arrangements, with workers provided little if any job security and few benefits. The growth of such atypical work arrangements poses major organizing challenges for unions, since part-time and temporary workers are normally a good deal more difficult to organize than full-timers.

The Public Sector Squeeze

The 1990s were particularly hard on public sector workers. In 1991, the federal government's imposition of a wage freeze caused the Public Service Alliance of Canada to launch its first-ever full-scale national public service strike (Swimmer, 1995). The strike was followed by a five-year suspension of collective bargaining; and even when bargaining resumed in 1996, salary arbitration remained suspended for five more years (Fryer, 2001). At provincial levels as well, most public sector workers had to endure wage freezes if not outright rollbacks, and suspension of normal collective bargaining procedures (Fryer, 1995). Downsizing and program cuts meant that, as in the private sector, there have been fewer people to do the work needing to be done, which in turn led to increased overtime—much of it involuntary and unpaid. (See, among others, PSES, 1999 and 2002). Beyond that, large-scale health care and education restructuring initiatives in Alberta and Ontario led to massive layoffs. While different provinces took different approaches to the question of public sector restructuring, few public sector workers escaped unscathed. Governments' tough stance toward their own employees has undoubtedly been a crucial factor in the wave of public sector strikes that has been taking place over the past five years.

FIGURE 3.1

A SCHEMATIC OUTLINE OF EVENTS IN THE HISTORY OF TRADE UNION MOVEMENTS IN THE UNITED STATES AND CANADA

The United States

1869 *Knights of Labor*
— uplift unionism
— membership not restricted
— craft and mixed locals

1886–1955 *American Federation of Labor (AFL)*
— a loose federation of craft-oriented unions
— excluded Knights of Labor because of dual unionism
— little activity in politics
— each affiliate was autonomous
— preferred little government intervention

1938–1955 *Congress of Industrial Organizations (CIO)*
— unions expelled from AFL
— wanted to unionize unskilled labourers
— wanted industrial unions
— more active in politics than AFL
— organized mass production workers

1955 *AFL-CIO*
— merger of AFL and CIO affiliated unions
— no-raiding pacts between unions affiliated with each federation
— craft and industrial unions
— conservative philosophy
— supports Democratic party
— code of ethical practices
— little control over affiliates

Canada

1875–1910 *Knights of Labor*
— active in Que., Ont., and N.S.
— uplift unionism
— membership not restricted
— craft and mixed locals
— problems with R.C. Church in Que.

1908–1927 *Trades and Labour Congress (TLC)*
— included Knights of Labor, N.S. Provincial Workman's Assoc. and other Canadian unions
— nationalistic in orientation
— dominated by regional interests
— wanted more Canadian control

1919–1956 *One Big Union (OBU)*
— mainly in western Canada
— dissatisfaction with TLC
— opposed to craft unions
— felt TLC structure not suited to western Canada
— influenced by radical IWW
— played an active role in Winnipeg General Strike of 1919
— became part of CLC in 1956

1927–1940 *All-Canadian Congress of Labour (ACCL)*
— remnants of CFL (Canadian Federation of Labour) of 1908, OBU, and CBRE (Canadian Brotherhood of Railway Engineers)
— wanted industrial unions
— critical of American control
— critical of TLC's conservative philosophy of TLC

1940–1956 *Canadian Congress of Labour (CCL)*
— Canadian branches of CIO unions
— remnants of ACCL
— wanted to unionize unskilled labourers
— wanted industrial unions
— active in politics
— organized mass production workers
— wanted less control from U.S.
— wanted more government action than TLC

1956 *Canadian Labour Congress (CLC)*
— merger of TLC and CCL affiliated unions
— no-raiding pacts between unions affiliated with each federation (not always observed)
— craft and industrial unions
— less conservative philosophy than AFL-CIO
— has supported NDP, but link now being revisited
— code of ethics
— little control over affiliates
— minimum standards of Canadian control apply to Canadian branches of U.S. international unions operating in Canada

1982–1997 *Canadian Federation of Labour (CFL)*
— formed by construction unions, but others also affiliated
— wanted more voting power in CLC
— non-partisan political stance and closer ties with government than CLC
— folded in 1997 ▶

Figure 3.1 (continued)

1991 *Federal Public Service Strike*
— sign of increasing public sector militancy
— result of government imposition of wage freeze
— PSSRB found Treasury Board guilty of bargaining in bad faith with PSAC

2001 *Nationwide health care strikes*
— result of years of salary freezes, cutbacks to health system
— also result from restriction of health care workers' bargaining rights
— N.S. premier threatened end to arbitration, backed off and sent dispute to final offer
— contract imposed in B.C. dispute (Aug., 2001)

2004 *Nationwide public service strikes*
— Wages, allowances the main issue
— deals ratified despite bargaining team's recommendation to reject

1998–2005 *Attempts to organize private service sector*
— serious bid to organize private service sector employers such as Starbucks, Wal-Mart, McDonald's. etc.
— limited success in wake of fierce employer opposition, increasingly harsh economic and political environment.

Union Developments in Quebec

1900 *Major strike in Quebec City, arbitrated by Archbishop of Quebec*
— confessional unions formed across the province
— meetings dominated largely by clergy
— influenced by Papal encyclicals

1921–1960 *Canadian and Catholic Confederation of Labour (CCCL)*
— founding convention in Hull, Quebec, in 1921
— brought workers together into a confederation
— wanted to keep workers Catholic and French-speaking
— dominated largely by clergy until 1940s
— adhered largely to teachings of Papal encyclicals

1947 *Asbestos strike*
— a turning point in Quebec's economic and social history
— broke ties between government and church
— lay leaders began to play major role in unions after mid-1940s

1960 *Confederation de syndicates nationaux (CSN)*
— dropped Catholic from name
— has about ten sectors
— became radical during the 1970s, but more pragmatic during the 1990s
— smaller than Quebec Federation of Labour (provincial arm of CLC)
— part of "Common Front" in 1972 and 1982
— QFL and CSN cooperate and raid

1991 *Social Contracts*
— response to recession of early 1990s
— signed by both CSN and QFL unions
— mainly in metal and pulp and paper industries
— guarantee long-term labour peace in return for employment stability, joint union-management administration of the agreement

1998 *Politcal Protests*
— major demonstrations and protest against P.Q. government cuts to health, education

Source: *The System of Industrial Relations in Canada* by Craig and Solomon, p. 111–112, 1996, Prentice Hall. Reprinted with permission by Pearson Education.

Union Consolidation

The 1990s also saw the consolidation of Canada's previously highly fragmented union movement, mainly through a variety of mergers (Heron, 1989; Murray, 1995). The most notable of these involved the Communications Workers of Canada, the Energy

Communications, Energy and Paper-workers Union of Canada (CEP)
National, socially conscious union formed as a result of mergers in the communications, energy, and pulp and paper industries.

and Chemical Workers Union, and the Canadian Paperworkers Union, which in 1992 joined forces as the **Communications, Energy and Paperworkers Union of Canada**, or **CEP**. The Canadian Auto Workers and Steelworkers were also heavily involved in merger activity during the decade (Murray, 1995:178; Craig and Solomon, 1996:190–193). The rationale behind many of these mergers was that the new, larger unions are likely to be in a better position to carry out intensive organizing and otherwise provide a broad range of services to their members than the smaller ones they replaced.

Closely related to the merger trend, in fact a direct result of it, was the evolution of a number of industrial unions, including the Auto Workers and Steelworkers, into general or conglomerate unions claiming to represent all workers, not just those in a particular industry. Though the trend led to a number of jurisdictional disputes, it also increased representational possibilities for previously hard-to-organize private service sector workers. For example, the Steelworkers, who had already been organizing groups as diverse as zoo workers and security guards, hotel and restaurant workers, and Montessori teachers, increased their private service sector organizing following their 1993 merger with the Canadian section of the Retail, Wholesale and Department Store union (Murray, 1995:178). For its part, the CAW organized at least two British Columbia branches of the Starbucks coffee chain (Murdock, 1997).

Revisiting the NDP Link

Earlier, we indicated that the English-Canadian labour movement has generally relied on the New Democratic Party to help it achieve its political objectives, such as labour law reform or improved health and safety legislation. Union support was critical to the election of NDP provincial governments in Ontario, Saskatchewan, and British Columbia early in the 1990s. As in the past (Heron, 1989), these governments often proved disappointing to their labour supporters once in office (Lipsig-Mumme, 1995:207). This was especially true in Ontario, where, in 1993, the NDP government imposed a "social contract" suspending free public sector collective bargaining and forcing workers to take unpaid days off (Murray, 1995:189). Loss of labour support, especially from the public sector unions, was clearly a factor in the NDP's disastrous 1993 federal election showing and in its defeat in the 1995 Ontario election. Its continuing relatively weak showings both in Ontario and at the federal level[19] suggest that the tensions resulting from the "social contract" still haven't been fully resolved. Similar tensions have surfaced in Quebec regarding the labour movement's link to the Parti Québécois, as a result of provincial government cutbacks to health care and education. These tensions, too, have remained largely unresolved.

Labour Strategy in Quebec

In Quebec, the labour movement responded quite differently to the economic crisis of the 1990s than it did in the rest of Canada. During the 1970s, the Quebec labour movement was by far the most radical in the country. During the '90s, supported by a succession of provincial governments that took a far more active role in socio-economic planning than even most NDP governments in English Canada, its strategy became one of tripartite cooperation with employers and government in the interest of creating and maintaining jobs (Lipsig-Mumme, 1995; Boivin and Déom, 1995). The decade saw both the Quebec Federation of Labour (QFL) and Confederation of National Trade Unions (CSN) sign on to long-term peace agreements, agreements that, unlike the botched Ontario experiment, can legitimately be called social contracts, since the unions were full partners in negotiating and implementing them (Boivin and Déom, 1995:461). In return for a long-term guarantee of labour peace (generally for five years or more), the union receives employment security for its members and is given joint administration of the agreement. In addition, employees are provided with full information about the firm's financial situation. To help compensate the union for giving up its right to strike for five years or longer, most agreements allow for arbitration of monetary clauses after three years (Boivin and Déom, 1995). While it isn't clear just how widely the Quebec social contracts have been adopted, they do appear to have had a positive effect on labour–management relations in the province.

Canadian Labour at the Dawn of the New Millennium

The changes to the economic and political environment of the IR system over the past 15 years or so have not been merely cyclical ones. Rather, they represent a fundamental "sea change" in the way work is organized and scheduled, in employers' and unions' strategies, and in national governments' willingness and ability to regulate economic and IR-related issues.

As we noted earlier, many workers don't even have a regular workplace any more. A growing number work out of their homes or on short-term contracts—a situation that is likely to prevent them from forming relationships with fellow workers and makes it more likely that their response to what they perceive to be poor working conditions will be to quit rather than to stay and try to improve conditions where they are. Even those with more or less regular jobs often have little job security; many, particularly in the private service sector, work such irregular shifts that they may know few if any of their workmates by name. This makes it difficult for unions to organize service sector establishments. Even when they do try, employers' opposition is generally fierce.

Gone are the loyalty and sense of mutual obligation that were once not uncommon features of Canadian labour–management relationships. In some cases, even profitable firms have laid off large numbers of employees, not because they were performing badly but in order to pay higher dividends to shareholders (see Peirce, 2000a:89). In the federal government, large-scale reorganization and massive human resource modernization (which will be discussed in more detail in Chapter 8) have left unions scrambling to keep up in the highly uncertain minority government situation that has existed since 2004. Initial wage offers below the inflation rate and attempts to remove longstanding allowances were major factors in rotating nationwide public service strikes in 2001 and a general strike by the Public Service Alliance in 2004. In the former case, the strikes were called off following the terrorist actions of September 11, 2001. In the latter case, members ratified new four-year agreements providing average wage increases of about 2.4 percent despite some bargaining team members' recommendations to reject the deals.

With the formation of broader regional trading blocs, not just in North America but also in Europe and Asia, it's no longer possible for Canadian employers, workers, or unions even to pretend that Canada can insulate itself from larger world economic developments. As Richard Marsden (2001:76) has noted, unionized garment workers in Montreal now find themselves competing with workers in Romania and the Ivory Coast. Entire chains of production have become globalized, making it more difficult for unions to mount effective strikes against manufacturers. Furthermore, the labour movement has again been fighting against itself, as evidenced by the SEIU-CAW and CSN-PSAC disputes described earlier in the chapter, as well as by the Teamsters' Union's abortive attempt to raid Canadian Food Inspection Agency veterinarians represented by the Professional Institute (see Fryer, 2001).

Marsden sums up the current situation well when he notes (2001:76): "The foundation upon which the post–World War II industrial relations system was based—long-term employment expectations that provided incentive for employee voice and a degree of protection from the full forces of the marketplace—has proved ephemeral." Taken together, the economic, political, and social changes just described have arguably left the Canadian labour movement in its weakest position since the Great Depression. While Canadian unions have maintained their membership levels surprisingly well so far, particularly in comparison with their counterparts in the US (see Murray, 1995 and 2001), they will be increasingly hard-pressed to do so in the twenty-first century. Among their most serious challenges will be:

- That of providing representation to an increasingly diverse and geographically dispersed workforce—many of whom do not even have a regular workplace, and many others who would appear to have little use for unions.
- That of countering increasingly fierce employer opposition to unions, particularly in the private service sector—an opposition that has manifested itself in a growing willingness to use replacement workers, resort to injunctions and other legal tactics during strikes, close down outlets that succeed in certifying unions, and even (as in the case of the Falconbridge strike discussed in Chapter 11) resort to violence against strikers.
- That of countering growing schisms within the labour movement and of making the movement appear attractive to young people and service sector workers.
- That of finding an effective political partner to help with legislation and political advocacy, whether that partner be a renewed NDP or some other party.[20]

The Canadian labour movement's ability to maintain relatively steady membership rates, in the face of an increasingly difficult economic and political environment, suggests that it possesses considerable resiliency. It will need all that resiliency and more, however, if it is to meet the challenges it is likely to face in the decades to come.

Case 3.1

A TALE OF THREE ERAS

John Godard (2005:410) has identified two distinct eras in post-war Canadian labour history: In the first of those eras, from 1953 through 1973, unemployment was modest, family incomes rose along with per capita GDP, and union density rose somewhat. In the second era, from 1977 through 1997, family incomes were stagnant, unemployment rose sharply, and GDP growth was greatly reduced. Union density first stagnated, then gradually declined.

Use what you've learned in this chapter and elsewhere about Canadian labour history to speculate on the likely prognosis for the Canadian labour movement during the first two decades of the twenty-first century. Will those decades more closely resemble the first or second post-war period? Or will they represent a completely new and distinct era, bearing little resemblance to either of the two earlier ones?

The following questions should prove helpful to you in your explorations, which may be done in small or large group discussion.

Case Questions

1. What are some of the most important indicators you would want to trace in determining the overall health of the Canadian labour movement?
2. What developments were crucial in the change from the first era to the second?
3. Have there been equally important developments—defining moments, if you like—in the period since 1997? If so, what would some of those defining moments be, and how would they likely have affected the labour movement?
4. To what extent do you think evidence regarding the US labour movement's experience is relevant in examining this issue? If you think that evidence is at least somewhat relevant, what do you think it has to teach us here in Canada?
5. How can the labour movement help ensure that the first two decades of this century more closely resemble the earlier than the later post-war period? Or is this just another pipe dream?

QUESTIONS FOR DISCUSSION

1. What did you know about unions and Canadian labour history at the start of this course? What was your impression of unions and what they do?
2. What were some of the barriers to unions found in most industrialized countries? What were some barriers unique to Canada?
3. How did the Quebec labour movement develop differently from the English-Canadian one?

4. Why was the Canadian labour movement closely tied to the American one for many years? What factors contributed to the loosening or severing of many of those ties?

5. What was the significance of the Berlin Convention of 1902 to the development of the Canadian labour movement?

6. How did the industrial unionism introduced during the 1930s and 1940s differ from traditional craft unionism? Did it succeed in bringing unionization to all Canadian workers who wished to join? Why, or why not?

7. How did the unionization of government employees and other public sector workers in the 1960s and '70s change the character of the Canadian labour movement?

8. What effects have globalization and liberalized trade had on the Canadian labour movement? Do you expect those effects to continue?

9. How has the Canadian labour movement benefited from its affiliation with political parties such as the NDP? Do you expect the linkages between the labour movement and progressive political parties such as the NDP (or Parti and Bloc Québécois) to continue? Why, or why not?

10. Who are some of the groups Canadian unions must reach if they wish to retain their existing membership levels in the decades ahead? What are some strategies that might help them achieve this objective?

Suggestions for Further Reading

Heron, Craig. (1996). *The Canadian Labour Movement: A Short History.* Toronto: Lorimer. First published in 1989, this has become a classic thanks to its readable style and the vivid picture it portrays of the lives of Canadian working people. The introductory section provides an extremely useful discussion of the barriers to the formation of an independent Canadian labour movement.

MacDowell, Laurel Sefton, and Ian Radforth (Eds.). (1991). *Canadian Working Class History.* Toronto: Canadian Scholars' Press. An extremely useful collection of articles covering many different aspects of Canadian labour history, from pre-Confederation days right through to modern times. Contains a number of articles on the role of women and immigrants—information that is often hard to obtain elsewhere.

Morton, Desmond. (1990). *Working People: An Illustrated History of the Canadian Labour Movement.* Toronto: Summerhill. Another very readable history of the Canadian labour movement that has gone through several editions. Excellent illustrations. Those with a real taste for history may wish to compare Morton's institutionalist perspective with Heron's political economy one. Both books are well worth reading.

Pathy, Alexander C. (2004). *Waterfront Blues: Labour Strife at the Port of Montreal, 1960–1978.* Toronto: University of Toronto Press. Drawing on the author's own experiences as a management representative at the Port of Montreal, this book tells the dramatic tale of poisoned labour relations, bitter strikes, and repeated government interventions resulting from technological change in the shipping industry.

CHAPTER 4

UNION MEMBERSHIP AND STRUCTURE

Volunteer union officials, like the steward shown here talking to a member about whether he should file a grievance, put in hundreds of thousands of unpaid hours each year and are really what keep the organizations going in many cases.

LEARNING OBJECTIVES

After studying this chapter, you should be able to:

1. Describe some of the economic, political, and social justice activities in which Canadian unions engage.
2. Summarize the trends in union membership and density in Canada.
3. Describe recent changes in the composition of the Canadian labour movement.
4. Contrast union density trends in Canada with those in the United States.
5. Describe the basic structure of Canadian unions and labour federations.
6. Define union democracy, identify its components, and summarize its limitations and safeguards.

Unions are the organizations most directly responsible for representing the interests of Canada's working people. We begin this chapter with a brief look at what unions are and the functions they serve. Next we look at changing patterns of union membership and density, both for Canada as a whole and within different industries and provinces and amongst various types of employment. Among the issues considered here is the divergence between Canadian and American union membership rates. The chapter then considers the structure of the Canadian labour movement, looking at activities carried out at the local, provincial, and national level and at the role played by international unions based outside Canada, which is a distinctive feature of the Canadian labour movement. We conclude with a discussion of union democracy, or the extent to which unions are responsive to their members' wishes.

UNIONS: A BRIEF OVERVIEW

Unions have been defined as workers' associations formed to enhance their power in dealings with employers (Craig and Solomon, 1996:9), particularly in negotiating the terms and conditions under which work is performed and in handling workers' grievances; however, while collective bargaining and grievance-handling may be their core functions, Canadian unions do many other things as well. In Canada, as in most other countries, many unions are heavily involved in political action, which is often aimed at passing legislation that will advance the interests of all working people, whether union members or not. Many unions also serve on joint union–employer industry panels aimed at advancing the interests of a particular industry. Beyond that, union political activities may include joining coalitions with other organizations, such as community groups, women's groups, anti-poverty groups, groups focused on equity rights for gays and lesbians, and other equity-seeking organizations.

In recent years, unions have also become increasingly involved in publicity campaigns of various kinds—some focused on mobilizing support for specific bargaining items, others designed to call public attention to social justice issues or problems of a more general nature, such as ongoing cutbacks in the federal and provincial governments, the problems associated with the increasing number of Canadian children living in poverty, and the need for a national daycare system. Finally, many unions provide assistance to non-profit and humanitarian projects both in Canada and abroad. The Canadian Autoworkers' Social Justice Fund (SJF) and the United Steelworkers' Humanity Fund contribute to a variety of causes such as emergency relief following natural disasters, human development and anti-poverty activities in Latin American and Africa, housing and training projects for homeless youth, the removal of landmines in formerly war-torn regions, and a variety of community development projects both nationally and internationally. Thus, unions are far more than organizations aimed at improving the terms and conditions of employment for their members. **Social unionism**, the pursuit of broad "social and political strategies on behalf of the working class in general" (Godard, 2003:479), has long been an important aspect of the Canadian labour movement—certainly more so than its American counterpart, which focuses more primarily on the economic function of unions.

social unionism
Unionism that works for the good of workers as a whole and uses political action as well as collective bargaining to achieve its objectives.

UNION MEMBERSHIP
National Membership Trends

Except for brief periods of decline during the early 1920s, 1930s, and 1960s, Canadian union membership grew steadily throughout most of the twentieth century. In 1911

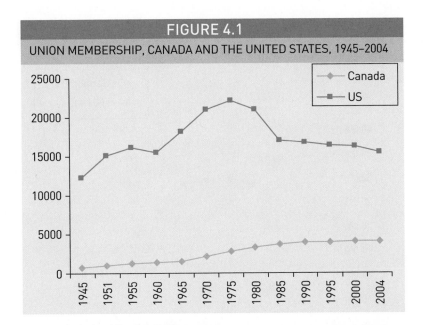

FIGURE 4.1

UNION MEMBERSHIP, CANADA AND THE UNITED STATES, 1945–2004

(Eaton, 1975), there were about 130 000 union members in Canada. By 1945, that number had grown to just over 700 000 and by 1977, 2.8 million Canadian workers belonged to unions. Between 1977 and 2003, union membership rose by 43 percent to just over 4 million. This increase, however, was not only below previous rates of union membership growth but was also below employment growth generally. The result has been a gradual decline in union density rates over the past two decades (Akyeampong, 2004).

Prior to 1984, **union density**, or the percentage of paid, non-agricultural workers belonging to unions,[1] had generally increased throughout most of the century, again excepting brief periods of decline during the early 1920s and 1960s. In 1921, the first year for which we have density data, Canadian union density stood at 16 percent (Eaton, 1975). This figure dropped to 12 percent through most of the 1920s, but rose steadily during the 1930s and soared during the Second World War, reaching a level of just over 24 percent by 1945 (see Figure 4.2). From 1945 through 1958, union density rose steadily to just over 34 percent. The next six years saw a decline, but then the rate started rising again, peaking at 38 percent in 1981. Union density again declined between 1989 and 1998 (Johnson, 2002a; Stats Can, 2005d), after which the union density rate stabilized around its current level of approximately 31 percent (Stats Can, 2005d).

Why have union membership and density rates risen and fallen as they have? As we pointed out in the previous chapter, labour shortages during both world wars increased workers' power relative to that of employers and made it easier for them to join unions. In addition, the extension of the *Industrial Disputes Investigation Act (IDI Act)* to all war industries encouraged union organization, especially during the First World War (Morton, 1995:139). The declines in membership and density levels during the 1920s were due largely to a determined employer anti-union offensive, facilitated by a post-war depression and by the government's dropping of wartime *IDI Act* restrictions against intimidation and harassment of union activists. The two major periods of growth during the post–Second World War period, those from 1945 to 1958 and 1965 through 1977, can be closely linked to legislative changes making it easier for workers to join unions. As we also noted in the previous chapter, *PC 1003*, passed in 1944, extended unionization rights to

union density The percentage of paid, non-agricultural workers belonging to unions.

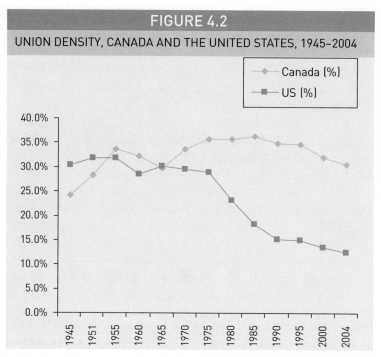

FIGURE 4.2

UNION DENSITY, CANADA AND THE UNITED STATES, 1945–2004

Notes: Union density is defined as the percentage of non-agricultural paid workers belonging to unions. No figure is reported for 1950 because the reference date of Labour Canada's survey was changed from Dec. 31 to Jan. 1 in that year. Data for Canada are not strictly comparable before and after 1978 because the number of paid non-agricultural workers was adjusted upwards after that year. Data for the United States are not strictly comparable before and after 1983 because of the different sources used by Kumar for US union membership figures. Figures for 1998–2004 are based on new series of non-agricultural paid workers, and hence differ slightly for years before 1988 and from those for later years appearing in the first edition of this book.

Sources: For Canada, 1946–1970, Eaton, 1975; for 1971–1976, Labour Canada, 1993, *Directory of Labour Organizations in Canada*, p. xvi, Table 1; for 1977–1987, HRDC, 1996 and 1997, *Directory of Labour Organizations in Canada*; for 1988–2001, *Workplace Gazette* 4:3, p. 36, Table 1; for 2004, "Fact Sheet on Unionization." *Perspectives on Labour and Income*. Statistics Canada. 2004; for the US, 1945–1992, Kumar, 1993; for 1993–2004, Bureau of Labor Statistics, US Dept. of Labor. The Dept. of Labor statistics are not entirely consistent with those used by Kumar; however, the differences are not great.

most blue-collar workers. The decade or so following the passage of this legislation saw the organization of large numbers of semi-skilled workers in heavy industries such as autos, steel, rubber, and meatpacking. Similarly, large numbers of government workers and other public sector workers such as teachers and nurses entered the labour movement during the late 1960s and early 1970s following the passage of major public sector legislation across Canada.

The lack of any major new legislative initiatives comparable to *PC 1003* or the more recent *Public Service Staff Relations Act* may be one reason why union growth has slowed over the past two decades. Another is that many of the legislative amendments that have been passed are less supportive of organizing. The introduction of mandatory vote certification systems in several jurisdictions is perhaps the best example of an amendment that has had detrimental effects on certification success rates and organizing (Martinello, 2000; Johnson, 2002b). The political shift to the right in recent years, which has seen the decline of the NDP and an increasing number of conservative provincial governments, has reduced the influence of unions on the passage of legislation and has had detrimental effects on union organizing and certification success rates, even independent of legislative impacts (Martinello, 2000).

Public sector downsizing, privatization, and contracting out have also taken their toll on union numbers. However, the most important factor behind the recent stagnation in union growth and decline in union density is most likely the loss of hundreds of thousands of manufacturing jobs, most in heavily unionized sectors (Morton, 1995:153), coupled with job growth in sectors, such as the private service sector, where unionization rates tend to be quite low. Organizing the service sector has presented a major challenge to unions and their successes have lagged significantly behind the growth of employment in this sector. Yet despite severe losses in traditional manufacturing strongholds, the Canadian labour movement as a whole has fared significantly better than those of many other industrialized countries, such as Britain, Japan, Australia, and the United States (Bamber and Whitehouse, 1993:310), all of which have experienced significant declines in union density since 1980.

Changing Union Membership Components

Growing Unionization of Women

While overall Canadian union density rates have remained relatively steady, this apparent stability masks many changes in the composition of the Canadian labour movement. Forty years ago, the typical Canadian union member was white, male, and employed full-time at a blue-collar job. Today, nearly half the country's union members are women (see Figure 4.3), and people from many different religious and ethnic minorities have joined the labour movement. Unionization has increased among part-timers and white-collar workers are now nearly as likely to be members as blue-collar workers.

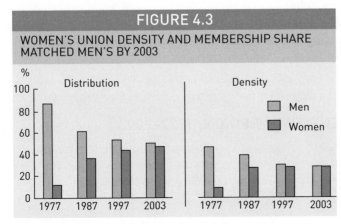

FIGURE 4.3

WOMEN'S UNION DENSITY AND MEMBERSHIP SHARE MATCHED MEN'S BY 2003

Source: Statistics Canada, *Perspectives on Labour and Income*, Catalogue 75-001, August 2004, vol. 5, no. 8, p. 6.

The most profound change in union membership in recent decades is the mix of men and women. From a mere 15.4 percent in 1962 (Stats Can, 1999), women's share of union membership jumped to 48 percent in 2003 (Akyeampong, 2004). Factors contributing to this phenomenon include women's increasing labour force participation rates—and especially their increasing presence in the public sector, within which unionization rates exploded through the 1960s and early 1970s. Also important is women's movement into traditionally male-dominated, highly unionized industries (Stats Can, 2005d). Increased unionization in certain service industries that tend to be female-dominated and increasing unionization rates amongst part-time workers have also facilitated this changing gender mix (Akyeampong, 1998). Finally, a shift in economic structure, from the male-dominated and once highly-unionized goods-producing sector, which accounted for about one-third of total union membership in 1987, to the service sector, has both increased union density rates for women and decreased union density rates for men. In 1977, women's unionization rate was about one-quarter of men's, but by 2004, women's unionization rate of 30.6 percent had edged past the men's rate of 30.3 percent for the first time ever (Akyeampong, 2004; Stats Can, 2004d).

Union Membership by Province

Union density rates vary between provinces, although not nearly to the same degree as they vary between states. In the United States, union density rates in 2004 varied from a low of 2.7 and 3.0 percent in North Carolina and South Carolina, respectively, to a high of 25.3 percent in New York (Bureau of Labor Statistics, 2005). In Canada, density rates varied in 2004 from a low of 24.1 percent in Alberta to a high of 40.6 and 40.7 percent in Newfoundland and Labrador and Quebec, respectively (Akyeampong, 2004).[2] The rankings by province have remained relatively stable over the last several decades, with Newfoundland and Labrador and Quebec leading the pack while rates in Alberta, Nova Scotia, Ontario, and New Brunswick tend to be the lowest. The one exception to this stability of rankings could be British Columbia, where density rates declined relatively steeply from 40.9 in 1977 to 32.4 in 2003 (Akyeampong, 2004).

The subject of what accounts for differing provincial union membership rates is one of increasing interest within the Canadian industrial relations profession. Over

Table 4.1

UNION DENSITY BY REGION, 1977–2003

	Total	Atlantic	Quebec	Ontario	Prairies	BC
1977	32.6%	34.1%	34.7%	31.0%	26.8%	40.9%
1987	34.2	36.9	39.6	31.0	30.1	38.6
1997	30.8	30.3	36.9	27.7	27.1	34.0
2003	30.3	29.3	37.6	26.8	27.1	32.4

Sources: Adapted from Statistics Canada, *Perspectives on Labour and Income*, Catalogue 75-001, August 2004, vol. 5, no. 8, p. 6.

the past two decades, there have been a number of studies that have shed light on various aspects of the question (see, for example, Maki, 1982; Meltz, 1989b; Ng, 1992; Martinello, 1996). To date, however, the definitive study on this important issue has yet to appear. Among the determinants most often identified are industrial structure, the type of labour legislation in place, and the presence, or absence, of pro-labour governments.

Certain industries, such as forestry and transportation, have traditionally been heavily unionized. Certain others, such as agriculture and finance, have traditionally had few unions. It follows that provinces with large numbers of heavily unionized industries should, other things being equal, have higher union membership rates than provinces with few such industries. The existence of strong forestry, pulp and paper, and, until recently, fishing sectors in Newfoundland and Labrador and British Columbia is likely one reason for these provinces' relatively high density rates.

An equally if not more important factor is the type of labour legislation a province has in place. Clearly, certain types of provisions can help union growth, while other types are more likely to retard it.[3] For example (Peirce, 1989), some provinces have relatively liberal exclusion policies governing who can and cannot join unions, barring only management and confidential labour relations personnel. Others have more restrictive policies that serve to prevent people such as professionals, domestics, and farm workers from joining unions in addition to the groups already mentioned. Not surprisingly, membership rates are generally higher in the provinces with liberal exclusion policies than in those with restrictive ones, since they have a larger pool of potential members.

Another relevant factor is the presence of a pro-labour government, such as the NDP or Parti Québécois, which can help the labour movement advance its cause in the political arena. As Maki (1982) has suggested, such governments can help increase union membership both directly, by passing legislation designed to make it easier for unions to attract new members, and indirectly, by improving labour's public profile, such as would occur when a union activist is appointed to a cabinet position, thus making union membership seem a more attractive proposition. Maki's study has directly linked the presence of NDP governments to higher union membership rates. In connection with this point, it is worth noting that except for Newfoundland and Labrador, all of the provinces whose union membership rates are above the national average have at some point had NDP or PQ governments. In contrast, only one of the provinces (Ontario) with below-average density rates has ever had an NDP or PQ government, and in that case the government served just one term, which may not have been long enough to have made a lasting difference.[4] Similar comparative studies (see Freeman, 1989; Bean, 1994) have linked support for labour or social democratic parties to increased union membership rates in various countries that are members of the Organisation for Economic Co-operation and Development (OECD).

Unionization Rates by Industry and Occupation

Union membership rates vary considerably more by industry than they do by province. In 2003 rates ranged from a dramatic low of 3.5 percent in agriculture to 71.0 percent in provincial administration. Federal administration at 69.2 percent, educational services at 69.0 percent, and utilities at 67.7 percent were close behind. Union density also tends to be relatively high in health care and in transportation and warehousing. Industries where union density tends to be low include professional, scientific and technical, real estate, accommodation and food services, finance and insurance, and other services. Historically, the goods-producing sector has tended to have considerably higher union density rates than the service sector; however, by 2003, the gap had virtually disappeared with 31 percent density in the former and 30 percent in the latter (Akyeampong, 2004).

Union density rates also vary considerably between occupations. Consistent with industry trends, nurses and other health care professionals tend to have high union density rates, as do teachers and professors in elementary, secondary, and post-secondary education. Managers and those who work in retail, wholesale, and food and beverage services tend to have density rates considerably below average. In recent years, union density rates for workers in child care and home support workers have posted fairly significant gains, bringing density rates for these workers to 38.6 percent (Akyeampong, 2004). In contrast, forestry and mining, industries that have traditionally had high union density, saw fairly precipitous declines between 1981 and 1998, falling from approximately 46 percent to just over 26 percent. Union density in construction and manufacturing, also traditionally highly unionized industries, fell by 13 percentage points each during that same period (Stats Can, 2005).

Other Union Membership Components

As has been the case for some time (see Rose, 1995), the public sector continues to be far more heavily unionized than the private sector. In 2003 (Akyeampong, 2004), more than 70 percent of Canadian public sector workers were unionized, as opposed to just 18 percent of the country's private sector workers. The extremely high unionization rates, in such sectors as education, public administration, and health care explains why 53 percent of the country's union members come from the public sector, even though fewer than one-quarter of all Canadians are employed there (Akyeampong, 2004).

As has also been the case for some time (see England, 1987), part-time workers are significantly less likely to be union members than full-timers. However, consistent with trends in employment, part-time workers' share of union membership rose from 8 to 14 percent between 1984 and 2003 and their union density rose from 18 to 23 percent. Meanwhile, full-timers' share of union membership declined from 92 to 86 percent and their union density rate fell from 39 to 32 percent (Akyeampong, 2004). Also consistent with overall employment trends, unionization rates have decreased slightly for permanent employees while for non-permanent employees rates rose from 22.7 percent in 1997 to 25.1 percent in 2003. Finally, between 1997 and 2003, union density fell 3.9 percentage points within large firms of over 500 employees and rose 0.7 percentage points within firms of fewer than 20 employees (Akyeampong, 2004).

Generally, union membership rates do not appear to be very strongly affected by an individual's age or educational attainment, except that very young workers (those aged 15 to 24) are far less likely than others to be union members. The likeliest explanations for the low density rate among young workers are the high proportion that work part-time and the frequency with which young people tend to change jobs. Recent trends, however, have seen union density rates increasing for young workers and those over 55 and decreasing for workers between the ages of 25 and 54. Owing to their growing concentration in industries that typically have low union density rates, the unionization rate of men aged 25 to 35 has fallen most dramatically in recent years, from 43 percent in 1981 to 24 percent in 2004. During that same period, unionization among women aged 45 to 64 increased by 8 percentage points, from 32 to 40 percent (Stats Can, 2005).

Union density rates tend to increase quite dramatically with job tenure, although recent data document losses in union density among longer tenure workers and gains among workers with tenure of less than five years (Akyeampong, 2004). Educational attainment appears to be of even less importance than age in determining a worker's union membership status. However, density rates are highest amongst workers with a university education or post-secondary diploma or certificate. This may reflect a high concentration of educated individuals in the heavily unionized public sector.

Canadian versus American Union Membership Rates

Many of the same factors that explain differing union membership rates in different Canadian provinces may also help explain differing Canadian and American union membership rates. While a number of studies of both Canadian and American union membership growth have found economic factors to be of great significance (Ashenfelter and Pencavel, 1969; Bain and Elsheikh, 1976; Eastman, 1983), economic factors arguably do little to explain the growing divergence in Canadian and American union membership rates over the past 40 years, a period when Canada and the United States have had roughly similar economic experiences and when their economies have become increasingly integrated.

In 1965, as Figure 4.2 shows, American union density was just slightly higher than that of Canada, both being around 30 percent. By 1980, the Canadian rate had risen to almost 36 percent, or more than half again greater than the US rate of just over 23 percent. Since 1986, the Canadian rate has invariably been more than twice that of the United States. Industrial relations scholars have put forward a variety of explanations for the growing divergence in the two countries' membership rates. One is differing public labour policy. In Canada, such policy has generally been more supportive of unions than it has in the United States. First, union security is more carefully guarded in Canada than in the United States. While the specifics of the union security clause may vary, every Canadian jurisdiction imposes upon employers a requirement to deduct union dues from employees' paycheques. In contrast, many US states have no union security protection in place. The existence of several "right-to-work" states, where union density rates are generally very low (Meltz, 1989b), may be the single most important difference in the Canadian and American labour policy environments.

Second, at least until recently, the process by which a union becomes certified has been quite different in Canada and the United States.[5] In the United States, a vote is mandatory in every certification and the procedure is often prolonged by objections, hearings, and other delays during which employer and union are locked in a heated battle for employees' hearts. Recent research suggests this reliance on mandatory votes explains 17 to 24 percent of the gap between Canadian and US union density (Johnson, 2004). In recent decades some Canadian jurisdictions have moved away from the simpler card-check systems and adopted mandatory vote certification procedures; however, this has only reduced the union density gap by about one percentage point (Johnson, 2004), most likely because Canadian mandatory vote procedures are significantly more expeditious than those in the US. Furthermore, limits on employer opposition behaviour during certification campaigns are both more strict and more strictly enforced in Canada than the United States.

Third, collective bargaining rights for public sector workers are generally a good deal stronger in Canada. In the United States, these rights were provided at the federal level through a 1961 executive order by President John F. Kennedy (Mills, 1989). They have generally not included the right to strike, and in the case of the federal public service, do not include the right to bargain over salaries. At the state level, as of 1996, 11 states had no legislation whatsoever to vest public employees with collective bargaining rights and 16 states restricted bargaining rights to only some public employees, leaving only 23 states and the District of Columbia granting bargaining rights to all public employees (Lund and Maranto, 1996). Only 11 states permitted state employees to strike and only 12 permitted education and municipal employees to strike (Lund and Maranto, 1996). As we will see in more detail in the public sector chapter, most Canadian public sector workers do enjoy the right to strike and, in general, possess more collective bargaining rights than their US counterparts. These greater rights appear to have made union membership a more attractive proposition for Canadian than for American public sector workers.

The political environment is also significantly different in the two countries. For the past 70-odd years, Canada has had a social democratic party (known first as the CCF and now as the NDP) dedicated to advancing labour's interests in the political arena. While not strong by European standards, the NDP has often held power provincially in Canada and on a number of occasions has held the balance of power federally. In all of these situations, it has been in a position either to pass union-friendly labour legislation directly, as it has done in BC, Saskatchewan, Manitoba, and Ontario, or to demand that its coalition partner pass such legislation as the price of continued NDP support. In Quebec, the Parti Québécois has generally played a similar role. Lacking a political ally, the American labour movement has often had considerable difficulty advancing its legislative agenda. Overall, the evidence suggests that the NDP and PQ have helped increase or at least maintain union membership rates in Canada, while conversely, the lack of a labour or social democratic party may help explain the recent decline in union density in the United States (see Bruce, 1989; Meltz, 1989b; Rose and Chaison, 2001).

Yet another difference is the extent of union organizing efforts in the two countries. Canadian unions have historically dedicated greater effort toward organizing unskilled workers than have their American counterparts (I. Robinson, 1990; Yates, 2000). The difference between Canadian and American organizing efforts was particularly great during the last years of George Meany's presidency of the AFL-CIO, which culminated in 1979. Like many conservative craft unionists before him, Meany cared little about the fate of unskilled workers and generally gave organizing a low priority. Indeed, he was quoted in a national news magazine as saying that the size of the American labour movement made no difference to him (Goulden, 1972; I. Robinson, 1990). Canadian unionists never shared this attitude towards organizing; not surprisingly, this country's unions greatly out-organized those of the United States, to the degree that in some years, despite the two countries' difference in size, Canadian unions actually signed up more new members than American unions did (Rose and Chaison, 1990).[6] Another difference between the two countries' labour movements that significantly affects organizing efforts is that in the US, it is the AFL-CIO that takes the leading role in organizing the unorganized, making its policies pivotal. In Canada, however, major organizing initiatives are spearheaded by individual unions, not by central labour federations (Yates, 2000). Thus, the strategic priorities of many different unions combine to focus organizing efforts on unorganized workers in a variety of industries.

Recently, the AFL-CIO's failure to adequately focus on organizing new members contributed to an historic rift in the federation, which saw a coalition of unions representing 7 million members call for a fundamental shift in the AFL-CIO's priorities. When that failed, the coalition formed a new federation, which held its founding convention on September 27, 2005, and pledged to focus more than 75 percent of its budget on organizing. Current Issues box 4.2 provides details.

UNION STRUCTURE

Canadian labour organizations conduct their business at local, provincial, national, and in some cases international levels. In general, the Canadian labour movement operates in a quite decentralized fashion, at least by international standards (see Rogow, 1989a:158–161 and Chaykowski, 1995:231). By international standards, as well, Canadian unions carry out a great deal of their bargaining at the union-local or plant level, a situation in sharp contrast to that prevailing in many European countries such as Germany and Sweden, where bargaining has normally been conducted at industry or even national levels (Fuerstenberg, 1993; Hammarstrom, 1993).

Canada's union structure is also generally considered quite **fragmented**. This means that by international standards, Canada has a large number of small unions. While Table 4.2 shows that some Canadian unions are quite large, representing upwards of 100 000 workers, many of these big unions are in the public sector. In the private sector, there is still a good deal of fragmentation, despite recent mergers such as that of UNITE HERE and a fair amount of diversification and expansion on the part of traditional industrial unions like the Canadian Autoworkers and United Steelworkers (see Murray, 1995). One result of such fragmentation can be **dual unionism**, or competition between two or more unions to represent workers in the

fragmented union structure A union structure marked by a large number of small unions.

dual unionism Competition between two or more unions to represent workers in the same sector.

Table 4.2	
TEN CANADIAN UNIONS WITH LARGEST MEMBERSHIP, 2004	
	Membership (000s)
Canadian Union of Public Employees - CLC	535
National Union of Public and General Employees - CLC	337
National Automobile, Aerospace, Transportation and General Workers Union of Canada (CAW) - CLC	260
United Food and Commercial Workers International Union - AFL-CIO/CLC	188
United Steelworkers of America - AFL-CIO/CLC	180
Public Service Alliance of Canada - CLC	153
Communications, Energy and Paperworkers Union of Canada - CLC	150
International Brotherhood of Teamsters - AFL-CIO/CLC	110
Fédération de la santé et des services sociaux - CSN	101
Laborers' International Union of North America - AFL-CIO/CLC	85

Note: CLC indicates the union is affiliated with the Canadian Labour Congress. AFL-CIO indicates the union is affiliated the American Labor Federation-Congress of Industrial Organizations, the labour federation in the United States. CSN indicates affiliation with the Confédération des sydicats nationaux.

Sources: Henry, Manon. (2004). "Union Membership in Canada." *Workplace Gazette* 7:3. Ottawa: Workplace Information Directorate, Human Resources and Skills Development Canada.

same sector. Such competition can lead to friction and internal dissent and may hinder the Canadian labour movement's attempts to form effective international sectoral alliances (Lipsig-Mumme, 1995). Finally, smaller unions often do not have sufficient resources to offer the same range of services—such as organizing, research, publicity, and legislative lobbying—as larger unions.

Union Locals

A union local usually represents workers in a given geographic area, most commonly a municipality. In some cases, it includes all workers represented by that union within the geographic area; in other cases, it includes only workers at a particular site. Public sector locals may represent all workers affiliated with that union throughout a municipal region or even an entire province (Godard, 2005). In some cases, a union local will not be affiliated with a provincial, national, or international parent union, in which case it is an **independent local** and the local constitutes the entire union. More often, however, the local will be affiliated with other locals of the same union and in this case, the local is the union's basic building block.

Locals in different types of unions tend to operate somewhat differently from each other. For example, in craft unions, which represent workers from a single occupation, such as carpenters or bricklayers, and in professional-employee unions, bargaining is often conducted at the local level (Chaison and Rose, 1989 [see Chaison 1982]). In such cases, the local will sometimes employ an individual known as a **business agent** to serve as chief spokesperson at negotiations, handle grievances, deal with members' problems, and liaise with other unions. Industrial and public service unions, where bargaining is often conducted at the industry, provincial, or even national level, as in the case of the federal public service, do not

independent union (or independent local) A union that is not affiliated with any labour federation.

business agent A staff member of a union who handles grievances, helps enforce agreements, and performs other tasks in the day-to-day operation of the union.

normally employ business agents, though these unions do often use provincial and national representatives to provide some of the same services as a business agent. In these cases, the local officers with whom members have most contact are **shop steward**s. Generally unpaid, shop stewards work for the union on a part-time basis. Their major responsibility is usually investigating grievances and representing members at grievance hearings; however, they may also be involved in such activities as recruiting new members or encouraging participation at meetings (Godard, 2005).

shop steward A union member elected to represent workers in a particular shop or department.

Whichever type of union a worker belongs to, the local is the level of the union with which he or she is generally most familiar. It is at the local's meetings, normally held monthly, where officers are elected, policies established, the broad outlines of bargaining strategy set,[7] and strike votes taken. Though attendance at monthly meetings is generally extremely low, meetings involving the election of officers or discussion of possible strike action will normally see a far better turnout.

As is the case with many other organizations, much of the local's work is done by a variety of committees. Typically a union will use both standing committees to deal with ongoing issues such as bargaining, grievances, pensions, and finances, and ad hoc committees created for a particular purpose, such as job action committees to plan strike strategy or strike committees to coordinate strike activities. Many of these committees entail a heavy time commitment on the part of participating members. While many union leaders are concerned, and rightly so, about the low attendance figures for most monthly meetings, these figures must be balanced against the hundreds of volunteer hours put in each month by the members of a typical union's many committees.

Most locals are affiliated with a **district labour council**, which is funded by a per capita tax on the locals and which functions to advance the labour movement's interests at the local and municipal levels (Craig and Solomon, 1996:156). In practice, this could mean anything from running an information booth at a Labour Day fair to providing a union perspective to the media on contemporary economic and political developments or lending support to a striking union in the area (Craig and Solomon, 1996). In larger centres, in particular, district labour councils can be a potent force. For example, the Toronto and District Labour Council was heavily involved in organizing protest actions against the Ontario provincial government in 1997 and 1998.

district labour councils Bodies designed to advance the labour movement's interests at local and municipal levels.

Parent Unions

The majority of Canadian union locals are affiliated with other locals of the same union in national, international, or provincial **parent union**s. These parent unions are essentially head offices that serve to: 1) coordinate the bargaining activities of the various locals; 2) provide assistance and expertise for bargaining and grievance handling; 3) provide financial and other support during strikes or lockouts; 4) organize additional locals (Godard, 2005). Most often, locals are affiliated with a parent because they were organized by that union and, therefore, were automatically affiliated. This expansion of membership is one of the most important functions of parent unions, especially in industries that are not highly unionized. As more and more workers within an industry become unionized, wages become a less

parent union A number of local unions affiliated under the same name and subject to a unifying constitution and structure.

Municipal and district labour councils such as this one help raise the profile of unions and the labour movement in communities all across Canada.

important aspect of competition between employers and unions are able to bargain more favourable terms and conditions of employment for their membership. Coordination of bargaining, especially within industries, is another important function of parent unions and involves either bargaining with multiple employers simultaneously or coordinating settlements to ensure similar wages and working conditions throughout the industry (Godard, 2005).

The organizational structure of a union local is usually replicated at the parent union level in that the parent has a number of elected officials. The president, vice-presidents, secretary, and treasurer of the parent union, however, are usually full-time, paid employees. To assist them in fulfilling their often extensive responsibilities, the parent union usually has a head office made up of multiple departments staffed with researchers, economists, and administrative support staff. The parent union also usually employs a large number of specialists assigned such tasks as organizing new members, training and education, coordinating bargaining, ensuring consistency in contract interpretation and grievance handling, pursuing equity goals, and political lobbying. These activities are funded by the member locals, each of which directs a portion of their members' dues to the parent union. The activities are coordinated through executive boards that include local union representatives and through the parent union's conventions and meetings (held either annually, biennially, or once every few years) where leaders are elected, the constitution is amended if necessary, policy directions are determined, and decisions are made regarding major funding initiatives. In addition to their intra-union affiliations, most local and parent unions are affiliated with provincial and national union federations. It is through these affiliations that unions exercise coordinated strength within a province, on the national scene, and even internationally.

National and Provincial Labour Federations

Some unions, most typically those representing professionals such as nurses (Boivin and Déom, 1995 [see Déom and Boivin, 2001]) or university professors, choose to remain completely independent of affiliations with other unions.[8] Most unions, however, see distinct advantages in joining forces with other unions at national and provincial levels. By far the most important labour federation in Canada is the **Canadian Labour Congress (CLC)**, which represents almost three-quarters of the country's union members (Henry, 2004). The organization's policies are established and constitution amended at its biennial conventions, attended by thousands of delegates from affiliates. It is also at these conventions that the CLC elects its officers and decides whether to admit, suspend, or expel individual unions. In between conventions, an executive council made up of the CLC's president, vice presidents, and secretary-treasurer is responsible for policy decisions (Godard, 2005).

Canadian Labour Congress (CLC) Canada's national labour federation, formed in 1956 from the merger of the Canadian Congress of Labour and the Trades and Labour Congress.

Functions of the Canadian Labour Congress

The CLC normally does not engage in collective bargaining and has little power over the unions affiliated with it, other than the power to expel, suspend, or reprimand them for offences such as raiding other unions. Its major functions are: (1) representing the Canadian labour movement politically, (2) providing services, such as research and organizing assistance, to its affiliated unions, (3) managing relations between its affiliated unions, (4) enforcing its ethical code, and (5) representing the Canadian labour movement internationally.

Political Representation

As we point out in the union action section of the next chapter, unions often become involved politically to influence the passage of the legislation affecting workers and their unions. Over time, the Canadian labour movement has found that it makes sense to coordinate much of its political activity in Ottawa, the seat of Parliament.[9]

The political activities of the CLC and provincial labour federations take a variety of forms. Among the most important of these is liaison with the labour movement's political partner, the NDP. In addition, labour federations use various other means in seeking to influence government legislation and policy. These include lobbying of Cabinet members and government officials, the issuing of press releases in response to economic developments, and the preparation of briefs or research studies on issues it considers of major importance, such as unemployment (Craig and Solomon, 1996:164). On issues they consider critical, labour federations will play a more active role in public debate; for example, in the case of the Canada–US Free Trade Agreement, the CLC issued numerous public statements and campaigned against the deal during the 1988 federal election campaign (Craig and Solomon, 1996). When the CLC feels its advice is being ignored, it will go even further, organizing demonstrations and publicity campaigns in the hope of spurring the government into action. This was the case in 1993, when the CLC organized a massive Parliament Hill demonstration to protest what it saw as the job-killing effects of the free trade agreements (Craig and Solomon, 1996:165).

Assistance to Affiliated Unions

The CLC provides a broad range of services for its members, many of whom lack the money or expertise to carry these services out for themselves. Such services can include labour education, research for collective bargaining, and organizing assistance (Godard, 2005).

Maintaining Relations Between Affiliates

Next to its political work, the CLC's most important activity is trying to maintain harmonious relations between its affiliated unions. Of particular concern here are jurisdictional disputes—or battles over which union will represent a given group of workers. Such disputes have become increasingly common in recent years as the big industrial unions, seeking to make up for the membership lost through deindustrialization and economic restructuring, have been forced to look farther afield for new members. In most cases, these unions have focused on organizing the unorganized, but on occasion they have attempted to sign up workers already belonging to another union, an action known as **union raiding**. Raiding is a serious concern to the CLC, since it not only saps the morale of many of those involved and wastes valuable money and human resources that should be directed elsewhere (Godard, 2005), but can also cause the entire labour movement major public embarrassment.

union raiding An attempt by one union to persuade members of another union to defect and join its ranks.

One recent and very public case of raiding took place in 2000 and is detailed in Case 4.1, at the end of this chapter. The CAW was accused of raiding the Service Employees International Union (SEIU) after some SEIU members who were seeking increased national autonomy from their international parent attempted to join the CAW. The CLC imposed sanctions which remained in effect until the parties resolved their dispute in May 2001 (CNW, 2001). Raids and attempted raids have also become more common in the public sector. For example, in 1999, the Teamsters' Union narrowly missed becoming the bargaining agent for a group of Canadian Food Inspection Agency veterinarians represented by the Professional Institute. In 2001, federal correctional officers shifted their allegiance from the Public Service Alliance to the CSN, after a lengthy battle between the two unions (PSSRB, 2000 and 2001).

Maintaining the Code of Ethics

To help ensure that its affiliates behave honourably, the CLC has written into its constitution a code of ethics. This code prohibits corrupt leadership practices and specifically guarantees union members the right to have honest and democratic elections, to run for union office, and to get fair treatment from their union's officials. The CLC's executive is charged with enforcing this code, although here, as in the case of union raiding, its powers are quite limited (Godard, 2005).

International Representation

Canada is active in a number of international labour organizations, including most notably the **International Labour Organization (ILO)** and **International Confederation of Free Trade Unions (ICFTU)**. The ILO is a United Nations agency that investigates workers' rights and working conditions all around the world and sets international standards, or conventions, that apply to all member countries. These conventions have been established for issues such as freedom of association, the right to strike, hours of work, and the abolition of forced labour (LaBerge, 1976). The ILO's powers are mainly limited to those of persuasion since, like the CLC, it lacks any real power to enforce its rulings (Godard, 2005; Craig and Solomon, 1996). The ICFTU is a confederation of national trade unions and federations, each of which links together the trade unions of their own country. The ICFTU is heavily involved in training unionists and in establishing and maintaining workers' rights in developing countries, where such rights are often far from a given (Craig and Solomon, 1996; Fashoyin, 1991). As the body representing the majority of Canada's unionists, the CLC represents the Canadian labour movement in these organizations, often playing a key leadership role.

International Labour Organization (ILO) A United Nations agency that investigates workers' rights and working conditions all around the world and sets international standards.

International Confederation of Free Trade Unions (ICFTU) A confederation of national trade unions, each of which links together the trade unions of that particular country.

Provincial Labour Federations

Provincial labour federations play an extremely important role in Canada, since most labour legislation is under provincial jurisdiction; hence the importance of maintaining a strong political presence at the provincial as well as federal level. The CLC has ten provincial and three territorial affiliates. Like the national federation, the provincial ones generally carry out activities that most unions lack the resources to carry out for themselves, such as political and legislative lobbying, research, and labour education. Their range of activities is often extremely broad. For instance, in one recent year (OFL, 1994), the Ontario Federation of Labour (OFL) submitted briefs on subjects ranging from workers' compensation and unemployment insurance to the possible incorporation of physicians and sustainable economic development. The Federation also carried out a substantial research program on health-related issues, successfully lobbied the provincial government to stop the introduction of user fees for drugs for seniors, organized an international symposium on the arts and labour, and held seminars on homeworking and teleworking, in addition to making plans for a joint conference with the Ontario Environment Network and helping to develop a dispute resolution process to deal with forest land-use claims.[10]

Quebec's Special Situation: Multiple Federations

Every province and territory except Quebec has a single provincial labour federation affiliated with the CLC. Like the other provinces, Quebec has its CLC affiliate, the Quebec Federation of Labour (QFL). There are, however, two important ways in which Quebec's union structure is different from that in other provinces: First, unlike any other province, Quebec has several different labour federations, as well as a sizeable number of independent unions not affiliated with any federation. The most important of the federations are the Quebec Federation of Labour and the Confédération des syndicats nationaux (CSN). Other Quebec-wide federations include the Centrale des syndicats démocratiques (CSD) and the Centrale des syndicats du Québec (CSQ).

Like many European countries, Quebec has a situation in which a number of different labour federations are actively competing for new members, both with each other and with the independent unions. The existence of multiple labour federations in Quebec has always been a source of friction and on occasion has resulted in violence, as in the case of the QFL's and CSN's pitched battles over the organization of James Bay construction workers during the 1970s (Boivin, 1982:431). At the same time, it cannot be denied that when the federations have pulled together, as they did during the 1972 Common Front strike, the result has been a provincial labour movement of unusual cohesiveness and strength.

The second distinctive feature of Quebec's union structure is the unusual degree of freedom granted the CLC's Quebec affiliate, the QFL. Unlike other provincial CLC affiliates, the QFL has always been in the position of having to compete for members, which almost by definition makes its situation a special one. When the debate over Quebec independence began to heat up, it was able to make the case that it would need special powers and more money than other provincial labour federations if it was to continue to attract new members. The CLC responded in 1974 by granting the QFL what amounted to partial autonomy, yielding its usual jurisdiction over labour education and local labour councils, and allowing the provincial federation to recoup funds for national services that provided Quebec members no tangible benefit, such as unilingual English newspapers (Boivin, 1982:433). Twenty years later, the CLC went even further, granting its Quebec affiliate what some have referred to as "sovereignty-association" status within the national federation. A 1994 agreement worked out at the Congress's convention in Toronto gave the QFL powers that would normally be granted only to a national labour organization, such as the right to designate its own representatives to activities held by international labour groups like the ILO and ICFTU. In addition, the QFL president was automatically made a voting member of the Congress's executive, and the QFL was given the right to observe its own protocols on matters such as internal jurisdictional disputes and labour education, as well as control over the money that the CLC would normally have allocated for these activities (Déom and Boivin, 2005).

National and International Unions

international union
As normally used in Canada, this term refers to unions headquartered in the United States but which also have Canadian members.

Canada is among the few industrialized countries to have a sizeable number of union members represented by unions headquartered outside the country. Generally known as **"international"** unions, these organizations are in reality American unions with Canadian branches. Their role in the Canadian labour movement has been controversial throughout the past century. It continues to generate controversy even at a time when some observers (for example, Lipsig-Mumme, 1995) have begun to argue for closer links between unions in Canada, the United States, and Mexico in response to the continental integration resulting from the Canada–US and North American Free Trade Agreements.

In the labour history chapter, we pointed out that there were good reasons for Canadian unionists in the late nineteenth and early twentieth centuries to choose to be represented by American unions. Bigger, more experienced, and stronger American unions could provide money and logistical and organizing support that simply were not available in this country. Moreover, at a time when many jobs were still seasonal, an American union card served almost as a meal ticket for many Canadian workers forced to seek employment in the United States (Lipton, 1973; McKay, 1983).

But if there were good reasons for the "internationalization" of the Canadian labour movement in the late nineteenth and early twentieth centuries, there have been equally good reasons for its more recent Canadianization, which has taken place mainly over the past 35 years. Numerically, the American labour movement is far weaker than it was during the early post-war period. Union density in the United States now stands at a mere 12.5 percent, down from 30.4 in 1945 (see Figure 4.2), and as a number of observers have pointed out, the decline in the size of the American labour movement has been mirrored by a decline in its political clout (see Lipsig-Mumme, 1989; I. Robinson, 1990 and 1994). Far from being stronger than the Canadian labour movement, as it was through the early years of this century, the American labour movement is now considerably weaker than its northern counterpart. This growing weakness has led many Canadian unionists to question the value of continued affiliation.

The precipitous decline of union density and power in the United States is not the only factor contributing to the nationalization of the Canadian labour movement. An equally important development has been the growth of public sector unionism in Canada. Almost by definition, public sector unions are **national unions**. It is difficult to imagine how a union based in another country could provide effective representation for Canadian government employees, schoolteachers, or health care workers. Indeed, any serious attempt by an American union to organize Canadian public sector workers, particularly federal or provincial government employees, would likely raise major concerns around issues of national sovereignty. Moreover, Canadian public sector workers would generally have little if anything to gain from affiliation with an American union, given the far less liberal public sector bargaining legislation in the United States (Craig and Solomon, 1996:183).

In the private sector, issues leading many Canadian unions to break away from their American internationals have included disputes over strike funding and bargaining strategy and political disagreements. More generally, the 1960s and 1970s were a time of growing nationalism and questioning of authority across Canada, a time when many Canadians were becoming increasingly displeased with the degree of American ownership of and control over this country's economy. To many Canadian unionists, a situation in which their unions were controlled outside the country had become unacceptable in itself—beyond specific disagreements over bargaining strategies or political affiliation. Taken together, the developments just described have

national union As normally used in Canada, a union whose headquarters and members are all in Canada.

Table 4.3

NATIONAL AND INTERNATIONAL UNIONS: PERCENTAGE OF CANADIAN UNION MEMBERS, SELECTED YEARS, 1962–2004

	National	International	Other*
1962	23.5%	72.0%	4.4%
1978	47.4	50.0	2.6
1990	63.6	31.8	4.6
1997	65.4	29.9	4.8
2001	65.5	29.5	5.0
2004	67.3	27.7	5.0

*"Other" refers to directly chartered unions and independent local organizations.

Sources: Workplace Information Directorate, HRDC. (1997). *Directory of Labour Organizations in Canada*, p. xii. (1962–1997); *Workplace Gazette* 4:3, p. 41, Table 6 (2001); Workplace Gazette 7:3, p. 45, Table 4 (2004).

transformed the Canadian labour movement from a primarily US-based one to a primarily national one. In 1920 (Chaison, 1982:152), international unions represented almost 95 percent of Canadian union members. As recently as 1962 (see Table 4.3), more than 70 percent of all Canadian union members still belonged to internationals. Today, the situation is reversed, with 67.3 percent of all Canadian union members belonging to national, rather than international, unions.

Current Issues 4.1

UNITE HERE!

In July, 2004, a new union was born from the merger of the Union of Needletrades, Industrial and Textile Employees (UNITE) and the Hotel Employees and Restaurant Employees (HERE). UNITE, itself a product of the 1995 merger of the Amalgamated Clothing and Textile Workers' Union and the International Ladies Garment Workers' Union, represented 25 000 workers in Canada and over 200 000 workers internationally. HERE, which represented hospitality, food service, travel, and tourism workers, received its original charter from the American Federation of Labor in 1891. UNITE HERE now represents more than 440 000 active members and over 400 000 retirees across North America, with the majority of them women and a high percentage of them African-American, Latino, and Asian-American workers. Its members are mainly service workers and come from several different industries including airport, apparel, distribution, retail, gaming, hotel, restaurant, and industrial laundry.

Both unions have a proud history of organizing, more recently using innovative strategies such as grassroots mobilization and corporate campaigns. They have fought to protect the rights of some of the most vulnerable workers in our economy, including sweatshop and immigrant workers. Their efforts have included the 17-year struggle to organize the JP Stevens workers that was portrayed in the Oscar-winning movie *Norma Rae*, and a strike in Las Vegas that lasted six-and-a-half years before workers returned to their jobs victorious with both seniority and back pension service credits. ▶

Although its founding unions have been around for over 100 years, UNITE HERE exemplifies the changing face of unionism in North America. Diverse, made up in large part of women, active in the service sector, aggressive and innovative in its organizing campaigns, and willing to participate in pioneering labour–management partnerships, it is a union both of the past and of the future.

Sources: Johnson, William. (2004). "The UNITE-HERE Merger: Is It a Step Forward...or Business as Usual?" Viewpoint. *Labor Notes* (April), p. 10, http://labornotes.org/archives/2004/04/articles/b.html; UNITE HERE websites: http://www.unitehere.org/ and http://www.unitehere.ca/, [March 22, 2005].

UNION DEMOCRACY

Union democracy is important to the labour movement for many reasons, not least because actual or even perceived lapses in democracy can hurt the movement's public image, causing it to lose much-needed support. Cynics sometimes say that the very notion of union democracy is an oxymoron. Others (for example, Craig and Solomon, 1996) suggest that, given the serious constraints under which unions often operate, their achievements in the area of democracy are admirable. Union democracy is not an easy concept to define. Anderson (1979) has suggested that it means, essentially, members' ability to influence decisions that are important to them and to participate effectively in its affairs. A more comprehensive definition by Edelstein and Warner has described democracy as:

> . . . a decision-making system in which the membership actively participates, directly or indirectly through its representatives, in the making and implementation of policy and in the selection of officials, for all levels, on the basis of political equality and majority rule. Furthermore, the system operates on the basis of the accountability of officials, the legitimacy of opposition, and due process for the protection of the rights of individuals and minorities (quoted in Chaison, 1982:166).

Achieving all these things is a tall order for any union. Indeed, a close reading of the definition reveals significant tension between a number of the objectives, such as operating through majority rule while still respecting the rights of individuals and minorities. If this is what is expected of unions, no wonder their actual achievements in the area of democratic operation often fall short of expectations. Indeed, one reason for some perceived lapses in union democracy is the tremendously high expectations people have for it. In part, this is the result of the way unions position themselves among the few democratic institutions in society willing and able to stand up to big business and other powerful and moneyed interests. And in part it is because, at the national or societal level, as the union impacts section of the next chapter will explain in more detail, trade unionism is clearly and closely related to democracy. With respect to unions' internal operations, however, things may turn out to be a bit different. Usually, union constitutions will provide that everyone be treated equally. In practice, though, some members and, particularly, some officials, may turn out to be more equal than others. The sub-sections that follow will attempt to provide some explanations for this apparent paradox, closing the discussion with a comparison of evidence of union democracy in Canada and the United States.

Components of Union Democracy

A review of the Edelstein-Warner definition just quoted reveals a number of key components, including membership participation, selection of officials, legitimacy of opposition, and due process.

Membership Participation

No two observers agree on exactly what proportion of union members attend meetings regularly; all agree that that proportion is very low. It is common to attribute poor attendance to apathy, or to union leaders' tight control over meeting agendas, which leads members to believe they will have little chance to provide meaningful input even if they do attend (see Chaison, 1982). Certainly many members do have an attitude that, if not apathetic, at best regards the union in an instrumental light: It is there if they need it, and they will turn out for strike votes and elections, but they have no wish to become involved in the organization's day-to-day operations. As for the issue of leaders' control over agendas, there is no doubt that this happens on occasion. Anecdotal evidence suggests that apathy, or instrumentalism, is a much more significant factor. Indeed, many leaders would dearly love to have better attendance in order to gain a better understanding of their members' interests and needs. Anderson suggests (1979:488) that attendance figures alone do not tell the whole story. What may be more important is whether those members who do attend meetings feel free to participate actively and without fear of being suppressed if their ideas run contrary to those of the leadership. The evidence suggests that turnout generally is high when important issues are at stake and that, contrary to popular belief, leaders do their best to get as much membership input as they can, particularly on those important issues. Whether members always feel free to participate in the way they would wish is another question, one to be taken up in the next section.

Selection of Officers and Legitimacy of Opposition

In a democratic union, at a minimum there should be regular election of officers. Those opposing the "official" or incumbent slate should have the opportunity to express their views to members through official union publications and in other ways. Finally, there should be at least a certain degree of turnover in union presidents and other officials, to ensure that the organizations receive the benefit of fresh thinking and to prevent ruling cliques from becoming unduly entrenched. While we would not expect incumbent union presidents to be defeated often, given the inherent advantages incumbents possess in unions as in most other political organizations, a situation in which they were never defeated would not augur well for union democracy.

Due Process

Unions possess a considerable degree of power over their members, including the power to discipline them. Penalties can include loss of union membership, which in turn can lead to loss of one's employment and livelihood in situations where only union members can be employed, or where hiring is conducted through the union, as in the building trades (Craig and Solomon, 1996:180–181). Organizations that have such great power over their members have the responsibility to use it wisely and fairly, especially in situations where someone's livelihood may be at stake. Ideally, those disagreeing with their union's disciplinary action should have the right to a prompt and fair hearing before a neutral third party or parties. In practice, it would appear that this ideal is seldom realized. The Canadian Auto Workers appears to be among the few Canadian unions that have established an impartial panel made up entirely of people from outside the organization to hear members' complaints about internal union actions (Craig and Solomon, 1996:181; Murray, 1995:182). What appear to be more common are internal procedures for handling such complaints, procedures that start at the local level and if not resolved there may end up before the union's executive board or even at its annual or biennial convention. Such a procedure is apt to be extremely time-consuming (Craig and Solomon, 1996:181). What is not clear is the extent to which unions may have developed speedier, more informal internal dispute resolution processes comparable to the expedited arbitration systems found in a number of industries and jurisdictions.

Limitations on Union Democracy

There are a variety of reasons why unions generally find it impossible to fully achieve the lofty democratic ideal suggested in the Edelstein and Warner definition discussed earlier. One argument often advanced (see Godard, 2005 and Murray, 1995) is the "iron law of oligarchy," one originally formulated by the political theorist Robert Michels. This theory argues that as political leaders stay in power, they become increasingly less responsive to their constituents and more concerned with simply staying in power. Godard (2005) points out that the "iron law of oligarchy" may be of particular relevance to union leaders, who unlike business leaders may have little or nothing to fall back on if they lose their jobs, except perhaps a shop-floor job, and for whom staying in office would thus appear to be of great importance.

Certainly there are some Canadian union leaders who may well be more concerned with getting re-elected than with formulating the wisest possible long-term policies for their organizations. At the same time, there is at least modest evidence to suggest that the "iron law" may not be working very strongly in Canada. Most Canadian union presidents appear to serve for fairly limited periods; the same is generally true at the national level, at least for CLC presidents, in stark contrast to the situation prevailing in the United States within the AFL-CIO. Moreover, it is also worth noting

One of today's most visible union leaders is CAW President, Buzz Hargrove, who has been a CAW staff member since 1975 and has served as National President of the union since his acclaimation in 1992.

that any union or federation wishing to prevent the "iron law" from taking effect has a number of options at its disposal, including term limits for leaders or stipulations that new people be regularly rotated onto their executives.

Other limitations to union democracy may be rather more intractable, since they have to do with the inherent nature of a union as a collective majoritarian political organization in which, at least occasionally, the wishes of the minority must be sacrificed to those of the majority. For example, an individual may perceive a lack of due process because the union has refused to carry a grievance forward; however, the union is perfectly within its rights to do so, providing it has considered the case on its merits and its decision is not the result of discriminatory treatment. Subject to the broad limitations of duty of fair representation, in order to represent the bargaining unit effectively, union officials must be given latitude in assessing the merits of a grievance and weighing its importance against the many other matters competing for time and resources.

Strikes are an even better example of situations where the wishes of the individual must often be subordinated to the needs of the membership as a whole. At such times, strict discipline is generally necessary. In particular, it is absolutely essential that a striking union be able to call its members out on picket duty and that those members obey the picket captain's orders. Failure to maintain an adequate picket-line presence could lead to the collapse of the strike; failure to follow a picket captain's orders could in certain situations lead to arrest, injury, or possibly even loss of life. Similarly, if enough members crossed a picket line and continued working, the strike could also collapse. This explains the fines and other forms of discipline that unions sometimes impose on members who cross picket lines, as well as the ostracism with which such workers are often greeted by co-workers once the strike is over.

Collective bargaining is yet another core union process that is arguably impossible for any union to conduct in a fully democratic fashion. A union may go to great lengths to solicit members' input on the initial bargaining package and almost all Canadian unions submit their tentative agreements to the membership for a ratification vote; however, bargaining, by its very nature, is a delicate process of give and take. If a union had to go back to the membership every time a demand was dropped or a position changed, the flow of negotiations would be seriously interrupted, and it is unlikely a settlement could ever be reached.

One other point must be made concerning limitations on union democracy arising from the nature of unions as political organizations. Not unlike other political associations, union leadership is not earned solely by merit; seniority also comes into the plan. To a degree, at least, individuals have to work their way up the ladder. Members generally also have to become known by key senior members and officials before being entrusted with leadership positions, no matter what skills and abilities they possess. To a degree, this sort of internal seniority system keeps unions from acquiring fresh ideas and new perspectives but it also decreases the risks and instability associated with excessive turnover of leadership.

Safeguards for Democracy

Although there are a number of limitations to how democratic a union can be, there are also a number of safeguards that, taken together, help to ensure active membership participation, the legitimacy of opposition, and the assurance of due process. First, as noted earlier, many leaders not only permit but encourage active participation on the part of their membership. As Godard (2005) notes, it is often in their enlightened self-interest to do so, since committed members are likelier to support strikes and a union with a reputation for encouraging member participation may have an easier time recruiting new members.

Second, members who are unhappy with their leadership have a number of options available to them. Most obviously, they may vote an incumbent slate out at the next election. In this regard, if an executive has been in office for a long time, even a close election can serve as a kind of warning and make the executive more responsive to the membership after the election.[11] Disgruntled rank-and-filers can also reject tentative contracts, engage in wildcat strikes, or in extreme instances move to have the union decertified. All of these actions can have serious consequences both for the leadership and for the union as a whole; thus the threat of any of them is something a wise union official will not take lightly.

Third, there are a number of legislative safeguards for union democracy, in addition to those contained in union constitutions and those of labour federations such as the CLC. Most jurisdictions have in place a duty of fair representation requirement that has the practical effect of forcing unions to consider each member's grievance in good faith and in a manner that is neither arbitrary nor discriminatory. In most cases, the effect of these duty-of-fair-representation provisions is to induce union officials to go to great lengths to not only be fair, but also to be perceived as fair.

(Chapter 7, which covers collective bargaining legislation, will deal with this issue in more detail.) A final safeguard against union officials acting in their own interest rather than in accordance with members' wishes is the requirement, in place in every Canadian jurisdiction, that the union conduct a secret-ballot strike vote before calling any strike.

Union Democracy in Canada and the United States

Overall, Canadian unions appear to be significantly more democratic than their American counterparts. To begin with, historically, corruption within American unions was a far greater problem in the earlier part of this century than within Canadian unions. Furthermore, there are profound differences in the ways in which the Canadian and American labour movements have operated, at least since the creation of the CLC in 1956. CLC presidents function as just that—presidents. That is to say, they are elected, serve for a relatively short period of time, and then move on to other things. In contrast, the presidency of the major American federations has in practice functioned more as a monarchy. At least two long-serving AFL presidents, Samuel Gompers and William Green, died in office. The first president of the merged AFL-CIO, George Meany, died shortly after his last convention, at which he was so ill that he had to be wheeled on and off the convention floor (A. Robinson, 1981). Only in 1995, when Meany's successor, Lane Kirkland, retired after serving as president for 15 years did one witness a change in the federation's presidency resulting from some cause other than the incumbent's death or disability. The AFL-CIO's current president, John Sweeney, has been in office for over 10 years, having been elected in 1995 and re-elected three times since.

With no serious possibility of an electoral challenge, AFL and AFL-CIO presidents have often conducted themselves in quite high-handed fashion. For example, under Gompers, the strong minority of AFL members favouring socialism and comprehensive industrial democracy was always ruthlessly suppressed (Galenson and Smith, 1978).[12] Despite such strong rumblings from the rank-and-file, Gompers appears never even to have considered the possibility of forming a labour party in the United States (Galenson and Smith, 1978). Later, under Meany, the AFL-CIO placed a low priority on organizing, despite many executive council members' obvious desire to expand the federation's efforts in this area (Goulden, 1972; Reuther, 1976; Winpisinger, 1989). As well, during the Vietnam era, Meany almost single-handedly put the federation firmly behind the government's policies (Goulden, 1972; Dulles and Dubofsky, 1984). When unionists dared oppose the Johnson administration's Vietnam policies, Meany not only cut them off at AFL-CIO conventions, he publicly attacked them as traitors and Communist sympathizers (Goulden, 1972).

Not only was the conduct of Gompers and Meany extremely undemocratic; there is reason to believe that it did not serve the country's union members and other working people at all well. For example, had the American labour movement established its own political party, as almost all other Western labour movements have, it might have been in a better position to combat the extreme anti-unionism of the Reagan administration. Meany's support of the Vietnam War and other reactionary foreign policies effectively severed the labour movement's ties to Congressional liberals (Peirce, 1995) as well as alienating young people from the labour movement (I. Robinson, 1990). Furthermore, had Meany devoted more money and resources to organizing, American union membership might well not have declined as sharply as it did even during the relatively prosperous 1960s and 1970s (see Figure 4.1), which again would have left unions in a better position to withstand the neo-conservative assault of the 1980s and would likely have prevented the 2005 splintering of the AFL-CIO that is detailed in Current Issues 4.2. It is hard to imagine any CLC president persisting in such misguided and undemocratic actions as those engaged in by Gompers and Meany, given the very real likelihood of defeat at the next election.[13]

Current Issues 4.2

CHANGE TO WIN COALITION

In a move that stunned observers of the US labour movement, on July 24, 2005, a coalition of unions announced they would boycott the AFL-CIO convention, scheduled to begin the next day. In the biggest schism in the US labour movement since the 1930s, the Change to Win Coalition's announcement was rumoured to be a prelude to a declaration the following day that the Service Employees International Union (SEIU), the International Brotherhood of Teamsters (IBT), UNITE HERE, and United Food and Commercial Workers (UFCW), together representing approximately one-third of the AFL-CIO's 13 million members, planned to withdraw from the federation. In fact, while all four unions boycotted the convention, only the SEIU and Teamsters announced their withdrawal, with other unions later following suit.

The dissident unions, along with three other unions, the Laborers' International Union of North America, the United Brotherhood of Carpenters and Joiners of America, and the United Farm Workers of America, formed the Change to Win Coalition in an effort to revive stagnant union membership. They claim the AFL-CIO has failed to stem the steep decline of the union membership in recent decades, which has caused a significant loss of economic and political power for the labour movement. The group of unions talked for months with the AFL-CIO leadership, urging them to take the necessary steps to modernize the federation's structure, function, and priorities. They demanded more money for organizing, the power to force the merger of smaller unions, and other changes they claim are key to labour's survival. The talks were to no avail, so the unions, with their very public action, took what they considered to be crucial steps to revive the US labour movement.

Ironically, a day after the SEIU's and Teamsters' departure, the AFL-CIO passed a resolution creating a $22.5 million fund for affiliates to use for organizing. The dissident unions claimed the move was too little too late and called for the ouster of President John Sweeney. Sweeney, who was running unopposed for another four-year term, condemned the dissidents' departure as "a tragedy for working people" (Chipman, 2005:4). Others claim this shake-up is just what the US labour ▶

movement needs and is perhaps the only way to reverse a long-term decline that has witnessed private sector union density plummet to below 8 percent, its lowest level since the 1920s. The tragedy may, in fact, be for the AFL-CIO as a federation since the Teamsters and SEIU together contributed $20 million annually in dues. Their departure necessitated the layoff of one-quarter of the federation's Washington staff.

Two months later, on September 27, 2005, the coalition of unions representing approximately 6 million union members held the founding convention of their new labour federation, Change to Win, pledging to revive the US labour movement and dedicate 75 percent of their budget, or $750 million per year, toward organizing new members. Their focus will be on groups of workers that remain largely unorganized such as school bus drivers, security guards, and Wal-Mart employees. They also pledged to engage in multi-union organizing campaigns and to unionize more minority members and immigrant workers in fast-growing sectors of the economy such as retail, hospitality, and health care. Already the new federation appears to be more representative of the workers of today: Anna Burger was elected chair of the new federation and Edgar Romney was elected Secretary-Treasurer, the first time in history either a woman or an African-American have been elected to high office in a US labour federation.

Sources: Fournier, Ron. (2005). "New Labor Group Aims to Boost Membership." *St. Louis Post -Dispatch* [St. Louis, MO]. July 26, p. A5; Chipman, Kim. (2005). "Teamsters, SEIU to part with AFL-CIO." *National Post*. July 26, p. FP4; Stern, Andrew. (2005). "Unions Reinvented: The AFL-CIO Has Failed to Recognize That Times Are Changing and Workers' Lives Are Evolving. That's Why the Labor Movement Must Split." *Los Angeles Times*. July 26, p. B13; Associated Press. (2005). "AFL-CIO Passes Resolution to Boost Organizing Efforts; Unions That Left the Organization Call the Move Too Little, Too Late." *Telegraph-Herald* [Dubuque, IA]. July 27, p. C8; Moberg, David. (2005). "Look Who's Walking." *The Nation*. July 26, http://www.thenation.com/doc.mhtml?i=20050801&s=moberg; Maher, Kris. (2005). "Breakaway Coalition of Unions Lays Out Strategy for Organizing: Focus Will Be on Wal-Mart, Workers Like Guards Who Mostly Lack Representation. *The Wall Street Journal*. September 28, p. B13; Change to Win website, http://www.changetowin.org/.

More research is clearly needed on specific aspects of Canadian versus American union democracy at the national level. It would, for example, be useful to know what happens to unofficial resolutions at AFL-CIO and CLC conventions, and more generally how policy is made in both federations. For now, the brief discussion provided should suffice to show that the Canadian labour movement has generally functioned a good deal more democratically at the national federation level than has its American counterpart and that this more democratic functioning appears to have benefited the Canadian labour movement.

CONTINUING CHALLENGES

In the early years of the twenty-first century, both the Canadian and US labour movements face many of the same issues that have always challenged them, such as maintaining and expanding membership numbers and safeguarding union democracy. However, the social, political, and economic contexts of the new millennium exacerbate many existing challenges and present some new ones: The ever-increasing globalization of markets and mobility of capital, for example, challenge unions to strengthen international alliances, yet the chasm between the Canadian and US labour movements has never been wider—and only time will tell whether the recent schism of the US labour movement will destroy or revive it. Widespread political moves toward conservatism make the climate ever less hospitable for unions, while the increasing diversity of union membership requires unions to meet a wider variety of membership interests and needs. The structural shift away from traditionally unionized industries such as manufacturing toward harder-to-organize industries such as those in the service sector is not a new challenge, but the increasing proliferation of non-standard forms of employment makes organizing new members even more difficult. To meet these challenges, the actions unions utilize to meet their objectives and maintain and expand their membership have evolved. The next chapter takes a look at these actions and their impacts and explores some of the ways unions' activities have changed in recent years.

Case 4.1

RAIDING OR DEMOCRATIC DECISION MAKING?

In 2000, the alleged raid by Canadian Autoworkers' (CAW) of 30 000 members of the Service Employees International Union (SEIU) ignited a firestorm of controversy within the Canadian labour movement. While most within the labour movement condemned the CAW for actions they considered cannibalistic and destructive of inter-union solidarity, a few praised the union for shedding light on what they termed "long-standing union collusion." Buzz Hargrove, the CAW president, claimed that raiding was not the issue. Rather, what was at issue was the right of Canadian workers to self-determination and national autonomy.

The roots of the controversy can be traced back to 1996 when Ken Brown assumed the role of International Vice-President, the top Canadian executive position within the SEIU. Brown was considered more progressive than the candidates who had previously long held the position. He spent the first couple years as international director trying to introduce new ways of operating and mounting publicity campaigns and aggressively organizing and representing workers. Brown also fought for greater autonomy from the US parent union and greater control over Canadian affairs. SEIU acknowledged shortcomings in their record of member service and examined internal democratic structures. In November 1998, SEIU Canada formed a task force that became known as the November Group; its mandate was to build a new Canadian structure, to unite Canadian locals, and to redefine the nature of their relationship with their US parent union. In February 2000, the plan that was to provide "full, democratic, Canadian autonomy," was laid out. While Brown voted in support of the plan, five days later he sent a letter to Andrew Stern, the International President in Washington, submitting his resignation as International Vice-President and informing Stern that he planned to merge his and seven other SEIU locals with the CAW.

Brown was dissatisfied with the plan for Canadian autonomy. He claimed it was more of "an exercise in keeping folks in line with the American vision" and concluded that it was unlikely he was ever going to be able to work within the SEIU to make real changes. His proposed merger with the CAW was rumoured to have been in the planning for some time but came as a complete surprise to the SEIU, which launched an aggressive counterattack suing Brown and 22 other executive officers for $5.5 million each and placing locals under trustees appointed by Washington.

In March, the Canadian Labour Congress (CLC) attempted to negotiate a settlement between the two member unions and appointed a neutral umpire, Victor Pathe, to assist the parties. No agreement was reached, however, and in July the CLC applied full sanctions, expelling the CAW and stripping their delegates of the right to vote in district labour councils, provincial labour federations, and other CLC bodies. Given CAW's rank as the third-largest union in Canada, this loss of dues revenue negatively impacted labour councils and federations in every province and territory and in some instances, such as for the Ontario Federation of Labour, resulted in layoffs of union staff.

Ken Brown claimed he tried to follow the CLC rules but they made it virtually impossible to move between member unions. Buzz Hargrove held firm to his convictions that the pact of non-aggression between CLC member unions worked against the goal of a vibrant, effective federation. This was a case of members democratically choosing one union over another, not of one union soliciting the members of another. New rules governing membership disputes between unions were required, he contended, and it was incumbent upon the Canadian labour movement to send a united message that Canadian workers have every right to leave international unions in favour of national ones. The CLC and most of its member unions, on the other hand, believed that the CAW's actions resulted in the type of internecine battle that saps the labour movement of time, energy, and resources but leaves it no better off in the end. They maintained that energy should be directed toward organizing new members, not fighting over existing members.

After a year and a half of recriminations and hard bargaining, the issue was eventually resolved when 10 000 workers voted 92 percent in favour of joining the CAW. Characterized by some as "one of the greatest crises in modern Canadian labour history," the SEIU–CAW dispute exposed a rift within the Canadian labour movement and raised questions regarding the CLC's rules governing membership disputes and the CLC's ability to address Canadian workers' desire for autonomy from international parent unions.

Sources: "Anatomy of a Raid: SEIU Canada tells its story." *Straight Goods*, http://www.straight-goods.com/Soloway/001030SEIU.shtml, [March 25, 2005]; Wheeler, Glen. (2000). "Anatomy of a Raid." *NOW* 19:53 (Aug. 31–Sept. 6); Niemeijer, Marsha. (2000). "Auto Workers Sanctioned Over Raiding Charges. Split Threatens Canadian Labor." *Labor Notes* (August), http://www.labornotes.org/archives/2000/0800/0800.html#story, [March 25, 2005].

Case Questions

1. In your opinion, did the SEIU–CAW dispute present more of a threat to labour unity and solidarity or to union democracy? Explain.

2. Visit the CLC's website and read their Disputes Protocol (under Official Documents, http://www.clc-ctc.ca/web/menu/english/en_index.htm). In your

opinion, does this protocol strike an appropriate balance between protecting labour solidarity and ensuring union democracy? Why or why not?

3. Describe some of the damages the Canadian labour movement might suffer due to disputes such as this.

4. Discuss the components of and limitations on union democracy that this case demonstrates. What changes would you recommend to the CLC and its rules in order to safeguard union democracy?

5. Discuss the issue of national autonomy from international parent unions. How might Canadian locals protect their national autonomy while still enjoying the benefits of membership in a large, international union?

QUESTIONS FOR DISCUSSION

1. Visit the Canadian Autoworkers' (CAW) website and the Canadian website of the United Steelworkers. Take a look at the variety of causes the CAW's Social Justice Fund (SJW) and the Steelworkers' Humanity Fund support. What motivates these unions to put their time and money toward these causes?

2. At which points did Canadian union membership increase significantly? At which points did it decrease? What were the reasons?

3. Explain how and why the mix of men and women within Canadian unions has changed.

4. In which provinces is union membership highest? In which is it lowest? Explain the reasons for this variation.

5. Thirty-five years ago, Canadian union membership rates were roughly the same as those in the United States. Now Canadian rates are more than twice those of the United States. Why has this situation changed? Do you think Canadian rates will continue to be significantly higher than American rates in the future?

6. Discuss the role played by union locals, municipal and district labour councils, and provincial labour federations.

7. Discuss the role played by provincial and national labour federations, particularly the CLC.

8. How does union structure in Quebec differ from that in all other Canadian provinces?

9. How would you define union democracy? Do you think the standards set by Edelstein and Warner in the definition discussed in the text are too high? Are there inherent limitations to union democracy? If so, how can unions be more democratic within those limitations?

Suggestions for Further Reading

Chaison, Gary. (1996). *Union Mergers in Hard Times: The View from Five Countries*. **Ithaca and London: Cornell University ILR Press.** A thought-provoking study of recent union mergers in the United States, Britain, Australia, and New Zealand, as well as Canada. Chaison's prediction is that in years to come Canadian union fragmentation will be greatly reduced and that large conglomerate unions such as the CEP and CAW will become "centers of mergers of activity and will come to rely on absorptions for continued growth."

Gindin, Sam. (1995). *The Canadian Autoworkers: The Birth and Transformation of a Union.* **Toronto: James Lorimer & Co.** A compelling essay on the history of one of Canada's largest and most influential unions written by a well-respected unionist who for 26 years helped shape CAW policy and strategy.

Strauss, George. (1991). **"Union Democracy." In G. Strauss et al. (Eds.).** *The State of the Unions. Madison: IRRA Press.* A useful discussion of a difficult concept.

CHAPTER 5

UNION ACTIONS AND IMPACTS

Delegates from the IBEW (International Brotherhood of Electrical Workers) meet with their Japanese counterparts from Tokyo Electric to discuss such issues as work culture, safety, utility deregulation, and workplace gender issues. With the globalization of business, international liaison has become an increasingly large part of many unions' agendas.

LEARNING OBJECTIVES

After studying this chapter, you should be able to:

1. Describe the range of actions Canadian unions take and have taken in support of their economic and political objectives.
2. Explain how Canadian union actions have been changing in recent years.
3. Identify unions' direct and indirect wage impacts.
4. Discuss the ways in which unions seek to achieve their wage goals.
5. Describe unions' effect on productivity and on the management of organizations.
6. Explain unions' overall effect on Canadian society as a whole.

Building on the discussion of the previous chapter, this chapter examines the kinds of actions unions take in support of their objectives and the economic and social impacts they have, both at the workplace and in Canadian society as a whole. We begin with a brief overview of union actions, and the way in which these actions have changed in recent years. We then take a more detailed look at a broad range of union activities from traditional ones, such as collective bargaining and political action, to modern ones, such as the creation of union-sponsored venture capital corporations and joint participation with management in a variety of employee-involvement schemes. Next, we examine unions' wage impacts, both on employers and on other, non-unionized workers. After a brief look at the ways in which unions achieve their wage goals, the chapter goes on to consider unions' productivity impacts and their effects on the management of organizations, before concluding with a discussion of their broader effects on Canadian society as a whole.

UNION ACTIONS

The question of the methods or actions that unions use to achieve their objectives has been of interest to industrial relations experts for more than 100 years. In a classic 1897 work entitled *Industrial Democracy*, Sidney and Beatrice Webb suggest that unions rely primarily on three methods: mutual insurance, collective bargaining, and legal enactment.[1]

As was pointed out in the labour history chapter, the mutual insurance function of unions was extremely important in the days before unemployment insurance, publicly funded health care, and sick and disability leave. Union benefit funds could help tide unemployed workers over periods of cyclical depression and support the families of workers killed or injured at work, or incapacitated due to illness. By representing themselves as "mutual benefit societies" or "friendly societies," unions were also able to get around harsh nineteenth-century legislation banning them as criminal conspiracies in restraint of trade (Forsey, 1982; Heron, 1989). Much of the unions' traditional mutual insurance function has been taken over by government. However, some elements of it survive, such as the Supplementary Unemployment Benefits contained in some collective agreements, which top up government EI payments to a level near the worker's normal wage (Craig and Solomon, 1996). A number of unions also now provide their members with such benefits as lower-priced auto and disability insurance (see among others PSAC, 2005).

Unions' collective bargaining activities are still generally carried on more or less as the Webbs envisaged, though the range of issues brought to the table is now often considerably greater. As for legal enactment, unions have been among the strongest supporters of higher minimum wages, health and safety legislation, anti-discrimination laws, and a broad range of social programs of benefit to all working people—not just union members. Again, this emphasis on working on behalf of all working people is in line with the Webbs' original emphasis.

Even today, the Webbs' three methods are at the core of what most unions spend a good deal of their time doing. But the range of union activity has expanded a good deal over the past century and to some degree its character has also changed. In the area of collective bargaining, for example, while most bargaining continues to be adversarial, a growing number of unions have entered into more co-operative arrangements with management. In some cases, unions have taken on what amounts to something approaching joint governance of the workplace—a role that would have been totally foreign to the unionist of 50 years ago and that continues to arouse considerable controversy within the Canadian labour movement even now (CAW, no date; CPU, 1990; USWA, 1991).[2] In the political arena, unions have also expanded their role, moving beyond support for specific pieces of labour-related legislation to more or less permanent alliances with parties such as the NDP and less formal arrangements with women's, environmental, anti-poverty, and church groups and other progressive organizations, as well as the creation of "humanity" or "justice" funds to support specific causes (Godard, 1994:218). They have also become adept at using publicity campaigns to help achieve their objectives and at using their members' savings and pension funds to promote local and regional development and job creation through a broad range of labour-sponsored venture capital corporations and pension pools (Boivin and Déom, 1995:459–460; Jackson and Lamontagne, 1995; Jackson, 1997 and 1998). Finally, Canadian unions have long been and continue to be involved in a broad range of educational ventures (CUPE, no date; Fisher and Peirce, 1995; R. White, 1995).

Thus, while their general objectives remain the same as those of unions in the past, today's unions tend to operate within a far broader context. They also have available to them strategies and technologies that the unionists of, for example, the 1940s could only dream about. The discussion that follows takes into account both that broader context and some of those strategies and technologies.

Collective Bargaining

Overall, the Canadian industrial relations system can fairly be described as voluntarist. This means that in unionized workplaces, most outcomes are left to be negotiated between the union and management—rather than being established through legislation, as is the case in some European countries such as France (Goetschy and Jobert, 1993). As a result, collective bargaining is, almost by definition, a core activity for virtually all Canadian unions.

The bargaining process itself will be considered in some detail in the chapter on negotiation, and thus need not be discussed here. But it may be worth taking a brief look at some of the ways in which that process has changed in recent years.

First, collective bargaining now addresses a far broader range of issues than it generally did early in the century, when agreements might be just one or two pages long and were usually limited to such core issues as wages, hours of work, holiday and overtime pay, and union security provisions (see Giles and Starkman, 2005). During the early post-war period, as was noted in Chapter 3, unions began to negotiate a broad range of **employee benefits** such as paid vacations, sick leave, pensions, and medical and hospitalization insurance (Heron, 1989; Giles and Starkman, 2001). More recently, demands from an increasingly diverse workforce containing growing numbers of women have caused unions to negotiate maternity and paternity leave provisions, flexible schedules, workplace daycare centres, and in some cases anti-discrimination and anti-harassment provisions that go beyond the requirements of human rights legislation. At the same time, the introduction of labour-saving technology into workplaces has caused unions to seek (albeit often unsuccessfully) to negotiate protection against job or income loss resulting from such technology. The introduction of new chemicals and other potentially hazardous substances has led to the negotiation of clauses regarding their use, as well as the employer's responsibility to provide appropriate safety equipment and training in

employee benefits (also sometimes referred to as fringe benefits) Non-wage benefits such as paid vacations or pensions, the cost of which is borne either wholly or in part by the employer.

the handling of such substances (see Giles and Starkman, 1995:367). Finally, growing concern for members' well-being both on and off the job has led unions to negotiate employee assistance programs to help employees with drug, alcohol, financial, or other personal problems, and in some cases wellness programs to provide employees with improved access to fitness facilities. The addition of this broad range of issues to such core issues as wages and hours of work has tended to make bargaining a longer and more complex process than it was in the past.

Second, while most collective bargaining continues to be adversarial, a growing proportion of it is now more problem-solving in nature (Downie, 1982 and 1989; Craig and Solomon, 1996). A problem-solving approach is most obviously useful in cases involving clear "win-win" issues, such as health and safety (Chaykowski, 1995:237); however, this type of bargaining has sometimes been more widely applied, even in cases involving monetary issues (Downie, 1982:323).

Joint Union–Management Ventures at the Workplace

The same types of challenges posed by a shift from adversarial bargaining to a problem-solving approach apply, to an even greater degree, to unions' participation in joint ventures with management designed to increase worker morale and productivity. Such ventures can range from single-issue labour–management committees to broad **gainsharing plan**s such as the Scanlon Plan (see Downie, 1982: 330–332). They can also include quality circles, self-directed work teams, and employee stock ownership plans (Verma, 1995).

gainsharing plan
Plan whereby the benefits of increased productivity and greater labour–management co-operation are shared by the employer and the employees or their union.

In a few cases, unions and management have negotiated joint governance arrangements whereby the union becomes, in effect, a full partner in management of the organization (Verma, 1995:299–300). These arrangements, which have been much more common in Quebec than elsewhere in Canada (Déom and Boivin, 2005), entail a radical transformation of the union's role, from that of workers' advocate to that of administrator and perhaps even manager of discontent. They also open up far greater possibilities for direct communication between management and employees—possibilities that run the risk of reducing the union's influence in the workplace (see Lemelin, 1989:452–455) and may even conflict with its advocacy role. If, for example, in its role as co-manager, a union has agreed with management on the need to cut costs, but rank-and-file members are pushing hard for immediate, up-front wage increases, what will union negotiators do at the bargaining table, and how will the demand for wage increases affect the union's continued participation in the joint governance scheme?

Moreover, participation in such schemes often requires union members and officials to learn new skills. Traditionally, motivational and political skills were most important for union leaders. But if a union is co-managing an organization, its officials and those of its members involved in joint governance committees will also need to learn business-related skills such as finance, economics, and accounting (see Verma, 1995:299).

Union participation in joint co-operation and employee involvement schemes has often proved quite controversial, within individual unions, in the Canadian labour movement as a whole, and among IR academics. Some regard increased employee involvement as inevitable, given globalization and increased competitiveness. Such writers argue that unions have no choice other than to participate in employee involvement programs. If unions don't participate, they suggest, management will introduce the programs anyway, and the interests of neither individual workers nor the union will have been well-served.[3] Others (e.g., Godard, 1991) are more skeptical, while still others (e.g., Wells, 1993) oppose any union participation in such ventures outright—on the grounds that for a union to assume any significant co-management role amounts to a conflict of interest with its core role as the workers' advocate. Within the labour movement, some unions (e.g., CAW, n.d.) have adopted policies of outright opposition to joint co-operation schemes, while some of the schemes' strongest supporters, such as the CEP and Steelworkers, have insisted on being given a major role as a condition of participation (Verma, 1995:297).[4] The economic environment of the past 15 years, which has seen many large-scale layoffs even in highly profitable organizations, has arguably made such joint ventures a dicier business from the unions' perspective. When large-scale layoffs occur despite unions' best efforts to increase productivity, even former supporters may wonder what the benefit of the schemes is for workers; at a minimum such layoffs serve to strengthen the hand of union "hawks" opposed to co-operation.

Joint Participation Outside the Workplace

Canadian unions are also involved in a variety of joint ventures with management outside the workplace. Among other things, unions and management groups have formed a number of sectoral councils to address such issues as training, economic restructuring, trade policy, and labour–management co-operation on an industry-wide basis. A large number of these sectoral partnerships have been formed in Quebec. In a recent (2003) *Workplace Gazette* article, Jean Charest provides a generally positive assessment, basing his conclusion on a study of some two dozen workplace sectoral committees from Quebec.

One of the first such councils was the Canadian Textile Labour–Management Committee (CTLMC), formed in 1967 in the wake of a bitter strike at the Dominion Textile plant in Quebec (Thomason, Zwerling, and Chandra, 1992:264). The joint union–management committee has not formally involved itself in collective bargaining as such but has sought to improve the bargaining process by ensuring that the parties are provided with accurate information about the real state of the industry (Thomason et al., 1992:266). In addition, the CTLMC has involved itself with issues ranging from domestic and foreign trade policies to productivity, occupational health and safety, and education and training. The committee appears to have been at least partly responsible for a major improvement in labour–management relations and a significant reduction in strike incidence in the textile industry (Thomason et al., 1992:264–266).

Another important sectoral initiative is the Canadian Steel Trade and Employment Congress (CSTEC), formed jointly by the major steel companies and the United Steelworkers of America (USWA) in 1985 (Verma and Warrian, 1992:124).

Since its formation, CSTEC has been heavily involved in trade issues, a special concern being the targeting of unfair foreign competition. The Congress's other major concern has been providing employment assistance for displaced steelworkers, of whom there have been a great many due to ongoing restructuring in the industry. Such assistance is provided under CSTEC's HEAT (Helping Employees Adjust Together) program, which (under an agreement with the federal government since 1987) has been provided with the same amount of per capita funding to assist displaced workers as would otherwise have been given to the Industrial Adjustment Service (Verma and Warrian, 1992). HEAT's services have included provision of job market information, training in starting a business, relocation assistance, and personal financial planning and retraining (Verma and Warrian, 1992:125).

tripartism Consultation or negotiations between representatives of labour, management, and government on matters of mutual interest.

Canadian unions have also been involved in a number of tripartite, or labour–management–government initiatives, although **tripartism** has never been as strong here as in many European countries, such as the Netherlands and Sweden (Adams, 1995a:506). While a fair number of tripartite consultative bodies were established during the 1960s and 1970s, in 1976 the labour movement withdrew its representatives from most of them, including the Economic Council of Canada, in protest over the federal government's imposition of wage-price controls (Craig and Solomon, 1996:138).[5] More recently, however, unions have joined with management and the federal government in launching the Canadian Labour Market and Productivity Centre (CLMPC) (Adams, 1995; Murray, 1995), recently renamed the Canadian Labour and Business Centre (CLBC). Much of this body's work has been on relatively non-contentious issues such as training and labour market information (Adams, 1995); however, over the past decade it has broadened its focus, doing important research on issues as varied as work hours (CLMPC, 1997), the impacts of labour-sponsored venture capital corporations (Jackson and Lamontagne, 1995), changing demographics, and women in the workplace (Craig and Solomon, 1996:54).

Political Action

Almost all unions engage in some kind of political action. This is because, to a large extent, unions' ability to achieve their objectives depends on the types of legislation and government policies in place. They can't possibly hope to influence legislation or government policy without in some way becoming involved in the political process, whether through lobbying government on specific issues or through more formal connection with a political party.

This said, the form of political activity taken varies greatly within the Canadian labour movement. Unions and labour federations have tended to differ, particularly with respect to the issue of affiliation with a political party. The Canadian Federation of Labour, for example, was always strongly opposed to any such affiliation (McCambly, 1990); in Quebec, a similar position has been taken by the Centrale des syndicates démocratiques (CSD), which during the 70s broke away from the CSN over this very issue (Boivin and Déom, 1995).

In the Canadian context, however, labour organizations such as the CFL and CSD have been probably the exception rather than the rule. Most Canadian unions are explicitly committed to social unionism, a type of unionism that believes that the role of unions is to further workers' well-being as a whole, outside the workplace as well as within it (Godard, 1994:217). Almost by definition, a commitment to social unionism entails some kind of affiliation with a political party, since acting on behalf of the working class as a whole necessitates winning passage of a broad range of legislation that will benefit workers and lower-income Canadians. This is something that's extremely difficult to do through ad hoc lobbying on specific issues. While affiliation with a political party is no guarantee of success, it does arguably improve unions' chances, by providing them with an experienced partner to assist them in their political ventures on a steady basis.

In English Canada, the labour movement has most often chosen the NDP or its forerunner party, the CCF, as its political partner. Unions are allowed a given number of delegate slots at NDP conventions (Godard, 1994:218) and many choose to affiliate directly to the party, a decision that allows them to play an active role in formulating its policy (Murray, 1995:189). In Quebec, most labour activists support the Parti Québécois, or the federal Bloc Québécois party (Boivin and Déom, 1995:458–459). The support, however, is typically of a more individual and ad hoc nature than the formal affiliation of unions with the English NDP. Only one Quebec central labour organization, the Quebec Federation of Labour (QFL), which is the provincial wing of the CLC, has formally endorsed the PQ (Boivin and Déom, 1995).

There's little doubt that the NDP-CCF and PQ have often been of great benefit to the labour movement. As we pointed out in the labour history chapter, the threat of a CCF victory was arguably the major factor responsible for the passage of Canada's first collective bargaining legislation, *PC 1003*. Later on, the NDP's balance-of-power position in a minority Liberal government was crucial in winning passage of the *Public Service Staff Relations Act*. More recently, NDP and PQ provincial governments have been responsible for a variety of pro-labour laws ranging from the removal of restrictive exclusions from unionization rights and the liberalization of certification procedures[6] to anti-strikebreaker bills, first-contract arbitration, and technological change provisions.

But there have also been many strains between the labour movement and the NDP or PQ, particularly when these parties have formed a provincial government and have been forced to make unpopular spending cuts directly affecting some of their union supporters. In 1982, the PQ government unilaterally imposed a 20 percent public sector salary reduction for the first three months of 1983, then unilaterally extended the existing agreements until the end of 1985 (Hébert, 1995:222). This action infuriated the public schoolteachers and other public sector workers, who had been among the PQ's strongest supporters, and caused much of the province's labour movement to withdraw support from the party in the 1985 election, which the PQ lost. Similarly, in 1993, Ontario's NDP government infuriated public sector unions by imposing a "Social Contract" providing for a three-year public sector wage freeze and unpaid days off. Public sector and many private sector unions withdrew their support from the NDP, which lost power in Ontario in 1995 and still hasn't recovered its former strength in that province. More recently, relations between the PQ and Quebec's labour movement were again severely strained by the government's large-scale cutbacks in health care and other social areas, which once again contributed to the PQ's electoral defeat in 2003. These conflicts have been among the many factors leading the labour movement to reconsider its role vis-à-vis its longtime political partners.

Not all politics is carried out in parliaments and legislative assemblies. As the economic environment becomes more globalized, many Canadian unions are finding themselves increasingly concerned with international development issues and with related problems of workers' rights, child labour, and the like, as well as with issues such as child poverty, hunger, and regional underdevelopment at home. As mentioned in Chapter 4, to help address these issues, a number of unions have established social justice or humanity funds. The Canadian Auto Workers' Social Justice Fund requires participating employers to donate one cent for each straight-time hour worked by each bargaining unit worker to a designated charity, food bank, or international relief effort (Godard, 1994:218). The Steelworkers' Humanity Fund, established on a similar checkoff basis, addresses itself to international labour issues, including support for core labour rights such as workers' freedom of association and reduction of child labour. More recently (2003), the PSAC also launched a social justice fund, based in part on employer contributions negotiated into collective agreements (PSAC, 2005). As globalization increases, such funds could well become a more prominent aspect of Canadian union activity, since they are potentially very useful vehicles for linking Canadian and overseas labour organizations.

Publicity Campaigns and Member Communication

Like most modern organizations, today's unions are finding that they have to spend an increasing amount of their time and energy communicating, both with their members and with the public at large. To keep members abreast of what they are doing, unions send out regular newsletters and other publications such as special pre-strike bulletins, develop telephone trees, and post notices on union bulletin boards. Virtually all large Canadian unions also have websites, which they use to communicate with members and publicize their activities. To tell their story to the general public, they use the full range of modern media, from traditional newspaper and magazine ads, to radio, TV, and the Internet.

Union publicity efforts serve a variety of purposes. In some cases, the purpose is to inform both the union's own people and sympathetic members of the general public about what the union is doing on a particular issue such as shorter work hours or health and safety. In other instances, the aim is to build coalitions with other stakeholders. In still other cases, like those of the Ontario Secondary School Teachers' Federation against education cutbacks or the CUPE ad against Ontario's two-tier health care plan, the aim is to protest government policy. While many union ads tend to be negative, at least insofar as they are critical of existing economic and political conditions and seek to change them, unions also run a variety of positive ads. For instance, a number of the union ads appearing in the *Ontario New Democrat* do not address specific issues but are designed merely to emphasize the unions' general support for the NDP.

A recent trend in union publicity efforts is the use of buses and bus shelters as vehicles for union advertising. In the city of Ottawa in 2001, buses carried numerous ads from both the PSAC and the PIPSC criticizing the government for inadequate salary offers during that year's round of bargaining. And while this edition of the book was being written, the Ontario Public Service Employees' Union (OPSEU) became embroiled in a dispute with the City of Ottawa over another round of transit advertising.

At issue was a series of ads which began "Lives depend on our public services" and featured photos of OPSEU members working for the Ontario public service. In early March 2005, senior officials at OC Transpo, the city's transit company, banned the ads as too political to appear in bus shelters. Mayor Bob Chiarelli initially sided with the OC Transpo officials, but later decided to review the city's policy allowing transit officials to ban ads they don't like. This, said OPSEU President Leah Casselman, represented a step in the right direction. At the same time, she warned that unless the city reversed its policy, the union might launch a Charter challenge to the ban. "OC Transpo has no business acting as a political censor," said Casselman. "Banning these ads is a clear violation of our members' free speech." (OPSEU, 2005).

The strongest and most controversial type of union publicity campaign is the **boycott**, or negative publicity campaign designed to induce the public not to purchase the goods or services of the company in question. Boycotts are frequently though not always launched in the context of a strike or lockout or union recognition dispute. Perhaps the best-known example is the grape-and-lettuce boycott undertaken by the late Cesar Chavez and his fledgling United Farm Workers (UFW) union in the United States during the late 1960s. The boycott, generally regarded as highly successful, was widely credited with helping the UFW win bargaining rights

boycott A negative publicity campaign aimed at persuading the public not to buy the goods or services of the company in question.

This ad taken out by the Ontario Public Service Employees Union (OPSEU) lets the public know in no uncertain terms what OPSEU members think of Ontario Premier Dalton McGuinty's policies with respect to the government's own employees.

*Let us never return to the days
when the wealthy enjoyed the best of care
and the poor entered through the back door.*

Treatment for the
POOR Only
No patients
received for clinics
after 9:30 A.M.
and 2:30 P.M.
Doors will be locked
at these hours

Yes to Canada's Health Care system,
with quality services for all.

Canadian Union of Public Employees

CUPE ad offers *Canadian Forum* readers a stark reminder of what two-tier
health care could be like.

for thousands of farm workers, mainly Mexican-American immigrants, who up to that point had been working under wretched
conditions for extremely low wages. A more controversial and
perhaps less successful campaign was one launched by the
Ontario English Catholic Teachers' Association against firms
found to have donated money exclusively to the governing Conservative party, to which the teachers were opposed because of the
education cutbacks leading to the fall 1997 Ontario teachers'
strike (Lakey, 1998).[7] The teachers' union boycott was particularly
controversial because it was a secondary boycott (a boycott of an
ally of one's adversary rather than the adversary itself)[8] and
because, in the eyes of some, it amounted to punishing people for
their political beliefs.

Unions in Business

The severe recession of the early 1980s caused many labour
organizations to start working proactively to create jobs and promote local and community development. It was at this time that
labour-sponsored venture capital corporations (VCCs) began to

United Farmworkers' grape and lettuce boycott was one of the most successful boycotts ever undertaken
and was widely credited with helping the union win bargaining rights for California farm workers.

appear. In a country where traditional financial institutions have often been reluctant to provide venture capital, especially to smaller or newer businesses (see Jackson and Peirce, 1990), the VCCs have played a key role. One recent study (Quarter, Carmichael, Sousa, and Elgie, 2001) estimates that such corporations are providing nearly half the venture capital in Canada. Most provinces have a single labour-sponsored investment fund organized by the provincial labour federation; however, in Ontario, where the Federation of Labour was split over support for such a fund, a number of different such funds have evolved (Quarter et al., 2001:95).

Among the first and by far the largest of the labour-sponsored VCCs was the Quebec Solidarity Fund, launched in 1984 with support from the Quebec government (Jackson and Peirce, 1990:42; Boivin and Déom, 1995; Déom and Boivin, 2001). Like other labour-sponsored VCCs, the Solidarity Fund offers investors a variety of tax credits, including an RRSP deduction as well as a provincial equity tax credit (Déom and Boivin, 2001:460). By 2004, the Fund had just over 550 000 investors and assets of approximately $4.6 billion Canadian dollars (World of Work, 2004). It is generally recognized that the Fund has been responsible for creating or saving many thousands of jobs in the province. Since its inception, the Fund has invested in a broad range of small and medium-sized enterprises in such sectors as communications, EDP software and service, and forest products, and has created specialized sectoral funds in biotechnology, environmental industries, and aerospace (Jackson and Peirce, 1990; Boivin and Déom, 1995).

The Solidarity Fund is far from being the only such organization in Canada. Other such VCCs include Working Ventures, founded by the Canadian Federation of Labour (Jackson and Peirce, 1990:43; Murray, 1995:188), First Ontario Fund, the Manitoba Federation of Labour's Crocus Investment Fund, and BC's Working Opportunities Fund (Jackson, 1998:4). The last three of these funds have been particularly interested in supporting employee-owned firms (Jackson, 1998). In addition, the Solidarity and Crocus Funds and BC's Working Opportunity Fund have, since the 1980s, directly supported a broad range of community economic development projects. For example, the Working Opportunity Fund invests in community loan funds serving small business (Jackson, 1998:10). In addition, unions and labour federations have been heavily involved in social housing projects across Canada (see Jackson, 1998 and Peirce, 2003:169).

Pension funds are another investment vehicle through which unions exercise considerable financial influence. Through their members' pension funds, unions control many hundreds of millions of dollars and an idea that has lately been gaining increasing currency both in the United States and, to a lesser degree, in Canada is that of using these funds to promote such socially desirable objectives as community development, affordable housing, and small-business growth (Jackson, 1997). The vehicle normally used for this purpose is an Economically Targeted Investment (ETI), a pooling mechanism that allows pension funds to channel a certain portion of their assets into such worthwhile ventures (Quarter et al., 2001). It is worth noting that in the US, the AFL-CIO has set up a housing trust for a similar purpose (ibid.:97).

In BC, the construction unions have engaged in ETIs by establishing development companies (e.g., Concert Properties) to which they channel a small portion of their investments. The construction unions, which benefited from the West

Coast real estate boom during the earlier 1990s, employ their own members through this approach, thereby increasing the amount of money available to their pension plan (ibid.).

In some cases, unions and their members have also bought significant or even controlling interests in the firms for which members work. Most often, this strategy has been used in single-industry resource towns where the corporate owners want to pull out even though the enterprise remains viable (Jackson, 1998:3). While many unions are critical of employee buyouts, arguing that it isn't the union's or workers' job to save management from the consequences of its own mismanagement, the Steelworkers have been a notable exception (Jackson, 1998:5). Since the early 1990s, this union has encouraged viable buyouts, both directly and through venture capital funds. By now, it has had enough experience to be able to provide support for those locals contemplating a buyout (Jackson, 1998).

Recently the Steelworkers' Union has become increasingly concerned about the growing number of steel and metal-related companies that have been going bankrupt. In response to the massive job loss and loss of vacation pay and benefits (including pensions) suffered by its members, the union has proposed major changes to Canadian bankruptcy law. A private member's bill introduced by an NDP MP stipulates, among other things, that no bankruptcy plan should be approved unless it provides protection for the wages and benefits of the company's current and former employees.

The preceding discussion has touched on only a few of the ways in which unions have begun to function, in effect, as business organizations, mobilizing their members' capital and in some cases using it to leverage other funds to create and save jobs, build affordable housing, and promote community development. Given government's growing reluctance to fund direct job creation schemes, this aspect of union action seems likely to expand in the coming years and will bear close observation by students of industrial relations.

Education

The labour movement has a long and proud record of involvement in education. As we noted in the labour history chapter, nineteenth- and early twentieth-century union halls often served as libraries, forums for public lectures and seminars, and venues for a broad range of educational and cultural activity. The tradition of union education has continued to the present day. Although there is not space in a general industrial relations textbook to do more than skim the surface on the subject of unions' educational ventures, even a cursory look will suffice to give some idea of the extent of their involvement.

While many union-sponsored courses focus on technical issues of immediate concern such as organizing, bargaining strategy, and shop steward training, others address broader issues such as women in the labour movement and unions and the environment (CUPE, no date; Fisher and Peirce, 1995). Over the years, the CLC has run weekend institutes and week-long summer programs covering a broad range of subjects (R. White, 1995). In Newfoundland, the Newfoundland Association of Public Employees (NAPE) has been a major player in this area, as has the Canadian Union of Public Employees (CUPE). NAPE's offerings have included training in public speaking and leadership, which has gone a long way towards building up members' confidence when placed in situations requiring them to speak in public (Fisher and Peirce, 1995). CUPE's courses, many offered in French as well as English, have included ones in political action, pay equity, technological change, and assertiveness training. The union has placed special emphasis on health and safety training; among its offerings, in addition to general health and safety courses, are specialized courses aimed at health care workers, municipal sewage-treatment-plant workers, social-service workers, and those who must deal with asbestos in the workplace (CUPE, n.d.).

A number of unions have begun to offer courses on contemporary political and economic issues of special relevance to their members. CUPE's offerings have included "Contracting Out and Privatization—Ways of Winning," a subject of obvious interest to the union's members given the wave of privatization that has taken place over the past two decades (CUPE, n.d.). The Communications Workers of Canada (CWC) and its successor union, the Communications, Energy, and Paperworkers Union (CEP), have also offered courses and developed educational materials on various "hot topics." During the early 1990s, the CWC conducted ongoing education on the subject of free trade (CWC, 1992). More recently, the CEP has developed a series of articles, videos, and other materials on work hours for insertion into its leadership development and steward training courses (J. White, 1997b).

A special area of interest for union educators is health and safety, due to Canada's appalling record in this area, as will be outlined in more detail in Chapter 6 (employment law). Recently, Canadian unions have begun supplementing formal course offerings in health and safety with informative articles on their websites. A recent visit to the Steelworkers' union website (uswa.ca) found an entire page devoted to health and safety. Interestingly, in addition to more "traditional" health and safety concerns such as diesel exhaust fumes, the page devoted much of its attention to the problem of Repetitive Strain Injury (RSI), a problem particularly prevalent in female-dominated clerical and grocery cashier jobs. Among the numerous articles on this subject, the Steelworkers' web site featured a promotion for RSI Day, February 28, 2005.

Current Issues 5.1

INTERNATIONAL REPETITIVE STRAIN INJURY (RSI) DAY: BECAUSE WORK SHOULDN'T HURT

Repetitive strain injuries are a serious occupational health concern across the world. February 28, 2005, marked the sixth annual International RSI Awareness Day.

What is an RSI?

Repetitive strain injury (RSI) is an umbrella term for a number of overuse injuries affecting the soft tissues (muscles, tendons, and nerves) of the neck, upper and lower back, chest, shoulders, arms and hands. Typically arising as aches and pains, these injuries can progress to become crippling disorders that prevent sufferers from working or leading normal lives. ▶

Why Should We Care?

Approximately 2.3 million Canadian adults have experienced a repetitive strain injury . . . serious enough to limit their normal activities, says a recent Statistics Canada study. These findings mark a significant increase in RSI over the five-year period between 1996 and 2001. The survey established [that] the majority of these injuries are caused by work-related activity. It also found a direct link between RSIs and stress.

In Your Workplace:

- Report RSI problems to your supervisor and your health and safety representative.
- If the work is unsafe, you have the right to refuse [it].
- Ensure ergonomics priorities are included in the priorities of your joint health and safety committee.
- Speak with your co-workers about RSIs.
- Circulate materials about RSIs in the community.
- Organize an RSI Awareness Day event in your workplace or community.
- Take part in RSI Day events and encourage others to attend.
- Speak with family and friends about RSIs.
- Send letters to the editor in community newspapers.
- Lobby local politicians for recognition of the day.
- Send a message to the federal Minister of Labour and Housing Joe Fontana asking him to bring forward federal regulations on ergonomics without delay.

Sources: Courtesy of United Steelworkers of America, http://steelworkers-metallos.ca/program/content/1992.php?lan=en&.

Unions' Expanded Scope of Action

As we have seen in the preceding pages, Canadian unions have greatly expanded their scope of action beyond such core activities as negotiating collective agreements, handling members' grievances, and seeking to achieve passage of pro-labour legislation. To begin with, they have entered into a broad range of partnerships with management, both within workplaces and beyond the workplace. Politically, their sphere of interest has widened, to encompass coalitions with anti-poverty and other social justice groups at home and with foreign unions and Canadian NGOs promoting economic development and human and labour rights overseas. And particularly over the past 15 years, many have entered the world of business, learning how to use available funds such as pension monies to promote job creation, community development, affordable housing, and other social objectives. In the field of labour education, a number of unions have expanded the labour "curriculum" beyond traditional core subjects such as collective bargaining and grievance handling, to encompass highly technical courses in specific areas of occupational health and safety and employment law and personal development courses in areas such as stress management and retirement planning (CUPE, n.d.). Supporting all these efforts has been an increasingly sophisticated publicity apparatus that makes use of the full gamut of media approaches, from traditional newspaper and magazine ads to direct mail campaigns and the establishment of websites on the Internet.

This new, expanded scope of union action has not been uncontroversial, either within the labour movement or outside of it. As noted earlier, some unionists feel a union has no business affiliating with a political party. A fair number might argue against a checkoff-based fund such as the Steelworkers' Humanity Fund, on the grounds that it should be up to the individual union member to decide which charities and non-profit organizations he or she will support. At least one major Quebec labour federation, the Centrale des syndicats démocratiques, has been skeptical about the merits of the Solidarity Fund (Boivin and Déom, 1995), and more national unions than not seem to be opposed to employee buyouts, even in cases where the rank-and-file strongly support the buyout (Jackson, 1998:5). Economically targeted investment vehicles for employee pension plans have been no less controversial (Jackson, 1997).

While the debates over these issues seem unlikely to end any time soon, the fact remains that most Canadian labour organizations have expanded their scope of action in one or more of the areas just mentioned. The areas into which a union or labour federation chooses to expand will depend on a variety of factors, including the organization's traditions and history, its membership composition, its members' interests, and the economic pressures facing the industry in which it operates. Some may wish (or need) to expand into more "new" areas than others. But in today's highly volatile economic and political environment, few if any unions can afford the luxury of simply burying their heads in the sand and concentrating solely on "minding the shop." While Canadian union membership rates have not declined anywhere near as sharply as those in the United States have, the pressures on Canadian union membership are nonetheless real (Murray, 2001; Lipsig-Mumme, 1995). In the coming decades, the ability to mount effective publicity campaigns and to use members' accumulated funds to create or save jobs may become increasingly critical to a union's survival. Our prediction, therefore, is that the scope of union action will continue to expand to meet the even stiffer challenges unions are likely to face in the coming decades.

UNION IMPACTS

Not surprisingly, given the broad range of activities in which we have just seen that they engage, unions have an equally broad range of impacts on their members' wages and working conditions, on the productivity and overall performance of the firms in which their members work, and on the Canadian economy and Canadian society as a whole. Many of these impacts, especially the wage impacts, have been studied extensively. A 1986 US review article (Lewis, 1986) considered more than 200 studies on wage impacts alone. Gunderson and Riddell (1993) review 11 Canadian studies on the same subject.

To a large extent, the union impacts likely to be of greatest interest to any given industrial relationist will depend on that person's overall perspective on IR (discussed in detail in Chapter 1). Pure economists and others of a neoclassical persuasion are apt to be most interested in unions' wage impacts. Students of organizational behaviour and other managerialists are likely to focus on the way unions affect management and overall firm productivity. Institutionalists may be most interested in positive productivity effects resulting from unionized workers' having a greater say in how firms are managed. For their part, reformists and people taking a political economy perspective are apt to emphasize unions' macro-level effects on Canadian society as a whole. Our view is that one must take *all* the above effects into account to have a good understanding of how unions operate in Canada today.[9]

Wage Impacts

Direct Union Wage Impact

direct union wage impact The premium a worker receives for union membership.

While unions are certainly about more than just money, it's unlikely that most people would remain members for very long if their unions could not negotiate a higher wage than they would otherwise receive. In simplest terms, a **direct union wage impact** is the premium a worker receives for union membership. It can be expressed as the difference between the wage a unionized worker and an otherwise equally qualified non-unionized worker would receive for doing the same job, as the following equation shows: $DUWI = W(uw) - W(nuw)$, where $W(uw)$ is the average wage for unionized workers doing any given job, and $W(nuw)$ is the average wage for non-unionized workers doing that same job.

To be sure, the question of how large any direct union wage impact is will typically be much more complex than the previous discussion would suggest. The whole assumption behind the calculation of direct union wage impacts is that other things, such as workers' experience and skill levels, are equal. Often they are far from equal. Because unionized firms generally offer higher pay and sometimes better working conditions as well, they tend to attract (and are able to hire) more highly qualified people than non-unionized firms. It may, therefore, be difficult to say to what extent a "union" wage impact is a simple premium for union membership, and to what extent it is a premium for greater skill or experience (Gunderson and Riddell, 1993:390–391).

Over the years, advances in statistical techniques have made it possible for researchers to "control" for differences in labour quality and job characteristics (Gunderson and Riddell, 1993; Gunderson and Hyatt, 1995:323). While there are still significant methodological problems[10] in determining the precise direct union wage impact for any country as a whole, the 11 Canadian studies reviewed by Gunderson and Riddell (1993:394–396) found that impact to be in the 10 to 25 percent range, a finding generally in line with earlier US studies (L. Reynolds, 1982:485–486; Lewis, 1986).

Since about 1990, however, the size of those impacts appears to have been decreasing. One recent study (Renaud, 1997) suggests that by 1990, the Canadian direct wage impact had declined from a peak of about 25 percent at the end of the 1970s to around 10 percent. Similarly, a 1999 study by Gunderson, Hyatt, and Riddell found that in 1997, Canadian workers covered by a collective agreement earned about 8 percent more than those not covered.[11] A still more recent study (Fang and Verma, 2002) found that the average union wage impact had dropped to about 7.7 percent. In most industries, the impact appeared to be in the 5 to 8 percent range.

Only in construction (19 percent) and retail trade (11 percent) was the impact found to be in double digits.

What are the explanations for this declining union wage impact? Both Fang and Verma (2002) and Gunderson and Hyatt (2001:393) suggest that the declining size of this impact may be due either to unions' declining power or their reorientation toward other, less costly objectives such as employment, job security, or union voice mechanisms. We, however, are by no means convinced that unions are any less interested in wage increases for their members than they were in the past. A more persuasive explanation, we believe, may be found in the increasingly large public sector share of Canadian union membership.

Given that public sector wages, particularly in lower-end jobs, tend to be significantly higher than comparable private sector wages (Gunderson, Hyatt, and Riddell, 1999), there is less room for a high union wage impact in that sector. As well, as we point out in more detail in the public sector chapter, public sector bargaining was severely restricted during much of the 1990s, making it extremely difficult for public sector unions to achieve significant (or in many cases any) wage gains for their members during that period. To the extent that this is a relevant factor in explaining the declining impact found by Fang and Verma, we should expect a modest increase in subsequent studies, as the results of renewed public sector bargaining flow into the overall wage pool.

In any event, it's clear that direct union wage impacts are not the same for every worker, or in every industry. In general, these impacts tend to be greater for blue-collar than for white-collar and for less skilled than for more skilled workers (Gunderson and Hyatt, 1995:325; Gunderson and Riddell, 1993:397; L. Reynolds, 1982:496–497). As Fang and Verma's study suggests, the impacts may be especially high in industries such as construction (see also Gunderson and Riddell, 1993:397; L Reynolds, 1982:485–486). In the United States, the evidence suggests that the impacts are greater for black workers and women than for white male workers (L. Reynolds, 1982:486); in Canada, there is some evidence of greater impacts for women, although this impact neither increases nor decreases the male–female wage gap since fewer women than men are covered by collective agreements (Gunderson and Hyatt, 2001:393). Finally, studies from both countries suggest that direct union wage impacts are generally greater in the private than in the public sector (Gunderson and Riddell, 1993; Gunderson and Hyatt, 2001).[12]

Impact on Employee Benefits

Most workers do not receive all their pay as up-front wages. Usually a portion of the total compensation package is paid in employee or non-wage benefits for such things as pensions, vacations, medical and dental insurance, holidays, and sick leave (Gunderson and Hyatt, 2001). Unionized establishments generally pay a greater portion of the total compensation package in employee benefits than do non-unionized ones; thus their impact on employee benefits is typically greater than their generally quite modest impact on up-front wages (Gunderson and Hyatt, 2005). There are a number of reasons for this. For one thing, being somewhat more highly paid, unionized workers can better afford to direct a portion of their pay packets toward non-cash remuneration. Secondly, unionized employers' compensation practices are a function of the demands the union forwards at the bargaining table. These demands reflect the preferences of the average, or median, voting member. The non-unionized employer, on the other hand, shapes compensation policies so as to influence marginal workers, those who can be convinced the join the employer's organization or persuaded not to leave by virtue of relatively small, or marginal, changes in compensation policies. Marginal workers tend to be younger, more mobile, less attached to one employer, and more likely to favour salary or wage increases over benefits. The median, or average, worker, on the other hand, is more likely to be older, with greater seniority, and more likely to have family responsibilities that would encourage him or her to invest in life, disability, and health insurance, and to favour pension improvements.

Finally, since unionized workers' rights, including the right not to be arbitrarily dismissed, are enshrined in a collective agreement, they have greater confidence in the eventual receipt of their benefits, many of which come in the form of deferred compensation. Pension benefits, for example, will not be paid out until many years after the employee begins contributions. Life, disability, and health insurance, as well as vacations and sick leave, are also forms of deferred compensation. Non-unionized workers, who have few protections against arbitrary dismissal and who may face great difficulty enforcing employment contracts, appear to find forms of deferred compensation a relatively less attractive option (Gunderson and Hyatt, 2005).

A recent (2002) study by Ernest Akyeampong found that unionized Canadian workers were almost twice as likely as their non-unionized counterparts to have extended medical coverage, a dental plan, or a life/disability insurance plan. Overall, about 80 percent of unionized workers were covered by each of the above plans, while slightly less than half of their non-unionized counterparts enjoyed such coverage. Unionized workers were also about three times as likely to have pension plan coverage as non-unionized ones (80 percent vs. 27 percent). Coverage was even higher in the public sector and in larger organizations. Another interesting finding was that unionized Canadian workers were about half again more likely to have a dental plan than their unionized American counterparts, although the rate of employer-sponsored pension plan coverage was roughly equal in the two countries.

Indirect Union Wage Impacts

indirect union wage impact The effect unions have on non-unionized workers' wages.

Indirect union wage impacts are the effects unions have on the wages of non-unionized workers. As various commentators point out (Gunderson, 1989; Gunderson and Hyatt, 2005), unions can affect the wages of non-unionized workers through a broad range of market, institutional, and legislative mechanisms. Pure economic theory would suggest that over the longer term, unions should reduce wages in the non-unionized sector, as employees from the unionized sector who are laid off when the unionized wage rises above the equilibrium level "spill over" into and crowd the non-unionized sector, thereby reducing wages there as well (Gunderson and Riddell, 1993:325–328). Institutional research suggests that, on the contrary, unions may well raise wages, if only by forcing non-unionized firms to raise their wages in a bid to forestall unionization or prevent valued employees from leaving. In practice, it's extremely difficult to determine the overall impact of unions on non-unionized workers' wages in Canada. In the past, the consensus was that this effect was modest but negative—probably less than 3 to 4 percent (Gunderson and Hyatt, 1995:327; Gunderson and Riddell, 1993:401). Other, including some more recent, studies cited by Gunderson and Hyatt (2005:403) have actually found a small positive effect. It would no longer be safe to say there is consensus even as to whether unions' overall effect on non-union wages was positive or negative, let alone on the size of that effect.

The reason why it's so difficult to come up with a single indirect union wage impact figure is that we're really talking about two quite different kinds of impacts, impacts that pull wages in different directions and apply to different types of workers. The depressing or so-called "crowding" effect predicted by economic theory (Gunderson and Riddell, 1993:385–386) will typically apply to lower-skilled workers with little labour market power. The so-called "threat" effect applies in situations where non-unionized employers increase their employees' pay, often to levels at or near those paid to unionized workers, in order to forestall a unionization drive or prevent employees with scarce skills from quitting and going to work in a unionized firm (Gunderson and Riddell, 1993:387–389). This type of indirect wage impact, also sometimes known as the "as-if-unionized" impact, most often applies in situations involving highly skilled workers such as professionals or skilled technical staff. In effect, this type of indirect union wage impact is a soft union-avoidance tactic since a primary aim is to reduce workers' demand for union services.

Unions and Wage Dispersion

In addition to increasing their members' wages relative to those of non-unionized workers, unions may affect national income distribution in various ways. Because unions tend to reduce wage differentials related to skill, age, experience, and seniority, there's less wage dispersion among unionized than among non-unionized workers (Gunderson and Riddell, 1993:402). To put it another way, there appears to be significantly less difference between the best-paid and worst-paid unionized workers than between the best-paid and worst-paid non-unionized workers. At the same time, unionization tends to increase overall dispersion by creating a wage differential between unionized and non-unionized workers (Gunderson and Hyatt, 1995:325). A number of studies from both Canada and the United States have shown that the former effect is stronger, which means that overall, unions tend to reduce wage dispersion throughout the economy as a whole (Gunderson and Hyatt, 2005; Gunderson and Riddell, 1993:402). Other things being equal, we would expect similar results from unions' efforts in the political arena, since they generally tend to support redistributive economic and social policies such as progressive taxation policies, high levels of unemployment insurance and welfare benefits, and pay and employment equity programs.[13]

How Unions Achieve Their Wage Goals

In Canada, collective bargaining is the major method used by most unions to achieve their wage objectives. This is not, however, the only method Canadian unions use. Some seek to keep wages up by restricting entry to the trade or profession (as by increasing entrance requirements for professional training or denying accreditation to those licensed in other jurisdictions). Others seek to fix non-union wages (as by supporting higher minimum wage or equal pay legislation) to reduce the relative cost of union as opposed to non-union labour, thereby maintaining or increasing the demand for union labour. Still others seek to change the environment within which bargaining is conducted (as by supporting changes in labour legislation that make union certification easier or supporting changes to a more centralized structure that will make it easier for the union to call an effective strike).[14]

Union Impact on Productivity

There is considerable disagreement within the industrial relations profession as to whether, on balance, unions serve to increase or decrease firms' productivity. The arguments on both sides have been usefully summed up by Freeman and Medoff (1979 and 1984).

Neoclassicists and others primarily interested in unions' economic impacts (the "monopoly" perspective described by Freeman and Medoff) argue that unions reduce productivity by raising wages above competitive levels, by reducing output through the strikes they call, and by forcing management to agree to restrictive work rules (Freeman and Medoff, 1979:75; Gunderson and Hyatt, 1995:328). Institutionalists and others primarily interested in workplace equity or equity within society as a whole argue that far from reducing productivity, unions often have positive effects on it. These include reduced quit rates and improved morale and worker–management co-operation resulting from union grievance processes and other mechanisms that give workers a sense that they have some say in what goes on in the workplace. Unions can also induce management to use more efficient production methods and even, perhaps, more effective personnel policies. In addition, they can increase productivity by collecting information about the preferences of all workers, information that can help the firm select better personnel policies and a more appropriate mix of wages and employee benefits (Freeman and Medoff, 1979:75). For their part, managerialists as well as some institutionalists argue that unions can have either positive or negative productivity effects, since what is most important is whether a union helps or hurts relations between workers and management. From this perspective, what may be of greatest interest are management's policy towards unions and the union's willingness to enter into a co-operative relationship with management (Godard, 1994:374–375). For example, if a union opposes an employee involvement initiative, the program's chances of success will clearly be reduced (Verma, 1995:297–298).

Which position is closest to the truth? The one thing almost everyone can agree on is that the question is an extremely difficult one to answer. As the previous discussion has suggested, some union effects are clearly positive, while others are clearly negative, and still others can be either positive or negative depending on the particular situation. Complicating matters still further is the fact that in many situations, particularly where what is being "produced" is a service rather than a tangible good, it may be extremely difficult if not impossible to measure productivity as such. In such cases, asking whether unions increase or decrease productivity may not be at all useful. Here (assuming we were trying to determine the effects of unionization in a recently unionized establishment), it might be far more useful to start by asking workers whether they found they were getting along better or worse with their supervisor than they were before the union came in, or whether they felt more or less confident than before about their ability to do their job. Even where productivity can be measured, the union's impact on the labour–management relationship may still be the most important factor. Where this is positive, it can lead not just to improved bargaining and communications (Gunderson and Hyatt, 1995:329), but to a broad range of problem-solving behaviour in all areas of workplace life, which in turn can result in reduced accident and illness rates, lower grievance and strike rates, and even reduced down time and spoilage.

Conversely, where the union's impact on the labour–management relationship is negative, the results can include greatly increased sickness, accident, and industrial conflict rates and increased down time and spoilage. At the end of the day, both positive and negative impacts of the less tangible variety described here may turn out to be more important than the generally modest union wage impacts discussed earlier.

Union Impacts on Management of the Organization

People from all different perspectives on IR agree that union impacts on the management of organizations are substantial. Where they disagree is on whether such impacts are beneficial. From a comparative perspective, these impacts appear to be greater in North America, with its detailed collective agreements regulating many different aspects of workplace behaviour, than in Europe, where agreements are apt to be more general (see Giles and Starkman, 1995:340) and unions do not generally have a significant effect on firms' day-to-day operations, a fact that may help explain North American managers' greater opposition to unions (Adams, 1995a:502). It is also worth noting that in many European countries, alternative mechanisms, such as works councils, are available to handle day-to-day problems on the shop floor.

In North America, unionization constitutes a significant limitation on management's freedom to run the enterprise as it sees fit. Here, management authority is specifically limited by any collective agreement provision; to counter such limitations, almost all management organizations insist that collective agreements contain management rights clauses, which generally have the effect of referring to management any matter not specifically addressed in the agreement. In Canada, unionization invariably brings with it a grievance process, since all jurisdictions' labour legislation requires collective agreements to include a process for the handling of disputes arising over the interpretation of the agreement (Carter, 1995:63).

Unions' most important impacts on the management of firms come through the aforementioned grievance processes, work rules laid out in collective agreements, and joint participation with management on various committees. For the average worker, and perhaps for management as well, it's the grievance process that is of greatest importance. Most significantly, the grievance process offers an avenue of redress for any worker who feels she or he has been unjustly dismissed. The chances of reinstatement following a dismissal grievance are more than 50 percent (McPhillips and England, 1995:81), whereas the non-unionized worker has no chance of reinstatement, except in the few jurisdictions offering the equivalent of a dismissal grievance process to certain non-unionized workers. The wish to avoid a costly and possibly embarrassing dismissal grievance process undoubtedly deters many managers from engaging in arbitrary dismissals. If managers are unduly timid, fear of a dismissal grievance may even keep them from firing people who should be let go. In lesser matters, as well, the grievance process serves as a brake on what might otherwise be capricious or arbitrary management behaviour.

Indeed, the threat of possible grievances typically causes management to operate in a very different way in a unionized establishment than it would in a non-unionized one. Now it must operate in accordance with two sets of rules: company policy and the collective agreement. As we noted in the management chapter, this makes the whole process of managing more formal and more legalistic. To the extent that the collective agreement brings a degree of certainty to what might otherwise be a confused, chaotic management process, the firm will likely benefit. To the extent that its work rules stifle creativity and innovation and cause people to become more concerned about legalistic observance of the contract than about doing their jobs better, the firm is likely to suffer.

No theory can tell us whether the positive or negative effects are more likely to prevail; the only way to tell is to go to individual workplaces and do detailed case studies. Here again, the nature of the individual labour–management relationship may be pivotal. Where there is a positive relationship, both sides may be willing to exercise some discretion in interpreting the collective agreement. Where the relationship is bad, both sides are more apt to "go by the book" in almost every instance, a process that can prove extremely counterproductive or even paralyzing if carried to extremes.

The work rules contained in collective agreements address a broad range of issues. Unless limited by legislation (as in the case of many public sector organizations) or by management rights provisions stating that layoffs and promotions are totally within management's discretion, collective agreement provisions are apt to use **seniority** as one of the criteria for promotion, and reverse seniority as the primary criterion for layoffs. Unions generally like seniority-based promotion and layoff provisions because they prevent management from promoting or laying people off in an arbitrary fashion (Godard, 1994:319–320). Without seniority provisions, employers facing an economic downturn might lay off more senior workers, because they would normally be earning higher wages, or might simply lay off any workers management didn't like. While the use of seniority to govern promotions is more controversial, relatively few collective agreements use seniority as the sole basis for promotion; much more common are provisions that state that seniority will be one criterion along with skills and ability (Giles and Starkman, 2005).

Other union work rules may apply more specifically to the work process. In some cases, workload itself may be limited. This was the case with the longshoring agreements of the 1960s, where a minimum gang size and maximum allowable load size might well have been stipulated (see Picard, 1967). More recently, it has

seniority An employee's standing in the organization, usually based on length of continuous employment.

often been the case with agreements in education. Public schoolteachers' agreements have sometimes limited class size; university professors' agreements have sometimes stipulated a normal or maximum number of courses a professor will be expected to teach.

Another important group of work rules has to do with procedures governing workforce reduction. In addition to provisions requiring that layoffs be in reverse order of seniority, unions may negotiate total or partial restrictions on management's ability to contract out work to outside firms. They may also negotiate restrictions on management's ability to implement technological change, such as requirements that the union be given a period of advance notice or that affected workers be provided with retraining opportunities. Finally, contracts may provide for a layoff notice period greater than that required by employment standards legislation or for training, job search assistance, or other benefits for employees facing layoff. In the federal public service, many agreements contain a separate workforce adjustment appendix outlining detailed procedures to be used in the event of large-scale reorganization or restructuring.

In addition to the impacts resulting from grievance procedures and the work rules contained in collective agreements, unions also affect the management of organizations through their joint participation, with management, in a number of committees or other forms of joint governance mechanism. The most important of these committees are the joint health and safety committees required in all jurisdictions. Here, unions often play a key role, both by educating and informing workers on the issues and by helping to ensure that the committee is not just a token. Unions also play an important role in the pay equity process through their involvement in job-evaluation procedures (Gunderson and Hyatt, 1995:330). Beyond that, collective agreements often provide for a variety of labour–management committees. While the scope and powers of these committees vary greatly, they do involve a good many workers, at least to some degree, in the day-to-day management of the organization—a development that most industrial relationists and many managers would probably regard as healthy.

Union Impacts on Society as a Whole

The previous discussion suggests that within the workplace, unions can have both positive and negative effects. For society as a whole, the situation is rather more clear-cut. Here, particularly in the social and political spheres, the impacts appear to have been almost entirely positive. It is largely thanks to unions, through their participation in politics, that Canadians have publicly funded medical care, unemployment insurance, public pensions, and other worthwhile social programs. Note here that the labour movement could not have achieved these results without a political partner (today the NDP, formerly the CCF), nor could the NDP or CCF have achieved them without the labour movement's active support. Earlier, we noted that the CCF and NDP have not only passed legislation providing for pro-labour legislation and social programs when they have been in government, they have also forced governments from other parties to pass such legislation when they have held the balance of power in minority governments, or when there has been a serious threat that those governments would lose to the CCF or NDP in the next election. It's important to note as well that the CCF, in particular, did not really get off the ground until it started attracting strong support from unionists during the Second World War (Heron, 1996). More recently, the NDP was strengthened by the increased support it started receiving from the CLC and affiliated unions beginning with the 1979 federal election (Morton, 1995; Murray, 1995). In the four federal elections held starting in 1979, the party posted some of the best results it had ever achieved. The critical role played by the labour movement within the NDP is also shown, in a negative way, by the party's relatively poor showing in all federal and Ontario elections since 1993 (the year of the social contract debacle), particularly in Ontario. Without strong, steady support from the labour movement, the NDP has little chance of remaining viable as a national political party.

The labour movement has made other important contributions to Canadian society. Over the years, it has done a great deal to raise the profile of health and safety issues, educating members, managers, and the general public alike. While Canadian workplaces are still far from safe, as the employment law chapter will show in more detail, they are safer than they would be without the work of unions, which have played a particularly important role in the joint health and safety committees required in all Canadian jurisdictions. Unions have also worked to bring in affirmative action, pay equity, and anti-discrimination legislation, and other human-rights measures benefiting all Canadians. Overall, we can only agree with Desmond Morton (1995:154), that "[m]uch that has made Canada a humane and civilized society has come from the social vision of its labour movement."

One other aspect of unions' broader impacts should be mentioned: their effect on the members who participate in their day-to-day operation and governance. More than 50 years after they had left the Knights of Labor (Kealey and Palmer, 1981), former members recalled their time in the Order as one that transformed their lives, giving them new vision and new hope. More recently (Murray, 1995:183), union activists have spoken highly of the impact that participation in the union has had on their personal development and understanding of society.[15] In some cases, union participation has marked the beginning of a worthwhile political career. In many more, union activists have taken the skills and self-confidence that they have learned through their participation and applied them to the problems faced by civic organizations such as school boards, zoning boards, or hospital boards. It would be an exercise in futility to attempt to measure the value of these activists' previous union participation through any sort of conventional cost-benefit calculus, but almost certainly that participation has helped make a difference to their communities.

ARE UNIONS STILL NEEDED?

Often, one hears the argument that while unions were very much needed in the late nineteenth and early twentieth centuries, when most workers were wretchedly paid and forced to work under appalling conditions, they have outlived their usefulness. Today, so the argument goes, almost all workers are well-paid, management has become totally enlightened, and working conditions everywhere are first-rate, thus making unions essentially redundant.

Those who have read the previous chapters with any care will immediately recognize the erroneous factual basis for such arguments. For example, Chapter 2 showed that many workers have found it difficult to keep up in today's brutally competitive economy. Chapter 2 also showed that in many cases management practice is becoming less, rather than more, enlightened than in the recent past. In addition, the health and safety section of Chapter 6, on employment law, will reveal some of the many health and safety problems continuing to face Canadian workers. All this is hardly evidence supporting the thesis that unions have outlived their usefulness. Even more significant than such blatant factual errors is the implicit assumption that Canadian society would somehow be better off without unions. It seems appropriate, in the circumstances, to ask what Canadian society would be like without unions, and what kinds of societies do not have free trade unions, in the sense in which we would understand them.

Since the second question is somewhat simpler, let's begin with it. Virtually every country we would consider democratic has free trade unions that advance their members' interests and, usually, those of the country's working people as a whole. On the other hand, fascist and other authoritarian regimes and military dictatorships generally do not allow unions at all, or at the very least constrain their activities severely (Kuwahara, 1993:223; Pellegrini, 1993:131; Fuerstenberg, 1993:178; Bean, 1994); while in Communist countries, such as the former Soviet Union, unions have most typically been absorbed into the larger state apparatus and given no independent role of their own in the IR system (Héthy, 1991). Quite simply, it would appear that free trade unions go hand-in-hand with democracy.

As for what Canadian society would be like without unions, the most immediate and obvious differences would be noticed at the workplace. To start with, many fewer Canadians would enjoy any real protection against dismissal or other arbitrary action by their employers. And many fewer would have any part in setting the terms and conditions of their employment. This would become a privilege enjoyed only by a select group of professionals, athletes, and middle- to upper-level managers. Health and safety laws would be less strictly enforced, even if the laws themselves did not change; the same would likely be true for human rights laws. Moreover, the already strong trend towards less secure work and more part-time, temporary, and contractual work would very likely accelerate without the brake now placed on it by union collective agreement provisions.

In addition to losing unions' workplace representation, working people would also lose political representation, since the one national party pledged to advance their interests, the NDP, would almost certainly cease to exist without a labour movement to support it. Publicly-funded health care might not disappear immediately, but support for it would certainly diminish, as would support for EI, social assistance, and other social programs, and public arts funding. Supporters of health care and public arts funding would definitely find their job much harder if they were forced to operate without the labour movement's financial support and the NDP's political support.

In a more general way, the question is perhaps best answered by two more. If there were no Canadian labour movement, what other group in contemporary Canadian society would be big enough and strong enough to provide a significant check to the economic and political clout of big business and the political right (Crispo, 1982)? And what other group would be in a position to advance the economic and political interests of the broad spectrum of ordinary working Canadians? Such questions are, admittedly, far from new or original. Expanded only slightly, they form much of the basis of the institutionalist perspective on industrial relations described earlier. They are nonetheless worth asking, given that the advocates of a union-free society have thus far had little to say in response to either one.

Fortunately, such questions are likely to remain purely hypothetical. As we pointed out earlier, the practical need for unions appears if anything to be increasing, rather than decreasing. From a broader perspective, a society without free unions would almost certainly be one in which few Canadians would care to live.

Case 5.1

WORKING TO PROTECT WORKERS AGAINST BANKRUPTCY

Bankruptcies are a common feature of economic life in Canada. Over the past five years, an average of about 10 000 firms per year have declared bankruptcy. During the first half of 2004 alone, the figure was 4980, with roughly 10 percent of these coming from the manufacturing sector.

Unfortunately, under current bankruptcy legislation, workers are last in line when a firm goes under. A company's taxes, lenders, and even its suppliers all get paid before its workers do. The result is that thousands of workers each year lose not only their jobs but their vacation pay, termination and severance pay, and even back wages for work they've already done. In addition, they lose their group insurance benefits. And if, as is often the case, the employer hasn't fully funded the pension plan, current workers and retirees will face cutbacks in their pension benefits as well.

The United Steelworkers of America (USWA) is a union whose members have been hard-hit by corporate bankruptcies in recent years. When the Fonderie Canadienne D'Acier in Montreal went bankrupt, the company's secured creditors recovered the $5 million owed them, but there was nothing left to cover an unfunded $260 000 pension fund liability, which meant pension benefits were cut.

Similarly, when Toronto's Ontario Store Fixtures went bankrupt twice in 2002–2003, over 1200 unionized employees lost their jobs. These employees were owed $800 000 in unpaid vacation pay and $11 million in statutory severance and termination pay. After lengthy negotiations with the firm's directors, the union won an agreement to pay the unpaid vacation claim and a small portion of the amount owed for severance and termination pay. But over $9 million owed to the firm's workers will never be paid.

For years, the USWA has been pushing to provide Canadian workers with better protection against bankruptcies. Now it appears their efforts may be about to bear some fruit, in the form of legislation which would put workers first in the event of corporate bankruptcies.

Sponsored by Pat Martin, an NDP MP from Winnipeg, Private Member's *Bill C-281* amends the *Bankruptcy and Insolvency Act* to provide that moneys owed to workers or that are for their benefit will be given first priority in the distribution of proceeds realized from bankruptcies. The bill also amends the *Employment Insurance Act* and *Regulations* to ensure that payments made to workers arising out of bankruptcy proceedings won't be deducted from benefits payable to employment insurance claimants. In addition, the *Canada Business Corporations Act* would be amended to provide an efficient way for former employees of a bankrupt corporation to press back wage claims against the corporation's directors.

Introduced late last year, Martin's "Workers First Bill" passed second reading in the House of Commons on May 5. It now goes to a House standing committee for further study and possible amendments before returning to the House of Commons for a final vote. If the bill becomes law, life will become a bit easier for the many thousands of workers whose lives are devastated each year by corporate bankruptcies.

Sources: Text of Bill C-281, An Act to Amend the Bankruptcy and Insolvency Act, etc.; NDP. (2005). "Standing up for Canadians' Pensions and Benefits," NDP home page, Campaigns, Workers First Bill, http://www.ndp.ca/node/1373, [Oct. 5, 2005]; Ken Neumann. (2004). "Unfair, Unclear, and Unworkable: Why Working People Need Changes in Canada's Bankruptcy Laws," USWA Canada home page, Bargaining, Campaigns & Political Action, Reform Canada's Bankruptcy Laws, October, http://steelworkers-metallos.ca/program/content/1708.php?lan=en&, [Oct. 5, 2005]; NDP. (2005). "NDP Celebrates First-Round Victory in Fight to Put Workers First," NDP home page, Campaigns, Workers First Bill, May 6, http://www.ndp.ca/page/1259, [Oct. 5, 2005].

Case Questions

1. What is a good rationale for legislation such as *Bill C-281?*
2. Why might the banks and other financial institutions object to such legislation? Do you agree with their position?
3. Why does *Bill C-281* take on particular significance at a time of global restructuring and trade liberalization?
4. How does this bill illustrate the importance of ongoing partnership between the labour movement and political parties?
5. If you were an MP, would you vote in favour of *Bill C-281?* Why, or why not?

QUESTIONS FOR DISCUSSION

1. If you are in a union, what kinds of activity does it engage in? What kinds have you, personally, been involved with? If you aren't in a union yourself, ask a friend or relative who is and find out what sort of things their union has been doing.
2. How has the range of union activities been expanding in recent years? Do you think this expansion has been healthy, overall?
3. Should unions engage in business ventures such as labour-sponsored venture capital corporations? Why, or why not? What about employee buyouts of failing businesses?

4. Why do public sector unions place such heavy reliance on publicity campaigns?

5. What are unions' major impacts on wages? In what ways, and why, have some of these impacts been changing in recent years?

6. What are some problems in evaluating union wage impacts?

7. What are unions' major impacts on productivity and management of the organization? Why are these impacts often extremely difficult to measure?

8. What are some of the major impacts unions have on society as a whole? How do they achieve these impacts?

9. Do you agree with those who argue that unions have outlived their usefulness in Canada? Why, or why not?

Suggestions for Further Reading

Akyeampong, Ernest. (2002). "Unionization and Fringe Benefits." In Statistics Canada, *Perspectives on Labour and Income* (fall), pp. 42–46. Brief but useful article outlining recent trends in unions' impacts on benefits. Contains some surprising findings.

Freeman, Richard, and James Medoff. (1984). *What Do Unions Do?* New York: Basic Books. Classic study of unions' impacts that implicitly argues that most economists have looked at union impacts from far too narrow a perspective. The comparison between the "monopoly" and "collective voice" perspectives on unions is particularly useful.

Quarter, Jack, I. Carmichael, J. Sousa, and S. Elgie. (2001). "Social Investment by Union-Based Pension Funds and Labour-Sponsored Investment Funds in Canada." In *Relations Industrielles* 56:1, pp. 92–113. Thorough review of these funds' numerous impacts through the end of the 1990s.

CHAPTER 6

EMPLOYMENT LEGISLATION

Family and friends of the Westray Mine victims march from the mine site in Plymouth, NS to the Westray Memorial Park in nearby New Glasgow to mark the fifth anniversary of the disaster.

LEARNING OBJECTIVES

After studying this chapter, you should be able to:

1. Identify some of the assumptions underlying the common law of contract and critique their application to the contract of employment.

2. Describe the implied rights and obligations the contract of employment is assumed to confer on both employees and employers.

3. Contrast the protections from wrongful dismissal that unionized employees enjoy with the protections afforded non-unionized employees in Canada.

4. Describe the purpose of, and the types of provisions contained within, employment standards legislation.

5. Describe three types of statutes that govern equity in employment in Canada.

6. Explain the system used in Canada to regulate occupational health and safety.

The laws that govern employment relationships in Canada can be divided into three interrelated legal regimes. The first, which governs non-unionized employment relationships, is the longest standing and is based on the common law concept of the contract of employment. The second, the collective bargaining regime, which will be covered in Chapter 7, applies only to unionized workers or those in the process of organizing a union at their workplace. The third legal regime, statutory regulation—or employment legislation—is comprised of the many pieces of legislation that set standards of employment that apply to both unionized and non-unionized employees. The focus of the first part of this chapter is the individual contract, or common law, of employment. Topics covered include the problems associated with applying the principles of contract law to the contract of employment, the implied contractual obligations of both employers and employees, termination of the employment contact, and both wrongful and constructive dismissal. The latter part of this chapter highlights various types of employment legislation, including employment standards, human rights protections, pay and employment equity, and occupational health and safety.

THE INDIVIDUAL EMPLOYMENT CONTRACT

While the majority of non-unionized employees never actually see their employment contract, since it is most often unwritten, every employment relationship is based upon the parties entering into a contract (LLCG, 2004). In a unionized setting, that contract is the collective agreement. In a non-unionized setting, the contract consists of the terms and conditions of employment to which the parties have agreed whether in writing, verbally, or by virtue of the exchange of salary or wages for services. The individual contract of employment is governed by the same common law principles that govern other commercial contracts (LLCG, 2004); thus, the legal presumption is that the contract was freely negotiated between parties with relatively equal bargaining power. The law also presumes the contract of employment was voluntarily entered into by two legally capable people, that an offer was made and accepted, and that consideration was exchanged. This exchange, or **quid pro quo**, is necessary to render the contract valid and binding, though the courts will generally not consider the fairness of the exchange but simply whether at least one of the parties tendered something in exchange for, or with the promise of, something in return.

> **quid pro quo** A term used in law to denote the giving of something for something, an exchange which is necessary to render a contract valid and binding.

Students who have held any type of employment will readily identify some of the problems inherent in applying the same principles to the contract of employment as are applied to contracts governing the buying and selling of commodities. The assumption of equal bargaining power is problematic. In reality, employers are far more likely to be able to offer terms and conditions of employment on a take-it-or-leave-it basis (LLCG, 2004); workers who are so in demand as to be able to dictate their conditions of employment are the very rare exception. Rare also are workers who are able to choose between many different job offers in the same manner as employers choose amongst job candidates. Furthermore, the hesitancy of the courts to examine the quantum or fairness of the employment bargain in a situation where the economic power of the parties is sometimes grossly unequal has led, especially during certain periods in Canadian history, to dreadfully poor terms and conditions of employment. Even today, for the vast majority of workers, the assumptions upon which contract law is based do not describe the reality of their situation, which more typically involves negotiating an employment contract in the context of an employment relationship based upon managerial authority and a labour market characterized by persistent unemployment. Finally, enforcement remains a problem. In light of the high costs and protracted delays associated with civil litigation, typically only high-level managers and professionals can afford to pursue enforcement of their rights through the courts. Thus, the common law notions of employment have largely failed low- to middle-income workers (LLCG, 2004).

Partially due to the failings of the common law to adequately protect the average worker, each jurisdiction in Canada has passed a range of statutes that set minimally acceptable terms and conditions of employment. While these statutes are of primary importance to employees who are not covered by collective agreements, they apply to all employment relationships and are generally enforced through specialized administrative tribunals designed to be more accessible, expedient, and less costly than the courts. Employment legislation will be covered in detail in the latter half of this chapter.

Implied Terms and Obligations

Beyond the assumptions already discussed, the common law contract of employment is also assumed to confer on both parties a number of implied rights and obligations. These implied terms reflect what have come to be regarded as reasonable expectations so pervasive as to form part of the "climate of contracting" that workers and employers are assumed to intend to govern their relationship. As societal and workplace standards gradually evolve, so too do these implied terms (LLCG, 2004; Carter, England, Etherington and Trudeau, 2002). Breach of these generally accepted expectations may provide adequate justification for dismissal (Carter et al., 2002). Thus, an employee must report for work punctually and regularly, perform his or her duties honestly and faithfully, obey lawful and safe orders within the scope of their contractual duties, and avoid gross misconduct such as drunkenness or insubordination (McPhillips, 2001). For professional and managerial employees, avoiding any conflict of interest—as would be created if an employee solicited his or her employer's customers—may also be an important element of the express or implied contract (McPhillips and England, 1995).[1]

Employers, in addition to abiding by any relevant statutes such as employment standards or human rights laws, must pay employees regularly and cannot change their duties, status, or level of pay significantly without the employee's consent (McPhillips, 2001). They must provide a reasonably safe workplace even for employees to whom the protections of occupational health and safety legislation do not extend. Employers are also obliged to provide reasonable notice of termination except in situations where employees have been guilty of misconduct or have performed their duties unsatisfactorily. The purpose of such notice is to cushion employees against the financial hardships associated with unemployment and to provide a period of time during which they can search for alternate employment. While the courts have refused to imply a general duty of fairness into all aspects of the employment contract,[2] employers are required to act professionally and in good faith when dismissing employees. Among other things, employers are expected to act in a procedurally fair manner, not to fabricate grounds for dismissal, and to conduct the dismissal in a manner that is not unnecessarily humiliating or psychologically harmful (England, 2005).

Termination of the Individual Contract of Employment

Contracts of employment generally are either for a limited term or, more commonly, for an indefinite duration. Contracts of the former type terminate at the end of the specified period of time. Contracts of the latter type are terminated only upon adequate notice or when one of the parties seriously breaches the contract. Thus, as mentioned above, unless the employee's conduct so seriously breaches the contract as to justify dismissal, the employer must provide adequate notice or payment in lieu thereof. In instances where the employee's conduct provides no justification for dismissal, the employer may terminate the contract at any time as long as adequate notice or pay in lieu is provided.

At common law, there is no right to retain employment against the wishes of the employer. This is perhaps the single most important difference between unionized and non-unionized employees. Unionized workers who are unfairly dismissed may seek redress under the grievance procedure of their collective agreement with a range of remedies available up to and including reinstatement with full pay for any time lost between the wrongful termination and the arbitration award. Non-unionized employees, on the other hand, must generally seek redress through civil action and the most they can expect is for the court to order the employer to pay damages, which in almost all cases amount to no more than the pay they would have received had adequate notice been provided. Since dismissal is considered the capital punishment of the workplace, unions tend to pursue such complaints vigorously, pushing them through to arbitration more often than any other type of grievance. Ordinarily in dismissal cases, the onus of proof is on the employer to demonstrate that the employee should be discharged and the standard of proof required by most arbitrators is high. Given these facts, a discharged unionized worker stands more than an even chance of being reinstated (McPhillips, 2001; Christie, 1980).

The substantial protection that union membership thus provides against arbitrary dismissal has frequently been cited in union-membership-joining and union-growth studies as a major reason why workers wish to join unions. Non-unionized employees, on the other hand, have little recourse should they find themselves arbitrarily dismissed. Even if they have the financial resources to pursue a wrongful dismissal suit through the courts, the legal costs can amount to more than the quantum of damages they hope to be awarded.

There are some notable exceptions to non-unionized workers' abysmally poor protection against unjust dismissal. Where the dismissal constitutes discrimination on grounds protected under the human rights legislation in that jurisdiction, the employee may pursue a complaint through the Human Rights Commission. While the process can be extremely protracted, reinstatement may be an option. Some jurisdictions, including Ontario, also offer protection for employees whose dismissal is the result of their employer's serious contravention of certain sections of the *Employment Standards Act*,[3] such as refusing to allow an employee to return following maternity leave or firing employees who attempt to enforce their rights under the *Act*; in such instances, an employment standards officer may order compensation, reinstatement, or a combination of the two.

Dismissal Adjudication for Non-Unionized Employees

Three jurisdictions, Nova Scotia, Quebec, and the federal jurisdiction, have included in their employment standards legislation an adjudication procedure that provides some protection from unjust dismissal for non-unionized employees. These protections are only available to non-managerial employees whose employment exceeded a specified period, which differs between jurisdictions. In the federal jurisdiction, for example, a minimum of one year of service qualifies employees for these protections.[4] Quebec requires two years' service,[5] while Nova Scotia offers protections only to those employees with greater than ten years of service with their employers.[6]

The adjudication process most studied is that carried out under the *Canada Labour Code*, which provides for adjudication of dismissal grievances of non-managerial, non-bargaining-unit employees with more than a year's service. Under this procedure, the adjudicator can either reinstate or award damages in lieu of reinstatement (McPhillips and England, 1989). One study (Eden, 1993) suggests that experience under this section of the *Code* has been more or less similar to experience in the unionized sector. Of 279 dismissal cases decided under this section of the *Canada Labour Code* between 1978 and 1989, 61 percent were sustained, a figure roughly comparable to that for dismissal grievances. In general, it appears that the same concepts of progressive discipline being applied by arbitrators in the unionized sector are being adhered to by adjudicators under the *Code*.[7]

It is not entirely clear why more jurisdictions have not followed the lead of the federal jurisdiction, Nova Scotia, and Quebec by providing some kind of adjudication procedure for non-unionized workers' dismissal grievances. Some writers have suggested that opposition from unions may be one reason, given that the availability of a dismissal grievance procedure for non-unionized workers might reduce workers' incentives to join unions. On the other hand, workers in various European countries, such as Germany, have a variety of options for handling grievances, including dismissal grievances, some of which also do not involve the union (Fuerstenberg, 1993) and there is little evidence that these countries' union membership rates have declined as a result. Given the fundamental importance to workers of having some kind of protection against arbitrary dismissal and the very real likelihood of stable if not declining Canadian union membership rates for the future, the issue warrants further investigation.

Constructive Dismissal

Dismissals may be of two types; outright dismissal, the refusal to continue to employ in any capacity, is easy to distinguish. The other type, constructive dismissal,

constructive dismissal Occurs when an employer unilaterally and fundamentally alters the terms and conditions of employment such that the change can be construed as equivalent to dismissal.

may not be so readily apparent. A **constructive dismissal** occurs when an employer unilaterally and fundamentally alters terms and conditions of employment such that the employee can construe the employer's action as equivalent to dismissal (Sproat, 2002). The change must be fundamental in that it must radically alter the nature of the employee's contract and it must be unilaterally imposed upon the employee (Echlin and Fantini, 2001). If the employee agrees to the change or implicitly condones it by not objecting, a constructive dismissal will not be established. The key is whether the employer fundamentally breached, or repudiated, the employment contract without the employee's consent.

In a case involving the Burns Foods Company,[8] a foreman named Baker was suddenly advised that his position had become redundant and offered alternative work at lower pay as a beef boner or security guard. When he refused, he was dismissed. The court ruled that Baker's removal from the position he had held for nearly 30 years constituted a constructive dismissal, since at no time did the company argue his work was unsatisfactory. But the notion of constructive dismissal does not apply to minor, or sometimes even fairly significant, changes such as lateral transfers, providing they do not involve lower pay or a demotion. In a case involving Lloyd's Bank,[9] a manager sued for constructive dismissal after being transferred from the bank's Vancouver branch to an equivalent position, at higher pay, at the bank's smallest branch in New York. In denying the plaintiff's suite, the court ruled this a lateral move rather than a demotion.

Reasonable Notice

The employer's implied obligation to give reasonable notice of termination has been formalized in each jurisdiction's employment standards legislation, within which minimum notice periods are outlined for dismissals in the absence of just cause. These notice periods apply to all dismissals not grounded in the misconduct or unsatisfactory performance of the employee, including layoffs for economic reasons. The notice periods generally graduate with the tenure of the employee but tend to be fairly short, even for employees with many years' service. For recent hires, it is all but non-existent (see Table 6.1). Every Canadian jurisdiction except Prince Edward Island also has special group termination provisions that take effect when a large number of workers are terminated in a short period of time, most often as a result of a plant closure or major downsizing. The special provisions are designed to take into account the hardship that may be faced not just by the affected workers individually, but by the entire community, particularly when the business being closed or downsized is the community's only or major employer.

As with all employment standards, these notice periods establish a floor; what is considered reasonable notice at common law is generally longer, sometimes substantially so. In determining what constitutes adequate notice under common law, judges still rely quite heavily on a 1960 case involving an advertising director named Bardal and *The Globe & Mail*.[10] While there was never any allegation of improper conduct or unsatisfactory performance, Bardal was summarily dismissed after refusing to resign with six months' notice and one month's salary. The factors used by the court in arriving at an award of a year's salary included the nature of the employment, the employee's length of service, his age, and the availability of similar

Table 6.1

TERMINATION OF EMPLOYMENT: EMPLOYER NOTICE PERIOD, ONTARIO

Length of Employment	Minimum Notice Period
Less than one year	1 week
One year or more and fewer than three years	2 weeks
Three years or more and fewer than four years	3 weeks
Four years or more and fewer than five years	4 weeks
Five years or more and fewer than six years	5 weeks
Six years or more and fewer than seven years	6 weeks
Seven years or more and fewer than eight years	7 weeks
Eight years or more	8 weeks

Sources: *Ontario Employment Standards Act, 2000* [S.O. 2000, c.41] s.57.

employment, as well as his experience, training, and qualifications. Courts will award longer notice periods to more highly skilled employees who can have difficulty locating suitably similar alternate employment; a longer notice period might also be justified by advancing age, which tends to impact negatively on employment prospects (Sproat, 2002). In addition to the "Bardal" factors, courts take into account whether the employee has made any attempt to mitigate the damages by seeking other, substantially similar work. Employees have the duty to mitigate; however, the onus is on the employer to prove that the employee has not made an attempt to find suitable work. More recently, courts have also awarded additional notice due to employers' unprofessional or bad faith conduct during dismissal.[11]

The longer notice periods at common law must be measured against the difficulty of enforcement. When a worker goes to court, the outcome is never certain, the process is normally quite long and stressful, and lawyers' fees can eat up a large portion of the award. The courts may not, therefore, be a realistic option for most workers other than professionals, managers, top-level athletes and entertainers, or those with extremely long periods of service. Still, awards have been increasing in recent years. Awards of 12 to 24 months' salary are no longer uncommon (McPhillips, 2001). Given the large amounts of money that may be at stake and the potential for damaging a firm's reputation and hurting the morale of other employees, it behooves employers to exercise extreme care when discharging employees. Dismissal is an extremely stressful experience in the best of circumstances. Employers and managers must take care not to aggravate an already emotionally loaded situation by such ill-advised and callous actions as termination in the presence of fellow workers, personal abuse, or false accusations of serious misconduct such as theft.

STATUTORY REGULATION: AN OVERVIEW

In each Canadian jurisdiction, an array of statutes provides a wide range of protections and establishes minimum standards of employment for all "employees," whether unionized or not. While the definition of employee may exclude certain workers in some jurisdictions, the intent of these legislative schemes is to provide a floor of standards that establish the minimum terms and conditions of employment deemed acceptable in current social and economic conditions. The basic statute, normally referred to as employment or labour standards, generally covers such things as minimum wages, maximum permissible hours of work, overtime pay, minimum annual vacation entitlements, paid holidays, termination notice periods, and maternity and parental leave. Provisions found in some, but not all, Canadian employment standards legislation also cover clothing or special apparel payments, child employment laws, minimum age levels for employment, bereavement and sick leave, and maximum permissible board and lodging charges (McPhillips and England, 1995; McPhillips, 2001). Statutory regulation also includes a variety of statutes that govern such things as occupational health and safety, human rights, pension benefits, pay equity, workers' compensation, employment equity, and even privacy of information. The federal employment insurance legislation, which has national coverage, might also be considered part of the general scheme of statutory regulation of the employment relationship (LLGC, 1998).

There are a number of reasons why legislation covering the broad spectrum of workers, not just those belonging to a union, is needed. First, as we noted earlier, only about one-third of all Canadian workers belong to a union. Many workers who do not belong to a union do not even have the legal right to join one. Other workers may have the opportunity, but not the propensity, to unionize. Considerations of fundamental equity suggest that some kind of legislation is needed to protect certain basic rights for all workers. For example, it seems unduly harsh to suggest that a worker should be required to join a union to be assured of a safe workplace or freedom from discrimination.

In addition, a number of important workplace issues, particularly human rights issues such as sexual harassment and religious discrimination, may be inherently difficult to regulate through collective bargaining alone. As we point out in Chapter 9, much collective bargaining is based on the notion of compromising on some middle ground between the parties' positions. Such a process does not lend itself well to protection of such fundamental rights as freedom from discrimination or the right to a safe workplace. Then too, what is gained at the bargaining table can also be lost there, particularly in a difficult economic climate. Furthermore, collective bargaining is a majoritarian process, through which the rights of certain groups of union members who may be in the minority are not guaranteed protection. At a minimum, collective bargaining over such issues needs to be supplemented by a process that applies to all workers.

Jurisdiction and Administration of Statutory Regulation

Like most labour relations legislation, most statutory regulation falls under provincial jurisdiction. The major exception is workers employed in undertakings of a clearly federal nature, such as the railroads, airlines, interprovincial transport companies, and chartered banks. These workers fall under federal jurisdiction and are covered by the relevant sections of the *Canada Labour Code* and *the Canadian Human Rights Act*. As for administration, employment or labour standards legislation is typically handled by a branch of the labour ministry, as is health and safety legislation. Human rights issues, pay equity, and employment equity are generally handled by separate commissions, as is workers' compensation.

This multiplicity of venues can be problematic since in some cases violations of employees' rights could involve proceedings under a number of different commissions or tribunals, each with different rules regarding filing of complaints, standards of timeliness, investigation procedures, and available remedies (England, Christie, and Christie, 1998). This patchwork of forums leads to a host of problems, not the least of which are the delay and cost associated with multiple proceedings and the added difficulty and confusion this imposes on employees seeking to enforce their rights. There has been some discussion regarding the creation of a single tribunal of comprehensive scope (a "mega tribunal," in effect) that could consolidate proceedings through a single process integrating all jurisdictions—although this has yet to come to fruition in any Canadian jurisdiction.

Employment/Labour Standards Legislation

As mentioned, employment or labour standards legislation covers a wide variety of terms and conditions of employment from such basics as minimum wages and maximum hours of work through to recent innovations such as whistle-blower protection and compassionate care leave. The multiplicity of conditions covered, the complexity of the associated regulations, and the large number of Canadian jurisdictions makes a comprehensive discussion or chart of Canadian employment standards tricky. Students are urged to consult the legislation and regulations in their jurisdiction as well as the very informative synopses available on the websites of Human Resources and Skills Development Canada and various provincial Ministries of Labour.

In today's economy, employment or labour standards legislation is of increasing importance, particularly to younger workers, part-timers, and those in low-skilled jobs in the burgeoning service sector, for whom unionization is generally not a realistic prospect. Others would argue that Canada's comprehensive net of minimum standards compromises employers' ability to compete on the global stage and argue for a scaling back of standards or at least greater flexibility in how they are applied. Indeed, some jurisdictions have amended their employment standards to facilitate employer flexibility.[12] On the other side of the debate, many argue that fair competition demands social clauses to link trade agreements with internal labour standards such as those established by legislation in Canada. They argue that these standards must be protected and enforced in order to avoid downward harmonization—otherwise called a "race to the bottom" or "social dumping" (Block, Roberts and Clarke, 2003).

Employment or labour standards legislation applies to most, but by no means all, Canadian workers. Some jurisdictions exclude certain groups completely from coverage under their employment or labour standards acts, while others do not apply particular provisions to certain groups. Overall, exclusions are not as broad as for labour relations legislation, nor do they appear to be quite as broad as they were in the early 1980s, when England (1987) found large numbers of workers falling outside the protection of many jurisdictions' employment standards laws. Still, the remaining exclusions raise significant equity concerns, particularly given that some of those excluded are among the country's least fortunate workers and some are also excluded from unionization rights under labour relations legislation. As an example, in Prince Edward Island and Alberta, farm workers are exempt from most sections of their employment standards acts while those employed in farming, ranching, or market gardening are completely exempted in Saskatchewan.[13] Home care workers are exempt from minimum wage and maximum hours of work protections in Prince Edward Island,[14] and, effective April 1, 2004, Alberta established distinct hours of work and overtime provisions for the home care and residential care sectors.

Beyond specific exclusions, labour standards legislation may also be failing workers simply due to the evolution of employment. As discussed in Chapter 2, the growth of non-standard employment has outpaced the growth in jobs that fit the traditional standard of full-time, full-year employment. Yet employment standards statutes have adapted little to ensure that all those employed in the increasing variety of non-standard arrangements are adequately covered. For example, New Brunswick is the only jurisdiction to establish a minimum wage for employees whose hours of work are unverifiable and who are not strictly remunerated by commission. Furthermore, while part-timers are generally covered under employment standards legislation, these positions often pay less per hour than, and do not provide the pensions or other benefits accorded to, similar full-time work. Indeed, employers often create a multitude of part-time positions specifically to cut labour costs. In recognition of this, Saskatchewan amended its employment standards regulations in 1995 to mandate, in essence, that whatever benefits are provided to full-time workers must also be provided, according to a specified pro-rated formula, to part-time workers. Quebec addresses this issue in a more limited way by outlawing the practice of paying employees lower rates of pay simply because they work fewer hours per week. (England, et al., 1998; Carter et al., 2002). Protections for part-timers are especially important to women, who are not only more likely to work part-time (Stats Can, 2003a) but are more likely to be involuntarily underemployed in part-time and other non-standard forms of employment (Kimmel and Powell, 1999). Indeed, the disproportionate representation of women in all forms of non-standard employment, especially part-time, temporary employment, which is the most precarious of all (Cranford, Vosko and Zukewich, 2003), suggests that the needs of many working women are not being adequately met either by current employment standards legislation or human rights protections.

Finally, the enforcement of employment standards legislation remains problematic. As with most other employment statutes, enforcement is complaint based, requiring that employees not only be familiar with their rights, but also willing to pursue a complaint. The ineffectiveness of enforcement mechanisms and the relatively low fines for violations provide employers little incentive to comply. Even though victimization of employees seeking to enforce their legal rights is prohibited, many employees hesitate to file a complaint against their current employer, partially due to fear of reprisal. Thus, not surprisingly, research suggests that the majority of awards occur after the employee has left their place of employment (Adams, 1987).

Table 6.2

CURRENT AND FORTHCOMING MINIMUM HOURLY WAGE RATES, EXPERIENCED ADULT WORKERS IN CANADA*

Jurisdiction	Effective Date	Wage Rate	Note
Federal[†]	18 Dec. 1996		The minimum wage rate applicable in regard to workers under federal jurisdiction is the general adult minimum rate of the province or territory where the work is performed
Alberta	1 Oct. 1999	$5.90	
British Columbia	1 Nov. 2001	$8.00	
Manitoba	1 Apr. 2005	$7.25	
New Brunswick	1 Jan. 2005	$6.30	
New Brunswick	1 Jan. 2006	$6.40	
New Brunswick	1 Jan. 2007	$6.60	
Newfoundland and Labrador	1 Nov. 2002	$6.00	
Newfoundland and Labrador	1 Jun. 2005	$6.25	
Newfoundland and Labrador	1 Jan. 2006	$6.50	
Newfoundland and Labrador	1 Jun. 2006	$6.75	
Newfoundland and Labrador	1 Jan. 2007	$7.00	
Northwest Territories	28 Dec. 2003	$8.25	Applies to all employees in the Northwest Territories.
Nova Scotia	1 Apr. 2004	$6.50	
Nunavut	3 Mar. 2003	$8.50	Applies to all employees in Nunavut.
Ontario	1 Feb. 2005	$7.45	
Ontario	1 Feb. 2006	$7.75	
Ontario	1 Feb. 2007	$8.00	
Prince Edward Island	1 Jan. 2005	$6.80	
Quebec	1 May 2004	$7.45	
Quebec	1 May 2005	$7.60	
Saskatchewan	1 Nov. 2002	$6.65	
Yukon	1 Oct. 1998	$7.20	

*In most jurisdictions, these rates also apply to young workers. More information is available on special rates for young workers under "Current and Forthcoming Minimum Wage Rates in Canada for Young Workers and Specific Occupations" on the HRDC website.

[†]Generally, the federal jurisdiction includes labour market sectors coming under federal authority by virtue of the *Constitution*, such as international and interprovincial transportation, telecommunications, and banking.

Sources: Human Resources and Skills Development Canada. (n.d.). "Current and Forthcoming Minimum Hourly Wage Rates for Experienced Adult Workers in Canada," http://www110.hrdc-drhc.gc.ca/psait_spila/lmnec_eslc/eslc/salaire_minwage/report1/index.cfm/doc/english, [February, 2005].

Equity Legislation

Human Rights Legislation

Every jurisdiction in Canada has human rights legislation. With regard to employment, the legislation is designed to ensure equality of both opportunity and of terms and conditions of employment. Employers and trade unions are prohibited from distinguishing between or excluding employees or members based on a number of enumerated grounds. Virtually all jurisdictions proscribe discrimination based on race, national origin, colour, religion or creed, marital status, disability, sex, or sexual orientation. Age is also a prohibited ground in every jurisdiction, but the definition of age varies. For example, some jurisdictions provide a general reference, whereas others will limit protections to those between certain ages such as 18 and 65 (Mason, Geddie and Dakai, 2004). Other protected grounds include such things as a criminal conviction for which a pardon has been granted and political belief, opinion, or conviction. Human rights legislation is normally enforced on the basis of individual complaints to the appropriate commission or council (McPhillips, 2001), although in a few cases proactive investigations may be conducted.

Current Issues 6.1

BANNING MANDATORY RETIREMENT

On August 18, 2004, the Ontario government announced its commitment to end mandatory retirement and its intention to hold public consultations regarding the anticipated impact of such a move. Ontario is not the first province to address this issue, which many argue constitutes discrimination on the basis of age and disproportionately disadvantages immigrants and women whose later start or career interruptions may necessitate working beyond normal retirement age. Both Manitoba and Quebec banned mandatory retirement in the early 80s and Alberta, the Yukon, and Prince Edward Island also outlaw it except in limited circumstances.

Employers, unionists, and labour economists have all argued against a ban on mandatory retirement, predicting that older workers would overburden payrolls, reduce the number of jobs available to younger workers, and mean a death knell for long-established deferred compensation practices that pay younger workers below and older workers above their productivity levels. Others argue that older workers may be the solution to impending skills shortages and expected pressures on public pensions as the population ages. However, in the provinces where mandatory retirement has been eliminated, older workers have not rushed en masse to continue toiling into their senior years. The average retirement age in Canada is 61 and while some Canadians will elect, or need, to work past normal retirement age, "Freedom Seventy-Five" is unlikely to hold mass appeal.

Sources: Ontario Ministry of Labour. (2004). "Ending Mandatory Retirement in Ontario," Backgrounder 04-92, August 18, http://www.gov.on.ca/LAB/english/news/2004/04-92b1.html; Kesselman, John. (2004). "Why Wasn't Mandatory Retirement Retired Long Ago?" *Globe and Mail*. Aug. 21, p. A15.

Direct versus Indirect Discrimination

Direct discrimination, intentionally distinguishing between employees based on a prohibited ground, has long been prohibited by human rights statutes. More insidious and difficult to address are practices and policies that do not directly differentiate; rather, they establish qualifications or set standards that have a disproportionately negative impact on members of a protected group. This **indirect** or **adverse effect discrimination** has come to be recognized as equally unacceptable and is prohibited in any aspect of employment. Thus, for example, establishing physical fitness standards that are not directly linked to job performance may be as prejudicial to women as expressly stating that they need not apply.[15] More recently, courts have abolished the distinction between direct and indirect discrimination and instead articulated a unified standard of review (Lynk, 2002).

Employers are not completely prohibited from establishing rules or standards that have the effect of differentiating between candidates on a prohibited ground; however, the rule or standard must be bona fide. In order to establish that a rule or standard is a bona fide occupational requirement or qualification (BFOR or BFOQ), an employer must demonstrate:

1. that the employer adopted the standard for a purpose rationally connected to the performance of the job;
2. that the employer adopted the particular standard in an honest and good faith belief that it was necessary to the fulfillment of that legitimate work purpose; and
3. that the standard is reasonably necessary to the accomplishment of that legitimate work-related purpose.[16]

Furthermore, the employer must also demonstrate that it would be impossible to accommodate individual members of protected groups without incurring undue hardship. Thus, members of protected groups must not bear the burden of a rule unless in the absence of that rule, the employer would bear an unreasonable burden.

Duty to Accommodate

Virtually all human rights statutes in Canada require employers and unions to make every reasonable effort to accommodate members of all protected groups, short of undue hardship (Lynk, 2002). In recent years, some of the most important developments in the area of human rights in employment have involved the duty to accommodate, especially as it relates to disabled employees. The most common issue is to what extent the workplace or workplace practices must be adapted before the point of undue hardship will be deemed to have been reached. While no formulae or thresholds are generically applicable, the courts have articulated a number of factors that will be considered:

- financial cost
- size of the employer's operations
- safety
- legitimate operational requirements of the workplace
- interchangeability of the workforce and facilities
- impact on the collective agreement, if one exists
- problems of employee morale[17]

Recently, the last two factors, the impact on the collective agreement and employee morale, have faded in importance. Collective agreement provisions,

direct discrimination Intentionally distinguishing between employees or job candidates based on a prohibited ground.

indirect (adverse effect) discrimination Occurs when an apparently neutral policy or practice has the effect of disproportionately disadvantaging members of a protected group.

including those involving seniority rights, are no longer considered sacrosanct.[18] Since employee morale is often influenced by discriminatory attitudes or misinformation, the more recent trend is to consider that undue hardship does not occur until the accommodation would substantially interfere with other employees' rights.[19]

Harassment Harassment is a form of discrimination that involves words, gestures, or actions that annoy or abuse (Black, 1983). Often the harassment is verbal, but not necessarily so. Sexual harassment is the most commonly recognized form and is described as

> any conduct, comment, gesture or contact of a sexual nature
> that is likely to cause offence or humiliation to any employee; or
> that might, on reasonable grounds, be perceived by that
> employee as placing a condition of a sexual nature on
> employment or on any opportunity for training or promotion.
> (*Canada Labour Code*, s.247.1)

Employers have a duty to do everything in their power to prevent harassment on any of the prohibited grounds and, where it occurs, to find the offenders and deal with them appropriately to minimize the likelihood of any recurrence. It is important to note that while employees are encouraged to identify behaviour they consider unwelcome, employers must take proactive steps to ensure that neither supervisors nor employees engage in behaviours that can reasonably be recognized as potentially offensive or unwelcome. The assumption is that hostility and offensive comments or conduct are inherently unwelcome; thus, an employee need not expressly or specifically identify such behaviours as offensive for there to be a violation of human rights. Furthermore, there is a growing recognition of harassment as a health and safety hazard that may contribute to a range of stress-related disorders—yet another reason to motivate employers to promote a healthy and tolerant workplace climate.

Remedies for Human Rights Violations Human rights are enforced through a process that first involves an officer of the commission or tribunal attempting to resolve the dispute and fashion a settlement that is acceptable to all parties. Should this fail, the dispute may be adjudicated before a tribunal or board of inquiry set up by the commission. Human rights commissions and tribunals have a broad range of remedies at their disposal. Their goal is to ensure the violation ceases and does not recur and to compensate employees for any losses they have incurred. Thus, they may order that employees be hired or reinstated, compensated for any quantifiable loss, or promoted to a position they were wrongfully denied. However, human rights commissions and tribunals generally also have a broader mandate and take a proactive role in promoting equality; thus, they may also order the employer to abandon discriminatory practices and adopt new policies, implement training programs, require that other employees be transferred or reassigned, and order proactive employment equity programs be implemented.

Case 6.1, at the end of this chapter, provides an example of the broad powers vested in human rights tribunals and commissions. However, it also illustrates the problem that threatens to render these agencies grossly ineffective. Protracted delays have come to be the norm, frustrating complainants and providing violators with a sense of impunity. One development has mitigated this problem for unionized workers: Recent court decisions have broadened the power of arbitrators to address alleged violations of employment-related statutes such as human rights legislation, thereby opening an alternate, more expedient, avenue of redress.[20] Non-unionized employees, however, must continue to rely upon the sluggish enforcement mechanisms of human rights commissions and tribunals.

Current Issues 6.2

WHAT YEAR IS THIS?

"The events you are about to read happened here, in Quebec, in the years 2000 and 2001," read the opening lines of a Quebec Human Rights Tribunal decision. The decision went on to describe the disgustingly squalid conditions endured by a group of 97 Haitian-born farm workers at one of Canada's largest commercial vegetable farms, the Centre Maraicher Eugene Guinois Jr, in Ste-Clotilde de Chateauguay, Quebec. What was even more astonishing was how dramatically these conditions contrasted with those provided for white workers at the farm.

It would have been shocking enough if the facts simply revealed that black workers were prohibited from entering the cafeteria designated as for white workers only. However, shock gave way to disbelief as evidence presented during the hearings revealed that while white workers enjoyed clean, modern, well-equipped cafeteria and restroom facilities, black workers were required to eat and change in a small, unheated, "green shack" that was never cleaned. The shack had no running water, no indoor toilets, no tables or benches, no lockers, and no hooks on which to hang clothing. The refrigerator did not work and the one functioning microwave was too dirty to use. Workers were forced to either sit on the shack's filthy floor to eat or use outdoor tables, even during inclement weather. The only available toilet facilities were poorly maintained outdoor chemical toilets and the only facility for washing was outdoor garden hoses. White foremen supervised white workers and black foremen supervised black workers. Black workers were told they were dirty and subjected to a barrage of racist invectives.

The evidence painted a picture of a racial divide so absolute and so extreme that it is incomprehensible it occurred in Canada in the years 2000 and 2001, rather than in South Africa during the apartheid regime. Yet, these conditions had persisted for years and, indeed, were only uncovered after the employer summarily dismissed four Haitian-born workers when one decided to leave after being victimized in a particularly offensive manner. The other three workers, who drove to and from work with this employee, obtained permission from their foreman to leave with him yet were fired two days later.

The four complainants were awarded a total of $62 500 in moral and punitive damages and the employer was ordered to immediately cease "all behaviour, speech, action, attitude [or] posting that constitutes discrimination or harassment based on race, colour and ethnic origin." In an almost surreal continuation of its ignorance, or perhaps arrogance, the employer applied for leave to appeal the Tribunal's decision claiming that the judge got the facts wrong: There were, in fact, clothes hooks in the "green shack."

Sources: Lancaster House. (2005). "Quebec Tribunal Condemns Segregation of Black Farm Workers," *Labour Law On-line*, May 12; *Quebec Human Rights and Youth Rights Commission v. Centre Maraicher Eugene Guinois Jr Inc.*, April 14, 2005.

Pay Equity

Through either their employment standards legislation or their human rights statute every Canadian jurisdiction prohibits paying women and men differently for performing substantially similar work for the same employer. On average, however, women still earn significantly less than their male counterparts. In 2003, women employed in Canada on a full-time, full-year basis earned 70.5 cents for every dollar earned by similarly employed males (Stats Can, 2005a), an abysmal increase of less than 11 percentage points in thirty years (Stats Can, 1995). Part of the problem lies in the method through which these provisions are enforced. Rather than requiring employers to perform an audit of their pay structures, it is left to employees to detect and file a complaint regarding pay discrepancies. A larger part of the problem, however, is that standard equal-pay provisions fail to address one of the most significant sources of the male-female pay gap: occupational segregation and the devaluation of women's work. Equal pay for work of equal value, or pay equity, seeks to address this source of pay discrimination through gender-neutral job evaluation systems that ensure female-dominated jobs are not paid less simply because of their gender composition.

Most jurisdictions have legislation that requires public sector employers to implement and maintain pay equity plans and two jurisdictions, Ontario and Quebec, also require this of private sector employers with at least 50 or 100 employees, respectively.[21] The federal jurisdiction utilizes a complaint-based process for achieving pay equity: The *Canadian Human Rights Act* prohibits differences in pay between male and female employees performing work of equal value (Mason et al., 2004). Nonetheless, the vast majority of Canadian private sector workers are not covered by any sort of requirement of equal pay for work of equal value.

Nor has pay equity legislation adequately remedied the situation for many public sector workers. No pay equity legislation of any sort exists in British Columbia, Alberta, or Saskatchewan. Even where legislation does exist, the fact that women tend to be segregated not only by occupation but also by industry has limited the effectiveness of pay equity analyses, which are performed on an employer-by-employer basis. In many instances, the employer has no male-dominated job classes that can be used for comparison purposes; only Ontario has addressed this shortcoming by permitting both proportional value methods of comparison and the proxy method of finding comparators.[22] In many instances, pay equity legislation explicitly permits employers to continue to perpetuate discriminatory pay systems for a period of time by limiting pay equity adjustments to predefined amounts such as, for example, one percent of the previous year's payroll.[23]

Although the limits on pay equity adjustments are less relevant now than when the legislation was first passed, a recent court decision affirmed the notion that financial exigencies trump women's right to equitable pay structures: The Supreme Court recently ruled that the government of Newfoundland's financial crisis justified violating the *Charter of Rights* by cancelling $24 million in pay-equity settlements it owed to provincial health care workers.[24] Even without such precedent-setting court decisions, however, the struggle to rectify discriminatory pay structures has been protracted and arduous. The pay equity complaint filed by the Public Service Alliance of Canada (PSAC) on behalf of 200 000 federal civil-service workers took

15 years of tribunal and court proceedings to resolve (England and Gad, 2002). Bell Canada's infamous legal wrangling to avoid paying up to $150 million in pay equity adjustments to workers, some of whom are owed up to $50 000, has dragged on for over a decade and is still not fully resolved.[25]

Employment Equity

Employment equity is another type of legislation designed to ameliorate discrimination in employment. Unlike pay equity, which specifically targets the undervaluation of women's work, employment equity targets four groups: women, Aboriginal people, people with disabilities, and visible minorities. Employment equity does not involve the imposition of specific hiring quotas (McPhillips and England, 1995). Rather, it mandates that employers undertake an analysis of their workforce to determine whether the proportion of target group members in their employ approximates their representation in the labour force. Employers are also required to audit their human resource practices to identify and eliminate sources of systemic discrimination and to implement proactive policies to achieve a representative workforce. Employers are not expected to assume undue hardship, create new positions, or hire or promote unqualified people. In fact, the opposite is true in that the audit of human resource policies is expected to uncover practices that overlooked or excluded qualified people.

The problem of lack of coverage that negates the effectiveness of pay equity applies even more so to employment equity. Ontario had employment equity legislation between September 1994 and December 1995 but it now only exists in Quebec and the federal jurisdiction (Mason et al., 2004). The federal *Employment Equity Act* applies to organizations that employ 100 or more employees on or in connection with a federal undertaking (Mason et al., 2004), while Quebec's legislation only applies to large public, municipal, educational, health and social service institutions.

Health and Safety Legislation

As Giles and Jain (2001:309) have aptly pointed out, "Work kills, maims, and sickens at a horrifying rate." For many, the seriousness of the situation with regard to occupational health and safety in Canadian workplaces was brought home by the 1992 Westray Mine disaster, in which 26 miners were killed in a coal mine explosion in Pictou County, Nova Scotia (Richard, 1997:I, vii). Judge Peter Richard, commissioner of the provincial board of inquiry looking into the causes of the tragedy, found "a complex mosaic of actions, omissions, mistakes, incompetence, apathy, cynicism, stupidity, and neglect," with a few "well-intentioned but misguided blunders" added to the mix (Richard, 1997:I, viii). Richard's report concluded that mine management disregarded critical safety factors and "appeared to regard safety-conscious workers as . . . wimps" (Richard, 1997:I, ix).

The issue of occupational health and safety is a complex one, as Judge Richard himself admits in his report. Many occupational accidents do not have any single or simple cause. Currently, over 900 Canadian workers each year die from work-related accidents or illness and one in 15 workers suffer a work-related injury (Ministry of

As the Westray Mine disaster demonstrated, unsafe working conditions remain a fact of life in far too many Canadian mining operations.

Labour, 2004; AWCBC, 2005). The toll on young, inexperienced workers has been especially high in recent years, prompting some governments, such as in Ontario and the federal jurisdiction, to launch Young Worker Awareness Programs specifically aimed at informing young workers about workplace hazards, their rights, and employers' obligations.

The Canadian approach to health and safety is twofold: prevention where possible, compensation where prevention fails (McPhillips, 2001; McPhillips and England, 1989:58). The two main preventive methods used are the "external system," whereby specified health and safety standards are established legislatively, and the "internal system," which mandates joint labour–management safety committees in virtually all Canadian jurisdictions[26] as a means of promoting safer workplace practices. The legislation is often contained in a specific health and safety statute applicable to all employers. It is sometimes supplemented by various statutes applicable to certain industries only and administered by different government departments (McPhillips and England, 1989).

The External System

There are two main components to the external system. The first is detailed laws, often geared to the circumstances of particular industries, compelling employers to operate in a safe manner. The second is a general "performance duty" imposed on both employers and workers, obliging them to promote health and safety at work (McPhillips and England, 1989). Safety legislation is often extremely detailed, specifying how many parts per million of a given substance may legally be discharged into the air or water or at what temperatures and under what conditions certain foods must be stored in restaurants. It also covers such issues as required sanitary facilities, the qualifications needed by workers to work in a given industry, and the manufacture and use of equipment. In some cases, it imposes specific obligations on workers, such as requiring that restaurant workers wash their hands after visiting the washroom or that construction workers wear hard hats on job sites. Legislation may also require training or successful completion of a test before workers are allowed to perform potentially hazardous work, such as operating certain types of heavy equipment or working on high construction scaffolds. In other cases, it requires periodic inspection of equipment, such as elevators.

Under the "performance duty," employers are obliged to ensure the health and safety of all workers on the site, whether they employ them or not. Employers are also obligated to notify the government of any serious accidents or illnesses that occur, as well as of any hazardous substances in use on the work site (McPhillips and England, 1989:58–59). Workers, for their part, are obliged to take reasonable care to protect their own health and safety and that of their co-workers while on the job. In some jurisdictions, the performance duty also confers an obligation on the suppliers of tools and equipment to ensure that the tools and equipment are in good condition and comply with the statutory safety standards (McPhillips and England, 1989:59).

Though external legislation has undoubtedly helped make Canadian workplaces safer than they would otherwise be, the system is far from perfect. Ultimately, any system of external legislation can only be as good as its enforcement mechanism. To suggest that health and safety legislation has typically been haphazardly enforced in Canada may be putting the matter charitably. In general, governments have preferred to accommodate employers rather than prosecute them for safety violations. Another problem is that inspectorates have been inadequately staffed, and inspectors have historically been reluctant to issue stop-work orders on large or politically sensitive projects, particularly those, like Westray Mines, backed by the provincial government, preferring to leave the hard decisions to their superiors. In recent years, provincial governments appear to have been taking a somewhat tougher line on chronic safety violators. Both in Ontario and elsewhere, the level of fines has increased. By the early 1990s, Ontario had begun to issue fines in excess of $10 000 in extreme cases, and criminal prosecutions, though rare, had occurred (McPhillips and England, 1995:93).

Another problem with health and safety regulation is that standards are not comprehensive, in that they fail to address a significant number of hazards that contribute to occupational injuries—a problem that becomes more serious all the time as new substances and equipment are introduced into Canadian workplaces. Still another problem is that the safety standards may be set too low to provide adequate protection against certain hazardous substances. As Edward Tucker (1986, in LLCG, 1991:1099–1100) points out, regulatory practice in Ontario has generally entailed bringing worst-practice firms in line with the industry average, thus serving to sanction existing exposure levels rather than improving them when new evidence suggests a tougher standard would be warranted. The main thrust of Ontario's regulatory concern is suggested, in Tucker's view, by the fact that the Labour Ministry has rarely selected standards that would lead to significant compliance costs for industry (Tucker, 1986, in LLCG, 1991).

A bill that came into effect in March 2004, may compensate for some of the shortcomings of provincial health and safety legislation. The *Westray Bill*, named in honour of the horrific explosion at the Westray mine, amended the *Criminal Code* of Canada to include the following:

> 217.1 Every one who undertakes, or has the authority, to direct how another person does work or performs a task is under a legal duty to take reasonable steps to prevent bodily harm to that person, or any other person, arising from that work or task.

This amendment extends responsibility for health and safety not just to committees but to virtually everyone in the workplace, including directors, officers, and managers. By articulating this responsibility in the *Criminal Code*, the bill increased the range of penalties for permitting unsafe working conditions to include not only significant fines but imprisonment and other remedies.

The Internal System

While external safety legislation is important, no legislation can cover every possible workplace situation. An important feature of Canada's health and safety system is, therefore, its "internal responsibility system," whereby management and labour both assume responsibility for workplace safety. A key assumption here is that prevention is more likely to occur when workers are actively participating in the process; the worker who operates a particular machine is often the one who best knows that machine's potential hazards and how to get around them (Swinton, 1983, in LLCG, 1991:1126). While the internal system is normally intended to work in tandem with the external one, Nova Scotia's health and safety act contains a unique provision stating that the internal system, encompassing all workplace parties, is the foundation upon which the act is based (CCH, 1998:551–1 to 551–2). The internal system's three major components, as outlined in Ontario's *Occupational Health and Safety Act*,[27] are joint health and safety committees, the right to refuse unsafe work, and the right to be informed about workplace hazards (CCH, 1998c:1125–1126).

Joint Committees Depending on the jurisdiction, joint worker–management health and safety committees are either mandatory, as is most common, or subject to ministerial discretion. Small workplaces, most commonly those employing fewer than 20 workers, are generally exempt from the requirement to form a committee and may instead have an individual health and safety representative. Committees are normally expected to be composed of between two and 12 members, at least half of whom must represent workers (Mason, et al., 2004). Usually they are required to meet at least once a month, though they are sometimes not required to do so more than quarterly. Their powers and functions are established through provincial legislation. In general, those powers are merely advisory, in that an employer cannot normally be forced to comply with a committee's recommendations unless mandated to do so by a government official (CCH, 1998c:1801). What the committee can do is call in a government inspector, who may issue a stop-work order or other directive if the work practice appears sufficiently dangerous. In most jurisdictions, employers are required to pay committee members for time spent preparing for and attending meetings and doing committee business (see CCH, 1998c:1922).

Committees are usually given a fair degree of latitude. In most jurisdictions, they have the power to handle employees' health and safety complaints, to establish health and safety training and education programs, to take part in health and safety–related inquiries and investigations, to access government and employers' reports relating to employees' health and safety at their work site, and to request any information necessary from an employer to identify existing or potential workplace safety hazards (CCH, 1998c). There is some variation in committees' functions in different jurisdictions. Under the *Canada Labour Code*, they are obliged to maintain records pertaining to the disposition of employees' health and safety complaints and to co-operate with any occupational health service established at the workplace. Other specific duties include accompanying government safety inspectors on "walkaround" inspections of work sites, investigating serious accidents, and helping to resolve work refusal cases (discussed in more detail below). In Quebec, committees have the additional responsibilities of designating a physician in charge of health services and working with the provincial Occupational Health and Safety Commission to develop recommendations for safe work practices (CCH, 1998c:1811).

A number of commentators (e.g., Bryce and Manga, 1985; McPhillips and England, 1989, 1995) have indicated that the presence of a joint committee seems to lead to a significant reduction in workplace injuries. Others, including Robert Sass (1993), a pioneer in introducing joint committees during the 1970s, have concluded that the committees are ineffectual. An obvious problem here is that many workplaces simply do not have committees. As McPhillips and England argue (1995:89), a minimum threshold of 20 employees may be too large, especially at a time when many jobs are in small and medium-sized businesses. A single representative may not be as effective as a committee in representing workers' health and safety interests—particularly a representative hand-picked by management. As well, it is generally recognized that committees need the active co-operation of top management if they are to operate effectively. While enlightened managers may be prepared to recognize that a strong health and safety committee is in their best interest, as well as their workers', not all managers are enlightened. Those opposed to committees may flout the law by simply refusing to establish one (McPhillips and England, 1989), by holding meetings infrequently, or by not granting the committee any budget or any real power.

Right to Refuse Unsafe Work A key component of any internal safety system is allowing workers the right to refuse any work they honestly consider unsafe, pending an investigation by a neutral third party, normally a provincial health and safety inspector. This right is granted to workers in all Canadian jurisdictions. Most jurisdictions require "reasonable" grounds or the "likelihood" of risk; in Alberta and Newfoundland, the right is more narrowly applied to situations of imminent or immediate danger (McPhillips and England, 1995:91). In most jurisdictions, anyone refusing unsafe work must formally report the situation to management (CCH, 1998c:601). Under the *Canada Code*, the worker must also notify the health and safety committee or representative where no committee exists. If management intervention fails to resolve the situation, the next step is for either the worker or employer[28] to notify a government safety inspector (CCH, 1998c). If the safety inspector upholds the worker's decision, she or he can continue to stay off work until the situation is corrected to the inspector's satisfaction; otherwise the employee must return to work. The one major exception, under both the *Canada Code* and provincial legislation, is that no one can refuse to work where the refusal would put someone else's life, health, or safety directly in danger (CCH, 1998c:1315). In some cases (police or correctional services work, for instance), a certain amount of risk is assumed to "come with the territory."

Though workers in most jurisdictions run the risk of loss of pay if no alternative work is available to them after a refusal, the worker is normally protected from discharge or other disciplinary action for exercising a legal right to refuse work under the health and safety act (CCH, 1998c:1316), providing the worker has duly notified the employer and, where appropriate, a government inspector. However, several studies (i.e., LLCG, 1984:4–359; McPhillips and England, 1989:62) find that, at least in Ontario, the vast majority of refusals to work occurred in unionized settings. Failure to exercise the legal right to refuse work in non-unionized settings could result from a fear of employer reprisal, simple ignorance of the law, or both. Whatever the reasons, the evidence suggests that unions have an important role to play in ensuring the adequate enforcement of safety legislation. It also suggests the need for stronger mechanisms to protect non-unionized workers, such as the equivalent of a dismissal grievance procedure in cases where a refusal to work triggered the dismissal.

Notification of Hazardous Materials (WHMIS) The third but far from least important component of the internal system is the right to know (Swinton, 1983), specifically, the right to be informed about the actual or potential danger posed by various hazardous substances that may be used in the workplace. Each jurisdiction has its own Workplace Hazardous Materials Information System (WHMIS) provisions. Under the federal *Hazardous Products Control Act*, suppliers are required to classify the products they sell according to the amount of risk entailed in handling those products. They are also required to provide appropriate labels that will enable workers to tell at a glance what kind of substance they are working with (CCH, 1998c:60, 560). These labels must include the product's brand or generic name, that of the supplier, appropriate hazard symbols indicating the type of hazard potentially posed by the product, information on how to handle the product safely, and any appropriate first-aid measures (CCH, 1998c). Material safety data sheets (MSDSs) must provide detailed descriptions of the product's chemical composition, any hazardous ingredients it contains, its fire or explosion hazard, its toxicological properties, and appropriate preventive and first-aid measures (CCH, 1998c:60, 820).

For their part, employers must ensure that controlled substances are labelled, must obtain and distribute material safety data sheets, and must educate workers about any hazardous substance used or produced at the workplace (CCH, 1998c:100). They are also required to provide workers and supervisors with a copy of the regulations (McPhillips and England, 1995:92). Under Ontario's law and that of most other jurisdictions, trade secrets can be exempted from WHMIS regulations. In Ontario (CCH, 1998c:14, 700), employers may apply to the Hazardous Materials Information Review Commission for an exemption for information contained on a label or MSDS that they believe to be confidential business information. However, even if the exemption is granted, the confidential information must be released to a doctor in a medical emergency (CCH, 1998c).

Workers' Compensation

Workers' compensation legislation is the major mechanism used to compensate the victims of workplace accidents or work-induced illness.[29] Normally, **workers' compensation** is under the control of a provincial board whose primary responsibilities are to collect levies from employers and pay benefits to disabled workers. The basic principle of the system is that it is "no-fault." This means that a worker need not prove employer negligence to be eligible for benefits, but workers are precluded from seeking further remedies through the courts. To be eligible for benefits, the worker must have suffered an accident or disease that arose out of and during the course of employment, disabled him or her beyond the day of the accident, and was not the result of his or her own willful misconduct, except in cases of death or serious disablement (CCH, 1998c:15.403).

Funds used to pay compensation benefits are drawn from a levy on employers, based on the nature of the industry and the size of the employer's wage bill (McPhillips and England, 1995:94). In high-risk industries, employers pay higher rates than in low-risk ones. In the past (see McPhillips and England, 1989), the tax was based on the number of claims filed by the industry as a whole. Such a system may actually have served as a disincentive to safe practice, since conscientious employers who did their best to maintain safe workplaces were forced to pay the same amount of tax as laggard or negligent ones. To correct this problem, most jurisdictions now use a system of "experience rating" whereby employers whose claims are above the industry average must pay higher premiums (CCH, 1998c:15,103), while those with good safety records pay less.

workers' compensation A no-fault insurance system paid for collectively by employers and governed by legislation in each jurisdiction that compensates workers in the event of work-related illnesses and injuries.

A RAPIDLY CHANGING FIELD

Unlike labour relations legislation, which has seen few major changes over the past 25 years, employment legislation has been changing constantly throughout most of that period. Human rights legislation, pay equity and employment equity, and joint health and safety committees are but a few of the more important innovations. Generally, the legislative changes have, from the workers' perspective, been positive, in that they have provided additional protections against discrimination and poor working conditions, although this has not always been the case. The fragmentation of Canadian employment law jurisdictions has facilitated evolution and experimentation, as provinces monitor the changes implemented in other jurisdictions before deciding whether to follow suit. For example, in an emerging area of employment law, workplace privacy rights, British Columbia seems to have blazed the trail. Other jurisdictions have only more recently turned their focus to this area.

Despite employment legislation's generally progressive evolution, there remain some serious concerns. First, despite the *Charter of Rights and Freedoms*, which has now been in force for about 20 years, many individuals and groups of workers continue to be excluded from even basic protection, particularly under employment standards legislation. Second, enforcement mechanisms have not only failed to keep pace with the evolution of new legislation; they have proved inadequate to enforce existing legislation. Among the most damning evidence is the extreme rarity with which the right to refuse unsafe work appears to be exercised in non-unionized establishments. Similarly, while human rights and other types of equity legislation have improved the lot of women, Aboriginal people, the disabled, and visible minorities, discrimination in employment, as well as in other aspects of our society, remains a tenacious fact of life. Finally, globalization and freer trade continue to challenge Canada's ability to enforce standards of employment that have evolved within the structure and affluence of Canadian society. The challenge for policy makers will be to balance the need for Canada's employers to remain flexible and competitive while ensuring that the benefits and protections of Canadian employment legislation are equitably extended to all Canadian workers.

Case 6.1

THE PROTRACTED BATTLE TO REMEDY OUTRAGEOUS DISCRIMINATION

Mike McKinnon began his employment as a corrections officer at the Metro Toronto East Detention Centre in 1977. He proved to be a dedicated, conscientious and meticulous employee, who received excellent performance reviews but who encountered difficulties with specific supervisors and co-workers who insulted and teased him due to his Native Canadian descent. Mike tolerated being referred to as "Chief," "Wagon Burner," "McInjun," "Geronimo," "Tomahawk," "Running Bear," "Crazy Horse," and "Big Canoe." McKinnon's wife, a correctional officer in the same facility, was referred to as "squaw." Co-workers posted caricatures of McKinnon and, on one occasion, a supervisor distributed feather headbands that were worn by co-workers when they greeted McKinnon with war whoops. Finally, McKinnon could tolerate the abuse no longer; in 1988 he filed a complaint with the Ontario Human Rights Commission, followed by another complaint in 1990, and a third complaint in 1992.

Forty-five days of hearings were held between February 1996 and October 1997; finally, in April of 1998, a board of inquiry found that the Detention Centre had violated McKinnon's right to equal treatment without discrimination because of race and permitted "a climate that was redolent with racist behaviour." The harassment and reprisal McKinnon suffered violated the Ontario Human Rights Code and he was awarded $20 000 in damages as well as compensation for salary lost due to stress-related leave. The Ministry of Correctional Services was ordered to award both McKinnon and his wife promotions the Ministry had told them they were denied because of his human rights complaint and to pay them the difference between the salaries they did earn and what they would have earned had they not been denied the promotions. The Ministry was also ordered to transfer one manager and ensure that neither he, nor the other managers who had participated in the abuse, were ever assigned to the same facility as McKinnon. The Ministry was also required to implement human rights training within six months and to read aloud the board of inquiry's orders at daily parade for five days.

Upon his return to work, McKinnon found that little had changed. The poisoned atmosphere continued unabated and he solicited the assistance of the board of inquiry to enforce and expand their redress. The Ministry of Correctional Services, however, argued that the incidents McKinnon complained of were new and necessitated the filing of new complaints. In 1999 the board rejected the Ministry's submission and the Ministry responded by applying for judicial review of the board's decision. Two years later, in 2001, the Ministry's application was dismissed. Another year and a half passed before the board of inquiry released their decision regarding McKinnon's request for additional remedies.

In its November 2002 decision, the board found that the Ministry had failed to comply with many aspects of the original order and the adjudicator, Albert Hubbard, stated:

> Having found that the orders have not been complied with, that the atmosphere of the Centre remains poisoned, that the complainant has suffered post-decision harms similar to those identified in the 1998 decision, I am obviously called upon to do something about it. In my opinion, since the Ministry failed to implement the original order, the authority I have under s. 41(1)(a) of the Code to direct it to do anything that, in my opinion, it ought to do "to achieve compliance with this Act in respect of the complaint and in respect of future practices" remains operative; and it is incumbent upon me to exercise it. In doing so I must address the root causes of the "problem at Metro East," the most critical of which continues to be "the indifference, ineptitude and bad faith of management at all levels" in dealing with race-based complaints and WDHP matters generally, and I must do so far more carefully, directly, and comprehensively than was done in the 1998 orders. Whether this process is described as "the crafting of new orders," or the generous amplification of existing orders, seems to me unimportant (para. 238).

In addition to remedies pertaining to the Toronto East Detention Centre, the board ordered Ministry-wide remedies including implementation of the recommendations of an external report urging a long list of system-wide changes designed to create an effective and accountable system for the investigation and handling of complaints. The board also ordered that the Deputy Minister, Assistant Deputy Ministers, Regional Directors, and senior management of the ministry attend training and that their compliance with the board's orders be included as a component of their performance appraisals.

Rather than complying with the orders, the Ministry again sought judicial review. When the Ontario Divisional Court dismissed their application in December of 2003, McKinnon could not be blamed for thinking the protracted battle was finally over. However, the Ministry appealed the court's decision. Finally, on December 12, 2004, the Ontario Court of Appeal found that the Ministry did not act in good faith in attempting to comply with the board's original order and endorsed the Divisional Court's view that "it was open to the Tribunal, as part of its ongoing obligation to oversee implementation, to recast its original orders to meet what it found to be a continuing problem." The decision breaks new ground in empowering tribunals to police their own orders, especially in cases where employers persistently demonstrate bad faith.

As for Mike McKinnon, the decision has yet to make a significant difference in his life. Both he and his wife remain on paid leave, although they both hope the day will soon come when they can return to work without fear of racism.

Sources: *McKinnon v. Ontario (Ministry of Correctional Services)* [1996] O.H.R.B.I.D. No. 13; [1997] O.H.R.B.I.D. No. 12; [1998] O.H.R.B.I.D. No. 10; [1999] O.H.R.B.I.D. No. 3; [2001] O.H.R.B.I.D. No. 22; [2001] O.H.R.B.I.D. No. 26; [2002] O.H.R.B.I.D. No. 22; Lancaster House. (2005). "Racism in Ontario's Jails: Court Upholds Sweeping Human Rights," *Labour Law On-line*, Jan. 5, www.lancasterhouse.com.

Case Questions

1. What is meant by a "poisoned work environment"?

2. Even though Mike tolerated the taunts of his co-workers, what actions should managers at Metro Toronto East Detention Centre have taken to ensure he was not harassed?

3. How can managers differentiate between harassment and good-natured teasing?

4. Using examples and facts from this case, describe two important problems regarding the enforcement of human rights legislation. What suggestions do you have for ameliorating these problems?

QUESTIONS FOR DISCUSSION

1. Outline the protections against unjust dismissal—including the avenues of redress and remedies—that are available to employees under each of the employment law regimes.

2. Why does a developed country like Canada need a network of statutes to provide minimum terms and conditions of employment? Shouldn't the labour market be allowed to operate freely to establish these standards through the forces of supply and demand?

3. In an increasingly global economy, Canadian labour standards may detract from the competitiveness of Canadian employers. To what degree should global market conditions be permitted to influence Canadian labour standards?

4. Most jurisdictions' legislation and regulations are readily available on-line. Visit the website of the Canadian Legal Information Institute (CanLII) at www.canlii.org or any other site that provides access to e-laws. Review the

regulations that accompany your jurisdiction's employment or labour standards legislation and list the types of workers who are either fully or partially excluded from coverage.

5. Discuss the three types of legislation aimed at ensuring equity in employment in Canada. Why don't more jurisdictions pass pay equity and employment equity legislation and why have these types of legislation been primarily confined to the public sector?

6. What is a bona fide occupational qualification (BFOQ)? List as many situations as you can think of where it would be legitimate to distinguish between job applicants based on protected grounds. Now consider how you might reasonably accommodate these job applicants. How many of your BFOQs are truly legitimate?

7. Explain the external and internal systems for regulating occupational health and safety. What role do joint committees play within the latter?

8. How does workers' compensation operate within most Canadian jurisdictions? What are some problems with it?

Suggestions for Further Reading

Block, Richard N., Karen Roberts, and R. Oliver Clarke. (2003). *Labor Standards in the United States and Canada.* Kalamazoo, MI: W.E. Upjohn Institute for Employment Research. Presents a new method for comparing labour standards across jurisdictions and uses this to compare labour standards in the United States and Canada. An important contribution to the debate regarding the impact of labour standards on a country's international competitiveness.

Eden, Genevieve. (1993). "Industrial Discipline in the Canadian Federal Jurisdiction," *Relations Industrielles* 48:1. A study of adjudication of dismissal grievances in the federal jurisdiction that suggests that experience under this system is roughly comparable to that under grievance arbitration in unionized establishments.

Fudge, Judy, and Leah F. Vosko. (2001). "By Whose Standards? Reregulating the Canadian Labour Market," *Economic and Industrial Democracy* 22:3, pp. 327–356. Offers a critical analysis of labour law and policy, given both the increasing participation of women in the workforce and the proliferation of non-standard forms of employment. The authors argue convincingly for an approach that embraces gender equity as a fundamental objective in regulation of the employment relationship and public policy design.

Richard, K. Peter (Commissioner). (1997). *The Westray Story: A Predictable Path to Disaster.* No place of publication given: Province of Nova Scotia. Not for the faint of heart! A chilling indictment of Westray management's callous disregard for workers' safety, and the Nova Scotia government's appalling lack of political will in enforcing its own legislation.

CHAPTER 7

COLLECTIVE BARGAINING LEGISLATION

Union and management representatives meeting with a conciliator from the Ministry of Labour. Compulsory conciliation has been a prominent feature of Canadian labour legislation since the early years of this century.

LEARNING OBJECTIVES

After studying this chapter, you should be able to:

1. Explain the need for and purpose of collective bargaining legislation.
2. Identify common features and major functions of collective bargaining legislation.
3. Compare and contrast card majority and mandatory vote certification procedures.
4. Identify the appropriate agencies and processes for resolution of labour relations disputes.
5. Describe how Quebec's collective bargaining legislation is distinctive from that of other provinces.

Collective bargaining, or labour relations, legislation is of pivotal importance in any industrial relations system. It addresses such issues as how a union can become certified, when a strike or lockout may legally occur, and what constitutes an unfair labour practice. In this chapter, we start by considering the need for regulation of union–management relations and take a brief look at the development of collective bargaining legislation in Canada. Next, we examine some of the common features of Canadian collective bargaining legislation and go on to explain its major functions, including certification and decertification of trade unions. The final sections of the chapter briefly highlight Quebec's special system of legislation and the major differences between the collective bargaining systems in Canada and the United States. Note that, in this chapter, we generally confine ourselves to private sector collective bargaining legislation. Public sector legislation is considered in the next chapter.

THE NEED FOR REGULATION

Regardless of which perspective on the employment relationship one holds (see Chapter 1), history and experience confirm that there will inevitably exist some conflicts between the interests of workers and their employers and that these conflicts will eventually manifest in one form or another. The question is not whether there will be conflict; it is rather what form it will take (see Hebdon and Stern, 1998; Godard, 2005). In the absence of legislation regulating industrial conflict or protecting workers' right to join unions, labour disputes may take on the character of pitched class warfare (see Kervin, 1984). Through the nineteenth century and most of the first half of the twentieth, as the labour history chapter shows, this kind of clash was far too common. It has remained common, even in the post-war period, in countries where governments fail to legitimate industrial conflict or accept workers' right to organize and bargain collectively.[1]

Recognizing the inevitability of conflict between labour and the owners of capital, labour relations legislation serves to suppress, control, and focus conflict so as to strike an appropriate balance between the rights and interests of both parties and ensure stability of labour–management relations and indeed of the capitalist system as a whole. (See Current Issues 7.1.) Thus regulated and with severe limits put on unfair practices by either side, labour disputes become less like class warfare and focus instead on specific issues such as the terms and conditions of employment or the level of employee support for unionization, rather than on more intractable issues such as the union's right to exist (see Kervin, 1984). In most cases, employers and unions are able to maintain reasonably effective long-term working relationships despite occasional disputes. Most conflict will eventually be resolved through collective bargaining, strikes, lockouts, and other activities of the IR system (Barbash, 1984). Indeed, there are those (e.g., Dubin, 1959) who would argue that conflict comes to play an essentially constructive role, once it has been regulated and limited by labour relations legislation.

Another important rationale for labour relations legislation and the collective bargaining it supports is the opportunity the latter provides for a degree of worker input into management decisions. As Paul Weiler (1980:29–32) notes, under collective bargaining, "[m]anagement must spell out its workplace rules; employees must be given a vehicle for collectively voicing their objections when their rights seem to be under siege." To Weiler, such an exercise is of value in and of itself, above and beyond the superior economic results it is likely to produce when compared to what most individual workers could likely obtain through individual negotiations with their employers.

To be sure, not everyone would agree with Weiler's positive assessment of collective bargaining. Over the years, it has often been criticized from both the right and the left. Neoclassicists like Milton Friedman (1962, in LLCG, 2004) see unions as an intrusion on individuals' freedom to choose. Managerialists (discussed in Freeman and Medoff, 1979, in LLCG, 1991) primarily resent the loss of control unions represent to employers and managers. On the left, reformists such as David Beatty (1983, in LLCG, 2004) criticize collective bargaining for leading to a tyranny of the majority, which takes little, if any, account of the needs of the "worst-off" classes in industrial society, such as domestics and farm workers. Further left, radicals such as Leo Panitch and Donald Swartz (1988, in LLCG, 2004) suggest that "free collective bargaining" is pretty much an oxymoron, given the coercive way in which the state has used its power in recent years, and its pronounced bias towards capital and business interests throughout the post-war period.

Despite these and other criticisms, such as the belief that unions gave away too much by giving away the right to strike during the life of the agreement (see Adell, 1988a), most Canadians, inside the labour movement and out, would probably agree that labour relations legislation and collective bargaining have helped produce a society in which workers are economically better off and have more workplace rights than those of their grandparents' generation. Imperfect though the Canadian system of collective bargaining legislation doubtless is, most believe that both workers and Canadian society as a whole are better served with it than they would be without it.

THE EVOLUTION OF CANADIAN COLLECTIVE BARGAINING LEGISLATION

As we noted in the labour history chapter, Canada was slow to develop collective bargaining and to pass collective bargaining legislation. Indeed, Canada was among the last industrialized countries to grant private sector workers the right to join a union, doing so only in 1944, several decades later than countries such as Sweden and Denmark, and almost a decade later than the United States.[2] In the case of Canadian public sector workers, most of whom did not receive full bargaining rights until the late 1960s or early 1970s, the lag was generally even greater. Among the major reasons for the slow evolution of unionism and collective bargaining in Canada were the country's comparatively late industrialization; its linguistically, regionally, and religiously fragmented labour movement; determined employer opposition; and a particularly unsympathetic federal government. Table 7.1 offers a brief synopsis of significant milestones in the evolution of Canadian collective bargaining legislation. Chapter 3 covers this history in much greater detail.

The Impact of the Charter

Chapter 3 details the evolution of Canadian collective bargaining legislation up to the late 1960s when public sector bargaining legislation was enacted. Since then,

Table 7.1

CANADIAN COLLECTIVE BARGAINING LEGISLATION: SIGNIFICANT MILESTONES

Year	Legislation/Decision	Effect
1872	*Trade Union Act*	Declared that the purposes of unions were not to be considered unlawful simply because they might be in restraint of trade.
1907	*Industrial Disputes Investigation Act*	Required all workers and employers in transportation, resources, and utilities industries to submit their disputes to a three-person conciliation board before starting a strike or lockout. Even after the board had issued its report, a further "cooling-off" period was required before any strike or lockout could become legal.
1925	*Toronto Electric Commissioners v. Snider*	Determined labour relations to be a matter that falls within the jurisdiction of provincial governments as outlined in the British North American Act and, in the absence of a national emergency, that division of powers must be respected.
1944	*Wartime Labour Relations Regulations,* or *PC 1003*	First Canadian collective bargaining legislation. Established process for union certification, prohibited certain employer practices, and established a labour board to administer and enforce the statute.
1946	Rand Formula	Justice Ivan Rand established the union security formula that compels employees in the bargaining unit to pay union dues but does not require that they join the union.
1948	*Industrial Relations and Disputes Investigation Act*	Collective bargaining legislation for federal jurisdiction, private sector. Later became the *Canada Labour Code.*
1944–1950	Various pieces of provincial private sector legislation	Provinces pass their own private sector collective bargaining legislation, generally following the "Wagner" model adopted in *PC 1003.*
1967	*Public Service Staff Relations Act* (PSSRA)	Legalized collective bargaining for federal public sector workers. Gave the union the right to choose between binding arbitration and the conventional conciliation-strike route of resolving disputes.
1944–1975	Various pieces of provincial public sector legislation	Legalized collective bargaining for provincial public sector workers.

Current Issues 7.1

RESTORING FAIRNESS AND BALANCE

Ontario Ministry of Labour
News Release
Communiqué

05-78

For Immediate Release
June 13, 2005

ONTARIO'S WORKPLACES RETURN TO BALANCED LABOUR RELATIONS
Labour Relations Statute Law Amendment Act, 2005 Receives Royal Assent

TORONTO—Bill 144, the Labour Relations Statute Law Amendment Act, 2005, restoring fairness and balance to the province's labour relations system, has received Royal assent and is now law.

"Since 1990, our labour laws have swung unfairly in favour of either employees or employers," said Labour Minister, Chris Bentley. "We have restored the traditional balance so all Ontarians can have equal confidence in our laws. This will contribute to the harmony and stability in the workplace that are vital for a prosperous, productive economy."

The Labour Relations Statute Law Amendment Act, 2005:

- Eliminates measures that promote unhealthy working relationships among employers and employees in Ontario. For example, employers will no longer be required to post de-certification information in all unionized workplaces, and unions will not have to disclose the name, salary and benefits of all directors, officers and employees earning $100,000 or more a year.

- Supports democracy by restoring to the Ontario Labour Relations Board (OLRB) the power to remedy the worst labour relations conduct by either side during an organizing drive, when that conduct effectively removes the workers' right to choose. For example, the OLRB will now be able—as a last resort—to grant union certification when an employer violates labour laws, or dismiss a certification application when a union violates the law.

- Re-establishes a card-based certification system for the construction sector in addition to the existing vote system. The card-based system will permit automatic union certification in the construction sector if more than 55 per cent of employees sign cards to join a union.

- Prevents consecutive strikes from paralyzing the homebuilding industry, as happened in 1998. The legislation makes permanent the special bargaining and dispute resolution regime set up in 2001 for residential construction in the Toronto area.

"Through these amendments, we are restoring fairness and we are restoring balance," said Bentley. "We are reasserting the principles that served as the foundation for Ontario's prosperity for decades, setting the stage for future prosperity." ▶

As this press release demonstrates, when regulating collective bargaining, governments attempt to balance the interests of employers and workers in order to facilitate the type of labour–management relationships conducive to economic stability and prosperity. Exactly how best to strike that balance is a matter of considerable debate. Social democratic or more liberal governments tend to enact amendments to collective bargaining legislation that offer relatively more support for workers who wish to access unionization and collective bargaining, as did the Ontario New Democratic Party in 1993. Amendments passed by conservative governments, such as those passed in Ontario in 1995, when the provincial Conservatives swung the pendulum in the opposite direction, tend to offer relatively more reverence for market forces and owners of capital. The Ontario Liberal government, author of the amendments referred to above, arguably aims for the middle ground.

Sources: Ontario Ministry of Labour. (2005). "Ontario's Workplaces Return to Balanced Labour Relations." OML website, News Releases, News Release Communiqué: 05-78, June 13, http://www.labour.gov.on.ca/english/news/2005/ 05-78.html, [Oct. 8, 2005]. © Queen's Printer for Ontario, 2005. Reprinted with permission.

apart from the politicization of collective bargaining legislation and the trend toward amendments that tend to favour the interests of employers rather than unions and employees, Canadian collective bargaining legislation has seen few important changes and no fundamental ones. This is not what most would have predicted following the enactment of the *Canadian Charter of Rights and Freedoms* in 1982. Many observers believed that the Charter would significantly affect the fundamental balance between legislatures and courts (see Carter, 1995). Some, notably David Beatty (1987; also Beatty and Kennett, 1988), thought the effect would be positive, as the courts used the Charter to strike down unjust labour laws. Others feared that unions would be the losers, faring less well before the courts than before labour boards, whose activities the courts might now severely circumscribe; this would have reversed a long-term trend towards granting more power to labour boards and less to the courts (Arthurs, 1988; see also Carter, 1982).

Neither the enthusiasts' hopes nor the skeptics' fears have been realized. The Charter's overall effect on Canadian labour relations might best be described as underwhelming. In the 1980s, a trilogy of Supreme Court cases[3] in which unions argued that the Charter's guarantees of freedom of association and expression entrenched workers' rights to unionize, strike, and picket were decided "with the score of management *three*, labour *nil*" (Arthurs, 2005:4). Another 1980s case saw a union member who objected to the union using funds for political purposes unsuccessfully challenge the constitutional legitimacy of the Rand formula.[4] Thus, although the labour trilogy decisions were extensively criticized by jurists and academic scholars (Arthurs, 2005), in general courts were reluctant to use the Charter to reshape the IR system (Carter, 1995:70; Swinton, 1995).

Recently a second trilogy of cases that on first reading all appear to forge new ground for labour turn out, upon closer examination, to continue the Supreme Court's reluctance to do anything that will alter the status quo; these decisions, in fact, do little more than place a requirement on legislatures to provide justification for the restriction of labour rights (Arthurs, 2005). The three decisions respectively upheld Quebec's requirement for compulsory union membership in the construction sector,[5] reversed a long-standing characterization of secondary picketing as illegal per se,[6] and struck down Ontario's wholesale exclusion of agricultural workers from collective bargaining legislation[7] (see Current Issues 7.2). The Supreme Court, however, declined to positively affirm labour rights; rather, it "instructed legislatures to carefully balance labour's Charter rights against economic exigency, public safety and private rights of property, person and reputation" (Arthurs, 2005; 4–5). Time will tell whether a recently launched Charter challenge will break new ground: the Canadian Union of Postal Workers and The Council of Canadians' Charter Committee on Poverty Issues[8] contend that the investment rules of the North American Free Trade Agreement (NAFTA) that empower foreign investors to challenge the actions of Canadian governments are unconstitutional on the grounds that they undermine the independence of Canadian courts and infringe rights and freedoms guaranteed by the Charter.

Current Issues 7.2

LABOUR'S CONSTITUTIONAL RIGHTS?

While workers' rights to unionize, bargain collectively, and go on strike were not formally entrenched in the *Canadian Charter of Rights and Freedoms,* many hoped that the courts would nonetheless use the Charter's guarantees of freedom of association and expression to protect and extend these basic rights. One recent Supreme Court decision, *Dunmore v. Ontario (Attorney General),* appeared to do just that when it ruled Ontario's complete exclusion of agricultural workers from collective bargaining legislation was unconstitutional in that it substantially interfered with agricultural workers' freedom to organize. The court recognized that unionization might be incompatible with the needs of a family farm but held that the continued exclusion of all agricultural workers was not justifiable, in part because it ignored the trend toward large corporate farms.

However, the Ontario Conservative government read between the lines of the decision, which at one point read, "I neither require nor forbid the inclusion of agricultural workers in a full collective bargaining scheme," and in response passed Bill 187 to create the euphemistically named *"Agricultural Employees Protection Act, 2002."* This act permits workers' associations but outlaws striking, and compels employers to do no more than receive and acknowledge workers' representations regarding terms and conditions of employment. It has been challenged by the United Food and Commercial Workers as a continued denial of agricultural workers' freedom of association.

Sources: *Dunmore v. Ontario (Attorney General)*, (2001) 207 D.LR. (4th) 193; quoting para 68.

COMMON FEATURES OF CANADIAN COLLECTIVE BARGAINING LEGISLATION

Legislative Fragmentation

To those familiar with other industrial relations systems, the most notable feature of the Canadian system of collective bargaining legislation is its extreme fragmentation. Unlike the situation prevailing in the United States, where private sector labour law is under federal jurisdiction, most Canadian workers fall under provincial jurisdiction, thanks to a British Privy Council decision in the 1925 Snider case (discussed in Chapter 3), which placed labour relations in the provinces' constitutional domain. As a result, each province has had to pass its own private sector labour relations act as well as various pieces of legislation governing their public sector workers.

The exceptions to the general pattern of provincial jurisdiction are workers in federal crown corporations; enterprises of an interprovincial or international nature, such as railways, airlines, interprovincial trucking, shipping, and telecommunications companies; the chartered banks; and works declared by Parliament to be of general advantage to Canada or to two or more provinces, such as uranium mining and grain elevators (HRSDC, 2005a). These workers, who together make up about 10 percent of the country's workforce, are governed by the *Canada Labour Code*. Federal government employees fall under the *Public Service Labour Relations Act*; provincial government employees and most other public sector workers, such as teachers and nurses, fall under a broad array of provincial public sector laws, which we discuss in the next chapter.

In all, there are several dozen different pieces of labour relations legislation in effect in Canada. Such extreme legislative fragmentation poses a number of difficulties, not least of which is the simple confusion of keeping all these laws straight (Carter, 1995). As well, provincial jurisdiction has definitely contributed to the emergence of a highly decentralized bargaining structure (see Anderson, 1982; Rogow, 1989a), for example, by making it more difficult for an industry to conduct negotiations at the national level (Carter, 1995). Given that Canada's decentralized bargaining structure has often been implicated as a cause of its relatively high incidence of strikes, the implications of provincial jurisdiction may be more profound than many realize. Moreover, in an economy where both labour and product markets are national or international, provincial autonomy may be little more than illusory. Indeed, it has been argued that Canada's global competitiveness may be better served by a system that could facilitate a national labour strategy (Arthurs, 2005). On the positive side, decentralization decreases the risk associated with policy experimentation and promotes innovation and change (Carter, 1995:56) as was the case with the many new dispute resolution procedures introduced in British Columbia while Paul Weiler (1980) was head of that province's labour board and which later spread to several other provinces.[9]

Majoritarianism and Exclusivity

The twin principles of majoritarianism and exclusivity apply democratic governance standards to the workplace. They require that the wishes of the majority determine outcomes such as whether workers will be represented by a union, go on strike, or ratify a collective agreement and that the union selected by the majority will be the exclusive representative for all employees in that group. A corollary to these twin principles is the prohibition of either individual bargains between employers and **bargaining unit** employees or bargains made between the employer and any trade union other than the one democratically chosen by that group of workers (Carter, England, Etherington, and Trudeau, 2002; LLCG, 2004).

bargaining unit The group of employees for which a trade union is certified or voluntarily recognized to act as the exclusive bargaining agent.

Right to Bargain for Union Security Provisions

Given their status as the exclusive bargaining agent, certified or voluntarily recognized unions have the right under Canadian collective bargaining legislation to bargain for provisions that protect their financial security and eliminate the problem of **free riders** (Carter et al., 2002:288–289). Several jurisdictions[10] mandate that should a bargaining agent request that the Rand formula, which requires the employer to deduct union dues from all employees in the bargaining unit and submit those dues to the union, be included in the collective agreement, the employer is obliged to comply. The formula is named after Supreme Court Justice Ivan Rand, who developed and applied the formula in 1946 while acting as arbitrator following a 100-day strike at the Ford Motor Company. Some jurisdictions simply require the employer to honour employees' written authorizations to deduct union dues. Saskatchewan is the only jurisdiction that requires employers to agree to **union shop** arrangements that not only require the employer to deduct union dues but also mandate that all employees maintain union membership as a condition of employment. Since joining or paying dues to a union violates some religious beliefs, the collective bargaining legislation in some[11] jurisdictions balances religious freedoms with the need to protect against free riders by exempting religious objectors from union membership as a condition of employment and permitting them to direct their union dues to a recognized charity (Carter et al., 2002:289).

The Duty of Fair Representation

The right to be the exclusive representative of all employees in the bargaining unit is balanced by the union's obligation to represent all employees fairly, non-arbitrarily and in a non-discriminatory manner. This **duty of fair representation** (DFR) addresses the paradox that arises from the twin principles of majoritarianism and exclusivity: "the need to protect individuals from the collective sanctioned to act on their behalf" (Bentham, 1991:2). The duty was first articulated in the context of racial discrimination through a 1944 United States Supreme Court ruling[12] and has since been statutorily imposed in most jurisdictions in Canada. In five jurisdictions[13] the statutory obligation applies only to unions' representational duties with respect to employee rights that arise out of an existent collective agreement. The statutes in Ontario, Quebec, and British Columbia explicitly extend this responsibility to all representations, whether with regard to existing rights or in the negotiation of new rights.

However, even in jurisdictions where the duty appears limited or is altogether absent,[14] the courts has recognized a common-law duty of fair representation with standards that parallel those imposed by statute[15] (Bentham, 1991). Thus, regardless of whether employees would be required to pursue their complaint through their jurisdictions' labour relations board or through the courts, they would have grounds for a complaint if their union failed to deal with them objectively, honestly, and without hostility or serious negligence.[16] The union is not bound to pursue every grievance to arbitration, nor is it prohibited from trading off one group of employees' bargaining requests in favour of another's (Bentham, 1991). Rather, a union has considerable discretion to balance competing interests, especially

free rider Someone who refuses to pay union dues, yet—by virtue of being in the bargaining unit—is entitled to the benefits and protections of union representation.

union shop A type of union security arrangement that requires employees to join the union as a condition of employment.

duty of fair representation Unions' duty to represent all members of the bargaining unit in a manner that is not arbitrary, discriminatory, or in bad faith.

with regard to the complex exercise of bargaining a collective agreement, as long as it is done in a manner that is "not arbitrary, capricious, discriminatory, or wrongful."[17]

Voluntarism and Emphasis on Process

A key assumption behind Canadian collective bargaining legislation is that it should operate primarily through free collective bargaining between employers and unions, with a minimum of government intervention. Rather than prescribing outcomes, such as a particular wage increase or set of working conditions, Canadian collective bargaining legislation delineates the *process* through which the parties interact to fashion an agreement that meets their particular needs and provides a variety of dispute-resolution procedures to assist the parties in resolving disputes "voluntarily and to the mutual satisfaction of both sides" (Godard, 2005:279). The major exception to Canada's generally voluntarist approach to dispute resolution is compulsory conciliation prior to a strike or lockout, a long-standing Canadian tradition still retained in many jurisdictions' labour relations acts.

Two types of provisions might seem to represent an exception to this emphasis on processes rather than outcomes. The first of these are first-contract arbitration provisions allowing for the imposition of an initial collective agreement in cases where the labour board believes an employer has failed to bargain in good faith with an eye to concluding an agreement. The second are provisions, now found in almost every labour relations act,[18] that allow labour boards to certify a union with less than majority support in situations where the board believes that the employer's unfair labour practices have prevented the employees' true wishes from becoming known. At first glance, both types of provisions may seem like heavy-handed government intervention in the collective bargaining process. Closer inspection, however, reveals that, far from stifling free collective bargaining, these provisions are designed to further it, by serving as a deterrent to grossly unfair labour practices, which if left unchecked would render the other party's statutory rights meaningless. And generally, labour boards will impose a first agreement or certify with less than majority support only as a last resort.

One other point should be made. The parties are not absolutely free to write any provisions they wish into collective agreements, because they are bound to abide by any relevant legislation, such as employment standards and human rights laws. Normally it is illegal for an agreement to contain any terms less favourable to employees than those found in the jurisdiction's employment standards legislation. For example, the parties cannot agree to a wage less than the provincial minimum or a shorter vacation period than that provided under employment standards. They also cannot agree to provisions that discriminate against any group, such as separate pay scales for women and men.

Specialized Tribunals

In every Canadian jurisdiction, the private sector collective bargaining legislation is administered and enforced by specialized tribunals, usually called labour relations boards, that derive their authority from the statute and are responsible for such matters as:

certification The process by which a labour relations board determines whether a union enjoys the support of a sufficient majority of employees in a bargaining unit and therefore acquires the right to act as their exclusive bargaining agent.

- union **certification** and **decertification**;
- facilitation of the right to organize and bargain collectively;
- regulation of internal union affairs; and
- the issuance of declarations and directions with respect to industrial disputes (Carter et al., 2002:69; Adams, 1993b:5-7).

In the federal jurisdiction and some provinces, labour relations boards are tripartite in composition, with neutral chairs and vice-chairs and board members drawn equally from employer and union ranks. The boards in other jurisdictions are composed of neutral members only (Carter et al., 2002:69).

Labour relations boards' powers are quite extensive and they enjoy considerable discretion to administer the statute in a practical manner that respects the complex nuances of labour–management relationships (Adams, 1993b:5-3). Thus, boards have the power to:

decertification The process by which a labour relations board determines that a trade union no longer enjoys the support of a majority of employees in a bargaining unit and therefore loses the right to act as their exclusive bargaining agent.

- subpoena witnesses and compel them to give evidence under oath;
- require any party to produce documents;
- accept such evidence as the board deems proper, whether or not that evidence would be admissible in the courts;
- require employers and unions to post notices;
- enter workplaces to inspect work processes and interrogate workers and managers;
- conduct representation, strike, and ratification votes; and
- bar applications for certification for a defined period.

They also have a broad range of remedies available to them, including the power to issue cease and desist orders and to order unfairly discharged employees reinstated with or without compensation. In every jurisdiction but Quebec,[19] boards also have the power to certify a union with less than majority support where egregious employer unfair labour practices prevent employees' true wishes from being made known. Especially in cases where employers' actions have adversely affected employees' attempts to unionize, boards have also demonstrated a willingness to develop innovative remedies such as requiring employers to write letters of apology that assure employees they will no longer interfere with their right to organize (Carter et al., 2002:246).

make-whole doctrine An approach adopted from civil law that requires the guilty party to right past wrongs and to restore victims to the positions they would have been in had the offence in question not been committed.

While most labour relations acts provide substantial fines for violations, punitive remedies are rare. Rather, the **make-whole doctrine** is adopted, which requires the guilty party to right past wrongs and to restore the victim to the position he or she would have been in had the offence in question not been committed (Godard, 2005:287). Indeed some would argue that boards' reluctance to impose punitive fines does so little to discourage illegal behaviours it is surprising more unfair labour practices are not committed (Godard, 2005). Criminal prosecution for some violations of collective bargaining legislation is a possibility, but boards seldom grant consent for such prosecution even for serious and willful violations, since it is seen as accomplishing little—other than to further embitter the parties (Carter et al., 2002:248).

Typically, labour board proceedings are more informal and less legalistic than proceedings before a court, though some have suggested that the gap between the two has narrowed (Arthurs, 1988:30). There is no requirement that parties to a labour board proceeding be represented by a lawyer, although an increasing number are (Arthurs, 1988:30). In general, labour boards are more concerned with finding practical and workable solutions that will win broad acceptance in the industrial relations community than with laying down long-term legal precedents. Toward this end, they usually take an accommodative approach in addressing workplace problems. Often a labour relations officer is assigned to a dispute, in the first instance, to help the parties resolve the problem on their own. If an accommodation is reached, the board will not hear the matter (Arthurs, 1988:68). As well, the board will sometimes refuse to act if the conduct in question has ended by the time of the hearing; in Ontario, it has had a policy of not issuing an order to remedy illegal strike or lockout action if the strike or lockout has ended before the hearing—except in cases where there has been a clear pattern of such misconduct (Arthurs, 1988).

An extensive jurisprudence of labour relations board decisions has developed, and while boards are not legally bound by prior decisions, they tend to follow established principles as these assist the parties in interpreting collective bargaining legislation and understanding board policies, especially where the statute itself is vague or couched in general terms (Carter et al., 2002:74). Board decisions are enforceable in regular courts as orders of the court and are subject to judicial review on limited grounds such as jurisdictional issues and adherence to fair procedures (Carter et al., 2002:29). Generally, however, courts have played a diminishing role in labour law in Canada; although they retain the power to enforce provincial statutes, interpret the Canadian constitution, issue injunctions,[20] bar picketing, and review the decisions of both labour boards and arbitrators, they have exercised increasing deference to specialized labour tribunals.

Labour boards have a number of advantages over the courts. In general, problems are resolved more quickly and expeditiously by boards. Since unions often have fewer resources than employers, this greater speed of resolution may be critical. In addition, labour boards have tended to be more even-handed than the courts, which overall have tended to favour employers far more often than labour (Arthurs, 1988:20; England, 1988:169). Some have also noted that because labour boards are made up of industrial relations practitioners and have expert staff available to them, they tend to be more knowledgeable about labour relations and more sensitive to its implications than are most judges, who may or may not have special training and expertise in the field.

No Mid-Term Strikes or Lockouts

Another key tenet of Canadian collective bargaining legislation is the "peace obligation" imposed on both unions and employers during the life of the agreement. Prior to World War II, Canadian workers used strikes to resolve virtually all their employment-related disputes. However, the need for continuous war production ushered in a new regime under *PC 1003*, where the only disputes for which strikes were legitimate were those involving the negotiation of collective agreements (LLCG, 2004:464). This regime persists to this day and timeliness is the most important factor in determining the legality of a strike. Thus, the collective bargaining legislation in every Canadian jurisdiction expressly prohibits strikes unless several conditions have been met including that the term of the collective agreement has expired.[21] Similarly, while employers are permitted to cease operations for legitimate business reasons, during the term of a collective agreement they are prohibited from attempting to resolve disputes by locking employees out. Rather, disputes regarding the administration, interpretation, or enforcement of the collective agreement are to be resolved through the grievance arbitration process. Most unions and employers negotiate the procedural rules for this multi-stage process into their collective agreements. However, where they fail to do so, the collective bargaining legislation in each Canadian jurisdiction outlines procedures to resolve such mid-term disputes (Carter et al., 2002:340). The grievance arbitration process is covered in detail in Chapter 12.

The Duty to Bargain in Good Faith

surface bargaining
A violation of the duty to bargain in good faith that involves going through the motions of the bargaining process but having no intention of actually concluding a collective agreement.

Consistent with Canadian collective bargaining legislation's emphasis on process, the duty to bargain in good faith is a concept designed to ensure employers do not subvert the process of collective bargaining by simply refusing to meet or by engaging in **surface bargaining**—that is, going through the motions with no intention of actually concluding a collective agreement. Also consistent with the emphasis on process, in assessing whether the parties have negotiated in good faith and made reasonable efforts to conclude a collective agreement, labour boards' scrutiny focuses more on the manner in which negotiations are conducted than on the content of negotiations (Carter et al., 2002:300). Furthermore, while actions in isolation may constitute bad faith bargaining, in many instances the determination is made in light of a pattern of behaviours including such things as:

- refusing to provide justification of a bargaining demand;
- reneging on agreements;
- repeatedly cancelling meetings or being persistently unavailable;
- insisting upon illegal or inappropriate demands;
- failing to respond to specific requests for relevant information;
- failing to disclose certain relevant information such as an impending closure; or
- attempting to circumvent the union and negotiate directly with employees (CAUT, 2002).

Statutory Freeze Following Notice to Bargain

Another common feature of Canadian collective bargaining legislation is the requirement that the parties "freeze" the terms and conditions of employment, as well as other employment-related rights, privileges, or duties, during their efforts to negotiate or renegotiate a collective agreement. The intent is to insulate collective bargaining from opportunistically timed unilateral actions and to maintain existing patterns, including periodic wage increases (Carter et al., 2002:289–290). Thus, for example, the employer is precluded from pressuring the union or sending not-so-subtle messages by adjusting pay scales or revoking benefits or privileges. Generally, this "business as usual" period ceases after a specified period of time has elapsed, either party has acquired the right to strike or lock out, or the union's bargaining rights are terminated.[22]

MAJOR FUNCTIONS OF CANADIAN COLLECTIVE BARGAINING LEGISLATION

Acquisition and Termination of Bargaining Rights

Certification

Regulating the process of certification is arguably the most important function of Canadian collective bargaining legislation. Before the Wagner Act in the United States and *PC 1003* in Canada, North American unions could win bargaining rights only by pressuring the employer (Craig and Solomon, 1996:213). As was noted earlier, strikes over recognition tended to be long and bitter and often resulted in bloodshed. Thus the establishment of a procedure through which unions could obtain legal recognition of bargaining rights was crucial to bringing about some measure of labour peace. The certification procedure remains the cornerstone of North American labour law and the relative ease of acquiring and retaining bargaining rights has critical impacts on both the percentage of employees able to gain the protections and advantages of collective representation (Bentham, 2002) and the overall strength of the labour movement. While it is possible for employers in every jurisdiction but Quebec (Carter et al., 2002:46) to voluntarily recognize a union as the bargaining agent for a group of employees, this tends to occur only in well-established union–management relationships in highly unionized industries where, for example, the employer is expanding into new locations.

Prior to 1977 (Riddell, 2001), every jurisdiction in Canada utilized the same system for certification of bargaining agents. Referred to alternately as **automatic certification** or the **card-majority system**, unions could tender evidence of majority support in the form of signed union membership cards. Since 1977, when Nova Scotia amended its legislation, five[23] Canadian jurisdictions have at one time or another instituted a certification system modelled on that used in the United States: the **mandatory vote system**. In the former system a union must demonstrate majority support only once. In the latter system, a union must not only submit a sufficient number of signed membership cards but, regardless of the level of support evinced, employees must reaffirm their support through a secret-ballot vote. Touted as a method of ensuring that unions do not coerce or intimidate employees and as an opportunity for employees to express their true wishes, the mandatory vote system has proven more to be an opportunity for employers to make their objections to unionization known, especially in the United States where long delays are typical. In fact, research clearly points to employer opposition and the failure of certification procedures to adequately protect employees' right to unionize as one of the most salient contributors to the precipitous decline of organized labour in the United States (Bentham, 2002).

Until very recently, it was widely accepted that even in Canadian jurisdictions that require a vote, expedited procedures and limits on employer behaviour during the certification process, which are both more strict and more strictly enforced than in the United States, limit both the prevalence and the impact of employer opposition

automatic certification 1) card-majority certification system; or 2) labour relations boards' power to certify a trade union even without evidence of majority support in instances where employer interference has been so egregious as to make it impossible to discern the true wishes of the employees.

card-majority certification system A system for certification of trade unions whereby the labour relations board accepts signed membership cards as evidence of majority support and certifies the trade union without need for a representation vote.

mandatory vote system A two-stage system for certification of trade unions whereby the labour relations board first requires signed membership cards as evidence of sufficient employee support to trigger a representation vote and then mandates a vote in every instance.

in this country. However, recent evidence suggests that employer opposition in Canada may be neither as infrequent nor as innocuous as assumed (Bentham, 2002). Due to a combination of factors, including the move toward mandatory vote systems, the pre-certification incidence of employer unfair labour practices has increased in Canada, both absolutely and relative to the United States (Bruce, 1994). Evidence suggests that the vast majority of Canadian employers overtly and actively oppose union certification applications. Their actions have had significantly negative impacts on both the likelihood of successful certification (Thomason, 1994b; Thomason and Pozzebon, 1998; Riddell, 2001; Bentham, 2002) and on post-certification outcomes, such as whether the parties will conclude a first collective agreement and the probability that the union will be decertified within two years (Bentham, 2002). In fact, the notion that Canadian certification systems effectively insulate employees from the detrimental effects of employer opposition appears to have very little empirical support (Thomason, 1994a). More recent empirical evidence suggests that previously employed statistical analyses seriously underestimated the true impact of employer opposition in Canada (Thomason, 1994b; Riddell, 2001). While there is little question that the magnitude of the problem is considerably lower in Canada than in the United States, the weight of evidence demonstrates that this does not mean that Canadian employers' opposition to union organizing is not significant.

Thus, the implementation of mandatory vote certification systems has been either condemned or commended, depending on whether one supports the notion that unionization is a choice that should be made independently by employees or one with regard to which employers should have an opportunity to express their views. The issue, which has become part of the larger politicization of labour relations legislation, has proven so politically divisive that some jurisdictions replaced card-majority systems with mandatory vote systems only to revert to card-majority systems a few years later.[24] British Columbia even introduced a mandatory vote system for a second time in 2001, after having abandoned it in 1993.

Regardless of which system is in place, the certification process begins with an application from a union to the labour board to represent the workers in a proposed bargaining unit. If no union holds bargaining rights, a certification application will normally be entertained at any time—other than during a period of time immediately following a failed certification attempt. However, where another union holds bargaining rights, an application may only be filed during specific windows of opportunity. Typically these **open period**s occur during the two or three months immediately preceding the expiry of a collective agreement or at specific times during an especially long-term agreement.[25] The application, a copy of which is normally delivered to the employer, must include a description of the proposed bargaining unit and an estimate of the number of individuals in the unit. It generally must also include a list of the names of the union members in the proposed bargaining unit and evidence of their status as union members; however, this information is not given to the employer.

At this point, the labour board has two jobs to do: (a) determine the appropriate bargaining unit, and (b) ascertain the union's level of support. To assist it in determining the unit most appropriate for collective bargaining, the board will allow employers or, in some cases, individual workers who object to the union's proposed

open period A period of time when applications for decertification or for certification of an alternate union may be submitted, usually the two or three months immediately preceding the expiry of a collective agreement.

unit to submit a proposal for the unit they prefer. In making its determination, the labour relations board will take into account a number of factors including statutory limitations, ability to organize, the viability of the bargaining structure, traditional methods of union organizing, the nature of the employer's organization, the wishes of the parties, and the community of interest amongst employees in the unit (Carter et al., 2002:268–272; Adams, 1993b:7-3–7-5).

To become certified, unions in all Canadian jurisdictions must reach two threshold points: (a) a level of support that will entitle them to apply for certification, with evidence usually being in the form of signed membership cards and (b) a level that will entitle them to become officially certified as the representative for the bargaining unit in question, with evidence being either in the form of signed membership cards or votes, depending on the certification system. While 40 percent support is the most common level, application thresholds vary from a low of 25 percent in Saskatchewan[26] to a high of 45 percent in British Columbia.[27] In card-majority systems, membership card evidence that exceeds the application threshold level but does not meet the required majority will trigger a representation vote. However, where membership card evidence meets the requisite level, which may require a supra-majority as high as 65 percent, as in Manitoba,[28] certification will generally be granted.

In mandatory vote systems, a vote is required in every instance, regardless of the level of majority support evinced through membership card evidence. Unlike in the United States, where the certification vote may not take place for several months, Canadian jurisdictions require mandatory representation votes to be held expeditiously, usually within five to ten days.[29] This, along with limits on employer behaviours during union organizing campaigns, which, as mentioned earlier, are both more strict and more strictly enforced than in the United States, has helped curb both the incidence and impacts of employer behaviours designed to sway employee votes.

Regardless of which certification system is in place, when a vote is required, most jurisdictions, including Ontario, Alberta, British Columbia, Manitoba, Nova Scotia, Prince Edward Island, Saskatchewan, and the federal jurisdiction, allow certification based on a majority of those voting. Two jurisdictions, Quebec and New Brunswick, require support from a majority of bargaining unit members—a situation that in effect allows abstentions to count as negative votes. A few jurisdictions have developed compromise approaches. In Newfoundland and Labrador, the union must receive support from a majority of those voting but the Board may require that at least 70 percent of the members in the proposed bargaining unit have voted.[30]

Definition of the Bargaining Unit

An essential step in the process of certification is the determination of the unit of employees most appropriate for the purposes of collective bargaining, a determination which is arguably labour relations boards' most important mandate. Such decisions have critical implications for the scope and effectiveness of collective bargaining, the probability of industrial disputes, and for the viability and stability of the labour relations system as a whole.[31] With the rare exception of instances where the bargaining unit is defined by statute, the labour relations board in each

Table 7.2

CERTIFICATION PROCEDURES BY JURISDICTION, JANUARY 2005

Jurisdiction	System	Application Threshold	Support Required	Constituency (if vote held)
Federal	Card Majority	35%	Majority	Majority of votes cast - at least 35% of eligible employees must cast votes
Alberta	Mandatory Vote	40%	Majority	Majority of votes cast
British Columbia	Mandatory Vote	45%	Majority	Majority of votes cast - Board may order another vote if fewer than 55% of employees in the unit cast votes
Manitoba	Card Majority	40%	65%	Majority of votes cast
New Brunswick	Card Majority	40%	60%*	Majority of those eligible to vote
Newfoundland and Labrador	Card Majority if parties agree, otherwise vote required†	40%	Majority	Majority of votes cast - Board may require that 70% of employees in the unit cast votes
Nova Scotia	Mandatory Vote	40%	Majority	Majority of votes cast
Ontario	Mandatory Vote	40%	Majority	Majority of votes cast
PEI	Card Majority	When deemed necessary	Majority	Majority of votes cast
Quebec	Card Majority	35%	Majority	Majority of employees in the unit
Saskatchewan	Card Majority	25%**	Majority	Majority of votes cast

* Board *may* grant certification if satisfied that more than 50% of bargaining unit employees are union members in good standing.

† The legislation does not specifically mandate a vote but the Board's practice is to require a vote unless both the employer and union agree in writing that the vote is unnecessary.

** When another trade union is already certified.

Sources: Compiled from Human Resources and Skills Development Canada. (2005). "Summary of General Private Sector Collective Bargaining Legislation," January, http://www.hrsdc.gc.ca/asp/gateway.asp?hr=en/lp/spila/clli/irlc/01industrial_relations_legislation_canada.shtml&hs=lzl.

jurisdiction has exclusive responsibility to determine the shape and size of any bargaining unit for which a union will be granted exclusive bargaining rights. In making this determination, boards attempt to balance two, often countervailing, objectives: to protect the rights of employees to access collective representation; and to ensure the viability and stability of the bargaining unit once it is certified (Carter, 2002:267–269; Adams, 1993b:7-4). Unions tend to find it easier to organize smaller, more cohesive units (Carter, 2002:268) and a plethora of research studies confirms that certification success tends to decrease as bargaining unit size increases (see, for example, Thomason, 1994a; Scott, Simpson and Oswald, 1993; Farber, 2001). But while defining the unit narrowly may increase the probability of certification success, defining it too narrowly may result in the union lacking bargaining power and the employer incurring increased costs and administrative difficulties in dealing with multiple small bargaining units each with its own collective agreement. It may also result in industrial relations instability due to the proliferation of small, fragmented bargaining units. On the other hand, if the unit is defined too broadly, the union may have difficulty gaining the support of a majority of employees and, even if it succeeds in becoming certified, may find it impossible to balance the disparate interests of a heterogeneous group of employees with different professional concerns, pay scales, and bargaining demands.

As discussed earlier, labour boards will consider a number of factors in shaping the bargaining unit and one of the most important of these is "community of interest," a concept designed to group together employees who share similar economic interests and exclude those whose possess conflicting interests (Adams, 1993b:7-3). Typically, a bargaining unit will encompass all employees of a particular employer in one location. Alternately, depending on the industry and the employer's operations, a bargaining unit may include all employer locations within a municipality. In many industries such as health care and the university sector (see Table 7.3), it is more typical for one employer to negotiate with a number of different unions, each with its own bargaining unit, each representing different types of workers in that organization. As Table 7.3 so vividly demonstrates, this may result in a plethora of unions and bargaining units often so complex as to demand a cadre of industrial relations staff engaged in seemingly never-ending rounds of bargaining.

Workers Excluded from Collective Bargaining Legislation

As discussed earlier in this chapter, not all employees enjoy statutory protection of their right to unionize and bargain collectively. For example, all private sector Canadian collective bargaining legislation expressly stipulates that for the purposes of the statute, managers and those involved in a confidential capacity with respect to labour relations are not included in the definition of "employee." Many Canadian industrial relations experts consider these exclusions, which stem from the need for employers' representatives to maintain confidentiality and an arm's-length relationship from the union, to be justified. Others argue that collective bargaining rights can be extended to all but the most senior managers and potential conflicts of interest avoided by adopting the approach generally used in the public sector: isolating managers from the employees they supervise by designating separate bargaining units for supervisory personnel. Indeed, the legislation in both the federal jurisdiction and British Columbia expressly provides for this possibility (Carter, 2002:273). Separate bargaining units may also be used to protect security guards' ability to monitor other employees, to separate plant and office employees, and for professional employees or dependent contractors (Carter, 2002:272–274).

Table 7.3

UNIVERSITY OF TORONTO CERTIFIED BARGAINING AGENTS: GENERAL INFORMATION

There are over 8000 employees represented in the following bargaining units at the University of Toronto:

Carpenters and Allied Workers, Local 27 represents Carpenters located on all three campuses of the University (Scarborough, Erindale and St. George). Approximately 11 employees.

Canadian Union of Public Employees, Local 1230 (Full-time) (CUPE, Local 1230 F/T) represents Library Technicians. Approximately 186 employees.

Canadian Union of Public Employees, Local 1230 (Part-Time) (CUPE, Local 1230 P/T) represents part-time Library Workers employed in the Central Library System. Approximately 222 employees.

Canadian Union of Public Employees, Local 3261 (Full-time) (CUPE, Local 3261 F/T) represents service workers, including Caretakers, Food Service Staff, Grounds Staff, Drivers, Laboratory Animal Technicians, and Athletic Attendants. Approximately 575 employees.

Canadian Union of Public Employees, Local 3261 (Part-Time) (CUPE, Local 3261 P/T) represents casual and regular part-time service workers located on all three campuses. Approximately 257 employees.

Canadian Union of Public Employees, Local 3902 (CUPE, Local 3902) represents University of Toronto students working as Teaching Assistants, Teaching Laboratory Assistants, and a small number of part-time lecturers. Approximately 2500 employees.

Canadian Union of Public Employees, Local 3902 (CUPE, Local 3902) also represents a recently certified unit of sessional and stipendiary instructors working on all three campuses in most academic departments. Approximately 600 employees.

Canadian Union of Public Employees, Local 3907 (CUPE, Local 3907) represents Graduate Assistants at the Ontario Institute for Studies in Education of the University of Toronto (OISE/UT). Approximately 195 employees.

Canadian Union of Public Employees, Local 2484 (CUPE Local 2484) represents daycare workers. Approximately 16 employees.

International Brotherhood of Electrical Workers, Local 353 (I.B.E.W.) represents Electricians and apprentices, located in the University's Facilities and Services and Physical Plant Departments. Approximately 24 employees.

International Alliance of Theatrical Stage Employees and Moving Picture Machine Operators of the United States and Canada, Local 58 (I.A.T.S.E.) represents the one stage hand employee at the University of Toronto Hart House Theatre.

International Association of Machinists and Aerospace Workers, Local 235 represents employees at the University of Toronto working as Locksmiths and Machinists on the St. George Campus. Approximately 12 employees.

University of Toronto Workers, Local 2001 represents employees at the University of Toronto working on all three campuses as Stationary Engineers, Building Management Systems Technicians, Building Engineers and Maintenance-Related Engineers.

International Brotherhood of Painters and Allied Trades, District Council 46, Local 557 - currently no active staff.

United Association of Journeymen and Apprentices of the Plumbing and Pipe Fitting Industry of the United States and Canada, Local 46, represents employees at the University of Toronto working in and out of the Facilities and Services and Physical Plant Departments. Approximately 15 employees.

Sheet Metal Workers' International Association, Local 30 represents sheet metal workers at the University of Toronto working from the Facilities and Services and Physical Plant Departments. Approximately 2 employees.

Ontario Public Service Employees Union, Local 519 (OPSEU 519) represents the University of Toronto Campus Police located on the three campuses. Approximately 44 employees.

Ontario Public Service Employees Union, Local 578 (OPSEU 578) represents regular and sessional Research Officers at the Ontario Institute for Studies in Education of the University of Toronto (OISE/UT). Approximately 21 employees. ▶

Table 7.3
(continued)

United Steelworkers of America, Staff-Appointed Unit, Local 1998 (USWA 1998 Staff-Appointed) represents staff-appointed full- and part-time administrative and technical employees on all three campuses. Approximately 3103 employees.

United Steelworkers of America, Casuals Unit, Local 1998 (USWA 1998 Casual) represents non-staff-appointed casual administrative and technical employees on all three campuses. Approximately 1700 employees.

Hotel Employees and Restaurant Employees International Union, Local 75 (HERE 75) represents workers at 89 Chestnut Street, a former downtown Toronto hotel that has been converted to a student residence. Approximately 100 employees.

Canadian Auto Workers (CAW) represents operating engineers across all three campuses, who operate the central steam plant as well as heating, ventilation and air-conditioning equipment in campus buildings. Approximately 73 employees.

Source: University of Toronto. (2000). "University of Toronto Certified Bargaining Agents: General Information," Human Resources Department, Labour Relations, May 31, http://www.utoronto.ca/hrhome/bargain.htm.

The above list provides some sense of the complexity of managing relationships with a number of different bargaining agents who represent a large and diverse employee population. And when you consider that the above list excludes the University of Toronto Faculty Association, which is a voluntarily recognized association rather than a certified trade union, the task seems almost unmanageable.

Historically, many other types of workers were denied the right to unionize. Typical exclusions included professionals, domestics, agricultural workers, and, in some instances, dependent contractors. In the past, professionals were often self-employed and even where they were salaried employees the belief was that their interests were best forwarded by their own professional associations. More recently, however, a wide range of professionals, including nurses, engineers, teachers, and university professors, have embraced collective bargaining (LLCG, 2004:236) and the rationale for their continued exclusion is unclear. Nonetheless, Ontario, Alberta, and Prince Edward Island continue to deny bargaining rights to members of the medical, dental, legal, and architectural professions.[32] Ontario also excludes members of the land surveying profession,[33] while Alberta and Prince Edward Island exclude engineers.[34]

Ontario[35] and Alberta[36] also stand alone as the only two jurisdictions that continue to deny agricultural workers the right to unionize. Originally their exclusion was justified by the unique nature of employment on a family farm, but with the growth of agribusiness this exclusion seems rooted more in the desire to control labour costs. As discussed earlier in this chapter, this is the subject of an ongoing constitutional challenge. Quebec and New Brunswick have offered some protections for family farms, while extending bargaining rights to those employed in larger agricultural operations by requiring that bargaining units be composed of at least three or five members, respectively (Carter et al., 2002:256).

Finally, police, firefighters, teachers, and other public employees may be specifically excluded from general collective bargaining legislation, but their collective bargaining rights are generally outlined in separate legislation. Members of the Royal Canadian Mounted Police are not covered under any collective bargaining legislation and this exclusion has survived a constitutional challenge.[37]

"No place in the sun." Though they're among the country's poorest workers, agricultural workers continue to be denied the right to unionize in both Alberta and Ontario. To make matters worse, several provinces also exclude them from coverage under employment standards legislation.

Decertification

A union may abandon its right to be the exclusive bargaining agent for a group of employees through long-term inaction or may lose this right when an employer goes out of business. A union will also be decertified if it is determined that its certification was obtained by fraud, or if a majority of employees in the bargaining unit no longer wish to be unionized or wish to be represented by a different union (Carter et al., 2002:282–285). Any bargaining unit employee may apply to the board for decertification; however, the application will normally be entertained only during open periods or, in cases where the union has not managed to negotiate a collective agreement, within a specified length of time after certification. From this point, the process is quite similar to the certification process and a copy of the application for decertification must be delivered to the employer and the union. Normally the application threshold levels and the required support are the same for decertification as for certification, although the process may be somewhat less rigidly defined.

Protecting the Right to Organize

Organizing and being granted a certification order is only one aspect of the process of gaining and maintaining the protections and advantages of collective representation. Accordingly, collective bargaining legislation also empowers labour relations boards to adjudicate complaints that either the union or employer has engaged in practices that violate or frustrate the other's rights under collective bargaining legislation. Labour relations legislation generally prohibits employers from interfering with employees' right to join a trade union and participate in that union's lawful activities. Prohibited behaviours include using threats or promises to intimidate or coerce employees not to support the union, discharging employees for union activity, or supporting employer-controlled unions or otherwise participating in the union's formation or administration. Employers are also prohibited from suspending or moving operations for the purposes of avoiding unionization, hiring professional strikebreakers, or engaging in activities that violate an employer's duty to bargain in good faith.

Employers are free to dismiss employees for just cause or close a plant for legitimate business purposes; however, where employer actions are tainted by **anti-union animus**, even where legitimate business motives exist, an unfair labour practice will have been committed (Carter et al., 2002:236–243). Similarly, employers are entitled to express opinions regarding union organizing drives but must exercise this right cautiously; given the degree of control employers exercise over their employees' economic well-being, it takes little more than nuance to convey threatening intent. In fact, the often tense atmosphere during a union organizing campaign can heighten employees' sensitivity to even seemingly innocuous employer statements, especially if accompanied by other, more overt anti-union behaviours. Thus, labour relations boards will often look with suspicion on one-on-one communications or so-called **"captive audience" speeches** where employers deliver appeals at meetings held during working hours and for which attendance is compulsory (Carter et al., 2002:243). Even in Alberta, where an employer's right to express views regarding unionization is expressly protected within the legislation,[38] the labour board's procedure guide cautions that because employers are in a position of power over employees, their speech "can much more easily appear coercive or threatening than employee or union speech" (Alberta Labour Relations Board, 2003:2).

For their part, unions are barred from interfering with the formation and operation of employers' organizations as well as from interfering with other unions that have won the right to represent given groups of workers. Unions may not use intimidation or coercion to compel people to join, nor may they arbitrarily deny anyone union membership (Carter et al., 2002:240). They are also forbidden from suspending or otherwise disciplining members for refusing to engage in unlawful strikes.

Regulating Industrial Conflict

As mentioned at the beginning of this chapter, collective bargaining legislation serves to suppress, control, and focus the conflict that inevitably arises between employers and groups of employees. Processes are outlined for the resolution of disputes regarding unions' right to represent groups of workers, the enforcement of collective agreements, and the negotiation of terms and conditions of employment. It is only with regard to the latter that unionized workers are permitted to use the withdrawal of services as a pressure tactic to force concessions and even then, the parties must follow the processes outlined in each jurisdiction's legislation before a dispute can be said to have reached an impasse that justifies either a

anti-union animus The existence of anti-union motive. Employer actions designed to avoid or escape unionization may constitute unfair labour practices even if accompanied by some legitimate business reason.

captive audience speeches Employer speeches delivered to employees at meetings held during work hours and for which attendance is compulsory. Sometimes used by employers to discourage employees from supporting a union.

strike or a lockout. Generally the procedures require that the parties bargain in good faith and make reasonable attempts to conclude a collective agreement. Where these attempts fail, the parties must notify the appropriate authorities and, in most jurisdictions, this will usually result in the appointment of a conciliator or mediator. In most cases, a strike or lockout will be legal only after the mediator, conciliator, or conciliation board informs the Minister that they have been unable to resolve the dispute, the Minister has either released the board report or declared that no report will be released, and a certain length of time—normally 7 to 21 days—has elapsed.

Private sector labour law in the United States does not require conciliation prior to strikes or lockouts, nor does that of most other countries (Bean, 1994:116–7). However, conciliation has been a hallmark of Canadian collective bargaining legislation since the *Industrial Disputes Investigation Act* of 1907 and while full conciliation boards and conciliation reports are now rare, some process to assist the parties to resolve disputes prior to permitting a strike or lockout persists in almost all jurisdictions.

Canadian collective bargaining legislation also outlines a number of other processes for regulating industrial conflict. For example, all jurisdictions require employees' endorsement of a strike through a secret-ballot vote, and most require that a formal notice of strike or lockout be filed 24 to 72 hours prior to its commencement. During the course of a strike, a few jurisdictions permit the employer's final offer to be put to a vote of employees at the request of the employer or discretion of the board.[39] The legislation in most jurisdictions specifically protects the right of striking workers to be reinstated and prohibits dismissing workers because they have participated in a legal strike; some jurisdictions[40] also provide protections to workers who refuse to perform the work of employees who are locked out or on strike. Several jurisdictions prohibit employers from denying pension rights or benefits to which the employee would be entitled but for the fact that they are on strike;[41] Manitoba extends these protections to "insurance schemes"[42] and Saskatchewan extends the protections to health and medical benefits[43] (Carter et al., 2002:324).

Several jurisdictions[44] explicitly disallow the use of professional strikebreakers or persons employed for the purposes of undermining the trade union's representational capacities and British Columbia and Quebec specifically prohibit the use of replacement workers during either a strike or a lockout.[45] These anti-scab provisions, as they are colloquially called, are primarily intended to curb the violence that tends to erupt when replacement workers cross picket lines. As an added bonus, they also serve to preserve the rights of low-skilled workers for whom the right to strike would be meaningless if employers could simply replace the entire bargaining unit every time they attempted to negotiate improved terms and conditions of employment. Finally, in recognition that certification is but the first step in a collective bargaining relationship, several jurisdictions offer assistance to newly established union–management relationships by allowing or mandating arbitration of first–collective agreement disputes. These provisions have proven extremely useful (Sexton, 1987).

The prohibition or restriction of strike activity, especially where the services are deemed essential, is not uncommon in the Canadian public sector, but some jurisdictions also have special provisions for restricting certain private sector work stoppages and substituting alternative dispute resolution procedures. The legislation in British Columbia, for example, allows the government to designate as essential "those facilities, productions and services that the board considers necessary or essential to prevent immediate and serious danger to the health, safety or welfare of the residents of British Columbia."[46] The Alberta legislation provides for the establishment of a Public Emergency Tribunal to mediate disputes in emergencies that threaten damage to health or property or cause unreasonable hardship; where necessary, the tribunal may hand down a binding arbitration award.[47] In Newfoundland and Labrador, special provisions exist for ensuring the orderly shutdown and maintenance of offshore petroleum production platforms prior to the commencement of a strike and for designating as essential a proportion of workers employed in public utilities that generate and sell electrical power.[48]

Primary responsibility for the enforcement of procedures regulating industrial conflict rests with each jurisdiction's labour relations board. The board's remedial powers include the ability to issue cease and desist orders and award compensation. However, more so than in any other area of labour relations, the courts continue to play a role in regulating industrial conflict (LLCG, 2004; 482). Picketing, for example, is governed essentially by the law of tort (Carter et al., 2002:330) and can give rise to an action in civil courts or a labour relations board proceeding, or both (LLCG, 2004:482).

COLLECTIVE BARGAINING LEGISLATION IN QUEBEC

Special mention should be made of Quebec's collective bargaining legislation, since in some ways that province's collective bargaining procedures and administrative mechanisms differ quite markedly from the rest of Canada's. Here, we focus mainly on private sector legislation; features applying to the public sector will be discussed in the next chapter.

While Quebec is best known to the English Canadian industrial relations community for pioneering anti-strikebreaking legislation and the right to strike for public sector workers, the most distinctive feature of its legislative regime is arguably its decree system, whereby collective agreements are extended to the non-unionized sectors of an industry. Common in Europe (see Chapter 13 for more details), the decree system has been in effect since 1934 (Déom and Boivin, 2005:447). It was established to encourage collective bargaining and to eliminate competition over wages and working conditions among low-wage, highly competitive industries. Trade liberalization in recent years led the Quebec government to remove many industries from the decree sector, although decrees can still be found in the service sector, especially services that require geographical proximity such as security, building and auto maintenance, and hairdressing (Déom and Boivin, 2005;447). Agreements resulting from decrees are normally narrower in scope than standard agreements, since permissible provisions for an extension are limited to wages, hours of work, working days, vacations with pay, and classification of operations and of employers and employees. Quebec law also provides for special, highly centralized arrangements in the construction industry, formerly a decree sector but now subject to sector-wide bargaining (Adams, 2001).

Perhaps because of the decree system, which encourages a good measure of sector-wide negotiation, employers' associations play a much more prominent role in Quebec than they do elsewhere. Many of them are directly engaged in negotiating with unions. In 1969, most of those associations joined forces to create a confederation of employer associations known as the Conseil du patronat du Québec (CPQ), which now directly or indirectly represents employers whose workers together constitute 70 percent of the Quebec labour force. The CPQ does not engage in collective bargaining as such, instead focusing its energies on legislative lobbying, public relations, and research (Déom and Boivin, 2005:465). The existence of such a federation has arguably enabled the Quebec business community to speak with one voice to a far greater extent than is possible in any other province. The organization of Quebec's trade unions also differs from that in other provinces. Unlike other provinces where the main labour federation enjoys a virtual monopoly, the Quebec Federation of Labour (QFL) is but one of four major labour federations in the province (Déom and Boivin, 2005:464). This trade union pluralism as well as the cultural specificity of Quebec have contributed to the development of an unusual association between the QFL and Canada's national labour federation, the Canadian Labour Congress (CLC), whereby the QFL enjoys a unique independence (Déom and Boivin, 2005:462). Other labour federations within the province include the Confédération des syndicats nationaux (CSN), the Centrale des syndicats démocratiques (CSD), and the Centrale des syndicats du Quebéc (CSQ) (Déom and Boivin, 2005:462–464).

Finally, Quebec has differed significantly from other provinces in the way it administers collective bargaining legislation. In 1969, it replaced its labour relations board with a three-tier system comprised of certification agents, labour commissioners, and general commissioners to deal with certification and unfair labour practice issues. A Labour Court was also established to handle appeals of commissioners and general commissioners' decisions and to deal with criminal prosecutions brought under the *Labour Code* (Boivin, 1989:424–425). While similar to labour boards in many ways, the Labour Court had exclusive jurisdiction in penal prosecutions brought under the *Labour Code*—a power not possessed by labour boards, which are administrative tribunals (Carrothers, Palmer, and Rayner, 1986). The idea was that such a specialized tribunal, staffed with industrial relations and human resource specialists, would reduce recourse to the courts on labour-related matters. It proved unable to achieve this objective, however, and was also widely criticized for its lengthy delays in rendering decisions (Boivin, 1989:425). In addition, appeals of the Labour Court's decisions were much more frequent than appeals of labour board decisions (Carrothers et al., 1986:183). As a result, the Labour Relations Commission (LRC) was reinstated in 2001 and now operates in much the same manner as the labour relations boards in other jurisdictions (Déom and Boivin, 2005:465).

CANADIAN VERSUS AMERICAN LEGISLATION

Canadian collective bargaining legislation originally evolved out of the American *Wagner Act* (1935) and in many ways, it still strongly resembles its American ancestor. In other ways, it has taken some quite different directions. The fact of provincial jurisdiction may well have helped Canadian legislation to change more—and more often—than has been the case in the United States, where the legislation is under federal jurisdiction and any change can affect many millions of workers. Both countries' laws tend to emphasize processes rather than outcomes and to be relatively voluntarist in their overall orientation. However, the American legislation has remained truer to its voluntarist heritage.

First, almost all Canadian jurisdictions have compulsory conciliation provisions. Second, Canada's compulsory grievance arbitration, which is not part of the Wagner model,[49] represents a significant degree of government intervention in the IR system. Third, the United States has no equivalent of Canada's first-contract arbitration or anti-scab laws. Indeed, US law allows for the permanent replacement of striking workers (Carter, 1995), except in cases where a dispute has arisen over illegal activities, such as the employer's attempt to get rid of the union. In these cases, permanent replacements are illegal and strikers have a right to get their jobs back (Sims, 1996).

In other areas as well, Canadian law offers workers and unions significantly greater protection than does American law. For instance, union security is generally stronger in Canada, which has no equivalent to the "right-to-work" provisions of the 1947 *Taft-Hartley* amendments to Wagner. Where the card count still exists, union certification is significantly easier in Canada than in the United States. Even in those jurisdictions that have moved to the vote, the expedited voting process used in Canada offers less opportunity for employer interference in the process than do the United States' lengthy campaigns, and thus there is considerably less likelihood that the union will lose the campaign.

RECENT TRENDS IN COLLECTIVE BARGAINING LEGISLATION

As we noted earlier, there has been little *fundamental* change in Canadian collective bargaining legislation since the passage of the *Public Service Staff Relations Act* in 1967. Even the *Charter of Rights and Freedoms* has had but limited impact on labour-related matters. Nonetheless, changes of a more incremental nature *have* been occurring, and the pace of these changes appears to have picked up over the past few years.

While collective bargaining itself and the legislation that governs it have always endeavoured to strike a delicate balance between the rights of the collective and those of the individual, the 1980s ushered in an era that tilted the balance relatively in favour of the latter. As discussed in Chapter 6, the protections enshrined in provincial and federal human rights codes were expanded to offer protections to a number of previously excluded groups and court decisions made it clear that the existence of discrimination was to be judged by the impact of a rule or practice, not simply by its purpose. As was also discussed in Chapter 6, pay equity and employment equity legislation introduced new rules for determining whether reward structures and human resource practices were equitable and free of discrimination. Increasingly, unions, employers, and the collective bargaining system have had to adapt to include previously excluded groups, to ensure traditional processes and practices such as job evaluation and seniority-based job advancement do not adversely impact individuals in protected groups, and to balance the rights and strength of the collective so as to accord greater respect to the rights of individuals.

Another balance collective bargaining legislation has endeavoured to strike is that between the rights and interests of employees and their representatives and those of employers. Recent years have seen the balance tilting relatively in favour of employers, as best demonstrated by the trend toward mandatory vote certification systems. On the other hand, current collective bargaining legislation excludes fewer employees than in the past, extending the possibility of unionization to a somewhat larger pool of employees. Indeed, the UFCW's charter challenge will determine whether such rights will, for the first time, be fully extended to agricultural employees in Ontario.

While Canadian collective bargaining legislation has evolved over the years, it remains predicated on the model of employment that was the norm in the 1940s. Canada's workforce, however, is no longer predominantly blue-collar workers employed by a single employer in a full-time, full-year position. It can certainly be argued that the processes for certification and the practices for definition of bargaining units are no longer suitable for a workforce that is increasingly employed in the service sector, holding multiple jobs, often with very small employers, and in part-time, temporary, or contract positions working from a variety of sites, including their homes. The challenge will be to adapt Canadian collective bargaining legislation to not only serve the needs of today's employers and employees but to do so in a way that delicately balances the rights and interests of all stakeholders.

Case 7.1

SERVICE SECTOR STRUGGLES: ORGANIZING WAL-MART IN QUEBEC

Industrial relations experts generally agree that if the union movement wants to increase or even maintain its current membership levels, it will need to organize more workers in the private service sector. However, no one is pretending this will be easy.

A recent case involving the Wal-Mart Department Store chain shows just how difficult the unions' job will be. On February 9, 2005, Wal-Mart announced it would be closing a store in Jonquière, Quebec, 150 kilometres north of Quebec City. The summer before, the United Food and Commercial Workers (UFCW) had been certified to represent the store's nearly 200 employees. At the time, the Jonquière store was the only unionized Wal-Mart in North America; although there have been many organizing drives in both the US and Canada, and even some successful certifications, none have managed to survive long enough to conclude a collective agreement.

Union Busting Denied
On February 2, 2005, after four months of bargaining, the union requested first-contract arbitration, as it was entitled to do under Quebec's labour legislation.

On the 9th, Quebec's labour minister granted the union's request and just hours later Wal-Mart announced its decision to close the store. While Wal-Mart contends the closure decision was taken because the store was not profitable, both the timing of the decision and Wal-Mart's history of similar union avoidance behaviours suggest it was the imposition of first-contract arbitration that triggered Wal-Mart's decision. A Wal-Mart spokesman, Andrew Pelletier, denied that the closure was an attempt to bust the union. Noting that the company could have closed the store months earlier but chose not to, he said, "It's a business decision, it's an economic viability issue ultimately, but it's been exacerbated through added pressures."

Politicians and Quebec union leaders were quick to disagree. Bloc Quebecois MP Real Menard urged the government to pull anti-smoking ads it had previously placed in Wal-Mart stores to send the company the message that it doesn't agree with its corporate conduct. Ottawa NDP MP Ed Broadbent described Wal-Mart as the "most anti-democratic company in the world," while Ontario Liberal MP Mario Silva urged Canadians everywhere to "stand up" for the store's workers. In Hull, Quebec, industrial relations professor Renaud Paquet said the closure would have a chilling effect on all Wal-Mart employees in the province. In his view, the message the closure sent was: "If you exercise your right to organize under Quebec labour legislation, we'll close your store down."

Message Loud and Clear

This is far from the first time Wal-Mart has sent such a message. In at least six Canadian provinces and several US states, workers have attempted to unionize Wal-Mart stores; on each occasion, Wal-Mart has responded with aggressive tactics focused on dissuading employees by predicting dire consequences should the store become unionized. Simultaneously, Wal-Mart engages a team of legal experts who file countless arguments, objections, and actions challenging everything from the union's contact with employees to the constitutionality of collective bargaining legislation. For example, in 1996, the United Steelworkers of America filed a certification application for the Windsor, Ontario, store. Wal-Mart reacted with an aggressive campaign, which was later determined to include a number of unfair labour practices but which successfully cast a chill on employee support. A protracted legal battle ensued that eventually enmeshed the parties in layer upon layer of labour relations board and court proceedings. Recognizing that any victory would be pyrrhic at best, the union finally agreed to give up their bargaining rights if Wal-Mart dropped all its litigation.

In April 2000, after butchers in its Jacksonville, Texas, store voted to become unionized, Wal-Mart announced it would cut all meat-packaging operations at all 180 stores. Wal-Mart characterized the decision as part of a long-term plan to sell pre-packaged beef cuts but offered no explanation as to why it had recently invested $40 000 in a new meat-wrapping machine for the Jacksonville store. After a protracted three-year battle, Wal-Mart was ordered by a National Labor Relations Board judge to recognize the UFCW, to restore the reassigned butchers' meat-cutting duties, and to engage in collective bargaining, including bargaining over the impact of the company's decision to switch to pre-packaged meat; however, a collective agreement has yet to be concluded.

A Public Relations Disaster

Meanwhile, the company did little to help its cause by placing a full-page ad in several Quebec newspapers praising its employees as "the backbone of the company." The ad drew outrage from Quebec unionists. "It's like a guy who betrays his wife and beats his wife and then the next day gives her flowers for Valentine's Day," said the UFCW's Yvon Bellemare. "The best present for Valentine's Day. . . is respect. . . satisfactory salaries and working conditions." Another union official termed the ad insulting. "They've been threatening this closure ever since we got the accreditation," said union spokesman Marie-Josee Lemieux. "How can they now say they [employees] are its biggest strength?" Lemieux's is a sentiment echoed by more than 200 academics in Canada, the US, and Europe who have signed a petition denouncing Wal-Mart's contempt for employees and urging Wal-Mart to cease its opposition to unionization and abide by international human rights standards.

Employees at Wal-Mart's Windsor store, where another organizing drive was underway, were unwilling to risk that Wal-Mart would mend its ways and in early March voted against unionization. Employees from the Wal-Mart in Saint-Hyacinthe, who became certified in January, had hoped to commence first contract negotiations but were stymied when Wal-Mart filed an objection to the certification. UFCW Canada has also applied to represent workers at twelve other Wal-Mart locations across Canada.

Sources: *Ottawa Citizen*. (2005). "Wal-Mart to Union: Store's Closed," Feb. 10, p. B1; *Ottawa Citizen*. (2005). "Wal-Mart Ad Sparks Outrage from Union," Feb. 15, p. D1; *Ottawa Citizen*. (2005). "Politicians Lambaste Wal-Mart over Jonquiere Closing," Feb. 15, p. D4; *Le Droit*. (2005). "Pour contrer les Wal-Mart et McDo de ce monde," Feb. 15, p. 17; Cray, Charlie. (2000). "Wal-Mart Cuts the Union." *Multinational Monitor*. [Washington] 21:4, p. 4; *Multinational Monitor* [Washington]. (2003). "Judge to Wal-Mart: Bargain" 24:7/8, p. 4.

Case Questions

1. In 2004, Wal-Mart's profits exceeded $10 billion US while their workers in the United States earned, on average, $8 per hour, with few working more than 32 hours per week. Given the huge discrepancy in power and resources, is it possible for employees to successfully challenge Wal-Mart's determination to remain union-free? If so, how? Make recommendations to employees, unions, and Canadian policy makers regarding how to successfully exercise and protect retail workers' right to unionize and bargain collectively.

2. What type of industrial relations strategy (discussed in Chapter 2) has Wal-Mart adopted? What would adoption of this strategy theoretically imply for compensation policies and do Wal-Mart's compensation policies fit this strategy? If Wal-Mart is determined to stay union-free, what advice would you give it regarding compensation and other human resource policies?

QUESTIONS FOR DISCUSSION

1. Get a copy of your province's labour relations act. Read it. Pay special attention to its preface or introductory paragraphs explaining its purpose. Does its purpose seem to be more closely related to maintaining industrial peace and promoting collective bargaining or to promoting economic growth?

2. Why does government get involved in regulating the processes through which employees become unionized and engage in collective bargaining with employers?

3. What impact has the *Canadian Charter of Rights and Freedoms* had on collective bargaining law?

4. Explain the features—or principles—of collective bargaining legislation that are common to all Canadian jurisdictions.

5. Human Resources and Skills Development Canada (HRSDC) maintains a website that describes the jurisdiction of the federal and provincial governments with regard to industrial relations and summarizes major provisions of labour relations legislation from each jurisdiction. Go to the "Industrial Relations Legislation in Canada" page on the website, http://www.hrsdc.gc.ca/asp/gateway.asp?hr= en/ lp/spila/clli/irlc/01industrial_relations_legislation_canada.shtml&hs=lzl, and identify the legislation that governs labour relations in the jurisdiction and industry in which you are employed or in the university sector in your province.

6. Compare and contrast card-majority and mandatory vote certification procedures. Explain why you believe one or the other makes for better public policy.

7. Explain how the duty of fair representation and the duty to bargain in good faith are related to the twin principles of majoritarianism and exclusivity. Can you think of an alternative to these twin principles that would better serve the interests of employees, unions, and employers?

Suggestions for Further Reading

Adams, George W. (1993). *Canadian Labour Law* (2nd ed.). Aurora, ON: Canada Law Book. A loose-leaf reference book updated quarterly. Consult for more information and in-depth analysis of any of the aspects of labour law discussed in this chapter.

Adell, Bernard. (1988). "Law and Industrial Relations: The State of the Art in Common Law Canada." In G. Hébert et al. (Eds.), *The State of the Art in Industrial Relations.* Kingston and Toronto: Queen's University IRC and the University of Toronto Centre for Industrial Relations. Contains a very useful discussion of perspectives on labour law.

Carter, Donald D., Geoffrey England, Brian Etherington, and Gilles Trudeau. (2002). *Labour Law in Canada* (5th Ed.). Markham, ON: Kluwer Law International, Butterworths. Thorough, yet easily understandable, survey and analysis of the legal protections and remedies available to employers and workers in Canada.

Fudge, Derek and John Brewin. (2005). *Collective Bargaining in Canada: Human Right or Canadian Illusion?* Nepean, ON and Rexdale, ON: National Union of Public and General Employees and United Food and Commercial Workers. Available from either NUPGE or UFCW, this study looks at the increasing restrictions on collective bargaining rights of Canadians and at governments' tendencies to unhesitatingly override labour's rights when politically expedient. The authors argue that when free collective bargaining is viewed from a human-rights perspective, Canada's record is not enviable.

Weiler, Paul. (1980). *Reconcilable Differences: New Directions in Canadian Labour Law.* Toronto: Carswell. A lucid, often witty, and always thought-provoking discussion by a man who, as chair of the BC labour relations board during its glory days, was "present at the creation" of many major innovations in Canadian labour law.

CHAPTER 8

LABOUR RELATIONS AND COLLECTIVE BARGAINING IN THE PUBLIC SECTOR

"Sick System." Striking nurses and hospital support staff let the public know they think their province's health care system is urgently in need of intensive care.

LEARNING OBJECTIVES

After studying this chapter, you should be able to:

1. Explain the significance of the public sector to the Canadian IR system.
2. Identify who is a public sector worker.
3. Describe the distinctive evolution of Canadian public sector bargaining.
4. Discuss significant recent developments in public sector labour relations.
5. Explain the major distinctions between public sector and private sector bargaining.
6. Describe dispute resolution methods unique to the public sector.

The public sector is of critical importance in the Canadian IR system because of the often essential nature of the work it performs and because public sector strikes can have severe consequences for the general public. It is also significant because roughly half the country's union members work there. After noting these points and indicating who should be considered a public sector employee, we go on to discuss the evolution of public sector collective bargaining, paying special attention to the difficulties of the past two decades. Then we consider some special features of public sector bargaining, including employee and employer differences, legislative differences, the narrower scope of bargaining generally permitted in the public sector, and special dispute resolution methods such as conventional and final-offer arbitration and the controlled strike. We conclude the chapter with a look at future prospects for collective bargaining in the public sector.

THE IMPORTANCE OF THE PUBLIC SECTOR

The public sector is important to IR students for a variety of reasons. First and perhaps foremost is the often essential nature of the work it performs. Public sector workers teach our children, care for our sick, and look after the needs of social assistance recipients, in addition to performing a host of other jobs ranging from garbage collection and snow removal to issuing driver's and marriage licenses. In many cases, there is no readily available substitute for the services provided through the public sector (Gunderson and Reid, 1995:158). If a shoe factory goes on strike, it is normally easy enough to obtain another brand of shoe. But if public schoolteachers go on strike, parents can't simply turn around and find another school. Thus the effects of public sector strikes tend to be more severe than those of private sector ones (Gunderson and Reid, 1995) and also more readily apparent.

The public sector is also important because it makes up a sizeable share of the country's workforce and a very large share indeed of its union membership. Moreover, in recent years, public sector unions and leaders have played an increasingly important role in the Canadian labour movement (Rose, 1995:47). With their high proportion of female members, the public sector unions have become leaders in the fight for paid parental leave and employment and pay equity (Swimmer and Thompson, 1995).

Finally, the public sector is important to IR students because of the state of crisis it has been in, not just in Canada but throughout most of the industrialized world (Beaumont, 1995). During the 1990s, faced with growing and seemingly intractable deficits and increasingly unable or unwilling to balance the books by increasing taxes, governments everywhere sought to reduce the one cost seemingly within their control: that of public sector workers' compensation. Although there were some exceptions, cost reductions were generally obtained through legislative fiat rather than through collective bargaining (Swimmer, 2000; Fryer, 1995).[1] In addition, Canadian governments have adopted such cost-reduction strategies as privatization, contracting out, downsizing, reorganization of work, and a greater use of "atypical" work arrangements such as part-time or temporary work, fixed-term contracts, home work, and even volunteers (Rose, 1995:35).

Though the deficits of the 1990s have now turned into surpluses in most jurisdictions, the restructuring, cutbacks, and public sector pay and bargaining restrictions have largely continued (see Rose, 2004b). Over the past quarter century, wage increases in public sector collective agreements have lagged significantly behind private sector increases, particularly in the federal public service and in the education/health/welfare sectors (Thompson and Ponak, 2005:438). Public sector workers have also been angered by the heavier workloads resulting from governments' failure to replace colleagues let go in the earlier wave of downsizings. Not surprisingly, such government tactics have led to increased union militancy and a rash of public sector strikes all across Canada. The years between 1999 and 2003 saw a cross-country wave of health care disputes, some of them illegal strikes, involving nearly 200 000 health care workers (Haiven and Haiven, 2003) extending from Nova Scotia and New Brunswick to British Columbia. The year 2001 also saw a series of transit strikes in Calgary and various BC cities (including one in Vancouver that lasted four months), while 2004 was marked by a nationwide strike of the Public Service Alliance of Canada (PSAC) against the federal government that ended only when the membership ratified proposed tentative agreements against the advice of their leadership (PSAC, 2004).

Aggravating the situation is the aging of the public sector workforce. Across Canada, employers are increasingly being faced with the problem of replacing aging workers due to retire (CLBC, 2000). This problem is often even more severe in the public sector, given that in many jurisdictions, the public sector workforce is older than the overall workforce (see Lowe, 2001a; Auditor-General, 2000 and 2001). As a result, issues of recruitment and retention have come increasingly to the fore. Public sector managers, as well as union officials, have warned that continuing labour–management friction can only hurt recruitment at a time when government is facing increasingly severe competition from the private sector for talented

"We won't work for peanuts." The above demonstration, which took place during a recent Public Service Alliance strike, offers graphic evidence of federal government workers' anger at receiving wage increase offers below the inflation rate.

employees (see Fryer, 2000 and 2001). But whether Canadian governments have got this message yet remains to be seen.

Who Is a Public Sector Worker?

For purposes of this discussion, the public sector includes the federal and provincial civil services, municipalities, health care, and education.[2] Between 1977 and 2004, the percentage of working Canadians employed in the public sector remained relatively steady at between 21 and 24 percent; however, this apparent stability masks important changes that have occurred in many parts of the sector. Whereas in 1977, the three sub-sectors (public administration, education, and health care) were of roughly equal size (Rose, 1995), by 2004 health care employed almost half of all Canadian public sector workers, with education accounting for slightly over one-quarter and public administration, slightly under (see Table 8.1).

Between 1991 and 2000, there was a gradual but steady decline in the percentage of Canadians employed in the public sector, a decline driven mainly by an ongoing decline in public administration (direct government employment). However, during that same period, the number employed in education increased by about one-third, while the number employed in health and welfare increased by about 60 percent. The period from 2000 to 2004 saw substantial increases in employment in all three sub-sectors. The public sector accounted for about a third of the country's total employment growth during this period (see Table 8.1), thereby increasing its share of total employment for the first time in well over a decade (Table 8.1). Once

Table 8.1

EMPLOYMENT (IN THOUSANDS), CANADIAN PUBLIC SECTOR AND VARIOUS SUB-SECTORS, SELECTED YEARS 1977–2004

Year	Pub. Adm.	Education	Health/ Welfare	Total Pub.	Total	Pub. as % of total
1977	723.8	716.9	796.2	2236.9	9978.2	23.4
1981	793.3	732.1	931.2	2456.6	11 398.0	21.6
1987	769.4	788.4	1148.5	2706.3	12 320.7	22.0
1991	846.3	860.7	1312.7	3019.7	12 850.6	23.5
1996	810.2	908.4	1393.5	3112.1	13 462.6	23.1
1997	795.3	914.1	1390.6	3100.0	13 774.4	22.5
1998	781.2	935.0	1426.3	3142.5	14 140.4	22.2
1999	774.2	982.6	1444.4	3201.2	14 531.2	22.0
2000	761.7	974.8	1526.4	3262.9	14 909.7	21.9
2004	829.2	1038.4	1736.7	3604.3	15 949.7	22.6

Pub. Adm. = Public Administration

Total Pub. = Total public sector employment (sum of public administration, education, and health and welfare). Government enterprise employees are not included.

Note: Data used are unadjusted annual averages for the various years; some relatively minor differences in employment figures between the 1996 and 2000 editions of Historical Labour Force Statistics used in this table do not affect the overall trends shown above.

Source: Statistics Canada, Cat. No. 71-201-XPB (Historical Labour Force Statistics), 1996 edition (for 1977 and 1981); 2000 edition (for all other years through 2000); Employment by Industry and Sex, CANSIM table 282-0008, for 2004.

again, health care was the main driver, accounting for over 60 percent of all public sector employment growth since the start of the new millennium.

Because union density rates are far higher in the public than in the private sector—72 percent as compared to 18 percent in 2003 (Akyeampong, 2004)—public sector workers have long made up a much larger share of the country's union members than of its total workforce. In 2003 (Akyeampong, 2004), the public sector accounted for over half the country's union membership, as it has for some time (see Rose, 1995). While the public sector density rate could certainly decline in the coming years, public sector unionists are almost certain to remain a critical element of the country's labour movement for the foreseeable future.

THE DEVELOPMENT OF PUBLIC SECTOR UNIONISM

Why Public Sector Unionism Developed Slowly

Two important facts about the growth of Canadian public sector unionism should be noted at the outset. First, it came a good deal later than private sector unionism. Most Canadian public sector workers didn't acquire the right to join unions until after the passage of the *Public Service Staff Relations Act (PSSRA)* in 1967—23 years after private sector workers acquired that right through *PC 1003* (discussed in the labour history chapter). Such a time lag between the granting of private and public sector union rights is quite normal in Western industrialized countries. In the United States, the lag between the *Wagner Act* and President Kennedy's executive order granting federal government employees limited bargaining rights was 26 years (Mills, 1989). Likewise, there was a lag of several decades between private and public sector bargaining rights in such European countries as France (Lorwin, 1954) and Sweden (Johnston, 1962).[3] The reason for such a lag is that the problem of providing essential public services under an IR regime that permits public sector workers to strike is one that few governments seem ready to confront until they have had substantial experience with private sector disputes.

The second important fact about Canadian public sector unionism is that, in contrast to private sector unionism, which developed rather slowly, it "emerged full-blown in a very compressed time span" (Ponak, 1982:343). In 1960, aside from some outside municipal workers, public schoolteachers (Ponak, 1982:344), and those in the province of Saskatchewan, very few public sector workers had joined unions. By the mid to late 1970s, the vast majority had (Ponak, 1982:350). The extremely rapid evolution of public sector collective bargaining meant that certain growing pains were inevitable. In particular, finding appropriate bargaining structures and dispute resolution procedures proved (and continues to prove) extremely difficult (Ponak, 1982).

The Early Years: Public Employee Associations

There was some form of public sector employee organization as early as the late nineteenth century (Rose, 1995:31), and by the end of the First World War, associations of public employees had become fairly prominent (Ponak, 1982:345; Fryer, 1995:347). But these associations operated quite differently from trade unions. Among other things, they sought to avoid confrontation with employers, had no compulsory membership requirements, did not affiliate with labour federations, and included management personnel up to the most senior levels (Ponak, 1982:345). While the associations undertook various social activities, they also played a consultative role by presenting to government employees' concerns about wages and working conditions (Fryer, 1995).

Throughout the pre-war period and well into the post-war period, such consultation marked the limit of permissible collective action for the vast majority of Canadian public sector employees. Before the Second World War, with even most private sector workers effectively barred from joining unions due to employer opposition and the lack of protective legislation, any significant degree of public employee organization was out of the question.[4] After the war, labour relations legislation in every jurisdiction except Saskatchewan continued to exclude public sector workers, other than some municipal workers (see Graham, 1995) and a few public schoolteachers. Public employers were generally opposed to unionism on the grounds that collective bargaining would inevitably lead to strikes and thus to disruption of essential services and possibly even threats to public safety (Ponak, 1982:347).

Another, even more fundamental, basis for opposition to public employee unionization was the sovereignty notion (see Fryer, 1995), whose proponents maintained that government bodies such as legislatures are vested with certain powers, especially over fiscal matters, that cannot be shared or taken away. Collective bargaining would, it was argued, be unconstitutional in that it would diminish those powers by forcing revisions in government budgets (Ponak and Thompson, 1989:376–377). The clearest statement of the doctrine was made in 1964 by Quebec Premier Jean Lesage: "The Queen does not negotiate with her subjects!" Just a year after issuing this lofty pronouncement, Lesage found himself doing just that, as his province became the second, after Saskatchewan, to grant public sector workers full collective bargaining rights, including the right to strike.

In addition, many public sector workers, particularly white-collar and professional ones, didn't like what they saw traditional unionism as representing. Many were skeptical about the possibilities of collective action and most disliked the adversarial tone characteristic of union–management relations in industrial settings. Professionals generally believed collective action, especially strikes, to be unprofessional; historically most had worked under a collegial system whereby their views were incorporated into management decisions (Thompson, 1982) and felt they could rely on professional associations to protect their economic interests. Others believed that the nature of their public service obligations, including particularly the need to maintain continuous service, ruled out collective bargaining (Ponak, 1982:346). It should also be noted that, prior to the Second World War, most government departments and other public sector organizations were generally quite small. For the most part, those working in such organizations would have known their co-workers and immediate superiors and subordinates quite well. In such small, intimate organizations, it may have been easier to work out problems informally than it would be later on, when government departments and other public sector organizations grew into large, impersonal bureaucracies (see Heron, 1989).

Association-Consultation: The NJC Experience

Through the early 1960s, the most common form of public employee action was association-consultation, whereby members of employee associations would consult, either formally or informally, with public sector management to express employees' concerns regarding pay, working conditions, and other aspects of the employment relationship. Perhaps the best-known consultative body was the National Joint Council (NJC), established in 1944 to address the needs of federal government employees. Comprising representatives from about a dozen civil service staff associations (the staff side) and senior government officials (the official side), the NJC would meet when necessary to consider such issues as recruitment, training, hours of work, promotion, discipline, tenure, pay, health, welfare, and seniority (Ponak, 1982:348). When the two sides managed to reach agreement on an issue, a recommendation would be made to Cabinet. Since the Council included senior government officials, the idea was that its recommendations would be quickly accepted by the government. All too often, this did not happen. For one thing, the scope of discussable issues was narrower than the staff side had expected. Most notably, wages were outside the NJC's jurisdiction, which forced the associations to submit salary briefs directly to the government (Ponak, 1982). Another serious problem was the lack of any mechanism to resolve disputes between the two sides. If the official side said "No," the matter was determined unilaterally by government (Ponak, 1982). These and various other inherent weaknesses led to considerable frustration on the part of federal government employees (Ponak, 1982).[5]

By the 1950s, the NJC's lack of any real power had caused an increasing number of staff associations to question its value. Throughout the 1950s and into the 1960s, the lack of wage increases, the rapid growth of government departments into large, impersonal bureaucracies, and a general climate of social change and questioning of authority helped move most government employees away from association-consultation and towards conventional trade unionism (Heron, 1989; Ponak, 1982). Recognizing that consultation wasn't meeting their members' needs, the associations began deleting no-strike clauses, excluding management personnel, hiring full-time staff, and affiliating with major labour federations such as the CLC (Ponak, 1982). The "last straw" was when John Diefenbaker's minority Conservative government rejected an NJC-recommended wage increase as inflationary (Swimmer, 1995). After his government fell (over a different issue), public service bargaining rights became a major issue in the ensuing election campaign, and the Liberals, under Lester Pearson, promised that, if elected, they would grant those rights with binding arbitration (Swimmer, 1995:369).

Transition to Collective Bargaining

Elected in 1963, Pearson and his Liberals had struck a commission to develop a model for public service bargaining when they were overtaken by a series of events, of which the most important was an illegal nationwide postal strike in 1965 (Swimmer, 1995). The strike, to which most Canadians were reasonably sympathetic (Swimmer, 1995), apparently made government officials realize that, for many public employees, arbitration would no longer suffice. Another key factor was the Liberal government's tenuous minority position, with the balance of power held by the pro-labour NDP. When, after the success of the postal strike, many of the old associations began demanding the right to strike, the government (as a matter of political expediency) came up with the then-novel "choice of procedures" mechanism (Swimmer, 1995), which it later enshrined in the *Public Service Staff Relations Act (PSSRA)*.

The *PSSRA* and Its Impacts

Passed in 1967, the *PSSRA* gave federal government employees the right to join unions. Those unions were given the right to choose, at the start of each round of bargaining, between binding interest arbitration and the conventional conciliation-strike route. To protect the public safety, union members designated as essential were not allowed to strike nor was the employer allowed to lock workers out. The legislation also created the Public Service Staff Relations Board (PSSRB) to administer the act. One of the Board's major functions was to determine appropriate public service bargaining units. Those units were determined along occupational rather than departmental lines, which meant a complicated system of 76 bargaining units (*PSSRA*, section 78[1]).[6]

After passage of the *PSSRA* , public service unionization grew very quickly. There were several reasons for this. First, association members typically joined one of the public service unions en masse, eliminating the need for extensive membership campaigns (Ponak, 1982). Second, since public employers generally accepted unionization, certification could proceed quite rapidly once the unions had signed up the old association members. Finally, the *PSSRA* was to set in motion a wave of legislation providing first provincial government employees and then other public sector workers, such as teachers and nurses, with collective bargaining rights. By the early 1970s, every province had granted its employees the right to join unions (Fryer, 1995). Some provinces adopted a variation of the *PSSRA* providing the right to strike; others, including Alberta and Ontario,[7] adopted an administrative model with binding arbitration as the dispute resolution procedure (Fryer, 1995).

Public sector unionization had a dramatic effect on both the size and character of the Canadian labour movement. Between 1965, when Quebec gave its employees the right to unionize, and 1978, the end of the great wave of public sector legislation, Canadian union membership more than doubled, from 1.59 million to 3.28 million. The country's union density rate also increased sharply, from 30 to 39 percent (Chaison, 1982). No less dramatic was the change in the labour movement's character. In 1960, most union members were male and blue-collar (Ponak and Thompson, 1995). By the 1970s, many were women and many were white-collar workers or professionals. The Canadian Union of Public Employees (CUPE) had become the country's largest union (Morton, 1995). Its heavily female membership and those of other public sector unions would push demands for maternity leave, flexible hours, and anti-discrimination provisions, while professionals and white-collar workers pushed professional development issues, such as support for in-service education and travel to conferences (see Ponak, 1982:351).

From the 1960s through 1975, public sector unions negotiated significant improvements in wages and working conditions. Special attention was paid to the correction of long-standing salary anomalies in lower-paid, largely female-dominated job classifications (Fryer, 1995:349). Throughout most of this period, public sector collective bargaining operated quite well with only moderate government interference in the form of back-to-work legislation, much of that being in Quebec (Ponak and Thompson, 2001:435).[8]

End of the Golden Age

This "Golden Age" of public sector collective bargaining, as it has since become known, ended abruptly on Thanksgiving Day 1975, with the federal government's imposition of a three-year program of wage and price controls (discussed in Chapter 3). While the controls applied to all workers, they appear to have demonstrated to government the political advantages of restraining public sector compensation (Ponak and Thompson, 1995).

At this time, as well, a number of governments began to take a harder line in their approach to labour issues generally and public sector labour issues in particular.[9] Most notably, the federal government moved to restrict government employees' bargaining rights substantially in a series of amendments to the *PSSRA* introduced in 1978. While the amendments, including the restriction of the right to strike, an extension of managerial exclusions, the introduction of the lockout right, and the tying of arbitration awards to private sector compensation norms, were eventually withdrawn in the face of strong public opposition (Ponak and Thompson, 1995), they pointed the direction for future federal public service labour policy. At least in part, the government may have been responding to growing public outrage at the frequent, lengthy strikes in the Montreal Transit system and the post office, a feeling that the highly publicized "public be damned" attitude of certain postal union leaders did little to diminish (Swimmer, 1995:385–386). The late 1970s also saw sharp reductions in federal government employment levels, which up till then had been increasing steadily since the beginning of the decade (Swimmer, 1995:377, Table 3). In Quebec, the government took the first steps towards the comprehensive essential services legislation it passed in 1982 (Hébert, 1995).

Perhaps not surprisingly, public sector unions responded to these developments with a show of increased militancy. Beginning in 1976, the public sector share of total person-days lost to strikes began to increase (Gunderson and Reid, 1995:138–139). Starting around 1980, the percentage of disputes settled through arbitration began to decline, suggesting, among other things, a preference for strike action as opposed to arbitration on the part of public sector workers (Ponak and Thompson, 1995:437). The public sector also began to feature high grievance rates (Ponak and Thompson, 1995:429). Overall, public sector union members were starting to behave more like their private sector counterparts, due to an increasingly difficult economic environment, as well as the growing restrictions placed on their activities by governments across Canada.

The 1980s: Wage Controls and Restraint

In 1982, the federal government responded to a second wave of inflation by imposing another round of controls, unilaterally extending collective agreements for a period of two years (Rose, 2004b) with increases of 6 and 5 percent (the "6 and 5" program). This time the controls were applied exclusively to wages and only in the public sector. The legislation also eliminated the right to strike and access to interest arbitration and precluded negotiation even over non-monetary issues (Rose, 2004b). By 1983, every province had followed Ottawa's lead and limited public sector compensation in some way or another (Ponak and Thompson, 1989), with six provinces adopting formal control programs of their own (Fryer, 1995:350). The harshest measures were taken in Quebec, where public sector workers saw their pay rolled back by about 20 percent (Hébert, 1995:222), and in British Columbia, where a right-wing government not only imposed a public sector wage freeze but also made drastic (25 percent) cuts in government employment levels (Morton, 1989:177; Thompson and Ponak, 1992:308). In Alberta, where government employees and many other public sector workers did not have the right to strike, arbitrators were ordered to take the government's ability to pay into account in fashioning public employee arbitration awards (see Haiven, 1995:246).

The wave of retrenchment wasn't limited to compensation issues. In 1982, in the wake of a disagreement over designation levels in an air traffic controllers' dispute, the Supreme Court of Canada ruled that the government had the sole right to determine the level of service to be provided (Swimmer, 1995:381). The decision in effect removed most of the PSSRB's adjudicative role and led to a sharp increase in federal public service designation levels after 1982 (Swimmer, 1995:379–381). In 1983, the Alberta government passed legislation outlawing hospital strikes in the province (Haiven, 1995:254). Meanwhile, in Quebec, a government weary of the public sector strikes that it had often been forced to end through legislation, in 1982 established an Essential Services Council to manage and maintain essential services during public sector disputes (Boivin and Déom, 1995:471). Among other things, the essential services legislation compels the parties to come up with an agreement on the definition of essential services before any strike can become legal. Three years later, the Quebec government placed further restrictions on public sector unions with its 1985 *Act respecting the process of negotiation of the collective agreements in the public and parapublic sectors.* This act significantly increased restrictions on public sector strikes and removed the right to strike completely for all matters negotiated at the local as opposed to provincial level (Boivin, 1989:429).

The attack on public sector unions went furthest in British Columbia where, in 1987, a sweeping revision of labour relations legislation sought to shift the balance of power away from workers and unions and towards employers (Shields, 1990). Though the BC government's attack on labour was not confined to the public sector, its effects were felt most sharply there. Among other things, Bill 19 replaced the province's tripartite labour relations board with an Industrial Relations Council headed by a commissioner selected by the government (Shields, 1990:52). This "labour czar" was given sweeping powers to impose mediation, binding conventional or final-offer arbitration, or a public interest inquiry board on the bargaining process (Shields, 1990:58). With regard to essential services, the Labour Minister was given the power to declare a category of workers essential whenever a dispute posed a threat to the province's economy or to residents' health, safety, and welfare. In the public sector, collective bargaining was subjected to the "ability to pay" clause, which made the government's ability to pay the primary consideration in all public sector settlements. In effect, this marked the abolition of free public sector collective bargaining over wages and its replacement with a state of permanent[10] wage controls (Shields, 1990).

The 1990s: Retrenchment and Restructuring

The 1990s were to prove even more difficult for public sector workers than the 1980s. In addition to continuing the previous decade's public sector wage freezes and rollbacks and (in many cases) suspension of collective bargaining (Fryer, 1995:350), governments across Canada reduced the scope and size of their operations, driven partly by massive deficit and debt levels and partly by an ideological shift back toward free market economics. As a result, public sector bargaining systems all across Canada faced their most severe stresses since the beginning of widescale public sector collective bargaining (see Swimmer, 2000; Ponak and Thompson, 2001). Starting in the late 1980s, such developments as privatization, contracting out, and the use of short-term and temporary contracts all served to put public sector workers' jobs increasingly at risk (Rose, 1995). Not surprisingly, those unions began to take an increasingly militant line, urging their members to vote against governing parties in elections, waging aggressive publicity campaigns against the government policies that were costing members their jobs, and accounting for an increasingly large share of the country's strike incidence, even in the face of severe restrictions on their right to strike.

The Federal Government and the 1991 Public Service Strike

Once again, the federal government set the tone for public sector bargaining across the country. On February 26, 1991, Finance Minister Michael Wilson told federal government employees that any wage increases could only be achieved at a proportional cost in jobs (Swimmer, 1995:398).[11] Moreover, annual wage increases greater than 3 percent would not be considered for the next three years. This hard-line stance would lead to the first full-scale public service strike in Canadian history in September of 1991. The massive effort proved unavailing, however, as the government legislated its employees back to work and unilaterally extended the old agreement with a wage freeze for the first year and a 3 percent increase for the second (Swimmer, 1995).

While the union's tough stance may have won it both respect and improved pension and workforce adjustment benefits (Swimmer, 1995), it didn't change the government's wage control policy. Indeed, in November of 1992, just slightly over a year after the end of the public service strike, the government took an even harder line in unilaterally extending the wage freeze for a further two years. This meant that federal government employees had a wage increase of only 3 percent over a four-year period (Swimmer, 1995:401), a rate far below inflation even in the recessionary 1990s. Abandoning its traditional stance of political neutrality, the PSAC then vowed to work for the Conservatives' defeat in the 1993 federal election (Swimmer, 1995:400). But the Liberal victory in that election gave government employees little solace. Although they had pledged during the campaign to restore free collective bargaining in the public service, once the Liberals took office, their prescription for the public service was more of the same medicine provided by the Conservatives. Wages were unilaterally frozen for a further two years, until 1997; worse still, the government axed 45 000 civil service jobs, or nearly one-quarter of all federal public employment (Swimmer, 1995:405; Craig and Solomon, 1996:362). Those who remained had to work harder to do both their own work and that of their now-departed colleagues. In addition, thanks to changes resulting from the 1992 *Public Service Reform Act (PSRA)*, it became much easier for the government to replace full-time, permanent employees with short-term, temporary, or casual ones who would receive no benefits and not be eligible for union membership (Swimmer, 1995:397–398). In the face of these and other developments, not least of which was the government's appropriation of the entire federal public service pension surplus (see Fryer, 2000 and 2001), federal government employees found themselves beleaguered on almost every front as the millennium approached.

The Provincial Scene

Federal public service employees weren't alone in facing wage freezes, major downsizing and restructuring initiatives, and more difficult working conditions for those managing to keep their jobs. So extensive did the scope of unilateral government action become that across Canada during the 1990s free public sector collective bargaining was the exception rather than the rule. In all, 11 of 15 governments in power during the 1990s resorted to legislative action, either exclusively or in conjunction with hard bargaining (see Rose, 2004b).

In the generally depressed Atlantic region, federal cuts to transfer payments hit particularly hard, leaving already hard-pressed provincial governments with little or no room to manoeuvre. In Newfoundland, the provincial government imposed a one-year wage freeze in 1991, later extending the freeze for a further three years, slashing pension contributions, and imposing unpaid days off on its employees. In 1994, the government's actions in slashing pension fund payments to teachers, closing schools, and reducing teachers' job security provoked a three-week province-wide teachers' strike (Fryer, 1995:353–354). Nova Scotia took similar measures. And in Prince Edward Island, the government imposed an 8.5 percent rollback on all public sector compensation in 1994, even though public sector workers had voluntarily agreed to a 6 percent reduction for four months just two years earlier (Fryer, 1995:355).

In Quebec, governments got into the habit of unilaterally extending public sector collective agreements, with the result that no collective bargaining occurred over six years and public sector workers received only a 3 percent wage increase throughout that period (Hébert, 1995:226–227). In addition, the 1993 extension was accompanied by legislation ordering all public employers to reduce their wage bill by 1 percent in each of the next two years. As in the case of the Ontario "social contract" discussed below, the reduction was to be achieved by means of unpaid holidays, unless the unions were prepared to agree on other ways of achieving the savings (Boivin and Déom, 1995:476).

In the late 1990s, the PQ government's pursuit of its zero deficit target caused it to embark on widespread health care and education cutbacks. Along with a very unpopular series of municipal restructurings, these cutbacks hurt the government's credibility, and may well have been a factor in its defeat by the Liberals in 2003.

In Ontario, an NDP government under Bob Rae, faced with ballooning budget deficits, initially sought to recoup more than $2 billion in savings from its 900 000 public employees without resorting to layoffs (Craig and Solomon, 1996:362). Rather than unilaterally imposing legislation, the government first sought to achieve this objective through a "social contract" to which it hoped the public sector unions would agree (Fryer, 1995:357). When the unions did not agree, the government passed its "Social Contract Act" in 1993. The act, bitterly opposed by the province's labour movement and also by three of the party's own backbenchers, provided for a three-year wage freeze and up to 12 days of unpaid leave per year in the event the wage freezes did not achieve sufficient savings.[12] Perhaps the legislation's greatest effect was to seriously weaken, if not destroy, the relationship between the province's labour movement and the NDP—the party that had taken office with the labour movement's support and pledged to defend its interests. The NDP failed to win a single Ontario seat in the 1993 and 1997 federal elections and was soundly defeated by Mike Harris's Conservatives in the 1995 and 1999 provincial elections. Not until 2000 did it again win a federal seat in a province once considered one of its strongholds.

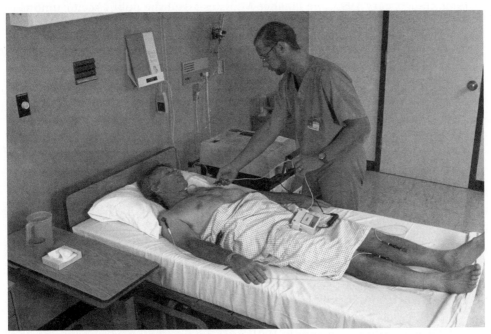

Health care workers like this nurse are coming under increasing stress due to cuts in health care budgets across Canada.

Still, draconian though it may have seemed in 1993, the Rae government's approach now appears almost benign when compared to that of the Conservative government that succeeded it. Abandoning a 50-year tradition of pragmatic, consensus-oriented conservatism in Ontario, the Harris government took office committed to implementing its strongly ideological "Common Sense Revolution" featuring large tax cuts, massive cuts in government spending, and major restructuring in health care and education. In 1996 and early 1997, public service cutbacks led to a series of province-wide one-day general strikes (*Collective Bargaining Review*, 1996–1997). Later in 1997, the province ushered in a new era of educational restructuring when it passed Bill 160. The bill eliminated local school boards, effectively concentrating control over the province's educational system in Toronto. The government also brought in shorter vacations, longer school days, and more classes with less preparation time for teachers (see Galt, 1998). In protest over these changes, the province's teachers staged a series of strikes in 1997 and 1998 (Green, 1998). In health care, the government's changes were no less dramatic. Major restructuring led to the closure of many hospitals, the merger of others, a reduction in the services offered patients, and the deinstitutionalization of many long-term patients (Marshall, 1998). Many services formerly provided in hospitals are now provided through home care of various kinds. On top of this, the government moved to contract out much of the home care service formerly provided by public sector workers (Marshall, 1998).

The Prairie provinces responded in various ways to the economic crisis of the 1990s. In Manitoba, the government froze public sector wages for a year in 1991. Though normal negotiations took place in 1992, resulting in a three-year contract (Fryer, 1995:356), the government did not allow that agreement to stay in place for long. In February 1993, the Finance Minister asked the public sector unions to accept a "voluntary" reduction in pay and benefits. When the unions did not agree, the government legislated 10-day unpaid layoffs for each of the next two years.

In Alberta, an ideologically driven Conservative government sought, in effect, to balance the provincial budget on the backs of public sector workers, cutting public expenditures by 20 percent to balance the budget over a three-year period ending in 1997. Cuts ranged from 8.3 percent in social services to 12.4 percent in education and 17.6 percent in health care (Fryer, 1995:360; Thomason, 1995:303). In education, the budget cuts resulted in the complete elimination of adult education funding, a 50 percent reduction in kindergarten funding, and a 5 percent cut in teachers' salaries (Thomason, 1995:303–304). These moves were accompanied by a major consolidation of public school boards and elimination of those boards' taxing authority (Thomason, 1995:280, 303).[13] In health care, still deeper cuts were made without consultation with the unions involved and with little consultation even with management (Haiven, 1995). Meanwhile, the government was equally hard on its own employees, initially forcing them to accept a 5 percent pay reduction comprising unpaid days off and a freeze on increments (Fryer, 1995:360), and later taking away four statutory holidays as well.

Initially, public sector collective bargaining fared better in Saskatchewan, where an NDP government took over in 1991. After a series of rotating strikes by government employees, their union agreed to accept a five-year agreement providing for modest wage increases and a cost-of-living adjustment in its late stages. The agreement expired in September 1996 (Fryer, 1995:359–360). Even here, however, with a government committed to maintaining free public sector collective bargaining, public sector workers have not been immune from restructuring, such as that resulting from the widespread closure of rural hospitals (Ponak and Thompson, 2001:418), or from frequent back-to-work orders when they did go on strike.[14]

In British Columbia, also an NDP province through most of the 1990s, a genuine social contract was arrived at through collective bargaining in the health care sector (Fryer, 1995; Haiven, 1995; Marshall, 1998). The "social accord" in health care, which was negotiated in 1993, broke new ground in Canadian public sector bargaining. The job reductions that the agreement provided for were to be achieved through attrition, early retirement, and a reduced workweek rather than layoffs (Haiven, 1995:268). Additional features included a modest (1.5 percent) wage hike, an early retirement fund, job security provisions, a labour adjustment program to help workers being transferred to community-care facilities, a guarantee of no expansion of contracting out, and the involvement of workers in decision making (Haiven, 1995:268–269; Marshall, 1998). Later, the BC government negotiated a new agreement with its own employees that didn't provide for a general wage increase, but did give the union considerable authority in improving work systems and redesigning service delivery (Fryer, 1995). However, with the defeat of the NDP government and its replacement by an ultra-right-wing Liberal government in June of 2001, public sector labour relations in BC took a hard turn back toward the adversarial mode that had dominated during the 1980s. Some of the measures taken by that new government are detailed in the next section.

The Twenty-First Century: Consolidation and Containment

By the late 1990s, most Canadian governments had moved from a deficit to a surplus position, and even in the remaining jurisdictions, the financial picture had generally brightened. Nonetheless, most Canadian governments have continued to take a tough stance toward their employees (Rose, 2004b). To be sure, employment has once again started to grow in the public sector, as we noted at the beginning of the chapter. But this growth has been quite modest compared to the country's population growth. In other ways, Canadian governments have tended to treat their employees pretty much as they did during the 1990s. It wouldn't be too far off the mark to refer to the past seven years as a period of "rightless recovery" for public sector workers and unions.

With the gradual resumption of "normal" collective bargaining in the late 1990s, public sector unions quite naturally sought to negotiate contracts allowing their members to make up for the years of purchasing power lost during the 1990s. For the most part, however, public sector employers have resisted the unions' attempts to catch up, though the unions did make a few very modest gains between 1998 and 2002 (Rose, 2004b:Table 3). Governments' actions helped to provoke the wave of public sector strikes described at the beginning of the chapter, leading to an increase in the public sector's share of total Canadian strike activity. Between 2000 and 2002, the public sector accounted for about half the total person-days lost to strikes (Rose, 2004b:286), despite the severe restrictions on public sector strikes in most jurisdictions.

As in the past, government's response was typically to resort to the legislative hammer. Back-to-work legislation was invoked in six provinces' health care disputes (see Haiven and Haiven, 2003) and three provinces' education disputes, as well as in utilities and municipal and urban transit (Rose, 2004b:285–287). In addition, BC's teachers and Ontario's ambulance workers were designated as essential, thereby restricting their right to strike. In Nova Scotia and BC, teachers saw their scope of bargaining reduced. Ontario also passed legislation limiting teachers' right to engage in such work-to-rule tactics as withdrawing from extracurricular activities (ibid., 287).

A growing problem related to the ongoing wave of provincial government cut-backs is the underfunding of community health care services and other community-based services such as group homes, women's shelters, and vocational training centres. While many services formerly provided by provinces have been devolved to the community level, all too often such devolution hasn't been accompanied by funding sufficient to enable already cash-strapped communities to provide these additional services. The result has been that many community-based workers, including those in both Ontario and Saskatchewan (CUPE, 2005a and 2005b), are paid substantially less than other public sector workers. Not surprisingly, this situation has led to high staff turnover (see Current Issues 8.1).

Current Issues 8.1

CARING FOR THE CAREGIVERS

In recent years, an increasing number of Canadians with developmental and intellectual disabilities, including some who in the past would have been confined to institutions, have been able to live with their families in their home communities thanks to supportive provincial programs and agencies.

Unfortunately, budget cuts have placed many of these valuable programs under severe stress. In Ontario, for example, community living agencies serving the developmentally disabled saw their budgets increase by only 0.5 percent in a year—a significant decline in real funding. The budget cuts come at a time when the agencies are facing increased demand for their services due to the aging of the population.

In Hamilton, local community living counsellors have warned that clients and front-line workers are paying the price for the continuing "woeful" underfunding of community living programs by the province.

While the previous Conservative government earned notoriety for its cuts to health care, the current Liberal government may not be doing much better. In fact, in the words of Ontario CUPE president Sid Ryan, "When it comes to providing adequate funding for services for people with developmental disabilities, the McGuinty Liberals' record is even worse than the predecessor Tories'."

An employer study has found community living workers underpaid compared to other social service workers, which has resulted in a high turnover rate in the sector, and a lack of continuity of care for those with developmental disabilities.

Ryan appeared at a press conference on March 22, 2005, with front-line community living workers and local NDP MPP Andrea Horwath in a bid to bring public attention to the impact of provincial underfunding on the community living sector. ▶

Ontario isn't the only province where people working in community-based sectors are under-paid. In Saskatchewan, provincial CUPE president Tom Graham has said that workers in group homes, child care centres, women's shelters, vocational training centres, and other community-based organizations are still being paid about $8 to $10 per hour less than other public sector workers doing comparable work.

"Now that Saskatchewan is considered a 'have' province," Graham said, there is no excuse for not closing these discriminatory gaps.

Sources: CUPE. (2005). "Underfunding by Province Hurting People in Hamilton with Developmental Disabilities . . . " press release, March 21; CUPE. (2005). "CUPE Gives Saskatchewan Budget Mixed Marks," press release, March 23.

Nowhere have the measures taken been more severe than in BC, a province which in 2001 cut the size of its civil service by about one-third in order to finance massive tax cuts (see Peirce, 2003:268). In addition to cutting the civil service and restricting its public schoolteachers in the ways described above, the province passed a *Health and Social Services Delivery Improvement Act* allowing health care employers to reorganize service delivery and contract out non-clinical services, even where this meant voiding collective agreement provisions dealing with contracting out and bumping rights (ibid.). Bill 29, which went well beyond even the most restrictive measures of the 1990s, has been characterized as arguably "the most severe government intrusion into collective agreements in Canadian history" (Thompson and Bemmels, 2003:108). A *Charter* challenge has since been mounted (Rose, 2004b:287).

While other Canadian governments haven't gone as far as BC, few have allowed their employees to share in the returning prosperity of the past five or six years. One reason why governments are maintaining their tough stance vis-à-vis their own employees may well be the lack of political fallout from continuing to do so (Rose, 2004b:287). This suggests that public sector unions will need to form coalitions with the users of public services if they are to have any hope of reversing their current sorry situation.

DISTINCTIONS BETWEEN PUBLIC AND PRIVATE SECTOR BARGAINING

By now, it should be clear that public sector bargaining differs from bargaining in the private sector in a number of important ways. In this section, we consider in more detail some of the many important differences between collective bargaining in the two sectors. The distinctions we focus on include employer differences, employee and union differences, and legislative and policy differences, including those affecting dispute resolution mechanisms.

Employer Differences

Government's Dual Role

The single most important employer difference between public and private sector bargaining is the dual role government plays—as the employer of public sector workers and as legislator. This dual role gives it a degree of power that private sector employers can only dream of possessing. Particularly in times of economic crisis, governments often find it irresistibly tempting to pass legislation to achieve objectives they haven't been able to achieve at the bargaining table (Haiven, 1995; Swimmer and Thompson, 1995). Government's desire to protect Canadians from the effects of public sector work stoppages has also resulted in frequent use of back-to-work legislation, particularly since 1975. From 1950 through 2002, the federal and various provincial governments resorted to such legislation on 90 occasions (Ponak and Thompson, 2005:435). Just since the start of the new millennium, there have been 19 such legislative interventions, 8 being from British Columbia (HRSD, 2005a). Moreover, even when governments haven't intervened, the threat of such intervention has often been enough to induce unions to accept a settlement proposed by the government, as in the case of the 1991 Toronto Transit strike (Craig and Solomon, 1996:412–413).

The vast power government possesses in its dual role as employer and legislator can be a source of considerable frustration to public sector workers and unions, who often spend months in painstaking negotiations only to see their hard-earned results overturned by a single stroke of the legislative pen. Government's power may also be a source of frustration to public sector managers, who sometimes find themselves forced to administer a government-imposed solution they don't like and had no hand in fashioning. In this connection, it is worth noting that a 1989 study by David Zussman and Jak Jabes found a significantly higher degree of frustration and lower degree of job satisfaction among public than among private sector managers.

Diffusion of Management Authority

Another key difference between private and public sector collective bargaining is the far greater diffusion of management authority in the latter. In most private sector organizations, management responsibility is well defined and clearly established (Ponak and Thompson, 1995:424). Unions can usually come to the table knowing with whom they are bargaining and (for the most part) where those negotiators stand.

In the public sector, on the other hand, there is typically a "bewildering fragmentation of authority among numerous management officials" (Ponak and Thompson, 1995). In some cases, this fragmentation is inherent. Government departments, for example, normally have both an administrative and a political role. While federal and provincial government employees typically spend most of their time on their administrative functions (e.g., program delivery or policy analysis), reporting to the deputy minister, they ultimately report to the minister, who may assign them to political chores having little to do with their administrative work or even in direct contradiction to it. Even where public sector workers do not potentially have political responsibilities, there is still typically a division of management authority between elected officials and the line management who administer public sector organizations on a daily basis (Swimmer and Thompson, 1995:5). Often this division of authority is not a happy one, as elected officials' political agendas or lack of labour relations and administrative experience may lead them into more or less serious conflict with line management (Swimmer and Thompson, 1995).

Such fragmentation is exacerbated by the fact that many public bodies are funded from several different sources, each of which is likely to want to influence how the money is spent. In urban transit, for instance, local transit commissions are generally financed through a combination of user fees, municipal subsidies, and provincial grants. Provincial governments, various municipal governments, citizen groups, and the transit commissions' management all seek to play some role in the collective bargaining process (Swimmer and Thompson, 1995). These groups' objectives may well differ. Citizen groups may be primarily interested in improving or at least maintaining the level of service, while provincial and municipal governments may be more concerned with keeping costs down. The existence of so many different claimants inevitably makes decision making and the collective bargaining process much more complex (Swimmer and Thompson, 1995). Not infrequently, the internal bargaining that must take place before the union's proposals can be seriously addressed is as complex as the bargaining between the management and union sides—if not more so (Swimmer and Thompson, 1995:425).

To bypass the difficult and time-consuming multilateral bargaining that normally ensues in such situations, public sector unions may seek (sometimes successfully) to do an "end run" around the management bargaining team to deal directly with a public official they believe will be more sympathetic to their cause, such as a mayor or provincial premier (Ponak, 1982:354–355). While such intervention can bring an end to the particular dispute in question, it may also impose excessive long-term costs on taxpayers in addition to being a source of frustration for public sector managers, who not unjustifiably resent the loss of authority and lack of trust implied by such actions. Even in cases where elected officials don't intervene in such a direct way, political competition between officials of different parties or representing different levels of government can aggravate the problem of management fragmentation still further (Ponak and Thompson, 1995:425), again making bargaining more complex and increasing the frustration of public sector workers and the unions representing them.

Where negotiations haven't been centralized at the federal or provincial level, a common phenomenon over the years has been phantom bargaining (Ponak, 1982:354), whereby formal negotiating authority is ostensibly vested in a management group, such as a health care employers' association, but the key player—in this case the provincial government—that controls the purse strings is not represented at the table. The absence of parties with any real authority from the bargaining table in such situations has sometimes led unions to refer to the government as the "phantom at the bargaining table" and to complain that without direct government representation, collective bargaining amounts to little more than going through the motions (Ponak, 1982).

In attempting to get around these various difficulties, Canadian governments have tried a number of different approaches. Quebec has customarily taken a highly centralized approach to public sector bargaining (Hébert, 1995; Haiven, 1995:240), although in recent years large-scale disputes resulting from that centralization have induced the government to bring in a degree of decentralization through a two-tier (provincial and local) bargaining system (Hébert, 1995; Grant,

2000; Ponak and Thompson, 2005). In health care in that province, and also in New Brunswick, the government actually sits at the bargaining table as the management representative (Haiven, 1995:244). For its part, Saskatchewan has taken a middle-of-the-road position, allowing the employers' association to represent management, but also having a government observer sit at the bargaining table (Haiven, 1995).

Overall, public sector bargaining structures have tended to become more centralized in recent years, as provincial governments have sought to save money and assert greater control over the process by consolidating bargaining units and streamlining collective bargaining (see Rose, 2004b). Perhaps the most significant recent changes have taken place in British Columbia, where the government has provided for negotiations in seven different public sub-sectors (Ponak and Thompson, 1995:445). Under the 1993 *Public Sector Employers' Act*, each sub-sector other than the provincial civil service has its own employers' association responsible for coordinating human resource activity within the sub-sector, including collective bargaining (Fryer, 1995:362). The government is directly represented in these employer associations and has representatives in each sub-sector's governing body and the power to approve bylaws (Fryer, 1995:362–363). In other changes, Ontario and, more recently, Quebec have been amalgamating their municipalities (see Rose, 2004b). Meanwhile, the province of Alberta recently amended its *Labour Relations Code* to streamline health care bargaining. Among other things, the amendments reduced the number of agreements in the sector from 400 to 36 (Rose, 2004b:282).

While the overall trend has been toward greater centralization, there may be limits to how far provincial governments are willing to go in this direction. As Rose (2004b:282) has pointed out, with greater budgetary control comes increased political accountability—and possibly greater political risks as well. For instance, the Ontario government's unwillingness to take those greater political risks could be one reason why it hasn't adopted province-wide bargaining in public education, despite its centralization of funding and amalgamation of school boards (ibid.).

Economics versus Politics

It's only a slight oversimplification to suggest that the currency of private sector bargaining is money, while that of public sector bargaining is political power. While private sector employers and unions are far from unconcerned about politics, at the bargaining table their major battles tend to be over monetary issues such as wages, benefits, hours of work, and levels of employment. In contrast, though public sector employers and unions are certainly concerned about money, particularly at a time of continuing government budget cutbacks and workforce reductions, public sector bargaining itself remains primarily an exercise in political rather than economic power (Swimmer and Thompson, 1995:2).

In private sector strikes, the union's aim is normally to induce employers to make a better offer out of fear of losing business and perhaps permanent market share. In public sector strikes, the aim is more often to turn public opinion against the government, with an eye to pressuring the government into changing those policies that the union feels are hurting its members.

Notably, the costs of disagreement tend to be quite different in the private and public sectors. While private sector strikes almost invariably impose monetary costs, in terms of lost profit and longer-term loss of market share, strikes may actually benefit public sector employers economically, since their revenues remain the same, but their expenses are reduced by the amount of the striking employees' forgone wages and benefits (Ponak and Thompson, 1995:425–426). In the public sector the costs are mainly political ones, particularly in the case of disputes that seriously inconvenience the public for a lengthy period of time, such as strikes of municipal garbage collectors. Irate at the loss of the service in question, angry residents will deluge ministers' or municipal officials' offices with letters, phone calls, faxes, and emails demanding the restoration of the service at any cost and threatening to vote the government out of power if it is not restored. Politicians' fear of not being re-elected may help explain why, in good times, striking public sector workers have sometimes received extremely, perhaps even overly generous settlements—and why in bad times they have often been legislated back to work.

A point not often enough made (see Gérin-Lajoie, 1993) concerns the lack of an economic "bottom line" in public sector bargaining and the effect such a lack may have on union–management relations and the bargaining process. In the private sector, if a firm is losing profits and market share, management and the union may not agree on the cause of the problem, but at least they'll be able to agree there is a problem. The recognition of this common problem and of a common interest in keeping the enterprise afloat may just be enough to get the parties to start thinking about innovative possible solutions. In the public sector, where there normally is no economic bottom line, and where revenues typically have no direct link to either the quantity or quality of the good or service produced (Ponak and Thompson, 1995:426), it's often much harder for the parties to agree on what their problems are, or even necessarily that there is a problem. With no decline in profit or market share to serve as a "wake-up call," public sector managers in times of crisis may see their employees coming into work and apparently doing their jobs as usual, without recognizing that serious morale problems resulting from government restructuring or downsizing have seriously affected the quality of service these employees are providing to the public.

Employee and Union Differences

Employee Differences

By and large, and increasingly so in today's tough economy, public sector workers have the same concerns as private sector ones (Ponak and Thompson, 2001). Job security, the maintenance of real income levels, work hours, and workload are of prime importance in both sectors.

This said, there *are* a number of significant differences between public and private sector employees, and also between the ways in which public and private sector unions tend to operate. Public sector union members are much more likely than their private sector counterparts to be female, professional, and white-collar. In this connection, it's worth noting that in 1998, 58 percent of all public sector union members were female, compared to 22 percent in the private sector (Akyeampong, 1999).

In addition, the public sector contains more than its share of unionized white-collar workers, and virtually all the country's unionized professionals (Ponak and Thompson, 2001:424). The high proportion of female members in most public sector unions has led pay and employment equity issues to be of prime concern for these unions. Similarly, the high proportion of professionals in many public sector unions helps explain these unions' concern with intrinsic issues around the nature of work. Teachers' unions have often bargained (or attempted to bargain) over such issues as class size and preparation time. Likewise, reimbursement of professional dues and fees is an important issue to many public sector unions.

Union Differences

The Importance of Publicity

While public sector unions are obviously concerned with specific issues of particular relevance to their members (class size for teachers, shift schedules for nurses), overall their bargaining agendas tend to be fairly similar to those of private sector unions—when they can bargain at all. What's different is the way in which they attempt to achieve their objectives. Given that members of the general public are important stakeholders in all public sector activity, both as consumers of public services and as taxpayers, public sector unionism is inherently political, with many of its efforts directed towards winning and maintaining public support both for public sector unions' specific rights and for the government spending that undergirds the services public sector workers provide. During the 1990s the relative importance of political action and publicity campaigns increased dramatically, due mainly to government restrictions on public sector bargaining activity.

As Swimmer and Thompson (1995:2) note, the media are far more important in public sector than in private sector bargaining, as both sides seek to win the hearts and minds of everyday citizens. This is particularly true during labour disputes. The media played a prominent role both in the 1991 federal public service strike (Swimmer, 1995:400) and in more recent disputes such as those involving Ontario's teachers and National Gallery employees. But public sector unions' publicity efforts are not confined to times when there is a work stoppage. Most are regularly involved in campaigns aimed both at the general public and their own membership (Lawson, 1998; S. Marshall, 1998). For example, in 1996 the PSAC responded to the federal government's privatization and contracting out of national parks with an article in the union's magazine, *Alliance* (Mitchell, 1996), following it up later in the year with a direct mail campaign featuring articles that showed the public, in a humorous way, some of the possible effects of the government privatization campaign. More recently, in fact even as this edition was being written, the Ontario Public Service Employees Union (OPSEU) was engaged with a dispute with OC Transpo, the City of Ottawa's bus service, over OC Transpo's refusal to allow its ads criticizing the provincial government to be placed in city bus shelters (OPSEU, 2005, Mar. 17).

While some observers, such as Warrian (1996), argue that political protest and other such pressure tactics will generally be futile, so long as restrictions on public sector bargaining prevent public sector unions from bringing many of their major concerns to the bargaining table, it is difficult to see what alternative they have.

Union Fragmentation Union structure can be quite fragmented in the public sector, particularly in health care and education. In large industrial settings like auto plants and steel mills, a single union typically represents all employees or at least the great majority of them (Haiven, 1995:241). For the most part, the industrial union model also holds in government departments, although in the federal government, the large number of occupational groupings under the *PSSRA* has led to fragmentation of a different sort (see Swimmer, 1995). This is not the case in health care. In hospital settings (Haiven, 1995), there are normally at least three unions representing health care workers: a nurses' union, a general service union for maintenance and support staff, and a "paramedical" unit for skilled technical staff like dietitians, X-ray technologists, and physiotherapists. To make matters even more complicated, several different unions may be competing for the right to represent the same group of workers (Haiven, 1995:241–242). CUPE represents many hospital maintenance and support staff, but it is far from being the only union in the field. The Service Employees International Union (SEIU), the International Union of Operating Engineers, and various government employee unions also represent many of these same workers (Marshall, 1998; see also Haiven, 1995:241–242). The result of this kind of "balkanization" is that bargaining becomes more difficult, since there is a rarely a single union that can come to the bargaining table representing all employees in a provincial sub-sector (Haiven, 1995:241–242). Similar if less pronounced fragmentation exists in the education sector. For example, university professors are generally represented by a certified independent staff association, while support staff are most often represented by a union such as CUPE or SEIU (see Table 7.3 in chapter 7 for a list of the many certified bargaining agents at the University of Toronto, for example).

Legislative and Policy Differences

There are a good many legislative and policy differences between the private and public sector. The two most important ones are the far greater degree of fragmentation and variation in dispute resolution methods found in the public sector, and the significantly greater extent to which governments restrict public sector unions' rights with respect to such matters as bargaining-unit determination and the scope of bargainable issues.

Legislative Fragmentation

For the private sector, each province has a single labour act more or less closely modelled after the American *Wagner Act* (Ponak and Thompson, 1989). While there are some minor differences in dispute resolution procedures, almost all jurisdictions require some type of conciliation before a strike or lockout can become legal.

In contrast, jurisdictions vary greatly with respect to the coverage of particular groups under public sector legislation. At one extreme is Ontario, with separate laws for almost every public sector group, including government employees, teachers, hospital workers, police, and firefighters. At the opposite extreme are the federal jurisdiction and New Brunswick, each of which has a single private sector act and a single public sector one. In between are provinces such as Saskatchewan and British Columbia, which apply their general labour acts to a number of different public sector groups, but have special acts for teachers (in both provinces), for police and firefighters (in Saskatchewan), and for provincial government employees (in BC). Quebec (see Hébert, 1995:201 and Boivin and Déom, 1995:473–474) has a hybrid system whereby all groups fall under the jurisdiction of the general labour act, but many groups also have specific legislation governing such things as bargaining structure, the scope of collective agreements, and in particular the maintenance of essential services (see Table 8.2).

The variation in dispute resolution procedures (see Table 8.3) is equally great. Most provinces do not permit police and firefighters to strike, but all grant that right to municipal employees and most grant it to employees of government enterprises. In between, there is little consensus. Seven jurisdictions permit their employees to strike; four (Alberta, Manitoba, Nova Scotia, and PEI) do not. Nine jurisdictions permit teachers to strike, while two (Manitoba and PEI) do not. Eight jurisdictions allow hospital workers to strike while three (Alberta, Ontario, and PEI) do not.

Most jurisdictions offer little in the way of consistent policy rationale for their choice of public sector dispute resolution methods. PEI, which has long had one of the most restrictive labour acts in Canada (Forsey, 1985; Peirce, 1989), doesn't allow any public sector workers except municipal employees to strike. At the opposite extreme are Saskatchewan and the federal jurisdiction, where all workers who have the right to bargain collectively have, at least in principle, the right to choose strike action (see Table 8.3), and BC, where all public sector workers have the right to strike, subject in most cases to essential service designations. In between, New Brunswick and Quebec allow all groups except police and firefighters to strike—an exclusion that has a certain logic given the essential nature of the work performed by these groups. Elsewhere, however, the right to strike seems to have been applied more or less randomly. Alberta, for example, allows teachers to strike, but not its own employees or hospital workers (see Table 8.3). Manitoba is just the opposite; there hospital workers can strike, but teachers and provincial government employees cannot. Ontario allows both teachers and provincial government employees to strike, but not hospital workers; in Nova Scotia, teachers and hospital workers as well as police can strike, but not provincial government employees.

How has such a fragmented, convoluted, and inconsistent system of public sector bargaining been allowed to evolve? At the end of the day, one can only speculate on the reasons for this bizarre evolution. Given the otherwise irrational, even contradictory nature of many of the provisions we have been discussing, it seems likely that local political considerations have played an extremely important if not pivotal role in that evolution (see Drache and Glassbeek, 1992:344).

Bargaining Unit Determination

Another key difference between public and private sector collective bargaining has to do with the way in which bargaining units are determined. In the private sector, this determination is normally made by the labour relations board, generally with

Table 8.2

PUBLIC SECTOR COLLECTIVE BARGAINING LEGISLATION

Jurisdiction	Municipal	Police	Firefighters	Hospitals	Teachers	Civil Service	Government Enterprise
Federal	*Canada Labour Code*	none (RCMP)*	*Canada Labour Code*, Par. 1	*Public Service Labour Relations Act (PSLRA)* (replaces the former *Public Service Staff Relations Act*)	*Public Service Labour Relations Act*	*Public Service Labour Relations Act*	*Canada Labour Code*
BC	general labour act; *Public Sector Employers' Act*[†]	general labour act; police/fire act	general labour act; police/fire act	general labour act; *Public Sector Employers' Act; Public Service Act; Health and Social Services Delivery Improvement Act; Health Sector Partnership Agreement Act* (If there is a conflict between *Public Service Act* and general labour act, the former prevails.)	general labour act; education act; *Public Sector Employers' Act*[†]	*Public Service Act*; general labour act	general labour act
Alberta	general labour act	police act	general labour act	general labour act[§]	general labour act; education act	*Public Service Act*	general labour act
Saskatchewan	general labour act	police act; general labour act	*Fire Department Act*; general labour act	general labour act	education act; *Teachers' Federation Act*	general labour act; *Public Service Act* (1998)	general labour act
Manitoba	general labour act	general labour act; *City of Winnipeg Charter*	general labour act; *Fire Department and Paramedics Arbitration Act*	general labour act; *Essential Services Act*	education act; general labour act;	general labour act; *Civil Service Act; Essential Services Act*	general labour act

Table 8.2
(continued)

Jurisdiction	Municipal	Police	Firefighters	Hospitals	Teachers	Civil Service	Government Enterprise
Ontario	general labour act	police act; *Public Service Act (OPP)*	fire act; *Public Sector Dispute Resolution Act*	general labour act; *Hospital Labour Disputes Arbitration Act; Ambulance Services Collective Bargaining Act*	education act; *Provincial Schools' Negotiations Act*	civil service act	civil service act
Quebec	general labour act	general labour act; police act+; *Public Service; Act‡*	general labour act‡	general labour act; *Public Service Act*	general labour act; *Public Service Act*	general labour act; *Public Service Act;*	general labour act; *Public Service Act;* civil service act
New Brunswick	general labour act	general labour act+	general labour act+	*Public Service Act; Nursing Homes Act*	*Public Service Act*	*Public Service Act*	*Public Service Act*
Nova Scotia	general labour act	general labour act	general labour act	general labour act	education act	civil service act; *Corrections Act*	general labour act
PEI	general labour act	general labour act	general labour act	general labour act	education act	civil service act and regulations	general labour act
Newfoundland and Labrador	general labour act	*Royal Newfoundland Constabulary Act*	general labour act; *St. John's Fire Dept. Act*	*Public Service Act; Interns and Residents Collective Bargaining Act*	education act; *Teachers' Association Act*	*Public Service Act*	*Public Service Act*

*The RCMP are excluded from unionization rights under both the Canada Labour Code and the *PSSRA*.

†The *Public Sector Employers' Act*, providing for public sector employer associations, applies to all public sector collective bargaining in the province except for the provincial civil service.

§Division 16 contains specific provisions for hospital employees.

+Sub-section 80.1 contains specific measures for municipal and regional police and municipal firefighters.

‡Unlike those covered by the main part of Quebec's *Code du Travail*, police and firefighters are forbidden to strike and must submit disputes to binding arbitration.

Note: Public service acts are general acts applying to several different branches of the public sector. Civil service acts, where applicable, apply only to the provincial civil service or (occasionally) to employees of certain government enterprises.

Source: "Statutes Governing Firefighters Collective Bargaining in Canada," http://www.hrsdc.gc.ca/asp/gateway.asp?hr=/en/lp/spila/clli/irlc/06Firefighters.shtml&hs=lzl; "Statutes Governing Public Servants Collective Bargaining in Canada," http://www.hrsdc.gc.ca/asp/gateway.asp?hr=/en/lp/spila/clli/irlc/02Public_servants.shtml&hs=lzl; "Statutes Governing Hospital Employees Collective Bargaining in Canada," http://www.hrsdc.gc.ca/asp/gateway.asp?hr=/en/lp/spila/clli/irlc/03hospital_employees.shtml&hs=lzl; "Statutes Governing Police Officers Collective Bargaining in Canada," http://www.hrsdc.gc.ca/asp/gateway.asp?hr=/en/lp/spila/clli/irlc/05police.shtml&hs=lzl; and "Statutes Governing Public School Teachers Collective Bargaining in Canada," http://www.hrsdc.gc.ca/asp/gateway.asp?hr=/en/lp/spila/clli/irlc/04teachers.shtml&hs=lzl. Human Resources and Skills Development Canada, 2005. Reproduced with the permission of the Minister of Public Works and Government Services Canada, 2005.

Table 8.3

DISPUTE RESOLUTION PROCEDURES IN VARIOUS PUBLIC SECTOR JURISDICTIONS

Jurisdiction	Municipal	Police	Firefighters	Hospitals	Teachers	Civil Service
Federal	strike (Yukon/NWT)	n/a	COP*	COP*	COP*	COP*
BC	strike*	strike*	strike*	strike*	limited strike*	strike
Alberta	strike	arbitration	arbitration	arbitration	strike	arbitration
Saskatchewan	strike	strike	strike or arbitration	strike	COP†	strike
Manitoba	strike	strike++	arbitration	strike*	arbitration	arbitration
Ontario	strike	arbitration	arbitration	arbitration	strike	strike*
Quebec	strike*	arbitration	arbitration	limited strike*	limited strike*	strike*
New Brunswick	strike	arbitration	arbitration	strike*	strike	strike*
Nova Scotia	strike	strike	strike§	strike#	limited strike**	arbitration
PEI	strike	arbitration	arbitration	arbitration	arbitration	arbitration
Newfoundland and Labrador	strike	strike††	strike‡‡	limited strike§§	strike	limited strike

Note: Most provinces permit government enterprise employees to strike. Arbitration is required in PEI and, for the most part, Alberta. Some provinces subject government enterprise employees to essential service designations.

COP = choice of procedures

* Essential services provisions stipulate that certain employees will be or may be required to continue working during a strike. In Manitoba, the City of Winnipeg's paramedics have had arbitration substituted for the strike right.

† Union choice of arbitration at the request of either party or strike.

+ Arbitration requested by either party is binding only if the constitution of the local union prohibits strikes.

++ Except for the city of Winnipeg, where the method is arbitration at the request of either party.

‡ In Quebec, health care and education workers are not permitted to strike over local and regional issues.

§ It should be noted that, at least according to Jackson (1995:317), there have been no recorded strikes by firefighters in Canada. Strikes by police have occurred, but only extremely rarely.

According to Thompson and Swimmer (1995:11), two large hospitals use arbitration instead.

** Nova Scotia schoolteachers are not permitted to strike over local and regional issues.

†† Arbitration is used for members of the provincial police force, the Royal Newfoundland Constabulary.

‡‡ Arbitration in St. John's, strike elsewhere.

§§ The union can demand arbitration if more than 50 percent of a bargaining unit is designated as essential and thus prohibited from striking. The same is true in the Nfld. civil service. Arbitration may be imposed if there is a state of emergency and the House of Assembly forbids a strike. Hospital employees may not engage in rotating strikes.

Source: "Collective Bargaining Dispute Resolution Process in the Public and Parapublic Sectors in Canada," http://www.hrsdc.gc.ca/en/lp/spila/clli/irlc/pub(e).pdf.

considerable input from the parties involved (see Ponak and Thompson, 1989:387). Indeed, where the parties agree, the labour board will not normally interfere. Where they do not agree, the board will base its decision largely on what seems likely to make for the most harmonious union–management relationship.

In contrast, public sector bargaining units are most often spelled out in public sector legislation (Fryer, 1995:345). Under the *PSSRA*, federal government employees were initially divided into some 76 different occupational groups (Swimmer, 1995:370), leaving the PSSRB little if any authority to determine bargaining units (Ponak and Thompson, 1989:387).[15] New Brunswick followed the federal government's lead, authorizing a number of occupationally-based province-wide bargaining units (Fryer, 1995:345). In contrast, BC's public service act spells out three bargaining units, and a single province-wide unit is named in the legislation of Alberta, Manitoba, Nova Scotia, Ontario, and PEI (Fryer, 1995). Some statutes go even farther, spelling out the only union that can legally represent government employees. While some analysts (e.g., Fryer, 1995:345) suggest that legislative determination of the bargaining agent appears to go against the Charter's "freedom of association" provision, various Supreme Court cases have made it clear that "freedom of association" does not include the right to choose one's own bargaining agent (Thompson and Ponak, 1995; Cavalluzzo, 1988).[16]

Scope of Bargainable Issues

Yet another important difference is the scope of issues that may be negotiated in the private and public sectors. In the private sector, the parties are free to negotiate pretty well any provision they want pertaining to the terms and conditions of employment, so long as it is not illegal. In most public sector acts, the scope of bargainable issues is severely limited. A modified form of the old sovereignty doctrine would appear to apply in some cases. For example, the *PSSRA* did not allow bargaining over any issue that would require parliamentary legislation, except for the appropriation of funds (Swimmer, 1995:371). In practical terms, this means that many issues central to private sector bargaining become management rights more or less by default (Swimmer, 1995). These issues include the criteria for appointments, promotions, and layoffs, job classification, and technological or organizational change (Swimmer, 1995:371–372). While some of these restrictions may be understandable, given the federal government's need to apply the merit principle to prevent favouritism in appointments and promotions, the merit principle does not explain the government's refusal to allow its employees to bargain over technological change, or the refusal of every province except Saskatchewan to allow its employees to bargain over pensions (Swimmer, 1995:371; Fryer, 1995:345).[17]

Most provincial public sector acts are only slightly more liberal than the *PSSRA* with respect to the scope of bargainable issues. Many do allow bargaining over technological and organizational change (Swimmer, 1995), but most prohibit bargaining over employee training programs, appointments, and promotions (Fryer, 1995). Somewhat more justifiably, perhaps, given the paramilitary nature of fire and police departments, both, in particular the latter, often forbid their employees to bargain over disciplinary issues and superior–subordinate relations (R. Jackson, 1995; Ponak and Thompson, 1995).

As Ponak and Thompson note (1995), such severe restrictions on the scope of bargaining may well hurt the bargaining process by creating frustration on the part of unions, thereby preventing trust from emerging. (See also Fryer, 2000 and 2001.) Indeed, the restrictions can themselves be a source of increased conflict, in that the parties may wind up wasting a good deal of time and energy bickering about what can and cannot legally be bargained over, rather than engaging in productive negotiations (Ponak and Thompson, 1995).

Dispute Resolution Procedures

To most Canadians, the single most important difference between public and private sector collective bargaining lies in the different procedures for resolving disputes in the two sectors. As noted earlier, the conciliation-strike routine is all but universal in the private sector. Only very rarely are other procedures, such as back-to-work legislation or binding arbitration, invoked, and then only in large federal-jurisdiction strikes with a substantial public interest component, such as railway or airline disputes.

In contrast, the essential (or allegedly essential) nature of much public sector work has led policy makers to devise a broad array of special dispute settlement procedures for that sector. As these procedures are dealt with in more detail in Chapter 11, they are discussed only briefly here. The alternative public sector procedures discussed here include conventional interest arbitration, final offer arbitration, choice of procedures, and the controlled strike. Other procedures, such as back-to-work legislation, have been left to Chapter 11.

Conventional Interest Arbitration

Conventional interest arbitration is the method normally used for resolving disputes involving police, firefighters, and other public sector workers whose services are considered so essential to the public health, safety, or welfare that they cannot be allowed to withdraw them. In addition, as noted earlier, it is also used for many government employees, teachers, and other public sector workers whose work may or may not be truly essential, but whom the government has nonetheless, for whatever reason, forbidden from striking.

Under conventional interest arbitration, arbitrators are normally free, within certain broad limitations, to fashion an award comprising the union's position, the management's position, or their own (Ponak and Thompson, 1989). Starting in the 1980s, some jurisdictions, notably Alberta (Ponak and Thompson, 1995:427), required arbitrators to take the government's ability to pay into account in arriving at public sector awards. In general, the ability to pay criterion is held in low repute within the arbitral fraternity (see Sack, 1991), both on the score of its subjectivity and because most arbitrators feel it ties their hands too much in fashioning awards.[18]

The major advantage of conventional, as opposed to final-offer arbitration (discussed below) is that, because arbitrators can "split the difference" in fashioning their awards, those awards are likely to be more acceptable to both sides (Ponak and Thompson, 1989:394). A major disadvantage is that, particularly in cases where parties use arbitration frequently, they can lose their ability to bargain, preferring to leave hard decisions to the arbitrator rather than making them themselves. Most evidence suggests that conventional arbitration systems lead to lower rates of negotiated settlement than systems that allow strikes and lockouts (Ponak and Thompson, 1989, 1995). While final-offer arbitration (FOA) appears to offer a way around this difficulty, it has not thus far been widely adopted in Canada.

During its eight years in power (1995–2003), Ontario's former Conservative government made a sustained and multi-pronged attack on interest arbitration, in

conventional interest arbitration A form of arbitration in which the arbitrator is free, within certain broad limits, to choose the position of one of the parties, some combination thereof, or fashion an alternative settlement.

the belief that controlling arbitration outcomes would help it achieve its objective of downsizing the public sector and slashing government spending. In 1996, Bill 26 established ability to pay as a permanent feature of public sector pay determination (Rose, 2000:261). In 1997, a new *Public Sector Dispute Resolution Act* went even further, specifying that arbitrators must take into account clauses of the act including those encouraging "best practices that ensure the delivery of quality and effective public services that are affordable to the taxpayer" (ibid., 263). A particularly controversial feature was a provision authorizing the appointment of retired judges in cases where the parties could not agree on an arbitrator. Fortunately for the independence of the arbitration process, CUPE was eventually successful in a court challenge of the appointment of a retired judge as arbitrator in a major hospital case.[19] The case went all the way to the Supreme Court of Canada (Re *CUPE vs. Ontario (Minister of Labour), 2003 SCC 29)*. In its decision, the Court pointed out, among other things, that "the appointment of an inexpert and inexperienced chairperson who is not seen as broadly acceptable in the labour relations community is a defect in approach that is both immediate and obvious" (see Ponak and Thompson, 2005:433).

The assault on arbitral independence was not confined to the health care sector. In public education, the government imposed even more severe restrictions on arbitration through Bill 62, the legislation ending the second wave of province-wide teacher strikes in 1998. This bill restricted arbitral discretion in a number of important ways. In addition to allowing either party to apply to have all remaining issues in dispute settled through mediation-arbitration, the bill stipulated that arbitral awards could not result in a school board incurring a deficit and required the mediator-arbitrator to demonstrate how the school board could meet any increased compensation costs resulting from an award. It also allowed the Labour Minister to appoint the mediator-arbitrator if the parties couldn't agree on one, which again meant the appointment of retired judges (Rose, 2000:275–276). Rose's stark conclusion is that " . . . the magnitude and restrictiveness of the statutory requirements stripped arbitrators of their independence" (ibid., 283; see also Rose, 2002). Here again, as was true in health care, the government's heavy-handed approach severely damaged its already fragile relationship with its public school teachers (see Rose, 2000 and 2002).

Final-Offer Arbitration (FOA)

final-offer arbitration (FOA) or final-offer selection (FOS)
A form of dispute resolution in which the third-party neutral must select either the proposal submitted by the union or that submitted by management, without alteration.

Under **final-offer arbitration (FOA)**, arbitrators have no discretion in fashioning their awards. They must choose either the union's or employer's position—for the entire package, if that is how the award is being made, or on an issue-by-issue basis. The idea behind FOA is that because the risk of "losing" is so great, particularly when the award is being made as a package rather than issue by issue, most parties would rather settle on their own (see Godard, 1994:353–354). FOA has been fairly widely adopted in American public sector legislation, and the evidence suggests that it generally achieves a significantly higher rate of negotiated settlements than does conventional arbitration (Ponak and Thompson, 1995:438). Nonetheless, it has seldom been adopted in Canada, one notable exception being its use in 2001 in settling Nova Scotia's health care dispute. One major criticism of this approach is that it can lead to bad collective agreements, at least in cases where both sides submit unreasonable proposals (Ponak and Thompson, 1995). Another is that it can foster a damaging win-lose mentality that will hurt the parties' efforts to build a more constructive relationship.

Choice of Procedures (COP)

Under **choice of procedures (COP)**, one party or the other (in Canada, normally the union) is given the right to choose between the traditional conciliation-strike route and binding arbitration. Initially devised for the *PSSRA*, COP soon spread to a number of provinces and US states (Ponak and Thompson, 1989:396–397). In Canada, the federal government's intention was to come up with a system that would give public service unions the right to strike, yet lead to arbitration in most cases. For the first decade or so of public service bargaining, COP generally fulfilled this expectation. However, after 1976, the public service unions' growing militancy and anger at the government's wage-price controls led them to choose strikes rather than arbitration most of the time (see Fryer, 2000). In addition, experience with arbitration boards and conciliation boards suggested that the latter were willing to address a broader range of issues, including some technically beyond the permissible scope of bargaining (Swimmer, 1995:375–376). For these reasons, the Public Service Alliance forbade its bargaining units to choose arbitration (Swimmer, 1995:377).

For many years, the federal government took a dim view of arbitration, fearing that arbitral awards could lead to costs it was not prepared to bear. When collective bargaining resumed in 1996, following a five-year hiatus, the government suspended interest arbitration for a period of three years. In 1999, the suspension was renewed for a further two years (Fryer, 2000 and 2001; Swimmer, 2000). Only recently has interest arbitration again become a "live option" in the federal public service, with recent awards providing settlements more or less comparable to those achieved through the conciliation-strike route.

choice of procedures (COP) Form of public sector dispute resolution in which one party or the other (normally the union) is given the right to choose between binding arbitration or the traditional conciliation-strike route.

Controlled Strikes

The **controlled strike**, based on the designation of certain employees who must remain on the job to provide essential services, has become the most common option in jurisdictions that permit public sector workers to strike. Indeed, every jurisdiction except Saskatchewan that permits public sector strikes now has some kind of designation procedure in place. Under the new *Public Service Labour Relations Act* that has just replaced the *PSSRA*, essential service agreements must be completed before a strike can become legal (see *Public Service Modernization Act*, Division 8). Elsewhere, the usual procedure is for the union and public sector employer to negotiate acceptable levels of designation, with the final decision left to a labour board or some other impartial tribunal in the event of a dispute (Thompson and Ponak, 1995:439). Often the negotiations over designation are long and difficult, sometimes as difficult as the actual collective agreement negotiations themselves (Thompson and Ponak, 1995:439–440).

controlled strike Public sector strike in which the public health and safety are protected by designating certain workers as essential, thus compelling them to continue working through the dispute.

In principle, the controlled strike should often be the most attractive option for governments, because it ensures the continuation of essential public services without removing unions' right to strike. In practice, administering such strikes has often been fraught with difficulties.[20] The most serious problem, particularly in hospital settings (see Haiven, 1995), is knowing how many employees to designate as essential. If the figure is set too low, public health and safety could be at risk. If it is set too high, the union may not be able to carry on an effective strike (Thompson and Ponak, 1995). Often, labour tribunals ruling on designation levels have erred on the side of caution, in some cases ludicrously so. During a 1989 hospital strike in BC, one hospital saw 110 percent of its usual nursing complement designated as essential (Haiven, 1995:256)! An option already in place in Newfoundland (see Table 8.3) that might prevent public sector employers from designating excessive numbers of employees as essential is to allow the union to take the dispute through to binding arbitration in cases where designation exceeded a certain level, such as 50 percent. The reason such an option could work elsewhere is that, in recent years, governments have been increasingly reluctant to submit public sector disputes to arbitration, disliking the loss of control and possible expense entailed in arbitrated settlements.[21]

THE FUTURE OF PUBLIC SECTOR BARGAINING: IS A TRANSFORMATION POSSIBLE?

As this chapter has shown, public sector labour–management relations have become extremely conflict-ridden over the past two decades. Wage freezes, rollbacks, and restrictions on collective bargaining have generally reduced public sector workers' real incomes, particularly since 1990. At the same time, workloads have increased and employees have come to feel far less secure in their jobs due to the ongoing wave of downsizing, restructuring, privatization, and contracting out described earlier in the chapter. While most Canadian governments are in a far stronger financial position than they were ten years ago, they have generally continued to maintain a tough stance on public sector compensation, making it impossible for their employees to make up for the real income losses suffered during the 1990s (Rose, 2004b). Not surprisingly, the result has been an escalation of the already severe tensions between governments and public sector workers (see Rose, 2002 and 2004b and Haiven and Haiven, 2003, for examples).

To help improve the deteriorating state of union–management relations in the federal public service, Treasury Board established the Fryer Committee,[22] a tripartite task force made up of equal numbers of government managers, union officials, and academics. As we noted in the previous edition of this book, the committee in its first report (Fryer, 2000) found a serious lack of trust and respect between the parties, resulting in large measure from the government's suspension of bargaining and arbitration during the 1990s as well as from the restrictive public service legislative framework. In its final report (Fryer, 2001), the committee concluded that the government and the public service unions will have to work together collaboratively if the system is to improve. Chief among the recommendations was that of a new institutional framework for labour–management relations, one that operates through institutions that involve employees, through their unions, in redesigning employment systems and that provide for effective dispute resolution systems.

More specific recommendations included revising and simplifying the *PSSRA,* expanding the scope of public service bargaining, and the consultation and co-development of policies at the service-wide, departmental, and workplace levels. The committee also recommended streamlining the process of designating essential employees and a major reduction in the exclusion of employees from collective bargaining rights. To help make public service bargaining more fact-based, the committee recommended re-establishing a Compensation Research Bureau (a previous Pay Research Bureau having been eliminated during the Mulroney administration).

With an eye to reducing the government's legislative intervention in collective bargaining, the committee recommended creation of a Public Interest Disputes Resolution Commission.[23] The commission, which would have been given a broad "toolkit" of remedies for solving disputes, was intended to replace the current "choice of procedures" mechanism for resolving public service bargaining disputes. The idea behind the commission was that it would turn both back-to-work legislation and strikes into unpalatable alternatives, thereby inducing the parties to work out their own solutions to disputes. (For more details on this commission, see Fryer, 2001 and Peirce, 2003:286–287).

After a long and sometimes tortuous gestation period, new public service labour legislation started to take effect just as this book was being written.[24] On April 1, 2005, a new *Public Service Labour Relations Act* replaced the *PSSRA.* The new legislation incorporated some, but by no means all of the Fryer Committee's recommendations. It didn't expand the scope of public service bargaining but it did make joint departmental consultation committees mandatory and encourage "co-development" (a kind of halfway stage between consultation and collective bargaining). A scaled-down version of the Fryer Public Interest Dispute Resolution Commission, a Public Interest Commission, replaces conciliation boards in the dispute resolution process. Exclusions have been reduced; in particular, Treasury Board employees and Justice Department lawyers are no longer excluded from union representation. Essential service agreements have replaced the cumbersome designation process. And the Public Service Staff Relations Board, renamed the Public Service Labour Relations Board (PSLRB), will once again carry out compensation research (the old Pay Research Bureau was part of the PSSRB).

Perhaps the greatest improvements are to the grievance process. Group and policy grievances (see Chapter 12 for more details regarding these terms), previously barred by the *PSSRA,* are now allowed. Human rights cases may now be grieved, which should make for a speedier resolution of many of these cases. In addition, adjudicators have been given the power to award interest in disciplinary cases. Informal internal complaint mechanisms (ICMSs) are now mandatory in all departments.

While on balance the new *PSLRA* probably benefits public service unions somewhat, one provision is of great concern: In addition to making strike votes mandatory, the new law allows non-member Rand deductees to vote, leading to the very real possibility that a union's position could be undercut at a critical stage in the bargaining process by people who have deliberately chosen not to join the union.

With regard to recourse from staffing decisions, the new regime, as laid out in the revised *Public Service Employment Act* (to take effect at the beginning of 2006), will definitely be a more restrictive one. The broad grounds for appeal under the old law are being replaced by just three grounds for complaint: abuse of authority, denial of the right to be assessed in the language of one's choice, or application of the *Canadian Human Rights Act* (i.e., discrimination on a prohibited ground). The new law also increases restrictions on federal government employees' political rights and moves resolution of staffing disputes from the Public Service Commission to a new Public Service Staffing Tribunal.

Overall, these legislative changes stop far short of helping to bring about a genuinely collaborative labour–management relationship in the federal public service. The greater degree of consultation stipulated in the legislation is welcome. It must, however, be recognized that at the end of consultation, management still has the right to act unilaterally. Notably, the legislation did not expand the scope of bargaining, nor did it do much else to fundamentally alter the existing balance of power between the parties, which as the first Fryer report noted has long been tilted in the employer's favour. Nor have we seen any evidence that other jurisdictions have done much more to redress the existing public sector labour relations power imbalance.

To the extent that a transformation has indeed occurred in private sector labour relations, the transformation has arisen out of a shared sense of urgency, a mutual recognition by the parties that if they didn't change their ways, economic disaster would almost certainly be the result. Driven by this sense of urgency, private sector unions have in many cases (see especially the "social contracts" discussed elsewhere in this book) moderated their wage demands and signed on to long-term peace guarantees. In return, private sector employers have, in effect, turned over a fair degree of control to their unions, often opening their books to them and giving them a substantial role in running the enterprise.

In many ways, the situation in the public sector is no less urgent. This is particularly true in the health care sector, where large-scale staff shortages are looming at a time of numerous public health crises. The past five years have seen the Walkerton water crisis, "Mad Cow" disease, SARS, and West Nile Virus, to name but a few. Even as we write, the horrific possibility of an avian influenza epidemic is becoming ever more real, with the confirmation of five human cases in China (CBC Radio News report, March 29, 2005). Unfortunately, with a few notable exceptions, the sense of crisis and urgency hasn't yet flowed through to the public sector labour relations system. In a highly complex twenty-first century world, the players remain wedded to a 1950s-style industrial approach to labour relations. How they will work their way out of this box is far from clear. It is difficult for the unions to "offer" wage moderation when it has already been imposed on them, often legislatively; at the same time, it's equally difficult for public sector managers to offer any sort of genuine power-sharing when their hands are tied by what are still, for the most part, very restrictive legislative frameworks for collective bargaining.

If the parties to public sector collective bargaining are to start to work out the creative solutions that have recently begun to appear in the private sector, they will need to be given something approaching the full range of bargaining tools available to their private sector counterparts. A necessary first step in any public sector transformation process is, therefore, to expand the scope of bargaining to include those many issues on which negotiation is not currently possible. If and when this happens, then progress may be possible on other issues. Otherwise, continuing and even increased public sector conflict would appear to be a virtual certainty.

Case 8.1

THE YEAR OF NURSES' DISCONTENT

In 1999, a wave of nurses' strikes began in Newfoundland, where nurses walked off the job on March 24. Years of government cutbacks had resulted in wage freezes and rollbacks, a decline in full-time employment, and huge workload increases. Newfoundland nurses were the lowest paid in Canada and had not seen a pay increase since 1991. Low morale and an aging workforce contributed to nursing shortages, which exacerbated the problems. On April 3, Premier Brian Tobin ordered the Newfoundland nurses back to work and imposed a settlement on them that was basically the same as they had rejected prior to the strike. Stiff penalties for violation ensured the nurses complied with the back-to-work legislation but did nothing to address the sources of the discontent.

Just days after the Newfoundland nurses returned to work, their Saskatchewan counterparts went on strike. Again, the most important issues included stagnating wages, burgeoning workloads, and critical personnel shortages. The NDP government of Roy Romanow exhibited an atypical lack of empathy for labour's plight and ordered the striking nurses back to work. Despite threats of stiff fines and jail sentences, however, members of the Saskatchewan Union of Nurses (SUN) defied the back-to-work legislation. The strike lasted 10 days, during which emergency patients were admitted, but surgeries were cancelled and expectant mothers had to travel to the US to give birth. Overwhelming public support for the nurses and a pending provincial election motivated Romanow to finally negotiate a deal with the nurses, including a 13.7 percent increase over three years and a pledge to hire more nurses and improve working conditions for those already employed. The government also agreed to reduce the penalties for the illegal strike. Not all nurses were pleased with the settlement. Indeed, some called for a second walkout when it appeared the government was backtracking on some of its promises. Many nurses were also of the opinion that while some progress had been made, core issues remained unaddressed.

The nurses' strike in Quebec that year was, however, the longest and most dramatic of all. It began in late June with two 24-hour walkouts that affected a handful of hospitals and then spread to every hospital in the province. As in Newfoundland and Saskatchewan, the main issues were wages, working conditions, and critical staff shortages. Lucien Bouchard's Parti Québécois (PQ) government responded to the walkout of 47 500 nurses with legislation that declared the strike illegal and imposed hefty fines. Undaunted, the nurses refused to return to work except to provide essential services. The public rallied behind them and, for the most part, laid blame squarely on the government's shoulders.

Bouchard's government faced a conundrum. It had hoped to keep government spending under control in order to balance the budget and bolster its chances of success in the upcoming sovereignty referendum campaign. In Quebec, all negotiations with public sector employees occur in the same year. Therefore, Bouchard wanted to avoid any settlement with the nurses that would detrimentally affect upcoming negotiations with teachers and other public sector workers; however, he also needed to maintain public support and avoid alienating public sector workers, whose votes could decisively affect referendum results. On July 18, a tentative agreement was announced that left the government's original salary offer unchanged yet articulated a commitment to review nurses' salaries and working conditions. Though their union recommended the deal, nurses overwhelmingly rejected it and the strike resumed. Union leaders scrambled to find a way to satisfy their members and still maintain public support. On July 24, the Quebec Nurses Union declared the strike over but refused to concede the battle. Nurses returned to work bitter and dissatisfied with both the government and the union, many of them planning to leave the profession or take job offers in the United States.

What is perhaps most interesting about Canadian nurses' extraordinarily public display of discontent in 1999 was that it could—and should—have been predicted by provincial governments across the country. While not all were hit with work stoppages, the vast majority faced exceedingly difficult negotiations in the late 1990s and early 2000s. Nurses' frustrations had been building for years as health care restructuring, undertaken to rationalize and streamline the delivery of services, resulted in staff shortages, staggering workloads, and an increase in involuntary part-time work and mandatory overtime. Shorter hospital stays meant that less seriously ill patients were sent home, increasing the proportion of acutely ill and post-operative patients. Hospital mergers and amalgamations resulted in wage disparities, as nurses previously represented by other public sector unions were amalgamated into the provincial nurses' associations—and increasing recognition of wage disparities between nurses and members of other professions further fuelled nurses' feelings of being overworked and undervalued.

Hospital mergers and amalgamations also served to increase the size and strength of provincial nurses' associations, seemingly offering nurses the means and opportunity to make their voices heard. In the end, however, while 1999—the year of Canadian nurses' very public discontent—resulted in increased public opposition to the dismantling of public services, it did not result in significant changes to nurses' working conditions.

Sources: "Overworked and Underpaid: Nurses Strike Back." *CBC News in Review*. September, 1999, http://www.tv.cbc.ca/newsinreview/sept%2099/nurses/flash.html; Sibbald, Barbara. (1999). "RN = Really Neglected, Angry Nurses Say." *Canadian Medical Association Journal*. May 18, http://epe.lac-bac.gc.ca/100/201/300/cdn_medical_association/cmaj/vol-160/issue-10/1490.htm.

Case Questions

1. Discuss how the various provincial governments' treatment of nurses in this case compares with this chapter's description of government's treatment of

public sector workers. In what ways did the provincial governments' actions contribute to the occurrence of the strikes and/or their continuation?

2. Based on this case, what purpose do strike bans and heavy penalties for disobeying back-to-work orders serve in health care labour relations?

3. What are some ways in which governments might help prevent a recurrence of these kinds of health care disputes in the future?

QUESTIONS FOR DISCUSSION

1. How (if at all) does work in the public sector differ from work in the private sector?

2. Why is the public sector important to any study of IR?

3. Discuss the main stages of the evolution of public sector collective bargaining.

4. What was the significance of the *Public Service Staff Relations Act*?

5. What are the main employer differences between the public and private sectors?

6. What are the main employee and union differences between the two sectors?

7. What are their major legislative and policy differences?

8. Why are special dispute resolution methods needed for the public sector? Discuss some of these methods, indicating which appear to you to be most promising, and which most problematic.

9. Why have Canadian governments thus far felt little political "heat" for continuing restrictions on public sector workers? What do you think public sector unions and the Canadian public in general can do to help change this situation?

10. How do you think the aging of the public sector workforce and other demographic changes described in this chapter will affect bargaining in the public sector?

Suggestions for Further Reading

Fryer, John (chair). (2001). *Working Together in the Public Interest: Final Report of the Advisory Committee on Labour Management Relations in the Federal Public Service.* Ottawa: Treasury Board of Canada. This report, based on thorough and detailed consultation with government managers and union officials, outlines a new, collaborative approach to federal public service labour–management relations. Together with the committee's first report, *Identifying the Issues* (2000), it offers insight into the problems affecting public sector labour relations across Canada, in addition to providing potential solutions for many of those problems.

Haiven, Judy, and Larry Haiven. (2003). "Health Strikes and Emergency Services in Canada: The Dilemma." *Workplace Gazette,* 6:2, pp. 73–83. Thoughtful and chilling chronicle of the decline of labour relations in the health care sector over the past decade. Policy makers and public sector managers alike should take careful notice.

Rose, Joseph. (2004). "Public Sector Bargaining: From Retrenchment to Consolidation." *Relations Industrielles*, 59:2, pp. 271–294. Perceptive account of recent developments in public sector labour relations, which suggests that despite the return of prosperity, governments generally remain wedded to the restrictive policies they adopted during the cash-strapped 1990s.

Swimmer, Gene, and Mark Thompson (Eds.). (1995). *Public Sector Collective Bargaining in Canada.* Kingston: Queen's IRC Press. Still probably the single most important source book for anyone with an interest in the public sector, though it should be supplemented with Swimmer's later (2000) collection listed in the References.

CHAPTER 9

COLLECTIVE BARGAINING STRUCTURES AND PROCESSES

Where public sector employers or large, private sector employers are involved, the outcomes of collective bargaining have the potential to affect many stakeholders and negotiations may draw significant media attention.

LEARNING OBJECTIVES

After studying this chapter, you should be able to:

1. Identify the types of bargaining structures commonly seen in Canada.
2. Identify the reasons for, and impacts of, Canada's decentralized bargaining structure.
3. Describe the four systems of activities identified by Walton and McKersie as comprising the process of collective bargaining.
4. Explain the concept of interest-based, or mutual gains, bargaining.
5. Explain the model of strategic negotiations.
6. Describe how union and management teams prepare for bargaining and establish their bargaining goals.
7. Identify the factors that influence unions' and managements' bargaining power.

The negotiating process is critical in the industrial relations system since in unionized workplaces, most outcomes are established through collective bargaining. We start this chapter with a consideration of bargaining structure, which has an impact on both the relative balance of power between the parties and the ease or difficulty of negotiations. Next, we look at the negotiating process itself, beginning with a consideration of some of the unique characteristics of collective bargaining. We explain the process of bargaining by examining its four sub-processes, highlighting recent process innovations, and summarizing the model of strategic negotiations. The processes union and management teams go through in preparing their bargaining mandate are described and the concept of a settlement zone is explained. After the stages of negotiation are briefly described, the chapter concludes with a discussion of the factors that affect both unions' and employers' bargaining power.

collective bargaining
The negotiation process through which the terms and conditions of employment of unionized workers are determined.

Collective bargaining is the negotiation process through which the terms and conditions of employment of unionized workers are determined. In non-unionized environments, employers unilaterally establish reward structures, including compensation, benefits, processes for promotions and transfers, and other conditions governing employment. While some individual employees may possess sufficient market power to demand superior conditions, for the most part, non-unionized employees negotiate their initial hiring salaries within the boundaries of employers' established policies and practices. Other than occasionally asking for raises, these pre-hire salary discussions are the only time most non-unionized employees will engage in negotiations with their employers. In a unionized environment, union and management meet on a regular basis to negotiate a wide range of terms and conditions of employment. Through this process, unionized employees have a voice in how rewards are structured, how disputes are resolved, and how employers deal with conditions such as technological change or business downturns. Employees' participation in decisions that affect their working lives democratizes the work place and establishes mutually understood rules and processes that are articulated in a collective agreement and upon which both employers and employees can rely.

Usually, the collective bargaining process occurs at regular intervals once every few years. A team of employer representatives will meet with a team of union representatives and each party will put forward a set of proposed changes to the collective agreement. During a series of meetings that usually extend over many months, the parties will discuss the proposed changes, explain their rationale, and attempt to persuade the other party to accept their proposals. This process of persuasion is a high-stakes and complex dance, during which the parties attempt to balance their respective and mutual interests, respond to changing environmental contexts and conditions, and manage the multitude of tangible and intangible factors influencing both the process and the outcomes of negotiations. Among the many factors that influence the process and outcomes of negotiation are bargaining structure, union and management goals and strategies, relative bargaining power, and the skill of the negotiators.

BARGAINING STRUCTURE

Bargaining structure refers to the number and type of employer and union groups who are party to the negotiations and are, therefore, bound by the resultant collective agreement. Other employer and union groups not directly involved in the negotiations but who are nonetheless influenced by their process and outcomes may also be considered part of the informal bargaining structure. Clearly, bargaining structure will influence the interactions between, as well as within, the parties. Bargaining structure has also been shown to influence the types of issues that will be brought to the table, the level of conflict and incidence of strikes, and the parties' relative bargaining power (Chaykowski, 2005). In Canada, the formal bargaining structure is most often a function of the certified bargaining unit, or the group of employees designated by a labour board as appropriate for collective bargaining. However, if the parties mutually agree, the formal bargaining structure may incorporate several different certified bargaining units. This would be the case, for example, if each of an employer's establishments were individually certified but the employer and union agreed to incorporate them all under one collective agreement in order to increase industrial relations stability and achieve administrative savings.

By international standards, the Canadian collective bargaining system is quite decentralized (Chaykowski, 2005; Rogow, 1989a), with negotiations most often occurring between a single employer and a single union; this has resulted in vast numbers of collective agreements in each jurisdiction and industry, with each covering relatively few workers. In many European countries, such as Germany and Sweden, bargaining structures tend to be much more centralized, with master agreements often negotiated on an industry-wide basis (Adams, 1995a). Moreover, at least in the private sector, Canada's tendency toward decentralization has been increasing in recent years, owing mainly to the breakdown of traditional multi-employer or **pattern bargaining** arrangements in several major industrial sectors (see Rose, 1986a; Forrest, 1989).

The single-employer, single-establishment, single-union structure is the most common in Canada. It usually occurs where the employer operates at one location only, has only one unionized establishment, or has different unions at different locations (Chaykowski, 2005). Another reason for its frequency is labour boards' tendency to use workers' community of interest as a major criterion in bargaining unit determination. This criterion generally pushes labour boards in the direction of smaller and more homogeneous units (Rogow, 1989a). Another common structure is the single-employer, multi-establishment, single-union type, which involves the negotiation of a single collective agreement across several different workplaces by the same employer and union. Offering useful economies of scale for both employers and unions in situations where the employer runs an integrated operation across a number of generally similar establishments (Chaykowski, 2005), it is most common in the public administration, transportation, and communications sectors.

Less common are the single-employer, single-establishment, multi-union structure and the single-employer, multi-establishment, multi-union structure. The former involves a negotiating partnership between two or more unions within the same workplace, as when production workers represented by an industrial union negotiate together with maintenance workers represented by a craft union. It is quite rare in Canada (Chaykowski, 2005), probably because in most situations where workers from different occupations within the same establishment feel they have enough in common to bargain together, they will already have joined the

pattern bargaining
A bargaining strategy whereby terms of the first, or target, contract are used as a pattern for subsequent collective agreements.

same union. The latter occurs mainly in the railway industry where operating union coalitions bargain as a group with each of the major railways (Chaykowski, 2005), and in certain other industries made up of a few very large employers and a larger number of small craft unions. As for the multi-employer, multi-establishment, single-union type of structure, it is most apt to be found in industries characterized by large numbers of relatively small employers and a single dominant industrial or craft union, such as in the trucking, fishing, and forestry sectors (Chaykowski, 2005). It is also found in health care, especially in bargaining with registered nurses, who typically are represented by a single, province-wide union (Haiven, 1995).

The highly centralized multi-employer, multi-establishment, multi-union type of bargaining structure is rarely one that Canadian parties choose for themselves. It is most often found in the construction industry, where it has generally been imposed by governments in a bid to bring labour peace following major disputes (Chaykowski, 2005; Rose, 1992). Under this type of structure, bargaining is normally conducted through a certified employers' association rather than by individual employers and in rare instances bargaining may be conducted by a province-wide council of trade unions, which is the union equivalent of an employers' association (Rose, 1992).

Current Issues 9.1

HISTORIC UFCW CANADA/LOBLAW NEGOTIATIONS

Three UFCW local negotiating committees made history in May 2005, when for the first time they met as one with management counterparts from Loblaw's, Zehrs, Fortinos, and Real Canadian Superstores. While their contracts were not scheduled to expire until 2006, negotiations for early renewal were a part of a December 2004 mediated labour relations board settlement over a dispute regarding the threatened closure of a Zehrs store in Strathroy, Ontario. The early negotiations were authorized by members of all three locals and any eventual agreement must be separately ratified by each local.

The negotiations come on the heels of Loblaw's announcement of disappointing first-quarter results that saw the company's earnings fall 19.3 percent due to one-time restructuring costs associated with the closure of several warehouses and the relocation of head-office employees. Even if the $55 million one-time restructuring charge were ignored, analysts found the Loblaw's results disappointing. The company is struggling to sustain profitability while sharing the market with "dangerously competitive" (Peterson, 2005) large, non-unionized retailers such as Wal-Mart who continue to put "unprecedented" (Flavelle, 2005) levels of new square footage into the marketplace. The result is global consolidation of the industry and ever increasing pressure to curb costs.

Loblaw Cos. Ltd. sought to reopen negotiations with UFCW in order to secure more flexible work rules and facilitate a "transformation" that will involve streamlining operations, closing several warehouses, and opening more big-box stores selling not only groceries but other general merchandise as well. The company wants to work with its unions to facilitate this much-needed change. The UFCW leadership is committed to bringing stability and security to the unionized retail sector and to bringing master bargaining to as many Loblaw Companies as ▶

possible; however, it wants to avoid any major concessions. "We want an agreement that protects our members' jobs and contract rights while not taking away from the employer's ability to compete," stated UFCW Local 1000A President Kevin Corporon. "We've managed to strike that balance with Loblaws for more than 60 years and I think it is entirely realistic that we can continue to do so again, this year or next" (UFCW, 2005b).

While the initial three weeks of negotiations failed to produce an agreement, the parties reconvened later in the summer after the Ontario Labour Relations Board ordered senior union and company officials to attempt to find a settlement with the assistance of board-appointed mediators. Several days of mediation resulted in considerable progress but by August 19, substantial issues remained unresolved. The mediators, Vic Pathe and David Joffe, expressed confidence in the parties' commitment to the process and desire to reach an agreement but given the number and complexity of outstanding issues, recommended a stand-down period of no more than 90 days, following which negotiations were to recommence.

Sources: Flavelle, Dana. (2005). "Loblaw Profit Falls 19.3 Percent: Food Giant Moves to Cut Labour Costs." *Toronto Star*, May 5, p. C1; UFCW. (2005a). "Historic UFCW Canada/Loblaw Negotiations Going Into Second Week." UFCW Loblaw Talks. http://www.ufcwloblawtalks2005.ca/, May 24; UFCW. (2005b). "UFCW/Loblaw Mediation Directed by Ontario Labour Relations Board." UFCW Loblaw Talks, http://www.ufcwloblawtalks2005.ca/, July 8; UFCW. (2005c). "Some Progress Made in UFCW/Zehrs Negotiations; Talks to Resume Within 90 Days." UFCW Loblaw Talks, http://www.ufcwlobllawtalks2005.ca/, Aug 19; Peterson, Scott. (2005). "Weston Cites Big-Box Stores for 20% Drop at Loblaw Profit: Expansion to Continue." *National Post*. May 5, p. FP5.

Reasons for Canada's Decentralized Structures

A key reason for Canada's generally decentralized bargaining structures is the fact of provincial jurisdiction over most labour relations matters. This tends to make national-level bargaining quite difficult (Chaykowski, 2005), except in interprovincial industries under federal jurisdiction. A second important reason is labour boards' tendency to determine bargaining units according to the community of interest criteria that generally favours the creation of relatively small, homogeneous bargaining units rather than larger, more heterogeneous, more broadly based ones (Rogow, 1989a). Another criterion often used by boards, that of facilitating unionization whenever a majority of employees wish it, has also tended to lead to the creation of small and relatively homogeneous bargaining units, since smaller units are generally more cohesive and easier to organize (Rogow, 1989a).

A third reason for this decentralization has to do with the attitude of North American employers, many of whom seem, on principle, to oppose broader-based bargaining, particularly any sort of multi-employer bargaining that would require them to surrender some of their control over bargaining to an employers' association (see Adams, 1995a). The fact that certain employers object to broad-based bargaining even in good times when it might help them by reducing unions' ability to **whipsaw** suggests that, at least for some, opposition to this type of bargaining may be rooted in something deeper than economic calculation (see Rogow, 1989a).[1] Nonetheless, the state of the economy *has* been the major reason for employers' growing support for more decentralized structures, which in turn has been one of the most important reasons for the increase in such structures in recent years.

whipsaw A bargaining tactic where either a union or an employer attempts to leapfrog, or improve upon, another settlement, using it as the minimum it is willing to accept.

Increased competition, driven sometimes by trade liberalization and sometimes by other factors, has led to the breakdown of many previously centralized bargaining structures and pattern bargaining arrangements over the past two decades. Sometimes one of the weaker firms in a centralized or pattern bargaining arrangement finds it can no longer meet the industry standard and remain competitive, with the result that it withdraws from the centralized arrangement. Soon other firms are likely to find themselves in a similar position and likewise withdraw. Once that starts happening, the demise of the centralized arrangement is virtually inevitable. In other cases, as in the case of General Motors' unsuccessful attempt to do away with pattern bargaining in its 1996 negotiations with the Canadian Auto Workers, an industry leader sets out with the avowed intention of ending the arrangement. Among the industries in which growing competitive pressures have led to the dissolution of employer associations or pattern bargaining arrangements are the railways, pulp and paper, trucking, and meatpacking (Rose, 1986a; Forrest, 1989).

One of the few major industries that have so far been able to resist the shift to decentralized bargaining structures is the auto industry (Kumar and Meltz, 1992). Here the pattern remains that for each round of negotiations, the Canadian Auto Workers (CAW) targets one of the big-three auto manufacturers for possible strike action. The settlement with that employer establishes the pattern the other two are expected to follow (Godard, 2005). One reason the industry has been able to retain its long-standing pattern bargaining arrangement is the bilateral Canada–US Auto Pact, which created an integrated continental market in auto products and parts manufacturing while maintaining previous levels of Canadian production and employment (Kumar and Meltz, 1992). However, in recent years even this most venerable of pattern bargaining arrangements has been put to the test. Only a determined struggle by the CAW in its 1996 strike against General Motors allowed pattern bargaining to survive that round of negotiations.

The Canadian industrial relations system has by no means been alone in this trend towards greater decentralization. All across the industrialized Western world, decentralization and flexibility have become catchwords over the past two decades (Scheuer, 1992). In the United States, a change in the product market and increased competition from non-unionized firms helped lead to the breakdown of pattern bargaining arrangements that had prevailed in the rubber tire industry since shortly after the Second World War (Kochan, McKersie, and Cappelli, 1984).[2] In Sweden, employers seeking more flexibility pushed bargaining from the national to the industry level, and even in some cases to the company level (Adams, 1995a; Hammarstrom, 1993; Kjellberg, 1992). Similar moves have taken place, generally at the behest of employers, in such countries as Denmark (Scheuer, 1992; Ferner and Hyman, 1992b), Italy (Ferner and Hyman, 1992a), the Netherlands, and Australia (Katz, Lee, and Lee, 2004). Even the German system, long considered among Europe's most stable, has made certain moves, albeit smaller ones, in the same direction (Jacobi, Keller, and Muller-Jentsch, 1992; Katz et al., 2004).[3]

The widespread downward shift in the locus of collective bargaining that occurred through the 1980s led many analysts to conclude that high-level, centralized negotiations that involved government in aggregate discussions with labour and management representatives were a thing of the past. Such **corporatism**, it was held, was too inflexible for today's highly competitive environments; however, the

corporatism Social arrangements in which bodies, or *corpora*, serve as political representatives and play a critical role in decision making. With regard to industrial relations systems, participation is tripartite: unions, private sector corporations, and government.

1990s saw a re-emergence of national-level social dialogue (Katz et al., 2004), even in countries where such policy making coordination had heretofore been weak. Financial crises and the need to conform to parameters required for participation in the European Monetary Union promoted social pacts and national-level dialogue in Italy, the Netherlands, and Ireland. Similar pressures prompted Korea to rely upon a tripartite commission to shape labour market and labour law policy reforms (Katz et al., 2004). Such national-level tripartite structures are absent in the United States and Canada and our collective bargaining structures are increasingly decentralized and individualized; however, in the United States a variety of regional tripartite mechanisms for coordination of collective bargaining have emerged, leading to what has been referred to as "coordinated decentralization" (Katz et al., 2004:211).

Effects of Different Bargaining Structures

In general, bargaining structures' effects on different parties tend to be different depending on whether the economy is weak or strong. In good times, private sector unions generally favour decentralized bargaining structures. Under such structures, at times when the demand for labour is high and employers are very much interested in maintaining labour peace, unions can often whipsaw employers, that is, use one settlement with one employer as the basis for obtaining similar or generally better terms with others (Gallagher and Wetzel, 1980). At such times, many employers are willing to give up some degree of control and enter into multi-employer bargaining agreements, because these will combat whipsawing by establishing a common wage scale throughout the industry (Gallagher and Wetzel, 1980). Indeed, some well-known centralized bargaining arrangements, including most notably the national-level bargaining that prevailed in Sweden from the 1950s through the 1980s (Kjellberg, 1992), have actually been started at the employers' behest, with an eye to moderating wage settlements. Other benefits employers may seek from multi-employer bargaining include a reduction in work stoppages and economies of scale in negotiations and contract administration, as well as reduced uncertainty about labour costs and, consequently, about product pricing (Rogow, 1989a).

In tougher economic conditions, private sector unions tend to favour centralized bargaining arrangements, while employers often seek to escape from them. Now, whipsawing is often done by employers, who may obtain concessions from the union in one negotiation and use this initial set of concessions as the basis for even greater ones in another negotiation. So long as the bargaining structure remains centralized, it is harder for an employer to force concessions on a union, and the costs of a strike are apt to be considerably greater. As well, employers have a harder time getting rid of their unions altogether under centralized than under decentralized bargaining (see Kochan et al., 1984; Rose, 1992). Ending centralized arrangements also means that employers are free to bargain based on their own particular circumstances. At a time of ever-increasing competitiveness, this kind of flexibility is increasingly important for many employers.

With regard to wages, market-driven decentralized structures generally lead to greater dispersion between higher- and lower-paid workers and greater union–non-union wage differentials (Katz et al., 2004). In contrast, centralized structures, which are marked by a significantly greater degree of government involvement both in the bargaining process and in any subsequent dispute settlement processes (Rogow, 1989a), generally lead to greater similarity of wages, benefits, and other terms of employment across industries or jurisdictions (Rogow, 1989a).

At the macroeconomic level, centralized systems have been associated with lower levels of inflation than decentralized ones (Tarantelli, 1986), at least in good economic times.[4] Again, more moderate settlements are likely to result—at least in part from unions' loss of the ability to whipsaw. In addition, there is often a different political dynamic at work in centralized systems, many of which have traditionally been found in countries with strong labour or social democratic parties with a good chance of forming the government, such as Sweden, Denmark, and Austria (see Tarantelli, 1986). When such a party forms the government, the labour movement will often be able to achieve much of its agenda politically and may well be induced to agree to lower wage settlements in return for pension and tax reform, price controls, a full employment guarantee,[5] or other government policies favouring workers and unions (Adams, 1989). The promise of favourable government policies can also induce unions to call fewer strikes than they otherwise would (Adams, 1989; Tarantelli, 1986). Thus, centralized structures offer a forum for addressing a variety of national-level policy and social welfare issues (Katz et al., 2004).

Another argument often advanced in favour of more centralized bargaining structures is that they lead to fewer strikes and less working time lost (Rogow, 1989a) and international evidence supports this contention (see Adams, 1989 and 1995a). Such a finding, however, seems almost axiomatic, given that such structures involve many fewer sets of negotiations at any given time than decentralized ones. In addition, larger negotiations with more at stake are likely to be conducted by more skilful and experienced negotiators (Rogow, 1989a) and managers with real decision-making authority are more likely to be at the table or at least in close contact with the management negotiating team (Rogow, 1989a). Furthermore, because of the relatively greater importance of centralized negotiations, governments are more apt to intervene both to prevent strikes and to end them quickly should they occur (Rogow, 1989a). Thus it is not centralization itself, but the shift in the locus of conflict that often accompanies it that seems to be the main reason for reduced industrial conflict levels in European countries with centralized structures (see Mishel, 1986 for more detail).

As for the bargaining process itself, the effects of greater centralization are somewhat mixed. On the one hand, centralization seems to make negotiations go more smoothly because of the more experienced negotiators generally conducting them and the presence or availability of senior management with real authority. On the other hand, because in centralized bargaining each side represents a greater number of union or management factions, internal or **intra-organizational bargaining** becomes more complex, with the result that negotiations as a whole tend to go more slowly (Mishel, 1986). There is also evidence that centralized negotiations may increase local union negotiators' and rank-and-file members' feelings of alienation from the negotiations and from the centralized negotiators, who are less likely to be closely attuned to specific local conditions and issues (Mishel, 1986). This, together with the fact that centralized negotiations by their very nature tend to encompass

intra-organizational bargaining Bargaining within each party in order to achieve internal consensus.

issues of general importance, thereby omitting issues of local concern, may well be a factor in the higher incidence of wildcat strikes found in centralized structures (Mishel, 1986). Two-tier bargaining systems with a master agreement that is supplemented by various agreements on issues of only local concern may be a way around this problem. These systems have long been used successfully in Europe, though in Canada they are confined mainly to the public sector (Adams, 1989; Gallagher and Wetzel, 1980; Hébert, 1995). While they are certainly no panacea, the evidence suggests such arrangements can help reduce a number of the problems associated with centralization, particularly when the union is careful to solicit local input throughout the bargaining process.

THE NEGOTIATION PROCESS

All negotiations share certain characteristics: They involve two or more interdependent parties who attempt to influence each other in order to gain something of value. Parties to negotiations usually expect some sort of give and take and favour that process over openly fighting or capitulating. They also usually believe that the process of negotiation can lead to more favourable outcomes than if they simply relied on a third party or higher authority to resolve the dispute. Finally, negotiations involve management of not only the tangible items under discussion but also of the intangibles, the underlying psychological motivations influencing the process (Lewicki, Barry, Saunders, and Minton, 2003). The intangibles are even more important when the negotiations are between parties to an ongoing relationship, as is the case in collective bargaining.

While collective bargaining is similar to other negotiations in many ways, it also has some very distinctive characteristics. To begin with, negotiations between union and management typically address a broader range of issues than most commercial contracts and the issues themselves are often more complex than those raised in the average commercial transaction. Given the many possible trade-offs, costing alone can be an extremely time-consuming process. Moreover, some issues, such as regulating the use of hazardous chemicals in the workplace or changing a pension plan, may be so technically complex as to require many hours of study by joint committees or even reliance on outside expertise. Finally, because of the breadth and complexity of issues involved in most labour–management negotiations, often more is at stake than in commercial negotiations and emotions can run high on both sides, particularly as a strike or lockout deadline approaches. This too can complicate bargaining, not just between the parties, but within each of the negotiating teams.

A second distinctive feature of collective bargaining is the degree to which the parties' responsibilities are statutorily regulated. For example, a union's need to ensure that it is complying with its statutory duty to represent all its members fairly may lead it to introduce a broader range of issues rather than just those endorsed by the majority of members. From another angle, the various dispute resolution processes imposed by labour relations legislation may slow negotiations down considerably. As we noted in Chapter 7, even in the private sector no union can strike or employer lock out until the agreement has expired and, in most cases, until some kind of conciliation or mediation process has been attempted and certain time limits have passed. As we note in Chapter 8, public sector legislation often imposes additional restrictions, such as further time limits or extra steps to the dispute resolution process. In some cases, strikes are barred altogether, forcing the parties to take their disputes to binding arbitration. When this happens, the result is often the so-called **chilling effect** whereby the parties refuse to make concessions, in the expectation, or at least hope, that the arbitrator will arrive at a middle position, thereby relieving them of the need to make hard decisions on their own. Whether strikes are permitted or not, the various dispute resolution processes often make negotiations take far longer than they otherwise would.

A third distinctive aspect of union–management negotiations is that they are conducted by representatives of the parties; thus, the negotiators must emerge with a settlement acceptable not just to their bargaining team but to their principals, who were not involved in the actual negotiations but who have the ultimate say as to whether the tentative agreement is accepted or rejected. Both union and management negotiators generally represent constituencies with diverse memberships whose interests are often conflicting; given that unions are democratic organizations and most collective agreements require ratification by the membership, this is especially true for union-side negotiators. All of this means that they must not only conduct negotiations with the other party but also within their own organizations. This intra-organizational bargaining not only lengthens the bargaining process, it may also increase the likelihood of a bargaining impasse or even a strike (Gunderson, Hyatt, and Ponak, 1995). As well, members of the various management or union factions will often be part of the bargaining team and will closely monitor the negotiators to ensure they are energetically representing the wide range of membership interests. In the eyes of some observers, it is the need to meet constituents' psychological as well as economic needs that explains much of the ritual and ceremony often connected to the negotiation process (see, for example, Sass, 1989).

Fourth, union–management relationships are generally long-term in nature. Most have a history; most will also have a future. In arriving at a settlement, union and management negotiators must try to come up with solutions that will not merely meet the parties' immediate needs but will help them build or maintain an effective working relationship over the medium to long term. Since such a process involves making projections and educated guesses about the future and gets into the parties' feelings and perceptions as well as objective economic issues, it will almost inevitably be more complex than a commercial negotiation that addresses only economic issues and that is often set at a single point in time, or at most involves projection over a relatively short time span. Where the relationship has been troubled in the past, there may be lingering issues to overcome and hurt feelings to assuage before the parties can move on to constructive negotiations over current issues.

Bargaining Strategies and Systems of Activities

The various approaches to conflict resolution have been characterized in many different ways, but the most relevant for industrial relations purposes was developed by Walton and McKersie (1965) and labels the competitive approach "**distributive**

---

chilling effect Refers to parties' hesitancy to make the concessions necessary to conclude a collective agreement when they anticipate arbitration and believe the arbitrator will choose a middle ground.

distributive bargaining System of activities focused on dividing limited resources. Functions to resolve pure conflicts of interest.

bargaining" and the collaborative approach "**integrative bargaining**." Distributive bargaining focuses on one's own substantive outcomes and is used when resources are fixed and the parties' interests are in conflict. This approach to bargaining is akin to dividing a resource in that a gain to one party represents a loss to the other. The best example of a distributive issue in union–management negotiations is wages, where increases are typically seen as a direct transfer of wealth from owners to employees. Matters of a distributive nature tend to engender competitive behaviour and the give-and-take concession trading we normally associate with union–management negotiations.

Integrative bargaining is the system of activities designed to resolve conflicts where the parties' interests are not fundamentally opposed. In this type of situation, the parties' interests can be integrated to some degree and solutions can be developed to issues of shared concern. Since one party's gains do not directly equate to the others' losses, parties are more willing to openly share information and interests and, thereby, collaboratively fashion a resolution. Furthermore, since optimal solutions require the co-operation of both parties, negotiators focus on both parties' goals and interests, not just on substantive outcomes for their own side. Both parties, for example, can benefit from open discussion and co-operation on issues regarding occupational health and safety or workplace training.

In truth, few conflicts fall squarely within the categories of irreconcilable versus shared interests. Most issues are characterized by a range of interests, some of which the parties may share and some that may be at odds. Negotiated wage increases, for example, do not in fact represent a simple transfer of funds from one pocket to another. Employers benefit from increased wages by being able to attract and retain more qualified candidates and properly structured compensation programs can increase productivity and focus employees' efforts. Thus, the benefits of higher wages offset the costs at least to some degree. Furthermore, most negotiations involve a mix of issues, some perhaps where the parties' interests are irreconcilable and some where they are shared—and this is especially true of collective bargaining, which involves a wide range of issues including wages, benefits, scheduling, vacations, job security, job advancement, technological change, occupational health and safety, procedures for dispute resolution, management rights, and mechanisms for employee participation in decision making, to name but a few. Finally, while distributive and integrative bargaining can be conceptualized as opposites, in truth they are interdependent, parallel sub-processes, each playing a part in bargaining even when one approach *appears* to be relied upon to the exclusion of the other. The mix of issues and the degree to which the parties' interests intersect are important determinants of bargaining approach; however, whether the parties adopt a primarily distributive or primarily integrative approach is also influenced by other historical, situational, and relationship characteristics and constraints (Lewicki et al., 2003).

In addition to the distributive and integrative approaches, or systems of activities, Walton and McKersie (1991) also identified two other parallel sub-processes: intra-organizational bargaining and **attitudinal structuring**. Intra-organizational bargaining occurs within each union or management team and functions to achieve consensus within each of these groups. Internal consensus with regard to bargaining goals serves to focus bargaining teams' efforts and bolster their bargaining power.

integrative bargaining System of activities focused on identifying resolutions to shared-interest conflicts that maximize joint gain.

attitudinal structuring Activities that influence the parties' relationship and attitudes toward each other.

Thus, both teams must conduct internal negotiations both while formulating their bargaining mandate and as their goals are shaped and reshaped through the negotiation process. Intra-organizational bargaining is an especially complex process for union teams who are the recipients of two sets of demands, one from across the table and one from their own members. One of their first steps when preparing for a round of collective bargaining involves canvassing members and synthesizing the multitude of diverse opinions into a relatively coherent bargaining mandate. Once bargaining commences, the union team must keep its members informed of their progress—and continually negotiate with them in order to bring their expectations into alignment with the realistic aspirations of those who have been privy to the bargaining process. Finally, once a deal has been concluded, the union bargaining team must usually present it to their members and ask for their support in a ratification vote. If the team is unable to convince the members that the deal represents the best mix and balance of issues achievable, it will be rejected. Thus, intra-organizational bargaining is an integral element of the collective bargaining process.

Also integral to the process is the system of activities that functions to shape the relationship between the parties, especially the degree of trust and whether the parties will interact competitively or co-operatively. This system of activities is referred to as attitudinal structuring (Walton and McKersie, 1991) and the parties often begin setting the stage long before negotiations begin. The parties may, for example, establish joint union–management committees during the term of an agreement, both as continuing problem-solving mechanisms and as forums for sharing information and building the trust and rapport that will facilitate integrative bargaining during the next round of negotiations. Alternately, one party may send the message to the other that the upcoming round of negotiations may be difficult and will concern issues with regard to which the parties have distinctly contradictory views. The imbroglio concerning a salary cap in the NHL, which is dealt with in the case at the end of this chapter, was just such an issue and the parties engaged in much posturing and attitudinal structuring both before and during the antagonistic negotiations.

Each of Walton and McKersie's systems of bargaining has unique functions and each demands a different set of actions and tactics. Indeed, much of the art of negotiations involves the balanced execution of what are often contradictory tactics. Distributive bargaining, for example, involves gathering information about the other party's goals and priorities while concealing information that might reveal your priorities or resistance points. In this system, parties stand firm on positions, usually only moving off them in exchange for a concession, and they attempt to discover the most favourable conditions under which a deal can be reached. Just as you would prefer not to pay $30 000 for a car if you could purchase it for $25 000, neither party wants to give more than is necessary to seal the deal.

mutual gains or interest-based bargaining (IBB)
A collective bargaining approach that incorporates integrative and principled bargaining.

Integrative bargaining, on the other hand, requires far more openness and information sharing regarding each party's priorities and the conditions under which they would accept a deal. Rather than standing firm on positions, the parties openly communicate to each other regarding their underlying interests and brainstorm to invent options that are advantageous to both (Walton and McKersie, 1991). **Mutual gains**, or **interest-based, bargaining** is a collective bargaining innovation that incorporates integrative bargaining techniques and **principled bargaining** (Fisher, Ury, and Patton, 1991). Principled bargaining encourages the parties to seek mutual gain in areas of shared interest and to use merit and objective standards to resolve issues where interests are in conflict.

While most collective bargaining continues to rely upon more distributive approaches, several union–management groups have found success in mutual gains bargaining, or as it is sometimes called interest-based, or win-win bargaining. Not only has mutual-gains bargaining sometimes served to improve the union–management relationship, but it has also been associated with improved productivity and flexibility (Chaykowski and Grant, 1995). However, in some instances attempts at mutual-gains bargaining have actually soured the union–management relationship and even where it is successful this approach to bargaining requires comprehensive change and high levels of trust, openness, training, and commitment of time and resources. While many union and management negotiators have experience with mutual-gains bargaining, its use is neither as sustained nor as diffused as might be expected given the substantial mutual gains predicted by proponents of this approach (Cutcher-Gershenfeld, Kochan, and Wells, 2001).

principled bargaining Process whereby the parties seek mutual gain in areas of shared interest and use merit and objective standards to resolve issues where interests are in conflict.

STRATEGIC NEGOTIATIONS

During the 1980s and 1990s, labour relations in the United States seemed to polarize around the opposite extremes of co-operation versus contention. According to Walton, Cutcher-Gershenfeld, and McKersie (2000), Walton and McKersie's systems of activities were still applicable to collective bargaining, but they proved inadequate in explaining the divergent shifts or in analyzing the many instances of negotiated change in union–management relationships. Collective bargaining processes and structures in an era of intensified market competitiveness seemed more varied and complex than Walton and McKersie's original conceptualizations. Therefore, Walton, Cutcher-Gershenfeld, and McKersie (2000) expanded the original theory to "fully capture the nature of contemporary change episodes" (2000:xiv). Their model of strategic negotiations was developed from 13 case histories in three industries and categorizes strategic approaches as falling into one of three categories: forcing change, fostering change, or escaping the relationship.

A forcing strategy combines a focus on distributive bargaining with attitudinal structuring designed to emphasize hostility and intra-organizational bargaining to maximize internal solidarity while exploiting any divisions within the other party's organization. Fostering focuses on integrative bargaining, attitudinal structuring emphasizing trust, and intra-organizational bargaining that builds consensus within both teams. A mixed strategy combines forcing with fostering, usually sequentially as goals and conditions change. Escaping the union–management relationship is not, in fact, a strategy for negotiated change, but employers may use threats of escape to compel unions and employees to engage in the negotiation process. Beyond simply relocating or transferring operations, some "escape" strategies employers may use are to systematically increase investments in their non-unionized locations, to contract out increasing amounts of work, to hire permanent replacement workers, or to attempt to decertify the union (Walton et al., 2000).

While a full explanation of the model of strategic negotiations is beyond the scope of this chapter, some elements can be broadly simplified and briefly summarized: First, in selecting a negotiation strategy, parties must consider their primary objectives or goals. In any set of negotiations, parties usually have both substantive goals and goals regarding the impact, or lack thereof, that the negotiations will have upon the parties' relationship. In the model of strategic negotiations, the latter are termed the **social contract outcomes**, the shared understandings "around the expected levels of trust, information sharing and mutual commitment" (Walton et al., 2000:viii). The model outlines two levels and various combinations of social contract outcomes. However, for our purposes the simplified lesson to be extracted is that the balance the parties strike between substantive and social contract goals is one of the most important predictors of negotiation strategy. A strong focus on substantive outcomes, with relatively little regard for relationship outcomes, will tend to steer the parties toward a competitive approach, while a relatively greater focus on social contract outcomes, such as employee co-operation and commitment, tends to lead to a more collaborative approach.

While negotiators' choice of strategy is both influenced and constrained by their goals, it is also determined by the anticipated feasibility of implementing a particular strategy. Some of the most important determinants of feasibility are the expected receptivity or resistance of the other party and their relative bargaining power. For example, if an employer expects the union to resist change even in the face of persuasive business rationale, a fostering approach would likely be ineffective. The employer may, therefore, elect to force the substantive change, but the anticipated effectiveness of this option would depend upon whether the employer is confident it has sufficient bargaining power to prevail.

Also of importance in the assessment of the expected feasibility of a particular strategy are a range of contextual factors that could either support or negate the strategy's effectiveness. For example, a union–management team with training in problem-solving skills and a history of successful collaboration would likely be much more successful at fostering change than one with a history of adversarialism and animosity (Walton et al., 2000). Or, if the cost associated with a strike has decreased due to automation that makes it feasible for managerial personnel to continue operations during a strike, the employer may be more willing to accept the strike risk that accompanies a forcing strategy.

Finally, negotiators need to ensure that the interaction systems, that is the negotiation processes and structures, are aligned with and support their chosen strategy. Characteristics of interaction systems that are exogenously determined—or outside the employers' control—such as mandatory participation in a centralized bargaining system, constrain negotiators' choice of strategy. In situations where interaction systems can be modified by the parties, influence runs in the opposite direction—in that changes in tactics, processes, and structures are a function of strategy. In such situations, negotiators can implement changes that facilitate their strategy and increase its effectiveness. For example, since decentralized structures and frequent interactions tend to facilitate fostering, in these circumstances, an employer and union team may create joint committees that tackle complex problems away from the main-table negotiations, or establish periodic forums for mid-contract dialogue (Walton et al., 2000).

social contract outcomes The shared understandings around the expected levels of trust, information sharing, and mutual commitment between the parties.

PREPARATION FOR BARGAINING

In Canada, whether employers adopt a strategic approach to negotiations or not, preparation for collective bargaining commences long before negotiations are scheduled to begin. There are a number of mandatory steps that must be followed as well as a number of common practices in which most parties engage. For example, before bargaining commences, it is usually the responsibility of the union to notify the employer of its intention to bargain a new or renewal collective agreement. In some jurisdictions, the employer may provide such notice to the union. Either way, the parties are statutorily required to commence bargaining in good faith following receipt of such notice, although the time period for commencement of bargaining varies between jurisdictions (see Table 9.1).

Prior to the parties' first meeting, and even prior to the bargaining notice, the parties engage in extensive preparations. Often success in negotiations can be

Table 9.1

BARGAINING FOR RENEWAL OF COLLECTIVE AGREEMENTS: PERIOD OF NOTICE AND REQUIREMENT TO COMMENCE BARGAINING

	Notice to Bargain	Bargaining Must Commence
Federal	4 months preceding contract expiry*	Within 20 days of notice[†]
BC	4 months preceding contract expiry[§]	Within 10 days of notice
Alberta	60–120 days prior to contract expiry**	Within 30 days of notice; proposals must be exchanged within 15 days following first meeting*
Saskatchewan	30–60 days prior to contract expiry	Immediately
Manitoba	30–90 days prior to contract expiry	Within 10 clear days of notice*
Ontario	Within 90 days prior to contract expiry[††]	Must meet within 15 days*
Quebec	Within 90 days prior to contract expiry[††]	Must begin and be carried on diligently
Newfoundland and Labrador	30–60 days prior to contract expiry[††]	Within 20 days of notice*
New Brunswick	30–90 days prior to contract expiry[††]	Within 20 days of notice*
Nova Scotia	2 months prior to contract expiry	Within 20 days of notice*
PEI	As per agreement, or at least 2 months prior to contract expiry	Within 20 days*

*Unless parties agree to a longer period.

[†]Unless parties agree otherwise.

[§]If notice is not given 90 days or more prior to expiry of the agreement, the parties are deemed to have provided notice 90 days prior to expiry.

**Or within a longer period specified in the collective agreement.

[††]Or in accordance with provisions in the agreement.

Source: Human Resources and Skills Development Canada. (2005). "Summary of General Private Sector Collective Bargaining Legislation." Industrial Relations Legislation in Canada, http://www.hrsdc.gc.ca/asp/gateway.asp?hr=en/lp/spila/clli/irlc/01industrial_relations_legislation_canada.shtml&hs=lzl, [April 7, 2005].

attributed to a team's superior preparation. Union and management teams generally start by canvassing their constituency or principals to determine the issues they would like to address, the relative importance of those issues, and whether they are prepared to stage or take a lawful work stoppage (Fisher and Williams, 1989). With the team's general objectives established, detailed preparations can begin. On the management side, this may well include monitoring workers' attitudes and concerns, getting a read on the overall economic and political environment within which negotiations will be conducted,[6] monitoring the union's developments, monitoring local or industry wage developments to get a sense of a reasonable ballpark figure for the final settlement,[7] and conducting background research aimed at developing proposals for non-wage issues (Godard and Kochan, 1982). Such background research may also entail conducting interviews or soliciting written submissions from line managers (Godard and Kochan, 1982), reviewing company policies and the administration of the current agreement, and examining any outstanding grievances or arbitration decisions resulting from the previous agreement (Williams, 1982). With this broad range of information in hand, the management team can start developing and costing specific wage and benefit proposals (Godard and Kochan, 1982).

A researcher pores over past settlements in her industry. In negotiations, good preparation is often half the battle.

For the union team, the overall objective of preparation is pretty much the same as it is for management: to obtain as thorough a knowledge of the general and specific economic and political environments as possible to arrive at bargaining proposals that are realistic and stand a reasonable chance of acceptance, in addition to meeting as many of the needs of the union's members as possible. However, because of the union's statutory obligation to represent members fairly, and because unions generally operate in a far more public and open fashion than do employer organizations, the *process* of preparation may be somewhat different. Like the management team, the union will solicit members' written input on contract proposals, and will conduct background research into comparable settlements in the area and in the industry. Then, both to receive further input and to help ensure members buy into any tentative settlement eventually negotiated, the union will typically hold one or more general membership meetings at which both general and specific bargaining objectives are discussed. At these meetings, the union leadership and negotiating team will normally take pains to ensure that proposals are put forward to address the needs of all major constituencies within the union. After these meetings, still further written input may be solicited, and the union may also inform members of ongoing developments through email messages or a series of "Negotiation Newsletters."

Developing the Bottom Line

Before the parties meet for their initial bargaining session, each side normally holds several private, pre-negotiation meetings during which the members of their committee plan, prepare, and among other things, develop their bottom line. At these meetings, committee members often divide issues into three categories: bottom-line issues, over which the team is prepared to strike or take a strike; trading issues, which are important but that can be bought by the other side in return for an equivalent concession; and "cannon fodder," or items of lesser importance that will be given up after a good fight (Fisher and Williams, 1989:200). Within these categories, individual issues are usually rank-ordered. Also, to the extent possible, the parties often attempt to classify the other side's anticipated demands in a similar fashion (Fisher and Williams, 1989).

Another purpose of the pre-negotiation meeting is to build teamwork and esprit de corps with an eye to ensuring that all team members understand, and remain committed to, the team's agreed-upon goals and objectives. At such meetings, team members may be assigned roles such as the taking of notes, collection of data, costing, or observing the other side's reactions (Fisher and Williams, 1989). Part of these meetings will likely be devoted to tactical decisions such as how to begin negotiations, or whether the chief negotiator will be the team's sole spokesperson and, if not, under what conditions others should speak. Especially if a generally distributive approach will be adopted, most teams find it best to allow the chief negotiator to do all the talking, except in the case of specific technical issues, such as costing, where the team member assigned to the role may be better informed and thus better able to help the team's cause (see Fisher and Williams, 1989).

Bargaining Goals and Outcomes

As discussed earlier, both union and management enter negotiations with both substantive goals and, often to a lesser extent, social contract goals. The degree to which the parties' goals overlap is an important determinant of bargaining outcomes. After categorizing their bargaining goals, each team will generally consider a range of potential outcomes for each issue and establish **target** and **resistance** points and formulate an **opening offer** (Lewicki et al., 2003). The opening, or initial, offer is generally the most optimistically anticipated outcome while the resistance point is the minimally acceptable outcome—or the point at which the party is willing to walk away from negotiations. For high-priority issues, the resistance point may represent the outcome the union is willing to go on strike to achieve, although strikes and lockouts are generally the result of a combination of issues. A target point is the hoped-for outcome, and effective negotiators establish target points that are realistically achievable.

In order for the parties to reach agreement on any of the wide range of issues under negotiation, their resistance points must overlap to some degree. This area of overlap, or **zone of potential agreement**, is the area within which most negotiation takes place, since anything outside this range would be rejected outright by either the union or management (Lewicki et al., 2003). For example, if the union's resistance point is an across-the-board increase of 3 percent and management is willing to go as high as 4 percent, the eventual deal will fall somewhere between 3 and 4 percent. This does not mean that the parties' opening offers will fall within this bargaining range. Indeed, it is very likely the union's initial demand will far exceed the eventual settlement. In some instances, a negative bargaining zone exits, in that the parties' resistance points do not overlap. If the previous example were reversed and the union was not willing to accept anything less than 4 percent but management was unwilling to go higher than 3 percent, the parties would not reach agreement unless and until one party or the other abandoned their resistance point, perhaps in exchange for an improved outcome on another issue.

In some instances where a positive settlement zone does not exist, it is not because the parties' resistance points do not overlap. Rather, it may be because the issue regards a fundamental principle that is not quantifiable and thus not amenable to the sort of trade-off inherent in the very notion of a settlement zone (Kervin, 1984). For this reason, disputes over such issues tend to be longer, more bitter, and far harder to settle than disputes over monetary issues. Often such disputes are only resolved after some kind of government or third-party intervention (Kervin, 1984). A union's right to exist, freedom from discrimination, or the right to a safe workplace are examples of matters that are of fundamental principle, which explains why they are regulated primarily through legislation, rather than being left to the vagaries of collective bargaining.

In many other instances where a positive settlement zone does not exist, the parties fail to discover this until well into the bargaining process (Lewicki et al., 2003). The parties begin discussions based on opening offers and as bargaining progresses through its various stages, it may become apparent that the union's opinion regarding how it would like to see an issue resolved is significantly at odds with management's perspective. However, the fact that there is no overlap between their resistance

---

target point The realistically anticipated and hoped for outcome.

resistance point The minimum outcome a party is willing to accept.

opening offer Initial offer, which is usually the most optimistic outcome one can anticipate.

zone of potential agreement The area within which the parties' resistance points overlap. Also called the bargaining range or settlement zone.

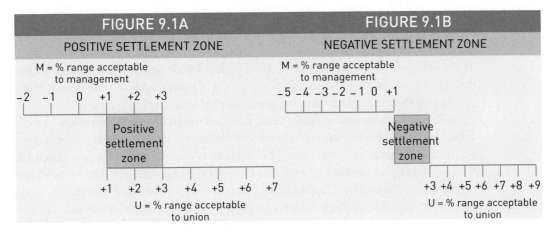

Source: Prepared from sketch by Jon Peirce.

points may not be discovered until after protracted negotiations. If the issue is not one of extremely high priority, one party might be persuaded to move its resistance point on one issue in exchange for the other party moving on another issue. On a high priority issue, if neither party is willing to re-evaluate its resistance point, they may call a strike or a lockout or submit the dispute to arbitration.

The Stages of Negotiation

Collective bargaining generally proceeds through four major stages: settling in, consolidation, finalization, and mopping-up (Fisher and Williams, 1989:189). Each stage contributes to the process and efforts to skip or rush through a stage can have detrimental impacts on both the process and the eventual outcomes. Attempts to push the other side too fast can result in unnecessary resistance; overly rapid concessions can lead to trouble on one's own side, and perhaps even to rejection of the tentative agreement if, for example, union members believe their negotiator capitulated unnecessarily.

Settling in, the first stage, is a time for the parties to familiarize themselves with each other (Fisher and Williams, 1989), particularly if the chief negotiators have no experience together. This stage also sets the groundwork for future success and parties may focus on integrative issues or distributive issues of relatively low importance or with regard to which the parties' positions are not diametrically opposed. Once a few minor items have been settled, teams are more likely to have developed the momentum needed to tackle the more major items, like wages and job security.

The second stage, consolidation, is normally by far the longest. It is here that each side more fully forwards its positions and arguments and learns more about the other side's priorities—often simply because the less important issues have been set aside, clearing the way for the "real" business. The consolidation stage often requires several team meetings, or caucuses, to allow each side to assess the other side's demands and priorities and come up with an appropriate response to them. It is common practice not to agree to anything important without calling a caucus

(Fisher and Williams, 1989). The overall aim of this stage is to hone one's own bottom line and develop an understanding of the other side's bottom line. While bottom lines may change in response to information exchanged at the table or changes in the economic or political environment within which negotiations are being conducted (Fisher and Williams, 1989), changes in a team's bottom line are not made lightly and should only be done in light of overall objectives.

Where a settlement zone does exist, it is discovered during finalization—or the actual reaching of a settlement (Fisher and Williams, 1989). Unlike consolidation, which usually lasts for a long time, finalization is normally quite quick. Often the final settlement is triggered by a corridor or washroom meeting of the two principal negotiators, followed by a last-minute concession or repackaging that makes a previously unpalatable package at least marginally acceptable to the other side.

Mopping up generally means drafting specific language for provisions to which the chief negotiators have agreed in principle. It may also entail attending to letters of intent or troubleshooting issues subsequently raised by one's constituency or principals (Fisher and Williams, 1989). It is important to attend to this stage carefully. Contract language that is not carefully drafted or does not reflect the true intent of the parties at the time of agreement can come back to haunt all concerned in the next round of negotiations, in addition to being fertile breeding ground for grievances and other types of union–management conflict during the life of the agreement.

THE ROLE OF BARGAINING POWER

Even the most co-operative union–management relationship will almost certainly feature a significant degree of competition over money (Kervin, 1989). In less co-operative relationships, competition is likely to permeate most, if not all, aspects of the bargaining process. Where competition is present, what chiefly determines bargaining outcomes is the extent to which each side is able to exert bargaining power over the other. The literature offers a number of definitions of the term *bargaining power*. One of the most widely quoted is that of Chamberlain and Kuhn (1986) who describe bargaining power as "the ability to secure another's agreement on one's own terms" (176). With regard to the union–management relationship, Chamberlain and Kuhn consider bargaining power a function of the cost of disagreeing with the other's terms versus the cost of agreeing to them. Godard (2005) states it slightly differently. In his view, each side has bargaining power, and therefore is likely to win concessions from the other side, to the extent that a work stoppage imposes direct and indirect costs on the other side. In essence, Godard focuses solely on the cost of disagreement.

Virtually all environmental or contextual factors can influence bargaining power by affecting the cost of agreeing to, or disagreeing with, a particular collective agreement term. Furthermore, these environmental factors are not static and relative bargaining power tends to shift over time. Economic factors tend to have greatest impact on relative bargaining power and include both broader macroeconomic factors, such as employment levels, and microeconomic factors, such as the degree to which the production process is labour-intensive. For example, periods of high unemployment will shift bargaining power in favour of employers as alternate employment becomes more difficult to find and the cost to workers of a strike rises. During good economic times, workers' bargaining power tends to increase as demand for goods and services increases and the cost to the employer of lost production due to a strike increases.

One of the most important factors in determining the cost of a strike is a firm's production technologies. All else being equal, a strike is more costly to firms whose production processes are labour intensive (Fisher and Waschik, 2000). Where the production process relies more upon capital, such as in the case of manufacturing processes that are becoming increasingly automated, employers may be able to continue at least partial production during a strike by reassigning managerial personnel. Similarly, unions' bargaining power is higher if workers are highly skilled, or if the bargaining unit covers the majority of the employers' operations, due to the difficulties these conditions pose for replacing workers and continuing operations during a strike. Highly integrated operations, especially those that rely on just-in-time inventory systems, may also shift power in favour of the union since a strike at one plant may cripple operations at other locations that depend on the struck plant for inputs. Another good example of a factor that influences bargaining power is the seasonal nature of an industry. Teachers, construction workers, agricultural workers, and even retail employees all experience fluctuations in their bargaining power at various times in the year.

The direct sources of management bargaining power relate to the economic cost to workers of a strike or lockout. Such direct bargaining power is reduced to the extent that workers can find alternate, comparable employment either permanently or during the course of a work stoppage (Godard, 2005). In most cases, however, there are costs attached to permanently changing jobs, as temporary jobs rarely pay anywhere near as much as regular full-time ones, and strike pay replaces only a small proportion of workers' regular wages or salaries. Therefore, this source of management power is likely to remain a potent one except in very good economic times, when striking workers may find it relatively easy to locate new full-time jobs, and when a firm may need to make up for production losses after a strike with large amounts of overtime (Godard, 2005).

Other environmental factors also influence bargaining power through their impacts on the relative cost of agreement versus disagreement. For example, legislation that prohibits the use of replacement workers during a strike shifts bargaining power in favour of workers, especially for those who might otherwise be easily and permanently replaced. The cooling-off period imposed by the *Industrial Disputes Investigations Act (IDI Act)* of 1907 shifted power in favour of employers, since it provided them an opportunity to stockpile inventory from which they could continue sales through a work stoppage. Not only did this decrease the direct cost of the dispute, but it also helped prevent the loss of market share that often occurs when customers are forced to seek alternate suppliers due to production shortfalls. Legislation that prohibits strikes or declares certain workers essential significantly shifts bargaining power in favour of the employer. Even if workers defy the law and withdraw their services, they will likely face fines or even imprisonment, so the cost of disagreeing is significantly higher for them than for workers who enjoy the unfettered right to strike.

Public opinion may also influence the cost of agreement or disagreement. In the public sector, public sympathy for strikers and the perception that the government's position is unreasonable may cause a corresponding loss of confidence in the government (Godard, 2005). In the private sector, striking workers may encourage the public to boycott the employer and their products. The greater the union's ability to impose such strike costs on management, the likelier management is to make concessions that will end the strike (Godard, 2005).

As the history of the Canadian labour movement illustrates, bargaining power can shift quite quickly. Often, such shifts in bargaining power are the result of large-scale economic and political trends. During the Great Depression, for example, with production severely curtailed and jobs at a premium, bargaining power swung very markedly towards employers. Once war was declared and most able-bodied young male workers were sent to the front, power shifted quite markedly in the opposite direction, although the government did what it could to mitigate the effects of this shift by imposing wage controls, freezing workers in essential employment, and limiting employees' right to quit or shift jobs (Morton, 1995). Through the 1970s, workers and their unions generally continued to enjoy a fair degree of bargaining power; however, things shifted quite quickly as a result of the recessions that came in the wake of the two major energy shocks of the 1970s and particularly the major recession of 1981–1983. In Canada, unemployment has been relatively high ever since and collective bargaining settlements have been correspondingly modest. Now, with the impending retirement of large numbers of workers who were born during the baby boom, the balance of power may be about to shift again, particularly in highly-skilled professional, managerial, and technical fields and in much of the public sector (see Galt, 2000; G. Lowe, 2001a; Auditor-General, 2000 and 2001).

COLLECTIVE BARGAINING: AN OVERALL ASSESSMENT

One of the fundamental criticisms of collective bargaining is that it assumes at least rough equality between the parties. In practice, this does not always exist, particularly in bad economic times, when, as it has in recent years, the balance of power tends to shift strongly in the direction of employers. Where such a balance of power does not exist, it becomes harder for unions to negotiate effectively, and the collective bargaining process does less well at defusing workplace conflict than it otherwise would. Should the power imbalance continue for any length of time, the conflict may well resurface in the form of increased grievance rates, higher quit rates, higher levels of official or unofficial strike action, or increased absenteeism and sick leave (see Shellenbarger, 1998), all of which may have severely negative consequences for both the organization and its employees. Furthermore, the recent trends toward globalization and fiercer international competition described in earlier chapters lead one to wonder how collective bargaining once every few years can realistically be expected to be frequent enough to respond adequately to an increasingly global economy marked by almost instantaneous transmission of information, rapid movement of goods, services, and capital across international borders, and constant fluctuations in exchange rates (Giles and Starkman, 1995).

Nonetheless, despite the validity of these criticisms—and others pointing out that real workplace democracy is seldom achieved through collective bargaining under the current system (see Giles and Starkman, 1995)—most workers are generally better off with collective bargaining than they would be without it. Unionized workers' wages and benefits are generally higher and their working conditions generally better than those of their non-unionized counterparts. As well, unionized workers enjoy a significantly greater voice in the workplace, thanks mainly to the grievance process. Thus, while it is far from perfect, collective bargaining is probably the best system currently available for determination of pay and working conditions. While the adversarial nature of the process and the length and complexity of most collective agreements are regrettable, they are likely inevitable so long as management continues to resist unions fiercely, and as long as bargaining remains highly decentralized, thus forcing most conflict to be worked out at the bargaining table rather than in the political arena. Unless and until either or both of these things change, collective bargaining seems likely to remain adversarial and conflict-ridden, and the collective agreements resulting from it will likely continue to be, for the most part, long, complex, and highly legalistic documents reflecting, to a considerable degree, the often bitter power struggles that have accompanied their drafting. We turn to these collective agreements in the next chapter.

Case 9.1

THE NHL FIASCO: HOW NOT TO NEGOTIATE

On February 16, 2005, the National Hockey League (NHL) earned the ignominious distinction of being the first North American professional sports league to lose an entire season to a labour dispute. Hockey fans, players, and owners alike all found it difficult to fathom how such a fiasco could have occurred. Talks to renew the collective agreement between the NHL owners and the Players' Association (NHLPA) had been under way since September 2003. A year later, in September 2004, the league locked the players out. Talks continued through the subsequent five-month lockout and progress had been made: The players had agreed to a 24 percent salary rollback and capitulated on the highly contentious salary cap issue, and the owners had abandoned the principle of a fluctuating cap that linked player salaries to revenues. It turned out, however, to be too little, too late and NHL Commissioner Gary Bettman proved willing to follow through on his threat to cancel the entire season. Bob Goodenow, head of the NHLPA, had hoped to avoid what he called "the unthinkable," but he stated that the "league's threats, ultimatums, take-it-or-leave-it tactics and refusal to negotiate ultimately prevented a deal here" (Campbell, 2005:C01).

In their postmortem analyses of the failed talks, many sports writers, labour relations specialists, and armchair athletes had to agree with Goodenow's assessment of the situation. In fact, many say the NHL 2003–05 negotiations serve as a lesson in the dangers of competitive bargaining. While the high-stakes contract between the NHL and their 750 players—who were scheduled to earn $1.5 billion (US) in the 2004–05 season—may be in a different league than most collective bargaining or commercial negotiations, the lessons that arise from their failure to reach a deal are relevant to anyone who negotiates.

Positions

One of the most important mistakes both the league and the players made was to formulate positions they knew were untenable to the other party and then refuse to budge from those positions. The league insisted on a salary cap, even though it had been unable to achieve this during the 1994–95 lockout and knew the players had pledged to never accept one. Rather than pitching a salary cap as the best way to achieve its objective of cost certainty, it held it out as the single solution to every problem. The league thus established a philosophical divide, yet offered the players no graceful way to cross that divide. Its insistence that a deal could not be reached unless the players caved virtually guaranteed an impasse. Even when the players finally did cave on the salary cap principle, Bettman and the league failed to capitalize on the opportunity to fashion an acceptable compromise. They seemed more intent on a victory than a deal.

Personalities

Another mistake that plagued the NHL talks is that the rancour between Bettman and Goodenow sometimes overshadowed the process. While each denied interpersonal animosity, their actions spoke louder than their words. Both behaved as personal enemies locked in a battle to the bitter end. Indeed, when it was announced the two would not attend last-minute discussions in Chicago, fans were optimistic that the change in dynamics would reveal a middle ground. Unfortunately, Goodenow and Bettman also excused themselves from last-ditch meetings with a US government mediator, instead sending a union senior director and the NHL's vice-president in their place. This absence of the two most important decision-makers likely doomed the mediation to failure.

Persistence

The process of collective bargaining is incredibly time-consuming. Collective agreements cover a broad range of complex issues and typically require many months of intense negotiations to conclude. And the NHL negotiations could have been expected to take even longer than most given the high stakes, the level of media scrutiny, and the need to resolve a long-standing and very contentious issue. Unfortunately, the meetings between the NHLPA and the league were few and far between, leaving talks at a standstill for weeks or months at a time. Each side seemed to wait for the other to make a move rather than persistently meeting to resolve issues one by one. Instead, it seemed their failure to see eye-to-eye on the salary cap issue discouraged them from successfully addressing other, less contentious issues, a process that might have allowed them to build on small successes.

Perspective

Difficult labour–management negotiations often culminate in last-ditch mediations with a third party who can offer an objective, fresh perspective. As often happens, the NHL and NHLPA become entrenched in their positions and seemed to lose sight of overall objectives. Had they fully participated in the process, mediation might have helped the parties agree on objective criteria against which to judge proposals or helped them to find common ground that could spark continued talks. A mediator might also have nudged the NHL and NHLPA toward an understanding of the situation that more objectively weighed proposed compromises against both the tangible and intangible costs of not getting a deal. Finally, a third party might simply have kept the parties talking—an absolute necessity if a deal was ever going to be struck.

After the cancellation of the entire season was announced, the NHL talks entered a new phase but tactics changed little. The NHL threatened to impose a collective agreement and hire replacement players for next season. Each side continued to stand stubbornly firm, painting themselves as the good guys and the other side as "a bunch of dastardly cheats" (Duhatschek, 2005). Neither the owners nor the players seemed ready to acknowledge their miscalculations and come up with a new game plan.

The sacrosanct salary cap was an element of the deal that finally ended the lockout in July. Not surprisingly, the players voted 87 percent in favour of the six-year agreement, likely recognizing continued resistance as futile. Goodenow was forced out as NHLPA head and while he was perhaps the most obvious casualty of the acrimonious negotiations, given the current health of the NHL union–management relationship, it's unlikely he'll be the only one.

Sources: Campbell, Ken. (2005). "'Regrettable' Day for the NHL: Bettman Shuts Down Loop, Vows a 2005–06 Return, Goodenow Slams Owners for Their 'Unthinkable' Move." *Toronto Star*. February 17, p. C01; Duhatschek, Eric. (2005). "In this new phase of the lockout, it's the same old posturing." *Globe and Mail*. March 2, p. S3; Kukec, Anna Marie. (2005). "NHL Fiasco Helps Teach Executives Key Lessons." *Daily Star* [Arlington Heights, IL]. February 22, p. 1; Panaccio, Tim. (2005). "Bettman Isn't Seeking a Deal, Only a Victory." *Winnipeg Free Press*. January 23, p. C6; Westhead, Rick. (2005). "NHL Talks: How Not to Negotiate." *Toronto Star*. February 18, pp. F1, F7; Woods, Allan. (2005). "Mediator Can't Save Talks: Secret Meeting Collapses: NHL, Union Can't Find Middle Ground in Washington." *National Post*. February 14, p.S1; Poddel, Ira. (2005). "NHL Owners Approve Labor Deal to End Lockout." *Advocate* [Baton Rouge, LA]. July 23, p. 2D.

Case Questions

1. Use Walton and McKersie's four bargaining sub-processes to describe the NHL negotiations.

2. Using Walton, Cutcher-Gershenfeld, and McKersie's categories of strategic bargaining, in what type of bargaining were the NHL owners and players engaged? Was this strategy appropriate? Why or why not?

3. If the strategic approach was appropriate, how might it have been more effectively implemented? If it was not appropriate, outline both a more effective strategy and the tactics that could be used to implement that strategy.

4. What should the NHL and the NHLPA do now to minimize the negative effect of the acrimonious negotiations on their relationship?

QUESTIONS FOR DISCUSSION

1. Distinguish between centralized and decentralized bargaining structures, and explain why private sector unions generally prefer decentralized structures in good times, but centralized ones in bad times. Also explain why Canadian private sector bargaining structures have generally become more decentralized in recent years.

2. In what ways does collective bargaining differ from other commercial negotiations? How might these differences account for differences in process, length of time required, and methods of dispute resolution?

3. Explain how union and management teams prepare for bargaining. Explain how and why the process is more complex for union teams.

4. Describe Walton and McKersie's four systems of activities or bargaining sub-processes. Describe an occasion during which you engaged in one or more of these bargaining sub-processes. Provide examples.

5. Discuss the concept of a settlement zone and identify some issues to which this concept would and would not apply. How might the size of a bargaining zone impact the process of negotiations and the likelihood of a bargaining impasse?

6. Explain some of the factors that influence bargaining power. Read Case 9.1 and discuss the factors that affected bargaining power in the NHL collective bargaining.

Suggestions for Further Reading

Fisher, Roger and William Ury. (1991). *Getting to Yes: Negotiating Agreement Without Giving In* (2nd ed.). New York: Penguin Books. The first edition popularized principled negotiation. The second edition replicates and expands upon the first edition's easy to read, uncomplicated—yet powerful—lessons on how to switch from adversarial bargaining to productive problem solving.

Lewicki, Roy J., David M. Saunders, Bruce Barry, and John W. Minton. (2004). *Essentials of Negotiation* (3rd ed.). New York: McGraw-Hill/Irwin. Exactly what its title suggests: an introduction to the essentials of negotiation including strategies and tactics, finding negotiation leverage, the role of perception and cognition, ethics in negotiation, and special considerations applicable to cross-cultural and international negotiations.

Walton, Richard E. and Robert B. McKersie. (1991). *A Behavioral Theory of Labor Negotiations: An Analysis of a Social Interaction System* (2nd ed.). Ithaca, New York: ILR Press. Originally published in 1965, this is the grandparent of collective bargaining theory. If you haven't read this, you're missing an important building block in your understanding of labour negotiations.

Walton, Richard, Joel Cutcher-Gershenfeld, and Robert McKersie. (2000). *Strategic Negotiations: A Theory of Change in Labor–Management Relations.* Ithaca, NY: ILR Press. Builds upon Walton and McKersie's pivotal work and uses case studies to develop a model of negotiated change to explain the polarization of labour relations in the United States around contentious or co-operative extremes. Parts I and IV are essential reading for anyone interested in labour–management relationships.

CHAPTER 10

THE COLLECTIVE AGREEMENT

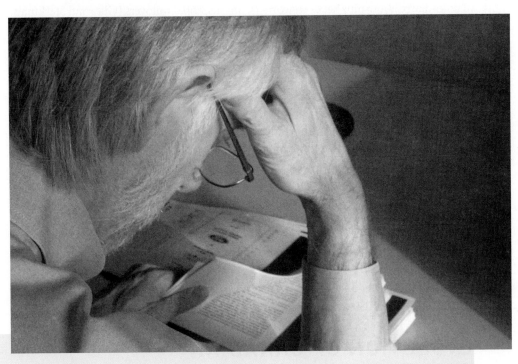

The Oxford English Dictionary? No. This document is in fact a collective agreement—though at first glance it may look like the OED and (for some) may be almost as difficult to read.

LEARNING OBJECTIVES

After studying this chapter, you should be able to:

1. Describe the evolution of Canadian collective agreements from the early twentieth century to the present.

2. Identify some functions of collective agreements.

3. Distinguish the various types of collective agreement provisions.

4. Explain how collective agreement provisions can reveal the character of a union–management relationship.

Collective agreements are closely related to the negotiating process discussed in the previous chapter, because they serve as a written record of negotiating results and a guide to future negotiations. In this chapter, we begin by discussing some of the functions served by collective agreements and the evolution of Canadian agreements through the twentieth century and into the twenty-first. From there, we go on to look at the most common types of agreement provisions. We conclude with a brief discussion of what collective agreements may say about a union–management relationship, and of the overall strengths and weaknesses of collective bargaining as a means of regulating workplace conflict.

Collective agreements—the tangible result of the negotiation process—are central to the Canadian IR system (Giles and Jain, 1989). The primary function of the collective agreement, at least from a legal point of view, is to set out the terms and conditions of employment to be followed by the union and management organization for a given period of time (Giles and Jain, 1989). These documents are of such importance because, in unionized establishments, they regulate many aspects of the day-to-day relationships between workers, unions, and employers (Giles and Starkman, 2001), including such important matters as workers' rates of pay and hours of work, their working conditions, and the processes for layoffs, promotions, and transfers.[1] They also spell out specific management and union rights and provide a mechanism (normally some kind of grievance procedure) for handling any disputes that may arise during their lifetime.

By European standards (see Adams, 1995a:503), most Canadian and American agreements are quite long and detailed. There are a number of reasons for this. Perhaps the most important is that, due in large measure to the relative political weakness of these two countries' labour movements (Giles and Starkman, 1995:341), they've concentrated most of their attention on collective bargaining and detailed regulation of work at the individual workplace level, rather than on political action, as is often the case in Europe. In addition, alternative mechanisms such as works councils, through which many workplace-level matters are regulated in European countries such as Germany and the Netherlands (Adams, 1995a:506), are rare here. As a result, the collective bargaining process takes on more importance and is forced to address a considerably broader range of issues than it does in most other industrialized countries.

EVOLUTION OF CANADIAN COLLECTIVE AGREEMENTS

In 1901, as Giles and Starkman (2005:295) note, Local 713 of the Carpenters' Union signed an agreement with Niagara Falls contractors that contained only eight brief clauses governing such basic issues as wage rates, hours of work per day, holiday and overtime pay rates, and security of employment for union members. Today, many collective agreements are far longer, often reaching several hundred pages and not infrequently containing a variety of appendices, letters of understanding, and wage schedules in addition to the main text. Also, unlike the Carpenters' agreement, written in plain English, many of today's agreements are written in complex, even convoluted legal jargon that makes them barely understandable to the workers and supervisors who must live by them on a daily basis (Giles and Jain, 1989). Why have Canadian agreements become so long and involved? And why must they be written in such complex language that even the people who work with them most closely and know them best have difficulty understanding them?

One reason, particularly for the greater length of today's agreements, lies in the growth of larger and more bureaucratic workplaces employing many different types of workers, including many unskilled and semi-skilled ones, and the industrial unionism that arose in response to this development. This has meant that collective agreements often must contain work rules and pay schedules applying to a dozen or more groups of workers, instead of just one as in the case of the Carpenters' Union. Another is the explicit incorporation into collective agreements of legal require-ments from work standards, health and safety, and human rights legislation to which the parties are required to conform (Carter, 1997). The incorporation of such provisions is a major cause of the "legalese" that often makes modern collective agreements hard to read and understand.

In recent years, as well, Canadian workplaces have made increasing use of a broad range of new technologies and chemical substances of various kinds. The increasingly rapid pace of technological change has led unions to negotiate provi-sions seeking to protect workers against the adverse effects of such change, such as loss of employment or income (Peirce, 1987). At the same time, the introduction of many new, potentially hazardous substances into Canadian workplaces has led unions to negotiate a variety of health and safety provisions governing the proce-dures for using such substances, the use of protective equipment, and the like. The growing emphasis on human rights in the workplace has also led some unions to negotiate clauses regulating such things as testing for AIDS and substance abuse and the monitoring of employees' email (Giles and Starkman, 2001). Again, these provi-sions, sometimes addressing quite complicated technical issues, have helped add to Canadian agreements' length and complexity.

Poor economic conditions are another reason for collective agreements' greater length and complexity. The growing numbers of layoffs arising from widespread downsizing and restructuring have led most unions to make job security a priority, negotiating employment and income security provisions when they can, and when they can't, negotiating severance pay provisions—or other ways of at least partially cushioning the impact of layoffs. The current environment has also led unions to demand greater control over pension plans (Giles and Starkman, 1995:349) and to negotiate increased involvement in the new forms of work organization that employers have often introduced in an attempt to make their firms more competi-tive (Giles and Starkman, 1995:343).

Yet another important source of collective agreement length and complexity has been the Canadian workforce's growing diversity. As large numbers of women entered the workforce and signed union cards, unions began negotiating parental leave and family leave provisions, anti-discrimination and anti-harassment clauses, and in some cases provisions establishing on-site workplace child care centres.[2] The entry of large numbers of professionals into unionized workplaces, many resulting from the widespread unionization of the public sector during the 1960s and 70s, resulted in provisions reimbursing employees for professional society memberships and committing employers to promote these employees' career development opportunities. Similarly, the entry of large numbers of ethnic and religious minori-ties into unionized workplaces has required unions to place additional emphasis on negotiating anti-discrimination and anti-harassment provisions, as well as provi-sions requiring employers to accommodate those of different religious backgrounds by providing time off for major religious observances or creating a different work schedule when necessary. And the hiring of increased numbers of people with disabilities has led unions to negotiate special provisions governing building accessibility or even redesigning jobs to allow them to be performed by those with disabilities (see Carter, 1997).

Finally, the prevailing Canadian doctrine of **residual management rights**, under which it's generally accepted by most arbitrators that any right not specifically granted to the union in the collective agreement is reserved to management, constitutes yet another source of collective agreement complexity. Particularly in view of many employers' continuing resistance to unions, unions have, in order to protect their members' interests, been forced to negotiate extremely detailed and comprehensive collective agreement provisions limiting the rights of management in the areas of greatest concern to those members. (See Giles and Starkman, 2005). Unions know that if they don't write specific language into the agreement on a particular issue, they're likely to lose any dispute over interpretation at arbitration and therefore generally prefer to write more rather than less into the agreement.

residual management rights The view that any rights not specifically laid out in the collective agreement are to be considered management rights.

MAIN TYPES OF COLLECTIVE AGREEMENT PROVISIONS

An Overview of Collective Agreements

One's first reaction, on looking at a typical Canadian agreement, is apt to be one of bewilderment or even despair at the array of clauses, sub-clauses, schedules, and letters of intent. After one has examined a number of collective agreements, though, one comes to see that, in many ways, most agreements resemble each other quite closely. Most begin with a brief statement outlining the agreement's general purpose and, if the document is at all complex, with a list of relevant definitions (Giles and Jain, 1989:321). Next comes a group of clauses outlining the rights and obligations of the parties (**management rights** and **union recognition clauses**), defining the bargaining unit, and, typically, providing for grievance procedures or (in some cases) other means of resolving conflict such as joint committees (Giles and Jain, 1989; Godard, 1994:305).

management rights clause Clause (or provision) in a collective agreement laying out areas specifically not subject to collective bargaining (e.g., hiring or the production process).

The second major group of clauses typically covers wages and hours of work. Included here are wage and hours schedules governing different groups of workers, provisions governing overtime pay, shift premiums for work at night, vacation allotments, and provisions for both paid and unpaid leave (Giles and Jain, 1989:321).

A third group of provisions (not always grouped together in the agreement) governs work rules, broadly defined. Here, in addition to rules governing how work is assigned and performed, one finds provisions governing technological change and the methods used for layoffs, transfers, and promotions (Giles and Jain, 1989).

union recognition clause Clause that identifies the union as the sole and exclusive bargaining agent for a particular group of workers.

The fourth and last major group of provisions concerns the work environment, again broadly defined (Giles and Jain, 1989). Such provisions may include disciplinary procedures, health and safety clauses, and anti-discrimination and anti-harassment clauses of various kinds.

If wage schedules are at all detailed and complicated, they are generally placed in an appendix, along with other issues considered too lengthy to be included in the main text (Giles and Jain, 1989). The agreement's back pages may also contain letters of intent or memoranda of understanding typically intended to spotlight issues to be addressed more fully in subsequent rounds of negotiations. A good example of such a letter of intent is the one on employees' use of frequent flyer points accumulated while on business-related travel contained in the 2000 agreement between the Canadian Commercial Corporation and the Professional Institute, which allows employees to use points acquired on business trips for personal travel.

Union and Management Rights and Conflict Control Provisions

These "ground rule" provisions, found in virtually all Canadian agreements, delineate the respective workplace rights of management and the union and provide for the handling of disagreements over interpretation, normally through a grievance procedure, but also sometimes through joint committees or other more proactive means. In addition, provisions in this group often specify the bargaining unit and members to whom the agreement applies, either directly or by listing members of excluded groups, such as management or in some cases professional staff or part-time employees.

Of greatest importance here are management rights and union rights and security provisions. Management rights provisions refer to clauses affirming management's right to run the enterprise as it wishes, subject to the limitations of the collective agreement. Such clauses may be either general or specific. In the latter case, they may spell out specific rights management reserves to itself, such as the right to hire, promote, transfer, or lay off workers, as well as to dismiss or suspend them. **Union rights and security provisions** officially recognize the union's place in the enterprise. In addition, they grant specific rights for union officials, such as stewards, and address the sometimes controversial issue of how dues are to be collected.

Beyond contract language generally recognizing their right to exist, unions need more specific provisions to ensure their presence is felt in the workplace on an ongoing basis. This means that their officials, in particular their stewards, need to be free to represent members' interests without management interference. With this in mind, unions will frequently seek to negotiate provisions allowing them access to company facilities, such as offices or bulletin boards, to enable them to carry out their duties. Along similar lines, stewards' rights provisions granting them time off to meet with members or accompany them to hearings have become fairly standard features of Canadian agreements. In some cases (Giles and Starkman, 1995:349), the company will reserve the right to limit the amount of time stewards can devote to union duties if it deems the time taken for such duties excessive.

Union security provisions address the issue of whether employees are required to be union members and if so, within what time frame. A number of types of union

union rights and security provisions Collective agreement provisions designed to protect the union's institutional authority and ensure its financial stability.

closed shop provision Collective agreement provision requiring all employees in a bargaining unit to be union members before being hired.

union shop provision Provisions requiring all employees to be union members within a specified time period after being hired.

modified union shop provision Provision stipulating that non-union members already employed need not join the union, but all new employees must join, and those already belonging to the union must remain members.

maintenance of membership provision Provision stating that no employee must join as a condition of employment, but that all who join voluntarily must maintain their membership for the agreement's duration.

open shop An enterprise in which union membership is not required as a condition of securing or maintaining employment.

security clauses are found in Canadian agreements. The strictest are the so-called "**closed shop**" **provision**s stating that the employer will hire only individuals who are already union members. Closed shops are most typically associated with the existence of hiring halls, organized and run by unions to provide employers with the number of workers they may need at any given time. Such arrangements are most common in industries like construction and longshoring, where the work is temporary in nature and the workers' real attachment is to their trade and union rather than to the firm. "**Union shop**" provisions do not require union membership as a condition of employment, but do require all employees to join within a specified time period after being hired. A "**modified**" **union shop provision** requires all those hired after a given date to join the union. The weakest type of union security provision, the so-called "**maintenance of membership**" **provision**, does not compel anyone to join the union or pay dues, but does require anyone who has already joined or joins in the future to remain in the organization (Giles and Jain, 1989:326). "Rand formula" clauses are a type of open shop provision. An **open shop** is an enterprise that does not require union membership as a condition for securing or maintaining employment. To prevent free riders from enjoying the benefits of the union's collective bargaining efforts, the Rand formula (discussed in Chapters 3 and 7) requires all bargaining unit members to pay union dues, regardless of their union membership status.

As of 2003 (Giles and Starkman, 2005:305-6), about 65 percent of all Canadian agreements imposed some type of union membership requirement. The commonest types were the union shop and modified union shop, with 40 and 14 percent, respectively. Closed shop provisions were found in just 8 percent of all agreements, and maintenance of membership provisions in a mere 2 percent. The remaining 35 percent of collective agreements contained open shop provisions.

Conflict-Control Provisions

Conflict-control provisions address the issue of how disputes arising during the life of the agreement will be handled. In some instances they also establish preventive mechanisms, such as joint committees, designed to reduce or redirect labour–management conflict. Conflict-control provisions also include "no-strike" clauses, whereby the union agrees it will not strike during the life of the agreement and management agrees it will not lock out, and provision for grievance arbitration as the mechanism for resolving mid-term contract disputes. Both types of provision are found in the vast majority of Canadian agreements and even where they do not exist, they are implied by legislation.

In many cases, grievance procedures are quite specific. Many agreements specify a list of acceptable arbitrators. Others provide for a single arbitrator instead of a three-person panel; still others name a standing umpire or establish various types of expedited arbitration procedures. The last of these is now found in about 16 percent of Canadian agreements, covering over a third of employees covered by those agreements (Bedard, 2004:46). Another reflection of the growing sophistication of Canadian enterprises' conflict resolution approaches is the growth in grievance mediation provisions. These also now appear in 16 percent of Canadian agreements covering about 30 percent of the employees affected by those agreements

(Bedard, 2004:44). The vast majority of agreements containing expedited arbitration and grievance mediation systems come from the public sector, which also accounts for over 90 percent of the employees covered by those provisions. (Bedard, 2004).

Another way in which unions and management seek to regulate conflict is through joint committees. The aim here is to address ongoing problems on a proactive basis, thereby preventing them from becoming formal grievances. As of 2003, such committees were found in over 90 percent of all agreements, covering more than three-quarters of all employees (Giles and Starkman, 2005:308). In a growing number of cases, unions and management organizations have gone beyond committees to negotiate broad, framework-style agreements, variously known as joint governance arrangements or social contracts (Verma, 1995; Giles and Starkman, 2005), normally involving a trade-off whereby the union agrees not to strike for a fairly lengthy period (typically for at least three years) and to moderate its wage demands in return for job security and increased involvement in organizational decision making. Often such agreements provide for continuous bargaining on work-related issues and allow for mid-term wage revision of pay rates, subject to binding arbitration if the parties can't agree (Giles and Starkman, 2005:307). These agreements mean that the union becomes, in effect, a full partner in managing the organization (Verma, 1995), and thus entail a fundamental transformation away from its traditional role as workers' advocate. Historically they have been particularly popular in Quebec, where they have been actively promoted both by provincial governments and by unions seeking to play a more proactive role in the workplace change process (Déom and Boivin, 2001:497-8).

Current Issues 10.1

LABOUR–MANAGEMENT PARTNERSHIPS

The Labour-Management Partnerships Program, a contribution program administered by the Federal Mediation and Conciliation Service, seeks to encourage more effective labour–management relations in the workplace or at sectoral levels by supporting efforts by unions and employers to jointly explore new ways of working, and of working together. Participants (a union and an employer or employer's association) must contribute at least half the project's total costs. In practice, participants generally contribute a good deal more than that. Projects can run up to two years and can be funded up to a maximum of $100 000.

In Ontario, Threads of Life is a non-profit organization that seeks to support families affected by workplace death or injury. It has entered into partnership with the Ontario Federation of Labour and the Industrial Accident Prevention Association of Ontario. Threads was launched in April 2003 during a Health and Safety Conference sponsored by the Association. At that conference, families from across Canada shared their experiences and took the first step towards building a national organization.

At the University of Sherbrooke, a project has been launched that seeks to develop a better understanding of how a union steward adapts to the role of working in a co-operative ▶

labour–management relationship. The larger aim here is to promote long-term partnerships between the university and its unions.

Other ongoing projects include joint ventures between the City of Toronto and its firefighters' association, NAV CANADA and the Canadian Air Traffic Control Association, and Westfair Foods and the United Food and Commercial Workers, Local 247. In addition, projects are taking place at Queen's University and the University of Calgary, while the Canadian Standards Association and the Conference Board of Canada are sponsoring ventures that extend beyond their own workplaces.

Source: *Workplace Gazette*, 7:4 (winter, 2004), pp. 53–56.

Wage and Hours Provisions

Since most people work primarily for the pay they receive, wages and hours are at the heart of the collective agreement. Compensation issues are normally among the more difficult items to negotiate and are typically left to the end of the negotiation process, after less contentious issues have been settled.

Wages

Most agreements contain various wage schedules detailing hourly, weekly, bi-weekly, monthly, or annual pay rates for workers in different groups. Production and other blue-collar workers are normally paid hourly wages, while office, white-collar, and professional workers are typically paid a weekly, monthly or annual salary (Giles and Starkman, 1995). Premium wages (most often 50 percent above the usual rate) are normally paid for overtime work (typically anything beyond 40 hours in a week or 8 in a day); sometimes an extra premium (normally at least twice the usual rate) will be paid for work on Sundays or holidays. Premium wages may also be paid for shift work, for work performed at night, or for unusually onerous or unpleasant work. In some cases, special clauses will provide "**standby pay**" for those who must remain on call or carry cell phones when off-duty, or "reporting pay" or "**call-back pay**" for those called into work for short periods (Giles and Starkman, 1995:353).

In addition to accounting for different jobs, wage schedules often take workers' length of service into account through a system of annual increments. Such "step increments" become particularly important when there is little opportunity for promotion (as in the case of much public sector work in recent years). Schedules often contain four to eight steps within each job category, with workers normally receiving a one-step raise each year providing their performance remains satisfactory.

The example in Table 10.1 illustrates a collective bargaining principle known as "front-end loading," whereby union members achieve a larger increase in the early part of the contract. Front-end loading is sometimes used by unions to make relatively low average wage increases appear more palatable to their members, by providing them with a larger immediate up-front increase. Had the increase been larger in the second year, then the principle used would have been "back-end loading." This approach is sometimes used by management to sell a somewhat larger average

standby pay Wage premium paid to those who must remain on call or carry a cell phone or pager when off duty.

call-back pay Wage premium paid to workers called back to their jobs after completing their regular shift and leaving the premises.

Table 10.1

HOURLY RATES OF PAY, GRAVEDIGERS, UNITED GRAVEDIGERS OF CANADA AND DRYASDUST MORTICIANS' ASSOCIATION

Gravedigger #1 (Spadeholder)							
Previous Rate	$8.94	9.32	9.70	10.08	10.46	10.84	11.22
Jan. 1, 2004 (3%)	$9.21	9.60	9.99	10.38	10.77	11.17	11.55
Jan. 1, 2005 (2%)	$9.39	9.79	10.19	10.59	10.99	11.39	11.78
Gravedigger #2 (Sodturner)							
Previous Rate	$11.50	12.00	12.50	13.00	13.50	14.00	14.50
Jan. 1, 2004 (3%)	$11.85	12.36	12.88	13.39	13.91	14.42	14.94
Jan. 1, 2005 (2%)	$12.09	12.60	13.14	13.66	14.19	14.71	15.24
Gravedigger #3 (Earthmover)							
Previous Rate	$15.00	15.60	16.20	16.80	17.40	18.00	18.60
Jan. 1, 2004 (3%)	$15.45	16.08	16.68	17.30	17.92	18.54	19.15
Jan. 1, 2005 (2%)	$15.76	16.40	17.01	17.65	18.28	18.91	19.53
Gravedigger #4 (Master Casketfitter)							
Previous Rate	$19.00	19.75	20.50	21.25	22.00	22.75	23.50
Jan. 1, 2004 (3%)	$19.57	20.34	21.12	21.89	22.66	23.43	24.21
Jan. 1, 2005 (2%)	$19.96	20.75	21.54	22.33	23.11	23.90	24.69

increase to their principals, on the basis that there will be immediate cost savings due to the lower first-year increase.

When inflation was high, as it was in the late 1970s and early 1980s, many unions sought to protect their members' real wages by negotiating cost of living allowance (**COLA) clauses**. The basic idea behind such provisions is to adjust wages to the inflation rate so workers' purchasing power is maintained through the life of the contract. COLA clauses typically provide some, though not complete, protection against inflation. Often they are triggered only at a certain rate of inflation (e.g., 3 percent or more). Also, some COLA clauses provide for less than full adjustment to the inflation rate. With the sharp decline in inflation since the early 1980s, COLA clauses have become far less common in Canadian agreements, accounting for only about 16 percent of all Canadian agreements in 2003 compared with 38 percent in 1981 (Giles and Starkman, 2005:316). Another consequence of the drop in inflation has been that few of the remaining COLA clauses have been triggered (ibid.).

While most unionized workers are paid a regular wage or salary, some are under incentive systems whereby they are paid wholly or partially on the basis on the amount of work performed. Unions generally dislike incentive systems, particularly individual systems that they typically criticize as "pitting worker against worker." As well, piecework systems are often difficult and costly to administer and can lead to considerable workplace conflict (Giles and Starkman, 1995:357). For these reasons, they have generally been uncommon in Canadian agreements, occurring in less than 5 percent of all Canadian agreements (Giles and Starkman, 2005:314), a significantly lower percentage than in the late 1980s (Fawcett, 1998). Where such arrangements do occur, it's most often in the clothing and forestry industries (Giles and Starkman, 2005).[3] Though individual incentive arrangements have become less common, it should also be noted that "team-oriented" incentive plans such as gain-sharing, group incentive plans, and, in particular, profit-sharing

COLA (cost of living allowance) clauses Clauses that provide workers with protection against inflation by allowing for wage increases based on increases in the inflation level.

plans, have increased since the late 1980s (Fawcett, 1998). In Canada as of 2003, 8.5 percent of all agreements covering just over 100 000 employees contained some type of provision relating pay to performance (Bedard, 2003a).

An emerging type of pay provision, which bears some resemblance to both profit-sharing and the old-fashioned COLA clause, can be termed the market price trigger bonus (see Aldridge, 2003). Such provisions, now found in mining and pulp and paper, provide either individual employees or the union with a bonus for each month or quarter that the average price of the product in question (e.g., nickel or newsprint) exceeds a certain level. For instance, the INCO-United Steelworkers agreement offers employees a lump-sum payment of 10 cents per hour worked in each quarter in which the company has net earnings and the average price of nickel is $2.25 US per pound (Aldridge, 2003:38). As of 2003, eight Canadian agreements covering about 15 000 workers contained a market price trigger bonus provision (Bedard, 2003a:30).

Still another form of compensation system is the "pay-for-knowledge" system whereby workers are paid a different hourly, weekly, or monthly rate depending on the number of skills they have mastered (see Halpern, 1984). Normally, mastery must be demonstrated by passing specific tests covering the skill or skills in question. Such systems are most common in socio-technical systems environments and other workplaces using self-directed work teams, where it is necessary for workers to have a broad range of skills to function effectively as team members.

Benefits

In addition to wages, compensation packages in collective agreements generally include a variety of benefits such as pension plans, disability and medical insurance, sick leave, extended health care, life and accident insurance, and dental insurance. Nationwide, such benefits comprise more than 30 percent of total compensation costs (Giles and Starkman, 2005), which makes the traditional term, "fringe benefits," something of a misnomer. In unionized establishments, the figure is almost certainly higher than 30 percent. Agreement provisions normally spell out the details of the various plans, the eligibility rules (often linked to **seniority**, especially in the case of pension plans), and the respective contributions to be made by the employer and employees towards the cost of the various benefit plans. Aside from benefits of the type listed above, some agreements also contain provisions entitling workers to a given number of days off a year for religious or unspecified personal reasons, or, in certain instances, to perform volunteer work.[4]

Vacation and holiday pay provisions state how much vacation workers at given seniority levels will be entitled to, which days will be considered paid holidays, and how much of a premium will be paid to those required to work on those holidays. Finally, the growing presence of women in the workforce has led to clauses providing parental leave beyond the minimum provided through employment insurance, the right to accumulate seniority while on parental leave, and the right to take time off to care for sick family members or attend to various parental responsibilities such as parent–teacher interviews at school (Giles and Starkman, 1995:354).

In recent years, there have generally been few new benefits, as cost-conscious employers have sought to reduce benefits or shift more of their costs to employees

seniority An employee's standing in the organization, based on his or her length of continuous service with that organization.

(Giles and Starkman, 2001). However, one new benefit that has been introduced with some regularity is prepaid legal services (Giles and Starkman, 2001). Another, perhaps in recognition of the growing stresses faced by workers in today's difficult economy, is the **Employee and Family Assistance Program (EFAP)**, which enables workers and their dependants to receive counselling on a broad range of issues, from alcohol- and drug-related problems to marital and financial ones. A third, increasingly popular since it can result in reduced sick leave usage, is the "wellness" benefit. Some "wellness" benefit provisions compensate employees for medical or drug costs not covered by provincial health insurance or by the organization's insurance plan. Others, like one negotiated in 2004 between the Professional Institute and its staff association, compensate employees a set amount for expenses directly related to physical or emotional well-being, such as athletic club memberships or the purchase of sporting goods.

Employee and Family Assistance Program (EFAP) Counselling services that offer employees assistance on a broad range of personal issues (e.g., alcohol or family problems).

Work Hours

Hours of work have been of enormous importance to the Canadian labour movement since the nineteenth century, when, as we noted in Chapter 3, demands for a nine-hour day helped mobilize the entire movement.[5] Hours provisions have taken on renewed importance in recent years, with the increased family responsibilities being shouldered by many workers and the growing recognition that shorter hours may be the best solution to persistent demand-deficient unemployment (Gunderson and Reid, 1998; Peirce, 2000b).

Most agreements stipulate normal working hours per week for those working on different jobs. The most common arrangements are still weeks of 35 to 40 hours during regular daytime hours; however, various alternative arrangements such as shift work and shorter or longer hours have been growing more frequent in recent years, so much so that only about 60 percent of all employed Canadians now work a standard five-day week in daytime hours (Giles and Starkman, 2005). In the case of shift work, agreements may provide for the rotation of shifts among employees or the scheduling of shifts by seniority (Giles and Starkman, 2001), which typically means that more senior employees can pick preferred daytime shifts. Other provisions stipulate the length of time allowed for lunch breaks, coffee breaks, and washroom breaks.

The growing presence of women in the workplace has contributed to demands for more flexible working hours to allow working parents to attend to family responsibilities. Flexible hours provisions allow employees to choose which hours they will work within a given core period (say between 7 a.m. and 6 p.m.), so long as they put in the requisite number of hours each day. **Compressed workweeks** most often give employees a day off every week or two weeks. In return, the employee puts in a slightly longer day, so that he or she works the regular number of hours over a one- or two-week period. In 2004, approximately 30 percent of Canadian workers covered by collective agreements could access some kind of flextime arrangement and about 27 percent were covered by compressed workweek provisions (Workplace Information Directorate, 2004a).

In a bid both to reduce unemployment and to allow workers to better attend to family responsibilities, European labour movements have been pushing shorter hours increasingly hard in recent years (see Peirce, 2000b). The Canadian labour

compressed workweeks An arrangement whereby employees work longer hours each day in return for a day off every week, two weeks, or month. The most common arrangement is one day off every two weeks.

movement has been somewhat ambivalent on the issue of shorter work hours (A. Jackson, 1997), in part because it represents many lower-paid workers who feel they need overtime pay to help make ends meet. For this reason, it has generally been reluctant to push for legislation reducing work hours, except to a certain extent in Quebec. However, a number of unions have taken the lead in negotiating agreements providing for reductions in either regular work hours or overtime hours or both in return for job creation. The unions that have done the most along these lines in recent years include the Canadian Auto Workers (CAW), United Steelworkers of America (USWA), and the Communications, Energy and Paperworkers' Union (CEP). (For a detailed discussion of these unions' activities with regard to work hours, see Peirce, 2000a and 2003).

Overall, recent evidence suggests that Canadian unions are generally putting a fairly low priority on shorter work hours. A survey conducted by Kumar, Murray, and Schetagne (1998:Table 9) found that reducing work hours was an extremely important priority for only 20 percent of the responding unions. If anything, reduced unemployment levels since the late 1990s (7 percent in 2004 compared to 9 percent in 1997 (Peirce, 2003)) may have made work hours even less of a priority now than they were seven or eight years ago.

Work Rules and Job Control Provisions

Without unions, management would have almost complete control over how work was organized and performed. At the bargaining table, unions seek to wrest some degree of control over **work rules** stating how work is to be done, as well as over the criteria for layoffs, transfers, promotions, technological change, and larger-scale workforce reductions. Since workers' belief that they are entitled to basic job rights almost inevitably conflicts with management's desire to maximize flexibility and control, job control and work rules provisions can be among the most bitterly contested in the entire agreement (Giles and Starkman, 2001).

work rules Collective agreement provisions regulating the production process and other on-the-job working conditions.

Hiring Process and Job Assignment

The strongest protection a union can achieve for its members is a "closed shop" provision (discussed earlier in the chapter) allowing only its members to be hired. Another, related form of control over job assignment may be obtained through the joint union–management dispatch systems that have often been used in longshoring (see Picard, 1967). Unions may also obtain a measure of control over hiring and, in some cases, over the number of people admitted to the trade through provisions establishing union–management apprenticeship programs, requiring vacancies to be filled from within the organization when possible, and preventing supervisors and other non-bargaining unit employees from performing jobs normally done by their members (Giles and Starkman, 1995:360). Management's strongest weapon here is the **probationary period**, found in about two-thirds of all major Canadian agreements (Giles and Starkman, 2001). Workers on probation, which normally lasts less than five months but may run for up to a year, can more easily be let go should management deem their work to be unsatisfactory.

probationary period An initial, generally rather brief, trial period during which the employee may be dismissed much more easily than after attaining indefinite status.

A probationary period thus allows management considerable control over the hiring process, even if the union has negotiated other sorts of restrictions (Giles and Starkman, 2001).

Work Rules

Work rules provisions get to the very heart of the production process. They regulate such things as the speed of assembly lines and production processes, the number of people who must be assigned to a given job, the maximum allowable workload, and the question of who is to be allowed to do certain jobs. Workload restrictions, for example, are an important part of bargaining in education. Teachers and university professors say that in order for them to provide quality education, there need to be restrictions both on the numbers of students they are asked to teach and on the numbers of classes or courses to which they are assigned. Such restrictions are needed, they argue, so that they will not be swamped with marking and preparation work. Additionally, public school teachers say they need time to "recharge themselves" during the school day. Workload was a major issue in both the 1997 and 1998 Ontario teachers' strikes (see Peirce, 2000a:121). It has remained a hot issue since then, as teachers have protested being forced to assume compulsory extracurricular duties such as coaching.

Job Control

Job control provisions govern the criteria to be used for changes in the firm's internal labour market, especially promotions, transfers, and layoffs. Like workload and work rule provisions, they're often the source of considerable conflict between workers and management, since management generally prefers to retain its control over such decisions, while workers and their unions fear that such decisions may be made arbitrarily and thus often prefer that such decisions be made on the basis of seniority (Giles and Starkman, 1995:362). Seniority provisions are used in two different ways: to determine a worker's status with respect to accrued benefits such as vacation time, severance pay, and pensions; and to determine his or her status relative to other workers in situations involving promotions, transfers, layoffs, choice of shifts, and the like (Godard, 1994:315–316).

The rationale behind seniority is that long-serving workers, who have invested much of their working lives in the organization, should be entitled to preferential consideration for promotion and transfers and greater security against layoffs (Giles and Starkman, 2001). Another argument in favour of seniority is that providing an objective, impersonal standard for personnel decisions eliminates the possibility of arbitrary or unfair management actions, which in turn can increase workers' morale and productivity (see Freeman and Medoff, 1979). Finally, seniority is a valid proxy for on-the-job experience, which is correlated—at least to some degree—with a worker's productivity. However, seniority provisions have come under increasing attack in recent years. For one thing, seniority-based layoff provisions may inadvertently discriminate against women, minority group members, and people with disabilities, who, as the "last hired," would of necessity be the first laid off and the last recalled under most existing layoff arrangements (Giles and Starkman, 2001). For another, the potential negative efficiency implications of such provisions, especially when applied to promotions where experience is not highly correlated to productivity, may be more severe now than in the past when, in many large industrial plants, workers and jobs might be more or less interchangeable. With fewer and fewer interchangeable jobs and more and more "knowledge-based" work in the economy as a whole, length of service has come to be a less reliable indicator, in many cases, of a worker's ability to do a new or different job. At the same time, the growth of part-time work adds a new twist to the debate over seniority. Part-timers will often support seniority provisions as a way of ensuring that they get to keep the precious hours and shifts they have earned, rather than seeing them go to preferred new hires with connections (see Frost and Taras, 2005:26).

Provisions stating that layoffs will be made in reverse order of seniority and that recalls will be in direct order of seniority have remained quite common; in 1999, they were found in about 65 percent of all major Canadian agreements (Giles and Starkman, 2001:302). Such provisions are favoured by almost all workers and indeed even by some managers, since they spare managers the necessity of making painful individual decisions as to who will be let go during economic downturns. More controversial is the use of seniority as a criterion for promotions. Nonetheless, provisions of this kind have also remained quite common in Canadian agreements; in 1999, they were found in about 55 percent of all major Canadian agreements, (Giles and Starkman, 2001:302). Seniority-based promotion provisions run the gamut from those that use seniority alone to clauses stating that it will be used only to break a tie in situations where the workers' skills and abilities are equal. In between, there is a broad range of provisions stipulating that some mix of ability and seniority will be used. Managers often dislike seniority-based promotion provisions because they may mean that the individual promoted is not the best person for the job, which over time may lead to reduced efficiency. Some workers also dislike these provisions, as well—particularly talented and highly-motivated ones who feel that the provisions may be limiting their opportunities for advancement.

bumping Exercise of seniority rights by more senior workers to displace more junior ones in times of layoff or the discontinuance of departments.

Many collective agreements also contain **bumping** rights that allow senior workers who have been laid off to take the jobs of more junior workers, who in turn may take the jobs of even more junior workers and so on down the line (Godard, 1994). Such bumping provisions were found in over half of all major collective agreements in 2003 (Giles and Starkman, 2005). Managers generally dislike bumping provisions, particularly those that set up lengthy organization-wide bumping chains, since they can lead to considerable uncertainty as to who will be doing which jobs within the organization.[6] As a result, most bumping provisions restrict bumping rights in some way or other, often by limiting them to certain locations or departments and requiring that "bumping" employees possess the ability to do the job within a minimal period of time (Godard, 1994:318–319; Giles and Starkman, 2005).

Technological Change

Workers and employers have battled over technological change from time immemorial (Peirce, 1987). On the whole, the Canadian collective bargaining system hasn't handled issues related to technological change very well. This really isn't too surprising, given that the purpose of collective bargaining is to fix terms and conditions of employment for a given period of time, whereas technological change is by its very nature destabilizing and often serves to change the balance of workplace power both between management and workers and among different groups of workers (Peirce, 1987; Cardin, 1967). Among the major consequences of such change can be layoffs, loss of income, and deskilling of jobs. In extreme cases, it can even lead to plant closures.

A study from the mid-1980s (Peirce, 1987) found that slightly over half of all Canadian agreements covering 500 or more workers contained some kind of technological change provision. However, in most cases the protection afforded was rather minimal, consisting primarily of advance notice or training and retraining provisions. Stronger substantive protection (i.e., employment security) was provided for in only about 20 percent of the agreements. Another significant finding was that agreements covering fewer than 500 workers were only about half as likely to contain technological change provisions as were those in the "large agreement" pool (Peirce, 1987).

Two more recent reviews (Giles and Starkman, 2001 and Bedard, 2003b) suggest that not a great deal has changed since the mid-1980s with respect to the handling of technological change through collective bargaining. To begin with, both studies found that over 40 percent of all agreements still contain no technological change provisions at all. Advance notice and consultation provisions are still found in fewer than half the agreements (48.5 percent in Bedard's study). Salary and layoff protection remains rare (16 percent and 6 percent of agreements, respectively, according to Bedard). The one bright spot is that training, learning, and upgrading provisions are now found in 36 percent of all agreements (Bedard, 2003b:28), a significant increase over the percentages found in both earlier studies. Nonetheless, it's clear that few Canadian unionized employees enjoy anything approaching comprehensive protection against the adverse effects of technological change.

Employers' unwillingness to relinquish any great measure of control over the pace of workplace change is undoubtedly one reason why workers don't enjoy more protection in this area (see Giles and Starkman, 2001:305). However, there's also reason to believe Canadian unions haven't always done enough to raise the issue at the bargaining table. The Economic Council's "Working with Technology" survey (Betcherman and McMullen, 1986) found that negotiations over technological change had occurred in only about 55 percent of the unionized establishments in which such change had taken place. When unions did raise technological change issues, they were successful about half the time, a finding that suggests that if unions were to raise these issues more often, collective agreement provisions addressing workers' interests would probably become more frequent (Peirce, 1987).[7]

Some (e.g., Cardin, 1967) have suggested that issues like technological change may be handled better under centralized bargaining systems that allow for political bargaining.[8] Others (Adams, 1985; ECC, 1987; Peirce, 1987) have suggested that collective bargaining over this issue should be replaced (or at least supplemented) with joint committees that would apply in all workplaces, unionized and non-unionized alike, and that would have the power to take issues through to arbitration if the committee were unable to arrive at a consensus. But despite the frequency with which this recommendation has been made, there has thus far been little sign that any Canadian government is prepared to act on it—nor does greater centralization of bargaining seem a realistic prospect in the foreseeable future.

Workforce Reductions

With the large-scale restructuring, downsizing, and layoffs that have been taking place in many industries in recent years, job security has become a top priority for unions. An issue of particular concern for many unions is contracting out, or the hiring of an outside firm to do a given job, rather than using existing employees or hiring new ones (Giles and Starkman, 1995:361). In many (perhaps most) cases, the firm to which the work is being contracted will be non-union, which may pose a threat to union membership levels as well as to members' jobs and incomes. In almost all cases, these firms pay their workers substantially lower wages than do the organizations that have contracted out the work to them. Contracting out has been a particularly hot issue in the public sector, as government departments, hospitals, and universities (to give just a few examples) have contracted out food operations, snow and garbage removal, and cleaning services with increasing frequency (Rose, 1995:36). Understandably, then, contracting out is an issue of considerable importance to many unions. Indeed, Kumar et al. (1998) found restricting it to have been the responding unions' fourth most important priority overall in their most recent round of bargaining. About 48 percent of all responding unions placed a high priority on this issue, while another 27 percent gave it moderate priority (1998:Table 10).

To help protect their members against the effects of contracting out, unions have negotiated a variety of prohibitions against the practice. Complete prohibitions are rare (Giles and Starkman, 2005). Much more common are prohibitions against moves that may lead to job loss, or prohibitions against contracting out of work to non-union firms. Other agreements contain provisions barring the contracting out of work so long as there are enough regular employees available to do that work. In recent years, unions have been moderately successful in negotiating **contracting out** prohibitions, which were found in about 65 percent of all major collective agreements in 2003 (Giles and Starkman, 2005:324), or more than double their 31 percent frequency in 1985 (Peirce, 1987:Table 7). Where unions are not successful in preventing job loss (as through the negotiation of contracting out prohibitions), they will, at a minimum, seek to cushion the impact of job loss through provisions requiring the employer to give employees notice of impending layoffs or to give severance pay packages to those being laid off.

Severance pay packages are a way of giving laid-off employees time to find a new job or adjust to retirement. They take on particular importance when a large number of employees are laid off simultaneously in a community, making new jobs hard to find. In some cases, the severance package may be a standard lump sum; more often, however, it is based on the number of years of service (Peirce, 1987), a typical formula being one week's pay for each year of service to a maximum of 26 weeks. In some cases, those being laid off may also receive career counselling, time off for job searches, or permission to use the employer's facilities in searching for a new job. Unions may also seek to negotiate the continuation

contracting out
Employers' use of workers from outside their own workforce to perform work previously performed by their own employees.

of employer-paid benefits for some time after layoffs have occurred (Giles and Starkman, 1995:361).

Work Behaviour and Work Environment Provisions

Work behaviour and work environment provisions address issues relating to the social and physical environment in which work is performed (Giles and Starkman, 2005). General rules governing work behaviour and disciplinary methods and more specific prohibitions on certain types of harassment relate to the social environment. Health and safety provisions are concerned with the physical environment.

Most collective agreements permit management to discipline or discharge employees provided there is "just cause" (Giles and Starkman, 1995:366). (Whether the employer has in fact shown just cause is something the union will often dispute, particularly in discharge cases). Other agreements state that an employee's disciplinary record may be "cleared" after a specified period of time (Giles and Starkman, 1995:366–367). Normally, specific disciplinary sanctions are not incorporated into the collective agreement. Rather, the appropriate sanction is determined with reference to not only the infraction itself but other relevant circumstances such as the employee's length of service and disciplinary record.

The handling of discharge and discipline cases by arbitrators represents the one significant modification to the doctrine of residual management rights that otherwise governs the interpretation of Canadian collective agreements. Though most agreements contain a provision that states that arbitrators do not have the power to alter an agreement term or substitute a new provision for an existing provision (Giles and Starkman, 1995), in discipline and discharge cases, arbitrators have broad discretion to substitute their own penalties for those imposed by the employer. In such cases, especially discharge cases, the onus of proof rests with the employer, and the standard required by arbitrators is generally high. Except in cases where an employee has been discharged for a single, extremely serious offence such as theft or assault, arbitrators normally expect employers to have imposed progressive, escalating discipline sanctions to give the employee a chance to mend his or her ways. Where progressive discipline was appropriate but not applied, the discharge will normally be overturned at arbitration. In such instances, it is common for the arbitrator to substitute a lesser disciplinary sanction such as suspension. Of those workers filing discharge grievances, slightly more than half are reinstated, many with some back pay (McPhillips and England, 1995). Collective agreements' grievance procedures thus offer workers quite substantial protection against arbitrary disciplinary action by employers.

A recent trend, resulting from the growing number of women in the workplace and their increasing prominence within many unions, has been the inclusion of sexual harassment provisions in collective agreements. While human rights legislation (discussed in Chapter 6) provides protection against such behaviour, incorporating harassment provisions into the agreement allows women who believe they have been sexually harassed to avail themselves of the agreement's grievance procedure as an alternative to the often cumbersome and time-consuming procedures established by the legislation. Similarly, the growing number of workers from ethnic and religious minorities has spurred demands for other kinds of anti-discrimination provisions, likewise enforceable through the grievance procedure.

As for health and safety, unions have long been leaders in pushing for safer workplaces. Their contributions in this area are among the most important ones they have made. Even though health and safety issues are the subject of legislation in every Canadian jurisdiction, unions continue to have an important role to play here, as we noted in Chapter 6, both through their role in enforcing legislation that governments might otherwise lack the resources or political will to enforce adequately and through their ability to enhance legislative standards at the bargaining table. In many cases, unions will insist on the inclusion of provisions allowing workers to be informed about, or to refuse, unsafe work (Giles and Starkman, 1995). While such provisions would seem to be redundant since these rights are provided in provincial and federal health and safety legislation, they again allow unions to avail themselves of their agreements' grievance procedures, which in practice may afford a speedier and more appropriate remedy than legislatively established procedures. Beyond that, unions can negotiate any number of industry- or firm-specific clauses, such as provisions requiring employers to cover all or part of the cost of safety equipment or establishing safety programs or training procedures governing the use of potentially hazardous equipment (Giles and Starkman, 1995).

Collective Agreements and the Union–Management Relationship

A collective agreement provision can tell a knowledgeable reader a good deal about the nature of the relationship between the union and management that have negotiated that provision. For example, rigid limitations on who can perform certain jobs or the number of people required to perform them are often found in highly adversarial union–management relationships, where there has been a long history of mistrust between the parties. Such provisions also appear to be characteristic of declining industries, such as longshoring and coal mining, where an approach based on maximizing short-term gains may actually be economically rational, given the short life expectancy of the firm and/or industry in question.[9] Conversely, provisions that allow the parties a greater degree of latitude, or suggest some significant sharing of workplace power or responsibility, are generally characteristic of more positive union–management relationships. Such provisions are more likely to be found in industries that are growing, or at least stable, such as telecommunications. The point here is that where collective agreement provisions impose increased costs on management (as many such provisions do), they are less apt to lead to serious union–management conflict in situations where at least part of the increased costs may be compensated for by a growth in revenues and profits.

Adapting and elaborating on some terminology devised by Godard (1994) to classify management attitudes towards unions, we would describe provisions in which the delineation of the union's and management's respective territory and rights is extremely detailed or minute as characteristic of an exploitive relationship between the parties. Here, the focus is quite simply on how much each side can extract from the other; there is generally little concern about the impact agreement provisions will have on the overall union–management relationship or even on the enterprise's long-term viability.

Agreement provisions that, without in any way suggesting a fundamental change in the nature of the employment relationship, are phrased in more general terms and allow some latitude in interpretation may be thought of as characteristic of accommodative union–management relationships. In such relationships, while the parties' interests may still diverge sharply in many cases, particularly when it comes to monetary issues, both are also concerned with the viability of the enterprise and with maintaining a good long-term relationship. In general, the parties to such relationships would tend to agree that extremely detailed and minute delineation of union and management "territory" in agreement provisions is not the best way to achieve such a relationship. A number of examples of such accommodative provisions may be found in the agreement between Bell Canada and the Communications Workers of Canada. For example, Article 12.01, on health and safety, states: "Both parties . . . recognize the need to ensure the safety and protect the health of all employees." Article 12.02 states that it is the company's responsibility to introduce "reasonable procedures and techniques" to provide for workers' health and safety, while for its part the union may make suggestions for improvements in this area. While leaving no uncertainty as to who is in charge of running the enterprise (as Article 12.02 in particular indicates), the provisions just cited point to a willingness on the part of Bell to accommodate workers' reasonable needs in the area of safety equipment and rest breaks for computer operators. Even more important, Article 12.01 suggests a willingness to share responsibility for health and safety issues and provides at least implicit recognition that here may be a "win-win" area for both parties. Normally the degree of trust needed to arrive at this kind of recognition must be built up over a number of years. Provisions of this kind are, therefore, generally characteristic of mature and stable bargaining relationships.

Occasionally (though rarely in Canada), one finds agreements that go beyond the accommodative approach just described to adopt an egalitarian approach. In place of detailed "control" provisions, such agreements tend to feature broad, rather general statements of principle. The best-known and most-studied Canadian agreement of this kind, that between the Shell Chemical Plant in Sarnia, Ontario, and Local 9-148 of the former Oil, Chemical and Atomic Workers Union, does not contain a management rights provision or a formal grievance procedure (Halpern, 1984). The agreement also contains no specific work rules or job control provisions, beyond a stipulation that layoffs will be made in order of reverse seniority, providing that the remaining employees are capable of meeting all job requirements (Halpern, 1984:73). A foreword making up about one-fifth of the agreement's very modest length states that its purpose is "to establish an enabling framework within which an organizational system can be developed and sustained that will ensure an efficient and competitive world-scale Chemical Plant operation and provide meaningful work and job satisfaction for employees" (Halpern, 1984:70). The agreement also reflects the management's and union's mutual commitment to a number of key principles, such as a belief that employees are responsible and trustworthy and are capable of making proper decisions related to their work arrangements "if given the necessary authorities, information and training" (Halpern, 1984). Such an agreement was adopted because both sides recognized that a collective agreement "composed of tight rules and regulations" would be inconsistent with the plant's workplace design, based on "minimal specification," encouragement of exploration, and a high degree of mutual trust (Halpern, 1984:51).

Beyond explicit contract provisions, the way in which parties interpret an agreement can offer important insights into their relationship. In mature, accommodative relationships, management and the union will tend to interpret the agreement judiciously and will not always seek to turn every apparent "violation" of the agreement into a formal grievance. Indeed, such relationships often feature proactive, problem-solving mechanisms like joint committees whose aim is to prevent most workplace problems from developing into grievances. In exploitive relationships, in contrast, each apparent "violation" of the contract is seen as a way to score political points against the other side. In extreme cases, grievances may be used as a political weapon by both sides (Stewart-Patterson, 1987; Godard, 1994:360). Such politicization of the grievance process, of which an excessively formal and legalistic interpretation of the collective agreement is often part and parcel, has frequently been associated with poor overall organizational performance (see Gandz and Whitehead, 1989:244).

EXHIBIT 10.1

A MEDLEY OF COLLECTIVE AGREEMENT PROVISIONS

As the following collection of collective agreement provisions indicates, creative management organizations and unions can use collective agreements for all sorts of purposes—from providing immunization assistance to encouraging employees' career and professional development aspirations or establishing procedures to be used when an employee is charged with a criminal offence.

(PIPSC AV Group and Treasury Board, agreement expiring June 17, 2007)

22.01   The Employer shall provide the employee with immunization against communicable diseases where there is a risk of incurring such diseases in the performance of the employee's duties.

(Memorial University Faculty Association (MUNFA) and Memorial University, agreement expiring Aug. 31, 1999)

19.25   In the event that an Academic Staff Member is accused of an offence which requires a court appearance, he or she shall be granted leave of absence without loss of benefits, and pay, to which he or she would otherwise be entitled, for the

▶

actual time of such an appearance. In the event that the accused Academic Staff Member is jailed awaiting a court appearance, he or she shall receive leave without pay . . .

19.28   The University shall encourage and participate in a professionally recognized and managed rehabilitation program for an Academic Staff Member who has been convicted. Participation shall include permitting the Academic Staff Member to return to employment, adjusting course scheduling or workload to permit rehabilitation, and other related accommodations. Participation shall not include direct financial support for a rehabilitation program.

(PIPSC AV Group and Treasury Board, agreement expiring June 17, 2007)

21.01   The Employer shall reimburse an employee for the employee's payment of membership or registration fees to an organization or governing body when the payment of such fees is a requirement for the continuation of the performance of the duties of the employee's position.

(MUNFA and Memorial University, agreement expiring Aug. 31, 1999)

27.04   Where an Academic Staff Member is party to a research or development contract which has explicit protection for patents and revenue sharing from such patents and an invention is made in the course of research or development supported by that contract, the provisions of that contract shall take precedence over this Collective Agreement.

27.05   The Academic Staff Member shall disclose in writing to the Administrative Head all potentially patentable inventions, discoveries or creations made by him or her. Within thirty (30) days of the date of disclosure, the University shall determine whether the invention, discovery or creation arose from University-related activities, and shall notify the Academic Staff Member in writing of its determination.

a)   If the University decides that the invention, discovery or creation arose from University-related activities, the Academic Staff Member shall assign to the University all proprietary rights for patents based on what he or she conceived, developed or embodied.

b)   If the University decides that the invention, discovery or creation did not arise from University-related activities, the Academic Staff Member may deal with the patent as he or she feels appropriate. The University shall relinquish all claims to the invention, discovery or creation at any time in the future . . .

(City of Sherbrooke, Quebec and CUPE, agreement expiring in 2001)

20.04   No permanent employee shall be fired or laid off, nor will a wage reduction be imposed following or because of technical or technological improvements or for whatever alterations or modifications may be brought to the City's structures or administrative system as well as to work procedures. ▶

(Miramar Con Mine Ltd. and USWA, Local 802, agreement expiring 2002)

Letter of understanding re: Gold bonus.

When the average gold price for a quarter falls within a specified range, each employee shall be entitled to receive a payout equal to the applicable percentage times their wage rate times all regular hours worked within that quarter.

Gold Price	Cumulative Payment
$US 339.99 or less	0%
$US 340.00 to $US 374.99	2%
$US 375.00 to $US 399.99	4%
$US 400.00 to $US 449.99	6%
$US 450.00+	10%

Source: For letter of understanding: Courtesy United Steelworkers of America.

COLLECTIVE AGREEMENTS AND COLLECTIVE BARGAINING: AN OVERALL ASSESSMENT

The excessively legalistic interpretation of collective agreements that appears to be characteristic of exploitive union–management relationships is just one of the problems associated with such agreements. Another is that even the most detailed agreement cannot possibly cover all possible workplace situations. In particular, as we noted already, technological change, plant closures, and other large-scale changes over which the union may have very limited control may alter the ground rules considerably.

The recent trends toward globalization and fiercer international competition that we described in earlier chapters lead one to wonder how collective bargaining can realistically be expected to operate in an increasingly global economy marked by almost instantaneous transmission of information; rapid movement of goods, services, and capital across international borders; and constant fluctuations in exchange rates (Giles and Starkman, 1995:342–343).[10]

In a recent article, Joseph Rose (2004a) has sought to answer this question empirically. The collective bargaining indicators Rose has selected for examination include union density, bargaining structure, duration of contract negotiations and length of collective agreements, wage settlements and the union wage premium, and strike activity. Among other things, Rose is interested in which of these indicators have changed significantly over the past quarter century, whether the fundamental balance of power between employers and unions has shifted, and whether growing international competition is primarily responsible for any changes observed.

His analysis suggests that while bargaining power has indeed shifted significantly in the direction of employers, Canada's collective bargaining system has remained quite robust and adaptable, particularly in the private sector. Despite a harsh economic and political environment, Canadian union density has remained quite stable, and there have been only modest changes in bargaining structure (toward greater decentralization in the private sector, but toward greater centralization in the public sector). The adoption of longer-term collective agreements and the decline in wage settlements and private sector strike activity are signs of employers' greater bargaining power. At the same time, we must note that the past 15 years have been marked by very low inflation, and that the longer-term agreements employers have sought in the private sector have often provided employees with increased job security, better benefits, and more involvement in the operation of the enterprise, as in the case of Quebec's social contracts. Such "quid pro quos" have helped increase the level of labour–management co-operation in the private sector.

In the public sector, in contrast, wage stability has been achieved not through "quid pro quo bargaining" but primarily through use of the legislative hammer. Even though most Canadian governments are now running surpluses rather than the deficits characteristic of the 1980s and early 90s, public sector wage levels have continued to lag behind the inflation rate (see Rose, 2004a:73). Perhaps not surprisingly, the result has been continued poor labour–management relations. During the 1980s, the public sector accounted for just over a quarter of person-days lost to strikes; it now accounts for about half. While there have been some exceptions, public sector union–management partnerships aimed at increasing co-operation between the parties remain rare.

As for the reasons behind the increase in employers' bargaining power, Rose suggests that while international competition has had some effect, that effect has been relatively modest. Far more significant, in his view, have been domestic factors such as economic recessions, low inflation, the rise of neo-conservatism and deregulation, and government wage restraint laws.

A fundamental criticism of collective bargaining that can be related to Rose's findings is that it assumes at least rough equality between the parties. In practice, this doesn't always exist, particularly not when (as it has in recent years) the balance of power tends to shift strongly in the direction of employers. Where such a balance of power doesn't exist, the collective bargaining process does less well at defusing workplace conflict than it otherwise would (as the recent history of Canadian public sector bargaining amply attests).

Nonetheless, despite the validity of these criticisms and others pointing out the lack of real workplace democracy achievable through collective bargaining under the current system (see Giles and Starkman, 1995:368), most workers are generally better off with collective bargaining than they would be without it. As we noted in Chapter 5, unionized workers' wages are generally higher than those of their non-unionized counterparts, and the former also enjoy significantly more workplace benefits. As well, unionized workers have significantly more workplace voice, thanks mainly to the grievance process. Thus, while it is far from perfect, collective bargaining is probably the best system available for determination of pay and working conditions. While the adversarial nature of the process and the length and complexity of most collective agreements are regrettable, they are likely inevitable so long as management continues to resist unions fiercely, and as long as bargaining remains highly decentralized, thus forcing most conflict to be worked out at the bargaining table rather than in the political arena. Unless and until either or both of these things change, collective bargaining seems likely to remain adversarial and conflict-ridden, and the collective agreements resulting from it will likely continue to be, for the most part, long, complex, and highly legalistic documents reflecting, to a considerable degree, the often bitter power struggles that have accompanied their drafting.

Case 10.1

ATTENDANCE

Read the Memorandum of Understanding, below, between General Motors and the Canadian Auto Workers, and then answer the questions appearing at the end of the case. Break into groups of three or four for discussion, if possible.

A Collaborative Attendance Management Approach: Beyond Punch-Clocks, Suspensions and Demerits
General Motors of Canada Limited and CAW-Canada,
2002–2005, 0194607
Memorandum of Understanding Concerning Attendance

During these negotiations the parties discussed problems associated with absenteeism and agreed that high levels of absenteeism are harmful to the success of the business in terms of cost, quality and efficiency. In addition, unnecessary and unexpected absences by a minority of employees create undue hardship on the majority . . . who attend work on a regular basis.

The parties recognize that the Company must accept sole responsibility for dealing with many aspects of the absenteeism problem. However, there are other aspects of the problem which could be addressed more effectively through jointly recommended initiatives. Such initiatives could include recommendations involving:

■ Ergonomics;
■ Rehabilitation of employees on long-term disability leave, or other personal medical conditions, and assistance in their return to productive employment;
■ Location of suitable work for medically restricted employees.

Accordingly, the parties agreed to establish a Committee for Attendance Improvement. This Committee will have six (6) members; three to be appointed by the President, National Union CAW, and three to be appointed by the Vice-President and General

Director of Personnel, General Motors of Canada Limited. Among its responsibilities the Committee will:

1. Achieve understanding of those attendance issues which can be dealt with jointly, and those which should continue to be solely the responsibility of the Company; and communicate this understanding to the local parties.

2. Analyze attendance data and other information on an ongoing basis to determine the underlying causes of absenteeism and recommend initiatives for improved attendance.

3. If the local parties decide, on their own, to develop joint attendance analysis or other initiatives, the Committee for Attendance Improvement will provide guidance and direction if requested.

Source: CAW Canada.

Absenteeism in the workplace is not a marginal phenomenon, and it will continue to increase in the years to come because of the aging population and the stress arising from work–family balance issues, among other causes. Now is the time for managers to determine the extent of the problem in their organization, and to adopt approaches designed to minimize its negative effects.

Case Questions

1. What type of union–management relationship is suggested by this Letter of Understanding?

2. Assuming you were a union representative and discovered that one of your members was missing about 30 percent of all scheduled workdays, including most Mondays and many Fridays, how might you use the Letter of Understanding to help address this employee's problems?

3. Now assuming you were a human resources manager, how would you use the Letter of Understanding to help address the problems of that same employee?

4. Based on your reading of this letter, would you favour the use of individual or group incentives to curb absenteeism if you were an HR manager? Why or why not? What would your position be if you were a union representative?

5. Describe some scenarios that might require ergonomic adjustments, as per this Letter. How do you see the union and management working together on these scenarios—or on ergonomic issues more generally?

6. Now construct an attendance policy that you see as being diametrically opposed in spirit to the policy contemplated by the Letter. What do you think would be some of the consequences resulting from that policy?

7. What are some possible dangers resulting from the policy envisaged through the Letter of Understanding? How, as a union or management representative, might you work to avert those dangers?

8. If you are presently employed, how does your organization's absenteeism policy compare to the one described in the Letter? Which do you prefer, and why?

QUESTIONS FOR DISCUSSION

1. Get a collective agreement. Read through as much of it as you can. Are you able to make sense of it? If not, why are you having difficulty?

2. List the four main types of agreement provisions and, using the agreement you read for question 1, try to identify one or more provisions of each type in that agreement.

3. Try to determine, from some key clauses of the agreement, what kind of union–management relationship the parties have.

4. Discuss the evolution of Canadian agreements. What has contributed to their growing length and complexity? In your view, has this evolution been healthy?

5. How does seniority play a role in Canadian agreements? Overall, is that role healthy or not, in your view?

6. Discuss some problems with collective bargaining and collective agreements. Might there be ways to get around some of those problems?

7. Do you feel collective bargaining is compatible with economic competitiveness? Why, or why not?

8. If you were in PIPSC, how would you try to strengthen the professional development provision contained in Article 21.01 in Exhibit 10.1 above? What arguments might you use to try to sell this stronger provision to the employer?

Suggestions for Further Reading

Kumar, Pradeep, Gregor Murray, and Sylvain Schetagne. (1998). "Adapting to Change: Union Priorities in the 1990s." *Workplace Gazette,* (fall). Extremely comprehensive study on Canadian union behaviour and priorities in the late 1990s.

Rose, Joseph. (2004). "Competitiveness and Collective Bargaining in Canada." *Workplace Gazette,* 7:1, pp. 68–77. Thoughtful study outlining ways in which collective bargaining has—and in some cases has not—adapted to today's more fiercely competitive economic environment.

Sack, Jeffrey and Ethan Poskanzer. (1996). *Contract Clauses: Collective Agreement Language in Canada.* 3rd Edition. Toronto: Lancaster House. A loose-leaf compendium of collective agreement clauses and their interpretation. Excellent resource for anyone negotiating or writing collective agreement language.

CHAPTER 11

STRIKES, LOCKOUTS, AND DISPUTE RESOLUTION

Members and supporters of the Sudbury Mine, Mill & Smelter Workers' Union, Local 598/CAW take part in a solidarity rally in Sudbury, Ontario, on January 27, 2001, almost six months after their strike against Falconbridge Mines began. However, scenes like this are rare. In most years, well over 90 per cent of Canadian agreements are negotiated without a work stoppage.

LEARNING OBJECTIVES

After studying this chapter, you should be able to:

1. Explain the significance of strikes and lockouts in the Canadian industrial relations system.

2. Explain how strikes and lockouts are identified and defined.

3. Identify the typical procedures parties must follow before a strike or lockout is legally permitted.

4. Identify the three policy approaches to strikes in the public sector.

5. Explain how strike activity is measured and identify recent trends in Canadian strike activity.

6. Summarize three theoretical models regarding the causes of strikes.

7. Identify a variety of processes typically used in Canada to help resolve collective bargaining disputes.

In this chapter we discuss the significance of strikes in the Canadian industrial relations system, as well as considering the causes of strikes and lockouts and some of the policy measures used to control them. We start by defining the terms strike and lockout as they are used in various labour relations acts. Next, we consider different types of strikes and discuss some of the problems involved in measuring strike activity. From there, we go on to consider the causes of strikes, including both economic and non-economic causes. This analysis includes a discussion of some recent Canadian labour disputes that have attracted widespread public attention. We conclude with a discussion of some of the dispute resolution methods used to help prevent or reduce the impact of strikes and lockouts, and with an explanation of recent trends in strike activity in Canada.

THE SIGNIFICANCE OF STRIKES AND LOCKOUTS

Partly for the wrong reasons, strikes and lockouts tend to be the aspects of the industrial relations system with which the average person is most familiar. Media coverage of industrial relations developments undeniably centres mainly on work stoppages, particularly the bitter, emotional type featuring violent picket-line confrontations. Quite simply, stories about conflict sell more newspapers and attract more viewers to TV screens than do stories about negotiation and compromise. As well, many journalists lack the training, the time, or the support from their superiors needed to provide in-depth coverage of industrial relations developments other than strikes and lockouts (Hannigan, 1986).

While perhaps inevitable, such media emphasis on confrontation can obscure the fact that, in most years, well over 90 percent of Canadian agreements are negotiated without a work stoppage. Moreover, even when there is a work stoppage, most employers do not attempt to bring in replacement workers, and the majority of strikes and lockouts are conducted peaceably. Sensationalist media coverage also tends to obscure the innovative preventive mechanisms being developed all across Canada, of which the various provincial preventive mediation programs are an excellent example.

The media's emphasis on work stoppages also gives uninformed readers and viewers the mistaken impression that strikes and lockouts are the only significant form of industrial conflict. As will be emphasized throughout this chapter, strikes are just one of many ways used by workers to send management the message that they are displeased with what is going on in the workplace. Other forms of conflict range from active ones such as grievances, vandalism, and sabotage, to more passive ones such as heavy use of sick leave or disability leave, unexcused absenteeism, alcohol or drug abuse, slacking on the job, or quitting. All result in reduced productivity; some, such as alcohol abuse or absenteeism, arguably lead to far greater productivity losses than do strikes, which have never cost the country as much as 1 percent of total working time, even in tumultuous years like 1919, which was marked by the Winnipeg General Strike, and 1976, the year of the nationwide Day of Protest against federal wage controls.

Clearly, then, strikes should not be considered as an isolated phenomenon. Rather, they should be viewed in the larger context of industrial conflict as a whole, of which they are just one manifestation—though certainly a dramatic one. This said, there *are* reasons why strikes are central to industrial relations. As was noted in the labour history chapter, Canadian labour relations law has developed largely in response to bitter, bloody strikes, with an eye to preventing the recurrence of such disputes, or at least making them less bloody. The *Industrial Disputes Investigation Act* of 1907, which made conciliation compulsory for the first time, was a direct response to a lengthy Alberta coal-miners' strike the previous winter (Morton, 1989). Similarly, *PC 1003*, the bill that, in 1944, granted basic collective bargaining rights to Canadian workers, can be linked to bitter wartime strikes in the gold mining and steel industries (MacDowell, 1978, 1982). Sizable portions of all Canadian labour relations acts are devoted to strikes and lockouts, including defining what constitutes a strike or a lockout, outlining when they may legally occur, and indicating which groups, if any, are denied the right to strike. Labour relations acts also address the issues of picketing, strikebreakers, replacement workers, third-party intervention and dispute resolution procedures, and what special restrictions may be placed on strikes in certain sectors. Indeed, it is probably not going too far to say that one of the central purposes of labour relations legislation is to regulate strikes and lockouts with an eye to protecting the public interest and maintaining public peace and order.

This emphasis is not misplaced. While labour disputes today are generally less violent than the pitched battles of the early twentieth century (Heron, 1989), they can still have extremely severe consequences, not just for the workers and employers involved, but also for third parties who may be seriously inconvenienced, especially in the case of public sector disputes. The deleterious impacts sometimes continue long after the dispute is resolved. For example, in the aftermath of a strike or lockout, particularly a lengthy one, firms may lose customers and market share, or in extreme instances be forced to shut down part or even all of their operations. Strikes or lockouts may also lead to lasting bitterness between unions and management, or sometimes even within unions. Given such a broad array of potentially serious consequences, work stoppages pose some difficult challenges for policy makers. Particularly in the case of public sector disputes (P. Weiler, 1980), they may be faced with balancing workers' right to strike in support of their demands with the public's need to continue receiving such essential services as health care.

While most people are familiar with the dysfunctional effects of work stoppages, fewer recognize that they can serve a useful function in the labour–management relationship. The ability to impose costs upon one another through a strike or a lockout is perhaps the most compelling reason collective agreements are resolved. Often it is the looming threat, or perhaps the actual experience, of a work stoppage that finally motivates the parties to compromise their positions sufficiently to make a deal they both find acceptable. Sometimes, as in the Toronto Transit Commission negotiations in 2005, neither party is particularly pleased with the deal but both are willing to accept it only because the alternative, a costly, divisive, and disruptive strike, is even less palatable.

Current Issues 11.1

TTC STRIKE AVERTED BY A DEAL NO ONE LIKED

"Do you want a deal or not?" shouted Toronto Transit Commission (TTC) chairman, Howard Moscoe. It was 5:00 p.m. Sunday, April 10, 2005, on the brink of a city-wide transit strike. Moscoe and Bob Kinnear, President of the Amalgamated Transit Union Local 113 were in a hotel hallway. The fate of over 600 000 TTC commuters and 8400 TTC employees hung in the balance. In a legal strike position for over a week, the union had announced that if it didn't have a deal by noon on Friday, it would cease negotiations over the weekend, and begin strike action on Monday morning. Only at the urging of the Ontario Ministry of Labour did the sides meet again on Sunday in a last-ditch attempt to avert the strike.

Commuters had been scrambling over the weekend to make transportation arrangements and businesses were braced for chaos, expecting the strike to impact every sector of the economy at virtually every level. Workers would be absent or late, meetings would be cancelled, and loads of goods would perish while trucks were stalled in traffic jams. A strike lasting more than a day was anticipated to have such dramatic negative impacts on Toronto's economy that many expected back-to-work legislation.

By 4:30 on Sunday afternoon, the union team was frustrated and ready to give up. Then, a phone call from Toronto Mayor David Miller convinced Kinnear to give it one last try. He hung up the phone and headed down the hallway. A few moments later, Kinnear's and Moscoe's raised voices could be heard. Tempers flared and accusations flew but the one that truly struck home was Kinnear's insistence that Moscoe was forcing a strike over "a couple hundred dollars." While a somewhat sarcastic underestimation of the pension issue to which he referred, Kinnear's statement drove home the significance of what was about to occur. Were their remaining differences really worth a massive transit strike that would paralyze the city, threaten Toronto's economic well-being, and perhaps cause the TTC to lose riders permanently? Within three minutes, everything changed. Realizing they were truly down to the wire, Moscoe and Kinnear changed their focus from finding a way to get more to finding a way to sell the deal to their respective constituencies. Suddenly, the deal no one wanted or liked only a half hour before became the deal they could both live with.

Sources: McGran, Kevin. (2005). "TTC Workers Vote on New Deal Today." *Toronto Star*. April 14, B1 & B4. McGran, Kevin. (2005). "A Deal No One Liked Averted Strike." *Toronto Star*. April 11, A1; McGran, Kevin and Raju Mudhar. (2005). "TTC, Union in Last-Ditch Talks." *Toronto Star*. April 10, A2; McGran, Kevin. (2005). "TTC Riders Face Chaos." *Toronto Star*. April 9, A1; McGran, Kevin. (2005). "Transit Strike Deadline No Worry to TTC." *Toronto Star*. April 7, B3; Teotonio, Isabel. (2005). "Labour Strife Could Turn Away Passengers for Good." *Toronto Star*. April 9, A4; Wong, Tony, David Bruser, and Sharda Prashad. (2005). "Business Braces for TTC Strike." *Toronto Star*. April 9, D1.

Beyond their function as a process or motivator for resolving conflict, strikes also serve a cathartic function, allowing workers to release pent-up frustration (Godard, 2005) that would otherwise be expressed through other means. Indeed, studies in both Canada (Hebdon and Stern, 1998) and the United States (Hebdon and Stern, 2003) show that far from suppressing conflict, laws that prohibit strike action simply redirect conflict into other forms such as grievances, publicity campaigns, and other types of job action. The open manifestation of conflict in the form of a strike or lockout may force the parties to admit the need for change and improvement in the union–management relationship and in their joint ability to deal with conflict. Both in Canada and in other countries, a number of creative joint problem-solving mechanisms have been introduced in the wake of strikes that convinced both sides they would need to restructure their relationship to prevent further strikes from occurring in the future.[1] Without the spur of the strike to prod them into action, the parties might never have developed those mechanisms.

STRIKES AND LOCKOUTS DEFINED

Unionized workers may engage in a range of behaviours to put pressure on an employer. For example, they may engage in a **work-to-rule** campaign, which means performing the job, but only as expressly outlined in the job description. Another tactic that is often included in a work-to-rule is to follow all work-related rules and procedures to the letter of the law, thereby effecting a work slowdown. For example, drivers in Regina, Saskatchewan, were pleased when, in 1988, members of the Regina Police Association decided to hit the city in the wallet by not issuing any traffic tickets and instead only issuing polite warnings to motorists. In 2005, Toronto City Police adopted a similar pressure tactic by responding only to calls for service rather than engaging in proactive activities such as patrolling. Teachers sometimes use the tactic of calling rotating "study sessions," often keeping secret the next school where teachers will walk off the job for the day. Another common practice is for teachers to refuse to participate in extracurricular activities or supervise lunchrooms.

> **work to rule** Collective refusal to perform duties not explicitly included in job descriptions and/or dogmatically following all rules to the letter, thus effecting a slowdown.

Given the range of pressure tactics in which unions engage, it is important to distinguish which meet the legal definition of a strike and are therefore subject to the rules outlined in labour legislation. The definition of a strike in most labour relations statutes contains three component elements. First, the action must constitute a refusal to work or cessation of work and, second, it must be by employees. Finally, the action must be "in combination or in concert or in accordance with a common understanding." (Carter et al., 2002:311). Thus an individual worker's refusal to work would not be considered a strike, regardless of whether or not that refusal was legal.[2] On the other hand, the withdrawal of services or refusal to work need not be complete. In general, Canadian labour relations acts state that a slowdown or other concerted activity designed to limit output is a strike. Under federal and provincial labour acts, such varied work actions as union-imposed overtime bans (Snyder, 1995), refusals to work new machines (Carter et al., 2002), rotating Canada Post strikes (Snyder, 1995), work-to-rule campaigns by railway employees, and a postal union's threat to order its members to stop verifying whether letters bore sufficient postage (Snyder, 1995) have all been deemed strikes. So, too, have collective refusals to cross picket lines, even in cases where the union-sanctioned refusal was based on a fear of picket line violence (Randazzo, 1995), and a union's refusal to handle work that was the subject of a legal lockout between a different employer and a sister local (Randazzo, 1995).

While the purpose of a collective refusal to work is usually to pressure employers to accept proposed terms and conditions of employment, this is not always the case. For example, unions may encourage their members to walk off the job to pressure political parties or protest legislation. Regardless, the element of purpose is no longer a significant component of the definition of a strike in any Canadian jurisdiction (Carter et al., 2002). Thus, such political protests will, if they possess the three component elements of a strike, be subject to all the legal rules and restrictions outlined in labour legislation. The same is not true, however, of a lockout. The critical element in determining whether an employer's closing of a place of employment or refusal to continue to employ union members is its intent. If, for example, the employer suspends operations due to legitimate business reasons, even if the closure occurs during bargaining for a new or renewal collective agreement, it will not be considered a lockout. It would be a lockout, however, if the employer suspended operations for the purpose of pressuring employees to agree to terms and conditions of employment. Suspending operations or refusing to continue to employ workers for the purpose of inducing or compelling them to abandon their rights under the *Labour Relations Act* also meets Ontario's definition of a lockout (Carter et al., 2002).

When Is a Strike or Lockout Legal?

In Canada, the most important element in determining whether a strike or lockout is legal is timeliness. Any strike or lockout that is untimely is illegal. It does not follow, however, that any strike or lockout that is timely is, therefore, legal. As will be discussed later, while there are few restrictions other than timeliness in the private sector, the right to strike in the public and para-public sectors is much more restricted. The most basic rule of timeliness is that strikes or lockouts are not permitted during the term of a collective agreement. The other rules of timeliness regard procedures the parties must follow both before and after a bargaining impasse is reached and these rules are laid out in the various jurisdictions' labour relations legislation. The initial step occurs even before bargaining begins, in that one party is expected to serve the other with notice of intention to bargain. The parties are then required to meet within a specified period of time and to continue negotiations in good faith and with the intention of concluding a collective agreement.

In the vast majority of cases, the parties conclude an agreement without resorting to economic sanctions; however, should the parties reach an impasse, they must go through a number of steps before a strike or lockout is considered legal. While every jurisdiction requires the union conduct a secret-ballot strike vote, beyond that each jurisdiction imposes slightly different requirements in terms of the process the parties must follow and the time periods that must pass. About half the Canadian jurisdictions require that the union or employer provide written notice to the other party and/or the Minister of Labour, with the notice period varying from a low of 24 hours in New Brunswick to a high of 72 hours in Alberta, British Columbia, and the federal jurisdiction.

In several jurisdictions, before the notice of an impending strike or lockout may be filed, one of the parties must provide notification to the Minister of Labour or the Labour Relations Board that they have failed to reach a settlement. In some jurisdictions, the parties then participate in a compulsory **conciliation** process and in some others conciliation may be required at the discretion of the Minister or the Board. In yet others, no such process is required. Where conciliation is required, the process generally provides that a conciliation officer confer with the parties and attempt to conclude a collective agreement. If that fails, the conciliation officer

conciliation A process, sometimes compulsory, during which a conciliation officer or a tripartite conciliation board attempts to assist the parties to resolve their bargaining impasse and avoid a strike or lockout.

reports to the Labour Relations Board or Minister of Labour, which then issues either a report on the dispute or a notice often referred to as a "no board report." In virtually all cases, it is the latter option that is followed and a countdown begins until a strike or lockout may commence. In Ontario, for example, 14 days must elapse after the Minister has released the "no board report" notice to the parties before they are in a legal strike or lockout position.

In some jurisdictions, including Ontario, the Minister has the discretion to impose a second conciliation process that utilizes a tripartite board to produce a report on the dispute. Although this option is quite rarely used in practice, it remains a part of the legislation in several jurisdictions. Finally, most jurisdictions provide the Minister discretion to appoint a special mediator to assist the parties, either as an alternative or an adjunct to conciliation. **Mediation**, while similar to conciliation, tends to be a voluntary process and also tends to be more interventionist, in that the mediator gets more actively involved in assisting the parties to shape a mutually acceptable settlement.

mediation A dispute-resolution process similar to conciliation, although mediation is more often voluntary, tends to be more interventionist, and may be used in either interest or rights disputes.

Strike Restrictions in the Public Sector

Free collective bargaining complete with the right to strike or lock out is one of the most important means through which the Canadian industrial relations system

Table 11.1

PREREQUISITES TO A LEGAL STRIKE

	Compulsory Secret-Ballot Strike Vote	Notice	Third-Party Intervention Before Strike or Lockout
Federal	Valid for 60 days.* Results determined by majority of those in the unit who vote. Not required if legal lockout has occurred.	72 hours	Notification of failure to settle required. Conciliation not required but conciliation officer, commissioner, or board may be appointed at discretion of the Minister.
BC	Valid for 3 months.* Results determined by majority of those in the unit who vote. Not required if legal lockout has lasted for more than 72 hours.	72 hours	Not required. Mediation at discretion of Board's mediation division, upon request from either party; or, a mediation officer may be appointed by the Minister.
Alberta	Valid for 120 days. Results determined by majority of those in the unit who vote.	72 hours	Mediator must be formally appointed before strike or lockout may be declared. Mediation at discretion of Director of Mediation Service upon request, unless required by the Minister.
Saskatchewan	Results determined by majority of those in the unit who vote.	48 hours	Not required. Conciliation or special mediation upon request or at discretion of Minister.
Manitoba	Results determined by majority of those in the unit who vote.	None required	Not required. Conciliation at request of either party; mediation upon joint request. Minister has discretion otherwise. ▶

Table 11.1
(continued)

	Compulsory Secret-Ballot Strike Vote	Notice	Third-Party Intervention Before Strike or Lockout
Ontario	Taken, at the earliest, 30 days before expiry of agreement.[†] Results determined by majority of those in the unit who vote.	None required	No strike or lockout unless conciliator or mediator appointed. Mediation and/or secondary conciliation process at Minister's discretion.
Quebec	Results determined by majority of the members of the union who vote.	None required	Not required. Conciliator appointed on request of either party or at Minister's discretion. Mediation at Minister's discretion.
Newfoundland and Labrador	Results determined by majority of those in the unit who vote.	None required	No strike or lockout unless a party has requested a conciliation board. Conciliation and mediation at discretion of Minister.
New Brunswick	Valid for one year. Results determined by majority of those in the unit.	24 hours	No strike or lockout unless a party has requested appointment of a conciliator.
Nova Scotia	Results determined by majority of those in the unit.	48 hours	No strike or lockout unless a conciliator or conciliation board has been appointed.
PEI	Results determined by majority of those in the unit who vote.	None required	No strike or lockout unless a conciliator, conciliation board, or mediator has been appointed.

*Unless the parties agree otherwise.

[†]If no agreement, 30 days from appointment of conciliator.

Sources: Compiled from Human Resources and Skills Development Canada: 1) Synoptic Charts on Legislation Pertaining to Certain Major Collective Bargaining Issues: Third Party Intervention in Collective Bargaining Disputes, http://www.hrsdc.gc.ca/en/lp/spila/clli/irlc/int(e).PDF; and 2) Strike Vote, Strike/Lockout Notice, Check-off of Union Dues and Ratification Vote, http://www.hrsdc.gc.ca/en/lp/spila/clli/irlc/votes(e).PDF.

attempts to strike a balance between the rights of employees and those of employers (Adell, Grant, and Ponak, 2001). Work stoppages in the private sector generally cause little more than inconvenience to any parties other than those directly involved. Work stoppages in the public sector, however, may result in the withdrawal of services that the public cannot access elsewhere and without which they may suffer significant harm. It is for this reason that many countries, including Canada, strive to balance the rights of the public with those of public sector employers and employees by either limiting or denying the right to strike to public sector employees.

As discussed in the public sector chapter, each jurisdiction in Canada has struck a somewhat different balance between free collective bargaining and ensuring the provision of essential services. However, each has applied, in various ways, some combination of three policy options: completely denying the right to strike; permitting the unfettered right to strike; or limiting the right to strike though some process of designation of essential services. Where the right to strike is denied, binding arbitration generally substitutes as a means for resolving bargaining impasses. The unfettered strike model permits the parties to exercise their relative power in resolving disputes and leaves it to them to determine which services, if any, will be provided during a work stoppage (Adell et al., 2001). The designation, or controlled strike, model either outlines which services are considered essential or designates a certain proportion of the normal complement of staff as essential. The union is permitted to withdraw only those services or members that have not been designated essential. The federal *Public Services Staff Relations Act* is unique in that it combines the no-strike and the designation model by providing the union the option to elect which one will apply to an upcoming round of bargaining (Adell et al., 2001).

While firefighters and police officers have the right to strike in Nova Scotia and Saskatchewan, throughout the remainder of Canada, they are either denied the right to strike or are subject to some form of designation model. On the other end of the scale are municipal workers and transit operators, who, throughout Canada, are either permitted the unfettered right to strike or are subject to the designation model (Adell et al., 2001). All three policy options are applied to teachers, health care workers, and civil service employees in the various jurisdictions, with Alberta's legislation being the most restrictive and Saskatchewan's the most permissive (Adell et al., 2001).

Even where public sector workers are permitted the right to strike, governments have shown great willingness to use ad hoc legislation to order them back to work. Since 1950, Canadian governments have legislated striking employees back to work on at least 100 occasions; three-quarters of those were when employees had been granted the unfettered right to strike and the remainder fall under the designation model. Such legislation is not unheard of in Canada's private sector, but is rarely used there, and then normally only in the case of disputes involving large, heavily regulated industries in the federal jurisdiction, such as the ports and the railways, where there is reason to believe that a lengthy dispute could cause innocent third parties serious harm. Generally, back-to-work legislation will provide for arbitration or mediation of the dispute but since the latter half of the 1990s, governments have been increasingly predisposed to avoiding arbitration and instead legislatively imposing terms and conditions of employment (Adell et al., 2001). This tendency has met not only with widespread opposition from union members but often also with open defiance of the legislation. Similarly, even where workers have been completely denied the legal right to strike, this has not prevented public sector unions from engaging in strike action, sometimes with great frequency.

MEASURING STRIKE ACTIVITY

It is generally agreed that Canada's strike record compares fairly poorly to that of most other Western industrialized countries. But what, exactly, is meant by this assertion? On what basis can we compare relative strike intensity in different countries, or, for that matter, in different jurisdictions or industries within Canada? The most basic measure of strike activity is *frequency*, or the number of strikes occurring in any given jurisdiction during any given period of time, normally a year. While it is useful to know how many strikes have occurred in a jurisdiction, by itself this statistic is of relatively little significance. Of particular importance are: 1) the *size*—or number of workers involved in any given dispute; and 2) the *duration*—or the length of time workers remain off the job. Clearly, the more workers involved and the longer the dispute lasts, the greater its impact will be.

Both average size and average duration have varied greatly over the years since the First World War (See Table 11.2). One reason for the variation is that both measures

Table 11.2

MEASURES OF STRIKE ACTIVITY, CANADA, 1919–2004

Year	Frequency*	Avg. Size†	Duration‡	Person-Days Lost**	As Percentage of Working Time
1919	336	443	22.8	3 400 942	0.60
1920	322	187	13.3	799 524	0.14
1921	168	168	37.1	1 048 914	0.22
1922	104	421	34.9	1 528 661	0.32
1923	86	398	19.6	671 750	0.13
1924	70	490	37.7	1 295 054	0.26
1925	87	333	41.2	1 193 281	0.23
1926	77	310	11.2	266 601	0.05
1927	74	301	6.8	152 570	0.03
1928	98	179	12.8	224 212	0.04
1929	90	144	11.7	152 080	0.02
1930	67	205	6.7	91 797	0.01
1931	88	122	19.0	204 238	0.04
1932	116	202	10.9	255 000	0.05
1933	125	212	12.0	317 547	0.07
1934	191	240	12.5	574 519	0.11
1935	120	277	8.7	288 703	0.05
1936	156	223	8.0	276 997	0.05
1937	278	259	12.3	886 393	0.15
1938	147	139	7.3	148 678	0.02
1939	122	336	5.5	224 588	0.04
1940	168	361	4.4	266 318	0.04
1941	231	377	5.0	433 914	0.06
1942	354	322	4.0	450 202	0.05
1943	402	543	4.8	1 041 198	0.12
1944	199	378	6.5	490 139	0.06
1945	197	488	15.2	1 457 420	0.19
1946	226	614	32.4	4 515 030	0.54
1947	234	442	22.9	2 366 340	0.27
1948	154	278	20.7	885 790	0.10
1949	135	347	22.1	1 036 820	0.11
1950	160	1200	7.2	1 387 500	0.15
1951	258	392	8.9	901 620	0.09
1952	219	513	24.6	2 765 510	0.29
1953	173	315	24.1	1 312 720	0.14
1954	173	327	25.3	1 430 300	0.15
1955	159	378	31.2	1 875 400	0.19
1956	229	387	14.1	1 246 000	0.11
1957	245	329	18.3	1 477 100	0.13
1958	259	425	24.4	2 816 850	0.25
1959	216	440	23.4	2 226 890	0.19
1960	274	180	15.0	738 700	0.06
1961	287	341	13.6	1 335 080	0.11
1962	311	239	19.1	1 417 900	0.11
1963	332	251	11.0	917 140	0.07
1964	343	293	15.7	1 580 550	0.11
1965	501	342	13.4	2 349 870	0.17
1966	617	667	12.6	5 178 170	0.34
1967	522	483	15.8	3 974 760	0.25
1968	582	385	22.7	5 082 732	0.32
1969	595	514	25.2	7 751 880	0.46 ▶

Table 11.2
(continued)

Year	Frequency*	Avg. Size†	Duration‡	Person-Days Lost**	As Percentage of Working Time
1970	542	481	25.0	6 539 560	0.39
1971	569	421	11.9	2 866 590	0.16
1972	598	1 180	10.9	7 753 530	0.43
1973	724	484	16.4	5 776 080	0.30
1974	1 218	487	15.6	9 221 890	0.46
1975	1 171	431	21.6	10 908,810	0.53
1976	1 040	1 525	7.3	11 544 170	0.53
1977	806	270	15.3	3 320 050	0.15
1978	1 057	379	18.4	7 357 180	0.32
1979	1 049	441	16.9	7 819 350	0.33
1980	1 028	427	20.8	9 129 960	0.37
1981	1 049	325	25.9	8 850 040	0.35
1982	679	684	12.3	5 702 370	0.23
1983	645	511	13.5	4 440 900	0.18
1984	717	261	20.8	3 883 000	0.15
1985	825	196	19.3	3 125 560	0.12
1986	748	647	14.8	7 151 470	0.27
1987	668	871	6.5	3 810 170	0.14
1988	548	377	23.7	4 901 260	0.17
1989	627	709	8.3	3 701 360	0.13
1990	579	468	18.7	5 079 190	0.17
1991	463	547	9.9	2 516 090	0.09
1992	404	377	13.8	2 110 180	0.07
1993	381	268	14.9	1 516 640	0.05
1994	374	216	19.8	1 606 580	0.06
1995	328	455	10.6	1 583 070	0.05
1996	330	835	11.8	3 269 060	0.11
1997	284	908	14.0	3 607 710	0.12
1998	381	641	10.0	2 443 870	0.08
1999	413	388	15.3	2 442 580	0.08
2000	379	379	11.5	1 656 790	0.05
2001	381	580	9.9	2 198 850	0.07
2002	294	571	18.1	3 033 450	0.09
2003	266	299	21.8	1 736 312	0 05
2004	298	869	12.6	3 254 559	0.09

* Number of strikes in existence during the year in question, whether they began that year or earlier.

† Average size is obtained by dividing the total number of workers on strike during the year by the frequency figure described in the previous note.

‡ Average days lost per worker on strike is found by dividing total person-days lost by the number of strikers involved.

** Product of frequency (number of strikes) times size and duration.

Sources: 1919–1975, Labour Canada, *Strikes and Lockouts in Canada,* various issues; 1976–1990 data provided by Work Stoppage Bureau, Workplace Information Directorate, Human Resources Development Canada; 1990–2004 data are from Human Resources and Skills Development Canada. (2005). *Chronological Perspectives on Work Stoppages in Canada,* http://www110.hrdc-drhc.gc.ca/millieudetravail_workplace/chrono/index.cfm/doc/english, [April 14, 2005].

have sometimes been greatly affected by single, large disputes. For instance, the average size of strikes in 1976 was more than three times what it had been the year before, in large measure because of the Day of Protest in October of that year. That one-day political strike also resulted in an average duration figure of 7.3 days, which was only about one-third of the previous year's 21.6 days. Similarly, lengthy Canada Post strikes in 1975 and 1981 were key factors in unusually long average strike durations for those years.

As Table 11.2 shows, the total person-days lost due to work stoppages has fluctuated greatly over time. In 1975 and 1976, more than 10 million person-days were lost due to strikes and lockouts, more than 100 times as many as were lost in 1930, during the Great Depression. Part of the difference results simply from an increase in the size of the Canadian workforce. Part of the difference can also be attributed to rising union membership rates. In 1976, Canada's union density stood at 37 percent, or nearly three times the rate it had been in 1930. We must also take into account economic conditions, the 1976 "Day of Protest," labour's generally stronger political position in 1975–1976, and the addition of large numbers of public sector workers to the ranks of workers eligible to strike.

One more piece of information is needed before we can meaningfully compare relative strike intensity in different jurisdictions or industries. Other things being equal, larger industries and jurisdictions lose more person-days due to strikes simply because there are more collective agreements expiring than in smaller industries and jurisdictions, and because these agreements cover a greater number of workers. Yet the number of person-days lost compared to the number worked may be minuscule in a large jurisdiction. It is, therefore, usual to divide the number of person-days lost by the number of person-days worked, so that the former can be expressed as a percentage of time worked. Such a figure facilitates more valid comparisons of strike activity in different Canadian industries and jurisdictions.

While interprovincial comparisons are relatively straightforward, comparisons between countries are somewhat more difficult due to differences in the measures that are used. For example, Canada's statistics include work stoppages involving a loss of ten or more person-days whereas some countries include work stoppages of any length and others do not include stoppages unless at least 100 person-days were lost. The United States has an unusually high threshold of 1000 person-days lost. This measurement difference alone results in the United States' record looking far better than it would were the Canadian definition of an official strike applied. Still other differences between countries' measures exist: Canada's work stoppage statistics include lockouts, yet in several other countries these are excluded. Some countries include in their tallies workers not directly involved in the labour dispute but whose work has been disrupted due to the job action, yet others, like Canada, do not. Canada's strike statistics include all industries, yet data for some countries exclude certain industries; for example, France excludes agriculture (Aligisakis, 1997). While Canada's statistics include both the public and the private sectors, some countries exclude all, or a portion of, their public sector. Finally, a few countries such as the United Kingdom, Turkey, and the United States exclude work stoppages staged for political purposes (Monger, 2004).

Temporal comparisons of strike data are somewhat less problematic but can be confounded by changes in measurements over time. For example, as mentioned earlier, since 1982 American strike statistics have been confined to work stoppages where at least 1000 person-days are lost, whereas prior to 1982 any stoppages involving six or more person-days were included (Gunderson, Hebdon, Hyatt, and Ponak, 2005). Despite these and other measurement problems, reasonably meaningful international or temporal strike comparisons can be made by using a measure such as percentage of working time lost or days lost per 1000 employees. Using the latter measure, Canada's strike record is still relatively high compared to other countries of the Organisation for Economic Cooperation and Development (OECD). Table 11.3 shows that in each year between 1993 and 2002 Canada's working days lost per 1000 employees was well above the OECD average and our country consistently ranked within the top five.

It must be kept in mind, however, that the measurement differences discussed above still plague these international comparisons even when using a measure such as days lost per 1000 employees. Nonetheless, some of the reasons that have been cited for Canada's relatively high strike activity include the influence of a few large industries that are subject to economic fluctuations and instability, our highly decentralized industrial relations system, and a politically weak labour movement that exercises little influence over government economic policies (Jamieson, 1979).

Trends in Canadian Strike Activity

Generally, strike activity in Canada has been declining since the early 1980s and especially since the early 1990s. While evident in both sectors, this trend has been more pronounced in the private than the public sector. (Gunderson et al., 2005). The mid-1990s evinced notable deviations from this trend: In 1996, the year of several short political-protest strikes, the proportion of working time lost due to strikes was more than double that of the previous year, at 0.11 percent. The following year, the figure increased again, to 0.12 percent. In both of these years, a high rate of public sector strikes helped fuel higher overall strike intensity. In 1996, 42 percent of all person-days lost to strikes in Canada were in the public sector. The following year saw the public sector accounting for 55 percent of person-days lost due to strikes. Between 1998 and 2000, the proportion of person-days lost to strikes in the public sector declined somewhat, ranging from 26 to 42 percent. However, the public sector still accounted for a majority of strikes and of workers involved, while the private sector accounted for more person-days lost because its strikes were generally of much longer duration.

Looking more generally at the pattern of Canadian strike activity since the end of the First World War, it is by and large true that strike activity tends to rise and fall with the business cycle, rising in inflationary periods and declining in times of recession or depression. This would appear to have been particularly the case with respect to strike frequency, perhaps somewhat less so with respect to duration. Certainly a desire to keep pace with rising inflation was an important factor in the wave of strike activity that followed the two world wars and also occurred in the middle and late 1970s and very early 1980s. Along similar lines, it is worth noting that strike

Table 11.3

LABOUR DISPUTES: WORKING DAYS NOT WORKED PER 1000 EMPLOYEES* IN ALL INDUSTRIES AND SERVICES, 1993–2002: OECD COUNTRIES

	1993	1994	1995	1996	1997	1998	1999	2000	2001	2002	Average† 1993–97	Average† 1998–2002	Average† 1993–2002	Percentage change 1993–97 to 1998–2002
United Kingdom	30	13	18	55	10	11	10	20	20	51	25	23	24	–8
[UK ranking]	[13]	[7]	[5]	[16]	[9]	[9]	[10]	[11]	[11]	[14]	[7]	[8]	[6]	
Austria	4	0	0	0	6	0	0	1	0	3	2	1	1	–50
Belgium	18	24	33	48	13	28	8	8	47	**	27	**	**	**
Denmark	50	33	85	32	42	1317	38	51	24	79	49	299	177	510
Finland	10	307	493	11	56	70	10	126	30	36	174	54	110	–69
France	48	39	300	57	42	51	63R	114	82R	**	98	**	**	**
Germany	18	7	8	3	2	1	2	0	1	10	8	3	5	–63
Ireland	68	27	132	110	69	32	168	72	82	15	82	73	77	–11
Italy	236	238	65	137	84	40	62	59	67R	311	152	110	131	–28
Luxembourg	0	0	60	2	0	0	0	5	0	**	12	**	**	**
Netherlands	8	8	115	1	2	5	11	1	6	35	27	12	19	–56
Portugal	25	30	20	17	25	28	19	11	12	29	23	20	22	–13
Spain	238	698	157	165	182	121	132	296	152	379	283	221	248	–22
Sweden	54	15	177	17	7	0	22	0	3	0	54	5	29	–91
EU average‡	69	98	96	53	37	53	35R	60	43	110	70	59	64	–16
Iceland	1	864	1887	0	292	557	0	368	1571	0	608	505	554	–17
Norway	19	54	27	286	4	141	3	239	0	72	79	91	85	15
Switzerland	0	4	0	2	0	7	1	6	6	6	1	4	3	300
Turkey	75	30	580	31	20	30	24	36	29	**	146	**	**	**
Australia	100	76	79	131	77	72	88	61	50	32	93	60	75	–35
Canada	132	137	133	280	296	196	190	125	162R	218	197	178	187	–10
Japan	2	2	1	1	2	2	2	1	1	0	2	1	1	–50
New Zealand	20	31	41	51	18	9	12	8	37	22	32	18	25	–44
United States	36	45	51	42	38	42	16	163	9	5	42	47	45	12
OECD average‡	48	61	77	51	41	46	29R	90	29	51	56	49	52	–13

* Some employee figures have been estimated.

† Annual averages for those years within each period for which data are available, weighted for employment.

‡ Greece no longer collects data on labour disputes; the European Union average therefore excludes Greece; EU and OECD averages exclude data for France, Belgium, Luxembourg, (EU and OECD) and Turkey for 2002 (OECD).

** No data available for 2002.

R Revised.

Sources: Monger, Joanne. (2004). "International Comparisons of Labour Disputes in 2002." *Labour Market Trends* (April), Newport, South Wales: Office for National Statistics, p. 146; for working days not worked: ILO, Eurostat, national statistical offices; for employees: OECD, except UK, Office for National Statistics; Crown copyright material is reproduced with the permission of the Controller of HMSO and the Queen's Printer for Scotland.

frequency fell off very sharply starting in 1982, a recessionary year that marked the end of the last significant wave of inflation seen in this country and the beginning of a second round of wage controls for most public sector workers.

At the same time, it is important not to overlook the various pieces of labour legislation, especially *PC 1003* (1944) and the *Public Service Staff Relations Act* (1967), which granted collective bargaining rights to large numbers of new workers. The increase in strike intensity immediately following the passage of these two pieces of legislation should not be considered simply a response to inflation. In part it was a reflection of the fact that more workers were now legally entitled to go on strike. As well, it may to some degree have reflected pent-up frustration over non-economic as well as economic issues, to which the newly unionized workers could now, for the first time, legally respond by striking.

It would probably be a mistake to attribute growing public sector strike intensity solely to structural factors. As a number of observers (Ponak and Thompson, 1995) point out, and as we pointed out in the public sector chapter, the decade of the 1990s was one marked by large-scale privatization, contracting out of government work, service cuts, and layoffs of public sector workers. Such developments were obviously the source of extreme frustration and stress for many public sector workers. One should also not overlook provincial and federal governments' all but nationwide imposition of public sector wage controls, which had the effect of taking away many public sector workers' ability to bargain over money. In the short run, the wage controls may have reduced public sector strike intensity, as appears to have been the case for the early 1990s; however, the wave of public sector strikes in 1996 and 1997 and the nationwide wave of health care and transit strikes in 2001 suggest that when added to the other frustrations and stresses of public sector worklife in the 1990s, the period of prolonged wage controls served, in the end, rather to spur renewed militancy, as public sector workers sought to make up some of the ground lost through years of wage controls, freezes, or in some cases even actual rollbacks (see Fryer, 2000 and 2001).

Overall, however, strike activity has declined significantly since the mid-1970s when 0.53 percent of working time was lost to strikes. Since the early 1990s that figure has exceeded 0.10 in only two years, 1996 and 1997. The decline has been more dramatic in the private sector, most likely due to the stronger impact of economic pressures. An increasingly competitive global economy has served, in many instances, to increase the relative cost of a strike or lockout. At the same time, innovative dispute resolution procedures and new bargaining arrangements such as Quebec's "social contracts," in which unions have signed long-term collective agreements containing no-strike clauses in return for job security and a guarantee of government investment in plant modernization, reduce the likelihood that negotiations will result in an irreconcilable impasse (see Déom and Boivin, 2001; Chaykowski and Verma, 1992).

SOME RECENT DISPUTES

In this section, we stop to take a closer look at three Canadian strikes that have occurred since 2000. While this section does not pretend to offer a representative treatment of all recent Canadian strikes, these three disputes should provide some sense of the kinds of issues of greatest concern to Canadian workers and their unions.

Falconbridge Ltd. and CAW/Mine Mill Local 598 (2000–2001)

Corporate mergers and shifting union structures played an important role in the seven-month strike between nickel giant Falconbridge Ltd. and CAW/Mine Mill Local 598, one of the longest and most bitter in recent Canadian history.

The strike began August 1, 2000, just weeks after Brascan Corporation took over majority ownership of Falconbridge's parent company, Noranda. In a bid to reorganize its business into two separate divisions, mining and smelting, the company sought to strip entire sections from the collective agreement, reducing the document by over 80 pages (OPSEU, 2000b). Among the areas in which the company was seeking major concessions were bumping and recall rights, union representation, and workplace committees, including health and safety (OPSEU, 2000b). The company's push for these major concessions combined with a management negotiator's reference to union members as "scumsuckers and bottomfeeders" left members feeling they had no choice but to go on strike (OPSEU, 2000b).

Breaking with a 75-year tradition, the company employed replacement workers to enable it to maintain at least partial production (SCSJ, 2001). While many striking workers would normally have had the opportunity to work for other contractors for the duration of the strike, Falconbridge blocked off this option by informing contractors that they would be blacklisted from future contracts with the company if they hired the strikers, which led contractors to demand a separation certificate before they would hire them (OPSEU, 2000b).

Viewing the strike as a "community crisis" that was inflicting serious economic and social harm on both the workers and the Sudbury Community, Sudbury Regional Council passed a resolution (OPSEU, 2000a) calling on the parties to resume bargaining, with the help of a provincial mediator if necessary. Regional Council was particularly upset at the company's use of replacement workers, a practice it claimed was not accepted by the Sudbury community, and called on the company to reverse its decision to employ such workers. Undeterred, the company not only continued to use the replacement workers but threatened to resume full production, with or without its striking workers (M. Lowe, 2001). Initially content merely to delay production vehicles and buses loaded with replacement and supervisory workers, frustrated strikers eventually forced a complete 12-day halt to production, whereupon the company responded by applying for, and being granted, an injunction limiting the number of picketers to 20 per plant gate. After a late January confrontation between strikers and their allies from other unions and local and Ontario Provincial Police riot squads armed with tear gas, pepper spray, attack dogs and truncheons, a second injunction in early February limited the number of pickets to five per line (M. Lowe, 2001).

The new collective agreement, ratified February 20, 2001, by 87 percent of those voting, provided the 1250 mine, mill, and smelter workers with a signing bonus, a wage increase, and various other economic improvements. But it also gave the company increased contracting out rights and the ability to eliminate certain job classifications and to force employees to do more than one job in different classifications. After the strike, the company announced that the total Falconbridge workforce would be reduced by 10 percent, but through retirements and attrition rather than layoffs (SCSJ, 2001).

The union declared that the end of the strike would not mean the end of the Falconbridge workers' struggle, merely that the struggle would take another form as the workers dealt with the implications of the new contract language (SCSJ, 2001). Meanwhile, at least one observer (M. Lowe, 2001) suggested that neither side emerged a winner. On the one hand, the company, despite its deep pockets, use of force, and numerous allies in powerful places, had failed to break the union's spirit. On the other hand, the new realities of globalized production meant that Falconbridge was able to maintain some production, obtaining feed for the strikebound Sudbury nickel smelter from a non-striking unit in Quebec and then shipping it to Norway for refining, a production chain that required the collaboration of half a dozen other unions including the Steelworkers, railway unions, and various longshoring and seafaring unions. A key factor here may have been the CAW's pariah status within the Canadian Labour Congress (the conflict between the CAW and the CLC was discussed in Chapter 4). Because of that status, the CAW was unable to invoke the assistance of CLC unions in obtaining a "hot goods" declaration that would have broken the international production chain and very likely allowed the strike to end much sooner than it did (M. Lowe, 2001). In Lowe's view, globalized production requires more rather than less solidarity among unions, and the price the CAW paid for its departure from the CLC was probably too high.

National Gallery of Canada and PSAC (2001)

Employees in the federal government's artistic community demonstrated considerable creativity during the course of a lengthy dispute with the National Gallery of Canada and the Museum of Contemporary Photography. Their efforts eventually bore fruit in a three-year agreement providing substantial wage and benefit increases.

The two-month strike, conducted against the backdrop of the Gallery's exhibition of the paintings of Gustav Klimt that opened on June 15, was preceded by a work-to-rule campaign and a variety of colourful protest tactics, including a lunch-hour march by employees and their dogs at which National Gallery management were requested to "Throw us a bone!" (PSAC Release, April 6, 2001). On May 10, the museum workers launched a full-scale strike after the failure of both conciliation and mediation (PSAC Release, May 10, 2001). The 2 percent salary increase that management had last offered was substantially below the regional inflation rate, and also below the 2.5 percent achieved, without a work stoppage, by their colleagues at the nearby Science and Technology and Aviation museums (PSAC Release, May 10, 2001).

During the strike, the museum workers kept up their colourful protest tactics. Most notable were the piles of red shoes frequently on display in front of the museums as well as in strike posters. Though the protests were entirely peaceful and the difference between the union's demands and management's salary offer was relatively small, the Gallery management took various legal actions against the strikers and made repeated requests for judicial injunctions to restrain the union's picketing, an aggressive tactic that did little to improve the already strained relations between the parties (PSAC Release, June 27, 2001). Nonetheless, on July 10 the parties reached a tentative agreement that was ratified three days later. The agreement provided a signing bonus, wage increases of up to 10.25 percent over a three-year deal, and improved vacation leave and parental benefits, as well as an assurance that there would be no reorganization during the term of the agreement. It also included a back-to-work protocol assuring employees that an "inclusive, respectful and supportive work environment" would await them upon their return. A key element of the protocol was the Gallery's agreement to withdraw all civil suits launched against its staff during the strike (PSAC Release, July 13, 2001).

Government of Nova Scotia and NSGEU (2001)

The year 2001 saw an almost unprecedented wave of strikes in the health care sector, from Nova Scotia to British Columbia. Fuelling these strikes were years of real income loss resulting from government-imposed wage freezes and rollbacks in the public sector. Other contributing factors included frustration over increased workloads, bed closures, and what the health care workers had come to perceive as a lack of respect and recognition from politicians. Also aggravating the situation was the higher pay being offered to nurses by recruiters from other countries, such as the US and Britain, as well as other provinces.[3]

The most bitter of these disputes took place in Nova Scotia, whose premier, ironically, is a former physician, Dr. John Hamm. Perhaps not so ironically, the Nova Scotia dispute started to heat up just as a similar strike in Saskatchewan, which had continued despite back-to-work legislation, was winding down. To make up for a decade of frozen wages, nurses belonging to the Nova Scotia Government Employees' Union (NSGEU) and their counterparts with the Nova Scotia Nurses' Union were demanding pay increases of between 20 and 25 percent over three years (CTV News, 2001). This was far higher than the 8.3 percent the government was prepared to offer. Fearful of the possible effects of a province-wide health care strike, the Hamm government on June 14 introduced a bill to take away health care workers' right to strike. Furthermore, the bill would have given Cabinet the power to impose settlements, prevented arbitration of health care disputes, and barred court challenges of any Cabinet-imposed settlement.

The government cited a $500 million deficit and $12 billion debt as its reasons for imposing the legislation. But unionists, nurses, and health care policy analysts said the legislation would only aggravate the already severe shortage of nurses in the province. Clearly, the legislation aggravated the friction between the parties, leading the NSGEU to reject a tentative settlement reached with the help of a mediator, and causing another public sector union, CUPE, to order its members to work to rule even though it had not yet even started bargaining. After a rally featuring national union leaders, the NSGEU's support workers, such as radiologists and lab technicians, launched full-scale strike action on June

27, supported by the union's nurses who honoured their picket line. When the NSGEU members were ordered back to work, most complied, but continued their protest by resigning *en masse*. Finally, the government withdrew the controversial legislation that had been the source of so many of the problems, and on July 5 it agreed to send its dispute with the NSGEU and NSNU to final-offer-selection arbitration. On July 17, local arbitrator Susan Ashley was appointed to settle the dispute. Ashley's ruling awarded the province's registered nurses, who had been the most poorly paid in the country prior to the award, their final demand of 17 percent over three years. But other health care workers received only the government's offer of 7.5 percent plus a lump sum payment (Lancaster, 2001 (25:7–8)).

Some Common Themes

Wages were clearly a factor in all three of the above disputes. This was particularly true in the case of the public sector disputes, where workers had seen their wages frozen for many years during the 1990s and as a result had experienced a significant decline in real income. By the same token, lack of respect and recognition must also be considered a significant factor, not just in the two public sector disputes but also in the Falconbridge strike. The Falconbridge management negotiator's derogatory slurs about union members were clearly inflammatory and insinuations by the Nova Scotia health minister to the effect that nurses were prepared to neglect patients in need of care infuriated many nurses. The use of injunctions and other hard-nosed legal tactics by the National Gallery's management had a similar effect.

Government restrictions on unions' bargaining rights were a prime factor in the Nova Scotia health care dispute, and may also have been at least an indirect factor in the National Gallery strike. Had the Nova Scotia government not introduced its legislation removing both the right to strike and access to arbitration, the NSGEU might have accepted the tentative mediated settlement. As it was, union president Joan Jessome noted that even some of those voting to accept felt they were doing so with a gun to their head, while those who voted to reject told her their dignity was not for sale. Workers at the National Gallery, in common with other federal government employees, were frustrated after years of suspension of bargaining, continuing suspension of interest arbitration, and numerous other restrictions on their rights as employees (see Fryer, 2000 and 2001).

Globalization and increased competition were clearly important factors in the Falconbridge dispute. A series of mergers and reorganizations led the company to try to "strip" the contract. Its globalized production chain also enabled it to maintain at least partial production despite the union's most valiant efforts. While the three strikes discussed above are all quite different from one another, it is worth noting that management took a tough line in all three cases. This was most evident in the Falconbridge strike, where the company brought in professional strikebreakers and used force to attempt to maintain production, but was also illustrated by the Nova Scotia government's bill banning both strikes and arbitration, and the National Gallery's repeated use of injunctions and other legal manoeuvres against the strikers.

WHAT CAUSES STRIKES?

Having looked in some detail at three recent Canadian strikes, and the causes for those strikes, we can now step back a bit and consider the issue of strike causes more generally. In very few cases, other than certain wildcat strikes, is the cause likely to be single—or simple. Leaving aside for the moment strongly inflationary periods, where strike action is often necessary to prevent rapid erosion of workers' real wages, experience suggests that most Canadian strikes appear to require: (1) serious medium- or long-term worker frustration, typically the result either of poor labour–management relations or an extremely difficult economic environment, or both; and (2) a triggering incident or incidents that can serve to channel that frustration, and around which union leaders can mobilize broad support for strike action. In many cases, wages are the triggering issue, but this issue alone is often insufficient to provoke a strike, particularly in deflationary periods. However, an employer's refusal to meet a union's wage demand will often prove to be the catalyst when antagonistic relationships marked by large accumulations of grievances or employer attempts to diminish the union's influence have already sown the seeds of conflict.

Beyond this, there is now a large body of literature correlating strikes with various economic factors: For example, empirical evidence quite consistently demonstrates that strike activity tends to diminish in periods of high unemployment and rise in inflationary periods or when real wages are eroded, although these relationships are somewhat weaker in Canada than in the United Kingdom or the United States (Gunderson et al., 2005). A smaller, but still significant, literature exists on such socio-political and cultural determinants as community cohesion, union leaders' values and ideologies, decision-making authority, and intra-organizational conflict within union and management organizations. Some attempts have also been made to link strikes to bargaining unit size and to the bargaining history of particular organizations.[4] Strike causation is undeniably a complex issue. In the final analysis, each bargaining relationship and set of strike issues is unique. To fully understand the causes of any given strike, one must know the players and the history of their interactions with each other, in addition to understanding the economic, political, and cultural environment within which those interactions are and have been conducted. Nonetheless, general frameworks have been developed to help explain some of the more common patterns of strike causation.

The Causes of Strikes: Models

While there exists an extensive literature on the theoretical causes of strikes, three basic models can be summarized: 1) the asymmetrical, or private, information model; 2) the joint-costs perspective; and 3) strikes as collective voice.

The Asymmetrical Information or Private Information Model

The asymmetrical, or private, information model treats strikes as a method of eliciting information from the employer. Typically, employers will rebuff unions' demands with statements regarding their dire financial position or expected product market conditions. These inability-to-pay arguments are often based on information to which the union is not privy and with regard to which the union may be justifi-able suspicious. Thus, the union may use the threat of a strike to test an employer's resolve. If the employer capitulates to the union's demands either before or shortly after the strike begins, it is clear the employer was bluffing, at least to some extent. If, however, the employer's financial situation is truly adverse, a strike, even one of long duration, will be a less costly option than a high wage settlement. Thus, the strike serves the purpose of confirming the employer's true financial position in relation to the general state of the economy (Gunderson et al., 2005). Any factors that decrease information asymmetry will tend to decrease the incidence of strikes. For example, a union representative on the board of directors may increase a union's confidence in the veracity of the employer's claims.

The asymmetrical information model can also help explain lockouts. In this case, the assumption is that the union members have the private information regarding whether or not the employer truly needs to increase wages in order to prevent workers from quitting and finding alternate employment. A lockout, or even a threat of one, is used to induce unions, whose members are not likely to find alternate employment at higher wage rates, to accept the employer's offer. On the other hand, the union's willingness to endure a relatively long lockout reveals to the employer the legitimacy of its claims that the workers' alternate wage rate exceeds the employer's offer (Fisher, 2001).

The Joint-Cost Perspective

The joint-cost perspective takes a different, yet complementary, approach in that it treats strikes and lockouts as but one way to resolve disputes. If the joint cost of resolving the dispute via a strike or lockout is higher than resolving it using other mechanisms that serve the same purpose, the parties will tend to avoid resorting to work stoppages. Instead, they may, for example, continue in conciliation, agree to arbitration, or utilize continuous bargaining. This perspective does not try to exam-ine what goes on within the black box of negotiations; rather, it aggregates the total joint costs associated with strikes or lockouts and compares these to the real resource costs and uncertainties associated with other dispute resolution mecha-nisms. If the joint cost of a work stoppage is relatively low, this option will be selected more frequently than if the joint cost were relatively high. Any factor that affects the cost of the strike for one party will influence the likelihood of a strike accordingly; however, if the factor affects the parties differently, any change will also affect settlement terms. For example, a legislative prohibition on using replacement workers increases the cost of a strike for the employer but has no influence on its cost for the union or employees. Therefore, the joint cost perspective predicts that the overall likelihood of strikes will decrease but this will likely occur in conjunction with employers agreeing to somewhat more generous contract terms in order to avoid a costly strike (Gunderson et al., 2005).

Strikes as Collective Voice

John Godard (2005) makes a distinction between strikes that result from mistakes, generally in the negotiation or ratification process, and those more appropriately regarded as union members' expression of their collective voice. In the former group Godard includes disputes resulting from immature or flawed bargaining relationships, as well as those caused by negotiators' lack of skill, inexperience with each other, or inability to get along. Another cause, often related to union intra-organizational conflict, can be individual workers' miscalculations, which may lead them to reject tentative agreements their leaders know are probably the best they can realistically hope for. The complexity of the situation itself can also be the source of mistakes that lead to strikes. Here again, intra-organizational conflict may lead to negotiating errors. More fundamentally, such errors are more apt to occur in situations where difficult issues are at stake, where bargaining structures are complex, or where many different occupations and classes of worker are being represented.

The strikes-as-mistakes perspective, which treats strikes as hazards of negotiations, can encompass both the private-information model and the joint-cost perspective. Both these models treat strikes as the means through which the parties come to appreciate each other's true positions. If the parties more effectively communicated their positions, they could determine and agree to the final settlement without incurring the costs of a strike. However, Godard holds that the strike-as-mistakes model offers an unduly narrow view of the reasons for strikes. By focusing only on how the parties maximize their economic well-being, this model discounts behavioural explanations and the role of non-economic motivations. A more comprehensive picture can be obtained if strikes are viewed, "first and foremost, as mechanisms of 'collective voice'" (2005:341).

Godard contends that the nature of the employment relationship is such that workers are inevitably in a position of subordination and that this position is not altered substantially through collective bargaining. This position of subordination, coupled with the conflicts that underlie labour–management relationships, causes workers to feel discontented with and distrustful of management. Strikes serve as a collective means to express this pervasive discontent and distrust. Factors that influence whether workers' collective discontent is expressed by means of strikes include the extent and intensity of worker discontent, union leaders' ability to mobilize that discontent, the extent to which the local community views strike activity as legitimate, the union's strike power, and management's willingness and ability to buy off discontent through generous wage settlements or progressive human resource policies. Also relevant are the availability and viability of other means of expressing discontent, such as quitting, and the presence or absence of cohesive community support, which may prove necessary, particularly in the case of a lengthy or bitter strike.

DISPUTE RESOLUTION METHODS

Canadian jurisdictions have developed a variety of dispute resolution methods for use in helping to prevent strikes, or, in some cases, as alternatives to strikes. Virtually all involve the use of a neutral third party. Facilitative dispute resolution mechanisms, such as conciliation, mediation, and fact-finding, aim to prevent a strike or lockout by assisting the parties to fashion a mutually acceptable settlement. Arbitration, on the other hand, substitutes for a strike or lockout and empowers the arbitrator to impose a settlement upon the parties. In establishing an arsenal of dispute resolution methods and in deciding which ones to use on any given occasion, Canadian governments seek to strike a balance between allowing the parties as much freedom as possible to settle their own disputes and protecting the public interest. For example, compulsory arbitration is virtually unheard of in the private sector. Its main use is with groups such as police and firefighters whose services are in many jurisdictions deemed so essential to public welfare and safety that they are denied the right to strike. Similarly, conciliation boards are now all but unknown in private sector disputes, though they are still used from time to time in high-profile public sector ones (Craig and Solomon, 1996; Godard, 2005).

Compulsory Conciliation

The labour relations acts in all Canadian jurisdictions display vestiges of the compulsory conciliation that was first introduced in 1907 in the *Industrial Disputes Investigation Act (IDI Act)*; however, the degree to which the legislation resembles the original two-stage, compulsory conciliation varies between jurisdictions. Ontario, Alberta, New Brunswick, Nova Scotia, Prince Edward Island, and Newfoundland and Labrador continue to impose conciliation; other jurisdictions have abandoned compulsory pre-strike conciliation and either impose conciliation only at the discretion of the Minister, as is the case in Saskatchewan, or allow the strike to commence prior to completion of the conciliation process.

Under compulsory conciliation, a government official, normally someone from the Ministry of Labour, meets with the parties to determine the possibility of settlement. Increasingly, conciliators have come to play active roles in attempting to resolve disputes, functioning more and more as mediators in fact if not in name. Indeed, in two jurisdictions, British Columbia and Alberta, mediators are used instead of first-stage conciliators. The second stage of the conciliation procedure, still on the books in several Canadian jurisdictions, is the conciliation board. Under this procedure, a tripartite board made up of a neutral person, a management representative, and a union representative is convened. Where used, the board operates more formally than a single conciliation officer, eliciting presentations from the parties and making recommendations as to the appropriate terms of settlement (Godard, 2005). However, as noted above, conciliation boards are increasingly rarely used, primarily because of the delays they cause and their tendency to interfere with the parties' willingness to negotiate a settlement on their own, the "chilling effect" discussed in Chapter 9. A number of jurisdictions have substituted mediation for the second stage of the conciliation process. Many argue that compulsory conciliation is highly interventionist by international standards and inconsistent with the general principle of voluntarism underlying the Canadian industrial relations system. While there may be some rationale for retaining the procedure in disputes with a substantial public interest component, it is not at all clear that there is any reason to involuntarily impose conciliation upon parties to private sector disputes that have little detrimental impact on the public.

Mediation

In theory, mediation involves more active intervention on the part of the third-party neutral than does conciliation, though the boundaries between them are becoming increasingly blurred in practice. Unlike conciliation, mediation is often voluntary and at the request of the parties. Depending on the nature of the negotiations and the experience of the negotiators, the mediator may be called on to do such things as meet with the parties to determine what their key issues are, discover where the settlement zone lies, act as a go-between, actively pressure the parties to compromise, and deal with the media both during negotiations and after a tentative agreement has been reached (Craig and Solomon, 1996; Downie, 1989; Godard, 2005).

Arbitration

interest arbitration
Process whereby a third-party neutral or board determines and imposes the terms and conditions of the collective agreement. Serves as a substitute for a strike or lockout.

rights/grievance arbitration Process to resolve disputes over the interpretation, application, or administration of rights articulated in a collective agreement.

voluntary arbitration
Parties have the right to strike or lockout but elect instead to submit the dispute to a third-party neutral or tripartite board to determine the terms and conditions of the collective agreement.

Interest arbitration, in which a neutral party acceptable to both sides or a tripartite panel chaired by such a neutral person establishes the terms and conditions of the new collective agreement, is often used in Canada's public sector, normally after the failure of one or more of the methods described above. Note that interest arbitration should not be confused with **rights** or **grievance arbitration**, which has to do with interpreting the existing contract. Note as well that compulsory interest arbitration is virtually never used in the private sector. In general, both management and unions prefer to negotiate their own contracts rather than turning the decision over to a third party. On occasion, however, **voluntary arbitration** is used. Not uncommon in the United States, where it has been tried in industries as varied as steel and major league baseball, it is rarer in Canada. However, it has been used in the Ontario clothing industry (Downie, 1989) and in some university settings such as the University of Ottawa (Craig and Solomon, 1996).

Binding interest arbitration is the normal method of resolving contract disputes involving essential employees whose services are considered so crucial that they cannot be allowed to strike. There are two main types of interest arbitration: conventional and final-offer selection (FOS). Under conventional arbitration, the arbitrator is given considerable latitude to pick and choose among the positions submitted by the parties or to fashion an alternative solution. With FOS, there is no such latitude. The arbitrator must choose either management's position or the union's. FOS may be used either on a total-package basis, or issue-by-issue. An intriguing variation (see Craig and Solomon, 1996:319) is tri-offer FOS, where, in addition to the positions advanced by management and the union, the arbitrator may pick the recommendations of a fact-finder.

The only type of arbitration commonly used in the private sector is first-agreement arbitration. The majority of jurisdictions provide this dispute resolution mechanism at the request of either party to a new collective bargaining relationship after they have reached a bargaining impasse. The rationale is that refusing to conclude a first agreement is sometimes used by employers as a union-avoidance tactic. Even where this is not the case, the parties' inexperience may detrimentally affect their ability to conclude a first agreement. Binding arbitration imposes the first contract and provides the parties an opportunity to build their relationship before they again engage in collective bargaining.

Conventional arbitration has been criticized on a number of counts. Some have been concerned at its cost, others at the slowness with which settlements are achieved through this method compared to settlements achieved in other ways. The two most common criticisms are (a) that groups that use it regularly may become so dependent upon arbitrators that they lose their ability to fashion their own settlements, the so-called "**narcotic effect**" and (b) that it inhibits genuine bargaining by removing the incentive for the parties to make hard choices, since they know the arbitrator is there to make the choices for them at the end of the day, the so-called "chilling effect." While there is no consensus in the literature on the extent to which such effects exist in Canada, there is at least some reason to believe they may be significant problems.

> **narcotic effect** Refers to parties' decreasing ability to resolve disputes on their own as they repeatedly refer disputes to, and become dependent upon, arbitration.

The use of FOS, especially in its total-package form, would seem to provide a good way around any possible chilling or narcotic effects. In principle, the possibility of having an arbitrator reject one's entire package and select that of the other side should be a very severe disincentive to unreasonable behaviour, and an equally strong incentive for the parties to settle on their own. Some evidence cited by Ponak and Thompson (1989) suggests that, under FOS, the rate of freely negotiated settlements is a good deal higher than under conventional arbitration. Nonetheless, FOS has found little favour in Canada, though it has become relatively common in US public sector bargaining.[5] One notable exception is the Nova Scotia health care dispute of 2001, where, as noted above, FOS arbitration was imposed after the provincial government withdrew its legislation suspending health care workers' right to arbitration.

Fact-Finding

Fact-finding is a type of dispute resolution process that is used less often now than in the past. The idea behind fact-finding is that if a neutral party has issued a report outlining the key issues, particularly if that report is made public, the parties will be more likely to settle. The process, which is more formal than mediation, typically involves the presentation of briefs by the parties and a hearing where they present their cases (Gunderson, Hyatt, and Ponak, 2001). The fact-finder then issues a report with recommendations; the report is often released to the public as well as to the labour relations board. However, the recommendations are never binding.

> **fact-finding** A dispute resolution procedure involving a neutral party investigating and reporting on the facts of the dispute.

Fact-finding was previously used extensively by Ontario's Education Relations Commission. Since the abolition of that body's separate dispute resolution functions, it has been used relatively infrequently in Canada; however, fact-finding was one of many options available in the "toolkit" approach to public service dispute resolution recommended by the Fryer Committee (Fryer, 2001).

Back-to-Work Legislation

Back-to-work legislation is used to end public sector strikes that have reached a point where government officials believe that, if they continued, they would pose significant risk to the public health, safety, order, or welfare. Such legislation is generally followed by a referral to arbitration or, increasingly, by the imposition of a settlement. While occasional use of back-to-work legislation is perhaps inevitable in any country that allows public sector workers to strike, the alarming frequency with which this legislation has been used in Canada suggests there is something seriously wrong with existing public sector bargaining arrangements.

SUMMARY

Overall, there appears to have been a gradual but significant trend away from formal investigative mechanisms such as second-stage conciliation, and towards more informal facilitative mechanisms such as mediation. The conciliation process itself has evolved into something very much like mediation in most jurisdictions. Within the public sector, arbitration, initially envisaged as the normal option under *PSSRA*'s "choice of procedures" approach, has recently found less favour. A number of jurisdictions that formerly used arbitration to resolve disputes with their employees have moved to the conciliation-strike route. In the public sector, federal and provincial governments continue to make frequent use of back-to-work legislation.

Members of the Public Service Alliance walk the picket lines in front of a federal building in Peterborough, Ontario, on Wednesday, August 15, 2001. The strike was one of many called across Canada in a series of "Workless Wednesdays" designed to draw public attention to federal government workers' contract demands.

UNDERSTANDING AND PREDICTING STRIKES AND LOCKOUTS

Much has been written on the topic of strikes and lockouts. Research is plentiful on how a variety of factors correlate with strike incidence and duration. A number of theoretical models attempt to explain the causes and functions of strike activity. Literature abounds regarding the efficacy of traditional dispute resolution procedures and the development of myriad alternatives. More newspaper column inches are dedicated to strikes and lockouts than to any other industrial relations topic. However, despite the volume and variety of information and research, strikes and lockouts are neither particularly predictable nor adequately understood; they remain perhaps the most mysterious and challenging of industrial relations topics.

Case 11.1

THE OPSEU STRIKE OF 2002: ESSENTIAL WORKERS?

Ontario's Conservative government, first led by Mike Harris and then by Ernie Eves, has the dubious distinction of having been at the bargaining table on both of the two occasions when negotiations with the Ontario Public Sector Employees' Union (OPSEU) broke down and the union went on strike. In 1996, the first strike in OPSEU's history lasted five weeks. The next round of bargaining, in 2002, resulted in a strike that lasted almost eight weeks.

According to OPSEU's president, Leah Casselman, by 2002 the Conservative government had weakened and fragmented the Ontario public service through six-and-a-half years of cuts, layoffs, privatization, and mismanagement. OPSEU members were fed up with increasing workloads, high stress levels, low morale, and lack of respect and recognition. Staff turnover was at an all-time high and recruitment into the public service had never been harder. The 2002 round of negotiations was more of the same, with government demands for concessions including the ability to rely increasingly on contracting out and short-term contract workers, the creation of a new classification of temporary employees, and control over OPSEU's portion of surplus pension funds. Members voted 88 percent in favour of strike action and withdrew their services on March 13, 2002.

While the negotiations affected 45 000 public service workers, only 30 000 walked off the job. The other 15 000 were employees in positions deemed essential and denied the right to strike. Included in this category were jail guards, ambulance dispatchers, staff in psychiatric hospitals, court workers, and workers in water and sewage treatment plants. OPSEU called these workers "inside strikers" and supported them in their refusal to do any work other than essential parts of essential jobs. By law, OPSEU was permitted to make frequent worksite visits to see what work was being done but they claimed that management often refused or terminated their visits.

Just two days into the strike, jail guards at nine correctional facilities around the province claimed to be locked out and unable to report for work. The government claimed the guards were not reporting for work in "a law abiding" manner. Although the Labour Relations Board ordered the guards back to work, the parties were back before the board within 24 hours, each asserting the other had failed to abide by an essential services agreement.

Just four days into the strike, prisoners from one of the Toronto Detention Centres failed to arrive for court appearances in Newmarket, leaving an irate Justice

John McIsaac blaming the union and citing union president Casselman for criminal contempt of court. A few days later the charges were dropped when the government's lawyer admitted in court that the decision not to transport the prisoners was made by corrections services management.

Soon 18 provincial jails became involved to some degree or another in the lockout, which the union claimed was part of the government's long-standing plan to bring in replacement workers. Toward the end of March, 92 jail guards from the Toronto West Detention Centre (TWDC) were suspended without pay and threatened with firing for allegedly not doing their jobs. The government claimed they were being insubordinate, disruptive, and verbally abusive and were refusing to provide medication to inmates or transport them to court. The union claimed it was management who was preventing workers from doing their job, not permitting them to search cells for contraband, and ordering that inmates not be transported to court. The suspensions were overturned by the Labour Relations Board two days later. However, throughout the remainder of the strike, "essential service" corrections employees often showed up for work only to be told their services were not needed. Managers struggled to operate correctional facilities safely but at least three escapes, a riot, a stabbing, and one death were blamed on untrained managers, improper monitoring, and infrequent patrols. One inmate apparently hopped the perimeter fence at the Ottawa-Carleton Detention Centre when cameras that normally monitored perimeter fencing were instead trained on picketers.

Similar, if not so dramatic, battles were also waged at the four provincial psychiatric hospitals where nurses who had been providing limited services throughout the strike were ordered by the Ontario Labour Relations Board to perform the full range of their duties. Other skirmishes involved ambulance dispatchers, court workers, and aggressive picketing—or what OPSEU termed "building invasions"—of buildings and the parking garages of those locations where the union claimed scabs were working. By the time the strike was over, the government had obtained over 150 picket line injunctions and union and management representatives had spent countless hours in Labour Relations Board hearings.

Finally, early on the morning of May 2, just hours before polls opened for two provincial by-elections—one of which was in the riding where then Premier Ernie Eves was seeking a seat that would allow him to return to the legislature—a deal was announced. While many OPSEU members saw the timing of the deal as suspect, Casselman stated, "I'll take a deal any time I can get it." Casselman was credited for her strong leadership during the acrimonious and gruelling dispute and she offered praise to Premier Eves, who had assumed the leadership of the Conservative party during the course of the strike. While Premier Harris had been seen as bent on destroying the union, Premier Eves adopted a more conciliatory style and expressed a strong desire to fashion a compromise that could end the dispute.

Sources: Brennan, Richard and Peter Small. (2002). "Jail Guards Threatened with Firing." *Toronto Star*. March 27, p. A18; Immen, Wallace. (2002). "Ontario Strike Sparks Prison Safety Fears." *Globe and Mail*. March 28, p. A10; Lawrence, Gary. (2002). "45,000 Ontario Strikers Fight Plans to Increase the Temporary Workforce." *Labour Notes* (May), p. 8; Mackie, Richard. (2002). "Eves Praised for Role in Ending OPSEU Strike." *Globe and Mail*. May 3, p. A8; Swainson, Gail. (2002). "Union Leader Cleared of Contempt Charges." *Toronto Star*. March 19, p. A21; Wilkes, Jim. (2002). "Strike's End Was Just a Call Away." *Globe and Mail*. May 3, pp. A1, A6.

Case Questions

1. Using the theory or theories that you think best explain the causes of the OPSEU 2002 strike, outline the factors or events that led to the walkout.

2. Explain how the designation of a proportion of the workforce as essential affects the viability of a strike as a means of putting economic pressure on an employer. Can you suggest an alternative way to balance the rights of employees, employers and the public?

3. Explain how the change in leadership of the Conservative party and the pending by-election may have affected the negotiations. Relate this back to your explanation of the causes of the strike.

QUESTIONS FOR DISCUSSION

1. Legally speaking, what is a strike? What is a lockout?

2. Describe the steps and processes unions and employers must follow before a legal strike or lockout may be declared.

3. Describe the three approaches toward public sector strikes. Keeping in mind that your definition must balance the rights of employees, employers, and the public, how would you define an essential service?

4. What is the most accurate way of comparing strike intensity across different jurisdictions, industries, or countries?

5. At which points in history was Canadian strike activity highest and lowest? Why?

6. What were the major causes of the three disputes described in this chapter? Apply the theoretical models of strike causation to each of the three disputes. Which of the models best explains each strike?

7. What factors would likely increase workers' collective discontent and distrust? In what ways could management address these factors in order to decrease the likelihood that discontent and distrust would be expressed through strike action?

8. What are some methods of dispute resolution used to prevent strikes or lessen their impact? Which ones are used mainly in the public sector? Which seem most effective? Are there serious problems with any?

9. Assume you are member of a job action committee for a teachers' union. You and your colleagues are all extremely frustrated at the slow pace of negotiations, and you have reached a legal strike position and taken a strike vote. At this juncture, someone says, "Maybe we aren't ready for a full-scale strike yet, but we could just not grade the final exams." Comment on the wisdom of this strategy.

Suggestions for Further Reading

Adams, Roy. (1995). "Canadian Industrial Relations in Comparative Perspective." In M. Gunderson and A. Ponak (Eds.), *Union–Management Relations in Canada* (3rd ed.). Don Mills, ON: Addison-Wesley. Contains a useful discussion of industrial conflict that suggests conflict may depend more on structures than on processes (such as dispute resolution systems).

Hebdon, Robert and Robert Stern. (1998). "Tradeoffs among Expressions of Industrial Conflict: Public Sector Strike Bans and Grievance Arbitration." *Industrial and Labor Relations Review,* 51:2. This study, which includes data from over 9000 bargaining units in Ontario, provides robust evidence of the trade-off between industrial conflict manifested in the form of strikes and conflict manifested in other forms. Similar subsequent research from Hebdon and Stern demonstrates the same phenomenon in the United States.

Kervin, John. (1984). "Strikes: Toward a New Typology of Causes." In *Proceedings of the 21st Annual Meeting of the Canadian Industrial Relations Association,* held in Guelph, ON. Offers an extremely helpful classification scheme for different types of strikes, including a discussion of policy approaches suitable for each. A useful corrective to the Panglossian optimism of those who think that all we need to do to prevent strikes is to be of good will and learn how to communicate better.

CHAPTER 12

GRIEVANCES: FUNCTION, RESOLUTION, AND PREVENTION

Grievance mediation can bring smiles to the faces of both sides—as well as lower bills.

LEARNING OBJECTIVES

After studying this chapter, you should be able to:

1. Explain what a grievance is and the general significance and function of grievances in the workplace.

2. Identify some typical workplace grievance procedures and some of the issues most commonly grieved.

3. Describe the arbitration process.

4. Identify some of the criticisms of conventional arbitration, as well as some modifications to the process that have been developed in response to those criticisms.

5. Explain the idea of alternative dispute resolution (ADR) and describe how it differs from conventional conflict resolution methods.

6. Discuss the grievance process within the broader context of workplace conflict.

The grievance process is important in that it provides a way other than a mid-term strike to resolve problems arising out of the interpretation of collective agreements. It also provides workers with a certain measure of workplace voice and a forum for expressing discontent about workplace conditions without fear of employer reprisal. We begin by examining the overall significance and functions of the grievance process. After a look at a specific case, we go on to examine grievance procedures and outcomes. We then consider some criticisms of the conventional grievance arbitration process and some innovative new mechanisms that have arisen in response to those criticisms—with a closer look at a specific alternative dispute resolution (ADR) process—before closing with a broad look at grievances in the overall context of workplace conflict.

Case 12.1

THE IKO CASE[1]

On April 12, 2001, Guy Lacelle, a millwright with 26 years' seniority and no previous disciplinary record, was suspended indefinitely from his job with IKO Industries Ltd. for sexual harassment and ordered to leave the premises immediately.

Twelve days later (April 24), Mr. Lacelle received the following letter . . .

Dear Mr. Lacelle:

This letter will confirm our discussion concerning the termination of your employment with IKO Industries Ltd. (IKO) effective immediately.

. . . The decision has been made to terminate your employment as a result of our investigation of a complaint [against your] actions, which are in breach of IKO's harassment and discrimination policy.

As a result of [this] investigation, IKO has determined that on April 11, 2001, you approached another employee and took certain actions which were . . . considered to be harassing by this employee. During our investigation it was clear that you understood that these actions upset your fellow employee. It is of particular concern to IKO that [this was neither] the first time that you have breached IKO policy, nor . . . the first that this employee has raised concern [sic] with respect to your actions . . .

[Although] you have been spoken to by the company or by fellow employees on three separate occasions, and despite our recent training regarding the company's harassment and discrimination policy, your actions on April 11, 2001, resulted in another breach of [that] . . . policy and the harassment of a fellow employee.

IKO considers that each of these actions is a breach of your obligations to IKO and/or fellow workers. Such actions cannot and will not be tolerated.

Under the circumstances, the decision has been made to terminate your employment for cause/wilful misconduct. While we regret the necessity of this decision, your conduct has left us with no other option . . .
Yours truly,

IKO Industries Ltd.

Per: Leonard Boyd

The Union and the grievor did not deny the April 11, 2001 incident referred to in the discharge letter, but submitted that, in all the circumstances, discharge was too severe a penalty for the grievor's actions and that it would be appropriate to substitute a period of suspension . . .

The Employer's view was that there were no mitigating circumstances which should cause this Board of Arbitration to substitute a lesser penalty than . . . discharge.

In whose favour do you think the Arbitration Board will rule? What facts and circumstances will be crucial to their decision? Stay tuned! As the case unfolds, you'll learn a good deal more about the way in which arbitrators arrive at their decisions.

GRIEVANCES AND THEIR SIGNIFICANCE

As we've pointed out throughout this book, worker–management conflict is a fact of life in most workplaces. Strikes, which are perhaps the most dramatic manifestation of such conflict, were discussed in Chapter 11. Here, we're concerned with grievances, a less dramatic but often equally profound manifestation of worker–management conflict.

What Is a Grievance?

Strictly speaking, a grievance (Gandz, 1982:289) is an allegation that one or more provisions of a collective agreement have been violated, and a claim for redress for any damages resulting from that violation. While one could apply the term to most types of employee complaints, such as those resulting from arbitrary supervisory practices (Gandz, 1982), using the term in its more general sense could result in ambiguity. We shall therefore limit the term "grievance" to allegations of collective agreement violation.

The Function and Significance of Grievances

The grievance process is of great significance in the Canadian IR system because it provides a forum for the resolution of disputes arising out of the collective agreement. Under Canadian legislation, mid-term strikes are banned,[2] although individual workers are, as we noted in Chapter 6, allowed to refuse work they believe unsafe. Otherwise, with a few exceptions, the rule is "work now; grieve later" (Godard, 1994:363). As we noted in the labour law chapter, collective agreements in every Canadian jurisdiction must contain procedures, culminating in binding arbitration, for the resolution of disputes over the interpretation and application of the agreement. Where such procedures are not explicitly written into an agreement, the labour board will normally deem them to have been included.

Because of the "work now, grieve later" rule, it's vital that aggrieved employees have a quick and relatively inexpensive mechanism for obtaining redress. It has been well established (see Rose, 1986b) that failure to address grievances quickly can lead to more serious labour relations difficulties (including wildcat strikes and other forms of industrial conflict) later on. Initially, in both Canada and the United States (Nolan and Abrams, 1997), grievance arbitration appears to have resolved most problems fairly expeditiously. However, since the early post-war period, it has tended to become lengthier, more formal, more highly legalistic, and a good deal costlier (Nolan and Abrams, 1997; Arthurs, 1988), as we'll see in more detail later on.

In addition to maintaining the agreement's integrity by providing a mechanism for ensuring that its terms are adhered to (Godard, 1994:359), the grievance process serves several other functions. First and foremost, it provides a system of industrial jurisprudence under which individuals can seek redress without fear of reprisal from superiors (Godard, 1994:360–361). By thus protecting workers from arbitrary treatment from superiors, the grievance process serves as an important mechanism of individual and group voice (Godard, 1994:360; Freeman and Medoff, 1984). Next to the higher wages that unions normally provide workers, the grievance process may well be the most compelling reason for people to join unions. Beyond that, the process can provide a forum for supplementary negotiations over items left vague in the agreement (Godard, 1994:359–360). It can also serve as a political mechanism for resolving intra-organizational conflict within both management and union sides. As Godard notes (p. 360), a union official may pursue a grievance more to satisfy a certain faction within the organization than out of any belief that the case has merit as such. Likewise, lower-level managers may encourage the union to pursue a certain grievance in the hopes of persuading senior management to change a policy they dislike or find unworkable.

The grievance process can also be used as a pressuring device to induce management to address issues not covered by the collective agreement (see Godard, 1994).[3] This use of the grievance process is problematic, since it can lead to large accumulations of grievances not arising out of the complaint of any individual union member. Habitual use of the grievance process for this purpose, as in organizations such as Canada Post (Stewart-Patterson, 1987), is generally a sign of very poor labour–management relations overall. Excessively high grievance rates can also affect a firm's bottom line, leading to a decline in both labour efficiency and product quality (see Ichniowski, 1986).

TYPES OF GRIEVANCES

It's useful to distinguish between individual, group, and policy grievances. As the name implies, an **individual grievance** involves the application of the agreement to one member. An example would be Mary Jones' contention that her three-day suspension for allegedly falsifying her time card violated the collective agreement in that the suspension was not imposed for just cause. A **group grievance** results from a combination of similar individual grievances seeking a common redress (University of Ottawa, 1994). For example, a group of workers might file a grievance alleging that the company had failed to pay overtime pay for work after regular working hours. A **policy grievance** involves a question of the agreement's general application or interpretation (University of Ottawa, 1994). Such a grievance might be initiated over large-scale technological or organizational change or a change in the pension

individual grievance A grievance involving the application of the collective agreement to one member.

group grievance A grievance resulting from a combination of similar individual grievances seeking a common redress.

policy grievance A grievance involving the agreement's general application or interpretation.

plan. While policy grievances are relatively infrequent, they're generally quite serious because they may involve millions of dollars or hundreds of jobs. Such grievances are often initiated at a late stage of the grievance procedure, where they can be dealt with by senior management and union officials (Gandz and Whitehead, 1989:241).[4] Discharge grievances may also skip one or more preliminary steps.

Let's look at an actual grievance case. We suggest that you read the following case now, then again when you have finished the chapter. See how your view of the case changes as a result of what you've learned.

Case 12.1 Continued

THE IKO CASE: SEXUAL HARRASSMENT

What's the appropriate penalty for sexual harassment, in a situation where the harassment has been repeated several times and the company's employees (including the harasser) have received formal training on harassment and discrimination? This case may shed some light on this matter. Please read the case thoroughly, then answer the questions at the end.

IKO Industries Ltd. (IKO) manufactures roofing shingles and roofing products and employs approximately eighty production and maintenance bargaining unit employees at its plant in Hawkesbury, Ontario. The complainant, Ms. M., . . . one of two women employed in a non-managerial capacity . . . is not a member of the bargaining unit . . .

Mr. John Brookes, a lawyer with a firm in Toronto . . . testified that he was contacted by Mr. Boyd, plant manager, in November 2000 and requested to . . . [investigate] . . . allegations of sexual harassment in the workplace. He met with Mr. Boyd and obtained background information as to the history of the plant, what harassment policies were in place, and information about a specific incident concerning Ms. M. and the grievor. Mr. Brookes met with Ms. M. who, while not wanting to name the other employee, indicated that [he] had, on a number of occasions, made her feel uncomfortable by standing too close to her and pressing his body against hers, saying he had a dream about her, and saying that she had a nice set of bears, when she was wearing a sweat shirt with bears on it.

She stated to Mr. Brookes that she had not complained to management previously about any of these incidents because, initially she was a temporary employee and subsequently very junior, and did not want to make waves. She [added] however that as the incidents increased . . . she was concerned that other employees would see it and that the incidents would spread.

Ms. M. told Mr. Brookes that she wanted the Employer to take some action to stop the incidents, but did not want to confront the grievor directly. Mr. Brookes testified that . . . he had concluded that the Employer's harassment policy may not have been distributed to bargaining unit employees, and that . . . [it] may not have been understood by all employees . . . it was [thus] determined that harassment training for all employees would . . . be appropriate.

On December 7 and 8, 2000, Mr. Brookes conducted harassment training for all employees. Throughout the day . . . he trained people as to what harassment was, how to respond to [it], and that persons could lose their job if they engaged in [it].

During the course of the training, reference was made to the Employer's harassment policy which provides in part as follows:

> In summary, sexual harassment occurs when one creates an environment that is intimidating, hostile or offensive because of unwelcome or unwanted sexually oriented conversations, suggestions, requests, demands, physical contacts or attention. Courteous, mutually respectful, non-coercive interactions between the employees that are acceptable to both parties are not considered to be sexual harassment . . . The Company will investigate and act firmly in dealing with persons harassing others . . .
>
> If an investigation confirms that an offence has occurred and remedial action is warranted:
>
> a) action shall be taken without delay;
>
> b) disciplinary sanctions imposed on the offender will be applied with an understanding of the seriousness of the misconduct and may include summary dismissal . . .

In April 2001, Mr. Brookes was again contacted by the Employer to investigate an incident between Ms. M. and the grievor, in which the grievor had pulled down on the hem of Ms. M's sweatshirt.

Ms. M. testified concerning this incident and . . . the history of her relations with the grievor. She has worked as a lab tech assistant for the past three years, and has been employed for a total of nine years by IKO . . . Her current job primarily involves gathering and testing samples and recording the information.

On April 11th, she had gone to the canteen . . . to get a glass of water. As she returned to the lab, she placed the glass . . . on a desk. The grievor entered behind her. She was not feeling comfortable, so she moved to the middle of the lab away from the grievor. Mr. Rejean Deslauriers, [her] supervisor, was adjusting the . . . oven in the middle of the lab, close to where Ms. M. was standing.

After using the telephone located near the entrance to the lab, the grievor walked . . . to the middle of the lab and stopped about two feet from Ms. M. He reached out and grabbed [her] sweatshirt by the lower hem and pulled it down and said, "[E]xactly what do you have written on your shirt?" Ms. M. grabbed the grievor's wrists and pulled his hands away and said "Don't touch the clothes." The grievor said "[W]hy?" Ms. M. pushed his hands away and turned and left the room crying. [She] testified that the grievor said "why" in such a way that she felt as if [he] was asserting a right to touch the clothes on her body.

Mr. Deslauriers did not see what the grievor had done. Ms. M. showed [him] and told him she could not keep coming to work and having this to deal with. She went to see Renee Bernatchez, the human resources coordinator. The following day . . . Ms. M. testified that she was approached by Mr. Deslauriers who said that the grievor had written a letter of apology and would she accept it. She said no because she felt that anyone who was truly sorry would apologize face to face.

Ms. M. also testified about an incident between herself and the grievor which had occurred in the first part of December 2000. Following the Christmas party, she was standing by the water fountain in the canteen. The grievor approached her from behind and poked her on both sides above the waist. Nothing was said at that time.

Ms. M. reported this incident to Mr. Horner, and they discussed what to do. Since this incident occurred only days following the harassment training, they determined to follow the instructions received during the training. Ms. M. went to find the grievor in the canteen, and they both went to the lab. Ms. M. advised the grievor that she did not appreciate being poked in the ribs, and that she wanted that sort of treatment to stop . . .

Ms. M. also testified concerning an incident in October 2000. She was testing at the mini-lab. The grievor approached and pulled her toward him. She had nowhere to go and felt trapped. She told the grievor she was not comfortable, and to give her some space. The grievor let go. Ms. M. reported the incident to Mr. Horner and he asked what [she] wanted done. Ms. M. advised that she would wait to see what happened.

Ms. M. also testified that in, in June 2000, the grievor approached and pressed up against her from behind, which left her feeling very uncomfortable.

In her evidence Ms. M. stated that, between December 2000 and April 2001, she had no incidents with the grievor and felt that the issues had been resolved. Following the April . . . incident, however, Ms. M. testified that she would feel uncomfortable if the grievor was reinstated to employment, and that, in such circumstances, she did not know if she could continue working. In response to questions from the Union's representative, Ms. M. stated that her purpose in reporting the incident to her supervisor was to have the behaviour stopped and to have something put into the grievor's personnel file.

Evidence concerning the grievor's behaviour was also given by Mr. Boyd. He stated that he met with the grievor on December 15, 2000 concerning an incident . . . that [had] occurred at an off-site training seminar. According to Mr. Boyd, Ms. Bernatchez had reported to him that, at this training seminar, the grievor had placed his hands on her shoulders and neck and massaged them, making Ms. Bernatchez feel uncomfortable.

The grievor testified that he did not remember the incident with Ms. Bernatchez but that if he did it, he was sorry and would apologize. Mr. Boyd advised that he was not going to document it but that he did not want the incident repeated.

The grievor testified that he also did not recall the incidents of October or June 2000 which were testified to by Ms. M. Concerning the incident of December 11, 2000, the grievor stated that he poked Ms. M. in the ribs in jest, and that after she told him she did not like it, he advised her that it would never happen again.

With respect to the incident on April 11th, the grievor stated that he recognized it was wrong, regrets it, and never intended it to be harassment of Ms. M. He stated that he went to to to the lab to telephone his wife to wake her up . . . He stated he approached Ms. M. out of curiosity to see what was written on her sweater. He acknowledged pulling Ms. M's sweater down by the bottom. He stated that he did not know what prompted him to pull her sweater down, except that he wanted to see what was written on it. He stated that he knew Ms. M. was upset by his actions.

He stated that he was called to Mr. Deslauriers' office where he was suspended pending an investigation and told to leave the premises immediately. He testified that he prepared a letter of apology which was typed by his daughter. He called a fellow employee. They met in the . . . parking lot and the grievor gave him the letter of apology for delivery to Ms. M. on his behalf. The grievor stated that he had been suspended and that if he had attempted to give the apology to Ms. M. personally it might only have made matters worse. The apology [read] as follows:

> April 12, 2001
> I realize my action disturbed you a lot and I realize you felt dis-turb [sic] and offended. It was not my intention to threaten you or make you feel uncomfortable. I sincerely apologize for my action and it will not be repeated.
>
> *Guy Lacelle*

In the Employer's submission, the grievor had engaged in conduct which amounted to sexual harassment, and there were no mitigating factors which would indicate that the penalty of discharge should be modified. In the Employer's view there must be identifiable and tangible factors to permit a board of arbitration to interfere with the [Employer's] decision . . . and no such factors existed in this case.

In the Employer's submission, despite [repeated] . . . warnings, the grievor still did not understand that his conduct was offensive and wrong, and therefore discharge was the appropriate penalty . . .

In the Union's submission, the issue is whether the grievor's conduct was such . . . as to indicate that he is beyond rehabilitation, or put another way, whether further progressive discipline was indicated so that the grievor would have an opportunity to correct his behaviour? According to the Union, the grievor's conduct was not of such gravity, nor was the grievor's disciplinary record so serious, as to indicate that the grievor could not be reintegrated into the workplace. The Union referred to the grievor's twenty-six years of seniority, that he had offered a letter of apology, and the grievor's evidence that he was truly sorry and that it would not happen again . . .

Case Questions

1. Do you think the employer's definition of sexual harassment is a reasonable one? Why, or why not?

2. Give some examples of interaction between employees which do you *not* think would be considered sexual harassment.

3. Explain why you do, or do not, consider the grievor's behaviour toward Ms. M. to constitute sexual harassment.

4. Do you think Ms. M. responded appropriately?

5. Do you think management responded appropriately? Why or why not? If you don't think management responded appropriately, please indicate what else you think management should have done.

6. What would likely be the penalty for an individual found to have behaved as Mr. Lacelle did in your workplace?

7. What would be some examples of "mitigating circumstances" which might induce an arbitrator to substitute a penalty less extreme than discharge? Do you think any such circumstances apply here?

8. How do you think an arbitrator will rule in this case? Please explain the basis for your view.

GRIEVANCE PROCEDURES

Collective agreements generally spell out grievance procedures in fairly consider-able detail. A 1978 study by Jeffrey Gandz (quoted in Gandz and Whitehead, 1989) found that Ontario grievance procedures had anywhere from two to seven steps, with three being the most common number. A verbal stage involving a discussion between the grievor (often accompanied by a union steward) and the supervisor appeared in about two-thirds of the procedures, often as the official first stage (ibid.). If the problem couldn't be resolved verbally, the grievance would then be put in writing and submitted to the next level of management above the supervisor. Most grievance procedures contained strict time limits for each stage; however, almost all also contained provisions allowing the parties to opt out of the time lim-its by mutual consent. A common feature was a semi-official "extra step" in which senior management and union officials would meet on a regular basis to review cases pending arbitration (ibid.).

Since 1978, the typical grievance process doesn't appear to have changed much. Most grievance processes that the author has examined contain either three or four official stages; many contain an additional unofficial stage either at the beginning or end of the process. The procedure in the University of Ottawa agreement discussed earlier is slightly more expeditious than some others in that it contains only one step between denial of the initial written grievance and refer-ral to arbitration: a meeting between the grievor (accompanied by a union repre-sentative) and the Dean to explore the possibilities of settlement. However, by allowing the parties to opt out of the time limits at any stage, the procedure has failed to address one of the major causes of delay noted in the literature (namely, failure to observe time limits).

The procedure outlined in Table 12.1, based on one described by Trotta (1976), would not be atypical, even today.

Table 12.1

A SAMPLE GRIEVANCE PROCEDURE

Step 1 **(oral discussion, filing of grievance).** Meeting between supervisor and aggrieved employee, accompanied by shop steward. If problem not satisfactorily resolved in three working days, grievance to be reduced to writing and Step 2 taken.

Step 2 **(discussion between shop steward and department head).** Shop steward to discuss grievance with department head. If grievance not satisfactorily adjusted within three working days, then Step 3 shall be taken.

Step 3 **(discussion between senior management and union officials).** Grievance committee consisting of four members appointed by the union to meet with plant manager or his or her appointed representative. The aggrieved employee and a representative from the international union may also be present.

Step 4 **(referral to arbitration).** If grievance not settled, dispute may be taken to arbitration providing either party has given written notice requesting arbitration within 15 working days after the end of the Step 3 meeting. The parties designate a mutually satisfactory arbitrator. If they cannot agree on one within three days after the arbitration request, then the appropriate government agency shall, at the request of either party, provide both parties with a list.

ISSUES MOST COMMONLY GRIEVED

Discharge and discipline are the issues most commonly grieved by unions. A study by Gandz and Whitehead (1989) of grievances in a basic steelworks found that about half of all grievances were of a disciplinary nature. Seniority accounted for another 15 to 20 percent of the grievances, the remainder being related to such issues as job postings, overtime, health and safety, and the performance of bargaining unit work by supervisors. For Ontario as a whole, a more comprehensive study by Adams (1978:40) found that discharge and discipline cases constituted 37 percent of all grievances sent to arbitration.[5] While management grievances against the union are rare, they do exist. Most typically (as in the case of the steelworks described by Gandz and Whitehead), such grievances would result from an illegal work stoppage. As for the causes of dismissal, both Adams (1978) and Barnacle (1991) found dishonesty, poor work performance, insubordination, poor attendance, alcohol, failure to get along, and union activity[6] to be the seven types of behaviour most commonly leading to dismissal.

THE ARBITRATION PROCESS

Panels versus Single Arbitrators

Arbitration decisions may be made either by single arbitrators or three-person panels. If a three-person panel is used, the union and management each select one member and a third party neutral (agreed upon by both the union and management) serves as chairperson of the panel. This effectively makes the chair the decision maker, since the panel need only reach a majority decision, not a unanimous one (Thornicroft and Eden, 1995:260). Indeed, even if neither nominee agrees with the neutral's decision, the chair's decision will generally be deemed to be the final award (Craig and Solomon, 1996:340).

Numerous studies have found that single arbitrators reach their decisions more quickly than three-person panels and that the single-person process generally costs a good deal less (Goldblatt, 1974; Rose, 1987; Button, 1990; Thornicroft and Eden, 1995). Other studies (i.e., Barnacle, 1991) have found little difference in grievance outcomes whether a panel or a single arbitrator was used. No doubt as a result, in recent years a decreasing percentage of cases have been heard by three-person panels. For example, in Ontario between 1980 and 1984, about 58 percent of conventional arbitration cases were heard by panels (Rose, 1986a). But by 1985–1986, panels were being used in only about a third of those cases (Rose, 1991). Recent trends towards expedited arbitration procedures (discussed later in the chapter) have almost certainly made panels still less common since then.

The Arbitration Hearing

Arbitration hearings are normally held in neutral settings (often hotel meeting rooms (Gandz and Whitehead, 1989:249)). While there is no requirement that parties be represented by legal counsel, unions and, especially, management organizations have been using such counsel increasingly in recent years (Arthurs, 1988; Barnacle, 1991). When the union doesn't use a lawyer, the case is most often presented by a business agent or a national or international representative (Gandz and Whitehead, 1989:249).

Often there will be preliminary objections to a grievance. These include allegations that the agreement's time limits have been breached, that the arbitrator lacks jurisdiction because the provision breached is not in the collective agreement but rather in a subsidiary document such as a letter of intent, or that the grievance has already been withdrawn, abandoned, or settled (Sack, 1994:75–76; Gandz and Whitehead, 1989:249–250). While the respondent may argue that the arbitrator should adjourn the hearing until the preliminary objection has been decided, the normal practice is for the arbitrator to reserve judgment on the preliminary objection, proceed to hear the grievance proper, and include his or her ruling on the preliminary objection in the final award, so as to avoid delay and additional expense (Sack, 1994:69–70,75–76).

Once any preliminary objections have been dealt with, the hearing normally proceeds as follows:

1. Each party makes an opening statement in which the nature of the grievance and the issues in dispute are raised (Gandz and Whitehead, 1989:249). Since the union is normally the party filing the grievance, the union will normally speak first. However, in discharge and discipline cases, where the onus of proof is on the employer, the employer will normally present first (Sack, 1994:70–71; Peach and Kuechle, 1975:248). The party making the first opening statement has the opportunity to reply to new points raised by the other party in their opening statement (Sack, 1994:77). The grievor's opening statement should include the remedy sought (e.g., reinstatement in the case of dismissal) and, if it is a dismissal grievance, the amount of income she or he has lost since the discharge, to guide the arbitrator in making a back pay award (Sack, 1994:79).[7]

2. The party on whom the onus of proof rests (normally the union, except in discharge and discipline cases) calls witnesses, who give evidence, generally under oath (Gandz and Whitehead, 1989:250). Each witness is cross-examined by the other party and then re-examined by the first party. Witnesses may also be questioned by the arbitrator and by the panelists if there is a three-person panel (Gandz and Whitehead, 1989). It's important to bear in mind that the rules about what kind of evidence an arbitrator can accept are much less strict than those applied to formal court cases. In general, labour relations legislation empowers arbitrators to accept any evidence they consider proper, whether or not such evidence would be admissible in a court of law (Sack, 1994:81–82). It's also important that no witness be "badgered" in cross-examination to the extent that that a witness feels unfairly harassed. Should this happen, the other side's representative or the arbitrator may intervene, and the arbitrator's ultimate decision may be negatively influenced (Sanderson, 1976: 66–67).

   In evaluating the evidence before them, arbitrators will hold the parties to different levels of proof, depending on the nature of the grievance (Thornicroft and Eden, 1995:258). In most cases, the standard of civil trials, proof on "a balance of probabilities," is required (Thornicroft and Eden, 1995; Sack, 1994:81).

This simply means that the side bearing the burden of proof must establish that its version of the facts is likelier to be true (Sack, 1994:81). However, in discharge cases, particularly those involving allegations of serious misconduct such as theft or dishonesty, the degree of probability that must be met is commensurate with the seriousness of the allegations and the quality of the evidence must be somewhat more convincing.

3. The responding party also calls witnesses, who then give evidence and are cross-examined and re-examined as in the case of the first party's witnesses.

4. Each side then presents its closing argument, normally in the same order as the initial presentation (Peach and Kuechle, 1975:247). Such closing arguments will often cite arbitration decisions made in similar cases (Gandz and Whitehead, 1989:250).

5. The arbitrator then adjourns the hearing. If sitting as the chair of a three-person panel, he or she confers with the other panel members. If acting as a sole arbitrator, he or she then prepares the award. If there is a panel, he or she prepares a draft award and seeks input from the panelists. The final written award is then sent to the parties (*OLRA*, section 48[9]). The arbitrator's or panel's decision is binding on the parties and on the employees covered by the agreement affected by the decision (*OLRA*, section 48[18]).

Enforcement

Most labour acts lay out a procedure for enforcing arbitration awards where either party refuses to comply. In Ontario, the award may be filed in the General Division of the Ontario Court (*OLRA*, section 48[19]) and enforced much as any other court judgment, through contempt proceedings for continued non-compliance (Sack, 1994:141). Thus, if parties continue to ignore the arbitrator's award after it has been filed with the court, they risk a fine or even imprisonment (Thornicroft and Eden, 1995:262).

Judicial Review of Awards

In general, Canadian jurisdictions are reluctant to use the courts to overturn arbitrators' decisions. A number of provinces attempt to limit judicial review of arbitration awards through a **privative clause** (Thornicroft and Eden, 1995). An example is section 101 of BC's labour act, which provides that except as noted in the act, any arbitration award or decision is final and not open to question or review in a court on any grounds whatever. Another section of the same act does grant the labour relations board limited power to review an arbitration award where a party has been denied a fair hearing or where the award is inconsistent with the principles of the labour act (Thornicroft and Eden, 1995; Sack, 1994:141–142). To date, most other provinces have not granted their labour boards this power (Sack, 1994:142).

In general, requests to appeal an arbitration decision are rarely granted, although, as we shall see later in the chapter, recent court decisions may have opened the door to an increased number of appeals. Appeals are most likely to be granted in cases where the arbitrator has shown bias, denied a party a fair hearing,

privative clause A clause in a labour relations act limiting or in some cases barring judicial review of arbitration awards.

or made an incorrect interpretation of a common law principle or a statutory provision lying outside his or her "core area of expertise" (Sack, 1994). Appeals will also be granted in cases where the arbitrator has made a jurisdictional error (i.e., an error relating to a legislative provision limiting his or her remedial powers).[8]

ARBITRATION OUTCOMES

To date, there has been no single, comprehensive study on all aspects of arbitration outcomes. There have, however, been a great many studies of a more limited nature seeking to relate arbitration outcomes to such factors as arbitrator characteristics, grievor characteristics, the type of issue grieved, and the use of legal counsel by the two parties.[9] Overall, the evidence appears to be fairly inconclusive as to whether arbitrator and grievor characteristics such as age, gender, education, and experience significantly affect the outcomes of arbitration cases (see Thornicroft and Eden, 1995:268–270). A much more significant issue may be the extent to which women, non-lawyers, and younger people find it possible to enter the profession at all. A 1988 survey by Brian Bemmels (see Thornicroft and Eden, 1995:264) revealed that only 7 percent were women, 63 percent held a law degree, and the average age was nearly 56. Similar results were obtained in several other studies reviewed by Thornicroft and Eden (1995). In principle, it would seem desirable to have a cadre of arbitrators whose demographic characteristics more closely approximate the diversity of the workforce. To the extent that the various provincial arbitrator development programs (see Thornicroft, 2005) allow more women, non-lawyers, and younger people to enter the field, they will be performing a very useful service indeed.[10]

Discharge Cases

Because the impact of discharge cases both on individual workers and on organizational morale can be so dramatic, these cases are of special importance in industrial relations. This may explain why they have been more intensely studied than other types of grievance cases. For the most part, except in cases involving a single extremely serious offence such as theft, assault, or sabotage, arbitrators expect employers to have applied **progressive discipline**, whereby the penalties have increased for each succeeding offence and the employee has been made aware of the possibility of further penalties up to and including discharge for any further offences (Adams, 1978; Thornicroft and Eden, 1995).[11] The purpose here is twofold: First, it informs employees that their conduct is unacceptable and states what the consequences will be should such conduct continue. Second, it allows them to correct the offending behaviour, where this is possible. The development of progressive discipline as the accepted norm for most dismissals arguably represents the single most important modification of the otherwise dominant doctrine of residual management rights. Slightly over half of all discharged employees who grieve their dismissals are reinstated, many with back pay (McPhillips and England, 1995:81).

Somewhat surprisingly, one's likelihood of reinstatement doesn't seem to depend very heavily on the type of offence one has allegedly committed. In George

progressive discipline A system of discipline whereby the penalties are increased for each succeeding offence and the employee is made aware of the possibility of further penalties should he or she repeat the offence in question.

Adams' 1978 study, 53.5 percent of grievors were reinstated. The proportion of employees reinstated for different categories of misconduct ranged from 38 percent for attendance and 39 percent for poor work performance and dishonesty to 58 percent for union activity and 55 percent for alcohol-related offences. A later (1991) study by Peter Barnacle yielded essentially similar results. Some 54 percent of all grievors were reinstated, and slightly over half (51 percent) of all dismissals for dishonesty were sustained, as compared to 25 percent of those for union activity and 35 percent of those for alcohol-related offences. Only 12 percent of all those discharged were exonerated (i.e., awarded full compensation).[12]

Of far more significance than the type of offence allegedly committed was the grievor's previous disciplinary record. Adams found that a full 94 percent of those with no previous disciplinary record were reinstated, as compared to just under 60 percent for those with a prior disciplinary warning, and only 39 percent for those with a previous suspension. Similarly, Barnacle found that dismissals were sustained for 68 percent of those with a prior record related to the dismissal offence, and 47 percent of those with some kind of prior record, but for only 23 percent of those with no prior disciplinary record. These findings point strongly towards arbitral use of progressive discipline as a criterion in determining the appropriate penalty for a given offence (see Thornicroft and Eden, 1995:269).

An all-too-familiar criticism of the IR system concerns the length of time it takes to bring most cases before an arbitrator. Adams's study in particular lends some support to this criticism. He found that the longer it took arbitrators to hear cases, the less likely a grievor was to be reinstated or to receive any back pay. In cases heard within three months of discharge, only 29 percent of the dismissals were sustained and 29 percent of the grievors were exonerated. However, in cases heard more than six months after the discharge, 62 percent of the dismissals were sustained and only 10 percent of the grievors exonerated (1978:50–51). Such findings lend support to the hypothesis, discussed in the labour law chapter, that expedited arbitration systems can be of considerable benefit to workers and unions.

Use of Legal Counsel

The use of legal counsel by management and unions has frequently been cited as the cause of delays in arbitration cases (Rose, 1987; Elliott and Goss, 1994; Thornicroft and Eden, 1995). Since lawyers are also expensive, the question naturally arises, why do parties continue to use them? The answer, as revealed by a number of studies (i.e., Goldblatt, 1974; Barnacle, 1991), is quite simple. If you have a lawyer and your opponent doesn't, you are more likely to win the case. If, on the other hand, your opponent has a lawyer and you don't, you're more likely to lose. Therefore, if there is any chance at all that your opponent will be using legal counsel, you would be well advised, from a purely practical perspective, to follow suit (see Barnacle, 1991:163). At the same time, since lawyers appear to make little difference to arbitration outcomes when neither party uses them or when both do (Thornicroft and Eden, 1995:265), the logical corollary is that both sides could achieve substantial time and money savings simply by agreeing not to use legal counsel at all.

Lawyers as Arbitrators

As we noted earlier, the vast majority of arbitrators come from the legal profession (Barnacle, 1991; Thornicroft and Eden, 1995). This raises the question of whether lawyer-arbitrators arrive at different outcomes than do arbitrators from other professions, such as economics or industrial relations. While space does not permit a detailed discussion of this issue, Barnacle's findings[13] suggest that the differences between lawyers and arbitrators from other backgrounds are generally rather slight. Similarly, Terry Wagar's 1994 study and Thornicroft and Eden's review of eight studies (1995:268) found little difference in outcomes between cases decided by lawyers and those decided by people from different backgrounds, a finding which lends further support to the notion that the quality of arbitration decisions would probably not suffer from opening up the profession to individuals from a broader range of backgrounds.

Other Outcomes

Dastmalchian and Ng (1990) found that grievances were more likely to be granted in organizations with a positive industrial relations climate than in those with a negative one. In another study, this one of the Canadian federal public sector (Ng and Dastmalchian, 1989), the same two authors found that grievances were more often settled at early stages of the internal grievance procedure, and that higher-status employees were more apt to have their grievances granted than lower-status employees.

A number of studies, including most notably one by Brett and Goldberg (1983), have found that grievances are rarely settled at the middle stages of internal grievance procedures. In effect, what seemed to be happening was that middle-level managers and union officials were simply rubber-stamping their subordinates' decisions and passing the matter up to someone with real power to decide the case. This finding has important implications for the development of grievance mediation systems and other alternatives to conventional arbitration.

CRITICISMS OF CONVENTIONAL ARBITRATION

There is by now a substantial literature on the failings of the conventional arbitration process. Most of this literature (i.e., Nolan and Abrams, 1997; Button, 1990) laments the transformation of grievance arbitration from an informal, speedy, and relatively inexpensive process to a slow, costly, and highly legalistic one. Another major criticism is that, because arbitration has become so slow and so costly, only a very small percentage of all grievances filed—2 percent or less, according to various studies (e.g., Foisy, 1998; Gandz and Whitehead, 1989:240)—are actually heard by an arbitrator. Still another criticism is that because the union "owns" the grievance process and individual workers cannot, for the most part, file their own grievances, the individual worker has little redress if the union decides not to file his or her grievance (Godard, 1994:360).

In this section, we examine the time delays, costs, legalism, and inaccessibility of conventional arbitration, leaving the broader and more systemic question of union ownership of the process to a concluding section.

Time Delays

If good labour–management relations are to be maintained, it's essential that grievances be resolved as quickly as possible. As the well-known case of Canada Post (see Stewart-Patterson, 1987) attests far too clearly, large backlogs of unsettled grievances often represent industrial relations "time bombs" waiting to explode. Unfortunately, the time required to settle grievances under conventional arbitration seems to be increasing. Various studies reviewed by Thornicroft and Eden (1995:267) found the total length of time from the action that inspired the grievance to the issuing of the arbitration award to be anywhere from six to fourteen months, with delays of eight to twelve months most common. Even more troubling, a 1996 study by Ponak, Zerbe, Rose, and Olson found that the average length of time from initial filing to issuance of the award had doubled over the previous two decades (see Thornicroft, 2005). At Canada Post, delays of more than a year have often been the norm, with delays of more than two years not uncommon (Stewart-Patterson, 1987). For obvious reasons, lengthy delays are of particular concern in discharge cases; employees who lose their job and cannot find another will almost certainly undergo considerable hardship. In addition, as was noted above, the longer the arbitration process takes, the less likely employees are to be reinstated.

Costs

Though arbitration may indeed be less expensive than litigation in the courts, it's still far from cheap. The total expenses for a single-arbitrator case where the hearing itself is finished in one day typically range from $2500 to $10 000 (Thornicroft, 2005); when the hearing is longer, the fees will obviously be proportionally higher. Where there is a three-person panel, panelists must also be paid, lodged, and fed. And when parties use legal counsel, they must pay lawyers' fees that can range from $100 to upwards of $300 per hour (Thornicroft and Eden, 1995). And this doesn't take into account the value of the time the parties themselves put into preparing and presenting the case. The mounting costs of the arbitration process have threatened, in the words of Thornicroft (2005:382) to make arbitration the more or less exclusive preserve of large unions and employers with the resources to afford it. Indeed, Thornicroft notes that the cost of arbitration may be a factor explaining the recent trend toward mergers of smaller unions.

Legalism

As Elliott and Goss (1994:12) have noted, arbitration hearings are all too likely to become bogged down in technical legal arguments, rather than concerning themselves with the merits of the grievance at issue. In their view, the problem has been exacerbated by the growing use of legal counsel in recent years and by the excessive number of cases that arbitrators and arbitration panels are forced to read, digest, and incorporate into their awards. Because of this excessive reliance on precedents, arbitrators take significantly longer to write their awards than they otherwise would, and the costs to the parties are greater. Moreover, when at long last awards are issued, they are often so weighted down with legal citations as to be very difficult for anyone but a lawyer to understand. The growing requirement that arbitrators apply "external" statutes such as employment standards and human rights legislation to their decisions will certainly do little to counteract the ongoing trend toward greater legalism in arbitration.

Accessibility

It isn't really surprising that so few cases are taken through to arbitration. With the cost of most arbitration cases running to four figures if not five, few management organizations and fewer unions could ever hope to take more than a tiny fraction of all grievances to arbitration. While some grievances may be resolved informally, many grievors, including some with very legitimate complaints, simply do not obtain a hearing for their cases. Such workers are likely to feel considerable frustration, and they can pose serious problems both for management and for their own union officials.

ALTERNATIVES TO CONVENTIONAL ARBITRATION

Growing awareness of the problems of conventional arbitration has led to the development of a number of innovative alternatives. Three of the most important for our purposes are **expedited arbitration**, which speeds up the arbitration process and reduces its cost, **grievance mediation**, where a third-party neutral helps the parties negotiate a solution to the grievance to prevent it from going to arbitration, and **preventive mediation**, where the parties seek to improve communications and develop proactive problem-solving mechanisms that will improve their overall relationship and thus prevent most problems from becoming formal grievances.

Expedited Arbitration

Most of the delay in arbitration cases results from cumbersome internal grievance processes, the use of three-person panels, dickering over the choice of an arbitrator or chairperson, the use of legal counsel at hearings, and long waits between the hearing and the issuing of an award. To counter these difficulties, a number of expedited arbitration systems have been developed both by governments and by unions and management working on their own. Though there are certain differences between the various systems, most observe the principles in Table 12.2, below.

The Canadian Railway Office of Arbitration (CROA) is a good example of a private sector arbitration system that has earned its spurs. This system, which has been in effect since 1965 (Button, 1990:30), uses a standing umpire who normally

expedited arbitration Any grievance arbitration system that has introduced mechanisms (e.g., the use of a single arbitrator, the use of a standing umpire, oral decisions or limits on the length of written decisions) to speed up the grievance resolution process.

grievance mediation A grievance settlement mechanism whereby a third-party neutral seeks to help the parties resolve the dispute themselves rather than sending it through to arbitration.

preventive mediation Voluntary third-party assistance aimed at improving the parties' communication and overall relationship with an eye to reducing grievance levels.

hears cases starting on the second Tuesday of each month (Button, 1990:36). The umpire will sit for up to three days if necessary (Button, 1990:39), hearing on average 13 cases at a sitting (Button, 1990:36). The grouping of cases means that where there is a delay in one case (as when the parties decide to try to settle the matter themselves) the umpire can simply move on to the next and return to the first when the parties are ready to proceed. Cases are presented in the form of written briefs, which reduces (though it hasn't completely eliminated) the use of legal counsel at hearings (Button, 1990:37).[14] In 1987–1988, the CROA simplified its procedures further by deciding to limit the use of counsel to discharge cases, unless the parties agreed otherwise (Button, 1990). The system has resulted in significant cost savings. For 1987–1988, the average cost per case was $1295 (Button, 1990:41), or 29 percent that of cases heard under conventional arbitration in the province (Rose, 1987). Best of all, the system has succeeded in doing what arbitration was originally intended to do: provide a quick, relatively inexpensive mechanism for resolving disputes over the interpretation of the collective agreement (Rose, 1987).

Though the CROA system of expedited arbitration is perhaps the country's best-known private sector system, it isn't the only one. An essentially similar grievance commissioner system was adopted in 1972 by Inco and two United Steelworkers locals (Thornicroft and Eden, 1995:273). And in Vancouver, the once strike-plagued longshoring industry has long relied on a "dockside arbitrator" who is on call 24 hours a day and, travelling by motor launch or helicopter if necessary, can be on the site anywhere in the port within an hour or two to render an instant on-the-spot decision orally (J. Weiler, 1984).[15] At various times, other expedited systems have been used in the garment, motor transport, and auto industry in Canada, as well as in numerous American industries (Gandz and Whitehead, 1989:251–252).

As we noted earlier (see Chapter 7), public expedited arbitration systems are in place in four provinces (BC, Manitoba, Ontario, and Saskatchewan). In three of them, expedited arbitration can be combined with prior grievance mediation,[17] further reducing costs and increasing the number of cases resolved. Section 49 of

Table 12.2

THE WAY TO QUICKER ARBITRATION DECISIONS[16]

1. Always use a single arbitrator rather than a three-person panel.
2. Where possible, have a standing umpire who will hear cases at the same time each week or month (e.g., the third Thursday of every month). This allows the arbitrator to hear a number of cases on the same day. It also ensures that the arbitrator "knows the business"—and may control costs in addition, since the umpire will be on monthly or annual retainer.
3. If a standing umpire isn't possible, then draw from a list you have agreed on in advance in an order you have agreed on in advance (e.g., alphabetical order).
4. Agree not to use legal counsel, or at least to restrict its use to complicated policy grievances.
5. Eliminate steps of the internal grievance procedure that don't seem to be producing any significant number of settlements, and consider replacing them with grievance mediation (discussed below).
6. Adhere strictly to time limits in any remaining steps.
7. Simplify procedural requirements as much as possible, by allowing oral decisions in straightforward cases, reducing the use of precedents, and requiring short written decisions very soon after the hearing.

the Ontario act sets out that province's expedited arbitration procedure. Under the *OLRA*, either party may apply to the Labour Minister for appointment of a single arbitrator. The arbitrator, drawn from a list maintained by the ministry, must schedule a hearing within 21 days of the request (section 49[7]) and issue an award within 21 days of the hearing. If both parties agree, the arbitrator may deliver an oral decision immediately after the hearing (Sec. 49[8]).

Over the years, expedited arbitration has become increasingly popular in Ontario. By 1992–1993, some 45 percent of all arbitration awards in the province were of the expedited variety, as compared to 19 percent in 1981–1982 (Thornicroft and Eden, 1995:272). The system has been shown to save both time and money. According to Rose (1991), between 1980–1981 and 1985–1986, expedited arbitration alone saved $2.2 million. Time savings were even greater, as the average elapsed time between the incident giving rise to the grievance and an expedited award was only four months, compared to eleven months under conventional arbitration (Thornicroft and Eden, 1995:272).

Grievance Mediation

One criticism of all arbitration systems, even expedited ones, is that they serve to foster an adversarial mentality by establishing a "winner" and a "loser," thus damaging ongoing relationships (Elliott and Goss, 1994). Grievance mediation, used either on its own or in conjunction with a system of expedited arbitration, can get around this difficulty by helping the parties to resolve their differences themselves. Instead of damaging the ongoing relationship, it can actually strengthen it by developing problem-solving skills that can later be applied to other areas of the relationship. In addition, its costs are quite low compared to those of arbitration.[18] And arbitration is still available should mediation fail. The process is confidential in that, unless both parties consent, nothing said or done there can be used as evidence in subsequent legal proceedings (Thornicroft and Eden, 1995:273). Normally no formal record of the proceedings is kept, except to record any agreement reached (Elliott and Goss, 1994:32). As well, settlements are without prejudice to either party, which means that no precedent created by the settlement can be used in any future cases (Thornicroft and Eden, 1995:273).

Mediation focuses on effective communication and negotiation skills (Elliott and Goss, 1994:27). The mediator's role is not to "settle" the dispute, but to help the parties communicate and negotiate more effectively, thus increasing the likelihood they will reach agreement on their own (Elliott and Goss, 1994). A typical mediation session might consist of the following four stages (Elliott and Goss, 1994:27–29):

1. Introduction. Here, the mediator explains the process and his or her role and seeks to create an atmosphere in which the parties feel free to speak openly. It is at this time that the ground rules for mediation are laid out.

2. Creating an agenda. Where the parties have not agreed on an agenda beforehand, one is established, normally through brief presentations by the parties outlining the issues they would like to see resolved. After the presentations, which would normally be followed by clarifying questions from the other side and the mediator, key points are identified to form the agenda.

3. Discussing interests. Here, each party has the opportunity to present its side of the story. The mediator will seek clarification of anything that appears unclear and will also seek to ensure that each party hears and understands the other's perspective, whether or not they agree with it. At this stage, common ground and agreed-upon facts are identified, in addition to any facts that may be in dispute. It is at this stage that the mediator seeks to reduce the dispute to its basic elements and to focus on the parties' underlying needs and interests.

4. Problem solving. Here, the mediator takes the information obtained in the previous stages and uses it to help the parties find a mutually agreeable solution, initiating suggestions for a possible solution where appropriate (Thornicroft and Eden, 1995:273). This may be done on either an issue-by-issue or "total package" basis.

The decision as to the best time to use mediation is often a judgment call. Ideally, it should be used at the earliest possible point in the dispute; where a relationship is very poor, it may even be used before the usual Stage 1 grievance meeting (Elliott and Goss, 1994:29). Often, the best stage can be determined empirically, from an examination of settlement rates at different points of the agreement's internal grievance process. If there is any step where settlement rates are particularly low, that would be a good place to insert grievance mediation (see Elliott and Goss, 1994:29–30). The Brett-Goldberg study (1983) cited below suggests that this place may well be somewhere in the middle of the process, where currently few cases are being resolved.

Grievance mediation has been used in four provinces, most often as a first stage in an expedited arbitration process. In Ontario, Rose (1991) found that voluntary grievance mediation had saved some $6.4 million between 1980–1981 and 1985–1986. As of the early 1990s (Craig and Solomon, 1996:351), about 80 percent of all expedited arbitration cases were being resolved through mediation. Unfortunately, the Ontario government has since discontinued this most useful and innovative program. However, it remains in effect in Alberta, Manitoba, and BC, where similar results have been obtained (Elliott and Goss, 1994:41–52), and in the private sector in the United States.[19] For example, in the American bituminous coal industry (Brett and Goldberg, 1983), an industry long notorious for its poor labour–management relations, 153 grievances were mediated between 1980 and 1982. Of these, 89 percent were resolved without arbitration. Likewise, of 2220 grievances mediated by the Chicago-based Mediation Research and Education Project between 1980 and 1982, about 85 percent were resolved without arbitration (Elliott and Goss, 1994:52).[20]

Current Issues 12.1

ALTERNATIVE DISPUTE RESOLUTION

ELEMENTS OF CONFLICT RESOLUTION (CR) AT DFO (THE DEPARTMENT OF FISHERIES AND OCEANS)

. . . When [seeking] to resolve a workplace conflict, the CR advisor will promote the use of informal conflict resolution processes that focus on the [parties'] needs and interests. ▶

Principles

. . . It is essential that all parties agree to share information openly, on a good faith basis, with the understanding that information disclosed during the conflict resolution process is provided on a without prejudice basis.

. . . The parties are encouraged to discuss their concerns and feelings openly while refraining from personal attacks. The CR advisor establishes ground rules to create a safe and respectful atmosphere . . .

. . . participation is voluntary . . . Either party may withdraw . . . at any time with no fear of retribution.

Formal Recourse Processes

In the first meeting with a CR advisor, the advisor will explore all alternatives to a negotiated settlement with the parties . . . The CR advisor will encourage the parties . . . to seek advice from union representatives and human resource advisors before agreeing to participate in an informal conflict resolution process.

The parties must agree to put all other recourse processes in abeyance in accordance with the rules of those processes and take no new steps in any other recourse process while using CR's informal process . . . Management will not invoke timeliness to deny a staff relations grievance when an individual has contacted and involved the CR office before their right to grieve has lapsed . . .

VICR's Informal Conflict Resolution Process

If all the parties involved . . . agree, one or both of the parties may be accompanied or represented by another person (e.g., a union representative, a human resource advisor or a colleague) during the informal conflict resolution process. If the issues in dispute revolve around the interpretation or application of a collective agreement, a union representative must be involved.

The CR advisor is an impartial and neutral party who . . . does not act as a judge [or] make a determination for the parties . . . The parties involved in the informal conflict resolution process talk to each other, not to the advisor. Discussions generally occur with everyone in the room. Occasionally, discussions may take place in "caucus" (i.e., a separate meeting) with the advisor. Unless the parties agree in advance that the confidentiality of the information disclosed in caucus will be protected, [this] information will normally be disclosed in joint sessions.

Settlement Agreements

. . . If the informal conflict resolution process does not result in a mutual agreement, the parties retain the option to pursue a formal recourse process.

The authority to resolve the conflict and to approve any agreement will be explored with the parties by the CR advisor. If the parties do not have the authority to finalize the agreement, they may agree that, upon resolution of the conflict, the informal resolution process will be adjourned to obtain the approvals necessary to finalize the agreement.

Source: "Elements of Conflict Resolution at DFO," Annex E, Informal Conflict Management System (ICMS) Resource Guide, PSHRMAC, draft prepared Nov. 2004. Reproduced with the permission of the Minister of Public Works and Government Services Canada, 2006.

Preventive Mediation

While it's good to save time and money through an expedited arbitration process, and better to use grievance mediation to prevent grievances from even being taken through to arbitration, it's best of all, where possible, to improve the labour–management relationship so that problems are handled proactively, as they arise, before they become formal grievances. This is where preventive mediation comes in. Designed to overcome the problems resulting from mutual mistrust and poor communications, preventive mediation programs in the federal jurisdiction and most provinces seek to help management and unions build and maintain constructive and co-operative working relationships (HRDC, 1994). To this end, a number of the programs, including those of Ontario (Bergman, 1988) and the federal jurisdiction (HRDC, 1994) use Relations by Objectives (RBO) workshops to help the parties hone their communications and joint problem-solving skills. A key principle of all preventive mediation programs is that they are purely voluntary (HRDC, 1994; Joyce, 1996).

The federal program includes six components: establishing a labour–management committee, negotiation skills training, committee effectiveness training, relationship by objectives, grievance mediation, and facilitation. The various provincial programs appear to have a fairly similar emphasis, although there are certain differences; for example, the Newfoundland program includes joint supervisor-steward training in collective agreement administration (Joyce, 1996).

Unfortunately, there has thus far been little in the way of evaluation of the various preventive mediation programs. However, some anecdotal evidence (e.g., Joyce, 1996) suggests that the programs have been effective and have found favour with both management and unions. On the RBO workshops that are an important component of many preventive mediation programs, a study by Bergman (1988) found that union–management relationships had improved after the workshops and that participants attributed at least some of the improvement to the RBO experience (Bergman, 1988; Downie, 1989:270).[21]

Emerging Trends in Grievance Arbitration: Bigger Scope and More Complexity

Even as the trends just described have been helping to reduce workplace conflict by steering cases away from conventional arbitration, that process itself has been growing even more complicated. Overall (see Lokan and Yachnin, 2004), it would be fair to say the scope of arbitral authority has been increasing, and arbitrators are now being expected to apply an increasingly broad range of statutes and fashion an equally broad range of remedies. One key tendency is the increased application of the duty to accommodate to the arbitration process. Another is the growing use of arbitration as the forum for resolution of most workplace disputes, whether or not they arise out of the collective agreement. Other important tendencies include the growing requirement for arbitrators to apply external legislation (e.g., employment standards as well as human rights law) to their decisions and the possibility of awarding aggravated or punitive as well as compensatory damages. Arbitrators are also being called on to decide growing numbers of harassment and defamation cases, many of which might previously have been heard in other forums. Complicating matters still further is the greater potential for judicial review of arbitration decisions resulting from recent Supreme and Divisional Court decisions. Finally, it should be noted that Canadian workplaces have not been immune from the growing violence afflicting almost every aspect of modern society. As a result, arbitrators have been called on to decide increasing numbers of cases involving actual or threatened workplace violence.

The Duty to Accommodate

Human rights legislation has had a major impact on the grievance procedure, where arbitrators have been obliged to interpret collective agreements in the light of anti-discrimination provisions contained in that legislation. Ever since the landmark *O'Malley v. Simpson-Sears* case (1986),[22] intent to discriminate need not be proved for a finding of illegal discrimination to be reached. Now, under the concept of "constructive" or "systemic" discrimination, workplace rules and collective agreement provisions can be found discriminatory, regardless of their intent, if they have a disproportionate effect on an individual employee due to the employee's status as a member of a protected group (Carter, 1997:188). This means that both unions and employers are required to accommodate affected employees up to the point of "undue hardship." The requirement has been construed to extend far beyond simple protection from sexual, religious, and racial harassment, to proactive measures such as the creation of different work schedules for members of religious groups whose beliefs forbid work on certain days, or the redesign of jobs to allow individuals with disabilities to perform them more easily (Carter, 1997:190–197). In some cases, it has even led to the rewriting of collective agreement provisions or the waiving of their application (R. Jackson, 2001).

Recent jurisprudence provides a somewhat clearer idea of just how far the "duty to accommodate" is now expected to extend. In the case of "innocent" absenteeism related to physical or mental disability or illness, it may sometimes mean tolerating what would otherwise be considered seriously excessive rates of absenteeism. For example, in two Canadian Human Tribunal cases dating from 2003, the *Desormeaux* and *Parisien* cases,[23] arbitrators' decisions upholding the employees' discharge for innocent absenteeism were overturned, on the grounds that the employers hadn't proved it would be impossible to accommodate the employees without undue hardship. In both cases, the employees were reinstated with compensation for lost wages, a top-up for increased income tax liability and interest, and an award for hurt feelings. The Parisien award was made even though the plaintiff had missed an average of over 90 days' work per year for a period of 18 years, due to post-traumatic stress disorder.

An arbitrator is most likely to rule that an employer has reached the limit of its duty to accommodate where there is little or no prospect the employee will be able to perform stated job duties in the foreseeable future. For instance, in New Brunswick, an arbitrator upheld the discharge for innocent absenteeism of a clerk who, despite a lengthy period of sick leave followed by a graduated return to work, retraining, and several attempts to place her in an appropriate position, remained unable to perform at anything approaching an acceptable level, and was eventually granted permanent disability benefits.[24]

Application of External Statutes

The requirement that arbitrators apply statutes outside of (external to) the collective agreement in interpreting the agreement is far from new. After all, it has long been accepted (see Chapter 10) that a collective agreement can't contain any provision that violates another law, such as a vacation entitlement below the minimum required by provincial employment standards law. If, for example, an arbitrator were called on to determine whether a particular vacation provision violated employment standards law, (s)he would, of necessity, be forced to apply that law in order to arrive at a decision.

What can be said is that in recent years, arbitrators have been expected to apply an ever broader range of external statutes, and to do so in situations far more complex than the relatively straightforward one just described. In some cases, arbitrators may apply such statutes as human rights legislation or employment standards law through provisions of labour relations legislation similar to Sec. 48(12(j)) of the *Ontario Labour Relations Act*, which specifically grants arbitrators the power to interpret and apply such statutes even when they may conflict with the collective agreement. But even in the absence of such a specific legislative provision, the obligation to ensure that a collective agreement provision did not violate human rights or employment legislation would usually be enough to give arbitrators jurisdiction over such issues.

The "duty to accommodate" cases discussed earlier, while increasingly frequent, are by no means the only way in which human rights concerns have entered the arena of collective agreement interpretation. With the *Parry Sound* case of 2003 (see Lokan and Yachnin, 2004), the Supreme Court of Canada has established that the *Human Rights Code* is an implied term of every collective agreement.[25]

The *Parry Sound* case arose when the Parry Sound Social Services Administrative Board dismissed a probationary employee shortly after her return from maternity leave (Lokan and Yachnin, 2004). When the union grieved the dismissal as discriminatory, the employer replied that a section of the collective agreement provided that dismissal of probationary employees was at the sole discretion of the employer. An arbitration board sided with the union, noting that Sec. 5(1) of Ontario's *Human Rights Code* prohibited discrimination in employment on the basis of family status and that Sec. 48(12(j)) of the *Labour Relations Act* granted arbitrators the power to apply human rights statutes. While the Ontario Divisional Court quashed the arbitral award, the provincial Court of Appeal restored it, whereupon the employer appealed to the Supreme Court of Canada.

In a 7–2 decision, the Supreme Court upheld the arbitral award and dismissed the employer's appeal, ordering the employee reinstated. Writing for the court, Justice Frank Iacobucci held that the *Human Rights Code* prohibited discriminatory discharges and therefore any allegation that a discharge was discriminatory would have to be considered arbitrable. Even had the parties intended to make discriminatory discharges inarbitrable—which Iacobucci doubted was the case—such a provision would have been void under Sec. 48(1) of the *Labour Relations Act,* which requires arbitration of all differences between the parties. In addition, Secs. 44 and 64.5 (1) of the province's *Employment Standards Act* rendered the dispute arbitrable because, as a result of those provisions, "each collective agreement is deemed to contain a provision that prohibits the discharge of a probationary employee because she took or intends to take pregnancy leave." In other recent cases (e.g., the *Serca Food-service* case of 2004),[26] arbitrators have found not only that they had an obligation to interpret employment standards legislation, but that the legislation took precedence over collective agreement provisions.

Tort-Based Claims

Simply put, a "tort" is a fancy legal word for a wrong done by one individual to another. In the past, many kinds of tort-based cases, such as those involving slander or other types of personal defamation, have been considered to be outside the purview of collective agreement arbitration, and have therefore generally been dealt with in other forums, such as the courts or in some cases a human rights tribunal.[27] More recently, the trend has been to consider such cases as falling within arbitrators' exclusive jurisdiction (Lokan and Yachnin, 2004:14). A key case here is the 1999 *Giorno vs. Pappas* one (see ibid., 9),[28] in which the Ontario Court of Appeal declined jurisdiction in a workplace defamation case, ruling that the case could have been brought as a health and safety grievance under the collective agreement (ibid., 14).

The effect of *Giorno* and similar cases[29] on the work of arbitrators has been threefold. First, it has complicated that work by including within arbitration many cases involving purely individual matters having little or no bearing on the union–management relationship which might previously have been taken to court (or settled out of court). Not only does this risk overloading the process; it may, at least in some cases, result in poorer union–management relationships, by politicizing purely individual disputes. Second, it has also facilitated better and fuller remedies, such as allowing for the removal from the workplace of supervisors found to have harassed their subordinates, a remedy which in the words of Lokan and Yachnin (2004:17) would have been "unimaginable" a few years ago. Third, and not unrelated to this last point, adding tort-based cases to arbitrators' workloads has also entailed adding tort-related remedies, such as aggravated or punitive damages for mental distress, to their toolkits. (Traditionally arbitrators have confined themselves to compensating or "making whole" the victims of workplace wrongdoing, almost invariably stopping short of awarding damages for mental distress aimed at "punishing" the perpetrator).

In the *Seneca College* case,[30] with the Ontario Court of Appeal's overturning of a supplementary arbitration award by Pamela Picher denying a reinstated grievor aggravated and punitive damages on the grounds that an arbitrator lacked jurisdiction to award damages for torts, it was clearly established that arbitrators do in fact have jurisdiction to award such damages. But even prior to *Seneca College*, arbitrators had begun to include punitive and aggravated damages in their awards. For example, in a 2003 case involving the Newfoundland Association of Public Employees,[31] arbitrator Peter Darby awarded $100 000 in punitive damages as part of an $800 000 compensation package for an employee, partially disabled from an earlier head injury, who was forced to leave his job after years of assaults, cruel practical jokes, and numerous other instances of harassment from co-workers—harassment the employer did nothing about. While only a few[32] other cases have resulted in awards anything like this large, there are now a number of cases in which smaller awards have been made for hurt feelings, lost dignity, humiliation, mental anguish, and the like (see Lancaster House, 2004b:3–4). More recently, arbitrators have demonstrated a tendency to recognize new bases for damages, including outsourcing, failure to consult, failure to accommodate, breach of inherent right, and harassment. Only time will tell whether these are fairly isolated cases or the tip of an emerging iceberg.

Lower Standards for Judicial Review

As we noted earlier, Canadian courts have traditionally been reluctant to overturn arbitrators' decisions, particularly in jurisdictions where the right of judicial review has been specifically circumscribed by a privative clause in the jurisdiction's labour relations act. The standard traditionally applied for judicial review has been that of patent (i.e., blatant) unreasonableness. Over the past two years, in a number of recent cases (among them *Voice Construction* and *Lethbridge Community College*),[33] provincial as well as federal courts have adopted a lower standard for review—that of simple unreasonableness (see Mullan, 2004). Thus far, the Supreme Court of Canada has continued to show a fair degree of deference to arbitral awards, restoring original awards that favoured the union in the *Voice Construction* and *Lethbridge* cases. Furthermore, a recent Ontario Court of Appeal decision, *Lakeport Beverages v. Teamsters, Local 938*, distinguished *Voice Construction* and *Lethbridge Community College* as unique to Alberta, where the labour relations legislation contains a relatively weak privative clause. Thus, while it is clear that the higher standard of patent unreasonableness continues to be the law in Ontario and other jurisdictions with relatively strong privative clauses, it is not entirely clear that the relaxed standard will not be used as a basis for overturning arbitral awards in other jurisdictions. This is a troubling possibility, at least for those who prefer to see judicial intervention in the IR system kept to a minimum.[34]

Workplace Violence: A Tougher Stance

Workplace violence has become an increasingly serious problem in Canada, with the result that arbitrators are being called on to decide a growing number of cases involving assault or the threat thereof, as well as harassment. Underscoring the importance of this issue, a recent ILO study (see Lancaster House, 2004:202–203) found that Canada had among the world's highest rates of workplace violence and harassment.

In cases involving workplace violence, it would appear that arbitrators are tending to take a tougher line than they might have prior to 9/11 and prior to such well-publicized incidents as the shooting of fellow employees by a deranged Ottawa-Carleton Regional Transport Authority employee a number of years ago. As veteran arbitrator Allen Ponak has said, "With all that's been going on in workplaces lately, I'm going to err on the side of caution."[35] Based on some recent decisions in workplace violence cases, it appears that Ponak's colleagues are inclined to agree, sustaining discharges particularly in cases involving actual physical assault or the threat of assault using a specific weapon (e.g., a gun or knife) or where the perpetrator has a previous history of violence. Often, even a long discipline-free record hasn't been enough to save the perpetrator's job.

For example, in a 2004 decision rendered by arbitrator Brian Etherington, a 21-year-veteran employee of a London, Ontario, wheel manufacturer was fired for shoving his supervisor three times in a row while "threatening to kick the s—t out of him" (Lancaster House, 2004, June 8).[36] Despite the existence of several mitigating factors, including a long, discipline-free record of service, documented stress and depression resulting from family, marital, and financial problems and the burning down of his house, and the employee's tendering of verbal and written apologies to the supervisor, Etherington declined to overturn the discharge. He was particularly concerned by the lack of provocation and the grievor's failure "to fully acknowledge and accept responsibility for his actions . . ." (ibid).

Even "offline" threats and abusive statements made in emails not intended to be read by management or co-workers may attract severe discipline, as a 2003 case involving a Manitoba publication company suggests.[37] In November 2002, the grievor, who had one reprimand on file for harassing a co-worker, was fired for sending a friend, via company email, a letter in which she said she was about to "drop the bomb of death" on another employee. The company's Internet policy gave management the right to read and record employees' emails without notice or permission. The company, which had been monitoring the grievor's email for months, was seriously considering suspending her for other abusive emails previously sent when it discovered the "bomb of death" email and terminated her.

Only the employer's failure to warn the grievor about her abuse of the company's email policy in an earlier letter of reprimand prevented the employer from being discharged, even though arbitrator Arne Peltz agreed with the union that the grievor was essentially harmless and unlikely to injure anybody. Because of this partial failure to maintain progressive discipline, Peltz reinstated the grievor subject to a psychological assessment, substituting for the discharge a six-month unpaid suspension, reassignment to the night shift, and a complete ban on any personal use of the employer's email system—still a severe penalty.

GRIEVANCES AND INDUSTRIAL CONFLICT: THE BIGGER PICTURE

While the grievance system appears generally to have worked reasonably well during the early post-war period, since then it has often been criticized for its slowness, costliness, and growing legalism, which taken together have meant that only a very small proportion of all grievances are ever taken through to arbitration. In response to these serious criticisms of the conventional arbitration process, governments, unions, and management have developed a broad range of innovative new dispute settlement mechanisms, of which the most important are expedited arbitration, grievance mediation, and preventive mediation. The evidence discussed earlier in the chapter suggests that these mechanisms, where applied, have led to speedier and less expensive arbitration decisions, a reduction in the number of grievances needing to go to arbitration, and improved union–management relationships with better communication between the parties.

Though these and other innovative new dispute settlement mechanisms[38] have contributed significantly to reducing workplace conflict in Canada, major sources of conflict remain unaddressed. One important source of conflict is unions' "ownership" of the grievance process. As noted earlier, an individual can't normally file a grievance independently; only a union can do so. Inevitably, unions' ownership of the process means that a certain number of grievances will be used for political purposes—perhaps to be traded off for other grievances or even for certain collective agreement provisions. Particularly where labour–management relations are already poor, it also means that large numbers of grievances may be filed simply as a pressure tactic, perhaps to protest the slow pace of negotiations or an arbitrary management action on some other front.[39] For its part, management may respond by stonewalling, that is refusing to deal with outstanding grievances for a more or less indefinite period of time. Such use of the grievance process increases labour–management conflict in a number of different ways. First, it overloads the grievance process so that legitimate and serious problems may not be addressed for far too long. Second, particularly when management stonewalls, it becomes extremely difficult to distinguish individual problems from broader political issues. Third, to the extent that individuals' grievances are not addressed in timely fashion, it decreases individuals' satisfaction with both the employer and the union, leading both to increased worker–management conflict and increased intra-organizational conflict within the union.

One could also argue that in the Canadian IR system, the grievance process is simply asked to do far too much. Not only does it serve as a vehicle for individual workplace voice; it must also serve as a vehicle for group and in some cases collective voice. In addition, as we noted earlier, it often serves as a forum for informal union–management negotiations and as a mechanism for helping to resolve intra-organizational conflict within both unions and management groups. Now, as we have just seen, it has become a kind of "one-stop shopping portal" for most workplace disputes, in recent years having been asked to handle cases previously addressed in the courts or through tribunals such as the Human Rights Tribunal. Perhaps all this is really more than should be asked of any single process.

One way to reduce some of the strain on the seriously overloaded grievance process might be to allow any worker to file a dismissal grievance independent of his or her union, on condition he or she was willing to bear half the costs. Unions and management might also, as Lokan and Yachnin have suggested (2004: 28) consider writing into collective agreements provisions exempting from arbitration certain types of work-related misconduct not directly related to the collective agreement (e.g., defamation). Another possibility might be a second-tier tribunal in some ways akin to Small Claims Court, which could handle relatively minor grievances, defamation claims and the like, without the legal formalities required in conventional arbitration or human rights tribunal claims. All this would help reserve "full-dress" arbitration for cases that really need it, thereby keeping the process from becoming even more overloaded than it already is.

Case 12.1 Continued

THE IKO CASE

You're probably wondering what happened to our old friend, Mr. Lacelle. Here is how the arbitrator ruled:

The grievor's actions . . . in particular his actions on April 11th, 2001, constituted sexual harassment . . . [This] is a demeaning practice, one that constitutes a profound affront to the dignity of employees forced to endure it. By requiring an employee to contend with unwelcome sexual actions or explicit sexual demands, sexual harassment in the workplace attacks the dignity and self-respect of the victim . . .

The issue of . . . sexual harassment, gives rise to particular difficulties. From the Employer's perspective . . . sexual harassment is such degrading and demeaning conduct, that anyone who engages in [it] is, ipso facto, not a person who can be rehabilitated by disciplinary action short of discharge . . . particularly . . . when the discharged employee has received training and at least two verbal warnings concerning the inappropriateness of his behaviour.

From the Union's perspective, while it is appropriate that sexual harassment be broadly defined, it must be recognized that the standards of acceptable and appropriate conduct in the workplace have been changing over the years. The grievor is a long service and middle aged employee, who may not have appreciated the seriousness of his actions . . . A suspension from work, as the next step in a policy of progressive discipline, [would] therefore [be] the appropriate penalty.

Having considered the evidence and submissions, I have determined that . . . the grievor should be reinstated to employment within fourteen days of the Employer receiving this award, without compensation, but without loss of seniority. The reasons for substituting this lengthy suspension for the discharge are . . . that the grievor's harassing conduct was not of such severity that a lengthy suspension will not have the desired effect of bringing to the grievor's attention the inappropriateness of his conduct, and cause him to modify his behaviour so it is not repeated. In arriving at this conclusion I have taken note of the grievor's employment record, his seniority, his admission of guilt and his offering an apology, the fact that the grievor and Ms. M. do not routinely work in close proximity to each other, and that the . . . acts of sexual harassment identified in the evidence are not of such a nature as to be just cause for automatic discharge . . .

In my view, the substitution of what amounts to an approximately eleven-month suspension, is a sufficient penalty to demonstrate . . . that conduct of this nature will not be tolerated, while at the same time giving the grievor one final opportunity to correct his behaviour. Any repeat of harassing behaviour by the grievor following his reinstatement . . . would certainly be grounds for discharge . . .

QUESTIONS FOR DISCUSSION

1. If you are in a union, read your collective agreement's grievance procedure. How many steps does it contain? Can time limits be waived? If a grievance is sent to arbitration, will there be a single arbitrator or a three-person panel? If you aren't a union member, find and read a collective agreement and answer the same questions.

2. What are some benefits of the grievance process to workers, unions, and organizations? What are some of the drawbacks? In your view, do the benefits outweigh the drawbacks?

3. Why has grievance arbitration become a lengthy, costly, and legalistic process?

4. List the steps in a "typical" grievance procedure.

5. Describe a typical arbitration hearing.

6. What seem to be the key factors in determining whether someone filing a dismissal grievance is reinstated or not?

7. Discuss some ways in which Canadian unions, management organizations, and governments have tried to speed up the arbitration process and reduce the number of grievances being sent to arbitration.

8. Based on your reading of the TRB case, explain why sexual harassment poses particular problems for arbitrators as well as for managers, workers, and unions.

9. Would you be more or less likely to reinstate Marcel Deschamps than you would have been after you first read the TRB case? If your position has changed, explain why.

10. Does the alternate dispute resolution (ADR) process outlined in Current Issues 12.1 (page 344) seem to you likely to reduce grievances and other forms of workplace conflict? Why, or why not? Would you consider applying such a process to the TRB case?

Suggestions for Further Reading

Brett, Jeanne and Stephen Goldberg. (1983). "Grievance Mediation in the Coal Industry: A Field Experiment." *Industrial and Labor Relations Review,* 37. A groundbreaking early study of grievance mediation in one of the United States's most conflict-ridden industries.

Lokan, Andrew and Maryth Yachnin. (2004). "From *Weber to Parry Sound*: The Expanded Scope of Arbitration." *Canadian Labour and Employment Law Journal,* 11, pp. 1–29. Thoughtful, very thorough discussion of recent trends in arbitration such as its handling of workplace defamation claims and the awarding of punitive damages.

Rose, Joseph. (1986). "Statutory Expedited Grievance Arbitration: The Case of Ontario." *Arbitration Journal,* 41:4. Important early study of the results of Ontario's expedited arbitration system.

CHAPTER 13

INDUSTRIAL RELATIONS AROUND THE WORLD

This Brazilian street vendor is one of many Third World people forced to earn a living outside the formal labour force. Throughout much of the Third World, the number of people forced to earn their living in this way has risen sharply in recent years.

LEARNING OBJECTIVES

After studying this chapter, you should be able to:

1. Explain the significance of international IR developments to the Canadian IR system.
2. Describe some traditional IR models.
3. Identify some recent challenges to traditional IR models.
4. Explain some of the key differences between IR in the developing world and IR in the developed world.
5. Discuss the significance of informal associations to IR in developing countries.
6. Explain how traditional views of IR need to be expanded to take accurate account of developments in developing countries.

In today's increasingly globalized economy, it is impossible to obtain a full understanding of the Canadian IR system without understanding developments in other countries. Over the past three decades, the changes on the international IR scene have been profound, especially in the developing world. The chapter begins by examining some traditional IR models. Next it looks at recent changes to those traditional models, particularly in Europe. It then considers the special situation of the developing world, where in many cases large segments of the population do not even participate in the formal labour force as such. Special emphasis is placed on the growth of informal workers' associations and informal associations of micro-entrepreneurs, and on the relationships some of these associations have formed with more formal bodies in their own countries and with unions and other organizations in developed countries. The chapter concludes with a brief examination of the question of whether traditional IR terminology and methodology can usefully be applied in the developing world.

INTRODUCTION: A NEW WAY OF LOOKING AT IR

Previous chapters have illustrated some of the ways in which the Canadian IR system has been changing over the past two decades. For example, we have pointed out how the balance of workplace power has shifted from workers and unions toward employers and managers. We've also noted that significantly fewer Canadians than in the past hold secure, full-time jobs, and have pointed out the increasing difficulties public sector unions are having representing their members in today's hostile economic and political environment.

Canada has by no means been alone in experiencing these kinds of changes. Most of them have been occurring around the world, in both developed and developing countries. In some cases, the changes have been significantly more severe and more abrupt elsewhere than they have here. In others, the impacts have been aggravated by extreme poverty, crushing debt loads, disease, or political instability (see Loxley, 1998).

Such developments pose serious questions as to the adequacy of our traditional industrial relations tools, particularly in the world's poorer countries. Until very recent years, few would have disagreed with Keller's (1991) characterization of workers and trade unions; managers, employers and their associations; and the state as the three key actors in virtually all IR systems. But such a characterization assumes, almost by definition, a society in which a fair amount of industrialization and economic development have taken place, in which a sizable share of the population works in more or less traditional employer–employee relationships, and in which the state has built up regulatory capacity sufficient to allow it to ensure that unions are able to function as workers' official representatives, as well as to administer employment-related legislation. In much of the developing world, none of these would necessarily be safe assumptions. In some countries, less than one-third of the population may even be in the formal employment sector, let alone officially employed (ILO, 1997:Table 7).[1] In others, a large number of self-employed workers or micro-entrepreneurs operate more or less illegally, without registering or paying taxes, either because they are ignorant of the regulations or because they can't afford the costs of complying with them (ILO, 1997:184–185). In still other cases, a large proportion of the population may be working without pay in family-run businesses, in which the distinction between "employer" and "employee" is virtually meaningless.

Such situations impose very real constraints on the ability of the traditional industrial relations actors to function as they would in a developed country. How, for example, can "official" unions effectively represent workers, such as rickshaw drivers or street vendors, who have neither an employer nor a regular workplace, and who may in some cases be operating illegally or even in such a way as to undercut the union's "regular" members (see ILO, 1997:203)? Even leaving aside the very real issue of resource constraints, how can governments regulate the wages, hours, or working conditions of such workers through employment legislation or health and safety laws? With respect to child labour, where do unions and other workers' organizations draw the line between work necessary to support the family and outright exploitation—and are they prepared to allow different standards in family-run businesses than in other types of business? And how can governments regulate family-run businesses employing unpaid workers in such a way as to prevent the abuse and exploitation of these workers, while at the same time respecting local or national traditions regarding the role of the family and not imposing such high regulatory costs that the businesses go under?

At a minimum, understanding these situations will require a new and broader conception of what industrial relations is. It also requires an appreciation of the role played by a broader range of actors than we are used to studying within the field of IR, including informal workers' associations, sector co-operatives, and associations of micro-entrepreneurs. As we'll see later in the chapter, while in many cases such organizations operate independently of the "official" IR institutions, such as trade unions or employers' associations, in others they have been incorporated into the larger, more formal organizations.

A key objective of this chapter, then, will be to describe in some detail the new, more complex model for international IR, whose outlines we have briefly sketched in the preceding paragraphs. Another will be to show how and to what extent the various IR actors—formal and informal alike—have succeeded in adapting to today's harsher global environment and what problems and challenges remain, in both developed and developing countries. But before we do either of those things, it will be necessary to consider a more traditional model of international IR, as well as to indicate some of the major forces that have served to undermine that model over the past two decades or so. Without an understanding of that model, we will find it difficult to appreciate the full significance of all the recent changes.

A TRADITIONAL IR MODEL

Unfree Systems

Traditionally, IR systems were divided into three groups: unfree, partially free, and free. Unfree systems were those in which unions had no effective role to play. In some cases, such as that of the Axis powers before and during the Second World War, this was the result of the outright dissolution of unions or a ban on their activities (see Kuwahara, 1993; Pellegrini, 1993; Fuerstenberg, 1993). Communist countries such as the former Soviet Union could hardly ban unions, since in theory these countries operated on the basis of control by the working class. At the same time, they were in no way prepared to accept a challenge to central state authority. In these countries, therefore, unions were not at all the independent workers' advocates we are used to. Rather, they served as a kind of "transmission belt," communicating official government policy to workers (Héthy, 1991:125–127) or at best carrying out modest social welfare functions.

With the gradual political liberalization that took place in Eastern Europe during the 1970s and 80s, the traditional Communist model loosened up somewhat. In countries like Hungary, public enterprises acquired a degree of autonomy from the government and there began to be an appreciation of the need for separate roles for employers and trade unions (Héthy, 1991). Elsewhere, in countries like Bulgaria and Poland, worker participation through self-management became more common. Nonetheless, there was little real collective bargaining until after the Soviet Union's collapse. Despite a general trend toward economic and political liberalization, governments remained reluctant to loosen their grip on wage determination, particularly in times of economic crisis, and there were few mechanisms available for solving labour disputes (ibid.:137).

Partially Free Systems

In general, partially free systems were found in the developing countries of Africa and Asia, particularly those that had only recently obtained their independence from a colonial power. They were also (and to a degree still are) found in a number of Latin American countries. In general, such systems allowed unions and labour centrals some freedom of manoeuvre, but would often limit that freedom, whether through legislation or through some form of outright repression (Fashoyin, 1991).

Often the leaders of newly-independent countries found themselves in a delicate position vis-à-vis their countries' unions. On the one hand, the unions had in many cases played a key role in the independence movement. On the other hand, unions and their leaders were sometimes perceived as a political threat to ruling elites. Moreover, once unions began operating more freely, engaging in collective bargaining and going on strike to support their demands, they were seen as interfering with national economic policies designed to attract outside investment that featured wage moderation and an absence of labour conflict (Fashoyin, 1991; Gladstone, 1980). Whether rightly or wrongly, free collective bargaining and strikes were often seen as luxuries that developing countries could not afford (see Peirce, 1996).

As a result, the governments of developing countries have at various times adopted strategies ranging from the substitution of compulsory arbitration and government wage-price controls for the right to strike to the co-optation of key unions and central labour bodies, even to the extent of giving union leaders important positions in the government (see Kassalow, 1963; Peirce, 1996; Park and Lee, 1995; Beng and Chew, 1995). Other countries have weakened their labour movements through fragmentation (as by refusing to allow a single major labour federation) or by failing to pass legislation protecting union organizers against arbitrary dismissal (see Kuruvilla and Arudsothy, 1995; Brown and Frenkel, 1993; Manusphaibool, 1993). Still others, such as Greece, have banned all political strikes (Fashoyin, 1991).

While not all developing countries have resorted to such drastic measures as the arrest and detention of union leaders and activists or the deregistration of unions found to be behaving in ways not to the government's liking, many have done so—at least on occasion. For example, military governments in Brazil and Argentina have routinely trampled on workers' and unions' rights (Fashoyin, 1991). In Singapore (Leggett, 1993), 1963 saw over 100 left-wing labour opponents of the government detained without trial and several unions deregistered.[2] In the Philippines (Jimenez, 1993), after President Marcos declared martial law in 1972, strikes and picketing in most key industries were banned. Violators were arrested and detained for the duration of the national emergency.

Free Systems

Free IR systems have, with some limitations, allowed unions to function as independent advocates for workers. The most important mechanism used by unions has been collective bargaining, whether at the national, industry, or enterprise level. But the unions of North America and Western Europe, where the lion's share of free systems are located,[3] have by no means confined themselves to collective bargaining. As we noted in Chapter 5, political action through both formal and informal channels has also been an important part of most Canadian unions' agendas. Political action has played an even more prominent role in many European countries (e.g., Sweden, Austria, and on occasion Germany) where the labour movement has been instrumental in helping to elect a sympathetic government and, once that government has been installed, in providing it with advice on appropriate social and economic policies.

It should be noted that many countries, particularly European ones, provide for workplace representation through some mechanism other than unions. In Europe, these mechanisms are generally known as works councils. In Canada, they are known as joint committees. (As we noted in Chapter 6, these committees are normally mandatory in the case of health and safety.) Works councils and joint committees operate in a somewhat different way than unions do. For the most part, their aim is to work out problems through consensus. The strike is virtually never used as a means of resolving disputes within the workplace-level body. Instead, disputes are normally resolved through arbitration, or, in the case of Canadian health and safety committees, through referral of the matter in dispute to a government safety officer.

Types of Free Systems

Over the years, several different types of free IR system have evolved. In decentralized systems, government normally plays quite a limited role, and unions' major activity is collective bargaining, most often at the enterprise level. In centralized systems, government's role is much more extensive. In addition to collective bargaining, most often at the national or industry level, unions are extensively involved in political action. Where the major thrust of bargaining is at the nationwide or industry level, it is often supplemented with a second tier of bargaining over local-level issues. As noted above, a prominent feature of most (though not all) such systems is a more or less consensual workplace-level mechanism such as a works council. Hybrid systems contain some features of each of the two preceding types. In the following paragraphs, we describe each of these three types in turn.

Decentralized Systems Countries with decentralized IR systems include the US, Canada, and, to a lesser extent, the UK. Economic activity is determined largely by market forces and collective bargaining is normally conducted at individual workplaces (Lipsig-Mumme, 2001). In the US and Canada, the collective agreements that result from this bargaining are generally extremely detailed and impose significant restrictions on employers' ability to manage. For this reason (although there are others as well), employers in these countries, the US in particular, tend to be more anti-union than their European counterparts, where bargaining is more apt to be at national and industry level and collective agreements are less detailed (see Adams, 1995a).

decentralized system An IR system characterized by large numbers of negotiations each involving relatively small numbers of workers, where most activity occurs at the workplace level.

While unions certainly go in for political activity in **decentralized systems**, their involvement is often of a more sporadic and ad hoc nature than in centralized systems; this is particularly true in the US. In Canada, much of the English Canadian labour movement is formally affiliated with the social democratic New Democratic Party. However, the NDP has never possessed anything like the power of labour and social democratic parties in Britain and on the Continent and in practice the labour movement's ties to it don't mean a great deal; on election day many rank-and-file members wind up voting for other parties, particularly the Liberals. Formal consultation is sporadic and carried out at the will of particular governments (Lipsig-Mumme, 2001).

In decentralized systems, union membership rates range from low (the US) to moderate (Canada and the UK). There is also a significant amount of exclusion with respect to the lack of protection of certain groups under labour relations and employment standards legislation. For example, farmworkers are excluded from unionization rights in the US and certain Canadian provinces (see Chapter 7 and Peirce, 1989). In the US, the *Taft-Hartley Act*, passed in 1947, effectively removed union security from many Southern and Midwestern states. It is thus extremely difficult for workers in these states to be able to join unions.

Within the group of countries with decentralized IR systems, the US stands out for a number of reasons. Its union membership rates, particularly in the private sector, are extremely low. The opposition of its employers to unions is particularly fierce, and the enforcement of labour legislation generally quite lax—so much so that many employers appear to be willing to commit unfair labour practices confident in the knowledge they probably won't be caught, or that even if they do get caught it probably won't matter since the damage to the union will already have been done and the union left without any meaningful remedy (Bruce, 1990). Some, notably Selig Perlman (1966), have attempted to explain the extraordinarily individualistic character of American labour relations as a result of the US's "exceptional" nature. Unlike most European countries, Perlman says, the US was never faced with the problem of winning the suffrage or the rights to a basic education for workers, and therefore the American labour movement never had to develop any sort of class-consciousness and tended to avoid politics, instead focusing itself more narrowly on bread-and-butter issues at the workplace. While there is undoubtedly some truth to Perlman's theory, there is much that it does not explain, including most notably the fact that Canadian unions, facing roughly the same conditions as their American counterparts, have often displayed quite considerable class-consciousness and have generally been more heavily involved in political activity (see Peirce, 1993).

Centralized Systems

Centralized systems feature significant government involvement in the economy and IR system. In such systems, bargaining has normally been conducted at the national level, as was traditionally the case in Sweden, or at the industry level, as in the case of Germany. The fact that collective bargaining isn't conducted at the workplace level and that in most cases supplementary mechanisms (works councils or multi-tier bargaining) are available to deal with workplace problems has had the effect of reducing industrial conflict in centralized systems well below its customary level in decentralized ones (see Adams, 1989). In effect, much conflict that would occur at the workplace in North America is moved into the political arena under centralized systems, thus accounting, in part, for these systems' lower level of conflict. Another reason for their lower level of industrial conflict is that because so much more typically rides on them than is the case with enterprise-level negotiations, negotiators are more expert, and generally senior management with real power will be at the table. Given how much is at stake in such negotiations, there is also an increased likelihood of government intervention if negotiations break down.

> **centralized system** An IR system characterized by a relatively small number of large negotiations each affecting many workers, and where activity often takes place at the national or industry as well as the workplace level.

Unions in centralized systems have normally devoted much of their effort to electing a favourable (labour or social democratic) government. Once such a government is elected, it will often establish tripartite (union–employer–government) consultation mechanisms that allow unions a significant voice in the formation of national social and economic policies. Often the unions will be induced to accept lower wage settlements and refrain from striking in return for pension and tax reform, a full employment guarantee, price controls, or other government policies favouring workers and unions (Adams, 1989). Such accords may be one reason for the generally superior economic performance found in centralized systems through the 1980s.

Economically, countries with centralized IR systems have tended to be more egalitarian and have a good deal less wage dispersion than countries with decentralized ones—in part because of the practice, in many European countries, of extending the wages negotiated in formal collective agreements to non-unionized firms, as a way of taking wages out of competition. For this reason, many European countries have a far higher rate of collective agreement coverage than union membership. In connection with the issue of wage dispersion, it's interesting to note that when Sweden, during the late 1980s and early 90s, moved away from its traditional national-level bargaining to bargaining at the industry level, wage dispersion in that country increased significantly (Kjellberg, 1992).

A number of researchers (see among others Tarantelli, 1986) have found that centralized systems generally perform better than decentralized ones with respect to unemployment and inflation as well as industrial conflict. Nonetheless, such systems have been falling into disfavour in recent years, largely because of the opposition of employers, who prefer the greater flexibility offered them under decentralized systems. This has been particularly true of multinational corporations (see Marginson and Sisson, 2002; Hyman, 2001). As we will see later in the chapter, even in Northern Europe, much bargaining has been devolved to lower levels, while in North America, many earlier centralized arrangements, such as pattern bargaining in the meatpacking and rubber industries (see Peirce, 2003:293–294) have broken down due to employer opposition.

Hybrid Systems Several IR systems do not fit neatly into either the centralized or decentralized category. These systems, including those of Japan, Australia, and Quebec, are perhaps best described as hybrid systems.

enterprise union A union whose membership is limited to employees of the individual firm or plant.

The most distinctive features of the Japanese system are its system of **enterprise unions**, whose membership is limited to employees of the individual firm or plant (Matsuda, 1993), and the "lifetime employment guarantee" provided to key employees of large, core firms—a group that never made up more than one-third of the Japanese workforce (Matsuda, 1993:192 and 201).[4] Under this system, in return for loyalty to the firm and a willingness to work very long hours by Canadian standards, employees are effectively guaranteed a job until mandatory retirement at age 60 (Matsuda, 1993; Adams, 1995a). While the government is heavily involved in economic planning, it plays little role in the IR system as such, and unions are not normally involved in the planning of social or economic policy.[5] Rather than serving as workers' advocates either in the political arena (as in centralized systems) or in the workplace (as in decentralized ones), Japan's enterprise unions play primarily an integrative role (see Tannenbaum, 1921 and 1951),[6] helping to link employees to the corporate culture (Lipsig-Mumme, 2001) and generally concerning themselves more with the company's productivity and profitability than with the problems of individual employees.[7]

Over the years, the Japanese IR system has been much studied and widely admired by Western observers. However, it must be said that the favourable working conditions it has provided for the few have been achieved only at the cost of harsh and insecure conditions for the many, including most of society's more vulnerable members. It should also be noted that in recent years, Japan's lingering recession and the Asian economic crisis have led to massive layoffs (Lipsig-Mumme, 2001).

Australia's is another system that is difficult to classify. While its economy has remained market-oriented, its IR system has often featured heavy government intervention, at least by North American standards. Labour market shortages in the early twentieth century led the government to establish a quite centralized IR system as a means of ensuring labour peace. A cornerstone of that system was the establishment of an arbitration court to set wages and resolve disputes. In an attempt to block low-cost foreign competition, the government also imposed severe immigration restrictions and provided tariff protection for manufacturers who could show they were paying "fair and reasonable" wages (Frenkel, 1993b:251). Unions thus had a strong incentive to register and seek members, so they could avail themselves of the arbitration tribunals. The tribunals encouraged unions to centralize their power at federal and state levels and facilitated generally high union membership rates (sometimes over 50 percent of the workforce). By world standards, Australian workers enjoyed very good working conditions, being among the first to achieve the 40-hour workweek

(Frenkel, 1993b:252). The system held up remarkably well until the late 1980s, when continuing economic deterioration led to the dismantling of tariff barriers, a weakening of the arbitration tribunals, and devolution of bargaining to industry and workplace levels (Frenkel, 1993b; Lipsig-Mumme, 2001).

Yet another hybrid system is that of Quebec. Like the rest of Canada, Quebec operates within a primarily market-oriented economy and has a system of labour legislation derived from the American *Wagner Act*. But there are important differences between IR in Quebec and in the rest of Canada. For one thing, Quebec governments have historically been far more prone than other Canadian governments to intervene actively in the economy (Déom and Boivin, 2005). For another, the Quebec labour movement plays a major role in social and economic planning in the province, unlike other provinces' labour movements, which have generally been marginalized except under NDP provincial governments.

Perhaps most important for our purposes, Quebec's IR system contains a number of features normally characteristic of European rather than North American systems. The most prominent and longstanding of these is the **decree system**, in effect since 1934, whereby the labour minister has the power to extend parts (especially monetary clauses) of collective agreements to non-unionized firms in the same sector. While the **extension of collective agreements** is not as common in Quebec as in many European countries, where collective agreement coverage may be several times the union density rate (see Peirce, 2003:Table 13.2), some 9000 employers and 71 000 employees were covered by decrees at the end of 2001 (Déom and Boivin, 2005). Other distinctive features of Quebec's IR system include its multiple labour federations, a direct legacy of the confessional unions set up by the Catholic Church early in the twentieth century to keep Quebec workers under the Church's sway, and the organization of large numbers of employers into formal employers' associations.[8] It should also be noted that Quebec has made more use than other provinces of European-style tripartite social accords (normally called social contracts) as a means of dealing with economic crises in particular industries. Under the typical Quebec social contract, in return for a long-term pledge of labour peace, unions are provided with a guarantee of employment security and joint administration of the agreement and employees are provided with full information about the firm's financial situation (Déom and Boivin, 2005; Verma and Warrian, 1992).

In recent years, there have been threats to certain aspects of the Quebec system. Most seriously, pressure from employers' associations has led the government to abolish decrees in sectors facing competition from outside the province. At the end of 2001, only about half as many employers and employees were covered by decrees as was the case in 1990 (Déom and Boivin, 2005:447). Nonetheless, despite severe economic pressures in recent years, most of the Quebec system's distinctive features have remained largely intact.

extension of collective agreements or decree system System whereby collective agreements negotiated for a few major firms in a given industry are extended to the entire industry by means of a government decree.

FORCES FOR CHANGE

Few if any of the "traditional" IR systems we have just been describing remain entirely intact; some have changed beyond recognition. In certain cases, most notably that of the former Soviet bloc countries, change has resulted from major political upheaval (in this case the breakup of the former Soviet Union). More often, though, the change has been driven by a combination of macroeconomic and local political forces, with the former coming to assume an increasingly prominent role.

Arguably the single greatest force driving change in national IR systems has been the globalization of the world's economy. As we'll see in the following sections, globalization is a far-reaching phenomenon that includes increasing trade, capital mobility, and the internationalization of product and labour markets. In its wake, globalization has left a world characterized by fewer steady, full-time jobs, more precarious employment, weaker national governments with reduced ability to regulate their domestic economies and IR systems, and reduced union membership rates. Firms, on the other hand, have significantly increased their autonomy in recent years. Globalization has also led to smaller public sectors and the widespread devolution of bargaining from the national or industry to the enterprise level.

In the next sections of this chapter, after taking a close look at globalization itself, we will examine the other developments described in the preceding paragraph. Special emphasis will be placed on seeing how different types of "traditional" IR system have managed to adjust to today's harsher global economic and political environment.

Globalization

Though the global economy has been interdependent for many centuries, the extent of this interdependence has increased sharply since the end of World War II. Perhaps globalization's greatest effect has been on labour markets. Liberalized trade, largely the result of the dismantling of tariff barriers, has meant that employers have been forced to place far greater emphasis on controlling labour costs, since they are no longer able to rely on protective tariffs to shield them from low-cost foreign competition (Gunderson and Riddell, 1993). Modular production processes such as those described by Giles (1996) have enabled firms, particularly multinational ones, to shift production to countries whose labour costs are lower. Nor need a firm actually shift production to a lower-cost country to achieve substantial labour cost savings. In many cases, the mere *threat* of relocating or contracting out production is enough to dampen unions' wage demands at the bargaining table—or even to rid the firm of the union altogether (ILO, 1997:76).[9] And firms can have the same effect on national governments seeking to raise corporate taxes or increase social welfare spending. In Germany, for example, where corporate taxes have fallen by 50 percent over the past two decades despite a 90 percent rise in corporate profits, a group of corporations including Daimler-Benz and Deutsche Bank thwarted the Finance Minister's bid to raise corporate taxes by threatening to move investment or production to other countries if the government's policy didn't suit them. Instead of a tax increase, the result was a further cut in the corporate tax rate (Hertz, 2001).

Regrettably, globalization has been linked to actual slavery in West Africa and other extremely poor regions (Bales, 2001). The United Nations' children's agency, UNICEF, has estimated that more than 200 000 children are trafficked in West and Central Africa each year. Elsewhere, as in Thailand, young girls are often sold into forced prostitution. As globalization drives rural people in poor countries into debt and into cities, they become unable to support their children. This makes them easy prey for slave-traders, who offer them a small amount of money and say their children will work on plantations and send the money home. Then the children disappear, never to be seen again.

Child labour is another phenomenon linked to globalization. The International Labour Organization (ILO) conventions on the subject define child labour as any work by children under age 12; work that prevents school attendance by children under age 15; or work by children under 18 that is hazardous to the child's physical or mental health. Using these definitions, the ILO estimates that in 2000 there were 246 million child labourers worldwide, nearly half of whom (110 million) were under age 12 (Indian NGOs, 2005a). While child labour is certainly not new, it has increased significantly in recent years, being particularly common in agriculture, textile and apparel production, and domestic service (ibid.). It is found in both developed and developing countries but is particularly common in the latter (see Table 13.1). One source estimates that India alone has about 110 million child labourers (CRY, 2005).

The growth of migrant labour can also be linked to globalization, as many migrant workers work for multinational enterprises around the world. The ILO has estimated that there are about 96 million migrant workers and dependents in the world today, a number some experts expect to double in the next two decades (Indian NGOs, 2005b). These workers, typically employed in low-wage, low-skill jobs, tend to be the most vulnerable class of employees. They often lack adequate training and language skills and may be subject to discrimination with respect to pay and other employment conditions as well as harassment on the score of their ethnic background or national origin. Some are held in virtual servitude, having to pay large deposits to their employers or even surrender their passports until they have worked a stipulated period of time. Workplace health and safety is a particular concern for migrant workers, since many are forced to work considerable overtime and are afraid to refuse for fear of employer reprisal (see Current Issues box below), while others want to work as many hours as possible in order to support families in their home countries. Female migrant workers tend to be particularly susceptible to physical and sexual harassment (ibid.).

Near the end of the chapter, we'll discuss various ways that labour organizations, non-governmental organizations (NGOs), and other bodies have been working to reduce child labour and ease the plight of migrant workers.

Regional Economic Integration

Closely related to globalization is the trend toward economic integration within specified geographic regions of the world. Over the years, a number of different patterns of regional economic integration have emerged, the aim being to promote liberalized trade within those regions. The two most important of these patterns, for our purposes, are the North American Free Trade Zone and the European Union (EU).

In 1994, the trilateral North American Free Trade Agreement (NAFTA) between Canada, the US, and Mexico took effect, following on the heels of an earlier (1989)

Table 13.1

EXTENT OF CHILD LABOUR, VARIOUS COUNTRIES

REGION,§ Country (Age)	No. of Child Workers	% of Age Group Working
AFRICA		
Benin (10–14, 2001)	14 319	13.9
Botswana (10–14, 2001)	2 488	1.2
Ghana (0–9, 2000)	323 024	5.8
(10–14, 2000)	424 180	18.8
Madagascar (6–9)	309 959	15.7
(10–14)	597 659	28.1
Mauritius (12–14)	1 600	N/A (0.2% of total employment)
Tanzania (10–14, 2000–01)	2 336 848	48.3
LATIN AMERICA		
Argentina (0–9)	450	*
(10–14)	8 986	0.4
Colombia (0–11)†	66 861	0.6
Costa Rica (10–14)	13 500	3.1
Ecuador (10–14)	72 580	7.9
El Salvador (10–14)	74 029	9.9
Mexico (12–14)	766 736	10.8
Peru (10–14)	9 262	1.2
ASIA		
Mongolia (0–15)	1 891	0.2
Pakistan (10–14, 2001–02)	2 181 000	12.0
OCEANIA		
Papua New Guinea (10–14, 2000)	155 413	25.0

Notes: Data are for 2003 unless otherwise noted.

This table significantly understates the extent of child labour. First, several countries known to have widespread child labour, most notably Bangladesh and India, reported no data at all. Second, other countries reported only aggregate labour force date and thus no breakdown on the extent of child labour is available. Third, as noted below for Colombia, some countries used age brackets which were not comparable to those of most other countries, and which therefore had to be excluded from the table. Finally, not all workers are "economically active." The term includes only those engaged in paid labour outside the household. It thus understates the extent of child labour by excluding the large number of children engaged in unpaid domestic or agricultural labour.

*Less than 0.1%

†Colombia's next age group, 12–17, could not be used, as it does not form a meaningful comparison to other groups used in the table and there is no way of knowing how many from this group were age 14 and under. Some 22.6% of this age group in Colombia were reported as economically active.

§No European country reported any labour being performed by children under age 15.

Source: ILO Yearbook of Labour Statistics, 2004, Table 1A, Economically Active Population. Copyright © International Labour Organization.

bilateral agreement between Canada and the US (Reid and Meltz, 2001). Since then, several other Latin American countries have been invited to join the agreement, and the intention is to extend the agreement throughout the Americas within the next few years.

It's difficult to measure the precise effects of the NAFTA agreement on the Canadian economy, because it took effect at the same time as other major macro-economic developments, including the economic recession of the 1990s, the implementation of the GST, and exchange-rate fluctuations (Reid and Meltz, 2001). Moreover, one must also consider what might have happened had the agreement not been implemented. It is entirely possible that in the absence of something like a NAFTA agreement, the US would have put up additional trade barriers that would have made it more difficult for Canadian firms to sell their goods in that country's markets.

Still, there is at best little evidence that either agreement has benefited the Canadian economy. Through the 1990s, unemployment was generally higher than it had been during the 80s. During that decade, hundreds of thousands of well-paid manufacturing jobs were lost. In addition, our country's social safety net is significantly weaker than it was 15 or 20 years ago. EI benefits have been reduced significantly, and there have also been major cuts to health care, social assistance, and other social programs.

The EU, which began in 1950, is the world's oldest system of regional integration. While it has traditionally favoured economic integration (including, now, a common currency) over the harmonization of social issues (Lipsig-Mumme, 2001), it has recently achieved some success in the latter area as well. Moreover, at least through the mid-1990s, it appeared that adjustment processes resulting from integration were generally less painful in the EU than under NAFTA because the disparities between member countries are less extreme in the EU.

The most recent evidence, however, suggests that even in "civilized, humane" Europe, adjustment processes resulting from regional integration have been far from painless. With European Monetary Union (EMU) increasing competition between firms, the multinationals in particular have begun forcing workers and unions to accept increasingly unfavourable working conditions, including Saturday work and loss of overtime premiums (Marginson and Sisson, 2002). Looking at recent European industrial relations more generally, Richard Hyman (2001) sees a growth (or resurgence) of market forces even in countries (e.g., Germany, Austria) where the "Rhineland" model of social protection had been strongest for the first half century after World War II. In his view, EMU has been a strong driver for the resurgence of market forces.

> "To meet the requirements of monetary union, governments across Europe have been spurred to impose new constraints on public employment and restrictions on the 'social wage.' The consequence has been an increasing pressure on the 'social partnership' typical of most European industrial relations systems . . . 'Deregulation' has also consolidated the rule of central banks and other financial institutions, imposing disciplines which are inherently antagonistic to the principles of social protection and social partnership which underlie most European industrial relations systems" (Hyman, 2001:288).

It is likely no accident that at a time when corporate decision making is increasingly being driven by "the products of a thousand MBA factories" who have little time for "such sentimentalities" as social partnerships, union membership rates in Austria and Germany have dropped precipitously (see Table 13.3), while throughout the continent national governments have limited will or capacity to impose employment regulation (ibid.:289). Perhaps the clearest sign of these new times is that a Labour Prime Minister (Tony Blair) could boast, after introducing proposed changes to his country's labour relations legislation, that even after those changes, Britain would still have the most lightly regulated labour market of any leading economy in the world (ibid.).

Coordinated Bargaining Efforts

Increasingly it is being recognized (Marginson and Sisson, 2002; Lipsig-Mumme, 1995) that the union movement must start to form transnational alliances if it is to have any hope of countering the massive power of multinational corporations. It is within the EU that unions have gone furthest in this direction, working through organizations like the European Trades Union Congress, which has become a respected player in social and economic policy formation in the region (Lipsig-Mumme, 2005). As well, the Maastricht Agreement makes possible Europe-wide collective bargaining and includes protection for the region's most vulnerable workers (ibid.). Other hopeful developments include a 1994 EU Directive providing for European works councils in multinational enterprises with at least 1000 employees, including at least 150 in each of two member states (ILO, 1997:139). But while the European unions are making some headway at coordinating their efforts, truly transnational union co-operation remains very much a work in progress (Lipsig-Mumme, 2005; Hyman, 2001). It's by no means clear whether the new "European" system will allow unions to make up the ground they have lost through the "hollowing out" of national IR systems related to European integration (Lipsig-Mumme, 2005; Ebbinghaus, 2002).

Growing Importance of Management and Employers

Few would dispute the ILO's contention that managers have effectively taken the initiative in reshaping industrial relations in the workplace and that individual firms are tending to exert greater influence in the conduct of industrial relations and in personnel management decisions. An example of management's more prominent role is the growing use of progressive human resource management policies (discussed in Chapter 2) such as profit-sharing pay schemes, merit-based pay, direct communication with workers, and total quality management (ILO, 1997:97–98). In such varied settings as India, Korea, Japan, Latin America, the US, and Britain, these progressive HRM policies have been found to increase workers' identification with management and reduce their desire to join or remain in unions (ibid.:96–99).

The growing importance of individual firms has had a number of significant effects on IR systems. Particularly given the trend toward an increase in the number of small- and medium-sized enterprises (SMEs), one impact has been a generally reduced role for formal employers' associations, which have tended to enjoy relatively good relations with unions in most countries.[10] Many small firms don't join the associations because they don't think the associations will be able to address their particular needs (ILO, 1997:61). The SMEs' relative growth in importance has been related to the decline in union density rates in some countries, given that these firms are significantly less likely to be unionized than larger firms. At the other end of the spectrum, a growing number of large, highly diversified firms that work in networks have also been breaking away from employers' associations. The major reason here appears to be that firms that work in networks find it difficult to take part in sectoral negotiations, a primary concern of most employers' associations (ibid.:62). More generally, it seems that in the current environment of heightened competition, most employers prefer to act autonomously, particularly in the export business (ibid.). The same desire has prompted many firms to move toward decentralized bargaining structures (discussed below).

At the macro level, a major consequence of firms' growing importance is the weakening of national governments' ability to regulate their domestic economies and IR systems as they otherwise might. This has been a particularly important phenomenon in Western Europe, where pressure from firms has by and large prevented a return to the Keynesian macroeconomic policies used to stabilize economies and keep unemployment down from the end of World War II through the early 1970s (ILO, 1997:11). Increasingly, the fear is that such expansionist macroeconomic policies, which generally depended on high levels of taxation, could trigger a "capital strike" that saw firms moving to countries where taxes and labour costs were lower, or at least outsourcing a sizable share of their production. Fearing such a "capital strike," governments of all political stripes have made price stability their major economic objective, leading many (including Labour and social democratic governments) to adopt austerity policies that impose real hardship on workers and their families (ibid.:11). This has left national labour movements effectively without a political partner, thereby contributing still further to their weakening.

If smaller enterprises have come to play an increasingly important role, so too have the multinationals, which now control an estimated two-thirds or more of all international trade (ILO, 1997:89). Since they are ultimately answerable to no national government, these enterprises pose a particularly serious challenge to national governments seeking to regulate their economies and IR systems. A recent trend within the multinationals has been the rationalization of product lines. Instead of attempting to produce the firm's full range of goods and services at each location, the multinationals now are increasingly setting up establishments specializing in specific production activities at each location (ibid.:91). This new approach has reduced the autonomy of national affiliates. So too has the growing tendency of multinationals to use the new information and communications technology to compare the economic performance of their different affiliates, a trend known as "coercive comparison," with an eye to "disciplining" the bargaining behaviour of local management and workforces alike (ibid.:93; see also Marginson and Sisson, 2002). A survey of 176 multinationals headquartered in Britain found that 70 percent of them make economic comparisons between their affiliates, and a number of major multinationals such as Digital, IBM, and Analog Device have adopted a corporation-wide approach to human resource management (ILO, 1997:93). In General Motors' European operations (Marginson and Sisson, 2002), the company would start by singling out one plant for changes in work organization or work hours. The agreement reached in the first round of bargaining was then presented to all others plants in the next round, forcing them to follow suit. As a result, unions have been forced to accept "overtime corridors" allowing for overtime work without the usual pay premiums, Saturday work, and the like. Such developments have further increased the stress on workers and the unions representing them.

Precarious Employment

Largely as a result of the sort of cost-cutting business strategies described in previous sections, employment has in recent years become more precarious in developed and developing countries alike. Throughout the world, fewer and fewer workers hold what could be called steady, full-time jobs. In manufacturing, firms have moved in the direction of "just-in-time" employment, with a small group of "core" permanent workers being supplemented by a larger group of peripheral workers brought in only at periods of peak demand. In the burgeoning private service sector—for example, in retail—just-in-time employment often takes the form of split shifts, whereby employees must in effect spend twelve hours in order to be paid for eight hours of work.

The trend toward increasingly precarious employment has had a number of different manifestations. First, throughout most of the world, unemployment rates have increased. In some cases, such as those of Argentina, the Scandinavian countries, and the Philippines, the increase since 1980 has been dramatic. While a number of countries, such as France and Spain, have seen improvement since 1995 (see Peirce, 2003:Table 13.4 for 1995 rates), others have worsened, particularly in Latin

Table 13.2

TRENDS IN UNEMPLOYMENT* RATES, 1980 AND 2003, VARIOUS COUNTRIES

Country	1980 Rate (%)	2003 Rate (%)	2003 Rate as % of 1980 Rate
Argentina[†]	2.3	15.6	678.3
Australia	6.1	6.0	98.4
Canada	7.5	7.6	101.3
Chile	10.4	7.4	71.1
Finland	4.7	9.0	191.5
France	6.4	9.6	150.0
Japan	2.0	5.3	265.0
Norway	1.7	3.9	229.4
Philippines	4.8	9.8[§]	204.2
Spain	11.4	11.3	99.1
Sweden	2.0	4.9	245.0
USA	7.0	6.0	85.7
Venezuela	5.9	15.8[‡]	267.8

*Unemployment is defined as percentage of the labour force unemployed.

[†]Data for Argentina for 1980 are for the Buenos Aires metropolitan area only.

[§]Data for Philippines are for 2001.

[‡]Data for Venezuela are for 2002.

Sources: ILO Yearbook of Labour Statistics *World Labour Report*; 1997, Table 8; 1980, Table 2.4; 2003, 2004 Table 3A. Copyright © International Labour Organization.

America. Brazil, Bolivia, Chile, Paraguay, Peru, and Venezuela are but a few of the Latin American countries that have seen an increase of at least 50 percent in their unemployment rates over the past decade (ILO, 2004:Table 3A). Second, in industrialized countries generally, as in Canada (see Chapter 2), a larger share of work is being done on a temporary, part-time, or contractual basis, or out of employees' homes rather than at a formal workplace.

It should also be noted that in developing countries, labour force participation has declined. A growing number of people support themselves through activities in the largely unregulated "informal" sector of the economy, working mainly for themselves or a family member, generally for extremely long hours and often under very poor, sometimes hazardous conditions. In recent years, the informal sector's influence appears to have been growing. While comparative data from the 1980s and 1990s are available for only eight countries, these data show that on average in those eight countries, formal sector participation declined by about one-quarter between the two decades (Peirce, 2003:Table 13.6). From this fact, we can infer that there has likely been a corresponding increase in the informal sector, and other evidence seems to bear this out. In Latin America, the informal sector accounted for over 80 percent of all new jobs created between 1990 and 1994, while in Africa it was estimated that by 1990 the informal sector accounted for over 60 percent of all existing jobs and that it would account for some 90 percent of all new jobs created during the 1990s (ILO, 1997:178–179). These developments have been linked to economic stabilization and restructuring programs that led to declines in public sector employment and large-scale downsizings by private sector firms (ILO, 1997:181).

More recent data (ILO, 2005) suggest continuing high rates of employment in the informal sector. The rates were generally highest in Asia (73 percent in Nepal, 46 to 56 percent in India,[11] 71 percent in Thailand, 63 percent in Indonesia) and in Africa (Ghana, 89 percent; Ethiopia, 50 to 74 percent; South Africa, 31 percent). However, a number of countries in the Americas had surprisingly high rates (Venezuela, 53 percent; Peru, 72 percent; Brazil, 35 percent; and Mexico, 32 percent). A number of eastern European countries such as the Russian Federation, Poland, Slovakia, Turkey, and Latvia had rates in the 5 to 25 percent range. Exceptional here was Lithuania, with a rate of 72 percent.

Long work hours (for those fortunate enough to be employed) are another feature associated with globalization. While the phenomenon is most prevalent in developing countries, even developed countries such as the US have recently experienced an increase in average work hours (from 41 hours in 1994 to 44.6 hours in 2003). In most Latin American countries, weeks of 43 to 50 hours remain the norm. In Asia, Japan has experienced a moderate reduction (to 42 hours), but most other countries are in the 45 to 50 hour range (ILO, 2004). Egypt, Jordan, and Thailand were among countries with an average workweek of 50 hours or more in 2003 (or the most recent year available from the ILO).

Declining Union Representation

Throughout most of the world, the proportion of workers represented by unions has declined over the past two decades. The sharp decline in union membership rates in countries such as Britain, the US, Australia, and New Zealand is by now fairly well known. Less well known, perhaps, but equally dramatic have been the rates of decline in Southern European countries such as Greece and Portugal, in African countries such as Kenya, Uganda, and Zambia, and in Latin American countries such as Argentina, Colombia, Costa Rica, Mexico, and Venezuela. Of 62 countries for which comparative 1980s–1990s data were available from the ILO, 52 saw their union density rates decline while only 10 experienced an increase,[12] several of these being newly-industrialized Asian countries which had previously had very low membership rates. The average decline for the 62 countries surveyed was 7.9 percentage points, or 17.7 percent (Peirce, 2003:Table 13.7). In the Americas, the decline was almost one-quarter (24.6 percent). Moreover, in over half (48) of the 92 countries for which 1995 data were available, union density was less than 20 percent in 1995 (ILO, 1997:7). The rate exceeded 50 percent in only 14 countries, many of these being in Northern Europe, where union membership rates have held up better than in most of the rest of the world.

Overall, the most recent period shows a continuation of the previous (1980–95) period's pattern of declining membership rates in some countries and stable rates in others. But the new millennium also shows some new and (from our perspective, at least) disturbing trends. Of particular note is the sharp decline in union membership

Table 13.3

UNION DENSITY RATES IN SELECTED DEVELOPED COUNTRIES, 1980–2002

Year	1980	1995	2002
Australia	50.0	28.0	23.1
Austria	59.6	51.6	35.0*
Canada	31.0	31.0	30.3
Denmark	77.8	81.9	81.7†
France	19.0	9.0	N/A
Germany	38.3	32.3	22.0*
Italy	49.0	38.5	37.0*
Japan	35.0	20.0	20.2*
Korea, Republic of	21.0	13.8	12.0*
Norway	55.0	56.0	54.0*
Sweden	82.0	83.0	82.0*
UK	55.8	32.1	29.0*
US	23.0	12.0	13.2

*Data for 2000

†Data for 2001

Sources: Lipsig-Mumme, Carla. (2005). "Trade unions and Labour-Relations Systems in Comparative Perspective." In Morley Gunderson, Allan Ponak, and Daphne G. Taras (Eds.), *Union-Management Relations in Canada* (5th ed.). Toronto: Pearson Addison Wesley; Ebbinghaus, Bernard. (2002). "Trade Unions' Changing Roles: Membership Erosion, Organizational Reform and Social Partnership in Europe." *Industrial Relations Journal,* 33:5, pp. 465–483.

rates in Germany and Austria, both countries with a long history of stable, relatively high membership rates, strong social democratic parties, and a tradition of a strong welfare state and tripartite co-operation between the government, employers, and unions. In the case of Germany, the economic difficulties related to the integration of East and West Germany have undoubtedly played a significant role (Lipsig-Mumme, 2005; Hyman, 2001). The explanation for Austria isn't as clear, but may well have something to do with the rise of the far right Freedom Party from a fringe group to junior partner in a centre-right government coalition (see Ebbinghaus, 2002).

One other factor worth noting is the continuing decline in membership in both the UK and Germany, despite the presence of Labour or social democratic governments for at least part of the most recent period. As we noted in the Introduction, the presence of such governments normally helps spur increased union membership. But in the case of the UK, Prime Minister Tony Blair's largely neo-liberal "New Labour" approach has done little to reverse the serious institutional damage caused by Margaret Thatcher's Conservatives, on whose watch British union density dropped by nearly half, from 55 to 29 percent. Even within the Labour Party, the labour movement's role has diminished significantly (Lipsig-Mumme, 2005:491). Much the same has been true in Germany. While Prime Minister Gerhard Schroder has taken principled progressive stands on foreign policy, such as by defying the US on Iraq, in economic matters he too has hewed to a neo-liberal line, cutting both social spending and corporate taxes significantly (Hertz, 2001).

Elsewhere, while tougher economic conditions have certainly played a role, other factors have also been at work. For instance, given that Australia is one of the world's more prosperous countries, it's hard to see how economics alone explains its more than 50 percent decline in union membership rates between 1980 and 2002. Indeed, there and in New Zealand, the decline in union membership rates was driven in large measure by deliberate government policy aimed at reducing the size of the public sector and at making it more comparable to the private sector (see Warrian, 1996) and by the replacement of collective bargaining with a system of individual contracts of employment (Haworth, 1993; Dannin, 1995). In these two countries, politicians modelled their approach quite deliberately on that of Britain, where the Thatcher and Major Conservative governments took policy measures quite deliberately aimed at weakening that country's union movement, such as legislation restricting strikes and making union recognition more difficult (Ferner and Hyman, 1992a; Lipsig-Mumme, 2001). In Eastern and Central European countries formerly belonging to the Soviet bloc, widespread privatization of previously state-owned enterprises (ILO, 1997:44–45) together with the removal of compulsory membership requirements go far toward explaining declining membership rates.[13] In developing countries, reductions in the size of the heavily unionized public sector have been a major factor in declining union membership rates. Equally important is the drop in formal sector employment, since employment in that sector is normally a prerequisite for union membership (ILO, 1997).

A phenomenon closely related to declining union membership is the decentralization of collective bargaining from national or industry levels to the level of the individual enterprise. In general, more centralized systems such as that of Sweden have higher union density rates and have dropped less sharply than decentralized systems such as those of the US, Britain, or Australia (see Peirce, 2003:Table 13.7 and

Lipsig-Mumme, 2001). Because decentralization of bargaining is such an important issue, it will be treated in a separate section.

Decentralization of Bargaining Structures

The movement toward bargaining at the level of the firm, rather than at national or industry levels, was already well under way by the early 1980s (Kochan, McKersie, and Cappelli, 1984); however, the trend has accelerated significantly since then. Driving this trend has been employers' desire for greater flexibility, a desire that also appears to have led to considerable weakening of employers' associations in traditionally centralized European countries (Ebbinghaus, 2002). This development should be of great concern to unions, since organized employers' associations are normally a strong force in support of collective bargaining (ibid.).[14]

In a group of 63 countries surveyed by the ILO (1997:Table 3.1), 18 saw an increase in bargaining at the national or sectoral (industry) level during the ten years preceding the survey. Eleven saw a decrease in bargaining at these levels, while in 23 bargaining at these levels remained relatively stable. Eleven countries provided no data for these levels. At the company level, 46 countries experienced an increase in bargaining, 3 saw a decrease, and 7 remained stable, the same number providing no data. Only in Africa was there an overall trend toward more bargaining at national or sectoral levels.[15] Elsewhere, the vast majority (87 percent) of countries providing data experienced an increase in company-level bargaining. Moreover, even in countries that the ILO traditionally listed as stable at national/sectoral levels, such as Sweden, Denmark, and Germany, there was some devolution of bargaining to lower levels. Similar trends have occurred in France, a country where collective bargaining was historically underdeveloped at the enterprise level (Goetschy and Jobert, 1993). Since then, there has been further decentralization and devolution of bargaining both in Europe and Japan (Ebbinghaus, 2002; Weathers, 2003).

Throughout much of Europe works councils are playing an increasingly important role in IR systems—another sign of the growing importance attached to enterprise-level consultation. Greece established works councils in 1988; Switzerland introduced mandatory participation in the private sector in 1994; and in the Netherlands, a 1996 act extended works councils to the public sector. In France (see above) as well as in Austria and Spain, the scope of works councils' activities has recently been widened (ILO, 1997:121). Perhaps because most works councillors are active unionists (see Adams, 1995a), there is some reason to believe that decentralization of bargaining structures doesn't have as severe an effect on union membership rates in countries with works councils as it does elsewhere, though the recent sharp decline in German and Austrian membership rates (see Table 13.3 above) suggests that this pattern may now be changing.

Overall, the evidence suggests decentralization of bargaining is likely to lead to weaker labour movements and an overall decline in workers' ability to solve workplace problems collectively, as has certainly been the case in Britain, the US, and Australia (to name but a few). In Europe, where industry-level agreements remain common, there is a growing threat that these agreements will be "hollowed out" until they are reduced to a few key minimum standards, with most terms and conditions of employment being established at the level of the individual enterprise (Marginson and Sisson, 2002).

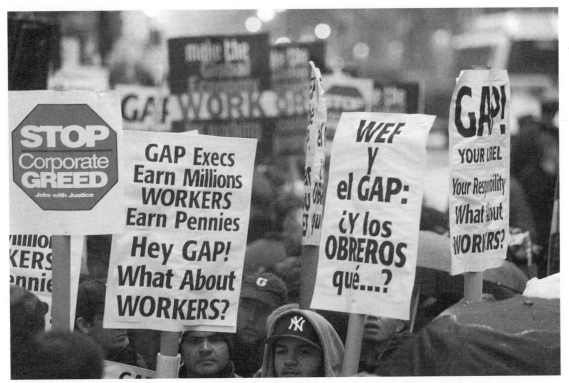

Workers and students demonstrate against clothing retailer The Gap in New York City as part of a January 2002 protest against the globalization of industry.

Liberalization of Former Soviet Bloc IR Systems

With the collapse of the former Soviet Union and the transition of former Soviet bloc countries from planned to market economies, these countries' IR systems have undergone a profound transformation. As noted earlier (see Héthy, 1991), some liberalization was already occurring, particularly in Hungary, prior to the collapse of the Soviet Union. Still, for the most part, unions continued to be closely tied to the state, serving largely as the transmitters of state policy and distributors of its largesse rather than as independent advocates for workers' interests (ILO, 1997:149), while for their part, employers other than the state had very little role to play.

Over the past decade, the role of all three major partners in the IR system has changed markedly, though there are variations in the type and rate of change due to such factors as differing rates of privatization of previously state-owned enterprises in different Central and Eastern European countries. The state's role in these countries' IR systems has been reduced, though it continues to be a major player in its new role as legislator and administrator of labour law and as the continuing owner of at least some business enterprises. More recently, this role has been further reduced by the growth of small- and medium-sized enterprises (SMEs), which in Hungary by 2001 accounted for nearly 70 percent of all employment (Martin and Cristescu-Martin, 2002).

The unions have begun to shift from a patronage role to a more conventional (in Western terms) collective bargaining role. Since the early 1990s, collective bargaining has increased dramatically if unevenly throughout the region. In Central Europe, in particular, most of that bargaining is now done at the enterprise level. An ILO survey of union branches (ILO, 1997:149) found that in Poland, over 96 percent of all wage bargaining was conducted at this level, while for the Czech Republic, Hungary, and Slovakia, the figures were 72 percent, 65 percent, and 60 percent, respectively. At the same time, industry-level bargaining has declined throughout most of the region (ILO, 1997:148). It is not at all clear that Central and Eastern European unions have adapted particularly well to their new role. Due mainly to such trends as privatization, deregulation, and globalization, union membership rates have declined dramatically throughout Eastern Europe over the past 15 years. For example, Hungary's largest union federation saw its membership drop by more than two-thirds between 1991 and 1996 (Frege, 2001). A study of unions in Hungary's garment industry revealed that most workers didn't believe their union could be effective in negotiating better wages and working conditions; a large majority also believed that the Communist union had been more effective in representing their interests. Relatively few identified with the union or expressed willingness to stand for union office. Along similar lines, a majority (60 percent) of union leaders surveyed didn't believe that the union or works council had any real power within the enterprise, and most appeared to regard themselves primarily as a connecting link between workers and management. Such findings lend support to the hypothesis that at least in clothing, Hungarian unions haven't yet developed an independent identity as advocates for workers in the eyes of a good many of their members (Frege, 2001).

During the first few years after the fall of the Soviet Union, national tripartite (government–employer–union) agreements assumed special importance in the former Soviet bloc countries. Often a response to a wave of major strikes, these tripartite agreements served a variety of functions, from setting minimum wages and establishing an economic and social council to protecting workers' claims in the event of insolvency of formerly state-owned enterprises (ILO, 1997:151). In several countries, tripartite agreements have resulted in major reforms in the laws governing collective bargaining and social protection. In Hungary, for example, the National Council for Reconciliation of Interests, founded during the last years of Communism, in early 1997 achieved an agreement aimed at promoting collective bargaining, facilitating the settlement of industrial disputes, and strengthening the application of labour legislation (ibid.:152–153). Tripartite committees were also responsible for settling major strikes in Hungary and the Russian Federation (ibid.:151).

More recently, tripartism appears to have been on the wane on Central and Eastern Europe. While many of the tripartite agreements still exist, a growing number appear to be little more than a hollow shell (Martin and Cristescu-Martin, 2002). Hungary, Poland, and Romania are among countries that have retained a formal commitment to tripartism but where little meaningful dialogue is carried out among the partners (ibid.).

The preceding sections have illustrated some of the changes to IR systems and to the actors within those systems resulting from today's tougher, more uncertain economic climate. In the next section, we look at strategies that different players have adopted in an attempt to adapt to the new, harsher environment. These include union recruitment and retention strategies aimed at women, the unemployed, and atypical workers generally, the formation of informal workers' associations, the creation of liaisons between workers' associations and the formal trade union movement, the growth of transnational unionism, the formation of associations of self-employed entrepreneurs, and publicity campaigns aimed at improving working conditions by inducing consumers not to buy from firms engaging in child labour or other exploitive practices. The chapter concludes with a brief assessment of the adequacy of traditional IR concepts in the current environment.

NEW STRATEGIES FOR A NEW WORLD ORDER

Unions

Confronted by steep declines in employment and membership in their traditional power bases, manufacturing and the public sector, unions are now looking more and more to groups with low levels of unionization, including women, young people, those employed in the private service sector, part-time workers, and even the unemployed, in an effort to bolster their ranks (ILO, 1997:31–32). In some cases, as we note in more detail in a later section, they have begun attracting members from the informal sector as well or forming alliances with informal sector workers' organizations. They are also offering their members a broader range of services and starting to engage in transnational campaigns aimed at correcting abuses such as child labour (ILO, 1997:40–44).

New Sources of Members and Methods of Organizing

Even in Canada, where unionization rights are relatively well-protected by world standards, those seeking to organize private service-sector workers face formidable obstacles. As we noted in Chapter 2, employer opposition to unionization in this sector is particularly strong, and the typically small size of bargaining units makes them expensive for unions to organize and service. Other obstacles include the low pay and high rate of turnover characteristic of this sector and in certain cases legal obstacles, such as bargaining structures that make it extremely difficult for a union to win certification or the outright exclusion of certain groups.[16] In developing countries, the obstacles are often far more severe. In general, the private service sector employs mainly women, and there are many developing countries in which women are far from enjoying equal rights in society at large—let alone in the workplace (ILO, 1997:32).

Despite these obstacles, there have recently been a number of successful efforts to increase union organization in the private service sector. In Canada, many of these efforts have resulted from the diversification of old industrial unions such as the Auto Workers and Steelworkers into general or conglomerate unions. The Steelworkers, for example, now represent security guards and hotel and restaurant workers

(Murray, 2001:99). In the US, there has been a growing recognition that the organization of women and ethnic minority group members requires different strategies than the recruitment of traditional male members in manufacturing. The Service Employees' International Union (SEIU), which represents large numbers of janitors and others in the highly unstable building services industry, has made significant use of those new strategies, based on empowerment and dignity rather than economic benefits, to bring in large numbers of women and minority group members, particularly Mexican-Americans in Texas and California (see Bronfenbrenner, 1992). Increasingly, too, the SEIU has realized that the site for organization must be the community as a whole, rather than simply the enterprise. Of particular note was its "Justice for Janitors" campaign, which bypassed National Labor Relations Board rules on bargaining structure and resulted in the city-wide organization of workers in such cities as Los Angeles, Portland, Denver, and Seattle (ILO, 1997:45–46).

A number of efforts have been directed specifically at women. In the Netherlands, for example, there are now separate women's trade unions that include equality of opportunity and treatment on their bargaining agendas (ILO, 1997:32–33). In Canada and the US, some unions have made particular efforts to organize women (ibid.:33). Unions and labour federations in Canada, France, Britain, and Italy have reserved certain management positions for women, and other unions have set up special women's departments. Other countries whose unions have made a special effort to take account of women's concerns or to integrate them into the union's management structure include Sweden, Uganda, the Netherlands, and Germany (ibid.:32–33).

Still other efforts have been targeted at specific groups of "atypical" workers. Unions in France, Germany, Japan, and Britain have made special efforts to reach out to part-time workers, while homeworkers have been targeted in Canada, Britain, the Netherlands, and Australia. Unions have also managed to conclude collective agreements for temporary workers sent out by agencies and other casual workers in Germany, France, and the Netherlands, as well as Canada. In Canada, certain artists and performers in the federal jurisdiction can now bargain collectively under the *Artists and Producers Professional Relations Act*. Since the act was passed in 1993, a number of collective agreements have been concluded by groups such as the Periodical Writers' Association of Canada. The act has been held up as a model for collective representation of freelance workers offering their services to a variety of different clients, but on essentially similar terms (Sims, 1995:241). Artists and performers have also achieved collective representation in France and Japan (ILO, 1997:35). In Canada, as well, certain types of self-employed individuals such as taxi drivers and fishers have been able to obtain collective representation under "dependent contractor" provisions in various jurisdictions' labour relations legislation. In France, there are collective agreements between oil companies and the tenant managers of service stations and inter-occupational agreements for commercial travellers and sales representatives (ILO, 1997:35).

Collective representation of retirees and the unemployed has been uneven, in part because of legal restrictions on union membership for members of these groups in countries such as Chile (ILO, 1997:35). Europe offers a more favourable environment for such representation, since all organizations affiliated to the European Trade Union Federation allow workers who have lost their jobs to retain their membership. In several northern European countries, union con-federations have set up special departments to address the needs of the unem-ployed and have launched programs aimed at other target groups such as migrants and young people. In addition, they have attempted to stay in touch with their retired members (ibid.).

New Union Services

In an attempt to retain existing members, unions have begun offering these members a broader range of direct assistance. The supplementary unemploy-ment benefits found in many collective agreements are a direct legacy of unions' "mutual insurance" function, as described by the Webbs (see the beginning of Chapter 5). Other unions have begun providing their members with legal and financial services and career counselling and other kinds of employment advice (Murray, 2001:101; ILO, 1997:31). An increasingly common benefit of union membership is the "affinity" credit card, whereby members pay lower fees and receive reduced interest on outstanding balances. Such cards are now available to union members in Britain, the US, and Canada (see ILO, 1997:31). Some British and American unions also offer their members discounts on loans and insurance premiums and run their own travel agencies and even retirement homes. In Japan, the "trade union identity" movement has established "total well-being" programs (ibid.).

Transnational Unionism

The emergence of multinational enterprises and the formation of regional eco-nomic blocs have made it increasingly important for unions in different countries to work together. Often, such international collaboration is difficult to achieve. To begin with, there are the obvious linguistic, religious, and cultural barriers. Beyond that, in several African countries (Nigeria, Cameroon, and Kenya), legislation either prohibits or severely restricts unions from affiliating to international confederations (ILO, 1997:37). In Britain, the US, and Brazil, the scope of international union action is limited by legislation restricting secondary boycotts; in other countries, it is limited by restrictions on sympathy and solidarity strikes (ibid.:38). Elsewhere (as within the European Union), the diversity of national labour relations regimes may prove a barrier to international co-operation.

Despite these barriers, international co-operation between unions has been increasing. Such co-operation has been most prominent in Europe, where regional economic integration has the longest track record and where the European Trade Union Congress (ETUC) plays a prominent role as a coordinating body (ILO, 1997:44). There, too, the International Trade Secretariats (ITSs) for different sectors have played an important role in bringing together the unions of the subsidiaries of multinationals, such as Honda and Fiat, into committees to exchange information or prepare for negotiations with the company's central management. Like other regional and international labour organizations such as the ETUC and International Confederation of Free Trade Unions (ICFTU), the ITSs also help facilitate bilateral relations between national trade unions and represent these unions in bodies such as the ILO (ILO, 1997:39). Trade unions have become particularly interested in forming bilateral and even multilateral cross-border co-operation initiatives to counter the multinational firms' "coercive comparisons" described earlier in the chapter. These initiatives become even more important as European Monetary Union (EMU) heightens competition among multinationals, which in turn forces them to seek to impose even more stringent conditions on their workforces (Marginson and Sisson, 2002).

Genuine international collective agreements are rare, but examples do exist. In 1988, the Danone Company and the IUF (International Union of Food, Agricultural, Hotel, Restaurant, Catering, Tobacco and Allied Workers' Associations) signed an agreement covering the promotion of equality between the sexes, skill training and development, and union rights (including unions' access to information). In 1995, the same union signed an agreement with the Accor Hotel group guaranteeing full freedom of association in all the group's establishments (such as the Novotel Hotels). There have also been agreements at the sectoral level (ibid.:43). For example, in 1995, the ETUC organization for the textiles, clothing, and leather sector and the European Confederation of the Footwear Industry signed an agreement whereby the Confederation's member companies undertook not to employ children in manufacturing anywhere in the world, either directly or through indirect subcontracting arrangements (ibid.:44).

Where international collective agreements have been reached, they've often been the result of broad-based publicity campaigns involving a broad range of partners such as religious, consumer, women's, and students' organizations as well as labour groups (see ILO, 1997:43, Box 2.3). Such campaigns are of particular importance in developing countries, where repressive labour legislation may make it extremely difficult for workers to form unions or for them to assert their rights in any meaningful way even if they do manage to form a union. In such cases, particularly when confronting a multinational enterprise, appealing to those enterprises' customers may be the only way to bring about positive change.

Recently, heightened competition has made many multinational firms more concerned than before about their public image. For this reason, the threat of loss of business can often bring about results more effectively than traditional union action at points of production. As the box below indicates, modern publicity campaigns are often highly sophisticated and multifaceted exercises involving a variety of different players.

Current Issues 13.1

BLOOD, SWEAT, AND PENNIES

As most of the world's TV screens focused on the 2004 Athens Olympics, a broad-based coalition led by the development agency, Oxfam, was seeking to focus public attention on the conditions of the men and women who made the athletic shoes and clothing athletes were wearing at the Olympics. Oxfam was joined in its campaign by the British Trade Union Council (TUC), global unions, the Clean Clothes Campaign, and Labour Behind the Label. ▶

Oxfam researchers found that wretched pay, appalling and unsafe working conditions, and suppression of union activity were the order of the day for the hundreds of thousands of people (mainly women) working in athletic shoe and garment factories.

A 22-year-old Thai worker noted that 16 or 17-hour shifts were routine. "Sometimes we want to rest, but our employer forces us to work," she said. "We cannot refuse overtime work as our standard wages are so low." The seven-day week is also the norm in the sportswear and garment industries, particularly at peak times like the run-up to the Olympics.

Despite the noisy working environment, the Thai worker said management didn't provide workers with masks or earplugs or educate them on how to protect their health.

In Indonesia, sportswear factory workers seeking to form a union were subjected to the full gamut of intimidation techniques, from badmouthing union activists in the workplace or firing them to hiring local thugs to beat up union leaders. [Shades of Henry Ford—authors' note.]

According to International Confederation of Free Trade Unions (ICFTU) general secretary Guy Ryder, the Olympics are supposed to be "a showcase of fairness and human achievement. But the exploitation and abuse of workers' rights endemic in sportswear is violating that spirit."

"We want companies to talk to us so we can work together for workers in the industry," said TUC general secretary Brendan Barber.

Initial reaction from the sportswear industry was mixed. Nike said it welcomed the Oxfam report and was working to improve working conditions, while Adidas said it already had a code of conduct in place requiring its suppliers to abide by core labour standards. Puma was "skeptical" of Oxfam's findings regarding its clothing sources, while a UK sportswear firm had no comment.

Meanwhile, one company that has often been the target of protests and negative publicity campaigns found itself praised by labour activists for its openness. In early August 2004, the retail clothing company The Gap released a self-critical study of conditions in its network of 3000 factories that supply its popular range of casual clothing. The study found that about 90 percent of its suppliers failed The Gap's initial evaluations, and that over half of its sites in sub-Saharan Africa were operating machinery without effective safety equipment.

Source: Gary Flood. (2004). "Gold Medal for Exploitation," on UNISON website, http://www.unison.org.uk/features/features (Aug.).

There are a number of different types of trade union publicity campaigns, and various roles that a union may take in such campaigns. In some cases, the aim is to assist an affiliated union, typically, though not always, in a developing country. Here, the union may coordinate local demands, enter into partnerships with other international unions, lobby politicians, apply pressure on targeted companies, or even threaten to apply trade sanctions based on workers' rights provisions of national trade law.

In other cases, the objective may be broader, such as the abolition of child labour or the overall improvement of working conditions in a particular country or industry (ILO, 1997:43). Here, a tactic sometimes used is the awarding of a "social label," as a sign that the goods in question have been manufactured under acceptable conditions. As an example, in 1997 several major American clothing firms, including Nike and L.L. Bean, concluded an agreement with trade unions and human rights groups in which they agreed to implement basic rules governing wages and working conditions and apply them to subcontractors, as well as their own subsidiaries. The agreement provided for a label, to be attached to clothes manufactured by the companies' subsidiaries and subcontractors, and established an association to verify implementation (ibid.:41, 43).

The pace and variety of publicity campaigns conducted by unions, central labour bodies, and their allies have increased in recent years, due to the continued spread of globalization and the continuing dominance of the political right. A major project has been the attempt to end the use of child labour in the manufacture of soccer balls in India and Pakistan (Cohn, n.d.). Earlier this year, the global union Union Network International (UNI) tied up its head offices in Nyon, Switzerland in white ribbon as part of a global campaign to end poverty (UNI, 2005). Earlier, metalworking unions, acting in unity, held a European Day of Action on Oct. 19, 2004, to protest General Motors' plans to cut 12 000 jobs in Europe (IMF, 2004). And in Colombia, the international trade union movement banded together to protest the expulsion of four international union representatives from that country, on orders of President Uribe (Global Unions, 2004). In addition to writing Uribe, the protest took the form of complaints to the ILO, their national governments, and intergovernmental and regional bodies including the European Union.

WORKERS' ASSOCIATIONS

We noted earlier that in many developing countries, a majority of workers do not belong to the formal sector, but rather work in the informal sector of the economy. The ILO has identified six different types of informal sector worker: owners or employers of micro-enterprises with a few paid employees or apprentices; self-employed workers; wage labourers employed in micro-enterprises; unpaid family workers; paid domestic workers; and wage workers who work in a place of their own choosing—normally at home (ILO, 1997:181). Many such workers do different categories of informal sector work during a given year. For example, they may work as paid labourers during peak agricultural harvesting seasons, then spend the rest of the year as self-employed entrepreneurs, selling goods they have made at home (ibid.). Although there is considerable variation from country to country in the relative importance of the different classes of informal sector worker, the ILO (1997:182) suggests that the self-employed, either working alone or aided by unpaid family members or apprentices, make up the largest group.

While it was formerly believed that the informal sector was a "transient phenomenon destined to disappear with economic modernization" (ILO, 1997:217), as discussed earlier, more recent evidence suggests that far from disappearing, the informal sector is growing, particularly in Africa and Latin America. By 1995, it comprised more than half the non-agricultural labour force in 14 of 17 Latin America countries (ILO, 1997:237, Table 1.3).

There are major barriers to the organization of informal sector workers, including the diversity of their employment status, which makes it difficult for them to find common cause; the fact that family or ethnic loyalties are often more important than working-class solidarity; and the small size and instability of informal sector units (ILO, 1997:181–183).[17] Yet another problem, which makes it particularly difficult for governments to regulate informal sector activities, is the blurring of the usual employer–employee distinction. Organization is also hindered by these units' tendency to operate on the fringes of, if not outside, the law, and by their lack of access to credit, training, and sometimes even such basic public services as sanitation, electricity, and running water (ibid.:184–186, 192–193). While it is difficult to estimate the extent of informal sector organization, it appears to be extremely low; estimates range from 1 percent in Bogota, Colombia, to 20 per cent in Dar-es-Salaam, Tanzania. Moreover, existing organizations don't appear to be growing very rapidly (ibid.:195).

Typically informal workers' associations are made up primarily of self-employed (own-account) workers or micro-entrepreneurs, who are generally in a stronger negotiating position than casual labourers or unpaid family workers (ibid.). The associations may be either trade- or neighbourhood-based. Examples of the former include a rickshaw-pullers' union in Nagpur, India, which has achieved some improvements in the legislation governing rickshaw licences, and a Tanzanian association of repair service businesses. The latter has developed codified skills profiles for its various trades in order to be able to regulate access to business and contract negotiations collectively, thus reducing competition from ill-qualified newcomers (ILO, 1997:198–200).

Neighbourhood-based or area-based multi-trade associations may be more cohesive than trade-based ones, as their members tend not to be competing for the same business (ILO, 1997:197). In some cases, they may play something of the same role as business associations in North America, ensuring that surroundings are kept clean and seeking to create an attractive environment for business while avoiding official harassment or theft (ibid.:198). But they also may play a more overtly political role, as in certain Latin American and African cities, where they helped coordinate protest riots against increases in the price of staple foods (ibid.). In the Philippines, the Apitong Neighbourhood Association (ANA) managed, despite some setbacks, to develop the land it had acquired through a government-sponsored community mortgage program for housing in urban areas. In addition to developing road, drainage, and water systems, ANA provided management training and helped obtain credit for members seeking to set up small businesses (ibid.:197).

Women have played a key role in many informal workers' associations. As the ILO notes (1997:195), these organizations have often been of particular benefit to impoverished women workers, since they have provided services that have helped increase women's opportunities in the labour market and made them more aware of their legal rights. It has also been observed that governments tend to regard women's organizations as less politically threatening than male-dominated groups, and that the former are less vulnerable to corruption because they have less experience in dealing with public institutions (ibid.). For example, the Cissin-Natanga Women's Association of Burkina Faso was initially organized by a group of women attending a literacy course. In 1985, with help from the country's central trade union congress, it was transformed into a more formal association. It has built craft and literacy centres for its members in which members are trained in various trades (ibid.:205). In Thailand, Chiangmai HomeNet began as a co-operative of home-workers' groups. Its achievements include the establishment of a credit union and a co-operative (ibid.:196, 202).

Workers' Associations and the Union Movement

The growth of the informal sector has proven a serious challenge for labour movements in developing countries. On the one hand, feelings of solidarity and humanity make unions eager to help workers who, in general, are in an even more difficult situation than their own members. On the other hand, unions recognize that the growth of the informal sector reduces their bargaining power and threatens the rights and conditions of workers regularly employed in the formal sector. At a time when their own membership is declining, often severely, some unions fear that the added burdens posed by informal sector workers would simply be too great. As well, established unions often find it difficult to obtain financial support to defend informal sector workers' interests because of competition from non-governmental organizations (ILO, 1997:203). (This appears to be less of a problem for international unions, perhaps because as international organizations they are not in direct competition with the associations or the NGOs.)

Despite these obstacles, co-operation between the organized labour movement and informal workers' associations has been increasing. In some cases, a union will provide specific technical or political assistance to a workers' association. In Ghana, for example, the Industrial and Commercial Workers' Union (ICWU) has been training members of the Ghana Hairdressers' and Beauticians' Association in occupational health and safety (ILO, 1997:188); while in Brazil, the central trade union congress has lobbied for policies that would make it easier for small-scale producers, craftspeople, and other self-employed workers to pursue income-generating activities (ibid.:203).

In other cases, the association may form a special department (e.g., women's department) of a union, or its members may simply be invited to join the larger organization. In India, the now well-known Self-Employed Women's Association (SEWA) began as the women's wing of the Textile Labour Association before evolving into an independent union and forming alliances with international unions and federations (ibid.:204–205); while in Ghana, union constitutions have been revised to allow informal sector workers to join. Latin American unions appear particularly open to informal sector workers, in part because of legislation in such countries as Brazil and Peru allowing self-employed workers to form or join unions. The self-employed have assumed such importance in Brazil that the country's central trade union congress has established a separate branch specifically to address their concerns (ibid.:204).

An association strategy in between seeking specific assistance from trade unions and seeking to allow informal sector workers to join the unions is that of forming long-term alliances with them. We have already referred to the Indian organization SEWA, which has long enjoyed such alliances internationally with the IUF union and ICFTU confederation. In Caracas, Venezuela, the Coordinating Body of Informal Sector Retail Workers (CONIVE) has obtained legal advice and political support from two regional Latin American unions, the Latin American Central of Workers and the Latin American Federation of Retail Workers, in a bid to strengthen its bargaining position vis-à-vis the municipal authorities. With the help of its partners, CONIVE has sought to persuade the authorities to create a public market area in which small retail traders might operate and to rescind a draft municipal order barring vendors from city streets (ILO, 1997).

In a few instances, informal associations have succeeded in bringing about change at the national political level. One such case involves PATAMBA, the Philippines' network of homeworkers' associations. Largely through PATAMBA's efforts, a National Steering Committee on Home Work was established in 1991. Gaining greater visibility through its participation in the Steering Committee, PATAMBA was later invited to take part in a National Tripartite Conference, which resulted in an Administrative Order providing significant improvements in homeworkers' legal status and working conditions, including the right to form or join associations of their own choosing (ILO, 1997:210).

ASSOCIATIONS OF MICRO-ENTREPRENEURS

Small-scale entrepreneurs, who are numerous throughout the developing world, face special difficulties. These typically include lack of marketable skills, lack of access to capital and credit, low levels of literacy, and lack of access to training and technology. These barriers tend to be even more formidable in the case of women, whose literacy levels are generally lower than those of men and who have less experience in the wider world (ILO, 1997:189). While institutions such as Bangladesh's Grameen Bank and Indonesia's Bank Rakyat have been successful at granting credit to micro-entrepreneurs, overall the demand for small-scale credit continues to outrun the supply (ibid.:190).

Like workers' associations, micro-entrepreneurs' associations may operate on a trade, neighbourhood, or area basis. And like the workers' associations, the micro-entrepreneurial ones may also link up with larger, more established employers' associations or trade bodies to obtain technical, legal, or lobbying assistance. Often, established employers' associations have supported the establishment of micro-entrepreneurs' associations. In a number of African countries, including Kenya, Nigeria, and Uganda, the employers' associations provide active assistance to the informal associations, as by offering "Start your business" and "Improve your business" programs aimed at the informal sector (ILO, 1997: 206–207).

A good example of a trade-based micro-entrepreneurs' association is the Panorama Rancho Estate Tricycle Operators and Drivers, Inc., or PARETODA, which has been operating in the Philippines since 1980. Eventually, PARETODA decided to join the Marikna Tricycle Operators' and Drivers' Association to benefit from the experience of the larger group's 60 other members. Thanks to the advice provided by more experienced members, local authorities granted PARETODA's request for a tricycle terminal (ILO, 1997:202, 207).

In Central America, with the decline in the state's role throughout most of the region, associations of micro-entrepreneurs have been playing an increasingly important role in economic renewal and the rebuilding of civil society after years of devastating wars. In 1992, associations of micro-entrepreneurs from seven Central American countries formed a Committee of Central American Micro-entrepreneurs (COCEMI), with an eye to coordinating efforts to upgrade the development of micro-enterprises and increasing affiliates' bargaining power at the country level (ILO,

1997:207). Through networking and lobbying, COCEMI promotes its affiliates' interests with national, regional, and international agencies. It also seeks to act as a conduit for technical and financial support to its national members' organizations (ibid.:208).

Elsewhere, informal sector associations are pooling their resources in an attempt to increase their productivity and bargaining power. In the African country of Benin, some 1600 micro-enterprises comprising a broad range of trades have established about 60 mutual savings and loan associations. Over time, the associations have had a high rate of recovery and good observance of repayment schedules. Recently they have begun to loan out their accumulated savings, thus further contributing to local economic development, and have also begun looking at ways to manage their assets jointly (ILO, 1997:207–209).

SUMMARY

Our review of IR systems and economic and working conditions suggests that in most of the developing world, workers face problems of a different order of magnitude than those generally faced in the developed world. In the latter, what we might refer to as industrial citizenship, including the right to join a union, bargain collectively, and if need be go on strike, remains restricted in many cases. This is certainly true in the developing world, as well. But there, workers also face restrictions on what we might call their economic citizenship, which can be defined as the ability, given a reasonable degree of effort, to hold paid employment in the formal labour force. For the most part, these restrictions are economic ones, resulting from a lack of sufficient economic opportunities in the formal economic sector. In some cases, such as the limitations put on women's labour force participation in certain countries, the restrictions are of a cultural nature. Whatever the cause, rural poverty levels of 30 to 80 percent throughout most of Africa and Latin America and much of Asia (see ILO, 1997:Table 6), together with the low labour force and formal sector participation rates to which we have already referred, attest to the developing world's "economic citizenship" crisis.

In closing, it seems appropriate to revisit the question of whether traditional IR terminology and mechanisms can usefully be applied to developing countries. We should admit from the outset that IR can't possibly be the same in the typical developing country as it is in Canada or the US or a European country. To give just one example, the state's role is inevitably more limited (and also more ambiguous) in a country where a majority of workers are not employed in the formal sector. To many informal sector workers, state regulation, however well-intentioned, is more apt to be seen as harassment than as an attempt at protection. This said, the traditional IR institutions such as unions, employers' associations, and government agencies *do* operate, even in the developing world. The traditional institutions' enduring power is suggested by the fact that informal sector organizations such as workers' and micro-entrepreneurs' associations often seek to emulate them, and in some cases even to join them. Moreover, when a country's economic or political situation improves (as in the case of South Africa since the end of apartheid), there is a strengthening of the traditional institutions.[18]

Still, although there is much about employment relationships that traditional IR can explain, even in developing countries, there is also much that it cannot explain. For instance, in considering how workers' associations operate, we're apt to find that the neighbourhood or city is a more appropriate level of analysis than the workplace. And the tactics of sophisticated modern publicity campaigns aimed at bettering Third World employment conditions extend far beyond the picket line.

Clearly, full-fledged industrial citizenship remains the goal, for workers in the Third World as well as the First. In the former, however, most would probably agree that industrial citizenship means little in the absence of basic economic citizenship—the ability to earn a living in the formal labour force. It thus seems fair to say that economic citizenship is a necessary pre-condition of industrial citizenship. A logical corollary is that to understand the full range of employment relationships in developing countries, the modern industrial relationist's toolkit must include an understanding of economic, community, and regional development. Without these additional tools, the resulting analysis will of necessity be limited to the more fortunate members of society, and will therefore be of little value from a practical perspective.

Case 13.1

FROM SEWING MACHINES TO SCRIBBLERS: THE ATTACK ON CHILD LABOUR IN BANGLADESH'S GARMENT INDUSTRY

The garment industry has been in sharp decline recently in developed countries, as manufacturers seek to pay wages below even statutory minima in Canada or the US. One of the beneficiaries has been Bangladesh, which saw its garment exports increase more than 100-fold, to $4 billion US, between 1983 and 1999. The garment industry accounts for almost two-thirds of the country's export earnings, and nearly half of all exports are to the US. Employment in the industry increased even more rapidly than exports, from about 10 000 to 1.5 million, 80 percent of whom were women.

In 1993, in response to growing concerns about the number of children employed in garments and other industries in the developing world, US Senator Tom Harkin introduced a bill banning the importation of goods produced wholly or in part by child labour. To avoid jeopardizing their lucrative US trade, Bangladeshi garment manufacturers began dismissing their child workers *en masse*. To help maintain family incomes, the former garment workers were often forced into even harder and more dangerous work, such as stone-crushing.

In 1994, the ILO and UNICEF received a written appeal from 53 Bangladeshi children. In response, they urged the Bangladesh Garment Manufacturers' and Exporters' Association (BGMEA) not to fire their child workers until a school system and other protective measures were in place. After almost a year of intense negotiations, the three parties, actively supported by the US Embassy and the government of Bangladesh, signed a Memorandum of Understanding (MOU), "The Placement of Child Workers in School Programs and the Elimination of Child

Labour." The MOU provided for an initial fact-finding survey, a special education program for former working children, monitoring and verification in the garment factories, income compensation for children attending school classes, skills training, and micro-credit and entrepreneurship training.

The survey found some 9500 children employed in the garment industry. While this number was minuscule compared to the numbers employed in agriculture or the informal sector, the ILO and UNICEF believed that due to the industry's importance to the country's economy, reductions in child labour here would provide considerable leverage for the ILO's Program for the Elimination of Child Labour (IPEC) and other organizations to reduce child labour elsewhere in the country.

UNICEF took responsibility for a three-year Non-Formal Educational component, in partnership with two national NGOs. A verification system was set up through the BGMEA/ILO/UNICEF Child Labour Project. ILO monitors were trained to carry out unannounced visits in all BGMEA member factories and verify school attendance. A monthly stipend was agreed on for each child withdrawn and placed into the informal education program. To oversee and coordinate implementation of the MOU, a local Steering Committee was set up with members from BGMEA, UNICEF, and ILO, and observers from Bangladesh's Ministry of Labour and the US Embassy. Among other things, the committee's objective was to deal decisively with non-compliance.

All child garment workers in the rehabilitation program are entitled to receive basic primary education at various non-formal schools established by the two partner NGOs. Children aged 14 and over are able to attend school as well as work, or receive skills training, under the "Earn and Learn" program. It appears that in most cases, the monthly stipend of about $8, paid to all those who attend school regularly, pretty well replaces the children's former earnings.

In 2000, the three original parties signed a second MOU aimed at continuing the social protection program and transferring the monitoring and evaluation system to a local entity to ensure sustainability.

Results

Between 1995 and 2000, the percentage of garment factories using child labour dropped from 43 percent to 5 percent. Some 2000 children were enabled to continue their formal education, and over 8200 received non-formal education. Another 680 received vocational training, while a further 148 were scheduled to do so. IPEC developed a database to provide a system for the random selection of factories to be visited each day by project managers. Between 1996 and 1999, the number of factory visits increased more than fourfold.

The program has been held up as a model for other programs aimed at eliminating child labour. In fact, an agreement by the Sialkot Chamber of Commerce and Industry, the ILO, and UNICEF to phase out child labour in Pakistan's soccer ball industry is considered a replication of the BGMEA model. The project has served as a model for similar ventures in seven other developing countries and has also inspired a large European-based fashion company to set up a skills training centre for former child workers in the garment industry, who are then placed in the company's factories on completion of the program.

One key to the project's success was BGMEA's ability to convince most of its members to co-operate with the monitoring teams. Another was the composition of the teams and the social and communication skills of the 50 monitors. Each team was made up of one government inspector, along with one BGMEA and two IPEC monitors. The aim was always to persuade, rather than pressure the factory owners into compliance. As part of the monitoring process, teams would advise manufacturers on how to comply with the program and would also inform them of the program's potential benefits to them.

A third key success factor was awareness-raising. Publicity campaigns were mounted both in Bangladesh and outside, attracting international interest in the new program model.

One of the featured speakers at a joint ILO–US Labor Department conference on the elimination of child labour, held in 2000, was Julekha Akhter, a former child garment worker from Bangladesh. Julekha was initially forced to take work in a garment factory at age 9, when she was in third grade, due to her father's illness. Thanks to the BGMEA program, Julekha was able to leave the factory at age 12 and continue her schooling, receiving a stipend sufficient to pay the family's rent. In addition to the "3 Rs," she took part in cultural activities like singing, dancing, acting, and reciting poems. On reaching age 14, she lost her stipend, but after taking further skills training, was able to obtain a job with Dragon Sweater, at a wage that has helped raise her family out of poverty. At the same time, she continues her studies under an "Earn and Learn" program.

Sources: Primary source: ILO/US Department of Labor. (2000). *Advancing the Global Campaign against Child Labor: Progress Made and Future Actions*, a report of a conference hosted by the US Department of Labor in collaboration with the International Labor Organization (ILO) on May 17, 2000, in Washington DC. The case study on Bangladesh's garment industry, one of 32 included in the report, was drawn on extensively. Also used: Grant, Michel. (2000). "Industrial Relations in the Clothing Industry: Lessons for Survival." In R. Chaykowski and A. Verma (Eds.), *Industrial Relations in Canadian Industry*, Toronto: Dryden.

Case Questions

1. How do First World boycotts of products produced by children help benefit people in the developing world?
2. What are some possible drawbacks of the boycott approach to child labour?
3. What were the key elements to the BGMEA program's success?
4. Do you see any potential difficulties with the approach taken in this case?
5. How might the project be improved for the future?

QUESTIONS FOR DISCUSSION

1. Have a chat with a classmate from a country other than your own. Compare his or her experiences with work and the IR system to yours. Pay particular attention to the role played by the labour movement in the two countries.
2. Distinguish between unfree, free, and partially free IR systems.

3. Distinguish between centralized and decentralized IR systems and give at least two examples of each.

4. Within Canada, what's distinctive about Quebec's IR system? Do you think these distinctive traits will likely last much longer?

5. How have the two free trade agreements affected the Canadian economy and IR system? Why has the impact been particularly great on low-wage industries?

6. How has globalization given more power to firms and managers?

7. Discuss the different ways in which employment has become more precarious in developed and developing countries.

8. Explain briefly why labour movements in centralized IR systems have generally fared better in recent years than those in decentralized systems.

9. Why is it now harder than in the past for national governments to introduce Keynesian economic policies that stimulate the economy and benefit workers and unions?

10. In what ways do you think informal workers' associations are an adequate substitute for trade unions? In what ways do they fall short? In your view, is it realistic to expect wide-scale mergers of the two in developing countries?

11. Are unions doing enough to build bridges with their counterparts in other countries? If you think they aren't, what else should they be doing?

Suggestions for Further Reading

Adams, Roy. (1995). "Canadian Industrial Relations in Comparative Perspective." In M. Gunderson and A. Ponak (Eds.), *Union-Management Relations in Canada* (3rd ed.). Don Mills, ON: Addison-Wesley. An excellent brief introduction to comparative IR, focusing mainly on systems in developed countries.

Hyman, Richard. (2001). "The Europeanisation—or the Erosion—of Industrial Relations?" *Industrial Relations Journal*, 32:4, pp. 280–294. A masterful essay linking theoretical concerns about the nature of industrial relations to recent practical developments in Europe. Must reading for anyone with a serious interest in the European IR scene.

International Labour Office (ILO). (1997). *World Labour Report*, 1997–98. Geneva: ILO. Offers an extremely thorough (sometimes chilling) account of labour relations and working conditions around the world at the turn of the millennium. Contains a particularly thorough discussion of the new "informal" sector. Extremely useful statistical tables.

CHAPTER 14

KEY THEMES AND ISSUES

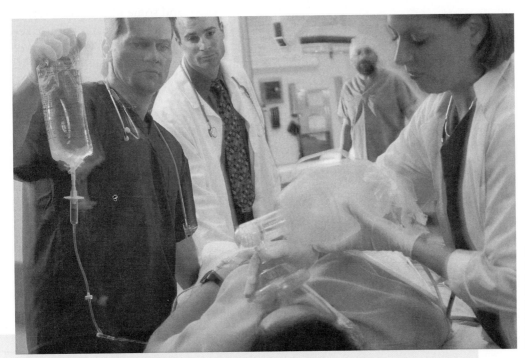

Continuing budget cuts are making it even more difficult for these community health care workers to do their jobs protecting public health.

LEARNING OBJECTIVES

After studying this chapter, you should be able to:

1. Explain the significance of each of the five key themes to the IR system as a whole.
2. Describe the key findings in support of each of the themes.
3. Discuss the policy options advanced.
4. Identify major areas where further IR research is needed and why.

In this chapter, we step back from the examination of specific issues and topics that has dominated the previous chapters, with an eye to seeing where the Canadian IR system as a whole has been going, and where it may be headed in the years to come. The chapter focuses on five key themes that, in our view, raise critical issues of public labour policy. It features a look at these five key themes and at some important findings related to each, as well as a discussion of policy suggestions arising out of each theme. The chapter closes with a discussion of areas where further IR research appears most urgently needed.

FIGURE 14.1

FIVE KEY THEMES

1. The impending demographic crisis.
2. The increasingly precarious nature of work.
3. The special problems facing immigrants to Canada.
4. The continuing lack of meaningful representation.
5. An overloaded conflict resolution system.

This book has tried to provide an introductory survey of industrial relations that is both comprehensive and comprehensible. In this chapter, the aim is to try to put the pieces together, and to take a broader look at the Canadian IR system and some of the directions in which it appears to be heading. We will do this through an examination of five key themes that, at least to some extent, appear to cut across the specific treatment of various topics in the previous thirteen chapters and raise important issues for IR policy makers.

In what follows, we start by looking at the themes themselves, as well as key findings related to those themes. You will note that the themes are often interrelated. For instance, Theme 4, the continuing lack of meaningful representation, may be linked directly to Theme 2, the increasingly precarious nature of work. Likewise, Theme 3, the special problems facing immigrants, may be directly linked to Theme 1, the demographic crisis, as immigration is one of the means policy makers are using in an attempt to solve the demographic crisis. If you read the previous (international) chapter, you'll also recognize that many of the problems facing Canadian workers and their unions are pretty much the same as those facing workers and union around the world.

KEY THEMES AND FINDINGS

The Demographic Crisis

In our previous edition, the impending demographic crisis was a key theme. (See Peirce, 2003:441–442). The situation doesn't appear to have changed much since then. This impending crisis already had significant effects on Canadian workplaces. As more baby boomers retire, these effects will likely become more serious. By 2015—less than a decade from now—it's estimated that 48 percent of the population age 15 and over will be between the ages of 45 and 64 (FLMM, 2003) and over 15 percent will be 65 and over (Duchesne, 2004a). Indeed, after 2016, the working age population is expected to decline. Currently the country's fertility rate is well below replacement level, and its birth rate is at an all-time low (Seward, 2005).

Potential skill shortages have been a concern for both management and union officials for some time (see CLBC, 2000; CLBC, 2004; Seward, 2005). In addition to the shortages in the public sector and in scientific areas discussed in our previous edition,[1] it now appears that Canada also faces serious skills shortages in manufacturing, a sector where the median retirement age is 61 (Seward, 2005). As of 2003, 11 percent of all manufacturing employees, including 15 percent of all managers and 13 percent of all skilled tradespersons, were over 55 and thus rated to be likely candidates for retirement by 2009 (ibid.). Manufacturing employers have already been relying heavily on immigrants to meet their needs for labour. The number of immigrants employed in the sector grew by over 200 000 over the past decade, a period when the sector as a whole grew by just 125 000 (Beauchesne, 2003). With the forecast one of continuing decline in Canadian birth rates, this dependence on immigration to meet the manufacturing sector's needs for workers can only increase. While we lack specific data for skill needs in other sectors, the situation is likely to be the same in many of them, as well.

The stress on the public pension system is likely to be particularly severe, as a much smaller number of prime-age workers struggles to support a much larger number of retirees. In addition, the health care system is likely to be severely stretched, both because of the growing demand for health care resulting from an aging population and because of the growing difficulty in attracting new recruits into medicine and nursing. In this connection, the tough stance taken by several Canadian governments in recent disputes involving their health care workers (see Chapter 8) will do little to make health care occupations appear more attractive to bright, dedicated young Canadians. While the education system will not be stretched in the same way, it will be faced with meeting the needs of a growing number of immigrants for language instruction. In particular, additional resources may need to be devoted to the instruction of adults.

Even positive aspects of the demographic situation, such as increased life expectancy, may have unanticipated side effects. One of them is Alzheimer's Disease, which afflicts an estimated 10 percent of the population aged 65 and over and nearly half of those 85 and over (*World Almanac*, 2002:745). With more and more Canadians living into their 80s and even beyond, the incidence of Alzheimer's increases significantly—and so does the strain on caregivers and the health care system.

Precarious Employment

The increasingly precarious nature of work is a theme that has appeared in every edition of this book. Regrettably, while the Canadian economy has improved somewhat since our first edition, the work situations of far too many Canadians

---

FIGURE 14.2

SOME KEY FINDINGS

1. Sharply declining birth rates mean Canada will become dependent on immigrants for many of its labour force needs.

2. Women and immigrants make up a large proportion of those facing precarious non-standard employment situations.

3. Many immigrants don't have their foreign credentials recognized in Canada.

4. A disproportionate number of recent immigrants are either unemployed or underemployed.

5. Private service-sector employers continue to resist unionization fiercely.

6. The adoption of "one-stop shopping" dispute resolution means that some workers are left without meaningful redress of any kind.

have not. Due to such developments as globalization, trade liberalization, and deindustrialization, employers have increasingly sought alternatives to standard full-time, full-year jobs wherever possible (Kalleberg, 2000). Over the past 30 years, there has been a large increase in such forms of non-standard employment as part-time, temporary, and contractual work as well as self-employment. Home work and moonlighting have also become more prevalent.

Admittedly, not all those employed in non-standard arrangements are poorly paid or badly treated in the workplace. Non-standard employment can encompass a wide range of situations, from lucrative per diem contracts for professionals to highly exploitive piecework arrangements for garment workers working at home. Common to almost all non-standard employment, however, is a lack of job security and a lack of employment-related benefits, such as paid vacations, sick leave, dental care, and pensions. In some service industries, such as retail, many workers may not know when their shifts will be, or even how many shifts they will have from one week to the next; many others must work "split shifts" which make their working day far longer than it would otherwise be. Such uncertainty makes it all but impossible for these workers to make financial plans or to have any sort of meaningful personal life. Not surprisingly, the result of such an uncertain working life is increased stress—stress that results in increased incidence of musculoskeletal disorders, migraines and other forms of headaches, absenteeism, turnover, and workplace conflict (Cranford, Vosko, and Zukewich, 2003; Zeytinoglu, Moruz, Seaton, and Lillevik, 2003).

The numerous stresses associated with non-standard employment are particularly likely to affect women, over 40 percent of whom were working in non-standard situations, compared to 29 percent of men (Townson, 2003). Recent immigrants of both genders are also apt to suffer from these kinds of stress, given the likelihood that even highly-qualified immigrants will be forced into low-paying, insecure menial work due to a lack of recognition of their professional or trade credentials acquired outside Canada. Overall, while there have recently been modest declines in the proportion of part-timers and self-employed workers (Townson, 2003), non-standard work arrangements remain a reality for a large proportion (34 percent) of all employed Canadians, up from about one-quarter in 1990. For far too many Canadian workers, non-standard work means not only substantially lower pay, but poorer (or no) employment benefits, reduced likelihood of eligibility for EI, minimal job security, and even less safe workplaces (see Cranford et al., 2003; Zeytinoglu et al., 2003).

Special Problems Facing Immigrants

The problems faced by recent immigrants have come to the fore at a time when Canada's declining birth and fertility rates are forcing it to place growing reliance on immigration for labour force growth and replacement of retiring workers (Seward, 2005). Immigrants already account for about 70 percent of the country's population growth (CLBC, 2004). Within another decade or so, they will account for all of it. It's estimated that by 2017, immigrants will account for over 22 percent of Canada's population and about one Canadian in five will be a member of a visible minority group, compared to 13 percent reporting themselves as such in 2001 (Stats Can,

2005b). Even now, immigrants make up a majority of the population of 17 federal ridings in the House of Commons.

Unfortunately, though Canada badly needs highly-trained immigrants to promote its economic growth, the evidence suggests that it is not exactly putting out the welcome mat for them. The problems faced by recent highly-educated immigrants—those whose skills should presumably be in greatest demand—include an unemployment rate several times that of native-born Canadians with equivalent educational attainment (Simpson, 2004); lack of recognition of foreign professional or trade credentials, which leads to severe underemployment; linguistic barriers; and in all too many cases, outright discrimination. For example, the unemployment rate for immigrants in 2001 was far higher than it had been twenty years earlier, even though the national unemployment rate fell during that time (ibid.). In addition, immigrants received less employer-supported training than did native-born Canadians (CLBC, 2004). It has been found that about 60 percent of recent immigrants aren't employed in occupations that use the education and skills they acquired abroad (CLBC, 2004). After six months in Canada, only 14 percent of those with one or more foreign credentials had had their credentials accepted (Simpson, 2004). As a result, many highly-trained immigrants either don't find work at all or are forced to take menial jobs just to pay the bills. At a time when so many workplace skills are at a premium, Canada can ill afford to continue this tragic and costly waste of its human resources.

In its 2004 *CLBC Handbook: Immigration and Skills Shortages,* the Canadian Labour and Business Centre (CLBC) noted that about 70 percent of recent immigrants had reported difficulty finding employment. Not surprisingly, lack of Canadian work experience, linguistic barriers, and non-recognition of foreign credentials were the three major reasons cited for these difficulties.

Between 1981 and 2001, the country's overall unemployment rate fell slightly, from 7.9 to 7.4 percent. But for immigrants in their first year in Canada, it rose sharply, from 17.4 to 29.7 percent. Immigrants who had been in the country between one and five years and between five and ten years also experienced significantly higher unemployment rates than they had twenty years previously. The so-called "transition penalty" for moving to Canada now dogs immigrants for more than a decade. Not until they have been in Canada more than ten years does their unemployment rate approximate that of native-born Canadians. By contrast, in 1981, it took less than five years for immigrants to achieve a lower than average unemployment rate (CLBC, 2004:18–19).

Worse still, the "transition penalty" increases with education. For example, immigrants with graduate degrees are nearly four times as likely to be unemployed as native-born Canadians with graduate degrees (Simpson, 2004). At the bachelor's level, three times as many immigrants (12 percent compared to 4 percent native-born Canadians) were unemployed (CLBC, 2004:19–20).

Lack of Meaningful Representation

The continuing lack of meaningful worker representation is another theme that has appeared in every edition of this book. Fewer than one-third of all Canadian non-farm workers are union members, and the prospects for further growth do not appear good. Despite the *Charter*, a number of groups including domestics and, in some jurisdictions, agricultural workers and professionals still don't even have the legal right to join a union. In the private service sector, many workers would like to join a union, but the determined and sometimes extra-legal opposition of firms like Wal-Mart, whose activities were discussed in Chapter 7 and will be discussed again later in this chapter, has made it very difficult for unions to make much headway. Elsewhere, the proliferation of non-standard work arrangements such as part-time, temporary, and contractual work, home work, and self-employment poses equally severe challenges for unions. In the public sector, membership rates have remained high, but governments' restrictions on union members' bargaining rights have continued despite the improved economy—a situation that has led to the high levels of conflict described in Chapter 8.

Perhaps the most significant finding is that there has been little change in the often-restrictive legislation that has made it difficult for Canadian unions to organize and attract new members in recent years. Exclusion provisions preventing domestics, agricultural workers, and professionals from joining remain in place in several jurisdictions, as do employer "freedom to communicate" provisions which could help employers intimidate workers seeking to form a union. And as was the case three years ago, a majority of Canadian workers live in jurisdictions where a union must win a vote in order to become a duly certified bargaining agent. Even the defeat of Ontario's Conservative government in 2003 and its replacement by a supposedly more labour-friendly Liberal government has not led to the repeal of the mandatory vote provision brought in by the previous government other than in the construction industry.

Private service sector employers have maintained their tough anti-union stance, frequently, as in the case of Wal-Mart, not hesitating to resort to tactics that bring them into conflict with labour boards and even the courts. In its attempts to prevent the United Food and Commercial Workers from representing its workers, Wal-Mart has proven itself to be remarkably resourceful, utilizing the same sort of questionable tactics in Saskatchewan (see box below) that it had tried earlier in Quebec.

Current Issues 14.1

WAL-MART IN THE WEST

You have to give the retail giant Wal-Mart an "A" for effort when it comes to the question of trying to keep their stores union free. In February of 2005, it announced it would be closing a store in Jonquiere, Quebec, that had been unionized several months earlier and had applied for first-contract arbitration. Around the same time, Wal-Mart was censured by the Quebec labour board for intimidating employees at another store.

The company's image has recently taken a black eye over its response to unionizing efforts at its stores, charges that it pays low wages, alleged sex discrimination, and alleged use of illegal workers, among other things. Indeed, Wal-Mart was starting to look so bad that it took out costly ads in US newspapers in a bid to improve that image.

In early April, its CEO H. Lee Scott even held a two-day media event to answer critics. But if you think all this would have stopped the company from continuing its "war of attrition" against union organizers—think again. ▶

In Saskatchewan, the United Food and Commercial Workers (UFCW) have been seeking to represent workers at stores in Weyburn and North Battleford. In its bid to keep the UFCW out, Wal-Mart developed an internal document entitled *A Manager's Toolbox to Remaining Union-Free.*

When the province's labour relations board started to probe Wal-Mart's conduct during the organizing drive, it ordered the company to give it a copy. Wal-Mart said the order violated its right to privacy, calling the documents irrelevant to the labour board's investigation.

Initially a provincial judge agreed. He dismissed the order as a "fishing expedition." But Saskatchewan's Court of Appeal overturned that decision. Then, on April 7, 2005, the Supreme Court of Canada sided with the union and the Court of Appeal. It refused to hear the company's argument that the labour board had no right to see the "toolbox" and a host of other company documents. This means that the parties now go back to the labour board to continue the certification process.

Company spokesman Andrew Pelletier expressed disappointment with the Supreme Court's decision, but noted that the labour board itself could still rule that the "toolbox" and other documents aren't relevant to the certification decision.

"Hopefully there's no more obstacles for Wal-Mart to hide behind in denying these workers their right to join a union," said UFCW local president Paul Meinema.

Given the company's past conduct, in Saskatchewan and elsewhere in Canada, one can only suggest that this remains to be seen.

Sources: Peter Brieger. (2005). "Wal-Mart Loses Fight over 'Union Prevention' Book," *Financial Post,* April 8; CBC. (2005). "Supreme Court Won't Hear Wal-Mart Appeal," unsigned CBC.ca article, April 7.

As we noted in Chapter 8, there has also been little change to public sector legislation restricting public sector workers' bargaining rights. In the federal public service, while human resource modernization brought some modest improvements to grievance and informal conflict resolution processes, it did not broaden the scope of bargaining by allowing the parties to bargain over key issues such as job classification, staffing, and pensions. The failure of the modernization task force to allow the parties to bargain over these issues means that the public service is likely to remain conflict ridden for the foreseeable future.

Overloaded Conflict Resolution System

Our fifth and final theme, an overloaded conflict resolution system, arises directly out of the developments described in Chapter 12. As we noted there, even prior to the new millennium, it was taking grievance cases an unconscionably long time—often more than a year—from filing until the issuing of the arbitration decision. Arbitration had also become tremendously costly. Even with expedited arbitration and grievance mediation available to reduce the burden on the regular arbitration system, only a tiny fraction of grievance cases filed were destined to reach arbitration, or indeed to receive any kind of neutral third-party hearing at all.

Over the past few years, arbitration has effectively become a kind of "one-stop shopping plaza" for the resolution of workplace disputes. Arbitrators are now expected to take into account a broad range of external legislation, including employment standards as well as human rights law, in arriving at their decisions. In fashioning awards, they must now also consider whether or not to award punitive or aggravated damages, a possibility that basically didn't exist a decade or so ago. Moreover, they are being asked to hear a much broader range than hitherto of harassment- and defamation-related cases, including many that would previously have been heard in other forums. The result of all this is that the process of arriving at a decision and writing an award has become even more complex than it was previously, thus further increasing the strains on an already overloaded arbitration system. There could also be a significant increase in the number of cases going to arbitration, a development which would likely mean still further delays. In addition, the use of the arbitration process in what are essentially private disputes over alleged defamation and the like will arguably do little to promote healthy union–management relationships.

So far it's too early to tell what the precise impacts of "one stop shopping" dispute resolution will be on the arbitration system (see final section for research suggestions). What we do know, from the *Vaughan* case (below), is that there will be instances where judicial insistence on keeping workplace disputes out of the courts will effectively mean that employees are denied any meaningful redress whatever.

In *Vaughan*,[2] the appellant, a former Public Works employee, sued the government when in 1995 it denied him the early retirement incentive (ERI) benefits it was offering under Program Review (Schmitz, 2005) and subsequently laid him off (case, p. 3). Vaughan sued rather than filing a grievance because under the *PSSRA*, issues around the ERI benefits, unilaterally provided under government regulation rather than through the collective agreement, could be grieved but not taken to independent adjudication. The Federal Court's prothonotary struck out his action; her decision was upheld on appeal.

Justice Ian Binnie, writing for the majority, held that "Where, as here, Parliament has created a comprehensive scheme for dealing with labour disputes, the process set out in the legislative scheme should not be jeopardized by permitting parallel access to the courts." His view was that Vaughan should have used the three-stage internal grievance process culminating in a decision by the Deputy Minister. In his view, the absence of access to independent adjudication through this process did not justify judicial intervention. While the lack of access to adjudication was "a consideration," Binnie held that "there is nothing on the facts of this case to take it outside the general rule of deference to the procedure mandated by Parliament" (case, p. 5).[3] It is quite easy to believe that over time, many other employees could similarly fall through the cracks of the dispute resolution system and be left without meaningful redress.

POLICY SUGGESTIONS AND PROPOSALS FOR ACTION

The following policy suggestions and proposals for action (see Figure 14.3 for a list of some of the most important ones) arise directly from the findings just discussed. While some of these proposals do seem to buck recent trends toward smaller government, it's important to note that recent economic and political

FIGURE 14.3

SOME KEY POLICY SUGGESTIONS AND ACTION PROPOSALS

1. Eliminate mandatory retirement in all jurisdictions.

2. Pro-rate employment benefits for part-timers.

3. Enforce employment standards legislation more strictly.

4. Establish national and provincial boards to speed recognition of recent immigrants' credentials.

5. Give tax credits to employers who provide language training or skills retraining to immigrants.

6. End all exclusions from unionization other than those of management and confidential IR personnel.

7. Return to the card count as the standard method of establishing union certification.

8. Establish "small-claims" labour tribunals to handle easier cases and take the load off the arbitration system.

developments have imposed serious hardship on many Canadians in addition to leading to increased workplace conflict. It should also be noted that a number of these proposals have already been put forward elsewhere, and most are of a fairly incremental nature.

With regard to the demographic crisis, there are limits to the measures policy makers can take, since demographic situations are by their very nature long-term and also involve factors over which governments don't have very much control (e.g., birth rates). Still, there are things that can be done to help ease impending skills and labour shortages. The first, and perhaps most obvious, is the abolition of mandatory retirement. It has long since been abolished in Quebec and Manitoba (see Reid and Meltz, 2001), and plans for its abolition are under way in Ontario (Ontario Ministry of Labour, 2004b). In addition, it no longer applies in the federal public service. Nonetheless, it still applies in most Canadian jurisdictions.

In addition to being discriminatory as such, and therefore no more justifiable than policies discriminating on the base of race, religion, or ethnic origin, mandatory retirement policies are clearly economically counterproductive at a time of growing skills shortages and increased strains on public pension systems. Beyond that, mandatory retirement works undue hardship on women, who frequently take a number of years out of the workforce to raise children and thus face significantly reduced pension benefits if forced to retire at a fixed age; the same is true of career-changers, who may not have all their years of service in their different jobs vested for pension purposes. All in all, we believe that mandatory retirement is at best an idea whose time has long since passed.

With an eye to retaining institutional memory in their organizations longer, employers should consider phased-retirement or part-time arrangements for older workers. Many are ideally suited to mentor younger workers, who would clearly benefit from the institutional knowledge passed on to them.

There are quite a number of things that could be done to ease the plight of those working part-time or in other non-standard work situations. The first is pro-rating of employment benefits (including pensions). As was noted in an earlier CBC Video Case on the Netherlands (Peirce, 2003:482–483), that country has managed to make part-time work a reasonably attractive prospect by ensuring that part-timers receive the same perks and benefits, including pensions, as their full-time counterparts. To date, just one Canadian jurisdiction, the often-pioneering province of Saskatchewan, has pro-rated benefits for its part-timers. It's high time the rest of the country followed suit.

Another policy shift that could benefit those in precarious work situations would be experience-rating of EI premiums. Under experience-rating, employers who rarely or never resorted to layoffs would pay significantly lower premiums than those making frequent layoffs, and thus imposing a significant burden on the system. Over time, this could result in a lower level of layoffs and unemployment.

In every edition of this book, we have emphasized the inadequacy of enforcement of minimum wage, work hours, and other employment standards legislation. Lack of enforcement has hit recent immigrants particularly hard. Often suffering from linguistic barriers, many haven't been aware of their legal rights, and even many of those who have been have often been afraid to complain about violations, for fear of dismissal or deportation (Peirce, 2000a:47; Arnopoulos, 1974). With immigrants forming a larger and larger part of the country's labour force, the issue of inadequate enforcement assumes added importance. The country's enlightened self-interest, not to mention considerations of basic decency and fairness, demands nothing less than full enforcement of the minimal employment standards laws currently in force.

Finally, we've already noted that women are at a disadvantage when it comes to pension benefits. In addition to the end of mandatory retirement, a policy measure that could prove helpful would be allowing women to count time spent off work raising children toward their Canada Pension entitlements.

The current situation with respect to recent immigrants—particularly highly-trained ones—is nothing less than shocking. Steps must be taken immediately to halt the waste of these people's valuable skills and talents. The top priority must be ensuring that new immigrants' skills and credentials are evaluated promptly. This in turn will ensure that those who are ready to operate in their new country can do so without undue delay, while others receive the necessary upgrading of their skills to ensure that their time away from their chosen field is as short as possible. To this end, we propose that national and provincial boards be established to provide prompt evaluations of new immigrants' credentials and, where necessary, to make recommendations for appropriate retraining and upgrading.

Close behind is the matter of linguistic training. As we noted earlier, about 30 percent of all highly-trained immigrants arrive in this country without a knowledge of either English or French. Many others, while perhaps possessed of sufficient linguistic skill to function to some degree, still need to improve if they are to communicate effectively with colleagues, employers, and clients in their new language. To help remove linguistic barriers to recent immigrants' full economic integration into Canada, we recommend that to the extent possible, Canadian embassies overseas encourage prospective immigrants to receive language training before leaving their native countries. In addition, employers should be given tax credits for establishing training programs to help recent immigrants develop or upgrade their language skills, as well as for technical retraining.

It must also be noted that while Canada has taken a number of commendable steps to help eliminate racism, such as the passage of broad-based human rights legislation, the sad reality is that racism and discrimination continue to exist in this country. As we pointed out earlier in the chapter, an alarmingly large number of visible minority group members report having been the victims of racism or other forms of discrimination. To give just one example, the most recent federal public service survey revealed that about 15 percent of all federal government employees believed they had been victims of discrimination over the three years prior to the survey, many on the score of their race or ethnic origin (PSES, 2002). Through strict enforcement of human rights legislation and whatever other means are necessary, Canada must work toward the elimination of racism in order to ensure that immigrants, the vast majority of whom are now members are visible minority groups, feel welcome here.

As regards the right to meaningful representation, we have twice before recommended the removal of all exclusions from unionization rights of all groups other than managers or confidential IR personnel. At present, these groups include domestics, agricultural workers, and professionals. We can do no more than repeat that recommendation here. In our view, the right to join a union is a basic right of industrial citizenship. Such a right should not be denied lightly. Only compelling policy rationales such as the many conflicts of interest that could result if managers and confidential IR personnel were allowed to join unions (particularly the same unions as those representing other workers in their organizations) justify preventing any group of workers from joining a union. At a more practical level, restrictive exclusion policies have been clearly identified with lower membership rates in the provinces (e.g., Alberta and Ontario) maintaining such policies. If the labour movement is to have any hope at all of increasing its membership, restrictive exclusion policies need to be removed from labour relations legislation across Canada.

We do not believe that the 2001 *Dunmore* decision (see Godard, 2005 and Peirce, 2003) granting Ontario's agricultural workers the right to legal representation before their employers but not the right to bargain collectively or to strike goes anywhere near far enough. On what basis should these highly vulnerable workers be denied the protection afforded to most other groups of workers under the *Ontario Labour Relations Act?* Indeed, with Roy Adams (1998), David Beatty (1987) and others, we would argue that the time has come to make the right to join unions and go on strike a constitutionally protected right under the *Charter.* Such a move would bring Canada into line with the mainstream of European countries that have long since enshrined such protection in their constitutions. In addition, it would, quite frankly, give Canada a better image in the world, particularly when it comes to situations where Canada is criticizing other countries' human rights violations.

We also see no reason why a vote should automatically be required to establish whether a union can be certified. Using a vote to establish certification rights sets up a "political campaign" situation where the employer becomes involved. This, in our view, is precisely what should not happen. The decision as to whether there will be a union in a given workplace or not should be solely that of the employees in that workplace. In the US, where votes have been required since the passage of *Taft-Hartley* in 1947, employers have ample opportunity to influence employees, sometimes through intimidation or harassment and sometimes through subtler means (see Weiler, 1983a). For this reason, the move to the vote has been associated with lower membership rates in the US (Bruce, 1990; Ng, 1992). Accordingly, we would propose that all jurisdictions utilize a simple card count as the normal method for establishing union certification, reserving formal votes for situations where the employees' wishes can genuinely not be determined through the card count.

Other areas of labour relations legislation deserve some attention, as well. In our previous edition, we noted that employer freedom-to-communicate provisions appear to open up the possibility of employers interfering with unions, particularly at vulnerable times such as during certification drives. This in our view is sufficient reason for such provisions to be eliminated. We have also noted that first-contract arbitration can protect vulnerable new unions (e.g., as in the service sector) by helping them establish a foothold against employers unwilling to negotiate a collective agreement with them. For this reason, we would recommend that all jurisdictions adopt first-contract arbitration provisions. In addition, the Wal-Mart cases discussed earlier conclusively demonstrate the need for continuing strict enforcement of labour relations legislation. In particular, labour boards need to retain the power they still have in most Canadian jurisdictions to certify unions with less than majority support in cases where employers' unfair practice has prevented the employees' true wishes from becoming known.

Finally, in the public sector, which in recent years has accounted for an increasingly large share of person-days lost to strikes in Canada, little or nothing appears to have been done to address the root causes of conflict. The new *Public Service Labour Relations Act* provides some improvements, notably to the grievance process, but does little to redress the fundamental power imbalances illuminated in the two Fryer reports (2000 and 2001). In our view, this can't happen until the parties can bring to the bargaining table something approaching the full range of issues they can address in the private sector, including such things as job classification, staffing, and employee pensions. The result of the current public sector bargaining restrictions is that most bargaining takes place over essentially peripheral issues and major problem areas go largely unaddressed at the table. Accordingly, we recommend that public sector labour legislation be amended to broaden the scope of bargaining substantially, so that collective bargaining can serve the purpose it does in the private sector of helping the parties work out mutually acceptable solutions to problems.

With respect to conflict resolution, while the expanded jurisdiction of arbitrators is in some respects a positive development, it also risks overloading the already heavily burdened arbitration system, perhaps to the point of breakdown. To prevent this from happening, we would propose that in the private sector, employers and unions and, in the public sector, governments establish something like a "small claims labour court." In such a forum, relatively straightforward minor grievance cases and possibly the sort of harassment or defamation case that arises from misunderstanding rather than genuine ill will could be heard, without the need to employ witnesses or produce elaborately reasoned decisions. Elaborate, full-dress arbitration could be reserved for terminations, policy grievances, and other complex matters genuinely requiring it. As is the case in some existing expedited arbitration systems (e.g., that of the Public Service Labour Relations Board), decisions would not have precedential value.[4] We would also urge arbitrators and judges alike to recognize that there are still cases not well-suited to arbitration, cases that would more appropriately be dealt with in other forums. Finally, we would urge arbitrators and judges to ensure that, in their zeal to avoid duplication of conflict resolution forums, they do not leave large numbers of employees without any meaningful redress at all.

SUGGESTIONS FOR FURTHER RESEARCH

Both in this chapter and throughout the book as a whole, we've indicated various issues that seem to us in need of further research. The list below (see Figure 14.4), while by no means exhaustive, covers some of the areas where such research seems to us most urgent from a public policy perspective.

Given the growing likelihood of skills shortages and of a serious drain on the pension system, governments and employers need to look for ways to help retain older workers and their institutional memory. Phased retirement plans and systems whereby older workers mentor younger ones are two approaches that have already been tried. Research is needed to see how these and other possible approaches might work in practice. In addition, since it's becoming increasingly clear that Canada will be relying on immigrants for a great part of its labour force needs for the foreseeable future, research is needed into how to more effectively assimilate recent immigrants into the workplace.

As the comparative chapter indicated, precarious employment is a global problem. It is also not a problem that will be solved overnight. In the long run, this problem needs to be tackled at the international level, through organizations like the UN and ILO. In the shorter term, we need to study how to reduce some of the most serious impacts of non-standard employment—impacts which, as we noted earlier, can include physical and mental illness, absenteeism, and high turnover. In this connection, the Netherlands is a country where part-timers enjoy much if not all of the status of their full-time counterparts. The situation there is favourable enough for part-timers that many people appear to be quite happy to work part-time for long periods.

FIGURE 14.4

SOME KEY RESEARCH ISSUES

1. What are some ways to help keep older workers with scarce skills on the job?

2. What are some ways to assimilate recent immigrants more effectively into Canadian workplaces?

3. What can we learn from other countries about ways to improve the situation of part-timers and others working under non-standard arrangements?

4. What can we learn from other countries about how to speed up the process of recognizing immigrants' foreign credentials?

5. What effects have provincial exclusion and union certification policies had on union membership rates in Canada?

6. What effects is expanded arbitral jurisdiction having on the speed and cost of conflict resolution?

Research is needed into the ways that the Netherlands and other socially conscious countries have managed to provide relatively decent working conditions for part-timers and other non-standard workers.

With regard to immigration, for a country that has always had fairly high immigration levels and has frequently made considerable use of immigrants to meet its labour force needs, Canada has, frankly, a poor track record in recognizing immigrants' credentials. Now, at a time of growing skill shortages, research is urgently needed into ways that other Western countries have managed to deal with the issue of recognizing foreign credentials. This might also be a good time to conduct research into the feasibility of providing prospective immigrants with English and French language training or training about Canadian culture before they leave their native countries.

In the area of labour law, it would be very useful if we could have specific, up-to-date studies on the impacts of exclusion policies and certification vote provisions on union membership rates. And while this may be a difficult thing to do, it would also be a good time for comparative public–private sector studies specifically relating restrictive public sector bargaining policies to that sector's increased strike incidence.

As for conflict resolution, we noted earlier that we can't as yet say what the precise impacts of "one stop shopping" conflict resolution will be on the arbitration system. It is important that studies be done to determine just what those impacts are, with an eye to modifying the system if need be. Comparative examinations of other countries' conflict resolution systems would also be in order. It would be particularly useful to know if internationally, duplication of conflict resolution forums is considered a problem to the same degree it is here. (Germany, in particular, has a history of not only permitting but encouraging multiple forums for resolution of workers' grievances (see Adams, 1995a).) It would also be good to know more about how long it takes to resolve workplace conflicts in other countries and what the cost is, both monetarily and in terms of person-hours.

The above list should be considered suggestive rather than definitive. No doubt many of you will have your own ideas about where further research is most urgently needed. The one thing that can be said with certainty about the rapidly changing field of IR is that it offers almost limitless research opportunities for people of intelligence and imagination with an interest in public policy issues.

Case 14.1

PLAR IN MANITOBA: MAKING SURE EVERYONE'S SKILLS GET RECOGNIZED

PLAR (Prior Learning Assessment and Recognition) is a way of recognizing the professional or trade credentials of immigrants from other countries, of mature learners who have been out of school for many years, or of people wishing to receive academic credit for practical life experience. In Manitoba, Red River College has been providing prior learning assessment since the 1980s. The province has been involved since 1995, when it gave the college funding for a PLA facilitator. Two years later, Manitoba Education and Training, in partnership with Red River College and Human Resources Development Canada (HRDC), established the Manitoba Prior Learning Assessment Centre (PLA Centre). In addition to providing advisory services to unemployed or underemployed individuals, the centre mounted a number of demonstration projects to validate the use of prior learning assessment. Federal funding continued until 2000; provincial funding, until 2001.

In 2000–2001, as part of a broader review of the way in which adult learners were able to access high school upgrading and post-secondary education, the province designed a new, decentralized PLAR framework. The aim was to expand the network of practitioners and make expertise and access available throughout the province, while connecting PLAR to other major educational initiatives. The province used the funds that had previously paid for the PLA Centre's operating costs to develop a comprehensive practitioner training program, which combines on-line instruction with formal classroom training. It also provided funding for three years for a new position specifically dedicated to PLAR at each of its publicly-funded post-secondary institutions. In order to access the funds, each of the institutions was asked to develop a specific PLAR-related initiative. All the institutions will also contribute to an annual report on institutional-based PLAR activities. The report will be a public document, which should help raise the profile of PLAR significantly.

In addition to working with educational institutions, the province is actively supporting Adult Learning Centres (ALCs) located in communities throughout the province. These centres are designed to provide individuals not yet enrolled in college or university who are seeking appropriate credentials for employment or post-secondary education with a broad range of "walk-in" services. The eventual aim is to have 40 to 50 ALCs offering PLAR services across the province.

In addition, PLAR-trained staff are placed in designated employment centres throughout the province. Finally, in conjunction with industry, the province has mounted a number of industry-related PLAR development programs.

Manitoba's new PLAR framework provides a sustainable and cost-effective funding mechanism for all areas of PLAR activity, a province-wide delivery system for advisory services, a program profile that is higher than that of a stand-alone program, and increased institutional capacity for PLAR across the post-secondary system. It is also leading to the development of a comprehensive and sustainable system of basic and advanced practitioner training.

Among the success stories is Stewart, an industrial electrician from England who came to Manitoba for a vacation, fell in love with it, and decided to move there with his family. To ply his trade in Manitoba, he would need to have his British certification recognized there. He was able to win recognition of his credentials after a lengthy interview and verification of documentation with the Apprenticeship Branch's PLAR coordinator. This enabled him to write the Inter-Provincial Certification Industrial Electrician exam. After moving to Manitoba in 2003, he passed the exam and is now employed in his trade in Selkirk.

Sources: *Manitoba's Policy Framework for Prior Learning Assessment and Recognition (PLAR)*, Nov., 2001, Government of Manitoba, no specific author or place of publication given; *PLAR Stories from Manitoba*, Government of Manitoba, no date, specific author or place of publication given.

Case Questions

1. Why has recognition of people's prior learning and experience become such an important issue today?

2. In addition to recent immigrants, what are some groups that can benefit from PLAR?

3. What are some of the advantages of the decentralized PLAR delivery system Manitoba has recently moved to?

4. Are there possible concerns that employers, the general public, or unions might have with PLAR? How could a well-designed PLAR program address such concerns?

QUESTIONS FOR DISCUSSION

1. Do you agree with the authors' choice of five key themes summarizing the main directions of Canadian IR today? If you do, which seem to you most important and why? If you don't, what other themes would you prefer to see discussed?

2. Do you think that the incidence of part-time work and other forms of non-standard employment is likely to increase, decrease, or stay about the same in the near future? What factors would be most likely to lead it to increase or decrease, in your view?

3. Why are issues around immigrants and immigration so important? What do you think governments, employers, unions, and ordinary citizens can do to improve the lot of recent immigrants? Do unions face potential conflicts in this area?

4. Do you agree with the choice of issues for further research? If you don't, what are some of the issues you would choose instead?

5. Overall, what would you say are some of the most important things you've learned from this book? If you plan to take further IR courses, what would you like to learn from those courses?

Suggestion for Further Reading

Rose, Joseph and Gary Chaison. 2001. "Unionism in Canada and the United States in the 21st Century: The Prospects for Revival." *Relations Industrielles,* 56:1 (pp. 34–65). A very thorough examination of most of the key factors underlying potential union growth and decline in these two countries. The authors' prognosis for the labour movement is grim, particularly in the US.

Endnotes

Chapter 1

1 For a useful discussion of recent trends in atypical employment, see Richard Chaykowski, "Non-Standard Work and Economic Vulnerability," *Canadian Policy Research Networks*, March, 2005.

2 One can learn a good deal about this insecurity by reading the so-called "GenX" fiction written by and (especially) aimed at people under 35. See, for example, Douglas Coupland's *Shampoo Planet*.

3 This same definition has been usefully adopted by Adams (1993).

4 On this point, see also Wood et al. (1975). For an even broader and more thought-provoking discussion of the ideas considered in this paragraph, see George Strauss, "Is IR Research Returning to Its Roots?" in *Perspectives on Work*, 3:1 (1999), pp. 59–60.

5 For a useful discussion on the distinction between conflict over fundamental issues of principle and what might be described as "instrumental" conflict over issues like wages, see Kervin (1984).

6 This may have been a logical corollary of Dunlop's rather strict separation of the economic and IR subsystems.

7 This point is very much worth considering in connection with the 1985 break-away of the Canadian Auto Workers from its parent American union. The break-away is frequently ascribed to Canadian workers' greater militancy. We would argue that CAW leaders simply engaged in some quite rational calculation, saw that they could do far better by Canadian members in a separate Canadian environ-ment, and acted accordingly. Whether Canadian workers are possessed of inherent traits making them "tougher" than their American counterparts seems quite beside the point.

8 As is noted in more detail in Chapter 7 (labour law), the Supreme Court of Canada has recently come around to Beatty's point of view, at least with regard to Ontario's exclusion of agricultural workers.

9 As we'll see in Chapter 7, Beatty's belief in the remedial powers of the Charter is shared by few other Canadian legal scholars or industrial relationists. However, the recent Supreme Court decision overturning Ontario's agricultural exclusion may perhaps win him some new allies.

10 For a useful if brief discussion on Marxism and its application to industrial rela-tions issues, see Godard (1994:36–45). I am indebted to Godard's discussion for much of the material in this paragraph.

11 Much of the material in this paragraph has been drawn from Anderson et al. (1989).

12 Readers should note that the term "political economy" is defined somewhat differently here than in Gunderson and Ponak (1995), who use the same term. Those authors don't have the equivalent of this book's reformist or Godard's liberal reformist perspective. Thus, Gunderson and Ponak's political economy perspective includes the work of many people whom Godard and the author would place in the reformist camp. The political economy perspective described in the first chapter of Gunderson, Ponak, and Taras (2000) is one of only two perspectives used there, and is in no way comparable to any of the five perspectives used in this book.

Chapter 2

1 EI regulations allow recipients to earn up to 25 percent of their benefits or $50, whichever is higher, without changing the amount of their EI benefits.

2 Here and elsewhere in the chapter, the term "unemployment rate" refers to the standard official measure label R4 by Statistics Canada, except as noted otherwise.

3 In Canada, these trends appear to have been somewhat less pronounced. Godard does not offer evidence on productivity. However, his chart (1994:95) shows a significant reduction in strike intensity and in union membership rates, but not in the actual number of union members, during the decade. Of course, it may well be that welfare capitalism was less widely adopted in Canada than in the United States. Further research is needed in this area.

4 Hunnicutt notes that New Deal era investigators looking into conditions in Southern textile plants in the early 1930s found widespread use of child labour and work weeks of 50 to 60 hours.

Chapter 3

1 As noted by Heron (1989:13), similar legislation was passed by the Canada West legislature in 1847.

2 As Morton notes, railway workers and others in positions where public safety was involved were excluded from the amended act's protection; these workers still had no legal right to strike. The exclusion thus set in motion the beginnings of the pattern of differential regulation of private and public sector workers still in effect in most of Canada today.

3 Since the First World War, Berlin has been known as Kitchener.

4 In fairness, Gompers' dislike of dual unions was not without cause. In 1885, according to Morton and Copp (1980:58), his own Cigar Makers Union had been undercut in a strike by the Knights, who had imposed their own rival union label.

5 This contention seems logical enough, given that Canada was the last major western industrialized country to grant its workers collective bargaining rights.

6 As Morton (1995:138) notes, the nickname is somewhat ironic, given that the plan was invented by none other than Canada's own Mackenzie King, during his stint as labour consultant to the Rockefellers.

7 As Boivin (1982:437) notes, between 1915 and 1936, the Catholic unions accounted for only nine, or less than 2 percent, of the strikes officially called in Quebec.

8 That is, 11 private sector jurisdictions. When the various public sector jurisdictions are taken into account, the number becomes several times that.

9 In 1931 alone, according to White, there were more than 7000 deportations. Between 1903-1928, deportations had averaged slightly more than 1000 per year.

10 The bill's official title is the *National Labor Relations Act*; however, it is usually referred to as the *Wagner Act* in honour of its main drafter, Senator Robert Wagner of New York.

11 Domestics and farm workers were excluded, as was management.

12 On early post-war Atlantic labour law, see Forsey (1985). On Alberta's law, see Finkel (1986).

13 I am indebted to Forrest (1997) for many of the ideas contained in this paragraph.

14 See Morton and Copp (1980:233-234). In 1959, these disclosures would lead to the passage of the *Landrum-Griffin Act*, which imposed substantial restrictions on unions' internal operations with an eye to preventing further union racketeering.

15 Through 1985 (Peirce, 1987:69), the Canada Labour Relations Board had accepted only one of 25 technological change applications brought before it under the federal legislation.

16 On a similar note, see Crispo (1982).

17 For much of this discussion, I'm indebted to Heron (1989:103–104).

18 As readers will recall from the discussion of alternative measures of unemployment in Chapter 2, the actual numbers of workers and families affected by unemployment during any given year would have been far higher.

19 The NDP did win one Ontario seat in the 2000 federal election, in a Windsor-area riding.

20 This challenge appears even more daunting than before, now that the NDP has been crushed by the Liberals in BC and reduced to a minority government in its long-time stronghold, Saskatchewan.

Chapter 4

1 In Canada, union density is normally defined as the percentage of paid non-agricultural workers belonging to unions. A rationale for excluding agricultural workers from the union density "denominator" is that such workers have often been excluded from unionization and in any case seldom join. However, as Murray (1995:162) points out, this rationale is not entirely consistent since members of other groups excluded from unionization rights, such as managers and confidential IR personnel, are counted as part of that denominator.

2 Aggregate union membership rates used in this book are generally higher than the disaggregated rates drawn from Akyeampong's Labour Force survey data. In note 1 of his 1997 article, Akyeampong explains the difference as follows: "CALURA density rates in the construction industry in particular have traditionally been higher than those captured by household surveys like the Labour Force Survey, mainly because CALURA union membership includes both the unemployed and retired, and the household surveys do not."

3 For a more detailed look at legislative provisions and their effect on union growth, see Ng (1992), Martinello (1996), Godard (2003), Johnson (2002b) and Johnson (2004).

4 The four NDP or PQ governments in provinces with above average density levels served for at least 10 years.

5 In the United States, private sector labour legislation is under federal jurisdiction.

6 In fairness, Meany's successors, Lane Kirkland and more recently John Sweeney, have given considerable attention to organizing (on Kirkland, see Winpisinger, 1989). However, by the 1980s, years of benign or not-so-benign neglect had left the American labour movement in such a weakened condition that many unions lacked the money and the people to mount effective organizing campaigns and instead made a conscious decision to devote their resources to protecting the interests of existing members (Chaison and Rose, 1991). For a more detailed discussion, see Lipsig-Mumme (1989).

7 Specific bargaining tactics are more often planned by the local's negotiating committee. However, the negotiating committee must make sure it is in sync with the general membership's wishes, or it will have an extremely difficult time arriving at an agreement that the membership is willing to ratify.

8 In the case of university professors, it should be noted that the profession's national organization, the Canadian Association of University Teachers, provides at least some of the same services that a labour federation would.

9 Similar political functions are carried out by provincial labour federations in provincial capitals.

10 Environmental issues, most of which involve multiple stakeholders, offer an excellent example of how the labour movement can put its specialized expertise (in this case, knowledge of negotiating strategy) to use in other public forums. In recent years, a special type of bargaining, known as multilateral negotiation, has evolved to address such environment-related issues as Native land claims and cleanup of toxic waste sites.

11 On the other hand, a close election may make an incumbent executive unduly conservative and fearful of pursuing new initiatives, particularly those involving cooperation with management. Such an executive may find it necessary to put up a show of toughness in a bid to shore up sagging support.

12 It is instructive to remember that a 1902 AFL convention saw a full 46 percent of the delegates voting in favour of a motion advocating socialism and cooperative industrial democracy, and that a decade later a socialist candidate opposed Gompers for the federation presidency and won a full one-third of the vote. (Galenson and Smith, 1978:51).

13 See Lipsig-Mumme (1989) for a much more detailed discussion of these points from a strategic choice perspective.

Chapter 5

1 For a useful if brief discussion of the Webbs, see Craig and Solomon, (1996:76–80).

2 For a useful overview of the key issues here, see Verma (1995).

3 Anil Verma tends to fall into this camp, as, with some reservations, does Maurice Lemelin (1989).

4 It is generally accepted throughout the industrial relations literature that the union must be involved as a full partner in any joint co-operation schemes if the schemes are to succeed. For a classic and still very useful statement, see Kochan (1979, quoted in Downie, 1982). Another useful list can be found in Lemelin (1989).

5 In an eerie echo of the 1970s, the Public Service Alliance, in August 2001, withdrew from all consultative bodies as a protest against the federal government's failure to offer its members better contract terms. It rejoined those bodies once it had signed new collective agreements with the government.

6 In British Columbia, the Social Credit government in 1984 instituted the requirement of a certification vote (Craig and Solomon, 1993:145). That requirement was removed by an NDP government in 1992 (Craig and Solomon, 1993:215), but then reinstated by a new Liberal government elected in 2001.

7 This strike was described in detail in the first edition of this book on pp. 445–446.

8 In connection with this point, however, it must be noted that when your adversary is the government itself, only a secondary boycott is possible; no one can realistically boycott a government (other than, perhaps, by leaving the province or country in question).

9 For an interesting and much more detailed discussion of the issues raised in this paragraph, see Godard (1994:210–221). An equally interesting discussion from a quite different perspective may be found in L. Reynolds (1982:492–498).

10 These problems raise technical statistical issues that in our view are far too complex to be discussed in an introductory industrial relations textbook. Students with an extensive background in labour economics and statistics who wish to pursue these issues further will find useful discussions in Gunderson and Riddell (1993:388–397) and Gunderson and Hyatt (1995:322–324).

11 In Canada, the impact of collective agreement coverage is a reasonably good approximation for a union wage impact, since there aren't many non-unionized workers covered by a collective agreement, except to some extent in Quebec (see Akyeampong, 2001).

12 To Gunderson and Hyatt (2001:393), this finding is surprising. To us, it is far from surprising. Union membership rates are so much higher in the public than in the private sector that in Canada, in the former, unionized status is basically the norm. Moreover, as in the federal government, where excluded workers often receive the same salary and benefits as their unionized counterparts, it is often the case that the benefits of unionization in the public sector spill over into the non-unionized part of that sector.

13 For a useful discussion around some of these points, see Godard (1994:217–219).

14 For most of the material in this paragraph, we are indebted to Gunderson and Hyatt (1995:318–322) and to Gunderson's discussion in the previous (1989) edition of the book, pp. 353–356. Some use has also been made of Murray (1995:184–190).

15 One of the authors has observed this same attitude in his industrial relations students, many of whom have been local union activists.

Chapter 6

1 For very senior people, especially those handling a financial portfolio, contracts may even stipulate that employees cannot solicit the employer's customers for a given period after they have left the employer's service.

2 *Wallace v. United Grain Growers Ltd.* [1997] 3 S.C.R. 701.

3 See, for example, *Ontario Employment Standards Act, 2000,* [S.O. 2000, c.41], s.104(1).

4 *Canada Labour Code,* [R.S. 1985, c. L-2], s.240(1).

5 *Quebec Labour standards, An Act respecting,* [R.S.Q. c. N-1.1], s.124.

6 *Nova Scotia Labour Standards Code,* [R.S.N.S. 1989, c. 246], s.71(1).

7 It should be noted that these findings do not please Eden, a critic of the whole notion of progressive discipline. For her detailed critique of this system of industrial justice, see (1992), "Progressive discipline: An oxymoron," *Relations Industrielles,* 47:3.

8 *Baker v. Burns Foods Ltd.* (1977), 74 D.L.R. (3rd) 762.

9 *Reber v. Lloyds Bank International Canada* (1984), 52 B.C. L.R. 90.

10 *Bardal v. The Globe & Mail Ltd.* (1960), 24 D.L.R. (2nd) 140.

11 *Wallace,* see note 2 above.

12 For example, an entirely new *Employment Standards Act* was introduced in Ontario in 2000 and increased flexibility was one of its aims. The 2003 amendments to British Columbia's *Employment Standards Act* were also grounded, at least partially, in the need for flexibility.

13 *Prince Edward Island Employment Standards Act,* [R.S.P.E.I. 1988, c. E-6.2], s.2.2., *Alberta Employment Standards Code,* [R.S.A. 2000, c. E-9], s.2(4) and *Saskatchewan Labour Standards Act,* [R.S.S. 1978, c. L-1], s.4(3).

14 *Prince Edward Island Employment Standards Act,* [R.S.P.E.I. 1988, c. E-6.2], s.2.3(a).

15 See, for example, *B.C. Government and Service Employees' Union v. B.C. (Public Service Employee Relations Commission)* [1999] 3 S.C.R. 3.

16 *B.C. Government and Service Employees' Union v. B.C. (Public Service Employee Relations Commission)* [1999] 3 S.C.R. 3., para. 54.

17 See *Central Alberta Dairy Pool v. Alberta (Human Rights Commission)* (1990), 72 D.L.R. (4th) 417 and *Central Okanagan School District No. 23 v. Renaud* (1992), 95 D.L.R. (4th) 577 (S.C.C.)

18 See *Bubb-Clarke v. Toronto Transit Commission,* Ontario Board of Inquiry (Human Rights Code), Alvin Rosenberg, Member, April 4, 2002.

19 *Kivela v. C.U.P.E., Local 21, and the City of Regina,* Saskatchewan Human Rights Tribunal (Human Rights Code), Roger Lepage, Member, October 10, 2003.

20 See, for example, *Weber v. Ontario Hydro,* [1995] 125 D.L.R. 583. [S.C.C.] and *New Brunswick v. O'Leary,* [1995] 125 D.L.R. 609. [S.C.C.]

21 Both Ontario and Quebec require employers with more than 10 employees to provide for pay equity in their workplaces but they are not compelled to file a pay equity plan.

22 For explanation of these methods and how they are utilized in Ontario, visit the Ontario Pay Equity Office's website at http://www.gov.on.ca/lab/pec/peo/english/about_us.html.

23 See, for example, *Ontario Pay Equity Act,* [R.S.O. 1990, c. P.7], s.13.

24 *Newfoundland (Treasury Board) v. N.A.P.E.* [2004] S.C.J. No. 61, S.C.C. 66, File No.: 29597.

25 Canadian Press. (2001, May 25). "Bell Canada Loses Pay Equity Battle," http://www.ctv.ca/servlet/ArticleNews/story/CTVNews/1027385611789_22794811?s_name=&no_ads=; see also "Bell Canada Pay Equity," on the website of the Communications, Energy & Paperworkers Union of Canada, Human Rights/Equity page, http://www.cep.ca/human_rights/equity/bell/bell_e.html.

26 In Alberta and Prince Edward Island, such committees are set up at the discretion of the minister (McPhillips and England, 1995).

27 Ontario's act was not the first providing for committees. In 1972 (Swinton, 1983), Saskatchewan's comprehensive *Occupational Health Act* provided for them. Earlier, a number of unions had obtained such committees through the collective bargaining process, and Canadian Labour Congress policy had stated that joint committees should be a cornerstone of occupational health and safety programs.

28 Both must do so under the *Canada Code.*

29 As various commentators note, it remains difficult to prove a relationship in the latter case. See, for example, CCH (1998:15, 406).

Chapter 7

1 In the Philippines, for example, as noted by Jimenez (1993:233), a major cause of increased strike activity during the 1960s was management's unwillingness to recognize unions or bargain with them.

2 In Sweden (Hammarstrom, 1993), basic bargaining rights were achieved in 1906. In Denmark and in Australia, recognition came even earlier, in 1899 and 1904, respectively (Scheuer, 1992; Davis and Lansbury, 1993). In the United States, recognition came in 1935 (Carter, 1995).

3 *Reference re Public Service Employee Relations Act* (Alberta), [1987] 1 S.C.R. 313; *Retail, Wholesale and Department Store Union, Locals 544, 496, 635 and 955 v. Government of Saskatchewan,* [1987] 1 S.C.R. 460; *Public Service Alliance of Canada v. Canada,* [1987] 1 S.C.R. 424.

4 On this point, see the *Lavigne* case, involving an Ontario community college instructor who did not like the fact that his union was using his dues for political causes with which he disagreed. The Supreme Court ruled in favour of the union, declaring that the union's freedom to spend dues for the collective good of the

membership constituted a reasonable limitation on the Charter's freedom of association provision. For a more detailed discussion, see Swinton (1995:66–8).

5 *R. v. Advance Cutting & Corning Ltd.*, (2001) 205 D.L.R. (4th) 385.

6 *Retail, Wholesale and Department Store Union, Local 558 v. Pepsi-Cola Canada Beverages (West) Ltd.*, (2002) 208 D.L.R. (4th) 385.

7 *Dunmore v. Ontario (Attorney General)*, (2001) 207 D.LR. (4th) 193.

8 See "Evidence Filed in Support of Constitutional Challenge to NAFTA Investment Rules" on the Council of Canadians website, Trade, NAFTA, UPS/NAFTA Challenge, http://www.canadians.org, [January, 2005].

9 Under the "laboratory of democracy" argument from political science implicitly advanced by Carter (1995:56), provinces or states are more likely to introduce legislative innovations than national governments because the risk in introducing the innovations at this lower level is far less. The "laboratory of democracy" argument also suggests that successful experiments will spread to other jurisdictions, as has indeed been the case in Canada. Some of Weiler's innovations, such as the use of grievance mediation in connection with expedited arbitration, have since spread to several other provinces.

10 Ontario, British Columbia, Manitoba, Newfoundland and Labrador, and the federal jurisdiction oblige employers to agree to include a Rand formula provision in the collective agreement. Quebec requires employers to deduct dues from every bargaining unit employee. New Brunswick, Nova Scotia, Prince Edward Island and Alberta simply require the employer to honour employees' authorizations to deduct union dues from their wages.

11 Canada, s.70(2)-(4); British Columbia, s.17; Ontario, s.52; Alberta, s.29(2); Saskatchewan, s.5(1); Manitoba, ss.76(3), 77.

12 *Steele v. Louisville & Nashville Railroad Co.*, 323 U.S. 192, (1944) (U.S.S.C.). A union that refused to grant membership to black employees was held to have not met its responsibility to represent all members of the craft fairly and without "hostile discrimination" when it negotiated a clause that granted greater job security to employees who were union members.

13 Alberta, Manitoba, Newfoundland and Labrador, Saskatchewan, and the federal jurisdiction.

14 New Brunswick, Nova Scotia, and Prince Edward Island.

15 See, for example, *Gendron v. Supply and Services Union of the Public Service Alliance of Canada, Local 50057 et al.*, (1986) 43 Man. R. (2nd) 123 Man. Q.B.); *Gendron v. Local 50057, Supply and Services Union of the Public Service Alliance of Canada and Public Service Alliance of Canada*, [1988] 1 W.W.R. 613 (Man. C.A.); *Canadian Merchant Service Guild v. Gagnon et al.*, (1984) 9 D.L.R. (4th) 641 (S.C.C.) 84 C.L.L.C. 14,043; *Centre hospitalier Regina Ltee v. Labour Court*, [1990] S.C.J. No. 56.

16 *Canadian Merchant Service Guild v. Gagnon* (1984), 9 D.L.R. (4th) 641.

17 Ibid., para. 36.

18 Ontario was a notable exception; this right was eliminated in 1998; however the Liberal government's amendments to the *Ontario Labour Relations Act* restored this power, effective November 1, 2005 (Ministry of Labour, 2005).

19 In 2005, *Bill 144* amended the O*ntario Labour Relations Act* to restore this power to the Ontario board. The previous Conservative government had removed this power following a Board certification order in respect of the Windsor Wal-Mart in 1997.

20 See, for example, *Aranas v Toronto East General & Orthopaedic Hospital Inc.*, 2005 Can LII 1056 (ON S.C.), January 19, 2005.

21 Some jurisdictions remove this condition in cases where the collective agreement contains a re-opener clause or designates provisions expressly subject to revision.

22 Saskatchewan is the exception, in that the *Trade Union Act* specifically stipulates that it is an unfair labour practice for an employer to unilaterally change rates of pay or conditions of employment without engaging in collective bargaining but makes no reference to any abridgement of this duty upon commencement of a strike or lockout. (R.S.S., 1978, c.T-17 s.11(1)(*m*))

23 As of January 2005, four jurisdictions mandated a vote in all instances: Nova Scotia (since 1977), Alberta (since 1988), British Columbia (reintroduced in 2001) and Ontario (since 1995) (Riddell, 2001; *Ontario Labour Relations Act*, 1995, c.1, Sched. A, s.8(2); *British Columbia Labour Relations Code*, 1996, c.244, s.24(1)). The legislation in Newfoundland and Labrador does not specifically require a vote but the Board's practice is to require a vote unless both the employer and union agree in writing that the vote is unnecessary; *Newfoundland and Labrador Labour Relations Act*, 1990, c.L-1, s.38.

24 Manitoba introduced the vote in 1997 and reverted to card majority in 2000. British Columbia introduced the vote in 1984, reverted to card-majority in 1993, and then reintroduced mandatory vote in 2001.

25 For example, in Ontario, the application may be made during the last three months of agreements of three years or less. For longer agreements, the application may be made during the last three months of the agreement's third and subsequent years (*OLRA*, section 63[2]).

26 This threshold level applies specifically to instances where the workers are already represented by one union and another union challenges majority support. *Saskatchewan Trade Union Act*, R.S.S., 1978, c.T-17, s.6(1) (b).

27 *British Columbia Labour Relations Code*, R.S.B.C., 1996, c.244, s.18(1).

28 *The Labour Relations Act, Manitoba*, C.C.S.M., c.L-10, s.40(1) (1).

29 Ontario and Nova Scotia require that votes normally be held within 5 days (*O.L.R.A.*, 1995, c.1, Sched. A, s.8(5); *N.S.T.U.A.*, 1989, c.475, s.25(3)). British Columbia normally requires votes be held within 10 days (*B.C.L.R.C.*, 1996, c.244, s.24(2). Alberta simply mandates "as soon as possible" (*A.L.R.C.*, 2000, c.L-1, s.34(3).

30 *Labour Relations Act*, R.S.N.L., 1990, c.L-1, s.38(2)c.

31 See *Kidd Creek Mines Ltd.* [1984] O.L.R.B. Rep. March 481.

32 *Ontario Labour Relations Act,* 1995, c.1, Sched. A, s.1(3)(a); *Alberta Labour Relations Code,* R.S.A., 2000, c.L-1, s.1(l)(ii), *Prince Edward Island Labour Act,* 1988, R.S.P.E.I., c.L-1, s.7(2)(a).

33 *Ontario Labour Relations Act,* 1995, c.1, Sched. A, s.9(4).

34 *Alberta Labour Relations Code,* R.S.A., 2000, c.L-1, s.1(l)(ii); *Prince Edward Island Labour Act,* 1988, R.S.P.E.I., c.L-1, s.7(2)(a).

35 *Agricultural Employees Protection Act,* 2002, S.O. 2002, c.16.

36 *Alberta Labour Relations Code,* R.S.A., 2000, c.L-1, s.4(2)(e)(i and ii).

37 *Gaétan Delisle c. Le procureur général du Canada et al.,* [1999] 2 S.C.R. 989.

38 *Alberta Labour Relations Code,* R.S.A., 2000, c.L-1, s.148(2)(c).

39 See, for example, *Canada Labour Code* (Part 1)(R.S., 1985, c.L-2), s.108.1(1); *Ontario Labour Relations Act,* 1995, (S.O. 1995, c.1), s.41 and s.42; *Saskatchewan Trade Union Act* (R.S.S 1978, c.T-17), s.45.

40 For example, Alberta and Nova Scotia. By virtue of their prohibition of replacement workers, British Columbia and Quebec also provide these protections.

41 *Canada Labour Code* (Part 1)(R.S., 1985, c.L-2), s.94.3(d); *Alberta Labour Relations Code,* R.S.A., 2000, c.L-1, s.155(l)(a); *Labour Relations Act,* R.S.N.L.,1990, c.L-1, s.24(2)(b); *Nova Scotia Trade Union Act* (R.S.N.S., 1989, c.475), s.53(3)(d).

42 *Manitoba Labour Relations Act* (R.S.M., 1987, c.L-10), s.17(a).

43 *Saskatchewan Trade Union Act* (R.S.S., 1978, c.T-17), s.11(1)(l)(i).

44 For example, the federal jurisdiction, Alberta, Manitoba, and Ontario.

45 *Quebéc Labour Code* (R.S.Q., c.C-27), s.109.1; *British Columbia Labour Relations Code* (R.S.B.C., 1996, c.244), s.68.

46 *British Columbia Labour Relations Code,* R.S.B.C., 1996, c.244, s.72(2).

47 *Alberta Labour Relations Code,* R.S.A., 2000, c.L-1, s.112–113.

48 *Labour Relations Act,* R.S.N.L.,1990, c.L-1, s.100.2 and s.22.

49 Significantly, Saskatchewan, the one province that adopted a more or less "pure" Wagner model, did not initially require grievance arbitration, changing its law to do so only in 1994.

Chapter 8

1 As noted by Fryer (1995:355), in 1994 the Prince Edward Island government unilaterally rolled back public sector pay by 8.5 percent—or roughly one month's pay per year, in a province where pay levels already lag behind those in most of the rest of Canada.

2 In principle, the public sector also includes the employees of government enterprises such as the CBC and Ontario Hydro (through 2001). However, data on the number of government enterprise employees are not available and therefore they have not been included for purposes of this discussion.

3 See Peirce (1989) for a more detailed discussion.

4 Rose (1995:21) notes that as of 1945, there were about 40 000 public sector union members, or roughly 5 percent of the country's total union membership. Almost certainly most would have been outside municipal workers, who faced less daunting legal obstacles to unionization partly because municipal workers have always been covered by general labour acts rather than by special, and generally more restrictive, public sector legislation. For a more detailed discussion of the evolution of municipal collective bargaining, see Graham (1995:181–183).

5 For a very thoughtful discussion of the NJC, see L.W.C.S. Barnes. (1975). *Consult and Advise: A History of the National Joint Council of the Public Service of Canada.* Kingston: Queen's IRC Press.

6 This structure has since been simplified considerably. The largest public service union, the Public Service Alliance of Canada (PSAC) now negotiates with the government at five bargaining tables.

7 In 1994, Ontario passed a new public service employment act granting its employees the right to strike (Fryer, 1995:346).

8 Between 1965 and 1974 (Ponak and Thompson, 1995:440), back-to-work legislation was invoked 12 times, or just slightly more than once a year. Six of the 12 back-to-work laws were in Quebec.

9 For a useful discussion of this change of attitude, see Godard (1994:262–263).

10 For as long as Bill 19 remained in effect. When an NDP government replaced Vander Zalm's Socreds in 1991, one of its first acts was to repeal this bill and the Compensation Stabilization program that had frozen public sector wages since 1982 (Craig and Solomon, 1996:365). The new government also did away with Bill 19's sweeping definition of essential services and replaced it with more limited essential services legislation roughly comparable to the Quebec legislation described earlier in the chapter (Craig and Solomon, 1996:235).

11 In other words, if federal government employees received a 1 percent wage increase, 1 percent of them would have to be laid off.

12 A "socialist" feature of this legislation was that those earning less than $30 000 per year were exempted.

13 Initially, the Klein government sought to eliminate taxing authority for all boards. It backed down following a threatened constitutional challenge by the Catholic boards (Thomason, 1995:280).

14 In January 1999, the province's health care support employees were embroiled in a dispute with the hospital associations. After staging a one-day strike during the first week of January, CUPE (the union representing the health care workers) agreed to return to the bargaining table and not to stage any more strikes (CBC Radio News, January 10, 1999).

15 In subsequent changes to the *PSSRA*, this number was reduced to 26 (Swimmer, 1995:390–391).

16 Whatever the merits of any Charter-based challenges to statutory designation of public sector bargaining agents, such designation appears to violate a key principle of Canadian labour legislation, namely that the employer should have no hand in the formation or operation of a union. Since government is ultimately the employer of all public sector workers, especially employees of its own departments, statutory designation of the bargaining agent amounts to its choosing which union will represent its workers. Somewhat similar provisions do exist in a few private sector labour acts; for example, Quebec's construction act (discussed in the previous chapter) specifies that construction workers must belong to one of five duly recognized associations.

17 The restriction on bargaining over pensions applies not just to federal and provincial government employees, but also to many municipal employees, teachers, and health care workers (Thompson and Ponak, 1995:431).

18 Among the most telling criticisms of "ability to pay" listed by Sack (1991) is the last of the seven he lists: that arbitrators are not in a position to measure public sector employers' ability to pay.

19 *CUPE vs. Ontario (Min. of Labour) (1999)*, 117 O.A.C. 340 (Div. Ct.).

20 For a fascinating if sometimes horrifying first-hand account of a controlled hospital strike in Vancouver, see Weiler (1980).

21 As Craig and Solomon (1996:315–316) note, the government of Quebec has long refused to submit most disputes in the public and para-public sectors to arbitration for just this reason.

22 The committee's official name was the Advisory Committee on Labour Management Relations in the Federal Public Service. However, it was generally referred to as the Fryer Committee, and in the interest largely of economy, I have stuck to that convention here.

23 This tripartite body, modelled closely after a recommendation in the 1968 Woods Commission report, should not in any way be confused with the abortive Dispute Resolution Commission proposed earlier by the Ontario government. As the Fryer Committee notes (2001:32–37), the idea was that such a commission should be chaired by an individual with a national reputation in public sector labour relations, and supported by union, management, and neutral members, all with significant experience in the field.

24 Except as otherwise noted, material for this discussion of public service human resource modernization has been drawn from "Human Resource Modernization at a Glance," on the PIPSC website, Labour Issues, HR Modernization, *Public Service Modernization Act*, http://www.pipsc.ca/english/labour/modernization/psma.pdf and http://www.pipsc.ca/english/labour/modernization/psma-pssra.pdf.

Chapter 9

1 Similarly, as Rogow notes, union leaders may favour centralized bargaining arrangements even at times when such arrangements are not in the union's economic interest because of their philosophical belief that such arrangements can better promote worker solidarity than more individualistic decentralized ones.

2 Through most of the post-war period, the "Big Four" tire manufacturers accounted for 85 percent of industry sales (Kochan et al., 1984:31).

3 For a very useful overview of these developments, see Ferner and Hyman (1992b), especially pages xx–xxii.

4 It is not likely that centralized systems would have such an effect in bad times. In connection with this point, it should be noted that most of Tarantelli's data were complied prior to the major recession of 1981–1983. At the same time, it should also be noted that inflation is generally of far less concern in bad times than in good.

5 Centralized systems have also been associated with lower levels of unemployment (Tarantelli, 1986). For one thing, the social democratic governments under which such systems are adopted have tended to follow full-employment policies as a matter of principle. For another, the political bargaining in which these governments often engage with labour movements often leads to trade-offs, such as those of the Swedish active labour market policy (Hammarstrom, 1993:200), which have led to full employment guarantees in return for the unions' pledge to restrain wage demands and in some cases strike activity.

6 If one's business is export-oriented, this may entail monitoring ongoing political developments and trade policies in the countries to which one is primarily interested in exporting.

7 Human Resources Development Canada puts out a number of publications listing various wage settlements, as do a number of provincial labour departments.

Chapter 10

1 As we noted in Chapter 8, these issues are typically treated as management rights rather than bargainable issues under most Canadian public sector bargaining legislation.

2 As well, violence and other forms of abuse, at home and on the job, are of growing concern to many unions, as well as government policy makers. To help address these problems, recent agreements signed by the Canadian Auto Workers have included provisions making workplace advocates available to support women facing harassment on the job or abuse at home (Giles and Starkman, 1995:359).

3 It may be worth noting that in logging and in the garment industries, the two industries that make the greatest use of piecework systems, most of the labour force is uneducated and many of the workers have few other options for gainful employment (Radforth, 1982; Grant, 1992:232–234). In the clothing industry in particular, extensive use has been made of immigrant women for whom the work is the "port of entry" into the Canadian labour market. These facts suggest that piecework systems would probably not be embraced voluntarily by the majority of workers.

4 All federal public service employees employed by the Treasury Board of Canada now receive one day off per year specifically to perform volunteer work, according to collective agreement provisions initially negotiated with the Public Service Alliance in 2001.

5 For a more detailed discussion of the evolution of shorter work hours, see Hunnicutt (1988) and Peirce (2000b).

6 Anecdotal evidence from my students suggests that many workers dislike bumping provisions for essentially the same reason—because they mean that

workers will not know for some time whether they have a job or what job they will be doing.

7 More research is needed to determine why unions have not, in fact, raised technological change issues more frequently than they have.

8 A good example would be the Swedish "active labour market system" whereby unions accepted management's right to hire and fire and to deploy new technology in return for income security and retraining rights. The system facilitated both occupational and geographic mobility (Kjellberg, 1992:96–97). For unfortunately brief discussions, see Kjellberg (1992) and Hammarstrom (1993).

9 In practice, as the reader may already have guessed, there is often considerable overlap between these two factors. The ultimate source of the long-standing mistrust between management and the union may well be the declining long-term economic position of the firm or industry in question.

10 For an extremely useful and much more detailed discussion of the points raised here, see Giles (1996).

Chapter 11

1 The point that a strike or other crisis can serve as a catalyst for introducing such mechanisms is well made by Verma (1995). For a discussion of this point within the American setting, see Woodworth and Meek (1995).

2 Such a refusal would be legal if the employee in question believed working conditions to be dangerous. See the employment law chapter for more detail on this point.

3 On June 14, 2001, just as the Nova Scotia dispute was starting to heat up, it was reported that about 3500 Ontario nurses per year were accepting jobs in these two countries (CTV News, 2001).

4 For a fairly detailed overview, see Gunderson, Hebdon, Hyatt, and Ponak, 2005.

5 For an interesting discussion see Ponak and Thompson (1989:395–396).

Chapter 12

1 This case is *Re IKO Industries Ltd. and United Steelworkers of America, Local 86580*, 104 L.A.C. (4th), 97-110. Reproduced from Labour Arbitration Cases with the permission of Canada Law Book, A Division of The Cartwright Group, Ltd. (www.canadalawbook.ca). Deletions have been made to save space; otherwise, the case is as originally published.

2 At least one recent Canadian writer (Haiven, 1990) is critical of the ban on mid-term strikes.

3 The grievance process is often used for this purpose in the public service or other branches of the public sector, where (as noted in Chapter 8), the scope of bargainable issues is generally considerably restricted.

4 At the University of Ottawa (University of Ottawa, 1994), such grievances are initiated at step three of the grievance procedure. As well, the potentially greater seriousness of group grievances is reflected by the fact that they are initiated at step two of the procedure.

5 This figure would almost certainly overrepresent the proportion of discharge and discipline-related grievances, given that unions send most discharge grievances through to arbitration.

6 For a useful if brief review of these studies, see Thornicroft and Eden (1995:262–265 and 268–270).

7 Sack also advises grievors to list their attempts to seek employment and the responses they have made, so they can prove to employers that they have made an honest attempt to mitigate (lessen) the damages resulting from the dismissal.

8 See Sack (1994:141–142) for an interesting and somewhat more detailed discussion of the issues covered in this section.

9 For a useful if brief review of these studies, see Thornicroft and Eden (1995:262–265 and 268–270).

10 Such programs have been established in four provinces: Newfoundland, Ontario, Alberta, and British Columbia. The Ontario one, however, is apparently no longer in existence. For a brief description, see Thornicroft and Eden (1995:264–265).

11 For an original and thought-provoking critique of progressive discipline and the assumptions behind it, see Eden (1992).

12 Interestingly, exactly the same proportion (12 percent) of those discharged for dishonesty were exonerated, a finding that suggests the arbitrators were not fully convinced the grievors hadn't committed the acts of which they were accused, since had the arbitrators been fully convinced, they presumably would have had no choice but to exonerate the grievors.

13 Admittedly, Barnacle's sample of non-lawyer arbitrators was very small, since more than 80 percent of his arbitrators were lawyers.

14 Counsel can, of course, be used to prepare the briefs, but this doesn't affect the length or cost of the hearing, though it does affect the cost of the process.

15 As Craig and Solomon (1996:352) note, the oral decision takes effect immediately, but must be confirmed by a brief written decision as soon as possible (normally within 48 hours).

16 This list is an adaptation and expansion of one developed by Rose (1987).

17 It is sometimes called something else, but the process is generally pretty much the same.

18 Elliott and Goss (1994:18) estimate that grievance mediation costs are less than 15 percent those of arbitration.

19 As Thornicroft and Eden (1995) note, there is little evidence available on private sector grievance mediation results in Canada.

20 For more detailed results of grievance mediation in the American private sector, see Feuille (1992). Feuille's study also includes cost and time data.

21 See Downie (1989) for a more detailed discussion of RBO and other related organizational development techniques.

22 This case is not included in the Lancaster House (2004) packet from which most materials in this section have been drawn.

23 *Francine Desormeaux and Canadian Human Rights Commission vs. Ottawa-Carleton Regional Transit Commission,* Canadian Human Rights Tribunal Decision, Jan. 14, 2003, in Lancaster House (2004:136–136a); *Alain Parisien and Canadian Human Rights Commission vs. Ottawa-Carleton Regional Transit Commission,* Canadian Human Rights Tribunal Decision, March 6, 2003, in Lancaster House (2004:136–136a).

24 *CUPE vs. Restigouche Health Services Corporation,* arbitral award made Nov. 12, 2003, in Lancaster House (2004:131–132).

25 *Parry Sound (District) Social Services vs. O.P.S.E.U., Local 324* (2003), 230 D.L.R. (4th) 257 (S.C.C.).

26 *Teamsters Local Union No. 987 vs. Serca Foodservice,* arbitral award made Jan. 21, 2004, in Lancaster House (2004:38–39).

27 One of the authors knows of a case in which one member of a union board had allegedly defamed a fellow board member by calling him a "scab" at a union meeting. The individual who felt himself defamed then filed an action in Small Claims Court.

28 (1999), 42 O.R. (3rd) 626 (C.A.).

29 See, among others, *Allen vs. Alberta,* (2002), 223 D.L.R. (4th), 385 (S.C.C.), and *Gaignard vs. Canada (Attorney General),* (2003), 232 D.L.R. (4th) 43 (Ont. C.A.), both discussed in Lokan and Yachnin (2004).

30 *OPSEU vs. Seneca College of Applied Arts and Technology,* Ontario Divisional Court review of arbitral award of Dec., 2001, [2004] O.J. No. 4440 (QL), issued Nov. 1, 2004.

31 *NAPE vs. Her Majesty the Queen in Right of Newfoundland and Labrador,* unreported arbitral decision of Feb. 17, 2003, discussed in Lancaster House (2004:387).

32 One that did was *Rees vs. Canada (RCMP),* an unreported Supreme Court of Newfoundland and Labrador decision in which an RCMP officer was awarded nearly $500 000, including $120 000 for pain and suffering ($30 000 of which constituted "aggravated damages") after he developed post-traumatic stress disorder as a result of ongoing harassment by his supervisor, and the judge concluded that the supervisor was retaliating against the officer for allegedly having "ratted" on him during an internal investigation, and that the RCMP had been negligent in failing to take steps to prevent the harassment. See Lancaster House (2004:297).

33 *Voice Construction Ltd. vs. Construction and General Workers Union, Local 92,* [2004] S.C.C. 23 and *A.U.P.E. vs. Lethbridge Community College,* [2004] S.C.C. 28. Both cases are discussed at some length in Mullan (2004).

34 A particular concern with the *Lethbridge* case is that the Alberta law under which the case was decided contains a privative clause, albeit a weak one (Mullan, 2004:137–138).

35 Statement made at a luncheon workshop, Lancaster House arbitration conference, Nov. 24, 2004.

36 *National Automobile, Aerospace, Transportation and General Workers of Canada (CAW-Canada), Local 27 vs. Accuride Canada,* [2004] O.L.A.A. No. 13 (QL) (Etherington). Case heard March 24, 2004 in Ontario.

37 *Media Union of Manitoba, Local 191 vs. Naylor Publications Co.*, unreported Manitoba Grievance Arbitration decision, April 7, 2003.

38 See Elliott and Goss (1994) for a detailed discussion of a broad range of these mechanisms.

39 Again, this has often been the case with Canada Post. Stewart-Patterson (1987) indicates that during the 1980s, a sizable portion of all grievances filed against the corporation had nothing to do with the collective agreement as such.

Chapter 13

1 In some Asian countries, as noted in Table 7, female labour force participation hovers at or even below 10 percent.

2 The perceptive reader will recall that deregistration has sometimes been resorted to in Canada, as well, as in the case of the 1959 International Woodworkers of America strike in Newfoundland, which ended in Premier Joey Smallwood's decertifying the IWA. To be sure, deregistration has been rare in Canada, at least since the full legalization of private sector collective bargaining in 1944.

3 "Free" systems are also found in such highly-developed Pacific Rim countries as Australia, New Zealand, and Japan. Since the end of the apartheid era and the modernization of its labour relations regime, South Africa has also qualified as a "free" system.

4 As Matsuda notes (1993:201), the rest of the work force, many of whom are women, have traditionally earned far less, enjoyed much less job security, and been more apt to be involved in work-related accidents than the "core" predominantly male work force.

5 Lipsig-Mumme's apt term for the role played by the Japanese government is "statist entrepreneurism."

6 For a brief discussion of Tannenbaum, see Craig and Solomon (1993). A much more far-reaching discussion may be found in Larson and Nissen (1987).

7 See Adams (1995:510–511) for an interesting and (to this observer at least) somewhat horrifying view of working life in a Japanese firm providing the guarantee of lifetime employment.

8 As Déom and Boivin note (2001:508–509), these associations have established a central body, the Conseil du Patronat du Québec, to provide the province's employers with a united voice particularly in its dealings with the provincial government. No comparable body exists anywhere else in Canada (see Adams, 1995a).

9 The ability of firms to use relocation threats as a bargaining tool has been recognized by industrial relationists for many years. This phenomenon is specifically discussed in the now-classic 1984 article by Thomas Kochan et al., "Strategic Choice and Industrial Relations Theory." What is new is the extent to which the threat of relocation, not just to another part of the country but to a different country, may now be a credible one.

10 For an interesting discussion on issues around this point, see Adams (1995).

11 Where two rates are given (as in the case of India), this means that the ILO provided two different figures for informal sector participation.

12 These figures are based on union density calculated as a percentage of the non-agricultural labour force. When union density is calculated as a percentage of wage and salary earners, we see some countries, such as Canada, Finland, and Sweden, whose density rates show a decline in Peirce 2003, Table 13.7, posting increases in their density rates. The reason for this is that these countries experienced increased unemployment between the two study periods and would presumably have had relatively fewer employed individuals (as a proportion of the working-age population) during the 1990s than they had had during the 1980s. Unfortunately, comparable two-period data for union density as a percentage of wage and salary earners were available for only a portion of the 64 countries listed in Peirce 2003, Table 13.7.

13 The removal of compulsory membership requirements may also help explain why union density rates dropped more sharply in Europe as a whole than one might otherwise have expected, given that continent's relatively strong support for unionism by world standards.

14 Ebbinghaus (2002) notes that while membership in the Chamber of Commerce remains mandatory for Austrian employers, their dues have recently been cut by a third, reducing the resources available to devote to collective bargaining.

15 The three countries that saw a decrease in company-level bargaining were all in Africa.

16 As we noted in Chapter 7 (labour law), these groups include agricultural workers and homeworkers.

17 As noted on p. 183 of the ILO study, a study carried out in Manila found that 4 percent of the city's informal sector units were less than a year old, and only 14 percent had lasted ten years or more.

18 As noted in Peirce 2003, Table 13.7, South Africa's union density rates increased by more than 40 percent between 1985 and 1995.

Chapter 14

1 Before coming to Canada, about 39 percent of male immigrants and 17 percent of female immigrants had been working in natural or applied sciences. Six months after arrival, those figures were 19 percent and 7 percent, respectively (CLBC, 2004:22).

2 *Vaughan vs. Canada,* [2005] S.C.C. 11.

3 Chief Justice McLachlin and Justice Bastarache dissented. In their view, "while avoiding duplication is an important policy consideration, resort to the courts in the case at bar is not truly duplicative because no independent adjudication is possible at the grievance level." In such cases, they argued, courts should retain residual jurisdiction.

4 Our idea might appear to be simply another expedited arbitration system. It should, however, be noted that our proposed forum would handle a broader range of cases than just grievances (e.g., the "simple" harassment and defamation cases referred to earlier). It should also be noted that a great many unionized workers don't currently have access to expedited arbitration.

CASE APPENDIX

Case HS.1 Health and Safety Case

SPIELBERG AND CN RAILWAY COMPANY

A skilled machinist returns from vacation to find his shop in a state of total chaos. Because of the slippery condition of the floor around his wheel reprofiling machine, he slips and falls, injuring his finger. The next day he refuses to work until the situation is remedied. Should he be penalized for this action?

Parties: Spielberg / Canadian National (CN)

Forum: Canada Labour Relations Board

Jurisdiction: Canada

The worker was a machinist who had been employed by CN for about 10 years. He had an unblemished employment history with CN and his expertise had been recognized. His specialized job involved essentially the reconditioning of locomotive wheels that had worn out and had deteriorated over time. He was expected to be able to reprofile three or four pairs of wheels during a normal shift if the machine used for the purpose was in good working order.

The worker was also an active member of the workplace health and safety committee, responsible for questions on health and safety in the shop. He had submitted written reports on several occasions disclosing shortcomings in the shop facilities, particularly in the wheel reprofiling section where he worked. Before he went on vacation, he had reported the fact that the platform around the wheel reprofiling machine was slippery and had no guardrail, which posed a danger to health and safety. On his return from vacation, he found the shop in a state of total disorder. The reprofiling machine required repairs and the dangers and deficiencies he had reported in writing had not been remedied. The worker refused to work because of the slippery condition around the machine, which had caused him to slip and fall the day before, resulting in injury to his finger. He requested that a Labour Canada officer be called to investigate the matter. The shop foreman refused and instead assigned the worker to perform other duties.

He later received a summons to a disciplinary hearing for alleged lack of productivity. The hearing led to the worker's being assessed 10 demerit points under the company's personnel management procedure known as the "Brown System" in disciplinary matters. Once an employee had accumulated a certain number of demerit points, he could be subject to dismissal.

Source: Adapted from Canadian Labour Relations Board Decision No. 757 Board File 950-99, 9/28/89, record #8994. © 1989, CCH Canadian Ltd. Reprinted from *Canadian Employment Safety & Health Guide* with permission. Some deletions have been made by the author for the purposes of this book and names have been changed.

The worker filed a complaint with Labour Canada alleging that his employer, in imposing the 10 demerit points against him, had contravened section 147(a) of the Canada Labour Code prohibiting any disciplinary or reprisal action against an employee who has exercised his rights under the Code or has sought the enforcement of any of the provisions of Part II of the Code. In this case, the complainant alleged that the disciplinary action taken by CN against him was the result of his insistence that safety standards should be complied with and of the fact that he had exercised his right to refuse unsafe work under Part II of the Code. The employer, in reply, essentially argued that the penalty imposed had no connection with the complainant's availing himself of the provisions of Part II of the Code.

Questions

1. Will the Board allow the machinist's penalty of 10 demerit points to stand? Why, or why not?
2. If you were the machinist's superior, how would you have handled this situation?
3. If you were senior management, in what light would you view the foreman's behaviour? How might you respond to the incident?
4. What might the machinist do, another time, to help ensure safe conditions without putting his own neck on the line to the same extent?

Case HR.1 Human Rights Case

MITCHELL AND SUBWAY SANDWICHES

Can an employer legally discharge an employee for pregnancy or medical complications resulting from pregnancy?

Canadian

C.H.R.R.

Human Rights Reporter

British Columbia

Pregnancy

Indexed as: *Mitchell v. Subway Sandwiches & Salads*

Monica Mitchell, the complainant, filed a complaint (Exhibit 1) in which she alleged that Subway Sandwiches & Salads ("Subway"), the respondent, discriminated

---

Source: Adapted from (2001), 39 C.H.R.R. D/102, 2001 BCHRT 2. Some deletions have been made by the author for the purposes of this book and names have been changed.

Note: This case will be useful in connection with Chapter 6 (employment legislation).

against her with respect to the terms and conditions of her employment and refused to continue to employ her because of her sex (pregnancy), contrary to what is now s.13 of the *Human Rights Code*, R.S.B.C. 1986, c.210 (as amended) (the "*Code*"). By letter dated March 20, 2000 (Exhibit 2), the Registrar of the Tribunal, in response to an application by counsel for the complainant, decided to add Sandra Stewart, also known as Sandra Olson, as a respondent to this complaint.

EVIDENCE

The complainant testified that she began working at Subway in April 1996. Her duties included making sandwiches, serving customers, dealing with the cash and cleaning the bathrooms. She worked the night shift from 7:00 p.m. to 2:00 a.m. with a co-worker, Arnold Patton, who told her that her supervisor was Alice. The complainant understood that Ms. Stewart was the owner of Subway. The complainant testified that she had very little contact with Ms. Stewart, who rarely came in during the evening. The complainant had a three-month probationary period.

On July 22, 1996, the complainant saw Dr. Brown because she believed that she was pregnant. The pregnancy was confirmed the next day. The complainant testified that, when she informed her supervisor, Alice responded that she knew the complainant would not be able to continue to work throughout her pregnancy because she, Alice, had not been able to. Alice told the complainant that the best thing to do would be to lay her off when she had enough weeks to qualify for unemployment insurance.

The complainant testified that, in mid-August, she had another conversation with Alice, who told her that she had been informed by Ms. Stewart that the complainant could not be laid off simply because she was pregnant. The complainant's evidence was that Alice then gave her two choices: either quit her employment after giving one month's notice, or Subway would make it very difficult for the complainant to get another job in the future.

The complainant's mother, Dottie Mitchell, testified that she telephoned the Employment Standards Branch (ESB) after the complainant told her what Alice had said. Ms. Mitchell's evidence was that she was informed by ESB that an employer could not fire an employee simply because she became pregnant, and that the complainant should continue to work and to document anything of importance. Ms. Mitchell passed this information on to her daughter.

The complainant testified that Alice continued to approach her and ask her when she was going to give her notice. The complainant testified that she put Alice off by saying that she had no time to deal with it or that she had forgotten.

The complainant began to work some day shifts in mid-August. She understood that Alice continued to be her supervisor. The complainant said that she did not deal with Carla Ledbetter, another manager at Subway.

On August 25, the complainant was not feeling well. She went to Emergency at the West Coast General Hospital (the "Hospital") at 1:30 a.m., where she was examined and discharged. She was not scheduled to work that day.

The complainant worked an eight-hour shift on August 27.

The complainant testified that, on August 29, she saw Dr. Wilson because she was experiencing bad cramping and vaginal discharge. Dr. Wilson gave her an undated note to take two days off work. The complainant was scheduled to work the night shift that day. Her evidence was that she took the note to Alice and informed her that she would not be able to work that evening. According to the complainant, Alice refused to take the note and told the complainant that she "better come to work" and that if she did not show up she would not have a job because Alice wanted to spend time with her daughter and some of the other employees were sick.

The complainant's mother testified that she drove her daughter to Subway so that she could give Alice the note from Dr. Wilson. Ms. Mitchell said the complainant came out of Subway crying. The complainant testified that, when she and her mother got home, her mother telephoned Subway and asked to speak to the manager. The complainant testified that her mother told her that the manager said that, if the complainant did not come into work, there would be no job for her. The complainant stayed with her mother on August 29 and did not work her shift. She said that this was the first shift she missed because of her pregnancy.

The complainant testified that she was absent from work on August 29 and 30. Her evidence was that, on August 30, her grandfather had a heart attack and was admitted to the Hospital in the evening. She and her mother went out to look for the complainant's brother to take him to the Hospital. The complainant's evidence was that, because her brother was "hanging out" with his friends, she and her mother had to drive around Port Alberni to look for him. Her mother gave similar evidence.

The complainant testified that her co-worker, Arnold Patton, told her that an employee of the respondent saw her in uptown Port Alberni that night when she was out looking for her brother.

On the morning of August 31, the complainant, who continued to feel ill, again went to Emergency at the Hospital. She was seen by Dr. Richardson, who advised her to take another one to two days off work. The complainant testified that she did not take this note to Alice because two days earlier Alice had refused the note from Dr. Wilson.

The complainant returned to the Hospital on the morning of September 1 when she was diagnosed with a threatened miscarriage and was sent home with another note that she should take a few days off work. She was admitted to the Hospital that evening and suffered a miscarriage.

The complainant's mother testified that she telephoned Subway from the Hospital. She believed that she spoke to Ms. Stewart. Ms. Mitchell told the woman she spoke to that the complainant was in the Hospital having a miscarriage. According to Ms. Mitchell, the woman told her that she did not care, that the complainant was fired, and that she should not show up for work. Ms. Mitchell responded that the complainant could not be fired for being sick. The woman told Ms. Mitchell that someone had seen the complainant the evening of August 30.

On September 2, Ms. Mitchell told her daughter that she had been fired. The Record of Employment issued to the complainant on September 3 states that her employment was terminated because she "failed to show up for shifts."

The complainant testified that she did not receive any written or verbal reprimands from either Alice, Carla Ledbetter or Sandra Stewart.

Sandra Stewart testified that she has been the sole owner of Subway since 1995. She stated that Carla Ledbetter took over as manager from Alice on August 12 and that this was communicated to the employees by word of mouth. However, Alice did not leave Subway until September 24. Ms. Stewart left hiring and firing decisions to the manager.

Ms. Stewart testified that it was Ms. Ledbetter's decision to fire the complainant because of her missed shifts. Ms. Stewart did not know any of the details surrounding the missed shifts. She stated that she was informed that there were concerns about the complainant's performance but she had no first-hand knowledge about them. Ms. Stewart testified that she never spoke to the complainant's mother.

Carla Ledbetter testified that the complainant telephoned just before her shift to say that she could not work because her grandfather was in the Hospital and that she had to find her brother. Ms. Ledbetter's evidence was that she later learned that this explanation was not true because the complainant was seen in uptown Port Alberni. Ms. Ledbetter understood that Alice told the complainant that two hours' notice was required when she could not work.

Ms. Ledbetter testified that, after the complainant's mother informed Arnold Patton that the complainant could not work because she was in the Hospital having a miscarriage, she telephoned the Hospital to check on the accuracy of the information. According to Ms. Ledbetter, she was told that there was no one by the name of Monica Mitchell there. Because Ms. Ledbetter could not confirm that the complainant was in the Hospital, her employment was terminated.

ISSUE

The issue before me is whether the respondents refused to continue to employ the complainant because of her pregnancy, contrary to s.13 of the *Code*.

DECISION

The complainant testified in a straightforward manner. There was no evidence to contradict her account of Alice's statement to her concerning her continuing to work during her pregnancy. Further, the evidence of the complainant's mother about her telephone call to ESB is consistent with the complainant's account of her conversation with Alice.

Ms. Ledbetter's evidence is that the decision was made to dismiss the complainant after she missed two shifts without providing adequate notice and for reasons which Ms. Ledbetter later determined to be untrue.

The complainant gave an account of her interaction with Alice on August 29 when she refused to accept Dr. Wilson's note and told the complainant that she "better come into work" or she would not have a job. I accept the complainant's testimony, which was not contradicted.

Ms. Ledbetter's evidence was that the complainant said that she could not come to work because her grandfather was in the Hospital and that Ms. Ledbetter later learned this was not true. This evidence is somewhat confusing because the complainant had a note from Dr. Wilson on August 29 that she was to take two days off work (Exhibit 4, tab 3). Therefore, on August 30, there would have been no reason for the complainant to say that the reason she could not come into work was because her grandfather had been hospitalized after a heart attack.

It seems to me more likely that the complainant's explanation on August 29 that she could not work because she was ill was doubted after someone from the respondent saw her in uptown Port Alberni on the night of August 30, when she was looking for her brother because their grandfather was in the Hospital. Her detailed account of the events that night, for example, her description of how her mother arranged pillows in the van so that the complainant would be comfortable, have satisfied me of the credibility of her evidence with respect to this incident.

Dr. Wilson's note refers simply to health reasons and makes no mention of the complainant's pregnancy. However, when her mother telephoned Subway on August 31, she advised them that the complainant could not work because she was having a miscarriage. While there is some confusion about whom the complainant's mother spoke to, Ms. Ledbetter's evidence makes it clear that she was aware of the content of the phone call.

Ms. Ledbetter's evidence was that she could not confirm this information when she telephoned the Hospital, and, as a result, the complainant's employment was terminated. Given the fact that the complainant was diagnosed as having a miscarriage on the morning of August 31, but was not admitted to the hospital until that evening, it appears that Ms. Ledbetter came to an incorrect conclusion about the veracity of the complainant's medical condition when she telephoned the Hospital and was informed that the complainant was not a patient there.

Discrimination on the basis of pregnancy constitutes discrimination on the basis of sex: *Brooks v. Canada Safeway* (1989), 10 C.H.R.R. D/6183 (S.C.C.). Adopting the reasoning that was applied in *Poirier v. British Columbia (Ministry of Municipal Affairs, Recreation and Housing)* (1997), 29 C.H.R.R. D/87 at D/91 (B.C.H.R.T.), I conclude that discrimination because of a miscarriage is a form of sex discrimination.

The respondents had an obligation to accommodate the complainant's pregnancy to the point of undue hardship. This legal obligation extends to accommodating a miscarriage, one of the possible outcomes of a pregnancy. It seems reasonable to me that such accommodation would require Subway to give the complainant both a reasonable opportunity to obtain and present medical confirmation of her miscarriage and also adequate time off to recover, if doing so would not amount to undue hardship.

Subway presented no evidence that accommodating the complainant would have amounted to undue hardship. Her position was not a skilled one that would have been difficult to fill. Indeed Ms. Ledbetter's evidence was that she returned to work to cover the complainant's absence. Ms. Ledbetter's unhappiness at having to return to work cannot be considered undue hardship.

Questions

1. What is the "duty to accommodate"? Why is it significant in this case?
2. Do you feel that the store management accommodated Ms. Mitchell to the point of "undue hardship"? Where would that point have come, in your view?
3. Had you been the adjudicator in this case, what would your decision have been, and why?

Case C.1 Certification Case

CUPE, LOCAL 79 AND CORPORATION OF THE CITY OF TORONTO

When a union is seeking to represent a bargaining unit containing large numbers of seasonal, part-time, and casual employees, who should be considered a bargaining-unit member for the purpose of determining whether the union has sufficient support to entitle it to a representation vote?

Canadian Union of Public Employees, Local 79 and The Corporation of the City of Toronto

Ontario Labour Relations Board, R.O. MacDowell, Chair; J.A. Rundle, Member; and H. Peacock, Member.

July 3, 1996.

J. James Nyman, for union.

E.T. McDermott, for employer.

No. 2603–95–R.

R.O. MACDOWELL, CHAIR

(H. PEACOCK, MEMBER, CONCURRING)

This is an application for certification in which CUPE Local 79 seeks to represent a large group of City employees who are currently unrepresented. A significant number of those employees have sought membership in the union and have indicated in a secret ballot vote that they want the union to represent them. The question in this case is whether the union is entitled to certification as their bargaining agent—that is, whether the Board can give legal effect to the wishes of employees recorded in the representation vote.

The union and the City are no strangers to the collective-bargaining process. CUPE Local 79 already represents some 2800 "white-collar" employees in the so-called "inside workers' bargaining unit." CUPE Local 43 (a sister local) represents a bargaining unit of 1800 "blue-collar" workers in the "outside workers' bargaining unit." Employees represented by the two CUPE locals work in proximity to the unrepresented workers affected by this application.

The two CUPE locals have been involved in collective bargaining with the City for decades. The issue in this case is whether another group of City employees is entitled to participate in that process.

Source: Adapted from OLRB, No. 2603-95-R, in 32 CLRBR (2nd), 1996, pp. 1–49. Some deletions have been made by the author for the purposes of this book and names have been changed.

The present application relates to a body of employees variously described as "part-time," "seasonal," or "casual," who work in the City's parks, community centres, and recreation programs. Their hours of work and work locations vary considerably, as does the actual work that they do. The number of casuals actively employed at any particular time also varies with the season and with the program mix offered by the City.

The parties are *agreed* that for the purposes of this certification application, the unit of employees appropriate for collective bargaining should be described as follows:

> all casual employees employed by the corporation of the city of
> Toronto in the Recreation Division of the Department of Parks and
> Recreation, save and except supervisors, persons above the rank
> of supervisor, and persons for whom the applicant or any other
> trade union held bargaining rights as of October 10, 1995.

However, the parties are *not* agreed on the number of employees in this unit for the purposes of the application. In other words, the parties agree on the *description* of the bargaining unit, but they do not agree on its *composition*.

The term "casual employee" (or "recreation casual") is used by the City for payroll purposes to describe these casual workers in a general way, and distinguish them from the "regular" inside or outside workers who are already represented by CUPE. For convenience, we will use the same terminology in this decision. However, it is important to note that the term "casual employee" (as used by the City and applied to a particular individual) does not necessarily connote a continuing employment relationship with the City, either in a common-law contractual sense, or for the purpose of certification under the *Labour Relations Act*, 1995. That is one of the issues that divides the parties. Since these "recreation casuals" work intermittently, there is a dispute about just how many of them actually were "employees" at the time the certification application was filed.

Counsel for the City advised that, over the course of the year, the City hires as many as 2400–2500 of these "casual workers" who work for various lengths of time in the parks, playgrounds, and recreation centres scattered throughout the City. The peak program period is during the summer months when, we were told, the City needs roughly 1500 additional employees to work as lifeguards, supervise wading pools, organize sports activities, administer camp programs, and so on. Many of these individuals are students employed during their school vacation period, so when the summer is over, their jobs end and they go back to school. They may or may not return the following summer.

In the fall, the complement of casuals drops considerably. Counsel for the City advised that, for the autumn programs, between 700 and 900 individuals are engaged for activities as diverse as square dancing, piano lessons, or Red Cross certification. In the winter, *yet another group* of workers is engaged in respect of indoor programs or outdoor winter sports activities at the City's parks, ice rinks, and arenas.

We were told that only a small group of "recreation casuals" are working continuously — primarily because they have a skill (for example, piano training) that is in constant demand for particular programs or at a particular recreation centre. However, that core group comprises only 200 to 400 workers (the parties disagree about the numbers). The rest of the recreation casuals come and go in accordance with the City's needs. There is no necessary carry-over between, say, those casuals who act as lifeguards or supervise the wading pools in the summer, and the casuals who clean the ice rinks in the winter. The composition of the casual group is continuously changing.

The City says that up to 75 percent of the summer casuals are hired again in the following summer (the union disputes the percentage). But there is no legal commitment to do so. Nor is there any obligation on the casual to return if asked. In this sense, the casual workers' situation is quite different from someone with enforceable "recall rights" under a collective agreement.

. . .   .

By any measure, there is a substantial turnover of casual employees, since the number and composition of the casual group depends upon the seasons, the program mix that the City chooses to offer, and, of course, their own availability to return to a program that has been offered before. Indeed, it is interesting to note that even the City had difficulty identifying the precise number of casuals who had been employed over the past year. We were told that compiling a list of casuals was difficult because the work locations were geographically diverse and many of the payroll records were kept manually.

This application for certification was filed on October 10, 1995—that is, precisely a month before Bill 7 came into effect. The material filed with the application therefore reflects the scheme of the Act that was in effect prior to November 10, 1995. However, because Bill 7 had certain retroactive features, it is agreed that the Board is obliged to apply the new Act to this application, even though it was filed "under the old system."

In support of this application for certification, the union has submitted 738 "membership" cards, and has estimated that, at the time the application was filed, the size of the bargaining unit was 840 persons. We were told that the union had been organizing for a number of months prior to the application, so its estimate is presumably based upon its contact with the various workplaces and its understanding of the ebb and flow of program activity. The union's estimate is generally consistent with the City's own estimate of the number of casuals *actively* working in the fall programs (see above).

In each case, the union card is signed by the individual worker concerned, is witnessed by another person, and indicates that the signer is applying for membership in the union. There is no real challenge to the form of this membership evidence either from the City or from any of the individuals who signed the cards. There is no reason to believe that the cards do not mean what they say: that the person signing the card wants to be represented by the trade union in a collective-bargaining relationship with the City.

The City has filed material in response to this application (which, as noted, was launched prior to the passage of Bill 7). The City's filing identified some 369 persons who were actively at work on Tuesday, October 10, 1995, the day on which the certification application was made.

The City has also filed a schedule of some 2455 other persons labelled "recreation casuals" who were not at work on the application date, but who had worked for the City at some point in the previous year. For the overwhelming majority of these individuals, the City has indicated that they were not scheduled to work on the application day, and that their expected date of return or recall was "unknown." The City's position is that all of these individuals (369 + 2045 = 2414) should be considered to be "employees in the bargaining unit" for the purposes of this certification application, *and further that if less than 40 percent of them have signed union membership cards, there can be no representation vote.*

It remains to be determined whether Bill 7 actually requires the kind of *pre-vote* arithmetic calculation proposed by the City, and, if it does, whether such calculation should be based upon the City's proposed list, material from the union, or some revised version of the City's list that emerges from inquiry or litigation. *The City asserts that an examination of this kind is required before any representation vote can be ordered.* The union's proposed interpretation of Bill 7 avoids this *pre-vote* exercise altogether—or, more accurately, shifts the focus to one of determining voter eligibility *after* the vote is ordered, rather than whether a vote should be taken at all. We shall have more to say about that later. At this point, it may be helpful to "do the arithmetic" in order to illustrate the dimensions of the problem.

For the 369 persons actively at work on October 10, 1995 (*i.e.,* literally "in" the proposed bargaining unit on the application date), the union has submitted 201 membership cards, which represents about 54 percent of the persons listed by the City as being at work on October 10. For the other 2045 persons not at work on October 10 (and for the most part not scheduled to return to work at any known date), the union has gathered a further 344 cards. Since the union's card-signing campaign took place in the weeks prior to the filing of the application for certification, it appears that by the time the application was filed, quite a number of the casuals who were working during the summer and had signed cards at that time, were no longer actively employed.

The union clearly has the support of the majority of the employees actively at work on October 10, 1995, and, therefore, unequivocally in the bargaining unit on the date the union applied for certification. Since the City says that there are around 900 individuals working in its fall programs, it is also clear that a significant proportion of them want to be represented by the union. However, if the bargaining unit actually contains 2400 to 2500 "employees" as the City claims, then the union's level of "card support" in that much larger group is only around 25 percent of this much larger number. And if the size of the bargaining unit is somewhere between 369 and 3000, it is currently impossible to determine the union's level of card support in percentage terms, without examining the actual situation of each person named on the employer's list to see whether such individual should be treated as an "employee" in the bargaining unit for the purposes of the certification process.

It is impossible to predict how long such analysis would take, particularly if the "facts" or their characterization are disputed, so that the Board would have to make specific determinations with respect to individual workers. But the union's estimate of "many months" is not at all unreasonable—especially if the test for inclusion in the bargaining unit for certification purposes ultimately turns on each individual's personal situation, his or her intention to return to work, or the likelihood that she or he will return to the program, position or location in which she or he had worked before. This could be a mammoth task, involving hundreds of individual inquiries, and by the time it was completed, the bargaining unit under review would likely have undergone significant change.

The nature of the inquiry urged upon us by the employer warrants some further elaboration, because it highlights what might be described as a "systemic concern" in the interpretation of Bill 7. The "process problem" raised by the City in this case is not at all unique. If the employer's interpretation of Bill 7 is right, quite a number of cases may require such pre-vote litigation to sort out the employee list. And that, in turn, may significantly impact on the way in which the Board handles certification applications under Bill 7. In other words, while the characteristics of this work group are a little unusual, the legal issue raised by the employer is extremely important for the way in which the certification process works generally—and ultimately whether the new system can actually deliver the five-day votes that are contemplated by the statute.

We should note that in this particular case, the union could not reasonably have known the precise number of "employees" in the bargaining unit, for, as we have already indicated, even the employer had some difficulty compiling a complete list. The union would have had some general information about the bargaining-unit size from its members in the field, from the casuals themselves and from an earlier application that was filed in the spring and later withdrawn. But the union would not know the precise number or identity of the employees in the bargaining unit in October, even where, as here, the bargaining-unit description was agreed upon. An agreement on the bargaining-unit *description* does not mean that there will be agreement on bargaining unit *composition*.

. . .   .

If uncertainty about the "employee list" is a basis for litigation, then there may be quite a lot of it. And if a "list dispute" of this kind can delay the "quick vote" contemplated by Bill 7, then there may be quite a few votes that are delayed—despite the terms of the statute.

. . .   .

On November 21, 1995, the Board (differently constituted) established a "voting constituency" for this application, based upon the agreed-upon bargaining-unit description. The Board also directed that a representation vote be taken, so that the "employees" affected by this application (whatever their number) could indicate, by secret ballot, whether or not they wanted to be represented by the union. In so doing, the Board took into account the material before it, its reading of what Bill 7 required, and the parties' agreement with respect to the bargaining-unit description. The Board was satisfied that the union's material demonstrated the requisite "appearance" of support required by section 8 of the Act, so that the union's right to certification depended on a test of employee wishes.

The City disagreed. The City took the position that no vote of employees *could* be taken, that no vote of employees should be taken, and further that if a vote were taken, the vote should not be counted and the wishes of employees should not be revealed.

The parties did not agree on the composition of the proposed bargaining unit, so they did not agree on the list of eligible voters in the voting constituency. The

City maintained that there were 2500 to 3000 persons who were "employees" in the bargaining unit entitled to participate in the vote, and apparently sent letters to those individuals (or many of them) advising them of the vote and urging them to exercise their franchise. The union's view was that the votes consisted of the 800 or so employees actually at work in the City's fall programs when the application was filed.

To avoid delay, the union agreed that a vote could be taken using the City's expanded voters' list. But the union's agreement was made without prejudice to its position that the City's list grossly overstated the number of employees in the bargaining unit and thus the number of eligible voters.

The union's position was that the City's list contained the names of a large number of persons who were no longer "employees" on the City's payroll. In the union's view, the City had "loaded the list" with a huge number of names in order to precipitate "front end" litigation over the list, and derail the quick-vote procedure contemplated by Bill 7. The union points out that delaying the vote was in the employer's interest because in a bargaining unit like this one employee turnover would erode the union's base of support. And on a more general plane, if a union had to meet a test of correctness with respect to bargaining-unit size, it would significantly impede any union's ability to organize employees.

··· ··· ···

The representation vote in the instant case was taken on December 8, 1995. There were four separate polls in various parts of the city, with voting hours extending to 8 p.m. so that any individuals interested in the process would have an opportunity to exercise their franchise. Voters were invited to signify by secret ballot whether or not they wished to be represented by the trade union in a collective bargaining relationship with the City.

The turnout was quite low—only 342 persons. The union says that this low turnout reflects the casual workers' lack of actual attachment to the workplace, whatever their notional "employment status" might be, and points out that, in any case, everyone had an opportunity to vote, whether or not they chose to do so.

··· ··· ···

In the result, a significant majority of the ballots cast in the representation vote were cast in favour of the union. In other words, all of the arguably eligible voters were given an opportunity to cast ballots, the ballots were counted, and the union "won" the vote.

The union is content with that result. The City is not.

··· ··· ···

None of the employees (or potential employees) in the bargaining unit affected by this certification application has raised any challenge to the Board's decision to direct that a representation vote be taken to test their wishes. No employee has raised any question about the manner in which the vote was conducted. Nor does any employee or potential employee oppose the union's request that a certificate should issue based upon that representation vote. This case is a contest between the "institutional parties."

··· ··· ···

THE SCHEME OF THE ACT UNDER BILL 7

Bill 7 was introduced into the Legislature in October 1995 and became law about a month later on November 10, 1995. Much of the Bill was directed to repealing features of "Bill 40." But in addition, Bill 7 made a number of other changes, including a revised certification process.

The new scheme no longer permits certification based on membership cards alone. A representation vote has now become the exclusive method of testing employee wishes and is a requirement in every case.

However, in opting for "a vote in every case," the Legislature has not simply reverted to the former process for obtaining and conducting a representation vote. Instead, the Legislature has created an entirely new and quite different mechanism, relying on very quick five-day votes, to measure the employee wishes, while at the same time limiting the employer's opportunity to improperly interfere with the employees' freedom of choice.

The secret ballot replaces the signed membership card as the means of testing the employees' appetite for collective bargaining. But like the previous card-based model, the new system is designed to avoid a protracted "campaign" where the union and employer compete for the loyalties of employees. Because of the tight time-frames, there is less opportunity for behaviour that could attract unfair labour practice charges (quite a number of these are filed each year). The new system makes it very clear that time is of the essence: it is not just "a vote in every case"; the statute contemplates a "*quick* vote in every case."

The five-day time-frame mentioned in the statute is the most critical characteristic of the new certification scheme. It not only defines the nature of the process, it also requires the Board to develop new administrative structures in order to meet the five-day target. Indeed, it is a target that we think the Board is required to meet if it can; moreover, it is a target that the Legislature must have intended that the Board *could meet* in most cases, applying the words of the new statutory scheme. The new certification process reflects a legislative trade-off: the elimination of the (relatively) *quick* card-counting model for certification, and the substitution of the *quick* vote model instead.

Questions

1. Why is the *City of Toronto* case potentially of great importance?
2. Whose arguments do you find more convincing: those of the employer or those of the union? Why?
3. What's the significance of "Bill 7," which has since been incorporated into the *Ontario Labour Relations Act*?
4. If you were the chair of the Ontario Labour Relations Board, would you allow the representation vote to stand? Why, or why not?
5. If you would not allow the representation vote to stand, how would you then proceed in this case?
6. There is considerable debate in the IR literature as to whether certification votes should be decided by a majority of bargaining unit members or a majority of those voting. Which do you think is the fairer standard, and why?

Case ULP.1 UNFAIR LABOUR PRACTICE CASE

CAW-CANADA AND MATRIX LOGISTICS

When a union activist is dismissed for smoking in the context of a recent union certification campaign, how is a labour board likely to view that dismissal?

National Automobile, Aerospace, Transportation and General Workers' Union of Canada and Matrix Logistics Services Ltd.

Indexed as: Matrix Logistics Services Ltd. and CAW-Canada

Ontario Labour Relations Board

Laura Trachuk, Vice-Chair

May 1, 2001.

DECISION OF THE BOARD

This is an application under s.96 [am. 1998, c.8, s.9; 2000, c.38, s.13] of the *Labour Relations Act*, 1995, S.O. 1995, c.1, Sch. A (the "Act"). The applicant [National Automobile, Aerospace, Transportation and General Workers' Union of Canada (CAW-Canada)] (referred to as the "union") alleges that the responding party [Matrix Logistics Services Ltd.] (referred to as the "company") violated ss.70, 72 and 76 of the Act when it terminated the employment of Joseph Conrad and Ian Fleming.

Facts

The Board heard evidence from nine witnesses. Much of the evidence was contradictory and few of the witnesses were able to provide testimony which was unaffected by self-interest. The Board has therefore based its decision on those facts which are not really in dispute or, where that is not possible, on the evidence which seems to be best supported by the undisputed facts or makes the most sense in the circumstances considering the balance of probabilities.

Background and History of Organizing Campaign

Matrix Logistics is a warehousing operation for drug store chains. It has a number of locations. The facts relevant to this application take place at the Mississauga warehouse. Both Mr. Conrad and Mr. Fleming were hired by the company in 1997. In the summer of 1999, Mr. Conrad and Mr. Fleming were given the newly created positions of "cleaners." The United Steelworkers of America ("USWA") commenced a union organizing campaign for the employees at the Mississauga location in 1999. Mr. Conrad was the key organizer. He was one of the initial contacts with the

---

Source: Adapted from 71 C.L.R.B.R. (2nd 2000) at 210. Some deletions have been made by the author for the purposes of this book and names have been changed.

USWA, he collected cards on the day shift and amassed the cards that had been collected by employees on the other shifts to return to the USWA. Mr. Conrad's position with the USWA was well known.

In September 1999, the company replaced its management team at the Mississauga location. In early October 1999, with the USWA representation vote pending, the new management team held a meeting with employees. John Lindsay, the company vice-president, asked the employees to vote against the union and give the company six months to resolve any concerns they had. Mr. Conrad spoke at the meeting in favour of the USWA. Mr. Lindsay told the employees that if the company did not live up to its six-month commitment he was sure that Joseph Conrad would be back with another organizing drive and they could vote "yes" then. The USWA lost the vote on October 5, 1999. Mr. Conrad was one of the scrutineers.

In March 2000, six months after the vote, Mr. Conrad commenced a new organizing campaign as promised. The members of the former Retail Wholesale Department Store Union, which had been affiliated with the United Steelworkers of America in 1999, had become affiliated with the applicant. It was the applicant which commenced the campaign in 2000. Mr. Conrad advised some of the company's team leaders that the campaign would be starting. Leaflets were distributed on a few occasions in March and April 2000.

Around the time that the new campaign began. Mr. Conrad was asked to attend a meeting with Ted Steele, the company's director of human resources, and Fred Forsyth, the maintenance manager. They warned him to stop harassing employees about the union. Mr. Steele testified that his operations manager had told him that three employees had complained that Mr. Conrad had approached them about joining the union and that they felt harassed. Mr. Steele would not tell Mr. Conrad the names of the employees but said that next time, if it went further, he would. Mr. Conrad claimed that Mr. Steele said "next time, when I fire you, I will tell you their names." At the hearing neither Mr. Steele nor Mr. Forsyth could recall the names of the employees who had allegedly complained. Dave Martini, the union's business representative, sent Mr. Lindsay a letter protesting against the meeting and an alleged threat to fire Mr. Conrad. Counsel for the company subsequently sent a letter to Mr. Martini in which he denied the allegations in Mr. Martini's letter and in which he took the position that the union was barred from making an application for certification for a year, i.e., until October 2000, as a result of the unsuccessful campaign the year before. A lawyer representing the union warned that the union would respond to any perceived reprisals against Mr. Conrad and indicated that the union would apply for certification when it saw fit. The largest percentage of the total number of cards collected was collected in March. Fewer cards were collected in April, May and June. In April the company hired approximately 100 new part-time employees.

Approximately a month after Mr. Conrad's meeting with Mr. Steele and Mr. Forsyth, the day-shift operations manager, Hans Schreiber, also warned Mr. Conrad that he had received complaints that Mr. Conrad was harassing employees about the union. Mr. Conrad advised him that he was just telling the new employees that there was an organizing campaign in progress and that they could speak to him if they wanted information. Apparently there was some discussion between Mr. Conrad and Mr. Schreiber as to whether that could constitute harassment. Mr. Schreiber advised Mr. Steele about the conversation. Mr. Schreiber acknowledged in cross-examination that prior to his conversation with Mr. Conrad, Michael Jackson, the site manager, had advised him that Mr. Conrad had been spoken to about talking about the union on company time. Mr. Schreiber testified that he also advised his team leaders that Mr. Conrad had been spoken to on the matter.

Approximately one week later, the general manager of Matrix Logistics Canada, Hoyt Steed, also told Mr. Conrad to stop talking to employees about the union.

In June 2000, Mr. Conrad, pursuant to the company's "open door policy," complained to Mr. Steed that one of the team leaders, Daniel Matthews, had been rude in directing him to clean up a water spill. Two meetings were held to discuss the matter. At some point in the first meeting, according to Mr. Steed, Mr. Conrad said something like, "I would not refuse to clean up the spill because you would fire me" and Mr. Steed said, "Well there's a thought." Mr. Conrad was again advised to stop talking to employees. The issue of the union was also raised at both meetings. Mr. Conrad said Mr. Steed raised it. Mr. Steed said that he could not remember who raised it but that it always came up between him and Mr. Conrad. Mr. Steed testified that he was not aware that there was an organizing campaign at that time but that he was not sure that there was not. Mr. Steele said the union issue was raised by Mr. Conrad who claimed they were complaining about him talking to employees because of his union organizing activities. Mr. Steele said that it was acknowledged at the meeting that Mr. Conrad was the chief union organizer but that they denied that was why they were telling him to stop talking. Mr. Steele said they told him to stop talking to employees because it was disruptive. Mr. Steele said that at the end of the meeting Mr. Conrad was told to go do his job and not talk so much.

Mr. Steele testified that aside from a few days of pamphleting in March 2000 he had heard neither "hide nor hair" of the union when he terminated Mr. Conrad. He testified that the company knew Mr. Conrad was the chief organizer on the day shift. However, they were not aware of any involvement that Mr. Fleming had with the union. He claimed that if Mr. Fleming had any interest in the union it was because he was a "follower."

Mr. Conrad testified that he stayed involved with the campaign after he was terminated and that he kept in touch with the union's organizers. He was aware that the union stopped receiving membership cards after his termination. Counsel for the employer objected that this evidence was hearsay as Mr. Conrad was provided with the information by other union organizers.

Cleaners' Duties

The company claims that it terminated Mr. Conrad and Mr. Fleming not because of union activity but because they were taking cigarette breaks outside of one of the doors to its receiving docks. Employees are allowed to smoke outside if they are working. However, the company says that Mr. Conrad and Mr. Fleming had no work duties outside. The question of what the cleaners' duties were is therefore a significant factor in determining the *bona fides* of the terminations.

There were three full-time cleaners, Mr. Conrad, Mr. Fleming, and Sean O'Shea. There was also a part-time cleaner, Peter Guernsey, who was on light duties. The cleaners reported to Mr. Forsyth, the maintenance manager. Mr. Conrad and

Mr. Fleming worked from 6:30 a.m. to 2:30 p.m. with one half-hour lunch and one 20-minute break. When they went out for lunch and breaks, they punched or scanned out. The cleaners' duties varied somewhat depending upon which warehouse they were working in, but essentially they involved driving around on vehicles called "double palette walkies," collecting cardboard and garbage and then putting cardboard in the cardboard compactor and garbage in the garbage compactor. They also did some cleaning and relieved the employee in the battery shop as needed.

The warehouse duties are divided into three contiguous areas, warehouse 10, warehouse 40/50, and warehouse 30. Until six to eight weeks prior to the termination, the three full-time warehouse employees would rotate into each area each week. However, six to eight weeks prior to the termination, Mr. O'Shea asked Mr. Conrad and Mr. Fleming if he could work exclusively in warehouse 30 because he was having health problems. They agreed to accommodate him. After that, Mr. O'Shea worked in warehouse 30, sometimes with Mr. Guernsey, who was on modified duties. Mr. Conrad and Mr. Fleming assisted them as needed. Mr. Conrad and Mr. Fleming rotated between warehouse 10 and warehouse 40/50. Mr. Forsyth testified that Mr. Conrad worked in warehouse 40/50 and Mr. Fleming worked in warehouse 10 and that that had been the situation since he started in February 2000. That was clearly not the case. Mr. Forsyth said the cleaners asked him if they could rotate and he said he would think about it. That was clearly not the case either. Mr. Forsyth never assigned them to any particular warehouse nor did he ever discuss a list of job duties with them.

Mr. Conrad and Mr. Fleming testified that the wind blew dust through a hole in the garbage compactor into the warehouse. The hole in the compactor was supposed to be covered by a steel plate but it was missing. Mr. Conrad and Mr. Fleming found that if they cut cardboard to fit the space and taped it on, it would stop the dust. However, the tape would not hold so it required daily repair. Mr. Fleming explained in cross-examination that there was a lip sticking out beneath the hole so the cardboard needed to be cut to fit. Mr. Fleming agreed the job could be done by one person but that it was easier with two because one could hold the cardboard up while it was cut and taped by the other. He testified that it was annoying to have to do this every day although it did provide an opportunity to have a cigarette. He said, however, that if it was not done, every time they dumped garbage in the compactor, dust blew back down the tunnel and in their faces. He said that he asked Mr. Forsyth for a mask because of the dust. He testified that cutting and putting on the cardboard took five to ten minutes. He also testified that since he became a cleaner he always went out to help "Randy." Randy was the driver for "UPAC," the company that collected the cardboard compactor. When the compactor was removed, a lot of cardboard pieces were left on the ground and had to be picked up. The company claimed that assisting Randy was exclusively the duty of the third cleaner, Sean O'Shea. However, all three of the cleaners testified that they all performed this task. Mr. Fleming said it took about ten minutes to pick up the cardboard.

Mr. Forsyth testified that he was aware of the hole in the compactor but that he never told Mr. Conrad and Mr. Fleming to cover it. He said that they had never filled out a maintenance requisition to have it repaired. However, he acknowledged that Mr. Conrad and Mr. Fleming had complained about dust and that Mr. Conrad had brought him to the compactor to show him how much dust there was. He said that he told Mr. Conrad it was not a perfectly sealed unit and that intake fans in the building caused negative air pressure which brought the dust in. He testified that he did not believe that covering the hole would stop the dust. He testified that he told them to use masks because of the dust and that he showed them where the masks were and they started using them. He also testified that Mr. Conrad came and asked for better dust masks and that he provided them.

Mr. Fleming also explained that there was a red light on the garbage compactor which would come on to indicate that it was full. However, it was possible to press another button to reset it. He testified that he would go outside to check the compactor when the red light came on before resetting it. Mr. Conrad explained that they went out to check the compactor to ensure that there was still play in the compactor arm so that it would not break. He testified that it had broken twice. Mr. Forsyth agreed that the compactor arm had broken.

Mr. Conrad testified that the cleaners also picked up garbage that fell on the ground outside when the garbage compactor was removed twice per week. This task sometimes involved a lot of sweeping. He also testified that they had to pick up cardboard that would slide underneath the compactor. Sometimes they shovelled snow and cleaned up around the shipping docks.

Mr. Fleming agreed in cross-examination that he went out door 11, which leads to the north receiving docks, three or four times per day. He said that that had been the case since they started the new conveyor system. He denied that he ever went out just to smoke a cigarette. He said that he always had some work to perform.

Mr. Conrad agreed in cross-examination that, except during the period in which he quit smoking, he more often than not lit up a cigarette when he went outside. He agreed that doing work outside provided an opportunity to smoke and that sometimes it provided an excuse to go outside and smoke. However, he said that he always performed some work that needed to be done when he went outside. He agreed that being able to smoke when he worked outside sometimes extended the period of time he stayed outside. He also agreed that it did not take two people to check the cardboard on the hole on the compactor.

Mr. Forsyth testified that the cleaners' duties had not changed since he started his position as maintenance manager in February 2000. His main concern from his arrival had been sorting out the material handling equipment and that he had not focused on the cleaners. Mr. Forsyth had no discussion with his predecessor, George Mitchell, about the cleaners or their duties. He testified in cross-examination that he accepted that the cleaners knew what they were doing and he did not feel it was necessary to review their duties with them. Nevertheless, Mr. Forsyth testified that the only cleaner who had a reason to go outside was Mr. O'Shea. Mr. O'Shea's only reason for going outside was to clean up the cardboard flaps that fall out when the UPAC driver took away the cardboard compactor. Mr. Forsyth testified that he told Mr. O'Shea that the person in warehouse 30 should go out and clean up the cardboard when the cardboard compactor was removed. He could not recall if Mr. Conrad or Mr. Fleming were there when he said that. He did recall that he did not say that no one else should go out to do that task. He acknowledged that Mr. Conrad and Mr. Fleming were to help Mr. O'Shea in warehouse 30 from time to time. During the period prior to the terminations, the UPAC driver was coming every day to remove the compactor. Mr. Forsyth testified that Mr. Conrad's only outside duty was to take out a garbage bin on the south side of the building (not outside door 11). It is not disputed that no one ever told Mr. Conrad and Mr. Fleming that they were not supposed to go outside.

Mr. Forsyth also agreed in cross-examination that he could not dispute that it was the cleaners' practice to cover the hole in the compactor with cardboard but he stated that no one told them to do it. Mr. Conrad said he had talked to Mr. Forsyth about the hole and that he had suggested covering it with cardboard.

On June 24, 2000, Mr. Forsyth held his first meeting with the cleaners on the day shift. As noted previously, he had never had a prior discussion with them about their duties. He had not assigned them their work or their work areas. At the meeting on June 24, 2000, Mr. Forsyth advised the cleaners that Jerry Flaherty was his assistant team leader. He also advised them that he was instituting a formalized break schedule, a copy of which he provided to them. He told them that they were taking too many unauthorized breaks and that a continuation of that behaviour could lead to discipline, including dismissal. There was no explanation at that time, or at the hearing, as to what he meant or what behaviour he was referring to, i.e., did he mean cleaners scanning out for more than one break? Did he mean going to the washroom too often? His agenda for that meeting says, "There has been many individuals taking more than one break and late lunch this is considered time theft and will not be tolerated anyone caught will be dismissed [sic]." Mr. Conrad denied that Mr. Forsyth said that at the meeting. Mr. Fleming could not recall but agreed it was possible it was said. Mr. O'Shea could not recall what was said was to happen, if the break schedule was not followed. Mr. Fleming testified that Mr. Forsyth said there had been complaints because they were in the lunchroom on breaks at different times than anyone else. However, the item is included on an agenda, which was identified by Mr. Forsyth and Mr. Flaherty and which was provided to the Board. The Board finds that unauthorized breaks were mentioned at the meeting. However, the agenda was never given to the cleaners. The cleaners were never given anything in writing except the break schedule. Nothing was posted. Many other points were also raised by Mr. Forsyth at the meeting. It appears that the break schedule was not popular and there was a lot of discussion about it because the cleaners thought it required them to take lunch too early.

In cross-examination, Mr. Forsyth testified that he understood that smoking was only permitted outside in designated areas and that the area outside door 11 was not a designated area. That view is not consistent with the company's policy, which permits smoking while working outside and is not restricted in any area. One would have expected that since Mr. Conrad and Mr. Fleming were terminated in Mr. Forsyth's presence for a violation of that policy he would have known about it. Mr. Forsyth's lack of knowledge on this point suggests that he and Mr. Steele never even discussed the theory upon which Mr. Conrad and Mr. Fleming were terminated. According to Mr. Forsyth, Mr. Conrad and Mr. Fleming should not have been smoking even if they were assisting Mr. O'Shea as it was not a designated area. He denied that if they were helping Mr. O'Shea it would have made a difference in whether they should be terminated because they were not "supposed to be there." He said that he considered it to be a firing offence for them to be outside their area and to be smoking outside the designated area. The company claims, however, that they were terminated for taking breaks outside.

Terminations

On July 12, 2000, Mr. Flaherty was walking by door 11. He saw Mr. Conrad and Mr. Fleming go out the door. He went and looked through the window and then immediately opened the door and told them to come back inside. They were outside for approximately one minute. Mr. Flaherty saw them standing at the bottom of the stairs from the door lighting up cigarettes. There was some dispute as to whether Mr. Fleming was actually lighting up; however, there was no dispute that he planned to do so. Mr. Conrad told Mr. Flaherty that they were going to check the cardboard that they placed over the hole in the garbage compactor to stop dust from blowing into the plant. Mr. Flaherty said something to the effect of "never mind the excuses and get back inside." They came back in. Mr. Flaherty testified that he then went to see Mr. Steele. As it was after 2:30, Mr. Steele said they would address it the next day. Mr. Steele said that he was considering suspending them at that point.

Mr. Fleming testified that around 1 to 1:30 on July 12, 2000, he and Mr. Conrad had just dumped some barrels into the compactor and were overwhelmed with dust. They had covered the hole in the garbage compactor with cardboard the day before so they went outside to check it. They just reached the bottom of the stairs when Mr. Flaherty came out. Mr. Conrad had a cigarette in his mouth. Mr. Fleming did not know whether he had had a chance to light it. Mr. Fleming was showing Mr. Conrad a $10 bill upon which, it appeared to him, an American flag was flying over the Parliament buildings. They were about to proceed to the compactor when Mr. Flaherty told them they should not be out there. They tried to tell him that they were going to look at the compactor but he said that he did not want to hear their excuses and he was not following them. Mr. Fleming then left while Mr. Conrad stayed behind and spoke to Mr. Flaherty. Mr. Fleming went to get more garbage bins. When he went to dump them into the compactor 20 minutes later, the dust was still blowing around. He therefore grabbed some tape and cardboard and went outside to tape up the hole.

The evidence with respect to the next day, July 13, 2000, is rather confusing and contradictory. Mr. Steele testified that when he came to work that day, he found Mr. Forsyth and Tom Walker, the manager of loss prevention, reviewing a surveillance tape of door 11. Mr. Steele testified that they told him that both Mr. Conrad and Mr. Fleming had made several entrances and exits through that door that morning. He also testified that he was told that Mr. Flaherty and Mr. Forsyth had seen *them* come in through door 11 at about 8:30. That appears to be the reason that they were reviewing the surveillance tapes. However the tapes show that Mr. Conrad and Mr. Fleming were *not* outside together that morning. The tape also shows no sign of Mr. Flaherty and Mr. Forsyth. Mr. Forsyth testified that he Mr. Flaherty decided to go down and look at door 11 on the morning of July 13th to see what number it was. When they got there they saw Mr. Conrad (and not Mr. Fleming) coming inside with a stick in his hand. Mr. Conrad apparently said "a good day for golfing" and walked by. They did not confront him or ask him what he had been doing. Instead, they decided to go and look at the tapes in the security office. The tapes they looked at showed the inside of door 11. There are cameras on the outside of the building as well. Mr. Forsyth testified that he wanted to see what the outside cameras showed but they were "broken or something." While Mr. Walker was getting ready to review the tapes, Mr. Steele came in. They told him they had seen Mr. Conrad coming in from outside. Mr. Steele testified that he did not stay at that point but arranged for a meeting to be held at 9:30. Mr. Forsyth said that they then viewed the tapes from the previous day and Mr. Conrad and Mr. Fleming came in and out so many times it was "ridiculous." (They came in and out three times.) He also said that they noticed that Mr. O'Shea had gone out the same door so they decided to bring all three of the cleaners in for an interview.

Mr. Steele's evidence was somewhat different. He said he reviewed at least some parts of the surveillance tapes of the inside of door 11 on the morning of July 13th prior to 11 a.m. He claimed that he reviewed the first exit on July 11th and possibly all of the exits on July 12th and the first one on July 13th. He testified that on the tape of July 12th they saw Mr. Fleming taking out a piece of plywood and then bringing the same piece back in. This appeared to be offered as support for his determination that something improper was going on. However, a close look at the tape shows that Mr. Fleming took out a piece of something that looks like cardboard and brought back a different shaped piece. Mr. Steele also testified that they were looking at the surveillance feed when they saw Mr. Conrad go out door 11 at 8:53. When he had not returned by 9:03, Mr. Steele ordered that the tape be pulled. No one went to see what Mr. Conrad was doing outside.

Mr. Conrad testified that he went outside on the morning of July 13, 2000, to see if there was enough play in the arm of the cardboard compactor. He said on Monday or Tuesday of that week the arm had become too tight and Mr. Forsyth had had to call UPAC to come and get the compactor right away. Mr. Conrad ascertained that there was enough room in the compactor arm and he came back inside. He went out again later and cleaned up with Mr. O'Shea and Mr. Walker when the UPAC driver came. He testified that later he covered the hole over the garbage compactor. On that occasion Mr. Fleming was with him. (That occasion must have been after the tape was removed as the tape does not show them going out together that morning.) On each occasion when Mr. Conrad went out, he lit a cigarette but he did not stay to finish it on the first occasion when he was checking the compactor arm.

Mr. Fleming testified that on the morning of July 13th at approximately 8 a.m. he was dumping cardboard when he heard a bang and thought it was Randy coming to take the cardboard compactor. He therefore went outside. When he went out he realized that Randy was not there and he came back inside. He testified that about 10:30 he went out with cardboard and tape to fix what he had done the day before to the hole in the compactor. He could not recall if Mr. Conrad was with him. He testified that the first time he went out he did not smoke but the second time he did.

Mr. Steele met with Mr. Forsyth at 11 a.m. on July 13th. He said they discussed the cleaners' duties. However, as noted above, it does not appear that the company's policy of permitting employees to smoke outside if they were working was discussed as Mr. Forsyth was unaware of that policy when he testified. Mr. Steele said that Mr. Forsyth advised him he had addressed the issue of "time theft" at the meeting of June 24, 2000. He reviewed the break schedule and the record showing that the employees had swiped out for their scheduled breaks. He said that he decided that they were engaged in "time theft" and that they should be terminated.

Mr. Steele testified that he asked Mr. O'Shea to come to a meeting on July 13th as he had been seen exiting door 11 right before Mr. Conrad and Mr. Fleming. (In fact only Mr. Conrad went out after Mr. O'Shea.) The meeting took place prior to the meetings with Mr. Conrad and Mr. Fleming. Mr. Steele said he asked Mr. O'Shea what he was doing outside and he said that he went to meet the truck (the UPAC vehicle). He asked him if he saw Mr. Conrad and Mr. Fleming out there and he said that he had. He asked him what they were doing and he said "standing smoking cigarettes." However, the surveillance tapes show that only Mr. Conrad was outside with Mr. O'Shea on July 13th. Mr. O'Shea was not outside when Mr. Conrad and Mr. Fleming went out on July 12th. This fact throws both accounts of this conversation into doubt. Mr. Steele knew that as he had just seen Mr. O'Shea go outside on the surveillance tape before Mr. Conrad but not Mr. Fleming.

Mr. O'Shea testified that he was asked what he was doing outside that morning. In cross-examination he could not remember what date they had asked him about. He said he was asked if he saw Mr. Conrad and Mr. Fleming outside and he said that he had. Again this was not true, and Mr. Steele and Mr. Forsyth would have known it as they just reviewed the tape. Mr. O'Shea said he was asked what Mr. Conrad and Mr. Fleming were doing and he said smoking. He was asked whether they were working at the same time and he said no. He was asked if he had seen them smoking outside before and he said he had. At the hearing he said he also went out there three times per day to work and smoke. He said they were allowed to do this as they were cleaners. In the hearing he also said that he saw them go out three to five times per day but did not know how long they were out there. In cross-examination he acknowledged that he did not actually see them going out but he would see double palette walkies near door 11. He also testified that there were many of those walkies in the plant and they were all painted the same colour. Sometimes the ones he saw at door 11 would have red or yellow bins on the back which would mean they came from the warehouse 30 and he would assume those were Mr. Conrad's and Mr. Fleming's. Mr. O'Shea testified in cross-examination that he warned Mr. Conrad and Mr. Fleming separately in September 1999 that they were going to get caught going outside so frequently. They both denied receiving such a warning from him. Mr. O'Shea confirmed that he had seen Mr. Conrad and Mr. Fleming covering the hole on the garbage compactor with cardboard and tape. He testified that that job should only need to be done about once per week and should not take more than a minute but that they took 10 to 15 minutes. However, he acknowledged in cross-examination that he had never done it himself and was just guessing. He agreed that it was part of Mr. Conrad's and Mr. Fleming's job to come out to assist him when the cardboard compactor was taken away. Sometimes one would help and the other would smoke, sometimes they would both work and he would smoke.

Mr. Steele and Mr. Forsyth asked Mr. Conrad to meet with them with the intention of terminating him after they met with Mr. O'Shea. There was considerable disagreement as to what was said at this meeting. As the company relied upon the exchange at this meeting as evidence of Mr. Steele's good faith and Mr. Conrad's culpability, it will be set out in some detail. However, it is hard to find that any account is entirely accurate. Ultimately what took place was Mr. Steele asked Mr. Conrad what he was doing outside, Mr. Conrad told him, Mr. Steele said he did not believe him and fired him. It is not disputed that Mr. Steele had decided to fire Mr. Conrad before the interview. Nevertheless, Mr. Steele testified that he asked

Mr. Conrad what he was doing outside on July 12th and he said he was going to cover the hole in the compactor because of the dust. Mr. Steele then said he asked how he was going to do that without tape or cardboard and that Mr. Conrad said "no comment." Mr. Conrad denies that. (If Mr. Conrad and Mr. Fleming went out on July 13th to tape up the compactor, it was after the surveillance tape had been removed so Mr. Steele would not know if they had cardboard and tape or not. The tape of July 12th does show them going out at one point with cardboard which apparently been [sic] out before they come back in.) Mr. Steele testified that he told Mr. Conrad that they had a large number of entrances and exits on tape and it was "time theft." He claims that Mr. Conrad said that if they had it on tape he would not comment. Mr. Steele said they then told him he was being fired for time theft, gave him a handwritten note to that effect, and walked him off the premises. It was acknowledged, however, that at some point Mr. Conrad said he had been cleaning up cardboard with Sean O'Shea but they told him the [UPAC] truck had left 35 minutes prior. (That did not make sense given what they had asked Mr. O'Shea. Furthermore, the tape for July 13, 2000, shows that Mr. O'Shea and Mr. Conrad were outside at the same time.) Mr. Steele said that he could not believe that Mr. Conrad was that stupid and that he had just given him cause to fire him. Mr. Conrad asked if he was supposed to get a warning and Mr. Steel said that Mr. Flaherty had given him a warning the day before. Mr. Conrad uttered a profanity and asked who Jerry Flaherty was. He said that he (Mr. Flaherty) might be Mr. Forsyth's assistant team leader but he was not his (team leader). He said that he had never seen a posting for that position. Mr. Steele said something like, "Thank you for saying that in front of us." At the time of this exchange Mr. Conrad already knew he was being fired. Apparently he made that comment about Mr. Flaherty as there had been no posting for his position according to the company's normal practice. Mr. Steele testified that he also told Mr. Conrad that Mr. Forsyth had warned him on June 24th about "time theft." Mr. Conrad denied that.

Mr. Forsyth testified in cross-examination that when Mr. Conrad was asked what he was doing outside, he described fixing the compactor arm and helping Mr. Fleming with the cardboard on the compactor and cleaning up the cardboard. Mr. Forsyth said they did not believe Mr. Conrad's explanation about the hole in the compactor. He said they did not believe his explanation about cleaning up after the cardboard compactor because the driver had left.

Mr. Steele and Mr. Forsyth then asked Mr. Fleming to come to a meeting. They had decided to terminate him before the meeting. Mr. Fleming did not know that Mr. Conrad had been fired. In examination-in-chief Mr. Steele claimed that he told Mr. Fleming that they had film evidence of him going out and taking breaks. Mr. Steele testified that he asked what they were doing and Mr. Fleming said "smoking." Mr. Fleming denied that. Mr. Steele said that he asked Mr. Fleming if he was begging to be caught and said, "I guess so." He asserted that Mr. Fleming said that if he had it to do over again he would not. Mr. Steele also said that he asked Mr. Fleming if he remembered Mr. Forsyth mentioning "time theft" at the meeting in June and that he remembered it was a serious issue. Mr. Steele told Mr. Fleming that he got himself caught up in a very unfortunate situation and that he could not treat him differently than any other individual in those circumstances so he was terminating him. Mr. Steele agreed that Mr. Fleming told him he was outside fixing the hole in the trash compactor. Mr. Steele also said, confusingly, that he did not discuss being outside on July 13th with Mr. Fleming. Mr. Steele said that was "moot" and they were only talking about July 12th. He said to Mr. Fleming, "I can't believe in your situation you would do this." (Mr. Steele was aware of some personal problems Mr. Fleming was having.) Mr. Steele acknowledged that he told Mr. Fleming that he was a good worker and that he had had high hopes for him and that he was caught up in a bad situation. He then offered to provide Mr. Fleming with an employment reference. Mr. Fleming called that evening to find out what kind of reference he would receive and Mr. Steele said that he would recommend him for employment.

Mr. Forsyth testified that they asked Mr. Fleming what he was doing outside and he said he was fixing the hole in the compactor. Mr. Forsyth said he asked him how he was going to do that without any tape. He also testified that Mr. Fleming said he went to see if the UPAC was there. Mr. Forsyth said they then asked him what he was really doing and he said "smoking." Mr. Forsyth then testified that they asked Mr. Fleming if he remembered what was said at the meeting (on June 24th) and he said he remembered being told about Mr. Flaherty and time theft and that if he had it to do over again he would not do it. Mr. Forsyth said Mr. Fleming was terminated because of time theft.

Mr. Fleming denied Mr. Steele's and Mr. Forsyth's account of the meeting. He testified that Mr. Steele asked him what he was doing outside and he said he was either helping Randy or taping up the garbage compactor. He believed that Mr. Steele was referring to the day the meeting was taking place, July 13th. He said that Mr. Steele did not believe he was outside doing what he claimed. He said that Mr. Steele asked him if he remembered Mr. Forsyth's warning about time theft at the meeting. He said he responded that he remembered the meeting but not what was said about time theft. Mr. Steele then said that "this is the part of the job I hate" and that it was one of the hardest decisions he had to make. Mr. Fleming testified that that is when he got nervous and asked if there was anything he could say to change Mr. Steele's mind. Mr. Steele said unfortunately Mr. Fleming was caught up in a bad situation and he could not "let go of one without the other." Mr. Steele then wrote his termination note and told him he was fired. Mr. Fleming said he called Mr. Steele later to find out what kind of reference he would give him. Mr. Steele said he was a good worker caught up in unfortunate circumstances and suggested he try "CFM" where they were hiring.

Again the Board does not find that any account of this meeting is very reliable. Mr. Fleming may well have acknowledged he was smoking but that was not an infraction of any rule or policy unless he was not working. It is clear he explained what tasks he was doing outside. Mr. Steele and Mr. Forsyth chose, or pretended, not to believe him for no apparent reason as neither had ever assigned duties to him or told him not to go outside.

Mr. Forsyth testified that when Mr. Conrad and Mr. Fleming said they were taping up the hole they were asked how they could do that without tape. In the hearing no one asked the witnesses if they actually had tape with them when they went outside. There did not appear to be any tape in their hands, but no one asked them if they had it somewhere else. The company did not rely in argument upon the apparent absence of tape as evidence of anything.

Mr. Steele testified that the only reason he terminated the two employees was because of their "theft of time." He claimed that he only considered Mr. Conrad's union involvement to the extent that it made him more cautious. He said that he considered suspending the two workers on July 12th for a "violation of policy" when they were "caught red-handed going out," but terminated them when he found it was a pattern. The Board queried Mr. Steele as to the policy to which he was referring. He said it was "going outside when they were supposed to be inside." Mr. Steele also testified that he believes Mr. Fleming to be a "follower" and that he would never have engaged in "time theft" on his own.

Mr. Steele testified that he went outside to look at the hole in the garbage compactor on July 12, 2000. There was no question that the hole was there and the Board was provided with a photograph of it. However, Mr. Steele claimed that he decided that it would not blow dust into the plant because of the "prevailing winds." However there is some question as to whether he did go out to look at the hole as there was no evidence that anyone told him on July 12th that that was the reason Mr. Conrad and Mr. Fleming gave for going outside that day. Mr. Steele testified in cross-examination that he had no idea how long the hole had been there nor whether it was usually covered with cardboard.

Mr. Conrad had no discipline on his file. The verbal warning he received in March 2000 was never recorded. Mr. Fleming also had no prior discipline on his file.

Decision

The company argued that demonstrating that a union organizer was terminated for serious misconduct is an important indicator of a company's good faith. The other side of that coin, however, is that terminating a union organizer who has essentially no disciplinary record for a minor offence is an important indicator of a company's bad faith. In *Hallowell House Ltd. and S.E.I.U., Local 183*, [1980] 1 Can LRBR 499 at pp. 504-505, [1980] OLRB Rep. 35, para. 19, the Board made the following comments:

> Seldom will an employer admit that it has been motivated by anti-union animus in discharging an employee. The Board, therefore, is required to draw its own conclusion as to the employer's motivation and in doing so must draw inferences from the evidence. In discharging an employee, the Board looks for a reasonable explanation for discharge. If the employer provides little or no explanation for terminating an employee and there is concurrent evidence of union activity the Board may, depending on the circumstances, draw the inference that the employer had an anti-union animus and acted in violation of the Act. If the employer establishes good cause for discharge on the other hand, the Board will normally require more cogent evidence of union activity, the grievor's participation in the campaign and the employer's knowledge of it before being willing to draw an inference of anti-union motivation. The evaluation of the adequacy of the employer's reasons for discharge is not aimed at determining whether the employer had just cause for discharge but is rather a step in the more complex

process of ascertaining the employer's motivation. While unfair discharge does not itself establish a violation of the Act, it may be evidence from which the Board will, in certain circumstances, draw an inference of anti-union animus.

In this case the company claimed that Mr. Conrad is guilty of "time theft." However, accusing Mr. Conrad of "theft" does not magnify what he did to a "serious industrial offence." At most he was guilty of wasting a few minutes in the same way that employees do every day in every workplace, in the same way that the two employees on the surveillance tape did when they stopped to chat for seven minutes. The Board did find that Mr. Forsyth warned the cleaners about "time theft" on June 24, 2000. However, there is no reason that the cleaners would have understood that to be a warning with respect to going outside to perform the tasks they had been performing regularly for a year. The evidence is that the cleaner's duties were assigned, or evolved, under George Mitchell, Mr. Forsyth's predecessor. There was no job description. When Mr. Forsyth started working in February 2000, he did not assign or change any duties. He held no meetings with the cleaners until June 24th. His evidence was that his focus was elsewhere. He did not even assign the cleaners to the areas in which they worked. The cleaners agreed to that themselves. Mr. Forsyth knew that he had never made either area or work assignments and he agreed that the cleaners knew their duties when he started his employment, so how could he be so certain that they had no duties outside? The answer is that he could not be certain. But he and Mr. Steele either refused to consider the possibility that Mr. Conrad and Mr. Fleming were telling the truth when they said they had duties outside, or they knew otherwise but chose to maintain that they had no such duties because they wanted to terminate Mr. Conrad. Yet the evidence demonstrated that Mr. Conrad and Mr. Fleming did have duties outside door 11. At the hearing, all three cleaners agreed that all three of them would help pick up when the UPAC driver came. All three agreed that Mr. Conrad and Mr. Fleming covered the hole in the garbage compactor. The evidence on the tape was that they did take cardboard out and bring back a different sized piece, consistent with the claim that they were covering the hole. Mr. Steele and Mr. Forsyth claim to have seen that on the tape. Mr. Forsyth agreed that they had complained to him about dust. There was no dispute that the arm on the compactor had broken twice, so trying to avoid that happening by checking the compactor was a good idea. No one claimed it was not.

Mr. Conrad and Mr. Fleming did go outside on a number of occasions on July 12th and 13th so the crucial factual question is whether they had work to do out there. The evidence with respect to July 11th is less reliable but the Board is prepared to assume they went out on a number of occasions that day as well. It is also undisputed that they often smoked cigarettes when they went out. However, it is the company's policy, well known to Mr. Steele, that employees are allowed to smoke if they are working outside. The company says that it terminated the employees because they had no work to do outside. However, the evidence disclosed that they did have work to do outside. The company ultimately argued that whatever tasks they were doing outside were not assigned to them or were excuses to go out and smoke. Certainly, Mr. Conrad and Mr. Fleming embraced opportunities to perform tasks outside. No doubt they were motivated to do so because they could smoke. However, it is hardly a termination offence for employees to do jobs they prefer or find to be easier rather than jobs they do not like or are more onerous when given the opportunity. The worst offence that Mr. Conrad and Mr. Fleming committed is that they both went out to check the hole in the compactor when one person could have done that.

Questions

1. What is your overall view of the way the company handled the union certification drive?

2. If you were a labour board chair, how would you respond to the evidence concerning Mr. Lindsay's speech of October 1999 on the subject of unionization at the company?

3. What is your view of the company's approach to health and safety issues, as illustrated in this case?

4. To the extent that the company had a significant problem with "time theft" caused by employees' smoking, how might it have addressed this problem, other than by dismissing certain employees?

5. Had you been the arbitrator or labour board chair in this case, what would your ruling have been, and why?

Case A.1 Arbitration Case

USWA, LOCAL 7884 AND FORDING COAL LTD.

Does an employer's prohibition of cellular phones in the workplace constitute an unreasonable infringement on employee's personal privacy?

Heard: November 5, 1997

Decision rendered: January 21, 1998; British Columbia; D.L. Larson

H. Alden, for the Union.

R.E. Lester, for the employer.

AWARD

The issue in this case is whether a rule established by the Company on September 11, 1996, that prohibits all employees from bringing personal cellular telephones into the workplace is valid.

The evidence relating to how the rule came about is not in dispute. Denis LeHoux, superintendent, employee relations, testified that the matter did not arise out of any

Source: Reproduced from Labour Arbitration Cases with the permission of Canada Law Book, A Division of The Cartwright Group Ltd. (www.canadalawbook.ca). (Adapted from 2-70 L.A.C. (4th 1998), pp. 33–43. Some deletions have been made by the author for the purposes of this book.)
Note: Instructors may find this case useful in connection with Chapter 6 on employment law.

particular incident, but that it was generally based upon concerns relating to safety, productivity, and efficiency. He testified that until the fall of 1996, cell phones were not a problem because they had not been a reliable means of communication in Elk Valley. However, when B.C. Tel established a new cell site and began to sell the service in the local mall, he concluded that it could become a problem and issued the policy.

When asked what was behind his safety concern, he replied that he became alive to the dangers of cell phones from news reports, combined with the fact that mining is inherently hazardous and that one must do everything possible to reduce the risk. He said that this mine encompasses a large geographic area with constant traffic on the haulage roads. It is an open pit mine with huge equipment, including 170 and 240 ton Wabco trucks, on roads that can have a pitch of up to eight degrees and that must share the roads with a lot of other smaller vehicles.

As for productivity and efficiency, Mr. LeHoux said that the mine is operating on very small margins, which requires maximum efficiency in order to remain profitable. He said that he could not even endorse the use of cell phones during breaks because that would be difficult to monitor and human nature being what it is, if employees were to have phones, they would use them during working time, particularly to take calls.

The Union conceded that there was good reason to be concerned with safety. Mike Park, national representative, testified that they concurred that employees should not be permitted to use cell phones while operating heavy equipment or working in the plant because there are already a significant number of accidents. But he said that the Union considered that it would be appropriate that shop stewards and safety representatives be permitted to carry them. He said that would involve only 20 to 25 employees, equal to about 3 percent to 4 percent of the total workforce, depending upon the number of active stewards. Further, he said they would be distributed into all areas of the property over three shifts.

Currently employees have access to the Company hard-wire phone system by permission. If a foreman is not immediately accessible, the procedure is that the employee may request a truck driver to call the foreman on his two-way radio. The foreman will normally then come around some time later and if he thinks that it is important, will either take the employee to a telephone or arrange for someone else to do it.

It is not without significance that the employees of outside contractors who work on the property are permitted to use cell phones. Mr. LeHoux explained that the Company tries not to interfere with the way they run their businesses. They usually have other customers who need to have access to them. On the other hand, he said that the allegations that Ron Carpenter, a management employee who works in the Purchasing Department, has been given permission to use a cell phone is incorrect and that what he has is a cordless phone that only works within a limited range from the base unit. Mr. Carpenter was not called as a witness and, since it involved a singular instance, even if true, I do not consider it to be sufficient to affect the integrity of the policy.

Del Pare, who is classified as Pit Utility in the Mine Production Department, was a shop steward from 1994 to 1995. She is currently a safety representative for the Union. She testified that her job is located at the "spoils," which is where the large Wabco trucks dump overburden. The spoils tend to be a fair distance from the actual mine, but a "dump shack" has been set up by the Company to provide shelter.

It has also been equipped with a two-way radio although Ms. Pare testified that the majority of the time it does not work. That was not disputed by the Company, which explained that the problem stems from the fact that the shack is on skids and is moved frequently.

She gave two examples of occasions when she was refused the use of Company phones in her capacity as a safety representative. She said that on December 18, 1996, she expressed concern to her foreman, Darren Kruchelinsky, that the shack had been placed on the opposite side of the road from the spoil. The problem was that it put her in a position of having to cross the road in the face of traffic. Her supervisor responded by giving her an alternate assignment of driving the buses that take employees to and from the mine. She said that she arrived at the mine at 1:30 p.m. during the lunch break. When Mr. Kruchelinsky came by she asked him if she could use the phone, to which he replied that he would have to ask Ken McAllister, a control foreman. Over the radio, Mr. McAllister asked if the call was for personal or union business. She said that when she told him that it was union related, he replied, "no," but he told her to take her lunch and wait for him. When he arrived at the dry, she said that she asked him why he did not permit her to use the phone during her lunch break. He explained that if she wanted to use the phone for union business she would have to book off work. But when she requested a union book off he refused it because there were too many off that day. She was then told to wait for Mr. Kruchelinsky to take her down to the buses. The result was that she ended up waiting a total of about 80 minutes including her lunch break, not being able to use the phone even though it was no more than 20 feet away.

The other example that she gave happened on July 6, 1997. On that day a rock went through the windshield of a front-end loader driven by John Gillespie. When it was reported to her, she asked for permission to go and see it. When she got there she felt that it was a dangerous occurrence that required investigation. In the course of the investigation she asked for permission to use the phone to call Ed Payne at home in order to determine whether a screen guard might be the solution. Mr. McAllister denied the request, stating that the investigation should be completed first, and that if she still felt that she would like to talk to Mr. Payne arrangements would be made. Based on that evidence, the Union took the position that a Company rule prohibiting all employees from possessing cellular phones on Company property is not reasonable in its application within the rule set out in *Re Lumber & Sawmill Workers' Union. Loc. 2537, and KVP Co.* (1965), 16 L.A.C. 73 (Robinson). While it conceded that there was a legitimate safety concern, specifically relating to employees using cell phones while working and operating machinery, it argued that the current rule is too broad and could not be supported by reference to any of the standard tests in the cases. Accordingly, it proposed that Union officials, including shop stewards and health and safety representatives, should be permitted to possess cellular telephones on Company property. Under the proposal, those officials would be entitled to use the phones in the following circumstances:

a. as of right, on their own time, without prior authorization;

b. as may be necessary on Company time, with authorization, which authorization would not be unreasonably withheld; and

c. as of right, during authorized leave for the purpose of conducting union business.

The Company takes quite a different position. On the authority of *Re British Columbia Railway Co. and C.U.T.E., Loc. 6* (1982), 8 L.A.C. (3d) 250 (Hope), Mr. Lester argues that the better view is now that an arbitration board does not have an inherent jurisdiction to determine whether a rule published by an employer is reasonable: *Bank of British Columbia v. Union of Bank Employees. Loc. 210* (1982), 133 D.L.R. (3d) 228 (S.C.), but can only monitor the application of the rule under its right to determine whether an employee has been disciplined for just and proper cause: *Re Religious Hospitallers of Hotel-Dieu of St. Joseph of the Diocese of London and Service Employees' Union. Loc. 210* (1983), 11 L.A.C. (3d) 1.51 (Saltman). As for the argument that the policy interferes with the administration of the Union, Mr. Lester says that, in point of fact, there is nothing in the policy that restricts the Union. He said that while the Union might like to be able to operate in a certain way, it has never had the right to use cell phones on Company property and that what it really wishes to do is enhance, facilitate, and improve the way that it carries out its functions. Since it is not a current right, he contends that the only way that it can be acquired by the Union is in the normal way, through collective bargaining.

Is the use of cell phones in the nature of a personal right similar to the right to privacy?

Ms. Alden took up that point by arguing firstly, that for the Company to suggest that the use of cell phones by employees would be an enhancement of their existing rights should not be accepted. Secondly, she said that prior to the policy, employees had a right to bring cell phones to work just as they have a right to bring a lunch and that, instead of the Union seeking to obtain enhanced rights, it is the Company that seeks to limit individual employee rights.

There would appear to be some support in the collective agreement that safety representatives are distinguishable from shop stewards and that they could be enabled to use cellular telephones, based upon the fact that their investigative responsibilities are not constrained in the same manner as shop stewards. Without deciding the matter, under Article 7.02 a steward must obtain permission from his supervisor in order to take time off from work "to attempt to resolve a grievance," although that provision equally provides that the supervisor will not arbitrarily or unreasonably withhold permission. By contrast, no similar requirement is imposed on safety representatives under Article 8. Article 8.02 requires that the foreman and safety representative will determine whether an investigation of an accident is required and if they cannot agree, the matter may be referred under subsection (c) to a referee process. In the event of a complaint that a condition is unsafe or an unusual hazard exists, a safety representative may investigate under Article 8.07 on the condition that a complaint must first be made and the employee is not satisfied with the decision of his or her supervisor.

In those circumstances, one could conclude that the use of cellular telephones by safety representatives could be more easily accommodated because they are less regulated. A safety representative is entitled to initiate an investigation depending upon certain objective conditions, while a shop steward may be refused permission to take time off work by the subjective decision of a supervisor that there are overriding operational requirements.

However, while safety representatives and shop stewards have been given different degrees of independence, nowhere does the collective agreement purport to give either of them a right to use cell phones. Further, there is nothing in the investigative procedures contained in Articles 7 and 8 that would permit me to imply such a right. Accordingly, I have no jurisdiction to determine whether the current policy that prohibits all employees from bringing cellular phones to the workplace is reasonable. Even more, I have no jurisdiction to decide whether the proposal put by the Union is better; nor can I mandate an alternative.

The fact is that the rule is not arbitrary in the sense that it is based upon considerations of safety, a matter which is conceded by the Union. Indeed, it is difficult to see how cell phones could be made completely safe by virtue only of the employee being a shop steward or a safety representative. The concern expressed by Mr. LeHoux was not that regulations could not be prescribed for when they could be used, as was proposed by the Union, but that these same employees will also be driving heavy equipment or operating plant machinery and that if they have them they will use them.

Questions

1. Why did management impose the ban on cellular phones in the first place? Do you think the ban was justified?

2. Is it reasonable for the union to argue that a ban on the use of cellular phones by union stewards and health and safety representatives constitutes interference with the union's workplace activities?

3. What would your decision have been had you been the arbitrator? Why?

4. Would the fact that outside contractors are allowed to use cellular phones, at least under certain conditions, affect your decision in this case?

5. The union has served notice that if this grievance is denied, it will challenge the ban as an unfair labour practice. Do you agree with this approach? If not, what alternative course might the union take?

Case A.2 ARBITRATION CASE

RWDSU, LOCAL 597 AND CITY CONSUMERS CO-OPERATIVE SOCIETY LTD.

Under what circumstances is a supermarket justified in dismissing an employee who fails to show up for a shift on very short notice?

Re City Consumers Co-Operative Society Ltd. and Retail, Wholesale and Department Store Union, Local 597

F.R. Woolridge, Q.C., L. McCormick, S. Marshall (Newfoundland)

June 15, 1982.

GRIEVANCE

The grievor claims her discharge for failure to work a scheduled shift was unjust.

FACTS

The facts are not in dispute.

The employer operates a large supermarket employing some 72 employees, including 21 cashiers, some part-time such as the grievor.

The store manager is Mr. Gibbon, the assistant manager is Mr. Clarke, and the head cashier is Ms. Chaytor, who is responsible for the shift scheduling of the part-time cashiers.

The grievor had been employed by the employer in September of 1981 and worked in the old store of the employer, where a notice was posted in the lunch room that forbade shift changes among the cashiers because it was a frequent occurrence, and sometimes for seemingly frivolous reasons in the eyes of management, and it was difficult to find replacements due to an unwillingness on the part of some cashiers to cover for a shift of another, or to work overtime.

In the new year, the employer moved operations to a new location on Topsail Rd. No such notice was posted there, and the rule was relaxed, but the employer requested that a reasonable period of notice be given before taking time off on a scheduled shift so that alternate arrangements to cover the shift could be made.

Some time in the month of February the grievor went to Ms. Chaytor and told of her plans to leave the province for two weeks to seek medical treatment. Absences of long duration such as this must be cleared with the manager, Mr. Gibbon, to whom she was sent. Gibbon was annoyed that the grievor was going in only two days' time, but because of the nature of the trip, and the fact that the grievor had travel plans already made, he agreed to the request, although he told her to give more notice in future.

The grievor was not told of any disciplinary consequences that would flow from any such future failure.

Commencing January 30, 1982, Mr. Clarke, the assistant manager, had commenced keeping records of cashiers who failed to show up for scheduled shifts. These records were kept for two reasons. Overtime under this agreement is not compulsory, and the employer was having difficulty finding employees prepared to do overtime work, which, while not compulsory, must not be unreasonably refused. These records would show the occasions of failure to report, and the reasons why, so that they would provide a history of the cashiers' record and provide evidence in the event that any disciplinary action was taken. Copies were given to the shop steward. One such record for employee Nolan (exhibit Consent 3) will serve as an example. It reads as follows:

> Department: Grocery
> Sent to: Arlene Nolan
> Date: Jan. 30/82
> Message:
> Jan. 6/82 Scheduled for work 5–9 but couldn't make it because she had company for supper.

Jan. 11 & 12/82 Late for work.

Jan.13/82 Couldn't make it from 1–5 or 6–9 because she had to take one of the boys out to the Dr.

Jan. 9/82 Asked to start work 1 instead of 1:30 but refused.

Jan. 18/82 Couldn't work today because she had to take one of the boys out to the Dr. Scheduled for 1–5.

Jan. 27/82 Scheduled for 1:30–5:30. Called 11 a.m. to say she wouldn't be in because of the snow.

Jan. 29/82 Scheduled for 9:30–1:30. Couldn't come because she never had any transportation.

On March 30, 1982, the grievor was scheduled to work the 1:30 p.m. to 5:30 p.m. shift for the next day. She went to Ms. Chaytor and asked permission to change that shift with one of the other cashiers because she had made a dental appointment for her children. Because such requests were again causing problems in scheduling, Ms. Chaytor had, some days or weeks before, gone to Mr. Gibbon and suggested they revert to the old system of prohibiting such changes. Gibbon had agreed. No notice had been posted but Ms. Chaytor feels that all the cashiers were notified. For that reason she told the grievor that there could be no change. The grievor then announced her intention to keep the dental appointment in any event and to miss the shift. She was not advised of the consequences of this action, because Ms. Chaytor was quite candid that she did not know what, if anything, the consequences would be.

Although Ms. Chaytor could not remember the incident, the grievor maintains that she called Ms. Chaytor at 12:15 p.m., March 31, 1982, one hour and 15 minutes before her shift was scheduled to start and confirmed that she would be absent. She failed to show up for the 1:30 p.m. shift, and another substitute cashier was found by 3:00 p.m.

At 3:00 p.m. or 3:30 p.m. on March 31, 1982, Ms. Chaytor notified Mr. Clarke that the grievor had not come to work. At that point Mr. Clarke decided to terminate the grievor, but in an effort to get her side of the story first, he telephoned her at home to see if she had an adequate explanation. When asked for an explanation the grievor pleaded the dental appointment had already been made. Mr. Clarke suggested that was no excuse because she should make such arrangements on her own time since they were not the concern of the employer, and that such absences caused obvious scheduling difficulties. The grievor responded that regardless of these considerations she would do the same in the future if the occasion arose, and went on to complain about the poor management of the Co-op. Clarke responded that if that was her attitude she need not bother to return to work. The grievor, then noticeably upset, thereupon announced her intention not to set foot in the store in future.

Shortly thereafter the grievor called both Ms. Chaytor and Mr. Clarke, still obviously upset, and complained of her disappointment over how she had been treated by Clarke. The grievor maintained that the employer was making a deliberate move to get rid of her, because other employees were getting away with the behaviour without penalty. Chaytor and Gibbon backed Clarke's decision and the grievor was discharged as of that date, and filed her grievance the next day.

CONSIDERATIONS

Was the grievor discharged for just cause?

By art. 25, the management's rights clause of this agreement, the employer has the unfettered right to " . . . plan, direct and control store operations . . . ," which obviously includes scheduling, and each employee owes the employer the obligation to work when scheduled, and the cases are too numerous to mention that a failure to fulfil that obligation will provide just cause for the employer to discipline or discharge the employee in question.

The employer argued that not only was the grievor absent without permission, but compounded the problem by wilfully disobeying a legitimate direct order and displaying a defiant attitude when she announced her intention to repeat the offence in future, all of which amounted to insubordination properly grounding discharge.

It suggests that she took no steps to find a replacement, and that given her attitude towards the job, particularly in the knowledge of the earlier warning in February, it would be pointless to reinstate her if she intends to disobey scheduling requirements.

The union does not condone this type of behaviour, but suggests the employer acted in a manner inconsistent with the way it treated other cashiers which amounted to discriminatory or arbitrary treatment of the grievor in a situation where it was never made clear to her that behaviour of this kind would suddenly lead to immediate discharge.

It points to exhibits Consents 4 to 9, which showed that since January 30, 1982, four cashiers have missed shifts ten times for reasons ranging from guests in to dinner to doctors' appointments for children and hospital visits, and says that in none of these cases was there ever imposed a more serious penalty than a reprimand memorandum placed in the employee's file. It therefore suggests that seeing this going on around her, it was not unreasonable for the grievor to reach the conclusion that regardless of what the stated rule was with respect to shift changes or missing shifts, the employer would only respond to such behaviour with a reprimand memorandum, and she accordingly had no reasonable apprehension that discharge would result.

We feel there is some merit in this suggestion. On the occasion of the February incident, an absence of long duration rather than one shift was involved and the evidence is that she was warned not to give short notice for such required long absences again, and there has been no recurrence.

That type of absence required the permission of Mr. Gibbon, and was treated quite differently from single shift absences or changes which were handled by Ms. Chaytor. Given the manner in which the employer elected to deal with such requests, it is not unreasonable for the grievor to conclude that an infraction of a single shift would be treated more leniently than for a long absence, and of course the best evidence available to the grievor as to how a single shift absence would be treated is how her fellow cashiers were treated when they committed the same offence.

The grievor had never been told such behaviour would lead to discharge—even Ms. Chaytor, her superior, was unaware of that. It would be wrong in principle to impose an unknown and unexpected penalty on an employee never made aware that a given infraction will reasonably attract that penalty, especially in a situation where an employer has acted in a manner to instill in the grievor's mind a belief that at most, she will receive a reprimand, and for these reasons we feel the penalty imposed was inappropriate.

Considerations of her insubordinate conduct are less easily resolved, since both before and after the scheduled shift the grievor made clear her fixed determination to disobey a legitimate direct order the employer had every right to make, and, moreover, made the quite unnecessary comment, even in the heat of the moment, that she fully intended to repeat the offence in the future.

Questions

1. What do you think of the supermarket's policy regarding shift changes? Does this kind of policy seem to you to be a good way to improve labour–management relations?
2. Does the grievor's attitude toward Mr. Clarke and the company (as shown during Mr. Clarke call to her on March 31, 1982) justify her termination, in your view? Why, or why not?
3. If you were Mr. Clarke, would you have conducted the March 31 interview with the grievor over the telephone? What might you have done differently this time?
4. Had you been a member of the store's management team, how would you have handled an employee exhibiting the kind of attendance record shown by the grievor?
5. Had you been the arbitrator, what would your decision have been in this case, and why?

Case A.3 Arbitration Case

HERE, LOCAL 75 AND DELTA TORONTO EAST HOTEL

When an employee is discharged without the union representation provided for in his collective agreement, will that discharge likely be sustained?

Re Delta Toronto East Hotel and Hotel Employees

Restaurant Employees Union, Local 75

[Indexed as: *Delta Toronto East Hotel and H.E.R.E., Loc. 75 (Manners-Sutton)* (Re)]

File No. Y-100782

Ontario

K.P. Swan

Heard: June 6, 2001

Decision rendered: June 8, 2001

Source: Reproduced from Labour Arbitration Cases with the permission of Canada Law Book, A Division of The Cartwright Group Ltd. (www.canadalawbook.ca). (Adapted from 98 L.A.C. (4th 2001), pp. 31–40. Some deletions have been made by the author for the purposes of this book.)

AWARD

A hearing in this matter was held in Toronto on June 6, 2001, at which time the parties were agreed that the arbitrator had been properly appointed pursuant to the collective agreement, and that I had jurisdiction to hear and determine the matter at issue between them.

The matter is the grievance of Mr. Robert Watson-Wright, #007/001/000, dated July 21, 2000. The grievance is to the effect that the termination of the grievor by letter dated July 20, 2000 was without just cause.

In addition to contesting the merits of the discharge, the Union also asserts that the circumstances in which the discharge was imposed constituted a breach of the collective agreement, specifically clause 12.6. That provision is as follows:

> 12.6 Suspension or dismissal:
>
> (1999) in the event that the Employer is contemplating a suspension or dismissal, the Employer will ensure that the employee will be provided the opportunity to have the assistance of a Shop Steward. Should the employee not wish to have Union representation he/she will sign a waiver.
>
> A claim by an employee that he/she has been unjustly suspended or discharged from his/her employment shall be treated as a grievance if a written statement of such grievance is lodged under step 1 of the grievance procedure within five (5) days of the beginning of the suspension or discharge.
>
> Such special grievances may be settled by confirming the management's action in dismissing an employee, or by reinstating the employee or by any other arrangement which is just and equitable in the opinion of the conferring parties.
>
> When an employee has been dismissed or if dismissal and resignation have been discussed, the Employer will inform the employee of his/her right to interview a shop steward for a reasonable period of time before leaving the premises.

The parties agreed that this issue should proceed as a preliminary matter, and they were essentially agreed on the facts on which the issue was to be determined. Those facts were placed before me by the opening statements of counsel and, there being no material dispute, the matter proceeded directly to argument.

It appears that, on July 19, 2000, the grievor was assigned to work as a Kitchen Guest-Contact employee. During the breakfast period, he was assigned to a food station where he prepared food items, including eggs, to the individual order of guests. A guest made a request of the grievor, and was sufficiently distressed by the grievor's response to fill out a comment card complaining about the incident.

It is not clear whether the Executive Chef, Mr. Raymond Taylor, contacted the grievor during the course of that day to discuss the incident. Mr. Taylor would normally have done so had the comment card come to his attention, but he has no specific recollection of doing so that day. The grievor's evidence would be that no such contact occurred. In any case, it is clear that whatever contact might have occurred would only have been an informal request for further information, made in passing.

In any event, the issue came to the attention of Mr. Scott Lannan, Director of Operations. The grievor has a significant disciplinary record of similar interpersonal difficulties with other employees, supervisors, and guests. Mr. Lannan concluded that the record, coupled with the customer complaint, would justify the grievor's termination, and he therefore had prepared the letter of termination dated July 20, 2000, for the signature of the Executive Chef.

On July 20, Ms. Anna Salvati, Director of People Resources, and the Executive Chef met in the Chef's office. The Chef then went to find the grievor to bring him back to meet with them both. The grievor's evidence would be that, on the way to the office, he asked the Chef what the meeting was about, and was told that he would find out when he got there. This exchange would apparently not be contradicted by any evidence from the Employer. Upon arrival at the meeting, the grievor was asked about the incident with the guest on the previous day, and offered some response. He was then informed that his employment was terminated, and the letter of termination, which had been at hand throughout the meeting, was given to him. At that point he asked something to the effect of "what about my union steward." Ms. Salvati asked if he would like a steward to be brought in, but the grievor responded in the negative. His testimony would be that it seemed to him to be too late, since he had already been terminated.

The Executive Chef then escorted the grievor outside the building, where the grievor stopped to smoke a cigarette. The Chef returned to the building, and brought the union steward to the grievor. The grievor then had the opportunity to discuss the matter with the union steward before he left, and the present grievance was filed. There is no dispute that the grievance was processed in the ordinary way through the grievance procedure, without any change in the Employer's position, and was properly referred to arbitration.

On this basis, the Union argues that the Employer was clearly in breach of the first paragraph of clause 12.6. This paragraph, in the Union's submission, requires that the Employer take steps to ensure that an employee is provided the opportunity to have "the assistance" of a shop steward, which is also referred to as "union representation" in the second sentence of the paragraph. The only way the Employer can escape that obligation is if the employee waives that right in writing, by signing a waiver of those rights.

While the Union acknowledges that the employee did have an opportunity to speak to the steward before leaving the premises, the Union argues that the circumstances of that interview might meet the requirements of the last paragraph of clause 12.6, but certainly cannot meet the requirements of the first paragraph. It is common ground between the parties that the first paragraph was added to the clause in the 1999 negotiations, the clause previously having consisted only of the last three paragraphs.

The Employer, on the other hand, argues that the purpose of the first paragraph is only to explain and augment the obligations of the Employer in respect of the last paragraph. It asserts that the Employer is required to ensure that employees are aware of the existence of the Union and the availability of shop stewards, but only for the purposes of the interview specified in the last paragraph, after termination and before leaving the premises. As to the requirement for a waiver, the Employer argues that this is merely to protect the Union against assertions of a failure of the duty of fair representation.

The Union relies on *Re Toronto (City) and C.U.P.E., Loc. 79* (1986), 24 L.A.C. (3d) 115 (T.A.B. Jolliffe); *Re Glengarry Memorial Hospital and C.U.P.E.* (1990), 11 L.A.C. (4th) 325 (Roach); and *Re Toronto (City) and C.U.P.E., Loc. 79 (Nzeakor)* (1995), 47 L.A.C. (4th) 197 (Charney). The last of these cases includes an extensive survey of the arbitral jurisprudence on the consequences of a failure by an employer to concede union representation rights in a disciplinary process. The Employer relies on the decision of the Ontario Divisional Court in *Cambridge Towel Corp. v. A.C.T.W.U.* (1988), 66 O.R. (2d) 793, and on three arbitration awards applying that decision.

In the *Cambridge Towel* case, the court quashed as patently unreasonable the award of an arbitrator which held that a failure to give three days' advance notice of a discharge to the union president, as required by the collective agreement, was a substantive right which could not be waived, and the breach of which resulted in the ensuing discipline being null and void.

The arbitrators in the three cases cited by the Employer all treat this decision as standing for the proposition that, in every case, an arbitrator should consider a purposive interpretation of the language of the collective agreement, to see what rights or protections are guaranteed to an employee, the extent to which those rights have been denied or withheld, the prejudice suffered by the employee by such a denial, and the appropriate remedy in all of the circumstances. With respect, I have no difficulty in accepting this as the correct way of interpreting any provision of a collective agreement, and in fashioning an appropriate remedy in all of the circumstances. Indeed, the arbitrators in the three cases cited by the Union appear to have taken a very similar approach.

Beginning with the purpose of the first paragraph of clause 12.6, despite the able submissions of counsel for the Employer, I am simply unable to accept that it has no other purpose than to provide structure for the rights specified in the last paragraph. Its placement at the beginning of the clause, separated from the last paragraph by two other paragraphs dealing with the grievance procedure, seems to me to highlight the obvious conclusion that the parties must have intended this to be an independent protection. It is also critical that the first paragraph speaks in a prospective mode, prescribing rights at a point when the Employer "is contemplating a suspension or dismissal." When contrasted with the language of the last paragraph, which applies when an employee "has been dismissed" or if dismissal or resignation "have been discussed," the only obvious conclusion is that the rights in the first paragraph must accrue before any disciplinary action has been taken which would involve either a suspension or a dismissal. There is no other rational interpretation of clause 12.6, read as a whole.

I note that other arbitrators have been able to infer the right to union representation from language which is not nearly as explicit as this, and have not hesitated to do so. In the two *Toronto (City)* cases cited by the Union, the language only defines the right as of "having . . . a shop steward . . . present at such meeting as an observer." Both arbitrators Jolliffe and Charney concluded, however, that this implied a right to union representation at that meeting. While the language before me does not expressly provide for a meeting or any other formality, it quite explicitly refers both to "assistance" and "representation," and sets the time for that to occur as when the Employer is still "contemplating" the discipline to be imposed.

The Employer asserts that the grievor suffered no prejudice. The Employer's assertion in this regard is unusual. It states that the decision to terminate the grievor's employment had already been taken by Mr. Lannan, that neither of the two individuals who were present in the meeting with the grievor had any authority to alter that determination, that the person who had made the decision was not even there, and that therefore nothing that the grievor or a union representative could say on his behalf could possibly have done any good. If such an argument were accepted, the Employer could completely avoid the obligations it has taken on in the first paragraph of clause 12.6 in every case, simply by making its decision in advance of, or instead of, affording the employee the representation rights bargained for. For an employer to say that nothing said to it could possibly change its mind is simply to deny the right specified in the collective agreement. As a matter of the reasonable interpretation of the collective agreement, an employer cannot be permitted to assert that arguments which it has never provided the opportunity to be made would not have affected its decision.

All of the cases relied upon by the Employer are cases where the right bargained for was something far less than a right to union representation. Each of them involves an obligation to provide timely written notice of some kind, and in each case it has been concluded that the purpose of the clause is only to alert the union of the action taken, presumably to permit grievance rights to be pursued, and not provide for union representation prior to the disciplinary action being taken. The present is a very different case, as I have found above. The right bargained for by the Union is one which arbitrators have repeatedly found to be a substantive right, fraught with prejudice to the grievor if denied.

Once an employee has been terminated, there are significant disincentives to reversing that decision. There are issues of management solidarity, questions of managerial authority, and financial consequences which increase day by day as the employee remains away from work without pay. To deny the right of representation at the time that the parties have bargained for it means that it is denied forever. It is for that reason, in my judgment, that arbitrators have regularly treated denial of such a critical right as depriving the employer of the right to rely upon the disciplinary events to found any discipline. That is why arbitrators have typically found that a termination after such a denial is void from the outset, and cannot be cured by either the grievance procedure or, for that matter, even by a full adversarial hearing before an arbitrator.

Questions

1. Why is union representation of employees facing discharge or other severe disciplinary action extremely important?

2. In the employer's view, the grievor in this case effectively waived his right to union representation. Do you agree? Why or why not?

3. Can you envisage circumstances that would justify the dismissal of an employee without union representation? What might those circumstances be?

4. How can the employer avoid having similar cases go to arbitration in the future?

5. Had you been the arbitrator in this case, what would your ruling have been, and why?

Annotated List of Websites Related to Labour and Employment

Canadian Sites

Statistics Canada

(www.statcan.ca)   If what you're after is basic economic and employment-related data, this is an excellent and very user-friendly site. The home page gives you the choice of an alphabetical index or a subject-related index. From there, it's easy to obtain basic data on such subjects as the unemployment and inflation rates, the labour force, earnings, and the incidence of full-time and part-time work. You can also, without much difficulty, find information on employment by industry or occupation and comparative international data on strikes and lockouts.

If you're looking for more detailed information or for historical data, the site becomes more problematic. In recent years, Statistics Canada has begun to operate on a "cost-recovery" basis, which means, in plainer English, that you have to pay for much of the data the agency has to offer. If you aren't careful, a search could end up costing you quite a bit of money. For historical data, you are best advised to start by consulting Statistics Canada's collection of hard-copy publications.

All in all, this is a very good site (and a fine complement to the HRDC site listed previously) for beginning industrial relations students. MBA students or others doing detailed research on a specific subject may find it less satisfactory.

Conference Board of Canada

(www.conferenceboard.ca)   This non-profit organization centres its attention on economic analysis, public policy issues, and issues around organizational performance. Its website, which is reasonably if not totally user friendly, offers buttons linking you to information on human resource management, leadership development, organizational excellence, education and lifelong learning, and management and e-business (among other things). The Conference Board frequently surveys both managers and union officials, and its website generally provides a pretty good sense of what these people expect the industrial relations outlook to be in at least the short term. Though not all industrial relations students will find this site useful, those with an interest in human resource management and organizational performance certainly will. The site is also a good place to get a quick read on the economic outlook at both federal and provincial levels. MBA students, in particular, will find it worth bookmarking.

Canadian Legal Information Institute (CanLII)

(www.canlii.org/index_en.html)   This invaluable website provides access to statutes and regulations, court and labour relations board decisions, and decisions of human rights and other tribunals from all Canadian jurisdictions.

Human Resources and Skills Development Canada

(www.hrsdc.gc.ca/en/gateways/topics/lzl-lal.shtml) This Government of Canada website consolidates information from all jurisdictions regarding industrial relations legislation and employment standards. It is updated regularly and presented in a clear, easy to understand manner.

Centre for Industrial Relations, University of Toronto

(www.chass.utoronto.ca/cir/library/hrirwebsites.html) The CIR Library offers an unsurpassed website with links to hundreds of human resources and industrial relations websites including employment and labour legislation sites, statistics and data sets, government information, research centres and professional associations, collective agreements, labour history, and a host of other IR/HR topics. If you only bookmark one website, this should be it!

Canadian Policy Research Networks

(www.cprn.ca) Like the Conference Board, but to an even greater extent, CPRN is a generalist organization addressing a wide range of policy issues. These include health, governance, and the family, in addition to issues around work and the workplace. CPRN's studies on work related issues are always well researched and balanced—favouring the viewpoint of neither management nor labour. Among the many first-rate studies available on its website are Graham Lowe's "Employer of Choice? Workplace Innovation in Government" and "What's a Good Job: The Importance of Employment Relationships," by Lowe and Grant Schellenberg. CPRN is generous in allowing people to download complete documents from its website. The site's one drawback is that it isn't always easy to navigate and some documents are available only in PDF format. Nonetheless, this is a good starting point for anyone with an interest in public policy issues, particularly issues around public sector industrial relations.

Union Sites

(Note: All are bilingual (French-English) unless otherwise indicated.)

Canadian Labour Congress

(www.clc-ctc.ca) A straightforward and easy-to-use site focusing on national-level political issues affecting the labour movement: health care, unemployment insurance, the privatization of public services, free trade, and workplace discrimination. From the front page, you can also access information about the CLC's upcoming convention and about the Congress' overall program.

Canadian Auto Workers

(www.caw.ca) This user-friendly site features a balanced mix of internal CAW business and discussion of broader political issues. Even as its members face devastating layoffs in the wake of widespread auto plant closures, the CAW remains interested in a full range of broader political and social issues, from the plight of the homeless in Toronto to the elimination of racism.

Canadian Union of Public Employees

(www.cupe.ca)   In some ways, the CUPE site reminds me of the HRDC one listed previously. No union site I have seen is richer in information, but the site can also be difficult—at times maddeningly frustrating—to use. Not unexpectedly, given CUPE's membership, the site focuses heavily on public sector issues, particularly health care. But it also contains an eclectic range of information on subjects of potential interest to any unionist, from how to communicate to members to how to set up a website. There is even a songbook containing a couple dozen of the time-honoured union classics such as "Joe Hill" and "Solidarity Forever." The two major drawbacks are: a) the difficulty of knowing what material a non-CUPE member can access and b) the difficulty of reading subheads printed in a font normally reserved for ads in the back pages of the Saturday paper.

Communications, Energy & Paperworkers Union

(www.cep.ca)   A balanced mix of internal business and regional and national news items of interest to members. A special feature of this site is its page devoted to the CEP's longstanding "Shorter Work Time Campaign." The home page contains a useful short statement of what the union is about overall. The site is generally, though not invariably, user friendly.

La Confédération des Syndicats Nationaux

(www.csn.qc.ca)   French-only, except for selected features ("Joining a Union"). An interesting contrast to most English-Canadian sites because of the international thrust of much of its news coverage. While the front page offers links to pages addressing internal union affairs, and while it contains news items about ongoing negotiations and developments in Quebec City and Ottawa, the extent of international news coverage is really quite striking.

Public Service Alliance of Canada

(www.psac.com)   Somewhat more inward-looking than the private sector union sites surveyed above, the PSAC site focuses mainly on collective bargaining developments and other internal union business. The home page does, however, contain a story on the UN Day for the Elimination of Racial Discrimination. An interesting special feature is the PSAC Youth Site, which, among other things, offers information on how young people can unionize their workplaces.

US SITES

Bureau of Labor Statistics

(www.bls.gov)   An extremely thorough listing of all kinds of labour- and employment-related information. Major topics are listed on the home page with major subheadings. They include: inflation and consumer spending; wages; earnings and benefits; productivity; safety and health; international labour; occupations (occupational outlook); demographics; employment and unemployment; industries; business costs; and geography (covering state- and municipal-level data). There's also a button devoted to publication and research papers, and even a kids' page listing career opportunities. In addition to the topical index found on the home page, an alphabetical index can easily be accessed as well. Wage settlements arrived at through collective bargaining can be found under "wages." Very user-friendly. Students interested in US labour information should start by consulting this site. (Note that information on household income and income inequality should be obtained from the Census Department website, and information on minimum wages from the Department of Labor website, both listed below.)

Department of Labor

(www.dol.gov)   Major headings on the home page include laws and regulations; statistics; research and publications; and doing business with the DOL. The minimum wage button takes you to a quite detailed and very interesting history of the development of minimum wage legislation in the US. There's also a detailed list of recent news stories related to labour and employment. Like the BLS site listed above, this one is quite user friendly. However, some of its information duplicates that found on the BLS site. On the whole, this site is probably less useful than the BLS for users who don't live in the US.

Bureau of the Census

(www.census.gov)   In addition to the topics listed above, this site contains information on employment-related subjects such as the labour force and working at home. A supplementary survey from the 2000 census is fairly easily accessed and includes economic, social, and housing information; this may be of somewhat more interest. Not difficult to use but not super-easy either. The logic of the various topic headings isn't always readily apparent. Give it about a 3 on a 5-point user-friendliness scale. Consider this as a supplement to the two previous websites rather than as a primary source of information about the US economy and labour scene.

AFL-CIO

(www.aflcio.org)   As might be expected of a national-level labour federation, this site places primary emphasis on national political developments affecting working people. A "Bush Watch" chronicles and analyzes all major legislation introduced during the current president's administration. There are also front-page news stories on unemployment insurance, steelworkers' fight on behalf of retirees, the American Labour Movement's "No More Enrons" campaign, and the AFL-CIO's "Agenda for America," a comprehensive political campaign aimed at mobilizing working families. The site's "Common Sense Economics" page features an "Executive Pay Watch" and stories about declining income equality, curbing corporate greed, and declining opportunities for young people in the new economy. The site is generally quite user friendly.

References

ABELLA, Irving. (1975). "Oshawa, 1937." In *On strike: Six key labour struggles in Canada 1919–1949*. Toronto: Lorimer. Reprinted in L.S. MacDowell and I. Radforth (Eds.). (1991). *Canadian working class history*. Toronto: Canadian Scholars' Press.

ADAMS, George. (2001). *Canadian labour law* (2nd ed.). Aurora, ON: Canada Law Book. Some use has also been made of the 1st (1998) edition of the same book.

ADAMS, Roy. (1998). "The human right to bargain collectively: A review of documents supporting international consensus." Society for the Promotion of Human Rights in Employment (SPHRE) Working Paper. Hamilton: McMaster University.

———. (1995a). "Canadian industrial relations in comparative perspective." In M. Gunderson and A. Ponak (Eds.), *Union-management relations in Canada* (3rd ed.). Don Mills, ON: Addison-Wesley. Some use has also been made of Adams' comparative chapter in the 2nd edition (1989) of the same book.

———. (1995b). *Industrial relations under liberal democracy: North America in comparative perspective*. Columbia, SC: U of South Carolina Press.

———. (1993a). "'All aspects of people at work': Unity and division in the study of labour and management." In R. Adams and N. Meltz (Eds.), *Industrial relations: Its nature, scope, and pedagogy*. Metuchen, NJ: Scarecrow Press.

———. (1993b). *Canadian Labour Law* (2nd ed.). Aurora, ON: Canada Law Book.

——— (Ed.). (1991). *Comparative industrial relations: Contemporary research and theory*. London: Harper Collins Academic.

———. (1987). "Employment standards in Ontario: An industrial relations systems analysis." *Relations Industrielles*, 42. Reprinted in LLCG. (1991). *Labour law: Cases, materials and commentary* (5th ed.). Kingston: Queen's IRC Press.

———. (1985). "Should works councils be used as industrial relations policy?" *Monthly Labor Review*, 108:7 (July).

———. (1978). *Grievance arbitration of discharge cases*. Kingston: Queen's U Industrial Relations Centre.

ADELL, Bernard. (1988a). "Law and industrial relations: The state of the art in common law Canada." In G. Hébert, H. Jain, and N. Meltz (Eds.), *The state of the art in industrial relations*. Kingston and Toronto: Queen's U Industrial Relations Centre and the U of Toronto Centre for Industrial Relations.

———. (1988b). "Introduction." In Ralph Cuervo-Lorens et al. (Eds.), *Labour law under the Charter: Proceedings of a conference sponsored by Industrial Relations Centre/School of Industrial Relations and Faculty of Law, Queen's University*. Kingston: Queen's Law Journal and Industrial Relations Centre.

ADELL, Bernard, Michel Grant, and Allen Ponak. (2001). *Strikes in essential services*. Kingston, ON: Industrial Relations Centre.

AKYEAMPONG, Ernest. (2004). "The union movement in transition." In *Perspectives on Labour and Income* (fall), pp. 39–47.

———. (2002). "Unionization and fringe benefits." In Statistics Canada, *Perspectives on Labour and Income* (fall) cat. No. 75-001-XPE, pp. 42–46.

———. (2001). "Fact-sheet on unionization." In Statistics Canada, *Perspectives on Labour and Income*, 13:3 (autumn), pp. 46–52.

———. (1999). "Unionization: An update." In Statistics Canada, *Perspectives on Labour and Income*, 11:3 (autumn), pp. 45–65.

———. (1998). "The Rise of unionization among women." *Perspectives on Labour and Income* (winter). Ottawa: Statistics Canada.

———. (1997). "A statistical portrait of the trade union movement." In Statistics Canada, *Perspectives on Labour and Income*, 9:4 (winter).

ALBERTA Labour Relations Board. (2003). "Unfair labour practices by employers." *Procedure guide*, http://www.alrb.gov.ab.ca/procedure/27(b).pdf.

ALDRIDGE, Bruce. (various years, 2001–2004). "Innovative workplace practices." In *Workplace Gazette*, various issues.

ALIGISAKIS, Maximos. (1997). "Labour disputes in Western Europe: Typology and tendencies." *International Labour Review*, 136:1, pp. 73–94.

ALLIANCE (Newsletter of the Public Service Alliance of Canada). Various articles, 1999 through 2001, connected with Goose Bay Canadian Forces Base and National Gallery of Canada strikes.

ANDERSON, John. (1989a). "The strategic management of industrial relations." In Morley Gunderson, Allan Ponak, and Daphne G. Taras (Eds.), *Union-management relations in Canada* (3rd ed.).

———. (1989b). "The structure of collective bargaining." In Morley Gunderson, Allan Ponak, and Daphne G. Taras (Eds.), *Union-management relations in Canada* (2nd ed.). Use has also been made of Anderson's bargaining structure chapter in the 1st edition (1982) of the same book.

———. (1979). "Local union democracy: In search of criteria." *Relations Industrielles*, 34.

ANDERSON, John and Morley Gunderson. (1982). "The Canadian industrial relations system." In Morley Gunderson, Allan Ponak, and Daphne G. Taras (Eds.), *Union-management relations in Canada* (1st ed.).

ANDERSON, John, Morley Gunderson, and Allen Ponak. (1989). "Frameworks for the study of industrial relations." In Morley Gunderson, Allan Ponak, and Daphne G. Taras (Eds.), *Union-management relations in Canada* (2nd ed.).

ARNOPOULOS, Sheila. (1974). Various *Montreal Star* articles, reprinted as "Immigrants and women: Sweatshops of the 1970s." In I. Abella and D. Millar (Eds.), *The Canadian worker in the twentieth century*. Toronto: Oxford U Press.

ARTHURS, Harry. (2005). *The rights stuff: Labour and the constitution*. Sefton Lecture, University of Toronto, January 19.

———. (1988). "The right to golf." In Ralph Cuervo-Lorens et al. (Eds.), *Labour law under the Charter*.

ASHENFELTER, Orley and John Pencavel. (1969). "American trade union growth." *Quarterly Journal of Economics*, 83.

AUBRY, Jack. (1998, July 30). "Windfall 'a long time coming' for underpaid workers." *Ottawa Citizen*, p. A1.

AUDITOR-GENERAL. (2000 and 2001). *Report of the Auditor-General of Canada*. Ottawa: Office of the Auditor-General.

AWCBC (Association of Workers' Compensation Boards of Canada). (2005). *National work injuries statistics program: Work injuries and diseases*, http://www.awcbc.org/english/NWISP_Stats.htm, February.

BAIN, George and Farouk Elsheikh. (1976). "Trade union growth in Canada: A comment." *Relations Industrielles*, 31.

BAIN, George and Robert Price. (1980). *Profiles of union growth: A comparative statistical portrait of eight countries*. Oxford: Basil Blackwell.

BAKER, William. (1983). "The miners and the mediator: The 1906 Lethbridge strike and Mackenzie King." *Labour/Le travailleur*, 11 (spring). Reprinted in MacDowell and Radforth (Eds.), *Canadian working class history*.

BALDERSTON, C.C. (1933). "Recent trends in personnel management." *Management Review*, 22:9. Reprinted in *Personnel and labour relations*.

BALES, Kevin. (2001, Nov.). "Slave owners making $12 billion a year from trafficking." *CCPA Monitor*, 8:6.

BAMBER, Greg and Russell Lansbury. (1993). *International and comparative industrial relations* (2nd ed.). London and New York: Routledge.

BAMBER, Greg and Gillian Whitehouse. (1993). "Appendix: Employment, economics, and industrial relations: comparative statistics." In Greg Bamber and Russell Lansbury (Eds.), *International and comparative industrial relations* (2nd ed.).

BARBASH, Jack. (1988). "The new industrial relations in the U.S.: Phase 2." *Relations Industrielles*, 43.

———. (1984). *The elements of industrial relations.* Madison: U of Wisconsin Press.

BARNACLE, Peter. (1991). *Arbitration of discharge grievances in Ontario: Outcomes and reinstatement experiences.* Kingston: Queen's IRC Research and Current Issues Series #62.

BARNARD, Robert D., D. Cosgrave, and J. Welsh. (1998). *Chips and pop: Decoding the nexus generation.* Toronto: DFait.

BEAN, Ron. (1994). *Comparative industrial relations: An introduction to cross-national perspectives* (2nd ed.). London: Routledge.

BEATTY, David. (1987). *Putting the 'Charter' to work: Designing a constitutional labour code.* Montreal: McGill-Queen's.

———. (1983). "Ideology, politics, and unionism." In K. Swan and K. Swinton (Eds.), *Studies in labour law.* Toronto: Butterworths.

BEATTY, David and Steve Kennett. (1988). "Striking back: Fighting words, social protest and political participation in free and democratic societies." In Ralph Cuervo-Lorens et al. (Eds.), *Labour law under the Charter.*

BEAUCHESNE, Eric. (2003, Aug. 25). "Immigrants behind in job market: Study." *Ottawa Citizen.*

BEAUMONT, P.B. (1995). "Canadian public sector industrial relations in a wider setting." In G. Swimmer and M. Thompson (Eds.), *Public sector collective bargaining in Canada.* Kingston: Queen's IRC Press.

BEDARD, Marie-Eve. (2004). "Grievance settlement system[s]." *Workplace Gazette*, 7:4, pp. 43–52.

———. (2003a). "Direct compensation in the workplace." *Workplace Gazette*, 6:4, pp. 28–37.

———. (2003b). "Clauses linked to technological change and labour reorganization in collective agreements." *Workplace Gazette*, 6:2, pp. 28–37.

BEMMELS, Brian. (1998). "Gender effects in discharge arbitration." *Industrial and Labour Relations Review*, 42:1.

BENG, Chew Song and Rosalind Chew. (1995). "The development of industrial relations strategy in Singapore." In A. Verma et al. (Eds.), *Employment Relations in the Growing Asian Economies.* London and New York: Routledge.

BENTHAM, Karen J. (2002). "The incidence and impacts of employer resistance to union certification: A study of eight Canadian jurisdictions." *Relations Industrielles*, 57:1, pp. 159–187.

———. (1999). "The determinants and impacts of employer resistance to union certification in Canada," PhD diss., Centre for Industrial Relations, University of Toronto.

———. (1991). *The duty of fair representation in the negotiation of collective agreements.* Kingston, ON: Industrial Relations Centre, Queen's University.

BERCUSON, David and David Bright (Eds.). (1994). *Canadian labour history: Selected readings.* Toronto: Copp Clark Longman.

BERGMAN, Paul. (1988). *Relations by objectives: The Ontario experience.* Kingston: Queen's IRC Research and Current Issues Series #55.

BERRIDGE, John. (1995). "The United Kingdom." In Ingrid Brunstein (Ed.), *Human resource management in Western Europe.* Berlin and New York: de Gruyter.

BETCHERMAN, Gordon and Kathryn McMullen. (1986). *Working with technology: A survey of automation in Canada.* Ottawa: Economic Council of Canada.

BETCHERMAN, Gordon, Kathryn McMullen, Christina Caron, and Norm Leckie. (1994). *The Canadian workplace in transition.* Kingston: Queen's IRC Press.

BETTER Times. (1997) and (1998). Various issues.

BLACK, Henry Campbell. (1983). *Black's law dictionary* (5th ed.). St. Paul: West Publishing Co.

BLAND, Susan. (1983). "Henrietta the homemaker, and Rosie the riveter." *Women's Study Journal, Atlantis.* Reprinted in MacDowell and Radforth (Eds.), *Canadian working class history.*

BLEASDALE, Ruth. (1981). "Class conflict on the canals of Upper Canada in the 1840s." *Labour/Le travailleur*, 7 (spring). Reprinted in MacDowell and Radforth (Eds.), *Canadian working class history.*

BLOCK, Richard N., Karen Roberts, and R. Oliver Clarke. (2003). *Labor standards in the United States and Canada.* Kalamazoo: W.E. Upjohn Institute for Employment Research.

BLS (Bureau of Labour Statistics). (2001). Information on US union membership drawn from BLS Website in December. (For more detailed information about the site, please see the Annotated List of Websites.)

BOIVIN, Jean. (1982). "Union-management relations in Quebec." In John Anderson and Morley Gunderson (Eds.), *Union-management relations in Canada.* Don Mills, ON: Addison-Wesley.

BRAVERMAN, Harry. (1974). *Labor and monopoly capital.* New York: Monthly Review Press.

BRETT, Jeanne and Stephen Goldberg. (1983). "Grievance mediation in the coal industry: A field experiment." *Industrial and Labor Relations Review,* 37.

———. (1979). "Wildcat strikes in bituminous coal mining." *Industrial and Labor Relations Review,* 32.

BRONFENBRENNER, Kate. (1992). "Seeds of resurgence: Successful union organizing strategies." Paper presented at 1992 Annual Meeting of the American Sociological Association.

BROWN, Andrew and Stephen Frenkel. (1993). "Union unevenness and insecurity in Thailand." In S. Frenkel (Ed.), *Organized labor in the Asia-Pacific region.* Ithaca, NY: ILR Press.

BROWN, H.F. (1934–1935). "Industrial relations activities survive a critical test." *Personnel Journal,* 13. Reprinted in *Personnel and labour relations.*

BROWN, Lorne. (1970). "Unemployment relief camps in Saskatchewan, 1922–1936." In *Saskatchewan history.* Saskatoon: Saskatchewan Archives Board. Reprinted in MacDowell and Radforth (Eds.), *Canadian working class history.*

BRUCE, Peter G. (1994). "On the status of workers' rights to organize in the United States and Canada." In Sheldon Friedman, Richard W. Hurd, Rudolph A. Oswald, and Ronald L. Seeber (Eds.), *Restoring the promise of American labor law.* Ithaca, NY: ILR Press.

———. (1990). "The processing of unfair labour practice cases in the U.S. and Ontario." *Relations Industrielles,* 45.

———. (1989). "Political parties and labor legislation in Canada and the U.S." *Industrial Relations,* 28 (spring).

BRUNSTEIN, Ingrid. (Ed.). (1995). *Human resource management in Western Europe.* Berlin and New York: de Gruyter.

BRYCE, George and Pran Manga. (1985). "The effectiveness of health and safety committees." *Relations Industrielles,* 40:2.

BULLEN, John. (1986). "Hidden workers: Child labour and the family economy in late nineteenth-century urban Ontario." *Labour/Le Travail,* 18 (fall). Reprinted in MacDowell and Radforth (Eds.), *Canadian working class history.*

BUREAU of Labor Statistics. (2005). *News: Union members in 2004.* USLD 05-112. January 27. Washington: United States Department of Labor.

BUTTON, Tony. (1990). *The Canadian railway office of arbitration alternative.* Kingston: Queen's IRC School of Industrial Relations Research Essay #29.

CAMERON, Dan. (2001). "The crisis in public-sector bargaining in Saskatchewan." *Policy Options* (Sept.), pp. 28–32.

CANADIAN Labour Congress (CLC). (1997). *Women's work: A report.* Ottawa: Author.

CARDIN, Jean-Real. (1967). *Canadian labour relations in an era of technological change.* Economic Council of Canada Special Study #6. Ottawa: Supply and Services.

CARPENTER, C.U. (1903, April). "The working of a labor department in industrial establishments." *Engineering Magazine,* 25:1. Reprinted in *Personnel and labour relations.*

CARROTHERS, A.W.J., E.E. Palmer, and W.B. Rayner. (1986). *Collective bargaining law in Canada* (2nd ed.). Toronto: Butterworths.

CARTER, Donald. (1997). "The duty to accommodate: Its growing impact on the grievance arbitration process." *Relations Industrielles,* 52.

———. (1995). "Collective bargaining legislation." In Morley Gunderson, Allan Ponak, and Daphne G. Taras (Eds.), *Union-management relations in Canada* (3rd ed.). Use has also been made of Carter's labour law chapters in the 1st (1982) and 2nd (1989) editions of the same book.

CARTER, Donald, Geoffrey England, Brian Etherington, and Gilles Trudeau. (2002). *Labour law in Canada* (5th ed.). Markham, Ontario: Butterworths.

CASSELMAN, Karen. (1998). Labour Relations Officer, Grievances and Arbitration Section, Canada Post. Telephone interview, December 21.

CAUT/ACPPU (Canadian Association of University Teachers). (2002). *Recognizing and responding to bad faith bargaining*, http://www.caut.ca/en/publications/bargaining/aug2002badfaithbargaining.pdf.

CAVALLUZZO, Paul. (1988). "Freedom of association: Its effect upon collective bargaining and trade unions." In Ralph Cuervo-Lorens et al. (Eds.), *Labour law under the Charter.*

CAW (Canadian Auto Workers). (n.d.). "CAW statement on the reorganization of work."

CCH. (1998, May). "Health and safety legislation" (including workers' compensation). In *Employment standards*. North York, ON: CCH.

CHAISON, Gary. (1996). *Union mergers in hard times: The view from five countries*. London and Ithaca: ILR Press.

———. (1982). "Unions: Growth, structure, and internal dynamics." In Morley Gunderson, Allan Ponak, and Daphne G. Taras (Eds.), *Union-management relations in Canada* (1st ed.). Use has also been made of the union structure chapter by Gary Chaison and Joseph Rose in the 2nd (1989) edition of the same book.

CHAISON, Gary and Joseph Rose. (1991). "The macrodeterminants of union growth and decline." In G. Strauss, D. Gallagher, and J. Fiorito (Eds.), *The state of the unions*. Madison: IRRA Press.

CHAMBERLAIN, Neil W. and James W. Kuhn. (1986). *Collective bargaining* (3rd ed.). New York, NY: McGraw-Hill.

CHAREST, Jean. (2003). "Workforce sectoral partnerships in Quebec: A positive assessment." *Workplace Gazette,* 7:3 (fall), pp. 61–67.

CHAYKOWSKI, Richard. (2005). "Collective bargaining: Structure, process and innovation." In Morley Gunderson, Allen Ponak, and Daphne G. Taras (Eds.), *Union-management relations in Canada* (5th ed.). Toronto: Pearson Addison Wesley.

———. (1995). "The structure and process of collective bargaining." In Morley Gunderson, Allan Ponak, and Daphne G. Taras (Eds.), *Union-management relations in Canada* (3rd ed.).

CHAYKOWSKI, Richard and Michel Grant. (1995). "From traditional to mutual gain bargaining." *Collective Bargaining Review* (May). Ottawa: Human Resources Development Canada, pp. 79–88.

CHAYKOWSKI, Richard and Anil Verma. (1992). "Canadian industrial relations in transition." In R. Chaykowski and A. Verma (Eds.), *Industrial relations in Canadian industry*. Toronto: Dryden.

CHRISTIE, Innis. (1980). *Employment law in Canada*. Toronto: Butterworths.

CLARKE, Oliver. (1993). "Conclusions." In Greg Bamber and Russell Lansbury (Eds.), *International and comparative industrial relations* (2nd ed.).

CLBC (Canadian Labour and Business Centre). (2004). *CLBC handbook: Immigration and skills shortages*. Ottawa: CLBC.

———. (2000). "Viewpoints 2000." Ottawa: CLBC.

CLEGG, Hugh. (1976). *Trade unionism under collective bargaining: A theory based upon comparisons of six countries*. Oxford: Blackwell.

CLMPC (Canadian Labour Market and Productivity Centre). (1997). *Changing times, new ways of working: Alternative working arrangements and changes in working time*. Ottawa: CLMPC.

CNW (Canada NewsWire). (2001, May 23). "Georgetti announces resolution of SEIU-CAW dispute."

COATES, Mary Lou. (1992). "Is there a future for the Canadian labour movement?" Kingston: Queen's IRC Current Issues Series.

COLLECTIVE *Bargaining Review* (CBR). (1996) and (1997). Various issues. Ottawa: HRDC.

COMMONS, John et al. (1918). *History of labor in the United States*. New York: Macmillan.

———. (1909, November). "American shoemakers: 1648–1895." *Quarterly Journal of Economics*, 24.

COWDRICK, Edward. (1934–1935). "Collective bargaining in 1934." *Personnel Journal*, 13:5. Reprinted in *Personnel and labour relations*.

CPU (Canadian Paperworkers' Union). (1990). "The team concept and the restructuring of the workplace." *CPU Journal*, 10:2.

CRAIG, Alton. (1986). *The system of industrial relations in Canada* (2nd ed.). Scarborough: Prentice-Hall Canada Inc.

———. (1967). "A model for the analysis of industrial relations systems." Paper presented to the Annual Meeting of the Canadian Political Science Association held in Ottawa.

CRAIG, Alton and Norman Solomon. (1996). *The system of industrial relations in Canada* (5th ed.). Scarborough, ON: Prentice-Hall. Some use has also been made of the 1st (1983) and 4th (1993) editions of the same book.

CRANFORD, Cynthia J., Leah F. Vosko, and Nancy Zukewich. (2003). "The gender of precarious employment in Canada." *Relations Industrielles*, 58:3, pp. 454–483.

CRISPO, John. (1982). "The future of Canadian industrial relations." In Morley Gunderson, Allan Ponak, and Daphne G. Taras (Eds.), *Union-management relations in Canada* (1st ed.).

CRY (Child Relief and You). (2005). www.cry.org, [Oct. 30].

CTV NEWS (2001). "N.S. nursing arbitrator hears final offers," CTV News with Lloyd Robertson, Aug. 4, CTV website, www.ctv.ca.

CUERVO-LORENS, Ralph et al. (Eds.). (1988). *Labour law under the Charter: Proceedings of a conference sponsored by Industrial Relations Centre/School of Industrial Relations and Faculty of Law, Queen's University,* Kingston, Sept. 24–26, 1987. Kingston: Queen's Law Journal and Industrial Relations Centre.

CUNNINGHAM, J.B., and T.H. White (Eds.). (1984). *Quality of working life: Contemporary cases.* Ottawa: Supply and Services (Labour Canada publication).

CUPE (Canadian Union of Public Employees). (2005a). "Underfunding by province hurting people in Hamilton with disabilities." CUPE Press Release, March 21.

———. (2005b). "CUPE gives Saskatchewan budget mixed marks." CUPE Press Release, March 23.

———. (n.d.). List of courses prepared by the CUPE education department.

CURRENT Scene: The current industrial relations scene in Canada. (1991). Kingston: Queen's University Industrial Relations Centre.

CUTCHER-GERSHENFELD, Joel, Thomas Kochan, and John Calhoun Wells. (2001). "In whose interest? A first look at national survey data on interest-based bargaining in labor relations." *Industrial Relations*, 40:1, pp. 1–21.

CWC (Communications Workers of Canada). (1992). Organization chart outlining the union's main activities.

DANNIN, Ellen. (1995). "Brother, can you spare a no-wage job? Labour law reform in New Zealand." In C. Gonick et al. (Eds.), *Labour gains, labour pains: socialist studies/etudes socialistes,* vol. 10, p. 405.

DASTMALCHIAN, Ali and Ignace Ng. (1990). "Industrial relations climate and grievance outcomes." *Relations Industrielles*, 45.

DAVIS, Edward and Russell Lansbury. (1993). "Industrial relations in Australia." In Greg Bamber and Russell Lansbury (Eds.), *International and comparative industrial relations* (2nd ed.).

DEERY, Stephen and Richard Mitchell (Eds.). (1993). *Labour law and industrial relations in Asia.* Melbourne: Longman.

DÉOM, Esther and Jean Boivin. (2005). "Union-management relations in Quebec." In Morley Gunderson, Allan Ponak, and Daphne G. Taras (Eds.), *Union management relations in Canada* (5th ed.). Toronto: Pearson Addison Wesley.

———. (2001). "Union-management relations in Quebec." In Morley Gunderson, Allan Ponak, and Daphne G. Taras (Eds.), *Union-management relations in Canada* (4th ed.). Use has also been made of the Quebec chapters written first by Boivin, then by Boivin and Déom, in the first three editions of this book (1982, 1989, and 1995).

DEUTSCH, Arnold. (1979). *The human resources revolution: Communicate or litigate.* New York: McGraw-Hill.

DOHM, Arlene. (2000). "Gauging the effects of retiring baby-boomers." *Monthly Labor Review,* (July), pp. 17–25.

DONNER, Arthur (Chair). (1994). *Report of the advisory group on overtime and hours of work.* Ottawa: Supply and Services.

DOWNIE, Bryan. (1992). "Industrial relations in elementary and secondary education: A system transformed?" In R. Chaykowski and A. Verma (Eds.), *Industrial relations in Canadian industry.*

———. (1989). "Union-management co-operation in the 1980s and beyond." In Morley Gunderson, Allan Ponak, and Daphne G. Taras (Eds.), *Union-management relations in Canada* (2nd ed.). Some use has also been made of the same author's chapter on the same subject in the 1st (1982) edition of the same book.

DOWNIE, Bryan and Mary Lou Coates. (1993). *The changing face of industrial relations and human resource management.* Kingston: Queen's IRC Current Issues Series.

DRACHE, Daniel. (1984). "The formation and fragmentation of the Canadian working class: 1820–1920." *Studies in Political Economy,* 15 (fall). Reprinted in *Canadian labour history.*

DRACHE, Daniel and Harry Glassbeek. (1992). *The changing workplace: Reshaping Canada's industrial relations system.* Toronto: Lorimer.

DUBIN, R. (1959). "Constructive elements of industrial conflict." In A. Kornhauser et al. (Eds.), *Industrial conflict.* New York: McGraw-Hill. Reprinted in *Labour law* (5th ed.).

DUCHESNE, Doreen. (2004a). "More seniors at work." *Perspectives on Labour and Income.* Statistics Canada. Catalogue 75-001-XPE. pp. 55–67.

———. (2004b). "The near-retirement rate." *Perspectives on Labour and Income.* Statistics Canada. Catalogue 75-001-XPE. pp. 68–72.

DULLES, Foster R. and M. Dubofsy. (1984). *Labour in America: A history* (4th ed.). Arlington Heights, IL: Harlan Davidson.

DUNLOP, John. (1958). *Industrial relations systems.* Carbondale, IL: Southern Illinois Press.

DUNNETTE, Marvin. (1971). "Research needs of the future in industrial and organizational psychology." Paper presented at 1971 American Psychological Association meetings, Washington, DC. Reprinted in *Personnel and labour relations.*

DUNNETTE, Marvin and Bernard Bass. (1963). "Behavioral scientists and personnel management." *Industrial Relations,* 2 (May). Reprinted in *Personnel and labour relations.*

DUXBURY, L., L. Dyke, and N. Lam. (1999). *Building a world-class workforce: Career development in the federal public service.* Ottawa: Treasury Board of Canada Secretariat.

DUXBURY, L., C. Higgins, C. Lee, and S. Mills. (1991). "Balancing work and family: A study of the federal public sector." Ottawa: no publisher.

EASTMAN, Byron. (1983). "Canadian union growth." *Relations Industrielles,* 33.

EATON, J.K. (1975). "The growth of the Canadian labour movement." *Labour Gazette,* 75.

EBBINGHAUS, Bernard. (2002). "Trade unions' changing roles: Membership erosion, organizational reform and social partnership in Europe." *Industrial Relations Journal,* 33:5, pp. 465–483.

ECC (ECONOMIC Council of Canada). (1987). *Innovation and jobs in Canada.* Ottawa: Supply and Services.

ECHLIN, Randall Scott and Jennifer M. Fantini. (2001). *Quitting for good reason: The law of constructive dismissal in Canada.* Aurora: Canada Law Book.

ECONOMIC Council of Newfoundland and Labrador (ECNL). (1989). "Equity capital and economic development in Newfoundland and Labrador." Ottawa: Economic Council of Canada Local Development Paper #8.

EDEN, Genevieve. (1993). "Industrial discipline in the Canadian federal jurisdiction." *Relations Industrielles,* 48:1.

———. (1992). "Progressive discipline: An oxymoron." *Relations Industrielles,* 47:3.

EHRENBERG, Ronald and R. Smith. (1985). *Modern labor economics.* Glenview, IL: Scott-Foresman.

ELLIOTT, David and Joanne Goss. (1994). *Grievance mediation: How and why it works.* Aurora, ON: Canada Law Book.

ENGLAND, Geoffrey. (2005). "The individual employment contract and employment legislation in Canada." In Morley Gunderson, Allan Ponak, and Daphne G. Taras (Eds.), *Union-management relations in Canada* (5th ed.). Toronto: Pearson Education Canada Inc.

———. (1988). "Some thoughts on constitutionalising the right to strike." In Ralph Cuervo-Lorens et al. (Eds.), *Labour law under the Charter*.

———. (1987). "Part-time, casual, and other atypical workers: A legal view." Kingston: Queen's U Industrial Relations Centre, Research and Current Issues Series Paper #48.

ENGLAND, Geoffrey, Innis Christie, and Merran Christie. (1998) *Employment Law in Canada* (3rd ed.). Toronto: Butterworths.

ENGLAND, Kim and Gunter Gad. (2002). "Social policy at work? Equality and equity in women's paid employment in Canada." *GeoJournal*, 56:4, pp. 281–294.

EPSTEIN, Abraham. (1932). "Employees' welfare: An autopsy." *American Mercury*, 25:99 (Mar.). Reprinted in *Personnel and labour relations*.

ERSKINE, Lillian and Trevor Cleveland. (1917). "New men for old." *Everybody's*, 36 (Apr.). Reprinted in *Personnel and labour relations*.

FANG, Tony and Anil Verma. (2002). "Union wage premium." In Statistics Canada, *Perspectives on Labour and Income* (winter), cat. No. 75-001-XPE, pp. 17–23.

FARBER, Henry S. (2001). "Union success in representation elections: Why does unit size matter?" *Industrial and Labor Relations Review*, 54:2, pp. 329–348.

FASHOYIN, Tayo. (1991). "Recent trends in industrial relations theory and research in developing countries." In R. Adams (Ed.), *Comparative industrial relations: Contemporary research and theory*. London: Harper Collins Academic.

FAWCETT, Blair. (1998). "Selected provisions in major collective agreements: Wage incentive plans, 1988 to 1998." *Workplace Gazette*, (fall).

"FEDERATION to end role as central labour group." (1997, August 22). *The Globe & Mail*, p. A8.

FERGUSON, G.V. (1935). "An Alberta prophet (1935 model.)" *Canadian Forum*, (Apr.). Reprinted in J.L. Granatstein and P. Stevens (Eds.) (1972). *Forum*. Toronto: U of Toronto Press.

FERNER, Anthony and Richard Hyman. (1992a). "Industrial relations in the new Europe: Seventeen types of ambiguity." Introduction to A. Ferner and R. Hyman (Eds.), *Industrial relations in the new Europe*. Oxford: Blackwell.

———. (1992b). "Italy: Between political exchange and micro-corporatism." In A. Ferner and R. Hyman (Eds.), *Industrial relations in the new Europe*. Oxford: Blackwell.

FEUILLE, Peter. (1999). "Grievance mediation." In A.E. Eaton and J.H. Keefe (Eds.), *Employment dispute resolution and worker rights*. Champaign, IL: IRRA Series.

———. (1992). "Why does grievance mediation resolve grievances?" *Negotiation Journal*, 8:2 (Apr.).

FINKEL, Alvin. (1986). "The cold war, Alberta labour and the Social Credit regime." *Labour/Le Travail*, 21 (spring, 1988). Reprinted in MacDowell and Radforth (Eds.), *Canadian working class history*.

FISCHER, Frank. (1968). "The personnel function in tomorrow's company." *Personnel*, 45:1 (Jan.–Feb.). Reprinted in *Personnel and labour relations*.

FISHER, E.G. and S. Kushner. (1986). "Alberta's construction labour relations during the recent downturn." *Relations Industrielles*, 41:4.

FISHER, E.G. and Brian Williams. (1989). "Negotiating the union-management agreement." In Morley Gunderson, Allan Ponak, and Daphne G. Taras (Eds.), *Union-management relations in Canada* (2nd ed.). Some use has also been made of Williams' negotiation chapter in the 1st (1982) edition of the same book.

FISHER, Roger, William Ury, and Bruce Patton. (1991). *Getting to yes: Negotiating agreement without giving in* (2nd ed.). New York: Penguin Books.

FISHER, Sandra and Jon Peirce. (1995). "Labour education in Newfoundland." *Workers' Education*, 10 (Oct.).

FISHER, Timothy C.G. and Robert G. Waschik. (2000). "Union bargaining power, relative wages, and efficiency in Canada." *Canadian Journal of Economics*, 33:3, pp. 742–765.

FITCH, John. (1917). "Making the boss efficient." *Survey*, 38 (June 2). Reprinted in *Personnel and labour relations*.

FLAVELLE, Dana. (2005). "Loblaw profit falls 19.3 percent. Food giant moves to cut labour costs." *Toronto Star*, May 5, p. C01.

FLMM (Forum of Labour Market Ministers). (2003). *Older workers in the labour market: Employment challenges, programs, and policy implications.* Winnipeg: Manitoba Education, Training and Youth Intergovernmental Relations Unit.

FOISY, C. (1998). "Is arbitration too slow and legalistic?" In M. Hughes and A. Ponak (Eds.), *Conference Proceedings of the 16th Annual University of Calgary Labour Arbitration Conference.* Calgary: Industrial Relations Research Group and University of Calgary.

FORREST, Anne. (1997). "Securing the male breadwinner." *Relations Industrielles,* 52:1.

———. (1989). "The rise and fall of national bargaining in the Canadian meat-packing industry." *Relations Industrielles,* 44:2.

———. (1986). "Bargaining units and bargaining power." *Relations Industrielles,* 41:4.

FORSEY, Eugene. (1985). "Labour and the constitution in Atlantic Canada." In E. Forsey (Ed.), *Perspectives on the Atlantic Canada labour movement and the working class experience.* Sackville, NB: Mount Allison University Centre for Canadian Studies.

———. (1982). *Trade unions in Canada, 1812–1902.* Toronto: U of Toronto Press.

FRANK, David. (1983). "The trial of J.B. McLachlan." In *Historical papers* (pp. 208–225). Reprinted in D. Frank and G. Kealey (Eds.). (1995). *Labour and working-class history in Atlantic Canada.* St. John's: Institute of Social and Economic Research.

FREEMAN, Richard. (1989). "On the divergence in unionism among developed countries." Washington: National Bureau of Economic Research Working Paper #2817.

FREEMAN, Richard and James Medoff. (1984). *What do unions do?* New York: Basic Books.

———. (1979). "The two faces of unionism." *The Public Interest,* 57.

FREGE, Carola. (2001). "Union weakness and post-communist identities in Eastern Europe: Evidence from the Hungarian clothing industry." *Industrial Relations Journal,* 32:4, pp. 295–312.

FRENKEL, Stephen (Ed.). (1993a). *Organized labor in the Asia-Pacific region: A comparative study of trade unionism in nine countries.* Ithaca, NY: ILR Press.

———. (1993b). "Australian trade unionism and the new social structure of accumulation." In S. Frenkel (Ed.), *Organized labor in the Asia-Pacific region.*

FROST, Ann and Daphne Taras. (2005). "Understanding the unionization decision." In M. Gunderson, A. Ponak, and D. Taras (Eds.), *Union-management relations in Canada* (5th ed.). Toronto: Pearson.

FRYER, John (Chair). (2001). *Working together in the public interest.* Final Report of the Advisory Committee on Labour Management Relations in the Federal Public Service. Ottawa: Treasury Board of Canada Secretariat.

———. (2000). *Identifying the issues.* First Report of the Advisory Committee on Labour Management Relations in the Federal Public Service. Ottawa: Treasury Board of Canada Secretariat.

FRYER, John. (1995). "Provincial public sector labour relations." In G. Swimmer and M. Thompson (Eds.), *Public sector collective bargaining in Canada.*

FUERSTENBERG, Friederich. (1993). "Industrial relations in Germany." In Greg Bamber and Russell Lansbury (Eds.), *International and comparative industrial relations* (2nd ed.).

GALENSON, Walter and R.S. Smith. (1978). "The United States." In J. Dunlop and W. Galenson (Eds.). *Labor in the twentieth century.* New York: Academic.

GALLAGHER, Daniel and Kurt Wetzel. (1980). "Centralized multi-employer negotiations in public education: An examination of the Saskatchewan experience in the public sector." *Journal of Collective Negotiations in the Public Sector,* 9:4.

GALT, Virginia. (2000, Nov. 3). "War for talent being waged on all fronts." *Globe & Mail,* p. B12.

———. (1998, Sept. 8). "Unions dispute claim work day below average." *Globe & Mail,* p. A12.

GANDZ, Jeffrey. (1979). "Grievance initiation and resolution: A test of the behavioural theory." *Relations Industrielles,* 34.

GANDZ, Jeffrey and J.D. Whitehead. (1989). "Grievances and their resolution." In Morley Gunderson, Allan Ponak, and Daphne G. Taras (Eds.), *Union-management relations in Canada* (2nd ed.). Some use has also been made of Gandz's grievance chapter in the 1st (1982) edition of the same book.

GANNON, Marvin. (1972). "Entrepreneurship and labor relations at the Ford Motor Company." *Marquette Business Review* (summer). Reprinted in *Personnel and labour relations.*

GEORGE, Claude. (1968). *The history of management thought.* Englewood Cliffs: Prentice-Hall.

GÉRIN-LAJOIE, Jean. (1993). "Quelques contrastes entre les secteurs privé et public au Québec." In *The industrial relations system: Proceedings of the 29th Annual Conference of the Canadian Industrial Relations Association.* Charlottetown, PEI.

GILES, Anthony. (1996). "Globalization and industrial relations," In *The globalization of the economy and the worker: Selected papers presented at the 32nd Annual Canadian Industrial Relations Conference.* Montreal.

GILES, Anthony and Akivah Starkman. (2005). "The collective agreement." In Morley Gunderson, Allan Ponak, and Daphne G. Taras (Eds.), *Union-management relations in Canada,* 5th ed. Use has also been made of the same authors' collective agreement chapter in the 4th (2001) and 3rd (1995) edition of the same book, and of the chapter by Giles and Hem Jaim in the same book's 2nd (1989) edition.

GLADSTONE, Alan. (1980). "Trade unions, growth and development." *Labour and Society,* 5:1, pp. 49–68.

GLASSBEEK, Harry and S. Rowland. (1979). "Are injuring and killing at work crimes?" *Osgoode Hall Law Journal,* 17, pp. 506–594.

GLOBAL UNIONS. (2004, Nov. 2). "Colombia: Global Unions condemn expulsion of international trade unionists." Global Unions Home Page, News, http://www.global-unions.org/displaydocument.asp?DocType=PressRelease&Index=991210835&Language=EN, [Apr. 15, 2005].

GODARD, John. (2005). *Industrial relations, the economy and society* (3rd ed.). Concord, ON: Captus Press.

———. (2003). "Do labor laws matter? The density decline and convergence thesis revisited." *Industrial Relations,* 42:3. pp. 458–492.

———. (2001). "Beyond the high-performance paradigm? An analysis in variation in Canadian managerial perceptions of reform programme effectiveness." In *British Journal of Industrial Relations,* 39:1, pp. 25–52.

———. (1994). *Industrial relations: The economy and society.* Toronto: McGraw-Hill Ryerson. See also the 2nd edition of this book (Toronto: Captus, 2000).

———. (1991). "The progressive HRM paradigm: A theoretical and empirical re-examination." *Relations Industrielles,* 46.

GODARD, John and Thomas Kochan. (1982). "Canadian management under collective bargaining." In Morley Gunderson, Allan Ponak, and Daphne G. Taras (Eds.), *Union-management relations in Canada* (1st ed.).

GOETSCHY, Janine and Annette Jobert. (1993). "Industrial relations in France." In Greg Bamber and Russell Lansbury (Eds.), *International and comparative industrial relations* (2nd ed.).

GOLD, Alan. (1993, May). Conversation with the author in Montreal.

GOLDBERG, Stephen. (1989). "Grievance mediation: A successful alternative to labor arbitration." *Negotiation Journal,* 5.

GOLDBLATT, H. (1974). *Justice denied.* Toronto: Labour Council of Metropolitan Toronto.

GOMEZ, Rafael, Morley Gunderson, and Noah Meltz. (2002). "Comparing youth and adult desire for unionization in Canada." *British Journal of Industrial Relations,* 40:3, pp. 521–542.

GOSPEL, Howard and C. Littler. (1982). *Managerial strategies and industrial relations.* London: Heineman.

GOULDEN, Joseph. (1972). *Meany.* New York: Atheneum.

GRAHAM, Katherine. (1995). "Collective bargaining in the municipal sector." In G. Swimmer and M. Thompson (Eds.), *Public sector collective bargaining in Canada.*

GRANT, Michel. (2000). "Quebec." In M. Thompson et al. (Eds.), *Regional differences in industrial relations.* No place of publication given: Canadian Industrial Relations Association.

———. (1992). "Industrial relations in the clothing industry: Lessons for survival." In R. Chaykowski and A. Verma (Eds.), *Industrial relations in Canadian industry.*

GREEN, Sara Jane. (1998, Sept. 9). "Catholic teachers angry at being on the picket line." *Globe & Mail*, p. A7a.

GUNDERSON, Morley. (1986). "Alternative methods for dealing with permanent layoffs and plant closings." In W.C. Riddell (Ed.), *Adapting to change: Labour market adjustment in Canada*. Toronto: U of Toronto Press. Reprinted in *Labour law*.

GUNDERSON, Morley and Douglas Hyatt. (2005) "Union impact on compensation, productivity, and management of the organization." In Morley Gunderson, Allan Ponak, and Daphne G. Taras (Eds.), *Union-management relations in Canada*, (5th ed.). Toronto: Pearson. Use has also been made of the same authors' chapter on the same topic from the 4th (2001) edition of the book, the 3rd (1995) edition of the book, and of Gunderson's chapter in the 2nd (1989) edition of the same book.

GUNDERSON, Morley and Allen Ponak. (1995). "Industrial relations." In Morley Gunderson, Allan Ponak, and Daphne G. Taras (Eds.), *Union-management relations in Canada* (3rd ed.).

GUNDERSON, Morley and Frank Reid. (1995). "Public sector strikes in Canada." In G. Swimmer and M. Thompson (Eds.), *Public sector collective bargaining in Canada*.

————. (1998). "Worksharing and working time issues in Canada." Montreal: Institute for Research in Public Policy.

GUNDERSON, Morley and W.C. Riddell. (1993). *Labour market economics: Theory, evidence and policy in Canada* (3rd ed.). Toronto: McGraw-Hill Ryerson.

GUNDERSON, Morley, Douglas Hyatt, and Allen Ponak. (2001). "Strikes and dispute resolution." In Morley Gunderson, Allan Ponak, and Daphne G. Taras (Eds.), *Union-management relations in Canada* (4th ed.). Use has also been made of the same authors' strike chapter from the 3rd (1995) edition of the same book, and of the strike chapter by John Anderson and Morley Gunderson from this book's 1st (1982) edition.

GUNDERSON, Morley, Douglas Hyatt, and Craig Riddell (1999). *Pay differences between the government and private sectors*. Ottawa: Canadian Policy Research Networks.

GUNDERSON, Morley, Allen Ponak, and Daphne Gottlieb Taras (Eds.). (2000). *Union-management relations in Canada* (4th ed). Toronto: Addison Wesley Longman.

GUNDERSON, Morley, Robert Hebdon, Douglas Hyatt, and Allen Ponak. (2005). "Strikes and dispute resolution." In Morley Gunderson, Allan Ponak, and Daphne G. Taras (Eds.), *Union-management relations in Canada* (5th ed.). Toronto: Pearson Addison Wesley.

HAIVEN, Judy and Larry Haiven. (2003). "Health care strikes and emergency services in Canada: The dilemma." *Workplace Gazette*, 6:2, pp. 73–83.

HAIVEN, Larry. (1995). "Industrial relations in health care: Regulation, conflict and transition to the 'wellness model.'" In G. Swimmer and M. Thompson (Eds.), *Public sector collective bargaining in Canada*.

————. (1990). "Hegemony and the workplace: The role of arbitration." In L. Haiven, S. McBride, and J. Shields (Eds.), *Regulating labour*. Toronto: Garamond.

HAIVEN, Larry, Stephen McBride, and John Shields. (1990). "The state, neo-conservatism, and industrial relations." In *Regulating labour*.

HALPERN, Norman. (1984). "Sociotechnical systems design: The Shell Sarnia experience." In J.B. Cunningham and T.H. White (Eds.), *Quality of working life: Contemporary cases*. Ottawa: Supply and Services (Labour Canada publication).

HAMMARSTROM, Olle. (1993). "Industrial relations in Sweden." In Greg Bamber and Russell Lansbury (Eds.), *International and comparative industrial relations* (2nd ed.).

HANNIGAN, John. (1986). "Laboured relations: Reporting industrial relations news in Canada." Toronto: U of Toronto Centre for Industrial Relations.

HAWORTH, Nigel. (1993). "Unions in crisis: Deregulation and reform of the Asian union movement." In S. Frenkel (Ed.), *Organized labor in the Asia-Pacific region*.

HEBDON, Robert. (1992). "Ontario's no-strike laws: A test of the safety valve hypothesis." In *Proceedings of the 28th Annual Conference of the Canadian Industrial Relations Association*.

HEBDON, Robert P. and Robert N. Stern. (2003). "Do public sector strike bans really prevent conflict?" *Industrial Relations*, 42:3, pp. 493–512.

HÉBERT, Gérard. (1995). "Public sector collective bargaining in Quebec." In G. Swimmer and M. Thompson (Eds.), *Public sector collective bargaining in Canada.*

HENEMAN, Herbert. (1969). "Toward a general conceptual system of industrial relations: How do we get there?" In Gerald Somers (Ed.), *Essays in industrial relations theory.* Ames, IA: Iowa State U Press.

———. (1960, July). "Manpower management: New wrapping on old merchandise." In U of Minnesota Industrial Relations Center "Special Release" 2. Reprinted in *Personnel and labour relations.*

HENRY, Manon. (2004). "Union membership in Canada." *Workplace Gazette,* 7:3. Ottawa: Workplace Information Directorate, Human Resources and Skills Development Canada.

HERON, Craig. (1996). *The Canadian labour movement: A short history.* Toronto: Lorimer.

———. (1989). *The Canadian labour movement: A short history.* Toronto: Lorimer.

———. (1984). "Labourism and the Canadian working class." *Labour/Le Travail,* 13 (spring). Reprinted in *Canadian labour history.*

HERTZ, Noreena. (2001, Nov.). "As governments abandon public sphere, corporations take over." *CCPA Monitor,* 8:6.

HÉTHY, Lajos. (1991). "Industrial relations in Eastern Europe: Recent development and trends." In R. Adams (Ed.), *Comparative industrial relations.*

HOLMAN, Worthington. (1904). "A 5000 brain-power organization." *System,* 4:2 (Aug.). Reprinted in *Personnel and labour relations.*

HRDC (Human Resources Development Canada). (1999, May 10). "Statistical analysis: Occupational injuries and fatalities, Canada." Ottawa: HRDC.

———. (1994). Federal preventive mediation program description.

HRSDC (Human Resources and Skills Development Canada). (2005a). *Chronological perspectives on work stoppages in Canada,* http://www110.hrdc-drhc.gc.ca/millieudetravail_workplace/chrono/index.cfm/doc/english, April 14.

———. (2005b) "Summary of general private sector collective bargaining legislation." *Industrial Relations Legislation in Canada,* http://www.hrsdc.gc.ca/asp/gateway.asp?hr=en/lp/spila/clli/irlc/01industrial_relations_legislation_canada.shtml&hs=lzl,April 7.

HUNNICUTT, Benjamin. (1988). *Work without end: Abandoning shorter hours for the right to work.* Philadelphia: Temple U Press.

HYMAN, Richard. (2001). "The Europeanisation—or the erosion—of industrial relations?" *Industrial Relations Journal,* 32:4, pp. 280–294.

———. (1983). "A critical view of industrial democracy systems." In *Essays in collective bargaining and industrial democracy.* Toronto: CCH Canadian. Excerpt reprinted in *Labour law.*

———. (1975). *Industrial relations: A Marxist introduction.* London: MacMillan.

ICHNIOWSKI, Casey. (1986). "The effects of grievance activity on productivity." *Industrial and Labor Relations Review,* 40.

ILO (International Labour Office). (2005). Data on trade union membership and informal sector membership provided electronically after personal request to ILO, April 11, 2005.

———. (2004). *Handbook of Labour Statistics.* Geneva: ILO.

———. (1997). *World Labour Report,* 1997–98. Geneva: ILO.

IMF (International Metalworkers' Federation). (2004, Oct. 15). "GM workers to hold European day of action." IMF Home Page, News Archive, http://www.imfmetal.org/main/index.cfm?n=47&l=2&c=9896.

JACKSON, Andrew. (1997). Chief Economist, CLC. Presentation at "32 Hours" conference, Toronto, November 22.

JACKSON, Edward T. (1998). "Worker ownership and community economic development." Paper presented to CLC conference on Jobs and the Economy, Ottawa, February.

———. (1997). "ETIs: A tool for responsible pension fund investment." *Making Waves,* 8:2.

JACKSON, Edward T. and François Lamontagne. (1995). "Adding value: The economic and social impacts of labour-sponsored venture capital corporations on their investee firms." Ottawa: CLMPC (Canadian Labour Market and Productivity Centre).

JACKSON, Edward T. and Jon Peirce. (1990). "Mobilizing capital for regional development." Ottawa: Economic Council of Canada Local Development Paper #21.

JACKSON, Richard. (2001). "Collective bargaining legislation." In Morley Gunderson, Allan Ponak, and Daphne G. Taras (Eds.), *Union-management relations in Canada* (4th ed.).

———. (1995). "Police and firefighter labour relations in Canada." In G. Swimmer and M. Thompson (Eds.), *Public sector collective bargaining in Canada*.

JACOBI, Otlo, Berndt Keller, and Werner Muller-Jentsch. (1992). "Germany: codetermining the future." In A. Ferner and R. Hyman (Eds.), *Industrial relations in the new Europe*.

JAMIESON, S.M. (1979). *Industrial conflict in Canada, 1966–1975*. Discussion Paper No. 142, Centre for Study of Inflation and Productivity, Economic Council of Canada. December.

JIMENEZ, Ramon. (1993). "The Philippines." In Stephen Deery and Richard Mitchell (Eds.), *Labour law and industrial relations in Asia*.

JOHNSON, Susan. (2004). "The Impact of mandatory votes on the Canada–U.S. union density gap: A note." *Industrial Relations*, 43:2, pp. 356–363.

———. (2002a). "Canadian union density 1980–1998 and prospects for the future: An empirical investigation." *Canadian Public Policy*, 28:3, pp. 333–349.

———. (2002b). "Card check or mandatory representation vote? How the type of union recognition procedure affects union certification success." *The Economic Journal*, 112 (Apr.), pp. 344–361.

JOHNSTON, T.L. (1962). *Collective bargaining in Sweden*. London: Allen and Unwin.

JOYCE, George. (1996). Conciliator, Nfld. Ministry of Labour. Statements made to various industrial relations classes at Memorial University concerning the Ministry's preventive mediation program.

KALLEBERG, Arne L. (2000). "Nonstandard employment relations: Part-time, temporary and contract work." *Annual Review of Sociology*, 26, pp. 341–365.

KASSALOW, Everett. (1963). "Unions in the new and developing countries." In E. Kassalow (Ed.), *National labor movements in the postwar world*. Chicago: Northwestern U Press.

KATZ, Harry C., Wonduck Lee, and Joohee Lee (Eds.). (2004). *The New structure of labor relations: Tripartism and decentralization*. Ithaca: ILR Press, Cornell University Press.

KEALEY, Gregory. (1985). "The Canadian working-class: Past, present and future." In *Perspectives on the Atlantic Canada labour movement and the working class experience*.

———. (1984). "1919: The Canadian labour revolt." *Labour/Le Travail*, 13 (spring). Reprinted in *Canadian labour history*.

KEALEY, Gregory and Bryan Palmer. (1982). *Dreaming of what might be: The Knights of Labour in Ontario, 1880–1900*. Cambridge: Cambridge U Press.

———. (1981). "Bonds of unity: The Knights of Labor in Ontario." *Histoire Sociale/Social History*. Reprinted in MacDowell and Radforth (Eds.), *Canadian working class history*.

KELLER, Berndt. (1991). "The role of the state as corporate actor in industrial relations systems." In R. Adams (Ed.), *Comparative industrial relations*.

KERVIN, John. (1989). "The science of bargaining." In A. Sethi (Ed.), *Collective bargaining in Canada*. Scarborough: Nelson.

———. (1988). "Sociology, psychology and industrial relations." In G. Hébert, H. Jain, and N. Meltz (Eds.), *The state of the art in industrial relations*.

———. (1984). "Strikes: Toward a typology of causes." In *Proceedings of 21st Annual Meeting of Canadian Industrial Relations Association*. Guelph, ON.

KESSELMAN, John. (2004, Aug. 21) "Why wasn't mandatory retirement retired long ago?" *Globe and Mail*, p. A15.

KILPATRICK, Ken. (1998, March 9) "Maple Leaf vote 'won on fear.'" *Toronto Star*, p. B1.

KIMMEL, J. and L.M. Powell. (1999). "Moonlighting trends and related policy issues in Canada and the United States." *Canadian Public Policy/Analyse de Politiques*, 25:2, pp. 207–231.

KING, Carlyle. (1944). "The CCF sweeps Saskatchewan." *Canadian Forum*, (July). Reprinted in *Forum*.

KJELLBERG, Anders. (1992). "Sweden: Can the model survive?" In A. Ferner and R. Hyman (Eds.), *Industrial relations in the new Europe*.

KOCHAN, Thomas. (1980). *Collective bargaining and industrial relations.* Homewood, IL: Irwin.

KOCHAN, Thomas and Paul Barrocci. (1985). *Human resource management and industrial relations: Text, readings, and cases.* Boston: Little Brown.

KOCHAN, Thomas, Robert McKersie, and Peter Cappelli. (1984). "Strategic choice and industrial relations theory." *Industrial Relations,* 23:1.

KUMAR, Pradeep. (1993). *From uniformity to divergence: Industrial relations in Canada and the United States.* Kingston: Queen's IRC Press.

KUMAR, Pradeep and Noah Meltz. (1992). "Industrial relations in the Canadian automobile industry." In R. Chaykowski and A. Verma (Eds.), *Industrial relations in Canadian industry.*

KUMAR, Pradeep, Gregor Murray, and Sylvain Schetagne. (1998). "Adapting to change: Union priorities in the 1990s." *Workplace Gazette,* (fall).

KUNDE, Diana. (1998, October 10). "Skilful salary negotiation can pay off for job seekers." *Ottawa Citizen,* p. K5.

KURUVILLA, Sarosh and Ponniah Arudsorthy. (1995). "Economic development strategy, government labour policy and firm-level industrial relations practices in Malaysia." In A. Verma et al. (Eds.), *Employment relations in the growing Asian economies.*

KUWAHARA, Yasuo. (1993). "Industrial relations in Japan." In Greg Bamber and Russell Lansbury (Eds.), *International and comparative industrial relations* (2nd ed.).

LABERGE, Roy. (1976). *The labour beat: An introduction to unions.* Ottawa: Media Algonquin.

LACEY, Robert. (1986). *Ford: The men and the machine.* Toronto: McClelland & Stewart.

LAFFER, Kingsley. (1974). "Is industrial relations an academic discipline?" *Journal of Industrial Relations,* 16 (Mar.).

LAKEY, Jack. (1998, May 14). "Winery boycotted for backing Tories." *Toronto Star,* p. B1.

LANCASTER House. (2005a). "Quebec tribunal condemns segregation of black farm workers" *Labour Law On-line,* May 12, www.lancasterhouse.com.

_____. (2005b). "Racism in Ontario's jails: Court upholds sweeping human rights." *Labour Law On-line,* January 5, www.lancasterhouse.com.

———. (2004). Labour Arbitration Conference 2004 (Toronto): Programs, Cases, and Materials. Except as noted, all cases in the "Emerging Trends in Grievance Arbitration" section come from this packet.

_____. (2001). Various issues of Lancaster House's *Collective Agreement Reporter,* containing analyses of changing labour legislation.

LARSON, Simeon and Bruce Nissen (Eds.). (1987). *Theories of the labor movement.* Detroit: Wayne State U Press.

LAWSON, Chris. (1998). Communications Specialist, CUPW. Personal interview, September 8.

LAXER, James. (1986). *Leap of faith: Free trade and the future of Canada.* Edmonton: Hurtig.

LEACY, F.H. (Ed.). 1999. *Historical statistics of Canada.* Ottawa: Statistics Canada.

LEGGETT, Chris. (1993). "Singapore." In Stephen Deery and Richard Mitchell (Eds.), *Labour law and industrial relations in Asia.*

LEMELIN, Maurice. (1989). "Quality of working life and collective bargaining: Can they co-exist?" In A. Sethi (Ed.), *Collective bargaining in Canada.* Scarborough: Nelson.

LEWICKI, Roy, David Saunders, and John Minton. (1997). *Essentials of Negotiation.* Chicago and Toronto: Irwin.

LEWICKI, Roy J., Bruce Barry, David M. Saunders, and John W. Minton. (2003). *Negotiation* (4th ed.). New York: McGraw-Hill/Irwin.

LEWICKI, Roy J., David M. Saunders, Bruce Barry, and John W. Minton. (2004). *Essentials of negotiation* (3rd ed.). New York: McGraw-Hill/Irwin.

LEWIN, David. (1999). "Theoretical and empirical research on the grievance process and arbitration: A critical review." In *Employment dispute resolution and worker rights.*

LEWIS, Gregg. (1986). *Union relative wage effects: A survey.* Chicago: U of Chicago Press.

LIPSET, Seymour Martin and Noah Meltz. (1998). "Canadian and American attitudes toward work and institutions." *Perspectives on Work*, 1:3.

LIPSET, Seymour Martin, Noah Meltz, and Rafael Gomez. (2004). *The paradox of American unionism: Why Americans like unions more than Canadians do but join much less.* Ithaca, N.Y.: ILR Press.

LIPSIG-MUMME, Carla. (2005). "Trade unions and labour-relations systems in comparative perspective." In Morley Gunderson, Allan Ponak, and Daphne G. Taras (Eds.), *Union-management relations in Canada* (5th ed.). Toronto: Pearson Addison Wesley.

———. (2001). "Trade unions and labour relations systems in comparative perspective." In Morley Gunderson, Allan Ponak, and Daphne G. Taras (Eds.), *Union-management relations in Canada* (4th ed.).

———. (1995). "Labour strategies in the new social order: A political economy perspective." In Morley Gunderson, Allan Ponak, and Daphne G. Taras (Eds.), *Union-management relations in Canada* (3rd ed.).

———. (1989). "Canadian and American unions respond to economic crisis." *Journal of Industrial Relations*, 31.

LIPTON, Charles. (c. 1973 [1967]). *The trade union movement of Canada, 1827–1959.* Toronto: NC Press.

LLCG (Labour Law Casebook Group). (2004). *Labour and employment law: Cases, materials, and commentary* (7th ed.). Toronto: Irwin Law.

———. (1991). *Labour law: Cases, materials and commentary* (5th ed.). Kingston: Queen's IRC Press. Use has also been made of the draft 4th edition (1984) of the same book.

LOGAN, Harold. (1948). *Trade unions in Canada.* Toronto: Macmillan.

LOKAN, Andrew and Maryth Yachnin. (2004). "From *Weber* to *Parry Sound:* The expanded scope of arbitration." *Canadian Labour and Employment Law Journal*, 11, pp. 1–29.

LORWIN, Val. (1954). *The French labor movement.* Cambridge: Harvard U Press.

LOW, Stephen. (1963). "The role of trade-unions in the newly independent countries of Africa." In *National labor movements in the postwar world.*

LOWE, Graham. (2001a). *Employer of choice? Workplace innovation in government: A synthesis report.* Ottawa: Canadian Policy Research Networks.

———. (2001b, May 16). "Job quality: The key to attracting, developing and retaining workers of all ages." Keynote address to the IMPA-CANADA National Training Conference, Fredericton, NB, Ottawa: Canadian Policy Research Networks.

———. (1980). *Bank unionization in Canada: A preliminary analysis.* Toronto: U of Toronto Centre for Industrial Relations.

LOWE, Mick. (2001, Apr. 3). "Solidarity? Whatever..." In *Straight Goods.*

LOXLEY, John. (1998). *Interdependence, disequilibrium and growth: Reflections on the political economy of north-south relations at the turn of the century.* Ottawa: IDRC.

LUND, John and Cheryl L. Maranto. (1996). "Public sector labor law: An update." In Dale Belman, Morley Gunderson, and Douglas Hyatt (Eds.), *Public sector employment in a time of transition.* Madison, WI: Industrial Relations Research Association.

LYNK, Michael. (2002). "Disability and the duty to accommodate: An arbitrator's perspective." *Labour Arbitration Yearbook*, 1:51, pp. 51–122.

MacDONALD, Robert. (1967). "Collective bargaining in the postwar period." *Industrial and Labor Relations Review*, 20:4 (July). Reprinted in *Personnel and labour relations.*

MacDOWELL, Laurel Sefton. (1982). "The 1943 steel strike against wartime wage controls." *Labour/Le Travailleur*, 10.

———. (1978). "The formation of the Canadian industrial relations system during World War II." *Labour/Le Travailleur*, 3. Reprinted in MacDowell and Radforth (Eds.), *Canadian working class history.*

MacDOWELL, L.S. and I. Radforth (Eds.). (1991). *Canadian working class history.* Toronto: Canadian Scholars' Press.

MacLEOD, Leslie. (2000). *Ontario management board secretariat final report on the Grievance Administration Project*. Toronto: Management Board Secretariat.

MAKI, Dennis. (1982). "Political parties and trade union growth." *Relations Industrielles*, 37.

MALLES, Paul. (1976). *Canadian labour standards in law, agreement, and practice*. Ottawa: Supply and Services.

MANLEY, John. (1986). "Communists and autoworkers: The struggle for industrial unionism in the Canadian automobile industry, 1925–1936." *Labour/Le Travail*, 17 (spring). Reprinted in *Canadian working class history*.

MANUSPHAIBOOL, Supachia. (1993). "Thailand." In Stephen Deery and Richard Mitchell (Eds.), *Labour law and industrial relations in Asia*.

MARGINSON, Paul and Keith Sisson. (2002) "European dimensions to collective bargaining: New symmetries within an asymmetric process?" *Industrial Relations Journal*, 33:4, pp. 332–350.

MARSDEN, Richard. (2001). "Labour history and the development of modern capitalism." In Morley Gunderson, Allan Ponak, and Daphne G. Taras (Eds.), *Union-management relations in Canada* (4th ed.).

MARSHALL, Katherine. (2001). "Part-time by choice." In *Perspectives on Work and Income*, (spring), pp. 20–27. Ottawa: Statistics Canada.

MARSHALL, Stan. (1998). Research Officer, CUPE. Telephone interview, September 9.

MARTIN, Roderick and Anamaria Cristescu-Martin. (2002). "Employment relations in Central and Eastern Europe in 2001: An emerging capitalist periphery." *Industrial Relations Journal*, 33:5, pp. 523–536.

MARTINELLO, Felice. (2004). "Fact sheet on unionization." *Perspectives on Labour and Income*, 5:8, Ottawa.

———. (2000). "Mr. Harris, Mr. Rae and union activity in Ontario." *Canadian Public Policy*, 26:1.

———. (1996). "Correlates of certification application success in British Columbia, Saskatchewan, and Manitoba." *Relations Industrielles*, 51.

MASON, Rita, Janine Geddie, and Carol Dakai (Eds.). (2004) *Canadian master labour guide* (18th ed.). Toronto: CCH Canadian Limited.

MATHEWSON, Stanley. (1931–1932). "A survey of personnel management in 195 concerns." *Personnel Journal*, 10:4. Reprinted in *Personnel and labour relations*.

MATSUDA, Yasuhiko. (1993). "Japan." In Stephen Deery and Richard Mitchell (Eds.), *Labour law and industrial relations in Asia*.

MAXWELL, Judith (2001). "Rethinking institutions for work in the new economy." Presentation to Canadian Industrial Relations Association, Quebec City, May 27.

MAY, Kathryn (1998, July 30). "Two hundred thousand share in landmark award." *Ottawa Citizen*, p. A1.

McALASTAR, Trish (2001, Jan. 18). "Making the grade." *Globe & Mail*.

McCALLUM, Margaret. (1986). "Keeping women in their place: The minimum wage in Canada, 1910–1925." *Labour/le Travail*. Reprinted in MacDowell and Radforth (Eds.), *Canadian working class history*.

McCAMBLY, James. (1990, August 21). "Why Canadian labor needs to stay politically neutral." *Globe & Mail*, p. A15. Reprinted in A. Craig and N. Solomon. *The system of industrial relations in Canada* (4th ed.).

McCORMACK, Ross. (1975). "The industrial workers of the world in Western Canada, 1905–1914." *Historical Papers*. Reprinted in MacDowell and Radforth (Eds.), *Canadian working class history*.

McINTOSH, Robert. (1987). "The boys in the Nova Scotia coal mines, 1873–1923." *Acadiensis*, 16:2 (spring). Reprinted in *Labour and working-class history in Atlantic Canada*.

McKAY, Ian. (1991). "None but skilled workmen." From *The craft transformed*. Reprinted in MacDowell and Radforth (Eds.), *Canadian working class history*.

———. (1983). "Strikes in the Maritimes: 1901–1914." *Acadiensis*, 13:1 (fall). Reprinted in *Canadian labour history*.

McKINLEY, Patrick. (1997, August 22). "Labour group to fold." *Winnipeg Free Press*, p. B1.

McPHILLIPS, David. (2001). "Employment legislation." In Morley Gunderson, Allan Ponak, and Daphne G. Taras (Eds.), *Union-management relations in Canada* (4th ed.). Some use has also been made of the employment legislation chapter by McPhillips and Geoffrey England in the 2nd (1989) and 3rd (1995) editions of the same book.

MELTZ, Noah. (1989a). "Industrial relations: Balancing efficiency and equity." In J. Barbash and K. Barbash (Eds.), *Theories and concepts in comparative industrial relations*. Columbia, SC: U of South Carolina Press.

———. (1989b). "Interstate versus interprovincial differences in union density." *Industrial Relations*, 28.

———. (1985). "Labor movements in Canada and the United States." In Thomas Kochan (Ed.), *Challenges and choices facing American labor*. Cambridge: MIT Press.

MILLS, D. Quinn. (1989). *Labor-management relations* (4th ed.). New York: McGraw-Hill.

MINISTRY of Labour. (2005). "Ontario's workplaces return to balanced labour relations: *Labour Relations Statute Law Amendment Act*, 2005 receives Royal assent," News Release, June 13, 05-78, http://www.labour.gov.on.ca/english/news/2005/05-78.html, [Oct. 10, 2005].

MISHEL, Lawrence. (1986). "The structural determinants of union bargaining power." *Industrial and Labor Relations Review*, 40:1.

MITCHELL, Nancy. (1996). "Coming to a national park in your area: ETOs." *Alliance*, (summer).

MITTAL, Anuradha and Frederic Mousseau. (2005, Apr. 6). "The poor get poorer." *Ottawa Citizen*, p. A17.

MONGER, Joanne. (2004). "International comparisons of labour disputes in 2002." *Labour Market Trends* (Apr.). Newport, South Wales: Office for National Statistics.

MOOGK, Peter. (1976). "In the darkness of a basement: Craftsmen's associations in early French Canada." *Canadian Historical Review*, 58. Reprinted in MacDowell and Radforth (Eds.), *Canadian working class history*.

MORISSETTE, René and Julio Miguel Rosa. (2003). *Alternative work practices and quit rates: Methodological issues and empirical evidence for Canada*. Ottawa: Statistics Canada. Business and Labour Market Analysis Division.

MORTON, Desmond. (1995). "The history of the Canadian labour movement." In Morley Gunderson, Allan Ponak, and Daphne G. Taras (Eds.), *Union-management relations in Canada* (3rd ed.). Use has also been made of Morton's labour history chapter in the 1st and 2nd (1982 and 1989) editions of the same book.

MORTON, Desmond and Terry Copp. (1980). *Working people*. Toronto: Deneau & Greenberg. Some, although less, use has also been made of Morton's 1984 and 1990 editions of the same book.

MOUAT, Jeremy. (1990). "The genesis of Western exceptionalism: British Columbia's hard-rock miners, 1895–1903." *Canadian Historical Review*, 71. Reprinted in MacDowell and Radforth (Eds.), *Canadian working class history*.

MUIR, J. Douglas. (1971). "Decentralized bargaining: Its problems and direction in the public education systems of Ontario and the Western provinces." *Relations Industrielles*, 26.

MULLAN, David. (2004). "*Voice construction:* One swallow does not a summer make?" *Canadian Labour and Employment Law Journal*, 11, pp. 113–138.

MURDOCK, Rebecca. (1997). "Organizing the service sector: The fight for 40 at Starbucks." *Canadian Dimension*, 31:6 (Nov.).

MURRAY, Gregor. (2001). "Unions: Membership, structure, actions and challenges." In Morley Gunderson, Allan Ponak, and Daphne G. Taras (Eds.), *Union-management relations in Canada* (4th ed.). Some use has also been made of Murray's chapter on unions in the 3rd (1995) edition of the same book.

MURRAY, Thomas. (1971, March). "It's hell in personnel." Reprinted in *Personnel and labour relations*.

NAUMETZ, Tim. (2001, Aug. 8). "PS hopes to boost morale with free tuques." *Ottawa Citizen*.

NELSON, Joyce. (1998). "The art of the deal." *Canadian Forum*, April.

NG, Ignace. (1992). "The probability of union membership in the private sector." *Relations Industrielles*, 47.

NG, Ignace and Ali Dastmalchian. (1989). "Determinants of grievance outcomes: A case study." *Industrial and Labor Relations Review*, 42:3.

NIVEN, M.M. (1967). *Personnel management, 1913–63: The growth of personnel management and the development of the institute.* London: Institute of Personnel Management.

NOLAN, Dennis and Roger Abrams. (1997). "Trends in private sector grievance arbitration." In J. Stern and J. Najita (Eds.), *Labor arbitration under fire.* Ithaca and London: Cornell U ILR Press.

NYLAND, Chris. (1989). *Reduced worktime and the management of production.* Cambridge: Cambridge U Press.

OFL (Ontario Federation of Labour). (1994). *Annual program report.* Toronto: OFL.

O'HARA, Bruce. (1993). *Working harder isn't working.* Vancouver: New Star.

ONTARIO Ministry of Labour. (2004a). *Backgrounder: Labour Relations Statute Law Amendment Act, 2004.* 04-120.

———. (2004b). "Ending mandatory retirement in Ontario." Backgrounder 04-92, August 18, Toronto: OML, http://www.gov.on.ca/LAB/english/news/2004/04-92b1.html.

OPSEU (Ontario Public Service Employees' Union). (2005, March 17). "OPSEU welcomes Ottawa mayor's change of heart on ad ban policy, considers Charter challenge," OPSEU Online, News Releases, http://www.opseu.org/news/Press2005/mar17b2005.htm.

———. (2000a, Oct. 3). "Mine mill remains determined to resist concessions." From OPSEU Cambrian College Local 655 website.

———. (2000b, Sept. 27). "Resolution passed by Sudbury Regional Council." From OPSEU Cambrian College Local 655 website.

OSTERMAN, Paul. (1988). *Employment futures: Reorganization, dislocation, and public policy.* New York: Oxford University Press.

OSTRY, Sylvia and Mahmood Zaidi. (1979). *Labour economics in Canada* (3rd ed.). Toronto: MacMillan.

OWEN, John. (1989). *Reduced working hours: Cure for unemployment or economic burden?* Baltimore and London: Johns Hopkins U Press.

OWEN, William. (1940–1941). "Decentralize personnel work." *Personnel Journal,* 19. Reprinted in *Personnel and labour relations: An evolutionary approach.*

PACHOLIK, Barb. (1998, April 3). "Ruling confirms gays entitled to same benefits as heterosexuals." *Saskatoon Star-Phoenix,* p. A3.

PALMER, Bryan. (1986). "Listening to history rather than historians: Reflections on working-class history." *Studies in Political Economy,* 20 (summer). Reprinted in *Canadian labour history.*

PANITCH, Leo and Donald Swartz. (1988). *The assault on trade union freedoms: From coercion to consent revisited.* Toronto: Garamond.

PARK, Young-Bum and M.B. Lee. (1995). "Economic development, globalization, and practices in industrial relations and human resource management in Korea." In A. Verma et al. (Eds.), *Employment relations in the growing Asian economies.*

PATTERSON, John. (1901). "Altruism and sympathy as factors in works administration." *Engineering Magazine,* 20 (Jan.). Reprinted in *Personnel and labour relations.*

PEACH, David and David Kuechle. (1975). *The practice of industrial relations.* Toronto and New York: McGraw-Hill Ryerson.

PEIRCE, Jon. (2003). *Canadian Industrial Relations* (2nd ed.). Scarborough: Prentice-Hall.

———. (2000a). *Canadian Industrial Relations* (1st ed.). Scarborough: Prentice-Hall.

———. (2000b). "The case for a shorter work week." Ottawa: Carleton Centre for the Study of Training, Investment and Economic Restructuring.

———. (1998a, May 14). "Plenty of militancy left in Canadian unions." *Toronto Star,* p. A14.

———. (1998b, March 20). "Jobless rate still far too high." *Toronto Star.*

———. (1996). "The sad saga of the late and little-lamented Newfoundland 'white paper' provisions on labour relations." In *Proceedings of the 1995 Canadian Industrial Relations conference.* Montreal.

———. (1995). "George Meany and the decline of the American labour movement." St. John's: Memorial U School of Business, working paper.

———. (1993). "An end to American exceptionalism?" In *The industrial relations system: Proceedings of the 29th Conference of the Canadian Industrial Relations Association.* Charlottetown, PE.

———. (1989). "Exclusions from collective bargaining legislation in Canada." Unpublished Master of Industrial Relations essay. Kingston: Queen's U Industrial Relations Centre.

———. (1987). "Collective bargaining over technological change in Canada: A quantitative and historical analysis." Ottawa: Economic Council of Canada Discussion Paper #338.

PELLEGRINI, Claudio. (1993). "Industrial relations in Italy." In Greg Bamber and Russell Lansbury (Eds.), *International and comparative industrial relations* (2nd ed.).

PERLMAN, Selig. (1966 [1929]). *A theory of the labor movement.* New York: Kelley.

PETERSON, Scott. (2005, May 5). "Weston cites big-box stores for 20% drop at Loblaw profit: Expansion to continue." *National Post*, p. FP5.

PICARD, Laurent (Chair). (1967). *Report of the inquiry commission on the St. Lawrence ports.* Ottawa: Department of Labour.

PIPSC (Professional Institute of the Public Service of Canada). (2001, Dec. 17). "Canadian food inspection veterinarians walk off the job." PIPSC press release.

PONAK, Allen and Morley Gunderson. (1995). "Future directions for Canadian industrial relations." In Morley Gunderson, Allan Ponak, and Daphne G. Taras (Eds.), *Union-management relations in Canada* (3rd ed.).

PONAK, Allen and Corliss Olson. (1992). "Time delays in grievance arbitration." *Relations Industrielles*, 47.

PONAK, Allen and Mark Thompson. (2005). "Public-sector collective bargaining." In M. Gunderson, A. Ponak, and D. Taras (Eds.), *Union-management relations in Canada* (5th ed.). Toronto: Pearson (Addison-Wesley).

———. (2001). "Public sector collective bargaining." In Morley Gunderson, Allan Ponak, and Daphne G. Taras (Eds.), *Union-management relations in Canada* (3rd ed.). Use has also been made of the same chapter in the first three editions of this book (1982, 1989, 1995), written by one or both of the same authors in each case.

PONAK, Allen, W. Zerbe, S. Rose, and C. Olson. (1996). "Using event history analysis to model delay in grievance arbitration." *Industrial and Labor Relations Review*, 50, pp. 105–121.

POSNER, R. (1977). *Economic analysis of the law* (2nd ed.). Toronto: Little Brown. Excerpts reprinted in *Labour law.*

PPF (Public Policy Forum, 2000). *Levelling the path: Perspectives on labour management relations in the federal public service.* Ottawa: Public Policy Forum.

PRICE, Robert. (1991). "The comparative analysis of union growth." In R. Adams (Ed.), *Comparative industrial relations.*

PSAC (Public Service Alliance of Canada). (2005). "What we do," PSAC Home Page, http://www.psac-afpc.org/what/what-e.shtml, [Oct. 5, 2005].

———. (2004, Oct. 15). "PSAC negotiating teams recommend rejection of Treasury Board offer: One more settlement negotiated." PSAC website, News Releases, http://www.psac.com, [Oct. 19, 2005].

———. Various articles drawn from PSAC website, www.psac.com, 1999 through 2001, on National Gallery of Canada and CFB Goose Bay strikes. For more detail on the PSAC website, please see the Annotated List of Websites.

PSES (Public Service Employee Survey). (2002). Ottawa: Treasury Board of Canada Secretariat.

———. (1999). *Turning results into action.* Ottawa: Treasury Board of Canada Secretariat.

PSSRB (Public Service Staff Relations Board). (2001). *Union of Canadian Correctional Officers–CSN (Applicant) and Treasury Board (Correctional Service Canada) (Employer) and Public Service Alliance of Canada (Intervenor).* 2001 PSSRB 25, File 142-2-356. Before J.W. Potter, Deputy Chairperson.

———. (2000). *Union of Canadian Correctional Officers–CSN (Applicant) and Treasury Board (Correctional Service Canada) (Employer) and Public Service Alliance of Canada (Intervenor).* 2000 PSSRB 106, File 142-02-356; 150-02-49. Before Yvon Tarte, Chairperson.

QUARTER, Jack, I. Carmichael, J. Sousa, and S. Elgie. (2001). "Social investment by union-based pension funds and labour-sponsored investment firms in Canada." In *Relations Industrielles*, 56:1, pp. 92–113.

RADFORTH, Ian. (1991). Statements made during various labour history classes, U of Toronto, fall semester.

———. (1982). "Woodworkers and the mechanization of the pulpwood logging industry of Northern Ontario: 1950–1970." *Historical Papers/Communications historiques*. Reprinted in *Canadian labour history*.

RANDAZZO, Daniel. (1995). *The 1995 annotated Ontario Labour Relations Act*. Scarborough, ON: Carswell.

RAVENHORST, A.M. (1990). "Industrial relations in Korea: The backdrop to the current drama." *Comparative Labor Law Journal*, 11:3. Quoted in Park Young-Ki. (1993). "South Korea." In Stephen Deery and Richard Mitchell (Eds.), *Labour law and industrial relations in Asia*.

REID, Frank. (2001, Nov. 1). Talk on HRDC's short-term compensation policy (worksharing) at Canadian Institute conference.

———. (1982). "Wage-and-price controls in Canada." In Morley Gunderson, Allan Ponak, and Daphne G. Taras (Eds.), *Union-management relations in Canada* (3rd ed.).

REID, Frank and Noah Meltz. (2001). "Social, political, and economic environments." In Morley Gunderson, Allan Ponak, and Daphne G. Taras (Eds.), *Union-management relations in Canada* (4th ed.). Use has also been made of the same authors' chapter on the economy from the same book's 3rd (1995) edition, and from its 2nd (1989) edition, cited in the text as Meltz and Reid (1989).

REID, Frank, Noah M. Meltz, and Rafael Gomez. (2005). "Social, political, and economic environments." In *Union management relations in Canada* (5th ed.). Morley Gunderson, Allen Ponak, and Daphne G. Taras (Eds.). Toronto: Pearson Addison Wesley.

RENAUD, Stephane. (1997). "Unions and wages in Canada." In *Selected papers from the 33rd Annual Canadian Industrial Relations Conference*. Quebec City: CIRA.

REUTHER, Victor. (1976). *The brothers Reuther and the story of the UAW*. Boston: Houghton Mifflin.

REYNOLDS, David. (1995). "The right to strike in the public sector: A comparative analysis of Canada, Germany, Japan, and Sweden." Unpublished paper: St. John's, Nfld.

REYNOLDS, Lloyd. (1982). *Labor economics and labor relations* (8th ed.). Englewood Cliffs: Prentice-Hall.

RICHARD, K. Peter (Commissioner). (1997). *The Westray story: A predictable path to disaster*. Province of Nova Scotia (no place of publication given).

RICHARDSON, J. Albert. (1985). "The role of organized labour in today's Atlantic Canada." In *Perspectives on the Atlantic Canada labour movement and the working class experience*.

RIDDELL, Chris. (2001). "Union suppression and certification success." *Canadian Journal of Economics*, 34:2, pp. 396–410.

ROBB, Roberta. (1987). "Equal pay for work of equal value: Issues and policies." In *Canadian Public Policy*, 13. Reprinted in *Labour law*.

ROBERTS, Wayne and John Bullen. (1985). "A heritage of hope and struggle: Workers, unions, and politics in Canada, 1930–1982." In M. Cross and G. Kealey (Eds.), *Modern Canada 1930s–1980s*. Toronto: McClelland & Stewart. Reprinted in *Canadian labour history*.

ROBINSON, Archie. (1981). *George Meany and his times: A biography*. New York: Simon and Schuster.

ROBINSON, Ian. (1994). "NAFTA, social unionism, and labour movement power in Canada and the United States." *Relations Industrielles*, 49:4 (fall).

———. (1990). *Organizing labour: Exploring Canada–U.S. union density divergence in the post-war period*. PhD diss., Yale University, New Haven.

ROGOW, Robert. (1989a). "The structure of collective bargaining." In Amarjit Sethi (Ed.), *Collective bargaining in Canada*.

———. (1989b). "Collective bargaining law." In Amarjit Sethi (Ed.), *Collective bargaining in Canada*.

ROSE, Joseph. (2004a). "Competitiveness and collective bargaining in Canada." In *Workplace Gazette*, 7:1, pp. 68–77.

———. (2004b). "Public sector bargaining: From retrenchment to consolidation." *Relations Industrielles*, 59:2, pp. 271–294.

———. (2002). "The assault on schoolteacher bargaining in Ontario." Relations Industrielles, 57:1, pp. 100–128.

———. (2000). "The ghost of interest arbitration." *Canadian Labour and Employment Law Journal*, 8, pp. 253–289.

———. (1995). "The evolution of public sector unionism." In G. Swimmer and M. Thompson (Eds.), *Public sector collective bargaining in Canada.*

———. (1992). "Industrial relations in the construction industry in the 1980s." In R. Chaykowski and A. Verma (Eds.), *Industrial relations in Canadian industry.*

———. (1991). "The emergence of expedited arbitration." *Labour Arbitration Yearbook, I.*

———. (1987). "Innovative grievance arbitration systems." Hamilton: McMaster U Faculty of Business Research.

———. (1986a). "Legislative support for multi-employer bargaining: The Canadian experience." *Industrial and Labor Relations Review*, 40:1.

———. (1986b). "Statutory expedited grievance arbitration: The case of Ontario." *Arbitration Journal*, 41.

———. (1982). "Construction labour relations." In Morley Gunderson, Allan Ponak, and Daphne G. Taras (Eds.), *Union-management relations in Canada* (1ˢᵗ ed.).

ROSE, Joseph and Gary Chaison. (2001). "Unionism in Canada and the United States in the 21ˢᵗ century: The prospects for renewal." *Relations Industrielles*, 56:1, pp. 34–65.

———. (1990). "New measures of union organizing effectiveness." *Industrial Relations*, 29.

SACK, Jeffrey. (1994). *Winning cases at grievance arbitration.* Toronto: Lancaster House.

———. (1991). "The ability to pay in the public sector: A critical appraisal." *Labour Arbitration Yearbook*, 2, pp. 277–298.

SANDERSON, John. (1976). *Labour arbitrations and all that.* Toronto: Richard de Boo.

SASS, Bob. (1993). "The work environment board and the limits of social democracy in Canada." *International Journal of Health Services*, 23.

———. (1989). "The art of collective bargaining." In Amarjit Sethi (Ed.), *Collective bargaining in Canada.*

SAUVÉ, Robert. (1971). "La négociation collective sectorielle." *Relations Industrielles*, 26:1.

SCHELLING, Thomas. (1957). "Bargaining, communication, and limited war." *Journal of Conflict Resolution*, 1:1.

SCHETAGNE, Sylvain. (2001). *Building bridges across generations: A response to the aging workforce.* Ottawa: Canadian Council on Social Development.

SCHEUER, Steen. (1992). "Denmark." In A. Ferner and R. Hyman (Eds.), *Industrial relations in the new Europe.* Oxford: Blackwell.

SCHMITZ, Cristin. (2005, Apr. 1). "250,000 government workers do not have general right to sue." *Lawyers Weekly*, p. 1.

SCOTT, Clyde, Jim Simpson, and Sharon Oswald. (1993). "An empirical analysis of union election outcomes in the electrical utility industry." *Journal of Labor Research*, 14:3, pp. 355–365.

SCOTT, F.R. (1945). "Ode to a politician." Reprinted in M. Wilson (Ed.). (1969). *Poets between the wars.* Toronto: McClelland & Stewart.

———. (1932). "Communists, senators, and all that." *Canadian Forum*, January. Reprinted in *Forum.*

SCSJ (Sudbury Coalition for Social Justice). (2001, Feb. 16). "Injunction decision reflects bias towards Falconbridge-Noranda." From SCSJ website.

———. (2000, Oct. 11). "An injury to one is an injury to all." From SCSJ website.

SEEGER, Pete. (1972). *The Incompleat Folksinger.* Lincoln: U of Nebraska Press.

SETHI, Amarjit (Ed.). (1989). *Collective bargaining in Canada.* Scarborough, ON: Nelson.

SEWARD, Shirley. (2005). "Meeting the skills challenge: The case of the manufacturing sector." Presentation to Canadian Manufacturers and Exporters, Feb. 8.

SEXTON, Jean. (1987). "First contract arbitration in Canada." *Labor Law Journal*, 38:8, pp. 508–518.

SHELLENBARGER, Sue. (1998, October 7). "Time off is workers' answer to stress." *Ottawa Citizen*, p. G32. (Reprinted from *Wall Street Journal*).

SHIELDS, John. (1990). "Building a new hegemony in British Columbia." In L. Haiven, S. McBride, and J. Shields (Eds.), *Regulating labour*. Toronto: Garamond.

SIMPSON, Jeffrey. (2004, Dec. 22). "Canada's scandal of squandered skills." *Globe & Mail*.

SIMS, Andrew (Chair). (c. 1996 [1995]). *Canada Labour Code, part I, seeking a balance*. Ottawa: Minister of Public Works and Government Services.

SINGH, R. (1976). "Systems theory in the study of industrial relations: Time for reappraisal?" *Industrial Relations Journal*, 7 (fall).

SLICHTER, Sumner. (1929). "The current labor policies of American industry." *Quarterly Journal of Economics*, 43 (May). Reprinted in *Personnel and labour relations*.

SMITH, Anthony. (1993). "Canadian industrial relations in transition." *Relations Industrielles*, 48.

SNYDER, Ronald. (1995). *The annotated Canada labour code*. Scarborough: Carswell.

SOKOLIK, Stanley. (1969). "Reorganize the personnel department?" *California Management Review*, 11:3 (spring). Reprinted in *Personnel and labour relations*.

SOLOMON, N., P. Andiappan, and D. Shand. (1986). "Canadian union presidents: An empirical study." *Relations Industrielles*, 41.

SPROAT, John R. (2002). *Wrongful dismissal handbook* (2nd ed.). Toronto: Carswell.

STATS CAN (Statistics Canada). (2005a) "Average earnings by sex and work pattern (Full-time workers)." CANSIM, table: 202-0102. http://www40.statcan.ca/l01/cst01/labor01b.htm.

———. (2005b). *Population projections of visible minority groups, Canada, provinces and regions*. 2001–2017. Demography Division. Catalogue No. 91-541-XIE.

———. (2005c). Statistics Canada, CANSIM, Table 282-0002. http://www.statcan.ca/english/Pgdb/labor07a.htm. March 15.

———. (2005d). "Study: Diverging Trends in Unionization." *The Daily*. Friday, April 22.

———. (2004a). *The Canadian labour market at a glance*. Catalogue No. 71-222-XWE. http://www.statcan.ca/english/freepub/71-222-XIE/71-222-XIE2004000.htm. November 17.

———. (2004b). *Employment by age, sex, type of work, class of worker and province, seasonally adjusted*. http://www.statcan.ca/english/Pgdb/labour66a.htm. March 15.

———. (2004c). *Perspectives on Labour and Income*. 5:6 (June). Catalogue No. 75-001-XPE.

———. (2004d). "Fact Sheet on Unionization." *Perspectives on Labour and Income*. 5:8. Ottawa.

———. (2003a). Full and part-time employment. http://www.statcan.ca/english/Pgdb/labor12.htm.

———. (2003b). *Perspectives on Labour and Income*, 15:1 (spring). Catalogue No. 75-001-XPE.

———. (2002). "Fact-sheet on unionization." *Perspectives on Labour and Income*.

———. (1999). Unionization in Canada: A retrospective. Supplement, Catalogue no. 75-001-SPE. summer.

———. (1998a). "Labour force update." Statistics Canada, Cat. No. 71-005-XPB, winter. Ottawa: Stats Can.

———. (1998b). *Historical labour force statistics*. Catalogue No. 71-201-XPB.

———. (1997). "Labour force update: Youths and the labour market." Statistics Canada, Cat. No. 71-005-XPB, spring. Ottawa: Stats Can.

———. (1995). *Women in Canada: A statistical report* (3rd ed.). Catalogue No. 89-503E. Ottawa.

STATS CAN and Canadian Heritage. (2005). "Population projections of visible minority groups, Canada, provinces, and regions." Statistics Canada Cat. #91-541-X1E.

STEED, Judy. (1994, January 9). "Algoma's man of steel." *Ottawa Citizen*. Reprinted in *The system of industrial relations in Canada* (4th ed.).

STERN, R.N. and J.C. Anderson. (1978). "Canadian strike activity: Union centralization and national diversity." In J. Stern (Ed.), *Proceedings of the 30th Annual Meeting of the Industrial Relations Research Association*. Madison: IRRA.

STEWART-PATTERSON, David. (1987). *Post-mortem: Why Canada's mail won't move*. Toronto: MacMillan.

STOREY, Robert. (1983). "Unionization versus corporate welfare: The Dofasco way." *Labour/Le Travailleur,* (fall).

STRAUSS, George. (1999). "Is IR research returning to its roots?" In *Perspectives on Work,* 3:1, pp. 59–60.

———. (1991). "Union democracy." In G. Strauss et al. (Eds.), *The state of the unions.* Madison: IRRA Press.

SUMMERS, Clyde. (1991). "Unions without majorities: The potential of the NLRA." In *Proceedings of the 43rd Annual Meeting of the Industrial Relations Research Association.* Madison: IRRA.

SUNTER, Deborah (2001). "Demography and the labour market." In Statistics Canada, *Perspectives on Labour and Income,* (spring), pp. 28–39.

SUSSMAN, Deborah. (2000). "Unemployment Kaleidoscope." In Statistics Canada, *Perspectives on Labour and Income,* 13:1 12:3 (autumn), pp. 9–15.

SWIDINSKY, Robert and Michael Swidinsky. (2002). "The relative earnings of visible minorities in Canada." *Relations Industrielles,* 57:4, pp. 630–659.

SWIMMER, Gene (Ed.). (2000). *Public sector labour relations in an era of restraint and restructuring.* Toronto: Oxford U Press.

———. (1995). "Collective bargaining in the federal public service of Canada: The last twenty years." In G. Swimmer and M. Thompson (Eds.), *Public sector collective bargaining in Canada.*

SWIMMER, Gene and Mark Thompson. (1995). "Collective bargaining in the public sector: An introduction." In G. Swimmer and M. Thompson (Eds.), *Public sector collective bargaining in Canada.*

SWINTON, Katherine. (1995). "The Charter of Rights and public sector labour relations." In G. Swimmer and M. Thompson (Eds.), *Public sector collective bargaining in Canada.*

———. (1983). "Enforcement of occupational health and safety: The role of the internal responsibility system." In *Studies in labour law.* Reprinted in *Labour law.*

SWINTON, Katherine and Kenneth Swan. (1983). "The interaction between human rights legislation and labour law." In *Studies in labour law.* Reprinted in *Labour law.*

TANNENBAUM, Frank. (1951). *A philosophy of labor.* New York: Knopf.

———. (1921). *The labor movement: Its conservative functions and social consequences.* New York: Putnam.

TARANTELLI, Ezio. (1986). "The regulation of inflation and unemployment." *Industrial Relations,* 25:1.

TASK Force on Microelectronics. (1982). *In the chips: Opportunities, people, partnership.* Ottawa: Supply and Services.

TEPLITSKY, Martin. (1992). *Making a deal.* Toronto: Lancaster House.

TERKEL, Studs. (c. 1975 [1972]). *Working.* New York: Avon.

THOMASON, Terry. (1995). "Labour relations in primary and secondary education." In G. Swimmer and M. Thompson (Eds.), *Public sector collective bargaining in Canada.*

———. (1994a). "The effect of accelerated certification procedures on union organizing success in Ontario." *Industrial and Labor Relations Review,* 47:2, pp. 207–226.

———. (1994b). *Managerial opposition to union certification in Quebec and Ontario.* Working Paper. Faculty of Management, McGill University.

THOMASON, Terry and Silvanna Pozzebon. (1998). "Managerial opposition to union certification in Quebec and Ontario." *Relations Industrielles,* 53:4, pp. 750–771.

THOMASON, T., H. Zwerling, and P. Chandra. (1992). "Labour relations in the Canadian textile industry." In R. Chaykowski and A. Verma (Eds.), *Industrial relations in Canadian industry.*

THOMPSON, Mark. (1995a). "The management of industrial relations." In Morley Gunderson, Allan Ponak, and Daphne G. Taras (Eds.), *Union–management relations in Canada* (3rd ed.). Some use has also been made of his chapter on management in the 4th (2001) edition of the same book.

———. (1995b). "The industrial relations effects of privatization: Evidence from Canada." In G. Swimmer and M. Thompson (Eds.), *Public sector collective bargaining in Canada.*

———. (1982). "Collective bargaining by professionals." In Morley Gunderson, Allan Ponak, and Daphne G. Taras (Eds.), *Union–management relations in Canada* (1st ed.).

THOMPSON, Mark and Brian Bemmels. (2003). "British Columbia: The parties match the mountains." In M. Thompson, J. Rose, and A. Smith (Eds.), *Beyond the national divide: Regional dimensions of industrial relations.* Kingston: Queen's U School of Policy Studies.

THOMPSON, Mark and Allen Ponak. (2005). "The management of industrial relations." In Morley Gunderson, Allen Ponak, and Daphne G. Taras (Eds.), *Union–management relations in Canada* (5th ed.). Toronto: Pearson Addison Wesley.

———. (1992). "Restraint, privatization, and industrial relations in the public sector in the 1980s." In R. Chaykowski and A. Verma (Eds.), *Industrial relations in Canadian industry.*

THOMPSON, Mark and Gene Swimmer. (1995). "The future of public sector industrial relations." In G. Swimmer and M. Thompson (Eds.), *Public sector collective bargaining in Canada.*

THOMPSON, Mark, Joseph B. Rose, and Anthony E. Smith. (2003). *Beyond the national divide: Regional dimensions of industrial relations.* Kingston: School of Policy Studies.

THORNICROFT, Kenneth. (2005). "The grievance arbitration process: Theory and practice." In Morley Gunderson, Allan Ponak, and Daphne G. Taras (Eds.), *Union–management relations in Canada* (5th ed.).

THORNICROFT, Kenneth and Genevieve Eden. (1995). "Grievances and their resolution." In Morley Gunderson, Allan Ponak, and Daphne G. Taras (Eds.), *Union–management relations in Canada* (3rd ed.). Some use has also been made of Thornicroft's chapter on the same subject in the 4th (2001) edition of the same book.

TOWNSON, Monica. (2003). *Women in non-standard jobs: The public policy challenge.* Ottawa: Status of Women Canada.

TROFIMENKOFF, Susan. (1977). "102 muffled voices: Canada's industrial women in the 1880s." *Women's Study Journal, Atlantis.* Reprinted in MacDowell and Radforth (Eds.), *Canadian working class history.*

TROTTA, Maurice. (1976). *Handling grievances: A guide for management and labor.* Washington: Bureau of National Affairs.

TROY, Leo. (1992). "Convergence in international unionism et cetera: The case of Canada and the U.S.A." *British Journal of Industrial Relations*, 30.

UFCW. (2005, May 24). "Historic UFCW Canada/Loblaw negotiations going into second week." *UFCW Loblaw Talks.* http://www.ufcwloblawtalks2005.ca/.

UNDERHILL, Frank. (1932). "The cooperative commonwealth federation." *Canadian Forum*, August. Reprinted in *Forum.*

UNI (Union Network International) Global Union. (2005, Apr. 5). "UNI ties up offices to fight poverty." UNI Home Page, News Desk, Press Releases, http://www.union-network.org/uniinfo.nsf/58f61ccf5875fe90c12567bb005642f9/ec5d2a8ae7fdce97c1256fda002b1099?OpenDocument, [Apr. 15, 2005].

UNIVERSITY of Ottawa. (1994). Collective agreement between U of Ottawa and Association of Part-Time Professors, U of Ottawa.

USWA (United Steelworkers of America). (1991). *Empowering workers in the global economy, a labour agenda for the 1990s.* Papers prepared for a conference in Toronto, October 1991.

VERMA, Anil. (1995). "Employee involvement in the workplace." In Morley Gunderson, Allan Ponak, and Daphne G. Taras (Eds.), *Union–management relations in Canada* (3rd ed.).

———. (1992). Statement made in PhD seminar in advanced industrial relations topics. University of Toronto Centre for Industrial Relations, winter term.

VERMA, Anil and Richard Chaykowski. (1999a). "Employment and employment relations at the crossroads." In *Contract and commitment.*

———. (1999b). "Business strategies and employment relations." In *Contract and Commitment.*

VERMA, Anil and Daphne Taras (2001). "Employee involvement in the workplace." In Morley Gunderson, Allan Ponak, and Daphne G. Taras (Eds.), *Union–management relations in Canada* (4th ed.).

VERMA, Anil and Peter Warrian. (1992). "Industrial relations in the Canadian steel industry." In R. Chaykowski and A. Verma (Eds.), *Industrial relations in Canadian industry.*

VERMA, Anil and Joseph Weiler. (1992). "Industrial relations in the Canadian telephone industry." In R. Chaykowski and A. Verma (Eds.), *Industrial relations in Canadian industry.*

VERMA, Anil, T. Kochan, and R. Lansbury (Eds.). (1995). *Employment relations in the growing Asian economies.* London: Routledge.

WAGAR, Terry. (1996). *Employee involvement, strategic management and human resources: Exploring the linkages.* Kingston: Queen's IRC Press.

———. (1994). *Human resource management practices and organizational effectiveness: Evidence from Atlantic Canada.* Kingston: Queen's IRC Press.

WALTON, Richard and Robert McKersie. (1991). *A behavioral theory of labor negotiations: An analysis of a social interaction system* (2nd ed.). Ithaca: ILR Press.

———. (1965). *A Behavioral theory of labor negotiations: An analysis of a social interaction system.* New York: McGraw-Hill.

———. (1963). *A behavioral theory of negotiations.* New York: McGraw-Hill.

WALTON, Richard E., Joel E. Cutcher-Gershenfeld, and Robert B. McKersie. (2000). *Strategic negotiations: A theory of change in labor-management relations.* Ithaca, New York: ILR Press.

WARD, Bob. (1974). *Harvest of concern.* Toronto: Ontario Federation of Labour. Reprinted in *The Canadian worker in the twentieth century.*

WARRIAN, Peter. (1996). *Hard bargain: Transforming public sector labour–management relations.* Toronto: McGilligan.

WEATHERS, Charles. (2003). "The decentralisation of Japan's wage-setting in comparative perspective." *Industrial Relations Journal*, 34:2, pp. 119–134.

WEBB, Sidney and Beatrice Webb. (c. 1920 [1897]). *Industrial democracy.* New York: Longmans.

WEILER, Joseph. (1984). "Grievance arbitration: The new wave." In J. Weiler and P. Gall (Eds.), *The labour code of British Columbia in the 1980s.* Calgary and Vancouver: Carswell.

WEILER, Paul. (1983a) "Promises to keep." *Harvard Law Review*, 96:8 (June).

———. (1983b). "Protecting the worker from disability: Challenges for the eighties." *Report to Ontario Ministry of Labour.* Reprinted in *Labour law.*

———. (1980). *Reconcilable differences: New directions in Canadian labour law.* Toronto: Carswell.

WEINER, Nan. (1995). "Workplace equity." In G. Swimmer and M. Thompson (Eds.), *Public sector collective bargaining in Canada.*

WELLS, Don. (1993). "Are strong unions compatible with the new model of human resource management?" *Relations Industrielles*, 48.

WHITE, J.F. (1932). "Deportations." *Canadian Forum*, July. Reprinted in *Forum.*

WHITE, Julie. (1997a). "Changing times: Shorter hours of work in the Communications, Energy and Paperworkers' Union." Ottawa: CEP.

———. (1997b). Conversation with the author concerning the CEP's educational activities around work hours. December.

———. (1993). *Sisters and solidarity: Women and unions in Canada.* Toronto: Thompson Educational Publishing, Inc.

WHITE, Robert. (1995). "Workers' education builds strong rights." *Workers' Education*, 10 (Oct.).

WINPISINGER, William. (1989). "A machinist and a left-of-center progressive." In P. Quaglieri (Ed.). *America's labor leaders.* Lexington, MA: Lexington Books.

WOOD, S.J. et al. (1975). "The 'industrial relations system' concept as a basis for theory in industrial relations." *British Journal of Industrial Relations*, 3 (Nov.).

WOODWORTH, Warner and Christopher Meek. (1995). *Creating labor-management partnerships.* Reading and Don Mills: Addison-Wesley.

WORKPLACE Information Directorate. (2004a). Custom Reports from Human Resources and Skills Development Canada's collective agreement database.

———. (2004b) *Workplace Gazette*, 7:3. Human Resources and Skills Development Canada.

———. (2001). *Workplace Gazette*, 4:3. Human Resources Development Canada.

———. (1998). Data on strikes obtained from Work Stoppage Bureau, Human Resources Development Canada.

————. (1997). *Directory of labour organizations in Canada.* Ottawa: HRDC. Use was also made of the 1993 and 1996 editions of the same book.

WORLD Almanac. (2002). New York: World Almanac Books.

WORLD of Work. (2004). "Solidarity fund: Labour-sponsored solidarity funds in Quebec are generating jobs." *World of Work,* 50, http://www.caledonia.org.uk/papers/quebec-solidarity-fund.pdf.

WORTHY, James. (1948). "Changing concepts of the personnel function." *Personnel,* 25:3 (Nov.). Reprinted in *Personnel and labour relations.*

YATES, Charlotte. (2000). "Staying the decline in union membership: Union organizing in Ontario, 1985–1999." *Relations Industrielles,* 55:4, pp. 640–674.

YODER, Dale. (1962). *Personnel management and industrial relations* (5th ed.). Englewood Cliffs: Prentice-Hall.

YOUNG-KI, Park. (1993). "South Korea." In Stephen Deery and Richard Mitchell (Eds.), *Labour law and industrial relations in Asia.*

ZEYTINOGLU, Isik Urla, Josefina Moruz, M. Bianca Seaton, and Waheeda Lillevik. (2003). *Occupational health of women in non-standard employment.* Ottawa: Status of Women Canada.

ZUSSMAN, David and Jak Jabes. (1989). *The vertical solitude: Managing in the public sector.* Halifax: Institute for Research on Public Policy.

ZWERLING, Harris. (1997). "Obesity as a covered disability under employment discrimination law: An analysis of Canadian approaches." *Relations Industrielles,* 52:3.

Glossary

All-Canadian Congress of Labour (ACCL) and Canadian Congress of Labour (CCL) Small Canadian labour federations that sought to organize workers on an industry-wide basis and emphasized political action.

American Federation of Labor (AFL) US-based labour federation, the forerunner of the current AFL-CIO.

Anti-union animus The existence of anti-union motive. Employer actions designed to avoid or escape unionization may constitute unfair labour practices even if accompanied by some legitimate business reason.

Attitudinal structuring Activities that influence the parties' relationship and attitudes toward each other.

Automatic certification 1) card-majority certification system; or 2) labour relations boards' power to certify a trade union even without evidence of majority support in instances where employer interference has been so egregious as to make it impossible to discern the true wishes of the employees.

Autonomous work teams A team of employees empowered to make decisions typically made by managers or supervisors. The level of authority and responsibility can vary from simply ordering raw materials to being empowered to discharge team members.

Bargaining unit The group of employees for which a trade union is certified or voluntarily recognized to act as the exclusive bargaining agent.

Berlin Convention Crucial 1902 convention of the Trades and Labour Congress, which banned dual unionism and affiliated Canadian and American unions more closely.

Boycott A negative publicity campaign aimed at persuading the public not to buy the goods or services of the company in question.

Bumping Exercise of seniority rights by more senior workers to displace more junior ones in times of layoff or the discontinuance of departments.

Bureaucratic management Specialized, professionalized administration, in this case the IR and HR departments, where decision making is centralized and authority flows through multiple layers of management.

Business agent A staff member of a local union who handles grievances, helps enforce agreements, and performs other tasks in the day-to-day operation of the union.

Call-back pay Wage premium paid to workers called back to their jobs after completing their regular shift and leaving the premises.

Canadian Auto Workers Industrial union representing Canadian auto workers, which split away from the United Auto Workers in 1985.

Canadian Labour Congress (CLC) Canada's national labour federation, formed in 1956 from the merger of the Canadian Congress of Labour and the Trades and Labour Congress.

Captive audience speeches Employer speeches delivered to employees at meetings held during work hours and for which attendance is compulsory. Sometimes used by employers to discourage employees from supporting a union.

Card-majority certification system A system for certification of trade unions whereby the labour relations board accepts signed membership cards as evidence of majority support and certifies the trade union without need for a representation vote.

Centralized system An IR system characterized by a relatively small number of large negotiations each affecting many workers, and where activity often takes place at the national or industry as well as the workplace level.

Certification The process by which a labour relations board determines whether a union enjoys the support of a sufficient majority of employees in a bargaining unit and therefore acquires the right to act as their exclusive bargaining agent.

Chilling effect Refers to parties' hesitancy to make the concessions necessary to conclude a collective agreement when they anticipate arbitration and believe the arbitrator will choose a middle ground.

Choice of procedures (COP) Form of public sector dispute resolution in which one party or the other (normally the union) is given the right to choose between binding arbitration or the traditional conciliation-strike route.

Closed shop provision Collective agreement provision requiring all employees in a bargaining unit to be union members before being hired.

Co-operative Commonwealth Federation (CCF) Social democratic party formed during the Depression, the forerunner to the present New Democratic Party (NDP).

Coercive drive approach A management approach most common in the nineteenth century that sought to "motivate" employees primarily through fear and intimidation, with the aim of extracting the maximum possible amount of work from them.

COLA (cost of living allowance) clauses Clauses that provide workers with protection against inflation by allowing for wage increases based on increases in the inflation level.

Collective bargaining The negotiation process through which the terms and conditions of employment of unionized workers are determined.

Communications, Energy and Paperworkers Union of Canada (CEP) National, socially conscious union formed as a result of mergers in the communications, energy, and pulp and paper industries.

Compressed work weeks An arrangement whereby employees work longer hours each day in return for a day off every week, two weeks, or month. The commonest arrangement is one day off every two weeks.

Concession bargaining Situations in which the union is forced to agree to a wage freeze, wage reduction, or reduction in existing benefit levels in order to conclude a collective agreement.

Conciliation A process, sometimes compulsory, during which a conciliation officer or a tripartite conciliation board attempts to assist the parties to resolve their bargaining impasse and avoid a strike or lockout.

Confédération des syndicates nationaux (CSN) Quebec labour federation originating in the confessional unions of the early twentieth century.

Confédération des travailleurs du Canada (CTCC) Catholic confessional union federation launched in 1921.

Congress of Industrial Organizations (CIO) Industrial union federation established during the Depression to compete with the AFL.

Constructive dismissal Occurs when an employer unilaterally and fundamentally alters the terms and conditions of employment such that the change can be construed as equivalent to dismissal.

Contingent work-force Individuals who enjoy little or no job security because they are employed on a temporary, part-time, or contractual basis and can generally be laid off with little or no notice.

Contracting out Employers' use of workers from outside their own work force to perform work previously performed by their own employees.

Controlled strike Public sector strike in which the public health and safety are protected by designating certain workers as essential, thus compelling them to continue working through the dispute.

Conventional interest arbitration A form of arbitration in which the arbitrator is free, within certain broad limits, to choose the position of one of the parties, some combination thereof, or fashion an alternative settlement.

Corporatism Social arrangements in which bodies, or *corpora*, serve as political representatives and play a critical role in decision making. With regard to industrial relations systems, participation is tripartite: unions, private sector corporations, and government.

Craft union A union that limits its membership to a single craft (e.g., brickmaking).

Decentralized system An IR system characterized by large numbers of negotiations each involving relatively small numbers of workers, where most activity occurs at the workplace level.

Decertification The process by which a labour relations board determines that a trade union no longer enjoys the support of a majority of employees in a bargaining unit and therefore loses the right to act as their exclusive bargaining agent.

Demand-deficient unemployment An overall lack of jobs in the economy.

Direct discrimination Intentionally distinguishing between employees or job candidates based on a prohibited ground.

Direct union wage impact The premium a worker receives for union membership.

Distributive bargaining System of activities focused on dividing limited resources. Functions to resolve pure conflicts of interest.

District labour councils Bodies designed to advance the labour movement's interests at local and municipal levels.

Dual unionism Competition between two or more unions to represent workers in the same sector.

Dues checkoff Employer deduction of union dues at the source.

Duty of fair representation Unions' duty to represent all members of the bargaining unit in a manner that is not arbitrary, discriminatory, or in bad faith.

Employee Assistance Program (EAP) Counselling services that offer employees assistance on a broad range of personal issues (e.g., alcohol or family problems).

Employee benefits (also sometimes referred to as fringe benefits) Non-wage benefits such as paid vacations or pensions, the cost of which is borne either wholly or in part by the employer.

Enterprise union A union whose membership is limited to employees of the individual firm or plant.

Expedited arbitration Any grievance arbitration system that has introduced mechanisms (e.g., the use of a single arbitrator, the use of a standing umpire, oral decisions or limits on the length of written decisions) to speed up the grievance resolution process.

Extension of collective agreements or decree system System whereby collective agreements negotiated for a few major firms in a given industry are extended to the entire industry by means of a government decree.

Fact-finding A dispute resolution procedure involving a neutral party investigating and reporting on the facts of the dispute.

Final-offer arbitration (FOA) or final-offer selection (FOS) A form of dispute resolution in which the third-party neutral must select either the proposal submitted by the union or that submitted by management, without alteration.

Fragmented union structure A union structure marked by a large number of small unions.

Free rider Someone who refuses to pay union dues, yet—by virtue of being in the bargaining unit—is entitled to the benefits and protections of union representation.

Frictional unemployment Temporary unemployment due to time lost switching between jobs.

Gainsharing plan Plan whereby the benefits of increased productivity and greater labour–management co-operation are shared by the employer and the employees or their union.

Grievance An allegation by either party (union or management) that the other has violated the collective agreement.

Grievance mediation A grievance settlement mechanism whereby a third-party neutral seeks to help the parties resolve the dispute themselves rather than sending it through to arbitration.

Group grievance A grievance resulting from a combination of similar individual grievances seeking a common redress.

High performance work systems A system of work practices designed to empower employees, facilitate their participation in decision making, and grant them greater autonomy over job tasks and methods of work.

Independent union (or independent local) A union that is not affiliated with any labour federation.

Indirect (adverse effect) discrimination Occurs when an apparently neutral policy or practice has the effect of disproportionately disadvantaging members of a protected group.

Indirect union wage impact The effect unions have on non-unionized workers' wages.

Individual grievance A grievance involving the application of the collective agreement to one member.

Industrial relations system An "analytical subsystem of an industrial society" (John Dunlop) governing individuals' workplace behaviour.

Industrial unionism Broad-based, politically conscious unionism that seeks to organize all workers in an industry.

Industrial Workers of the World (IWW, or Wobblies) Radical, Western-based union of the early twentieth century.

Integrative bargaining System of activities focused on identifying resolutions to shared-interest conflicts that maximize joint gain.

Interest arbitration Process whereby a third-party neutral or board determines and imposes the terms and conditions of the collective agreement. Serves as a substitute for a strike or lockout.

International Confederation of Free Trade Unions (ICFTU) A confederation of national trade unions, each of which links together the trade unions of that particular country.

International Labour Organization (ILO) A United Nations agency that investigates workers' rights and working conditions all around the world and sets international standards.

International union As normally used in Canada, this term refers to unions headquartered in the United States but which also have Canadian members.

Intra-organizational bargaining Bargaining within each party in order to achieve internal consensus.

Knights of Labor Idealistic early labour federation, which organized on an industry-wide rather than craft basis.

Labour force All persons 15 years of age and over who are either employed or are unemployed but actively seeking employment.

Layoff Separation from employment as a result of a lack of work.

Lockout Closing of a place of employment or a suspension of work by an employer done to compel employees to agree to terms or conditions of employment.

Maintenance of membership provision Provision stating that no employee must join as a condition of employment, but that all who join voluntarily must maintain their membership for the agreement's duration.

Make-whole doctrine An approach adopted from civil law that requires the guilty party to right past wrongs and to restore the victim to the position he or she would have been in had the offence in question not been committed.

Management rights clause Clause (or provision) in a collective agreement laying out areas specifically not subject to collective bargaining (e.g., hiring or the production process).

Mandatory retirement Compelling employees to retire upon reaching a certain age, normally 65.

Mandatory vote system A two-stage system for certification of trade unions whereby the labour relations board first requires signed membership cards as evidence of sufficient employee support to trigger a representation vote and then mandates a vote in every instance.

Mediation A dispute-resolution process similar to conciliation, although mediation is more often voluntary, tends to be more interventionist, and may be used in either interest or rights disputes.

Modified union shop provision Provision stipulating that non-union members already employed need not join the union, but all new employees must join, and those already belonging to the union must remain members.

Moonlighting A situation where an individual holds more than one paid job at the same time.

Mutual gains or interest-based bargaining (IBB) A collective bargaining approach that incorporates integrative and principled bargaining.

Narcotic effect Refers to parties' decreasing ability to resolve disputes on their own as they repeatedly refer disputes to, and become dependent upon, arbitration.

National Labor Relations Act (NLRA) or Wagner Act First American collective bargaining legislation, passed in 1935.

National union As normally used in Canada, a union whose headquarters and members are all in Canada.

Non-standard employment A term generally used to describe any type of employment other than full-time, full-year employment contracts of indefinite term.

One Big Union (OBU) Short-lived Western-based socialist industrial union launched in 1918.

Open period A period of time when applications for decertification or for certification of an alternate union may be submitted, usually the two or three months immediately preceding the expiry of a collective agreement.

Open shop An enterprise in which union membership is not required as a condition of securing or maintaining employment.

Opening offer Initial offer, which is usually the most optimistic outcome one can anticipate.

Parent union A number of local unions affiliated under the same name and subject to a unifying constitution and structure.

Paternalistic management Human resource practices based on the notion that it is an employer's responsibility to take care of employees and determine what is in their best interests.

Pattern bargaining A bargaining strategy whereby terms of the first, or target, contract are used as a pattern for subsequent collective agreements.

Policy grievance A grievance involving the agreement's general application or interpretation.

Pre-industrial management A system of management used in pre-industrial societies—when most of those in employee status worked for friends or relatives—that operates on the basis of personal supervision, often by an owner-manager working alongside his or her employees.

Preventive mediation Voluntary third-party assistance aimed at improving the parties' communication and overall relationship with an eye to reducing grievance levels.

Price elasticity of demand The degree to which demand for a product or service is affected by its price.

Principled bargaining Process whereby the parties seek mutual gain in areas of shared interest and use merit and objective standards to resolve issues where interests are in conflict.

Privative clause A clause in a labour relations act limiting or in some cases barring judicial review of arbitration awards.

Probationary period An initial, generally rather brief trial period during which the employee may be dismissed much more easily than after attaining indefinite status.

Progressive discipline A system of discipline whereby the penalties are increased for each succeeding offence and the employee is made aware of the possibility of further penalties should he or she repeat the offence in question.

Public Service Alliance Canada's largest federal public service union, representing mainly secretarial, administrative, and operational employees.

Quality circles A gathering of employees for the purpose of identifying the root cause of a problem and finding a solution.

Quality of working life (QWL) A process using joint problem-solving approaches that is focused on improving labour-management relations, organizational effectiveness, and employees' work satisfaction.

Quebec Federation of Labour (QFL) Quebec division of the Canadian Labour Congress.

Quid pro quo A term used in law to denote the giving of something for something, an exchange which is necessary to render a contract valid and binding.

Rand Formula Union security provision whereby no worker is required to join the union but all must pay it an amount equal to its dues as a condition of employment.

Rank-and-file Ordinary union members, as opposed to the leadership.

Residual management rights The view that any rights not specifically laid out in the collective agreement are to be considered management rights.

Resistance point The minimum outcome a party is willing to accept.

Right-to-work states States which have passed legislation banning union security provisions. Most such states are in the southern or midwestern US.

Rights/grievance arbitration Process to resolve disputes over the interpretation, application, or administration of rights articulated in a collective agreement.

Scientific management (also known as Taylorism) A system of management launched by F.W. Taylor whereby tasks were broken down into their smallest possible components and quotas set on the basis of elaborate time-motion studies.

Seniority An employee's standing in the organization, usually based on length of continuous employment.

Shop steward A union member elected to represent workers in a particular shop or department.

Social contract outcomes The shared understandings around the expected levels of trust, information sharing, and mutual commitment between the parties.

Social unionism Unionism that works for the good of workers as a whole and uses political action as well as collective bargaining to achieve its objectives.

Standby pay Wage premium paid to those who must remain on call or carry a cell phone or pager when off duty.

Strategic choice framework (or theory) An industrial relations theory developed in the US by Thomas Kochan and his associates that stresses the linkages between a firm's industrial relations and human resources policies and strategies and its overall competitive strategies, and distinguishes three levels of industrial relations activity.

Strike A cessation of work by employees, in combination, in concert, or in accordance with a common understanding. May include a slowdown designed to restrict output.

Strikebreakers Those continuing to work during a strike or replacing striking workers.

Structural unemployment A situation in which there is a mismatch of available jobs and skills, or in which unemployed workers live in different locations from those where jobs are available.

Surface bargaining A violation of the duty to bargain in good faith that involves going through the motions of the bargaining process but having no intention of actually concluding a collective agreement.

Taft-Hartley Act Legislation, passed in the US in 1947 as a series of amendments to the Wagner Act, which severely limited the powers of the American labour movement. The most significant feature was the "right-to-work" provision, which allowed states to outlaw union security provisions.

Target point The realistically anticipated and hoped for outcome.

Total quality management A philosophy and set of practices aimed at continual improvement in managing quality, meeting customer requirements, improving production processes, and reducing costs.

Trades and Labour Congress Canada's first major labour federation, founded in 1886.

Tripartism Consultation or negotiations between representatives of labour, management, and government on matters of mutual interest.

Two-tier wage schemes Wage arrangements whereby newly-hired workers are paid substantially less than experienced ones.

Union acceptance strategy An industrial relations strategy in which employers do not actively resist becoming unionized or make attempts to rid themselves of existing unions.

Union density The percentage of paid, non-agricultural workers belonging to unions.

Union raiding An attempt by one union to persuade members of another union to defect and join its ranks.

Union recognition clause Clause that identifies the union as the sole and exclusive bargaining agent for a particular group of workers.

Union removal strategy An industrial relations strategy in which employers aggressively try to eliminate any unions that already exist within their operation and avoid any new certifications.

Union resistance strategy An industrial relations strategy characterized by acceptance of already existent unions but vigorous opposition to additional certifications or expansion of coverage of existing unions.

Union rights and security provisions Collective agreement provisions designed to protect the union's institutional authority and ensure its financial stability.

Union shop A type of union security arrangement that requires employees to join the union as a condition of employment.

Union shop provision Provisions requiring all employees to be union members within a specified time period after being hired.

Union substitution/avoidance strategy An industrial relations strategy in which the goal is to remain union free. This strategy usually involves implementing practices designed to substitute for union protections.

United Food and Commercial Workers (UFCW) International union representing large numbers of Canadian retail workers.

Voluntary arbitration Parties have the right to strike or lockout but elect instead to submit the dispute to a third-party neutral or tripartite board to determine the terms and conditions of the collective agreement.

Welfare capitalist management A system of management, most common between the two world wars, in which companies sought to cement employees' loyalty and remain union-free by providing a broad range of benefits and establishing in-house consultation systems.

Whipsaw A bargaining tactic where either a union or an employer attempts to leapfrog, or improve upon, another settlement, using it as the minimum it is willing to accept.

Wildcat strike A work stoppage carried out during the term of a collective agreement, normally without the union's authorization.

Work rules Collective agreement provisions regulating the production process and other on-the-job working conditions.

Work to rule Collective refusal to perform duties not explicitly included in job descriptions and/or dogmatically following all rules to the letter, thus effecting a slowdown.

Workers' compensation A no-fault insurance system paid for collectively by employers and governed by legislation in each jurisdiction that compensates workers in the event of work-related illnesses and injuries.

Workers' Unity League (WUL) Depression-era Communist labour federation.

Zone of potential agreement The area within which the parties' resistance points overlap. Also called the bargaining range or settlement zone.

Index